CANADA AND THE UNITED STATES
A MODERN STUDY

THE BACKGROUND OF OUR TIMES

SERIES II

Book I: The Foundations of the West
Book II: The West and a Wider World
Book III: Canada and the United States

GENERAL EDITORS:

KENNETH W. McNAUGHT, Ph.D.,
Professor of History, University of Toronto

RAMSAY COOK, Ph.D.,
Professor of History, York University

JOHN C. RICKER, M.A.,
*Professor of History, The College of Education,
University of Toronto*

JOHN T. SAYWELL, Ph.D.,
*Professor of History, Dean of Arts and Science,
York University, Toronto*

CANADA AND THE UNITED STATES

A MODERN STUDY

KENNETH W. McNAUGHT, Ph.D.,
Professor of History, University of Toronto

RAMSAY COOK, Ph.D.,
Professor of History, York University

MAPS BY ROBERT KUNZ

CLARKE, IRWIN & COMPANY LIMITED
TORONTO, VANCOUVER

ISBN 0 7720 0252 5

6 7 8 9 10 JD 75 74 73 72 71

Printed in Canada

CONTENTS

PART ONE: THE UNITED STATES

Introduction: The Foundations, 1500-1763   3
The Division of a Continent, 1763-1783   14

1. The Supreme Law of the Land   24
2. Federalists and Republicans   39
3. Nationalism and Sectionalism   52
4. Andrew Jackson's America   69
5. America and the Industrial Revolution   79
6. The Failure of Compromise   89
7. Civil War   108
8. Radical Peace and Bourbon Triumph   119
9. The Businessman's Revolution   129
10. Parties and Protests   146
11. "A Splendid Little War"   163
12. The Politics of Progressivism   175
13. Wilson's Dilemma   185
14. Farewell to Reform   196
15. F.D.R. and the New Deal   209
16. From Versailles to San Francisco   221
17. From Fair Deal to New Frontier   238
18. Foreign Policy in the Cold War   250

PART TWO: CANADA

19. The Question of Survival   267
20. The Growth and Defence of British North America   280
21. Post-war Expansion   291
22. Reaction, Reform and Rebellion in the Canadas   302
23. Durham's Report and the Triumph of Responsible Government   316
24. The Uneasy Union   328
25. Founding a New Nation   340
26. The Uncertain Nation   354
27. Railways, Riel and Sectionalism   366
28. Race, Religion and Victory for Laurier   379
29. Laurier and National Development   388
30. Canada, the Empire and the United States   400
31. The Trials of War   411
32. The Triumph of Mackenzie King   422
33. Depression Decade   435
34. Nationalism and Isolation   450
35. Canada and the Second World War   463
36. Canada in a World of Super Powers   475

LIST OF MAPS

	Page
The Northwest Territories in 1787	25
The Troubled Border, 1794	49
The Louisiana Purchase	57
Travel Routes to the West	63
The Missouri Compromise	65
Principal Railways, 1860	82
The Maine-New Brunswick Border Dispute	90
The Mexican War, 1846-1848	93
The Extension of Slavery, 1850-1854	100
The Alignment of the States in 1861	106
The Civil War	110
Cattle Trails and Railroads	138
The Election of 1896	161
The United States in the Pacific	165
The United States in the Caribbean	172
The Election of 1912	183
The Boundaries of Quebec, 1763-1774	271
Loyalist Settlements	276
The War of 1812	287
Western Expansion	292
The Oregon Boundary Dispute	335
The Expansion of Confederation	355
The Northwest Rebellion	372
Transcontinental Railways	392
The Alaska Boundary Dispute	405
The War in France, 1914-1918	412
The European Campaign	471

LIST OF CHARTS

The Federal Division of Powers	31
Checks and Balances in the American Constitution	33
The Legislative Process	34
Immigration to America, 1870-1900	142

ACKNOWLEDGMENTS

The authors and publishers wish to express their appreciation to the following organizations which have made available the illustrative material appearing on the pages listed.

E Bartholomew, Toyahvale, Texas (N. H. Rose Collection), 135

The Bettmann Archive, New York, 5, 7, 16, 19, 21, 39, 47, 76, 125, 136, 168, 169, 173, 181, 186, 192, 194

Brown Brothers, New York, 103, 144 (top), 151, 182, 189, 203, 217, 234

Buffalo and Erie County Historical Society, 317

Canada, Dept. of National Defence, 470

Canada, Dept. of Trade and Commerce, 322

Canada Steamship Lines (W. H. Coverdale Collection), 284

Capital Press, Ottawa, 407, 485

Cleveland Plain Dealer, 200

Culver Pictures Inc., New York, 28, 44, 73, 120, 122, 147, 149, 153, 156, 180

Ewing Galloway, New York, 198, 206

Gettysburg National Military Park, 112 (by Philoppoteaux)

Halifax Chronicle-Herald, 486 (by Chambers)

Library of Congress, 58, 140

Miller Services, Toronto, 216, 227, 259

Montreal Daily Star, 417 (right), 430 (both by Racey)

Museum of the City of New York, 84, 144 (bottom)

National Film Board, Ottawa, 482

National Liberal Federation, 399, 409, 414, 444, 445

Thomas Nelson & Sons Ltd., 275

The New York Historical Society, 61, 78, 87, 94, 96, 98

New York Public Library, 40, 43, 81, 92, 116, 123, 132

The Ohio Historical Society, 101

The Old Print Shop Inc., New York, 18

Ontario Archives, 283, 300, 350

Philadelphia Inquirer, 225

Public Archives of Canada, 12, 269, 273, 296 (by Bainbrigge), 298, 305 (by Bainbrigge), 307, 309, 312, 314, 325, 336, 337, 344, 345, 351 (from Macdonald Papers), 360 (from *Canadian Illustrated News*), 367 (by Weston), 373, 377 (from *Grip*), 380, 381 (from *Grip*), 383 (by Russell), 386 (top) (by Rostap), 391, 397 (all), 402 (from *Saturday Globe*, Nov. 3, 1900), 404 (from *Globe*, Oct. 17, 1900), 408, 417 (left), 419, 420, 425, 428, 465, 473; also cartoons by Bengough on 347, 361, 365, 374; also cartoons by Julien on 386, 389, 390, 416; also pictures from *Illustrated London News* on 330, 332, 342, 358.

Richmond Times-Dispatch, 219 (by Seibel)

Royal Ontario Museum, Canadian Gallery, 281, 320, 369

Society for the Preservation of New England Antiquities, 74

Toronto Daily Star, 427, 443 (by Callan), 448, 460 (by Callan), 490 (by Macpherson)

Toronto *Globe and Mail*, 456, 488

Toronto Public Libraries, John Ross Robertson Collection, 277, 289, 293, 295, 297, 311, 327, 333

Union Pacific Railroad Company, 130

Wide World Photos Inc., 117, 160, 190, 205, 208, 210, 211, 213, 223, 228, 230, 233, 239, 241, 243, 244, 247, 248, 253, 255, 258, 262, 462, 467, 468, 477, 480

Winnipeg Free Press, 452, 483 (both by Arch Dale)

Wisconsin State Historical Society, 177

PREFACE

Canada and the United States has been a long time in the making. Three years ago authors and editors sat down to plan a book for the new Grade 13 course in Ontario. At our first meetings we reached general agreement about the kind of book we wanted to write. We rejected the superficial narrative approach as satisfying none of the important purposes which history should serve and resolved that our book must come to grips with the hard core of North American history. We stressed particularly that narrative and interpretation, or analysis, must be so blended as to raise questions and to answer them; issues must not be overlooked because they were difficult but must be approached firmly and honestly.

A book constructed on these principles is not an easy book. Indeed history is not an easy subject. It is as complex and whimsical as the men who make it, as varied and impersonal as the environment in which men must live. History may be romantic, it may be tragic; it is sometimes sweet, it is often bitter. Historical events are sometimes obvious, more often obscure. Though men may seem to mould history, more often they merely struggle to keep their feet amid currents they cannot control and sometimes do not understand.

One fact emerges clearly from a study of history, however: the march of events, seldom tranquil, is accompanied by the noisy beat of economic rivalries, social tensions, conflicting ideas and competing personalities. It is this beat we have attempted to isolate and explain in *Canada and the United States*.

Working on this book with Ramsay Cook, Kenneth McNaught and John Ricker was exciting and challenging. Each brought to the task not only a different talent but often a sharply different point of view. Arguments were frequent and sometimes acrimonious; compromises were many and sometimes reluctant. From the collaboration, however, there emerged a work which is a mixture of the opinions of all four—not a bland mixture which might conceivably meet with agreement on every point, but a heterogeneous mixture which will, we hope, stir up discussion and debate.

JOHN T. SAYWELL

Toronto, May 15, 1963

ix

PART ONE: THE UNITED STATES

The Foundations
1500-1763

At the end of the fifteenth century several European states, of which Spain and Portugal were the most powerful, gave their support to maritime adventurers in the search for overseas wealth and possessions. Thus began the quest for empire and the expansion of Europe which was to last for over four centuries, and was to bring the entire world within the orbit of western civilization. For many of these adventurers the precious metals and luxurious spices of the Orient were the chief objectives. An English poet expressed this aim nearly a hundred years after the discovery of America:

> *I'll have them fly to India for gold,*
> *Ransack the ocean for orient pearl,*
> *And search all corners of the new-found world*
> *For pleasant fruits and princely delicates.*

That "new-found world" was the vast land mass that the fifteenth-century sailors had found lying in the path of a direct sea route to the wealth of Asia. Christopher Columbus, sailing under the Spanish flag of Ferdinand and Isabella, was the first adventurer to set foot on the continent later christened America. Columbus' son described the scene which took place in the autumn of 1492 on the coral island of San Salvador (Watling Island):

Presently they saw naked people, and the Admiral went ashore in the armed ship's boat with the royal standard displayed . . . [and] with the banners of the expedition on which were depicted a green cross with F on one arm and a Y on the other and over each his or her Crown. And all having rendered thanks to our Lord kneeling on the ground, embracing it with tears of joy for the immeasurable mercy of having reached it, the Admiral rose and gave this island the name San Salvador.

The Spanish laid claim to much of the then uncharted Americas, but they concentrated most on the central and southern sections of the New

3

World where they were to have great success. The unknown areas in the
north were left for the explorers, merchants, and fishermen of the countries
of northern Europe. But England and France were slow to join the
fifteenth- and sixteenth-century quest for empire. While Spain and Portugal were discovering America and charting the route around the Cape of
Good Hope, the people of England and France were occupied chiefly with
domestic political and religious conflicts. Not 'until the end of the sixteenth
century had both countries become sufficiently united and wealthy to turn
their attention to the struggle for empire, and that attention soon centred
on North America.

1. THE EARLY DEVELOPMENT OF CANADA

Five years after the discovery of America, John Cabot, an
Italian sailing under the English flag, had skirted the coasts of Newfoundland and Cape Breton Island. Fishermen followed his lead and discovered the enormously rich cod-runs off the Grand Banks. Explorers also
followed his path, hoping to find a route to the Far East. Many an intrepid
captain in a frail sailing-ship probed the indentations on the North American
coast for that elusive water-way through the land mass to the wealth of
the Orient. In 1534, one such adventurer, Jacques Cartier of St. Malo,
entered the Gulf of St. Lawrence where the Indians excited him with
tales of the quantities of gold and copper that lay up the great river.
Cartier never did find such wealth, but he did open up the interior of the
continent as far west as the Indian village of Hochelaga which over a
hundred years later became Montreal. Nevertheless, despite the explora-
tions of Cartier and others it was not until the end of the sixteenth century
that Frenchmen were ready to settle in their new lands and to develop
the trade in fish and furs.

Excluding the ill-fated settlement on Sable Island in 1598, where the
unhappy survivors waited five years to be removed, the first attempt to
start a permanent French colony in North America was the work of
Samuel de Champlain. In 1603 Champlain, the greatest of the early
French explorers and colonizers, reached Acadia, and in 1605 he founded
a colony at Port Royal in the Annapolis Valley. Champlain typified the
seventeenth-century French explorer. He was devoutly religious and
enthusiastically encouraged missionaries to come to the new country.
But he combined religious zeal with a burning desire to establish a thriving
French colony and prosperous commercial enterprise in Canada.

In 1608 Champlain founded Quebec as the centre of France's activities
in North America. It was a colony ruled by a commercial company, but
besides its activities in the fur trade the company assumed responsibility
for settlement. Of course, these two objectives were not always in harmony, for recruiting and transporting settlers was costly and the company
was anxious to protect its profits. Moreover, settlement forced the fur-
traders to travel farther into the woods to meet the Indian trappers. Yet

The colony at Jamestown, Virginia, was all but annihilated during its early years. The discovery of a method of curing tobacco assured it of a staple crop, however, and the community began to grow. In 1619 the 1,000 men in Virginia received a representative assembly, sixty unmarried women sent by the directors to seek husbands, and twenty slaves.

the colony could not exist without the fur trade for it was New France's chief economic resource.

The company was not the only power in the colony. Soon after the founding of Quebec, missionary priests began to arrive, first the Récollets and later the Jesuits. Living among the Indians was at best extremely uncomfortable, at worst extremely dangerous. Yet, filled with the zeal of the Counter-Reformation, these priests were dauntless. Every year the Jesuits sent a report of their work and of the colony's progress back to France, thus providing propaganda for the colony and for their own work. In 1636 the report, or *Relation*, described the missionary's life: "I say it without exaggeration, the five or six months of Winter are spent in almost continuous discomforts, excessive cold, smoke and the annoyance of Savages. . . . Add to all this, that our lives depend upon a single thread; and if wherever we are in the world we are to expect death every hour and to be prepared for it, this is particularly the case here." This was no exaggeration. After years of effort the Jesuits managed to establish a successful mission among the Hurons, one of the less nomadic tribes. But in 1648, just when years of religious work seemed to be achieving some results, the Iroquois attacked Huronia and within two years had wiped out mission, missionaries and Hurons. The martyrdom of Brébeuf and his brethren at Huronia, however, only increased the zeal of the Jesuit missionaries as they, like the tiny colony of New France, struggled against the hardships and dangers of the New World.

The heroic years from 1608 to 1663 were precarious ones for the colony. It suffered neglect and indifference from France and almost constant siege from the Iroquois. But somehow, with its 2,500 settlers spread out in a thin line in the areas surrounding Quebec, Three Rivers and, the most dangerous outpost of all, Montreal, it survived.

2. FOUNDATION OF THE AMERICAN COLONIES

A serious threat to the existence of New France was the growing power of the English colonies to the south. Like France, Britain had begun her colonizing venture early in the seventeenth century. Her first colony, Virginia, had been established in 1607, and, like New France, it was first ruled by a company of merchant adventurers. Settlers in Virginia found life difficult; they had expected to discover gold and acquire quick fortunes but they found instead the backbreaking labour of cultivating the soil. Tobacco, however, was soon developed into a staple export, and a lucrative source of income.

The charter of Virginia contained one clause of great significance for the development of the English colonies. All Englishmen in the colony, it said, "should have and enjoy all liberties, franchises and immunities . . . as if they had been abiding and born within this our realm of England." By 1619 a representative assembly known as the House of Burgesses had been established in Virginia. Thus from the earliest years of settlement, English colonists, unlike their French counterparts, enjoyed a form of government in which they could express their views about local matters. Even after Virginia was transformed from a chartered Company colony into a Royal colony in 1624, it was able to preserve and even strengthen the powers of the House of Burgesses.

Virginia was only one of several types of colonies that Englishmen established in America. The colony of Massachusetts was strikingly different from Virginia in both origin and organization. Primarily it grew out of the determination of English Puritans to escape the control of the Anglican Church in England and to build a society on the basis of their own religious principles, ruled by what they called "godly magistrates." In 1620 a dissenting religious group, the Pilgrims, some of whom had lived for eleven to twelve years in Holland, landed on the rocky shores of New England from their weather-beaten ship, the *Mayflower*. Nine years later the basis of a larger Puritan settlement was laid when wealthy English Puritans obtained a charter for the Company of Massachusetts Bay. By 1640, 25,000 persons had joined in the "Great Migration" to New England. The arrival of these religious dissenters in New England was in sharp contrast to the exclusion of dissenters in New France which was purposely maintained as a Roman Catholic colony.

The Puritans' objective was to establish a community where they could freely practise their religious beliefs. In Massachusetts the primary test for full citizenship became membership in the Puritan church. Within these limits—and they were narrow, for the Puritans did not tolerate differences of religious opinion—Massachusetts practised self-government free from outside control. The chief executive of the colony was the governor, elected by the board of directors. The charter, however, provided for the establishment of a "general court" which allowed for popular participation in government. In addition, Massachusetts pioneered in the development of local government, for each settlement had its "town meeting" where citizens gathered to discuss and settle local affairs. By the mid-seventeenth century Massachusetts was a thriving colony. While the rocky lands of New England were not well suited to farming, access to the sea meant that agricultural produce would be supplemented with fish. More important, such access gave energetic Puritan merchants an opportunity to join in the profitable trade which grew up between America, the West Indies and Great Britain.

Not everyone found the tight Puritan rule of Massachusetts to his liking. Roger Williams was one of those who resisted the strict standards of religious orthodoxy for citizenship. He insisted that the state and the church should be separated for they were concerned with quite different matters. All men, regardless of religious belief, should be allowed to participate in civil affairs, he argued, while the church should be restricted only to the chosen few, or "saints" as the Puritans called the converted. After a bitter dispute with the ruling oligarchy in Massachusetts, Williams was forced to flee and he organized a new colony at Providence, Rhode Island. In 1644 Williams obtained a charter for the colony of Rhode Island. The new colony's liberality was well described in the vigorous seventeenth-century prose of Williams himself: "We have long drunk the cup of as great liberties as any people we can hear of under the whole of heaven. We have not only been long free . . . from the iron yoke of the wolfish bishops, and Popish ceremonies. . . . We have not felt the new chains of Presbyterian tyrants, nor in this colony have we been consumed with the over-zealous fire of (so-called) godly Christian Magistrates." The separation of church and state made religious toleration possible, and this policy was accompanied by a governmental structure which permitted the popular election of the governor and barred no one from public life on religious grounds.

Protestants were not the only religious group which sought the freedom to live according to their beliefs in America. Roman Catholics found life in seventeenth-century England as insecure as did the Puritans. In 1634 the Roman Catholic nobleman, Lord Baltimore, made proprietor of a large tract of land by Charles I, began settling Catholic colonists in

A painting by G. H. Boughton shows Pilgrims going to church. The Pilgrim colony at Plymouth, started in 1620, grew very slowly, while the wealthier Puritan colony at Massachusetts Bay expanded rapidly. Finally, in 1691, Plymouth became part of Massachusetts Bay.

Maryland. Actually, the colony which was designed as a haven for Roman Catholics soon attracted settlers of various religious groups. In 1649 the Maryland Assembly passed a toleration act, which, with the exception of the years from 1654-58, remained in force throughout the colonial period. Although the act guaranteed religious toleration the Roman Catholics did suffer from political discrimination.

Thus, unlike New France, the English colonies in America exhibited a wide variation in origin, government, economic activity and religious policy. By the middle of the eighteenth century thirteen separate colonies had sprung up in America under loose British supervision. Some were founded on company charters, some were proprietary like Maryland, but most were or became Royal colonies with governors directly appointed by the Crown. Variety was equally characteristic of their economic life for tobacco, hemp, furs, agriculture, shipbuilding and overseas trade all contributed to the British colonies' well-being and economic growth. Despite these differences, however, all the English colonies had one feature in common which clearly distinguished them from their French rival. This feature was the measure of self-government which each British colony enjoyed. By the eighteenth century their assemblies, while by no means democratic in their composition, jealously guarded the rights they had been granted, and in some cases extended those rights to limit the powers of the governors and of the British government in North America. But as long as the French lay to the north and the colonies remained divided and economically dependent upon Britain, the British settlements in North America showed no desire to free themselves completely from the loose control of the motherland.

3. THE GROWTH AND EXPANSION OF NEW FRANCE

By the end of the seventeenth century France and England had become the chief colonial powers in North America. The Dutch, who had established themselves on the Hudson River, had been squeezed out by England in 1664. To the south, the Spanish had also found it impossible to maintain their extensive claims in the face of British expansion into the Carolinas and the establishment of French posts in Louisiana. The major question in the first half of the eighteenth century was whether the French and English could co-exist in North America, or whether one power would succeed in dominating the continent. Already by the beginning of the century conflict was growing serious. As French traders and explorers moved westward to the Great Lakes and then southward down the Ohio valley and the Mississippi River, the English colonists began to fear that they would be forever hemmed in on the Atlantic seaboard. Particularly bitter was the growing struggle for control of the fur trade carried on first between the Dutch and then the British merchants with their headquarters at Albany on the Hudson River, and the French merchants working out of Montreal.   After 1670 the French were faced with a new British threat, for in that year the British established themselves on Hudson Bay and reached out to gather in furs from the many Indian tribes living along the rivers, lakes and streams that spread out from the Bay.   But the greatest conflict emerged between Montreal and Albany.   Here the French had the advantage of the splendid natural transportation system of the St. Lawrence.   But they also suffered from the disadvantage of the hostility of the powerful and ferocious Iroquois who were allied with the traders on the Hudson River.   By 1663 New France was on the verge of extinction. Its population remained small, and the Iroquois had placed the colony in a virtual state of siege.   Only outside assistance could save it.

As Louis XIV turned his ambitious eye to the extension of French power and influence in Europe, he recognized the potential of his struggling colony in North America.   Under the influence of his brilliant minister, Jean-Baptiste Colbert, he decided in 1663 to take over full responsibility for the colony's affairs by placing it directly under the Crown.   A new, Royal government was established with a sovereign council led by three powerful figures: the governor, the intendant, and the bishop.   Now for a brief period the colony received the attention and assistance it required.   French troops were dispatched to North America and the Indian menace was temporarily ended.   Jean Talon, appointed the first Intendant, began a programme of vigorous colonization and inaugurated schemes for diversifying the colony's economy.   After the fur trade, agriculture became the most important economic activity, and the one which attracted new settlers.   Talon also made efforts to construct mills, build roads, open small mines, and provide such necessities as forges, bakeries and brick kilns.

In 1672 Talon returned to France and Louis XIV began to lose interest in his colony; New France was once more thrown back upon its own resources for survival.   By that time its population had grown to 9,000, and about 20,000 acres of land had been brought under cultivation.   But the fur trade was still the colony's economic mainstay.   Essential as it was, the trade weakened the colony.   Every year as many as three or four hundred young men went out from the colony to become "coureurs-de-bois" and to engage in the fur trade.   None of the government measures to prevent this damaging exodus of the colony's young men proved successful, both because the fur trade promised the coureurs-de-bois a life of riches and adventure and because the fur trade continued to remain the basis of New France's economic life.

The fur trade also weakened the colony in another way: it fostered disputes among the governing officials of the colony.   The Roman Catholic Church was suspicious of the fur-traders, for the priests believed that the Indians were corrupted by the gay, free-living coureurs-de-bois.   What was worse, the traders, to compete with the cheap goods and rum offered the Indians by the English, gave the Indians brandy in return for furs.   Under the leadership of the strong-willed Bishop Laval the Church repeatedly attempted to stop the brandy trade. But the Intendant, on his part, was eager to expand the colony's trade and he accepted the fur-traders' argument that if they didn't sell the Indians brandy the English would, and would thereby take away much of New France's fur trade. Thus he not only refused to help the Bishop end the brandy trade; he actually encouraged it. The endless quarrels between the Bishop and Intendant, arising on many occasions from the fur trade, weakened the colony at a time when only a united front could ensure its safety.

A final threat to the colony inherent in the fur trade was the trader's irresistible tendency to expand. As fur-traders and explorers pushed farther inland to find the best furs, they met increasing hostility from the British and their Iroquois allies; for as they moved inland the French fur-traders found themselves in closer and closer competition with the English fur-traders who were also moving inland in the search for better furs.

4. ANGLO-FRENCH RIVALRY

By the end of the seventeenth century Britain, as France had earlier, was showing a greater interest in her colonies, for the political and religious problems which had torn her apart in the middle years of the century had been settled by the Glorious Revolution of 1689 and Britain was free to embark on a career of commercial and territorial expansion. Yet even before the end of the century Britain had attempted to bring some order into her colonial affairs by adopting a series of laws governing Imperial commercial activities. These Navigation Acts were based on the economic theory known as mercantilism whose object was to promote the power of the mother country by developing colonies and confining their trade within the Empire thereby making the mother country economically self-sufficient. Beginning as early as 1620 and continuing into the years before the American Revolution, the British government passed laws which prohibited the colonies from selling goods to foreign countries or transporting their products in foreign ships. In the seventeenth and early eighteenth centuries these laws were undoubtedly beneficial to both Britain and the colonies for they not only ensured Britain's control over colonial commerce, but they guaranteed a market for the colonies' expanding production.

Britain's growing interest in her North American colonies during the last years of the seventeenth century was a symptom of the deepening European rivalry between France and Britain at the end of the seventeenth century. Both countries were anxious to defend and ambitious to extend their commercial and political power. Their colonies in North America quickly became part of a global competition that stretched from Europe to India; indeed, their fate depended upon the outcome of that struggle. In North America the odds against the French were higher, for their population was small and spread over a vast area that was dangerously open to attack from both land and sea. Nevertheless, throughout the latter years of the seventeenth century New France was able to defend her position. Yet the little French community was disastrously weakened not only by the increasing indifference of the mother country but by the rapidly growing power of the English colonies. Despite her heroic efforts to spread her influence westward along the St. Lawrence and southward down the Ohio valley, New France found herself increasingly hemmed in by the British in New England and New York to the south and on Hudson Bay to the north. In 1713, at the close of the War of the Spanish Succession, Britain's encirclement of New France was further extended when Acadia (Nova Scotia) was ceded to the British.

For another four decades New France managed to continue its precarious existence. Internally it developed at a quickened pace and largely on its own initiative. The amount of land under cultivation doubled and by 1719 the wheat crop reached 234,000 bushels and the colony was able to balance her trade with France. A few other industries, such as lumbering, small-scale shipbuilding and flour milling contributed a small amount to the colony's economic life. A high birth-rate caused the population to jump from 42,000 in 1720 to around 70,000 in 1758. But the fur trade still remained the life-blood of the colony. Every year competition with the British fur-traders grew more bitter. Finally, in 1744, war in Europe between Britain and France spread to the New World. The main target of the British in North America was the impressive fortress of Louisbourg which the French had constructed on Cape Breton Island following their loss of Nova Scotia to the British in 1713. The fortress represented a serious threat to the New England fishermen and the English colonists were naturally eager to destroy it. In 1745 that objective was achieved, at least temporarily. But by the treaty of Aix-la-Chapelle, which ended the war three years later, Louisbourg was returned to France in return for Madras, a city the French had taken from the British in India. The treaty of 1748 was, however, a truce rather than a real peace settlement, and during the following decade both sides engaged in war preparations.

5. THE SEVEN YEARS' WAR

In North America during the years of uneasy peace there was sporadic warfare along the undefined border which separated French from English colonies. By 1755 this border warfare once more exploded into open conflict, despite the existence of an official peace between Britain and France in Europe. When the war broke out the British took a harsh step to consolidate their position: the deportation of between six and ten thousand French-speaking Acadians who lived in Nova Scotia. These quiet but determined agrarian people refused to take an oath of allegiance which involved a promise to fight against France. Unwilling to accept a promise of neutrality from the Acadians the British authorities herded them onto ships and carried them to the southern colonies where many of them suffered extreme hardships. This tragic story, one of the most brutal events in the history of Britain's relations with the French in North America, formed the basis of the American poet Longfellow's poem "Evangeline."

The deportation of the Acadians was merely a prelude to official declaration of war between Britain and France in Europe and America. In 1756 the Seven Years' War was officially begun and North America became a major battleground. Indeed, William Pitt, the British Prime Minister, shrewdly recognized that France's greatest area of weakness was her American colonies and he determined to destroy the French empire overseas while Britain's European allies held France in check on the continent.

In 1756 the French commander in New France, Montcalm, had only 6,000 regulars and 10,000 militiamen under his command and he was faced with the problem of defending the long frontier of the colony. Quebec City alone was effectively fortified while the rest of the colony lay wide open to enemy attack either by the overland route from New England or down the St. Lawrence. Britain's great strength and France's great weakness in the colonial war was on the sea, for there the powerful, well-disciplined British navy was clearly master. The survival of New France depended upon massive reinforcements from the home government. But France was fighting for her life in Europe, and even when reinforcements were dispatched the troopships were turned back by the

When the British fleet was attacked by French fire-ships at Quebec in June 1759, a British officer wrote: "They were certainly the grandest fire works that can possibly be conceived, every circumstance having contributed to their awful, yet beautiful appearance; the night was serene and calm, there was no light but what the stars produced, and this was eclipsed by the blaze of the floating fires issuing from all ports and running almost as quick as thoughts up the masts and rigging." To meet the danger, the British ships lowered rowboats which took the blazing French vessels in tow, pulling them off into the current which carried them away from the sitting target.

British naval blockade. Without these reinforcements the little colony of New France could not hope to defend itself successfully.

Soon after the outbreak of war, despite the courage of the French-Canadian militia, it became apparent that the struggle was hopeless. "From all sides, dear brothers, the enemy is making immense preparation, its forces at least six times greater than ours," one Church leader announced, and the parish priests were ordered to sing the psalm, *Miserere mei Deus*. At Quebec in 1759 the British General, James Wolfe, led his army up the cliffs at the Anse-au-Foulon (Wolfe's Cove). Within five days Quebec City, the colony's major stronghold, capitulated. One year later Montreal fell into the hands of the invader. The struggle for North America had ended in the British conquest of New France.

The Division of a Continent 1763-1783

Britain's victory over France in the Seven Years' War brought nearly all of North America into the British Empire. But the competition between the colony on the St. Lawrence and the settlements to the south was not easily ended. The commercial centre of Montreal, now infused with new strength by the arrival of British capital and British traders, continued to struggle vigorously for control of the rich fur-trading areas of the western hinterland that stretched down through the Ohio valley. In this territory, as their French predecessors had, they met keen competition from the merchant groups operating out of Albany and along the Hudson River system.

The expulsion of France from the St. Lawrence area had another unexpected effect on North American affairs: it gave the American colonists a new sense of security. As long as the French represented a threat to the British colonists, the support of Great Britain was necessary to them. Now, with the French gone, the American colonists gradually lost their sense of dependence on the mother country. This growing sense of independence developed just at the time when the British government found it necessary to assert new measures of control over her Empire.

1. THE NEW IMPERIAL POLICY

For Britain, the successful conclusion of the long war with France brought two pressing needs. First, a new governmental and administrative system for her vast new territories had to be devised. Secondly, means had to be found to pay the enormous debt incurred during the war, which had risen to £140,000,000. Since nearly half of this staggering debt had been incurred in fighting the war in North America, it was not surprising that the British government looked to the colonies for new sources of revenue. It was out of the twin needs for administrative reorganization and sources of increased revenue that a new colonial policy was born.

The outlines of the new policy were quickly revealed. The Royal

14

Proclamation of 1763 established four new provinces in the New World, all with constitutions patterned on the experience of the thirteen colonies. The new provinces of Quebec, East and West Florida, and Grenada in the West Indies were each given a royal governor, an appointed executive council, and an elective assembly. (It is worthy of note that in Quebec the promise of an elective assembly was not kept.) Though the political settlement seemed satisfactory, many people in the thirteen colonies objected strenuously to the new territorial divisions, for the Proclamation drew a line running along the Ottawa River and down the crest of the Appalachians, and decreed that land sales and settlement beyond that line were forbidden until an agreement had been reached with the Indian tribes in the area. To traders, land-hungry settlers and speculators in the thirteen colonies, this plan had the appearance of a plot to turn this rich area into a preserve for the British and Canadian traders working out of Montreal.

If these new political divisions were obnoxious to many colonists, the programme for financing the North American empire and controlling its trade was even more so. The Navigation Acts had been fairly easily evaded prior to 1763, but now the Royal Navy was instructed to enforce them rigidly, and new courts were established in the colonies to try smugglers. Moreover, in order to raise one-third of the cost of maintaining 10,000 regular troops in the colonies for their defence, the British government began experimenting with new revenue acts. When the colonists failed to respond to British requests for suggestions as to the best method of contributing to their own defence, the British parliament passed a Stamp Act in 1765. The Act required that in the North American colonies revenue stamps be purchased and affixed to all legal documents, pamphlets and several other categories of business paper. Compared to taxation in England, this tax was very low. On the other hand, it was the first tax to be levied directly on the colonists by the British parliament.

At once colonial lawyers, businessmen and legislators protested that as Englishmen they could not be taxed by any legislature in which they were not represented. Their ringing cry "no taxation without representation" drew much support from farmers who constituted nine-tenths of the colonial population. In fact, the customs laws had involved taxation, but the colonists argued that these had been primarily for trade regulation, and that direct taxation was a different matter. Actually, the colonists did not want representation in the British parliament where they would always have been outvoted; what they wanted was to avoid both British taxation and responsibility for their own defence.

At a Stamp Act Congress in New York, delegates from nine of the colonies drew up a list of grievances and rights which they forwarded to London with a request for repeal of the Act. At the same time, non-importation agreements became popular in the colonies and groups calling themselves Sons of Liberty intimidated anyone who purchased British imports. Many royal officials, especially customs collectors, had their houses ransacked, their belongings stolen and their bodies tarred and

Philadelphia was the largest of the colonial towns, with a population of 25,000 on the eve of the Revolution. Its buildings and its trade already rivalled those of the leading towns in England.

feathered. This violence, together with the severe financial losses suffered by British merchants as a result of the boycott, caused parliament to repeal the Stamp Act.

Another device to raise revenue was tried in 1767, when the Townshend Acts placed special though not heavy duties on imports into the colonies of paint, tea, lead and glass. Although these duties were not "direct taxes" the revenue from them was to be used to pay royal officials in the colonies. Colonists, now deeply suspicious, saw tyranny lurking in this plan which they interpreted as an effort to remove judges and governors from dependence upon colonial legislatures for their salaries. Once again non-importation agreements were arranged among the colonists and smuggling became more widespread than ever. To reinforce the law, Britain sent extra troops to Boston in 1770. When a small detachment of these troops was taunted and snowballed by a crowd of Boston townsfolk, the soldiers opened fire, killing four of their tormentors and wounding several others. At once news of the "Boston Massacre" spread through the colonies, and in London it became clear that rebellion rather than revenue would result from further attempts to collect the new duties.

The Townshend duties were repealed in 1770 except for a three-penny tax on tea. Nevertheless, enforcement of the Navigation Acts was strengthened and throughout the colonies tempers flared as royal officials used general search warrants in their tireless search for smuggled goods.

Opposition to British policy, already well established, was further stimulated by the ingenious activities of Samuel Adams of Boston. Adams
established Committees of Correspondence so that scattered Massachusetts
towns could keep each other posted on the latest grievances as well as
on methods of resistance. Soon there were intercolonial correspondence
committees, then a central co-ordinating committee, and colonial leaders
became accustomed to working in concert. Adams, who was genuinely
dedicated to democracy, was found useful by merchants who were rather
more interested in loosening trade restrictions than in political thought.
Impecunious himself, he suddenly found his affluent backers ready to
supply him with the elegant clothes necessary for his new intercolonial
organizing work.

2. BACKGROUND TO REVOLUTION

Despite undercurrents of agitation there was relative calm
in the colonies for three years following 1770. Many prosperous merchants had been worried by the outbursts of mob violence. While they were
prepared to protest constitutionally they did not care to risk a rebellion
which might imperil their own property or even introduce a more radical
form of democracy. In 1773, however, another Imperial crisis induced
many men of property in the colonies to think once again of lawless action.
In that year the British government took drastic steps to save the great
East India Company from bankruptcy and thus safeguard an important
source of revenue. To bolster the Company's sagging finances, the government granted it the privilege of importing tea into the American colonies
without paying the customs duties normally levied in England when tea
was trans-shipped for the colonies. With this privilege the Company's
agents could sell tea in the colonies, even after paying the threepenny
Townshend tax, more cheaply than could any colonial importer. So
violent was the colonial merchants' reaction to the Tea Act that not a
single case of East India tea was landed. In Maryland, the Company's
ship was burned. At Boston, importers organized a gang of rowdies,
painted them to resemble Mohawks, and led them on board three tea
ships at anchor in the harbour. All the chests were dumped into the
December waters in one huge "tea party."

When news of the Boston outrage reached England early in 1774,
punitive legislation—which came collectively to be called the "Intolerable
Acts"—was quickly enacted. The port of Boston was closed until damages had been paid, the Massachusetts charter was suspended and town
meetings forbidden. In addition, officials accused of murder while enforcing the law were to be tried not in colonial courts, but in England, where
they were likely to receive easy sentences. At the same time, the Quebec
Act was passed by the British government. Although it had been long in
preparation and was designed to reconcile French Canada to the conquest,
the Act also had important meaning for the colonists south of the St.

This English illustration, which depicts the members of the Continental Congress as provincial bumpkins, reveals the lack of understanding which existed between the colonies and the mother country. It is interesting to compare this view with that of a French immigrant who wrote of his new country in 1782: "A pleasing uniformity of decent competence appears throughout our habitations. . . . Lawyer or merchant are the fairest titles our towns afford; that of farmer is the only appellation of the rural inhabitants of our country. . . . Our dictionary . . . is . . . short in words of dignity, and names of honour. . . . We have no princes, for whom we toil, starve, and bleed: we are the most perfect society now existing in the world."

Lawrence. Indeed, their darkest suspicions were aroused by three of its provisions. The Act extended the boundaries of Quebec to include the Ohio valley; it thus seemed to make permanent the exclusion of American colonists from that area, which had been decreed as a temporary measure in the Proclamation of 1763. Furthermore, the Act established for Quebec a provincial constitution which made no provisions for a legislative assembly and thus seemed to threaten colonial liberties. Finally, colonial leaders noted with horror that the hated Roman Catholic Church was to be recognized in the huge new province of Quebec.

Although Massachusetts was the centre of opposition to the "Intolerable Acts," other colonists rallied to the cause in the belief that all colonial liberties were in question. Twelve of the colonies sent representatives to a Continental Congress which assembled in Philadelphia in 1774. This first Continental Congress debated colonial problems for seven weeks, produced a stirring Declaration of Rights, and issued appeals to the King and people of Britain for redress of grievances. The petitions were rejected in England, while in the colonies radical spokesmen such as John Adams of Massachusetts and Patrick Henry of Virginia led in establishing a tight non-importation agreement known as The Association. Other leaders such as Samuel Adams and John Hancock began organizing

A crowd in New York tears down a statue of George III during an anti-Loyalist demonstration. In his best-selling **Common Sense**, Tom Paine expressed the prevalent mood: "Of more worth is one honest man to society, and in the sight of God, than all the crowned ruffians that ever lived." A New York newspaper reported in 1775 that a mob brought a suspected Loyalist "under the liberty pole and told him to go down on his knees and damn his Popish King George." When the Loyalist instead exclaimed, "God bless King George!" the mob "dragged him through the green, tore the clothes off his back, and robbed him of his watch."

colonial militia soldiers as "minute-men," and collecting stores of arms and ammunition. At Lexington and Concord, near Boston, British regular troops seized some of these stores, but were driven back upon Boston by colonial snipers. Although with wiser statesmanship and better communications war might still have been averted, this skirmish was in fact the opening battle of the War of American Independence.

3. THE AMERICAN REVOLUTION

One month after the skirmish at Lexington the second Continental Congress assembled at Philadelphia in May 1775. The Congress appointed George Washington, lately a colonel in the British colonial army, to command a Continental army, and issued a Declaration of the Causes and Necessity of Taking up Arms. The Declaration recounted the sins of the British parliament in taxing without representation, denying jury trial, permitting general search warrants, suspending constitutions and sealing off the West. It added:

We have received certain intelligence, that General Carleton, the Governor of Canada, is instigating the people of that province and the Indians to fall upon us. . . . We are reduced to the alternative of chusing an unconditional submission to the tyranny of irritated ministers, or resistance by force. The latter is our choice.

Although radical leaders were already pressing for independence of the American colonies, they did not gain a majority in the Continental Congress until early in 1776. Declarations continued to profess loyalty to Britain and to depict the armed resistance as being aimed at redress of grievances only. So slight was the demand for independence that while Washington's slowly growing army skirmished with British troops at many places, a toast to the King was drunk nightly in his officers' mess. After the failure of a desperate American assault on Quebec in December 1775, and in view of the indifference of most French- and English-speaking Canadians to appeals from the Continental Congress to permit themselves to be liberated, colonial radicals grew more insistent that the blood already shed must be justified by the achievement of independence. The radical cause was immensely aided by the appearance in January 1776, of a fire-eating pamphlet, *Common Sense*, by an English radical named Tom Paine.

Recently arrived from England, Paine was an extreme democrat. Written with a minimum of logic and a maximum of rhetoric, his pamphlet swept through the colonies and whipped up sympathy for the independence movement:

There is something very absurd in supposing a Continent to be perpetually governed by an island. . . . Of more worth is one honest man to society, and in the sight of God, than all the crowned ruffians that ever lived. . . . O ye that love mankind! Ye that dare oppose not only the tyranny but the tyrant, stand forth!

The Continental Congress, already angered by the growing numbers of hired German mercenaries in the British army in the colonies, and aware that foreign aid would be needed by Washington's army, took the fateful step in July, 1776. Hoping to attract French support by planning complete separation from the British Empire, and anxious to build greater intercolonial unity by defining its goals clearly and dramatically, Congress adopted a Declaration of Independence on July 4. The chief author of the Declaration was Thomas Jefferson of Virginia. At thirty-three this brilliant planter-lawyer was already noted for his literary style. He couched his argument in the popular philosophical terms of the eighteenth century, the terms of natural law and natural rights:

We hold these truths to be self-evident: That all men are created equal; that they are endowed by their Creator with certain unalienable rights; that among these are life, liberty, and the pursuit of happiness; that to secure these rights, governments are instituted among men, deriving their just powers from the consent of the governed; that whenever any

George Washington is portrayed here in heroic terms, encouraging his troops during the War of Independence. His achievement was the result of perseverance and consideration of the needs of his ragged, unpaid and underfed army. During the gruelling winter of 1777-78, shivering in winter quarters at Valley Forge outside Philadelphia, he fumed as the local farmers sold their produce at good prices to General Howe's British force comfortably lodged in the town.

form of government becomes destructive of these ends, it is the right of the people to alter or to abolish it, and to institute new government, laying its foundations on such principles, and organizing its powers in such form, as to them shall seem most likely to effect their safety and happiness. . . .

At one leap the Congress removed its case from one based upon the rights of Englishmen to one based upon the rights of man. Justifying this radical position by a philosophy of government which stemmed from the Englishman John Locke, the Declaration went on to list all the grievances, real and imagined, of the preceding years and to lay *all* of these at the door of George III. Having insisted for ten years that their allegiance was to the King, not parliament, the colonists had now decided to break even their connection with the Crown. The same session that approved the great Declaration also appointed a committee to travel to France to seek an alliance against Britain, and in 1778 Louis XVI signed a Franco-American treaty which bound each party to assist the other if attacked by Britain.

The War of Independence was also a civil war. Opinion in the colonies was divided about equally three ways among the radicals, or patriots, who controlled the Continental Congress; the Loyalists, or Tories, who remained loyal to Britain; and the uncommitted. Most of the Tories hoped to ride out the storm without losing their property; the rest left for England or took refuge in Quebec and Nova Scotia.

Immediately following the Declaration of Independence, colonial legislatures adopted new constitutions as independent states. The new states continued to send delegates to the Continental Congress, which was the central body responsible for directing the military resistance to Britain. The outstanding leader in the war was George Washington who, through the most distressing days and with completely inadequate supplies, kept an army in the field. Congress, lacking direct taxing powers, had to rely on state contributions, and on bonds issued to finance the war. Few states responded fully to requests for money, supplies or men.

Fortunately for the colonists, inadequate British leadership prevented the Empire from using its vastly superior naval and military resources against the disorganized colonial forces. In 1778 the colonial cause won support from France and Spain, and Holland soon joined with them, all three countries hoping to gain revenge for earlier defeats at British hands. In 1780 the French landed an army of six thousand in Rhode Island. In 1781, with the American treasury empty, disunity and suspicion rampant among the states, and desertions from the Continental army frequent, the decisive battle of the war was launched. The British General, Cornwallis, allowed himself to become hemmed in at Yorktown on Chesapeake Bay. There he expected to receive reinforcements from the Royal Navy. Instead, the French fleet successfully blockaded the harbour, while the combined French and American armies overwhelmed the beleaguered British forces. The victory at Yorktown put the seal on colonial independence. Although the war dragged on for another year and a half, the British government, disgraced by its handling of the war, was replaced by a ministry which favoured peace negotiations with the victorious colonies.

At Paris, the scene of the peace negotiations, the British and American negotiators met secretly to arrange a settlement. The Americans, Benjamin Franklin, John Adams and the brilliant New Yorker, John Jay, knew that the terms of their alliance with France prohibited negotiation by either ally of a separate peace settlement with Britain. However, they suspected that France had designs on the trans-Allegheny West, and they therefore outmanœuvred the French by signing a separate treaty with Britain.

In the Treaty of Paris, signed in 1783, the British agreed to a generous settlement. Their magnanimity flowed from a desire to re-establish their lucrative American trade, and to prevent the Franco-American alliance from becoming a permanent feature of world politics. Moreover, the British Whig government, which was responsible for the negotiations, was composed of men who had always been critical of the unbending Tory policies which, they claimed, had led to the American Revolution. By the treaty Britain recognized the independence of the colonies and ceded to them territory reaching from the Atlantic to the Mississippi and from Florida to the Great Lakes. The Floridas were not included, only because they had been recaptured by the Spanish forces during the war. In return for these concessions the Treaty committed the independent colonies to recommend earnestly to the various state governments that steps be taken to restore property confiscated from Loyalists, as those who had retained their allegiance to the Crown were called, and to place no obstacles in the path of Loyalists who sought repayment of debts owing to them.   The inability of the American Congress to fulfil this undertaking was to prove cause of serious Anglo-American friction in the future.

It remained for the Americans to organize, defend and develop their expansive continental empire.   No new nation had ever benefited more from the coincidence of European rivalries, nor had any stripling state been more eager to exploit its legacy.   Even before the war had ended, plans for the future were being laid, and if there was no unanimity about the shape of the future nation, the very multiplicity of plans and ambitions bespoke a formidable vigour.

CHAPTER 1

The Supreme Law
of the Land

The Treaty of Paris in 1783 ended the American War of Independence, but the survival of an independent United States of America was still very much in doubt. Old problems remained to plague the new nation. How were the Americans going to govern themselves? Would the central government and the new state governments, all extremely jealous of their independence, be able to establish a workable relationship? Would the Americans now really have free access to the trans-Appalachian West? If so, what authority would control that vast region? Would the United States government be strong enough to deal with great powers like Britain, France and Spain in disputes over trade and territories? In short, was the United States of America genuinely a new nation or was it a collection of thirteen separate states only loosely joined together? Between 1783 and 1789 American statesmen answered most of these questions.

1. THE ARTICLES OF CONFEDERATION

The first American federal constitution had been drafted by a committee appointed by the Continental Congress of 1777. The resulting constitution, the Articles of Confederation, was described by their principal author as a "firm league of friendship." With the Articles of Confederation the Americans embarked on a new and dynamic experiment in government; for the Articles created a federal union of states in which the citizens of the thirteen states were to have two governments, one for all the states combined and one for the state in which they lived. Although that constitution gave a considerable number of powers to the central government, it provided little power of enforcement. Under the Articles, there was a Congress which was composed of delegates from the states and was empowered to deal with foreign and interstate affairs, the post office, and public lands. But Congress was given no taxing power and therefore had to rely upon state levies both for defence and general revenue. In addition, there were no national courts and no clearly defined executive branch to put the laws of Congress

24

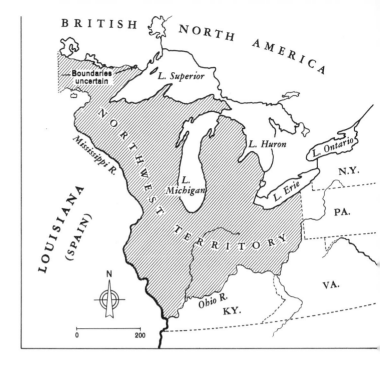

The
Northwest
Territories
In 1787

into effect. Moreover, since each state delegation in Congress had only one vote, and the enactment of important bills required a two-thirds majority, speedy transaction of business was almost impossible. Finally, amendments to the Articles themselves required a unanimous vote in Congress, but every proposed amendment found at least one of the thirteen states opposed.

In spite of these weaknesses, the Confederation Congress, that is, the Congress that came into being as a result of the Articles of Confederation, was not totally unsuccessful. It handled the problems of the West with efficiency and remarkable foresight. In 1785 it passed a Land Ordinance which provided that western lands should be surveyed in an orderly fashion and the proceeds from their sale be used to pay off the national debt. The surveyors were to divide the land into townships six miles square, with each township divided into thirty-six sections of one square mile each. In each township the money derived from selling the sixteenth section was to be used for founding public schools. Thus the Ordinance not only established a useful pattern for later western expansion, but guaranteed the early development of public education, and secured the land titles of the first settlers. Canada later adopted a very similar system in the surveying of her prairie West.

Even more significant for the future was the Northwest Ordinance of 1787 which dealt with the problem of government in the public domain. The 1787 Ordinance decreed that the Northwest Territory should never be open to slavery and that the pioneers should be granted self-government as soon as the population was sufficiently large. Not more than five nor less than three states were to be created there, and Congress might admit any of them into the Union "on an equal footing with the original states in all respects whatever," whenever the population of the particular region reached 60,000 free inhabitants. The Ordinance, which was the American answer to Britain's old Imperial problem of how to govern weak, unsettled areas, continued to be upheld by succeeding American governments.

But despite its successful western settlement policy, the Confederation Congress could not provide security against Indians on the frontiers, or against the threat posed by Spanish territorial claims to the south or the presence of British traders and troops in American fur-trading areas. Nor was it able to offer any naval protection for American commerce on the high seas. It could not effectively regulate trade between the states and foreign countries, or even among the various states themselves. Moreover, since Congress lacked the power to control currency, and since any bank could issue its own currency, money values fluctuated wildly and it became difficult to plan interstate business. While most farmers were satisfied with the slow economic growth which was inevitable under these conditions, businessmen were deeply concerned about the missed opportunities for expansion. Many blamed too weak a national government for the country's troubled and slow economic development. Some men even feared that without a stronger central government the entire federal experiment would collapse.

People who entertained such fears were particularly concerned about the public credit. Since first the Continental and later the Confederation Congress lacked taxing power, each had had to borrow large amounts of money. The bonds which represented the government's promise to repay these loans were held by merchants and bankers. By 1784 the government had issued more than $40,000,000 worth of bonds, but was unable to pay even the interest on them. In addition, state governments, which had issued $20,000,000 worth of bonds, were also in financial difficulties. In Massachusetts the problem produced a serious crisis, and an armed uprising.

At the centre of the crisis was the conflict between debtors and creditors over "hard money." The value of a dollar was measured by its gold or silver content, but the amount of coinage, or hard money, in circulation was very limited. Thus, gold and silver dollars were in short supply and of high value. Most people found it difficult to secure enough hard money to meet their obligations and argued for expansion of the money supply. In the absence of fresh gold and silver discoveries this could only be done by printing paper money which, because it did not have to be entirely redeemable in specie, made possible an expansion of the money supply. It also, however, had an inflationary effect, that is, it lowered the purchasing power (or value) of the dollar.

When the Massachusetts legislature levied a tax of twenty dollars a household (a considerable sum of money in the eighteenth century) to pay off the bonded debt, the conflict over hard money burst into the open.

Facing mortgage foreclosures and loss of their property, the already hard-pressed farmers argued that paper money should be issued to allow them to meet their debts more easily.   But creditors hated the idea of printing paper money because they would have to accept payments in currency of less value than that in circulation when they had advanced their original loans.   With the Massachusetts jails full of debtors, a rebellion formed under the leadership of Daniel Shays, a captain in the War of Independence, who now spoke for the western counties of Massachusetts. The farmers believed that the Boston businessmen who dominated the government had no right to tax them, and many decided to resist the tax collection.   Fighting between the rebels and state militia lasted from October 1786 to February 1787 when the rebellion was finally suppressed.   Although it had failed, Shays' rebellion had shocked the men of property in all the states, who realized that rebellion had a way of spreading.   To these men, a stronger national government seemed more desirable than ever.

Other matters like western expansion, trade problems, and foreign relations also seemed to require a strong central power.   American land speculators wanted the western frontier to be made secure against the Indians.   There was uneasiness also because in the southwest and the northwest Spain and England still maintained posts in territory that had been ceded to the United States by the treaty of 1783.   Manufacturers wanted protection against British goods which were flooding the American market, and merchants wanted a government strong enough to bargain with England for entry of American trade into the British West Indies. Always present, too, was the problem Benjamin Franklin voiced when he said: "We should I think be constantly on our guard and impress strongly upon our minds, that though Great Britain has made peace with us, it is not in truth reconciled either to us, or to its loss of us."   Historians have called these years the "critical period" of American history, and many contemporary Americans talked in a similar vein.   As one of them put it in 1787: "The American war is over; but this is far from being the case of the American revolution.   On the contrary, nothing but the first act of the great drama is disclosed."

2. THE NEW CONSTITUTION 1787

The second act of the great drama was the formulation of a new constitution under which Americans could more effectively rule their new nation.   In 1786 George Washington, Alexander Hamilton, John Jay, James Madison and others issued an invitation to the states to send delegates to a national convention at Philadelphia in May 1787 to discuss the problems of disunity in the country, for by 1787 the federal union was floundering.   The Confederation Congress reluctantly endorsed the invitation, stating that the convention would be "for the sole and express purpose of revising the Articles of Confederation."   The Philadelphia

This painting by J. B. Stearns shows George Washington presiding at a meeting of the Constitutional Convention. His reputation for patriotism did much to hold together the clashing interests at Philadelphia. Writing to his friend John Jay prior to this meeting, he revealed his fears and hopes: "It is much to be feared, as you observe, that the better kind of people, being disgusted with the circumstances will have their minds prepared for any revolution whatever. . . . Would to God, that wise measures may be taken in time to avert the consequences we have but too much reason to apprehend."

Convention, however, was to achieve far more than that "sole and express purpose."

Delegates to the Philadelphia Convention were generally conservative. Among them there was only one farmer; most were lawyers, plantation-owners, merchants, and bondholders. Well aware of the immense wealth and power that might be developed in North America with the help of a strong and purposeful central government, the conservative businessmen and lawyers were determined to equip their country with a framework of government that would enable it to secure the West, guard its own markets, and provide a native mercantilist system to replace that which had been lost by withdrawal from the protective British Empire. Their economic interests and sense of nationalism thus demanded a strong central government. So did their political philosophy, for most of the Fathers of American Confederation feared democracy and believed that the central government would be less likely to yield to popular demands than state governments, and, therefore, should have more power. For economic, national and political reasons, then, the Founding Fathers quickly agreed not just to amend the Articles of Confederation, but to write a new constitution.

The Virginia delegates, led by George Washington, were the first to arrive at the dignified Georgian State House in Philadelphia. They brought with them a plan for a strongly centralized government, which was not unlike that proposed for the later Canadian Confederation. It provided for a Congress of two houses to which the states would elect representatives in numbers proportionate to the size of the free (non-slave) population of each state. The great power which this "large state" plan obviously gave to the most populous states was further increased by the provision that the central government could disallow any law passed by a state legislature. Delegates from the smaller states were naturally not enthusiastic about the Virginia plan. In fact many of them (such as those from the state of Delaware which had a population of only 60,000) had been specifically instructed to oppose any plan that departed from the principle of equal representation and voting power for each state as such, regardless of its population.

The small states countered the Virginia plan with a proposal put forward by William Patterson, leader of the New Jersey delegation. The New Jersey plan retained the existing Congress with its equality of representation for states, but gave the central government power to regulate the tariff, levy its own taxes, and create an executive and judicial branch.

During the steaming June days debate on the two plans rose to fever pitch. A delegate from Delaware underlined the bitter suspicions aroused by the struggle over the issue of "equal versus proportional representation" when he warned: "The large states dare not dissolve the Confederation. If they do the small ones will find some foreign ally, of more honour and good faith, who will take them by the hand and do them justice." One delegate wrote of those days: "We were on the verge of dissolution, scarce held together by the strength of a hair."

Solution of the problem of representation in the central government came in the form of the "Great Compromise," which was worked out by a small committee along lines proposed chiefly by the aged and revered Benjamin Franklin. The compromise provided for a legislature of two houses. The lower house, or House of Representatives, was to be composed of members elected from each state on the basis of population; these members were to vote individually in the House, rather than on the old basis of one vote per state delegation. To mollify the small states, the compromise provided that the upper house, or Senate, was to be composed of two members from each state, regardless of population. In addition, the Senate was given almost as much legislative power as the House of Representatives, as well as certain special powers of considerable importance so that the small states would be assured of an effective voice in the government.

To some extent James Madison, one of the Virginia delegates, was right when he noted that the real division among the delegates of the Convention of 1787 "did not lie between the large and small states; it lay between the Northern and the Southern." This division was between people who drew their wealth from different kinds of property. Many

Northern businessmen wanted the central government to be able to foster industry by protective tariffs, and to regulate and encourage trade by other means. Southern planters, however, wished to remain free to buy and sell in whatever world markets were most advantageous to them, and felt that tariffs would restrict rather than extend their trade. Moreover, they were fearful that the federal government would use its powers over trade and commerce to interfere with the Southern slave trade. After bitter and prolonged debates on these topics, the delegates reached another compromise. The South agreed to give Congress control over commerce in return for a guarantee, written into the Constitution, that the slave trade would not be interfered with before 1808.

The Southern slave owners argued that slaves should be counted as property rather than as people for purposes of assessing direct federal taxes, which were to be levied in the states according to population. But state representation in the House of Representatives was also to be in proportion to population, and for this purpose the Southerners wanted the slaves to be counted as people. Here again a compromise saved the day. In any state, three-fifths of the slave population were to be used in determining both taxes and congressional representation. By another compromise the South secured a clause requiring free states to return fugitive slaves to their masters. These clauses were to become extremely important in later disputes, for they enabled Southerners to claim that the Constitution recognized slaves as property and thus that the federal government had a duty to safeguard the Southerners' right to hold slaves.

Most important, perhaps, of all the debates at Philadelphia were those concerning the nature of the American federal system. Every federation must be a compromise between those who desire a strong centralized government to serve the national interest and those who favour decentralized government to protect local interests. As the long debate over the Articles of Confederation had already revealed, on this question the American people were sharply divided. The bitter debate on the power of the central government was continued in Philadelphia.

To establish the Constitution's new and fundamental authority, its framers wrote:

> This Constitution, and the laws of the United States which shall be made in pursuance thereof; and all treaties made under the authority of the United States, shall be the *supreme law of the land.*

Despite the reservations held by many people, then and later, all else, including state laws and constitutions, were to rank below the Constitution in authority. All public officials and judges, both state and federal, would be bound by this "supreme law of the land." Under the Articles of Confederation the central government had had no real power over states or individuals. The new federal constitution provided that the states would give up many of their powers to the central government. These powers, together with the powers already possessed by the old Congress,

THE FEDERAL DIVISION OF POWERS

FEDERAL POWERS	SHARED POWERS	STATE POWERS
• Foreign relations, war and peace	• Taxation	• To establish local government
• Regulation of foreign and interstate commerce		
• To legislate on citizenship and immigration	• Borrowing of money	• To conduct elections
• To coin money		• Public education
• To operate postal system		
• To control patents and copyrights	• Establishing courts and penal laws	• To regulate business within state
• To maintain armed forces		
• To establish federal courts	• To charter banks	• Control of marriage and divorce
• To govern federal territories and admit states to Union		
		• Any power not granted to the federal government nor specifically prohibited by the Constitution
• To enact laws "necessary and proper" to carrying out its powers	• Expropriation of property in the public interest, with the just compensation	

were then "enumerated" in the Constitution as belonging exclusively to the central government, thus giving it direct power over the people of the various states. The central government was empowered to direct foreign affairs, matters of war and peace, and to regulate all commerce between the states and foreign countries as well as among the various states themselves. In addition, Congress was given sole authority to regulate the issuance of money, to raise money by taxation for federal purposes, to administer all non-state territories of the Union, and to regulate the admission of new states. To underline the amplitude of the new central powers, the Constitution declared that congressional revenues could be employed not only for the common defence and other enumerated powers, but, in a section often called the elastic clause, it provided that Congress could "make all laws which shall be necessary and proper for carrying into execution" the enumerated powers and "all other powers vested by this Constitution in the government of the United States or in any department or office thereof." Interpretations by the courts of the elastic clause and the interstate commerce clause have frequently been used to expand the powers of the central government beyond any point envisaged by even the most nationally-minded Fathers of the Constitution.

It was impossible, as it is in any federal constitution, to define beyond a shadow of a doubt the line separating central and local powers. Moreover, it was necessary to conciliate the defenders of states' rights, those men inside and outside the Convention who feared the growth of a distant central authority that might prove as despotic as they believed the British government in London to have been. Thus each state retained control over voting qualifications, education, intra-state businesses, criminal law within the state, marriage and divorce, local government institutions, and general "police powers" involving the safety and health of its citizens. Further, the Tenth Amendment to the Constitution, ratified in 1791, stated: "The powers not delegated to the United States by the Constitution, nor prohibited by it to the States, are reserved to the States respectively, or to the people." This Amendment lent weight to the views of those who, in later disputes over the balance of power within the Union, argued that the states remained sovereign and had merely delegated some powers to the federal government.

3. THE CONGRESSIONAL-PRESIDENTIAL SYSTEM

Within the central government itself no one branch was given supreme control; the system created in 1787 is said to be one of "checks and balances" or "separation of powers." One of the delegates from Massachusetts, and later President, John Adams, summed up the theory of checks and balances thus:

> A legislative, an executive, and a judicial power comprehend the whole of what is meant and understood by the government. It is by balancing each of these powers against the other two, that the efforts in human nature toward tyranny can alone be checked and restrained, and any degree of freedom preserved in the constitution.

To achieve this balance the Constitution divided the various powers within the jurisdiction of the central government among the three branches, made some powers (such as treaty-making) the joint responsibility of two branches, and created different sources for the authority of each branch— direct election, indirect election, and appointment.

The power to make federal laws was given to a Congress composed of the Senate and House of Representatives. To ensure the influence of the states in the federal government and to protect the states' rights, each state was given two members in the Senate. To make certain that the Senators would really represent the states, the Senators were to be elected by the members of the state legislatures. Senators were to remain in office for a term of six years, but to guard against too sudden changes in the Senate the terms of office were staggered, with one-third of the Senate retiring every two years. Members of the House of Representatives were to serve for two years only, and the number of Representatives for each state was to be in proportion to the population of the state.

To become law, a bill had to receive a majority vote in each house, as well as the signature of the President. Bills that required the expendi-

CHECKS AND BALANCES IN THE AMERICAN CONSTITUTION

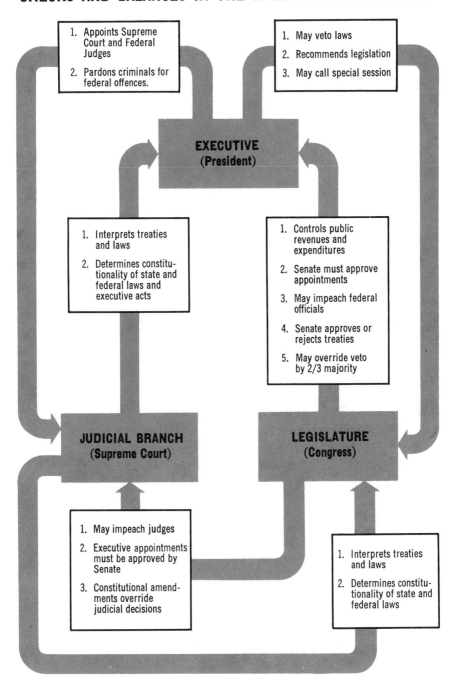

THE LEGISLATIVE PROCESS

(A bill, after being drafted by a member of Congress or a committee, is introduced either in the Senate or the House of Representatives. If it involves the raising and spending of money it must originate in the House as does the bill in this chart.)

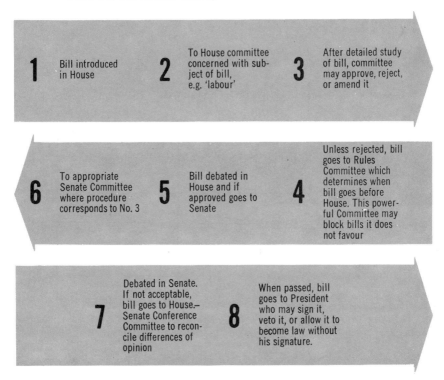

1 Bill introduced in House

2 To House committee concerned with subject of bill, e.g. 'labour'

3 After detailed study of bill, committee may approve, reject, or amend it

6 To appropriate Senate Committee where procedure corresponds to No. 3

5 Bill debated in House and if approved goes to Senate

4 Unless rejected, bill goes to Rules Committee which determines when bill goes before House. This powerful Committee may block bills it does not favour

7 Debated in Senate. If not acceptable, bill goes to House.— Senate Conference Committee to reconcile differences of opinion

8 When passed, bill goes to President who may sign it, veto it, or allow it to become law without his signature.

ture of public money had to originate in the House of Representatives, but all other bills could originate in either the House or the Senate. While the House of Representatives alone had the right to initiate money bills, the Senate also had its important special powers. It could refuse to endorse Presidential appointments of judges, diplomats and cabinet members, and no treaty could go into effect without approval by two-thirds of the Senators. Moreover, since the Senate could amend money bills it gradually came to exercise powers equal to those of the House in controlling public expenditures.

The separating and balancing of powers is most clearly seen in the office of President and in his relations with Congress. The Constitution made the President chief executive of the nation and charged him specifically with carrying out the laws of Congress and upholding the Constitution in all aspects. The President was to be chosen by state "electors" who were referred to collectively as the electoral college. The voters in each state elected a number of electoral college members equal to the number of Senators and Congressmen from that state. The electors then met in each state to ballot for a President. This provision had two objects: first, to prevent popular passions from being directly reflected in Presidential elections; and second, to enable the voters to select men from their state whom they could know and trust to charge with electing a President, because with the size of the country and the slow methods of transportation it was impossible for all the voters at that time to know and judge between rival Presidential candidates. After the establishment of political parties, however, it became the practice for candidates for the electoral college to run on "party tickets," which meant that they were committed to vote for the Presidential candidate nominated by their party.

The President's term of office was to be four years and as chief executive his powers were very great. He was commander-in-chief of the United States armed forces. He was to appoint the heads of the various executive departments of government which were charged with carrying out congressional laws: for example, he appointed the Secretary of State to head the State Department, and the Secretary of the Treasury to manage national finances. Each departmental head was to be responsible directly to the President, and collectively these men have come to be known as the President's Cabinet. The separation of powers is emphasized in the provision that neither the President nor anyone appointed to public office by the President could be a member of Congress. Thus, contrary to the British and Canadian parliamentary systems, American cabinet members were not to be able to defend their policies personally in the legislature. The President was also given large powers in defence and foreign affairs, since as well as commanding the army and navy he appointed all ambassadors and authorized the negotiation of treaties. But this power was also checked by the treaty-approving power of the Senate and by the Senators' right to withhold approval of Presidential appointments. The House, too, could severely limit any of the President's powers by refusing to vote the money to implement his policies. At the same time, the President was given the power to veto a congressional bill by returning it unsigned to the House in which it originated within ten days of receiving it. If he merely refuses to sign, the bill becomes law automatically after ten days, unless the congressional session ends in less than ten days. The latter case is known as a "pocket veto." However, if Congress repasses the vetoed legislation with a two-thirds majority in each House, the bill could become law despite the President's veto and without his signature.

The great authority of the President was enhanced by the fact that he was the only federal official in the nation to be chosen by "all the people." Furthermore, he could be removed from office before the expiration of his normal term only by the extreme procedure of impeachment. In order to do this, an indictment of the President for grave misdemeanours first had to pass the House of Representatives. Then a committee of the House would present the case before the Senate, which would act as a court to try the case. This drastic procedure has been attempted only once, in 1868, and on that occasion it failed.

The careful checking, balancing and separating of the federal government's powers reflected the determination of the framers of the Constitution to prevent any individual or "vested interest" from usurping power. Although many American observers, including some Presidents, have felt that this system inhibits effective use of national powers, most attempts to change it by amending the Constitution have failed. Succeeding generations have generally hesitated to lay hands on a system which, despite its admitted imperfections, has generally protected their basic liberties.

To judge legal cases involving the interpretation of the Constitution, and to clarify the meaning of congressional legislation, the Constitution authorized the establishment of a federal court system presided over by a Supreme Court. Under the Articles of Confederation, the central government had had to rely upon state courts, which were frequently hostile to federal policy, for the enforcement of its laws. The Supreme Court was the answer to this problem. While state courts were obliged to enforce federal laws, their decisions could now be appealed to the Supreme Court whose members were to be appointed by the President. Unlike the Canadian Supreme Court, the United States Court cannot give advisory opinions on problems referred to it by government; it judges only in actual cases arising under existing law.

While the Constitution was the supreme law of the nation, it was far from inflexible. Usage later changed many original provisions, and the document itself prescribed procedures for its own amendment. An amendment could originate as a resolution in Congress. If it passed by a two-thirds majority it was then to be sent to the various states for consideration. If three-quarters of the states ratified it, the amendment then became a part of the Constitution equal in strength to the original clauses. Although a great many amendments have been proposed over the years, only twenty-three have been ratified. The first ten of these are really a part of the original Constitution since they were promised as part of the campaign to ratify the Constitution in 1787-88. The party system has been more important than the amending procedure in making the Constitution flexible. By having representatives in both Houses of Congress, in state governments and in the Presidency, parties have considerably modified the original separation of powers. While a cabinet member may not sit in Congress, other members of his political party do sit there and, if liaison is good, help to implement Presidential policies.

At Philadelphia it was decided that the new Constitution would take effect as soon as it was ratified by at least nine of the thirteen states. At once, supporters and opponents of the Constitution began to organize their forces. In each state a convention was summoned to discuss ratification of the Constitution. The differences of opinion in these conventions were to produce two political parties whose membership was further clarified by later differences over financial and foreign policies. The supporters of ratification were called Federalists and their opponents were known as Antifederalists. The Antifederalists included supporters of states' rights, small farmers from the frontier townships, and artisans. In addition, some businessmen, worried about debts they had contracted, feared that the Federalists were conspiring to keep money in short supply and to impose heavy taxation, both of which policies would work to the advantage of creditors. The Federalists, who generally drew their supporters from the more well-to-do classes, mostly living in the older settled areas close to the seaboard, argued for stability, law and order, and the sacredness of contractual debts which they felt could be achieved only through a strong central government.

For years historians have differed about the reasons for the adoption of the Constitution. A famous American historian, Charles Beard, in his book *An Economic Interpretation of the Constitution*, argued that the men of property had triumphed over the majority of common people. It is now generally believed, however, that, as the ratification debates developed, the division of opinion reflected not only property interests but also local and sectional interests and ideas which were not necessarily the result of a person's class in society.

This was not in fact a particularly democratic age, and even those people who opposed the Constitution did not necessarily do so because it seemed to favour the rich. Nevertheless, the majority of Americans seemed to be Antifederalists and their position was well put by a farmer delegate to the Massachusetts ratifying convention:

> These lawyers and men of learning and moneyed men, that talk so finely, and gloss over matters so smoothly, to make us poor illiterate people swallow down the pill, expect to get into Congress themselves; they expect to be managers of this Constitution, and get all the power and all the money into their own hands, and then they will swallow up all us little folks, like the great leviathan, Mr. President; yes, just as the whale swallowed up Jonah. This is what I am afraid of.

Patrick Henry of Virginia typified another form of opposition to the proposed Constitution. He suspected that the Constitution was simply a device to seize power from the states, where the people were more directly influential in government, and centralize that power. "Who," he cried, "authorized them to speak the language of We, the People instead of We, the States?" This was the "states' rights" cry that was to be heard down through American history and which would eventually help to produce the bloody Civil War.

Ratification of the Constitution came largely because the Federalists had precisely the powers and advantages that the Massachusetts farmer had feared. Newspapers carried lengthy arguments in favour of the Constitution, ministers preached its virtues, and hundreds of pamphleteers supported it. The most famous of the pamphlets, known as *The Federalist*, was a collection of newspaper articles containing penetrating arguments in favour of a strong central government. The authors of *The Federalist* were John Jay, Alexander Hamilton and James Madison. Because all were "Fathers of the Constitution" and wrote from inside knowledge of the Philadelphia debates, their work has often been cited by American courts in later years to prove or disprove various interpretations of clauses in the Constitution.

In addition, the fact that very few poor men attended the ratifying conventions aided the Federalist cause. Even so, in several states the division was very close and in an effort to gain more votes for ratification some of the Federalists promised that if their conventions were to ratify the Constitution, a Bill of Rights would be added to it during the first session of the new Congress. This Bill was to be in the form of amendments to the Constitution guaranteeing specific rights to both individuals and states. The amendments would be introduced at the first session of the new Congress.

Despite the bitterest opposition, nine of the thirteen states had ratified the Constitution within four months after the Philadelphia Convention had ended in September 1787. Resistance in the key states of Virginia and New York gave way while North Carolina and Rhode Island followed soon after. While the Constitution was not, perhaps, what an English Prime Minister, W. E. Gladstone, later called it, "the most wonderful work ever struck off at a given time by the brain and purpose of man," it was a document of monumental importance. As decade followed decade, and generation succeeded generation, the work of the Philadelphia Convention assumed ever wider significance, until today it affects the destiny of the world itself.

CHAPTER **2**

Federalists and
Republicans

The choice of George Washington as first President of the
United States was unanimous, indeed almost automatic. By the time of
his inauguration on April 30, 1789 the new President could look back
on a most distinguished career in the British frontier military service, in
the long and arduous struggle to keep an army in the field during the Revolutionary War, and in the Philadelphia Convention. He was not a brilliant
man, but what he lacked in intellect he more than compensated for in his
quiet wisdom and devotion to his nation's welfare. Washington would
have preferred to remain on his peaceful estate on the Potomac rather
than to accept the office of President. As he said:

> My movement to the chair of government will be accompanied by
> feelings not unlike those of a culprit who is going to the place of his
> execution; so unwilling am I in the evening of a life nearly consumed
> in public cares to quit a peaceful abode for an ocean of difficulties.

It was certainly fortunate for the nation that a man of Washington's
temperament and lack of ambition was elected as its first President; for
Washington resisted every opportunity the novel republican experiment

A reception was held by
President and Mrs. Wash-
ington, shortly after the
election of 1789. Although
Washington liked to be
addressed as "Your Excel-
lency" Antifederalists were
mistaken when they sus-
pected him of monarchist
ambitions.

This engraving of the first American Cabinet gives some idea of the casual air of its meetings. From left to right: Knox, Jefferson, Randolph, Hamilton and Washington.

offered him to become the Cromwell or Napoleon of the American Revolution.

In the spring of 1789 the United States was in a truly critical position. The nation owed large debts both to Americans and foreigners, its trade was excluded from all British ports, pirates preyed on its ships, and its Indian frontiers were turbulent. Yet despite these problems the new government was launched with surprising leisure. On March 4, 1789 the church bells of New York rang out and the battery guns at the tip of Manhattan Island boomed their acclaim of the day appointed for the opening of the first Congress. It was a false start. Not until the first week in April had enough Senators and Representatives clattered and bumped their way to New York to provide quorums for both Houses.

Once established, however, the administration took a firm grip on the country, created governmental machinery and adopted major national policies, with a speed calculated to make up for lost time. Washington chose Thomas Jefferson as Secretary of State to deal with foreign relations, Alexander Hamilton for the Treasury, Henry Knox for War and Edmund Randolph of Virginia as Attorney-General. Although the department heads at first corresponded with the President by letter, they soon felt the need to meet together to exchange ideas and co-ordinate departmental policies. A Presidential cabinet thus came into being, although no mention was made of such a body in the Constitution.

1. HAMILTON AND THE FEDERALISTS

The thirty-three-year-old Hamilton was a dominant figure in Washington's first administration. Born in the West Indies, the illegitimate son of a French Huguenot mother and a Scottish father, he was brought to New York by an uncle who provided for his education. There, he achieved rapid success and some fame in college and at the bar. As an army colonel he had been Washington's aide during the last phase of the Revolutionary War. He was already well known as a lawyer and a student of public affairs by the time he helped organize the movement for the Constitutional Convention at Philadelphia in 1787. His share in writing the influential Federalist Papers had further enhanced his reputation. Although his faith in what he called "the rich and well-born" sat oddly on one of his origin, he nevertheless became the most eloquent spokesman in the United States of the right of the rich to govern. Always suspicious of democracy, he declared that "the people is a great beast" and that the common man "seldom determines aright." Democracy, to Hamilton, was chiefly a means of persuading the common man that the decisions of the natural leaders, or men of wealth, were best for the nation. Some years after 1789, reflecting on the Constitution, for whose adoption he had worked so hard, he described it as "a frail and worthless fabric" which would probably not last a generation, because it did not concentrate power sufficiently in the hands of the central government. In one or two crises, in exasperation, he even advocated a monarchy for the United States on British lines, and on occasion was tempted to return to the army and lead it to glory and quick power against the Spanish in the lower Mississippi valley.

Hamilton's personal code was as rigid as that which he advocated for the nation. In 1804, he was challenged to a duel by Aaron Burr, a bitter political enemy; he accepted the challenge although he disapproved of duelling. Refusing to fire, he allowed Burr's shot to end his life. Despite his premature death, Hamilton had lived long enough to leave an indelible mark on the political constitution and economic life of the United States, for this handsome and enigmatic man had formulated the major Federalist policies during George Washington's Presidency.

The most important of these policies arose from the need to deal with the huge legacy of debt from the revolutionary and confederation period. To establish the national credit, which he felt was necessary to the country's independence, he recommended paying the full value of the national debt, twelve million dollars of which was owned by foreign investors and forty million by Americans. This proposal had a two-fold aim: it would strengthen the financial credit of the United States abroad and at home, and it would secure the loyalty of the nation's businessmen to the central government. But at home most of the bonds were no longer held by their original purchasers. As the credit of the Continental and Confederation Congresses had declined, and as debtors found it more difficult to get money to repay their creditors, the bonds had been sold to speculators at a fraction of their value. Thus Hamilton's proposal to have the national treasury redeem them at their full value would enrich the bond speculators, some of whom knew in advance of Hamilton's proposal and had hard-riding agents scouring the back country, buying up bonds at less than twenty-five cents on the dollar. Despite the vehement opposition of many Antifederalists who argued that the government should redeem the bonds only at their market value, Congress approved Hamilton's plan.

The Secretary of the Treasury also recommended that the twenty-five million dollars of state debts, incurred during the Revolutionary War, be assumed by the federal government. This measure too would increase the support given to the central as opposed to the state governments. States like Georgia and Virginia with small debts, or states which had already paid much of their own debts, bitterly resented the fact that they would be taxed to help pay off the larger debts of states like Massachusetts and they strenuously opposed the proposal. To ensure the success of his measure in Congress, Hamilton made a bargain with Jefferson. Many Southern Congressmen who were followers of Jefferson wanted the nation's capital to be in the South. In return for a promise to move the capital from New York to Philadelphia and after ten years to the banks of the Potomac River, Jefferson secured enough votes from his followers to ensure the passage of Hamilton's Debt Assumption Act.

Hamilton next recommended the creation of a Bank of the United States to help the government safeguard its funds, sell bonds, and stabilize currency values. After another fiery debate, with Northern votes carrying the bill, Congress agreed to charter the new Bank for a period of twenty years. The Bank was to have a capital of ten million dollars and a bank-note circulation of seven and a half million dollars. While the Bank was to be privately owned, the government was required to purchase one-fifth of the stock and to ensure the Bank's stability. Not only could the Bank issue paper money, it could establish branches throughout the country which would have the same functions as the National Bank. Once again, Hamilton's opponents cried "special privilege" and "centralization." The private owners of Bank stock, they argued, would have a splendid guaranteed investment and great influence over credit throughout the nation; moreover the Bank would still further buttress the central government.

The differences of opinion over the Bank issue were so deep and so strong that Washington asked for opinions on the constitutionality of the Bank Bill from his Cabinet. The written opinions prepared by Hamilton and Jefferson clearly defined two opposing points of view on the interpretation of the Constitution. Jefferson voiced the "strict construction" argument: nowhere, he argued, did the Constitution empower the central government to charter a National Bank, and for that government to move beyond its specific constitutional powers was "to take possession of a boundless field of power, no longer susceptible of any definition." Hamilton stuck closely to his idea of the "executive impulse," that is, to the belief that a strong national executive must guide Congress and compel the "lesser" state governments to accept policies for "the good of the nation." Thus he argued for a "loose construction" of the Constitution by which the central government would possess powers "implied" by the elastic clause of the Constitution. He felt that since the Constitution gave the

Hamilton's excise tax on whiskey enraged the poor frontier farmers of Pennsylvania who often tarred, feathered and beat federal tax collectors. Rebellious frontiersmen were in complete agreement with their representatives who hurled this challenge at the federal government. "It [the excise] shall not be collected. We will punish, expel, and banish the officers who shall attempt the collection. . . . The sovereignty shall not reside with you, but with us. If you presume to dispute the point by force, we are ready to measure swords with you, and if unequal ourselves to the contest, we will call in the aid of a foreign nation [Britain]. We will league ourselves with a foreign power."

federal government control of currency it *implied* the right to charter a bank for the carrying out of that power. But Jefferson believed that to accept such "implied powers" in connection with the Bank would provide a precedent for the central government to expand *all* of its enumerated powers. This, he thought, would demolish states' rights, and since state governments were "closer to the people," would further limit democracy.

Washington signed the Bank Bill principally because he agreed with Hamilton that the central power should be strengthened. But tension steadily mounted as the rest of Hamilton's programme appeared, tension which rose to fever pitch over the excise tax question.

In order to raise revenue to pay the interest on the new government bonds which were being sold to replace the old debts, Hamilton decided to levy an excise tax on various products, including liquor. Congress passed the necessary act, and by the spring of 1791 tax collection was in full swing. But popular opposition was fierce; the tax was called "odious, unequal, unpopular, and aggressive." In the hills of western Pennsylvania, where farmers converted their bulky grain into distilled whiskey in order to reduce transportation charges across the mountains, the opposition broke into violence. Tax collectors and even federal marshals were tarred and feathered.

In this resistance Hamilton saw a golden opportunity to prove the strength of the new government and to show businessmen that the ghost of Daniel Shays had really been laid. Into the West rode Hamilton at the head of 13,000 soldiers whom he had persuaded President Washington to mobilize. Although there was no organized rebellion to crush, a hundred people were arrested and two of them sentenced to death. Hamilton had clearly demonstrated that the federal government could and would use force to collect revenue, the very thing that had been impossible under the Articles of Confederation.

Jefferson's magnificent home, Monticello, and the beautiful buildings of the University of Virginia bear eloquent testimony to the President's brilliant architectural and artistic talents. Though for a long time many people doubted that they were really Jefferson's work, it is now acknowledged that this versatile man created "a distinctive American style, classic but modern in the circumstances of the time, from which the history and profession of architecture in this country took their rise."

The excise taxes were but one part of Hamilton's revenue programme. In 1789 he had persuaded Congress to place tariff duties on imported goods. Three years later he argued successfully that these duties should be increased enough to protect American manufacturers against foreign competition. Farmers and merchants protested that this was unfair assistance to one small group, but again Hamilton won his point. Clearly, he wanted to establish a republic whose society and government would very much resemble English models: one which would rapidly become an industrial nation with real control situated in the Eastern cities. Since nine-tenths of the American people in the 1790's lived on farms, plantations or in very small towns, his plan was bound to run into serious opposition.

Two political parties emerged out of the effort to organize and express public opinion on these issues. The first of these was the Federalist party. The Federalists had been the chief promoters of the Constitution and they had won a majority of seats in the Congress. Once in power, they formed caucuses or party conferences in both Houses, made sure that their supporters received appointments to the courts and other lucrative offices, and extended their influence into the electoral districts. Both their power and their policies stimulated the growth of an opposition party.

2. JEFFERSON AND THE REPUBLICANS

Led by Thomas Jefferson and James Madison, the Democratic Republican party, often simply called the Republican party, also had very definite ideas about what was best for the nation. Madison's support of Jefferson gave the opposition party particular strength since Madison had been a principal author of much of the Constitution and of some of the most brilliant essays in the Federalist Papers. Both men were gravely alarmed as they saw the unfolding of Hamilton's full plan of centralized government.

Thomas Jefferson, unlike Hamilton, was born an aristocrat. Like George Washington, he was a Virginia planter with extensive estates. He had been an ambassador to France during the Philadelphia Convention and thus had had no direct influence on the framing of the Constitution. As the author of the Declaration of Independence, however, and as a political theorist in his own right, he was welcomed in the Paris salons and witnessed the first enthusiastic phases of the French Revolution. He deeply distrusted Europe and England, and deplored the early manifestations of the industrial revolution in those countries and the growth of ugly industrial towns. He believed that farms bred the most virtuous men while the great cities, about which Hamilton dreamed, debased men by depriving them of contact with nature and making them dependent upon others for the right to work. Moreover, Jefferson despised Hamilton's low view of human nature and believed that men were essentially good and trustworthy. He felt that evil and fickle men were largely the product of vicious social and political institutions, of systems which denied to them their natural independence and freedom of growth. As a legislator in Virginia and as its Governor from 1779 to 1781, he regularly assaulted the "artificial aristocracy of wealth and birth." Desiring an intelligent democracy he worked for a system of public education for all, a wide franchise and legal reform. Jefferson regarded an established church as one of the bulwarks of a privileged class and he campaigned vigorously for separation of church and state. While he did not think that a movement for abolition of slavery would gain sufficient public support to succeed, he did argue that "the day is not distant when [the public] must bear and adopt it, or worse will follow."

It was natural that this broadly cultured man should not remain quiet in the face of Hamilton's assault on the liberal principles in which he believed. In particular he opposed Hamilton's centralization of power and advocated a strict interpretation or "construction" of the Constitution and the upholding of the powers of the states. Jefferson believed that all governments tend to be interested in increasing their own power; that they should therefore be held in the closest check by an active and well-informed democracy. On one occasion he remarked: "If left to me to decide whether we should have a government without newspapers, or newspapers without a government, I should not hesitate for a moment to prefer the latter." Later in life he declared that he would not wish to live in a community in which there was not an attempted rebellion at least every twenty years.

It is small wonder that inside·Washington's Cabinet, Jefferson and Hamilton were constantly at loggerheads. In Congress the Republicans began their own caucus which quickly became even more disciplined than that of the Federalists. Throughout the country Jefferson and Madison developed permanent organizations of support for the party and enlisted such prominent men as Governor Clinton of New York, Albert Gallatin of Pennsylvania and Aaron Burr of New York. The party organization thus built up, and particularly the congressional caucus of the Republicans, was to control the Presidency from 1801 to 1825, under Jefferson, Madison and James Monroe respectively.

Curiously, although Washington sympathized with Hamilton's views in most matters, the Jeffersonians supported Washington for President in 1792 and he was thus unopposed and returned unanimously for a second term. The same year, however, saw the first open demonstration of party politics. Governor Clinton, the Republican candidate for Vice-President, took fifty electoral votes while John Adams, the Federalist, won with seventy-seven. In an election in the same year, however, the Republicans gained the majority of seats in the House of Representatives.

As the parties took shape, issues over which they were bound to disagree were plentiful. One of the most important of these concerned America's relationship to Europe and to European power in the New World, a problem which was to remain central to American party politics for a long time.

3. FOREIGN AFFAIRS AND PARTY STRIFE

The beginning of the French Revolution coincided with the launching of the American Constitution, and at first Americans welcomed "the end of French tyranny" wholeheartedly. The leading Federalist lawyer (and future Chief Justice) John Marshall wrote: "In no part of the globe was this revolution hailed with more joy than in America." Even in conservative Boston, Royal Exchange Alley was renamed Liberty Street, while throughout the United States there were popular celebrations and feasts to observe the fall of the Bastille. But by 1790 many Americans, and all Federalists, took a different view. They took note of Edmund Burke's *Reflections on the French Revolution* and agreed that the new ideas of the French democracy were more dangerous to men of property than was the *ancien régime*. They saw the single-chamber Assembly of the 1791 French Constitution as an attack on the checks and balances they themselves had erected against "unbridled democracy" in the United States.

With news of the execution of Louis XVI and the Jacobin Reign of Terror, the Federalists turned against France and showed a growing sympathy for England when France declared war on the British. Most Jeffersonian Republicans, on the other hand, continued to support the French drive for greater democracy and applauded *The Rights of Man*, a pamphlet by the political philosopher, Tom Paine, which argued vehemently for complete democracy, agnosticism in religious matters, and the levelling of social distinctions. In the spring of 1793 Republicans welcomed Citizen Genêt who arrived from France as ambassador of the new government. Genêt's main job was to organize American support in the war against England. He was a personable and confident young man and soon had commissioned a number of American ship captains to attack Brit-

This Federalist cartoon sees Jefferson being aided by the devil in his attempt to destroy the federal government. The devil is saying: "Pull away. Pull away, my son. Don't fear, I'll give you all my assistance." Jefferson says: "Oh! I fear it is stronger rooted than I expected, but with the assistance of my Old Friend and a little more brandy I will bring it down."

ish merchantmen. Hamilton and his Federalist colleagues in the Cabinet pointed out that Genêt's behaviour was highly irregular, and that he had not even bothered to present his credentials to the President before launching his campaign to whip up enthusiasm for France. Jefferson agreed that Washington should ask the French government to recall him. Genêt himself, however, decided that life was too precarious in France. He married a daughter of the Governor of New York and settled into a Hudson Valley estate. But his short career as France's ambassador had raised the temperature of American politics and led to a significant decision.

The French government wanted the United States to honour the Franco-American treaty of 1778, in which the United States had promised to help defend the French West Indies should they be attacked by Britain. Hamilton wanted to disavow the treaty because of the guillotining of Louis XVI. Jefferson, however, argued that the treaty should be honoured, or at least that the United States should bargain for commercial concessions from England as the price of repudiation. Washington finally decided to ignore the treaty and to declare the United States neutral in the European struggle. Jefferson argued that the President's action was unconstitutional. Since Congress had the exclusive power to declare war, he said, it must also have the sole authority to declare neutrality. As a result of this dispute, Washington lost confidence in Jefferson, and Hamilton's power increased proportionately.

As the French revolutionary war dragged on, relations between the United States and Great Britain grew steadily worse. Since 1783 American merchants had been excluded from all the ports of Great Britain and her colonies; in 1793 the British government issued an order to seize all ships of any nation trading with France or French colonies. In the United States the Republicans called for a stern response and open support of

France, but the Federalists refused to make a break with Britain for they owned most of the shipping and would pay most of the taxes if war were to break out. Moreover, almost ninety per cent of United States imports were produced in Britain. Finally, Federalists felt that Britain stood for the same kind of government and society that they wished to build up in America, while France stood for revolution, anarchy, terror and atheism. At the peak of this clash over foreign policy, Jefferson resigned and was succeeded as Secretary of State by Edmund Randolph, a leading Federalist, thus strengthening the Federalist party's hold on the executive and emphasizing the growing strength of the party system.

Meanwhile, events in the interior of the continent further damaged Anglo-American relations. In 1783 the British had agreed to surrender all their western fur-trading posts in American territory, including Detroit, Oswego, Niagara and Michilimackinac. The fur-traders in Canada naturally objected to such a course, for it would mean their exclusion from much of their traditional western trade. In the treaty of 1783 the Americans had promised to compensate the Loyalists for the damages the latter had suffered during the Revolutionary War, and when they delayed doing so the British used the default as an excuse to retain the western posts. The Americans believed that the British in the West encouraged and supported the Indians in their fierce opposition to the advancing American settlement south of Lake Erie.

Anxious to remove these causes of conflict with Britain, Washington sent John Jay to London in 1794 to arrange a treaty. The British were sympathetic, for they had no desire to force the United States into the arms of revolutionary France. Nevertheless, they proved to be hard bargainers. In the end Jay's Treaty provided that Britain would withdraw from the western posts and remove her troops by 1796; that the United States could trade with some parts of the Empire, but not with the British West Indies; and that joint commissions would discuss the questions of debts and boundaries. The British adamantly refused to abandon their policy of seizing American ships trading with France. While war had been averted and the troublesome western question temporarily solved, Jay's Treaty was unpopular in the United States. Jay was burned in effigy, flags were flown at half-mast, and Hamilton was stoned in the streets of New York. Republican strength increased rapidly. Even the defeat of the Indians by General "Mad Anthony" Wayne at the Battle of Fallen Timbers in 1794, which cleared the way for settlement westward from Lake Erie, did little to quell growing criticism of the Federalists.

Jay's Treaty, however, did encourage Spain to make concessions to the United States in the south, where Spain controlled Florida and the mouth of the Mississippi. Fearful that with the British threat removed in the north the United States might attack her possessions in the south, Spain signed the Pinckney Treaty in 1795 adjusting the boundary of West Florida as the United States wished and permitting the Americans to use the port of New Orleans and the lower Mississippi River.

The Troubled Border, 1794

Although they wanted much more, settlers in the trans-Allegheny West were encouraged by these treaties. By 1800, Kentucky, Tennessee and Vermont had been admitted to the Union as states and the Ohio country was being occupied. In the Northwest Territory there were already 45,000 settlers. Most of the Americans who were thus busy forming new societies in the West were Jeffersonian in politics. They distrusted the distant central government and the business leaders of the Federalist party. Interested in cheap or free land, easier credit and military help to hasten the reluctant Indian withdrawal along the frontiers, they looked to the Republicans as the party most interested in the frontiersmen and western expansion.

In the midst of the party struggle Washington decided not to run for a third term, thus establishing a precedent not broken until 1940. His farewell address, delivered in the face of a mounting attack on the Federalist leadership, advised the nation to keep neutral in foreign affairs and to avoid party politics.

> I have already intimated to you the danger of parties in the State. . . . Let me now . . . warn you in the most solemn manner against the baneful effects of the spirit of party. . . . The great rule of conduct for us in regard to foreign nations is, in extending our commercial relations to have with them as little political connection as possible.

4. ADAMS AND FEDERALIST DECLINE

In 1796 John Adams, a scrupulously honest man, was elected the second and last Federalist President. Adams was concerned about the democratic tendencies of the age as well as with threats to American national interests. When he saw that the French were trying to bribe American ambassadors and were seizing American ships in retaliation for the Jay Treaty and American repudiation of the Franco-American treaty, he supported military preparations in anticipation of a war with France. While a settlement was arranged with the French in 1800 and the war scare passed, the tension it had created was exploited for political purposes.

In 1798, alleging a dire threat of subversion by pro-French opinion in the United States, the Federalists passed the harsh Alien, Sedition and Naturalization acts. The latter prescribed fourteen years instead of the previous five as the period an immigrant must wait before naturalization. The Alien Act gave the President power to arrest and deport undesirable aliens, while the Sedition Act empowered the executive to imprison anyone who spoke or wrote in such a way as to bring the government into disrepute. Federalist judges decreed fines and imprisonment for seventy people brought to trial under the Sedition Act, while men like Judge Samuel Chase took the trials as occasions to preach violently against the Republican party. Many of the convicted men were Republican editors and one was a Republican Congressman from Vermont.

James Madison called the Sedition Act "a monster that must forever disgrace its parents." Across the country protest against the arbitrary acts mounted. Republicans declared that the acts violated the Bill of Rights and the legislatures of Virginia and Kentucky passed opposition resolutions, prepared by Madison and Jefferson. These "Virginia and Kentucky Resolves" defined the Republican position on states' rights by asserting that the Union was a compact. Since the sovereign states entered a voluntary compact to establish a central government for certain common purposes, it was argued that if the central government violated the agreement the compact would be broken. The resolutions declared that the powers of the central government were merely delegated to it by the various states and that the states had the right to declare any federal law "unauthoritative, void and of no force." While the resolutions did not specifically say how a state might make its veto effective they did give additional prestige to the doctrine of states' rights.

As the election of 1800 approached, opposition to the Federalist programme of centralization of power in the federal government and the arbitrary use of that authority increased in strength. The Federalist candidates for the Presidency and Vice-Presidency, John Adams and Charles Pinckney, lost to Jefferson and Aaron Burr. Jefferson was clearly the man the country wanted for President, but the electoral college did not distinguish between the votes for President and Vice-President, and Jefferson and Burr had both received the same number of electoral votes. Thus the decision was made by the House of Representatives, which reflected the will of the people and the electors by selecting Jefferson as President and Burr as Vice-President. To avoid a similar problem in the future the Twelfth Amendment, passed in 1804, provided that the electors would vote separately for the two offices.

The election of 1800 plainly showed that Republican and Jeffersonian ideas had the support of the great majority of ordinary Americans as well as of Virginia planters and some of the leading families of New York and Pennsylvania. The Federalists were disheartened. As one commented pessimistically after the election: "I cannot describe how broken and scattered your federal friends are! We have no rallying point; and no mortal can divine where and when we shall again collect our strength. Shadows, clouds and darkness rest on our future prospects."

Thomas Jefferson referred to the election as "the Revolution of 1800." It remained to be seen what new directions would be given to American government, business and society by the Republicans.

CHAPTER 3

Nationalism and Sectionalism

In his first inaugural address Thomas Jefferson appealed to his countrymen to unite in defence of their institutions and principles. Referring to the bitter conflict between Federalists and Republicans, he declared that "every difference of opinion is not a difference of principle. We are all Republicans, we are all Federalists. If there be any among us who would wish to dissolve this Union or to change its republican form, let them stand undisturbed as monuments of the safety with which error of opinion may be tolerated where reason is left free to combat it."

1. THE REPUBLICAN PROGRAMME

Jefferson's inauguration took place in 1801 in Washington, which had now become the capital of the United States. Although Hamilton was right in saying that the new President was "as likely as any man I know to temporize" rather than to attempt a drastic change, Jefferson did implement many of his election promises. In this he was ably assisted by James Madison whom he appointed Secretary of State and Albert Gallatin, a Pennsylvanian of aristocratic Swiss birth and great financial ability, who served as Secretary of the Treasury.

Jefferson dropped many Federalist customs which he believed had a flavour of monarchy. Instead of appearing before Congress to read his messages, like the king opening parliament, Jefferson communicated them in writing. Frequent informal levees at the White House replaced the occasional formal receptions at the "President's Palace." The conviviality of Jefferson's popular evenings was enhanced by the huge cellar of excellent wine which he had acquired while he was in France. The Republican administration repealed excise taxes, eliminated many public positions and allowed the Alien and Sedition laws to lapse. Jefferson not only curtailed government expenditures, but also allotted government funds for specific purposes, rather than have Congress provide lump sums to be spent at executive discretion.

All of this programme was "Jeffersonian" in that it reduced the growth of the central government's influence and power, and within the central government appeared to give more power to Congress and less to the executive. But in other ways the Republican President fulfilled Hamilton's prediction that he would temporize. Jefferson did not in fact touch the central core of the Hamiltonian system, satisfying himself, rather, by modifying its operation. Indeed, as a practical politician, Jefferson actually increased the power of the Presidential office, and through personal contacts he kept control over the Republican majority in Congress; for by keeping in close and friendly communication with Republican leaders in House and Senate he was able to get favourable legislative action on policies desired by himself and his cabinet. His predecessor, Adams, who had not had a majority following in Congress, had been unable to overcome the "separation of powers," and like many later Presidents had encountered grave difficulties as a result. In appointing men to the hundreds of public positions, from the foreign service down to postmasters, Jefferson took care to strengthen his party. The courts, however, remained mostly under Federalist judges. As Congressman William Giles of Virginia remarked: "The revolution of 1800 is incomplete so long as that strong fortress is in possession of the enemy."

A direct clash between the Federalists entrenched in the Supreme Court and the Republicans came in 1803 when Chief Justice John Marshall, Jefferson's cousin, delivered his judgment in the case of *Marbury versus Madison*. The significance of this decision was Marshall's assertion of the Supreme Court's power to invalidate federal legislation. He consistently upheld the principle that both state and federal laws were subject to constitutional review by the Supreme Court, and defended this assertion of judicial independence in these words:

> The particular phraseology of the constitution of the United States confirms and strengthens the principle, supposed to be essential to all written constitutions, that a law repugnant to the constitution is void, and that courts, as well as other departments are bound by this instrument.

The Jeffersonians were furious, and asked who was to check the courts and to whom the judges were responsible. They asserted that the executive could enforce laws even if they had been declared unconstitutional by the Supreme Court. The Judiciary Act passed in 1789, establishing the federal court system, had empowered the Supreme Court to interpret the Constitution but nowhere had the Constitution itself specifically given the Court this power. Thus, argued the champions of states' rights and a strict construction of the Constitution, the Supreme Court did not have the right of judicial review over state or federal legislation. They even argued that the legislature could impeach judges, relying on the will of the people as expressed in succeeding elections to decide who was right. There could be no final solution to this question, but in Marshall's thirty-four years as Chief Justice the claims of the Supreme Court to judge the constitutionality of both federal and state laws were steadily entrenched.

Despite his opposition to centralization and executive power, Jefferson was to take one step which would increase the power of both the central government and the President. In 1800 Napoleon Bonaparte had acquired the vast Louisiana territory from Spain and two years later prohibited Americans from using the port of New Orleans. Americans were alarmed by the closure of a port which handled forty per cent of their exports. They also suspected that Napoleon planned to re-establish a powerful French empire in North America and permanently exclude them from the trans-Mississippi West. Jefferson at once instructed his minister in Paris, Robert Livingston, to try to purchase New Orleans, and sent James Monroe of Virginia to assist him. A nervous Congress voted two million dollars for diplomatic expenses. While the Federalists called for war against France, Jefferson sent a secret note to the French government, warning it that the French move "completely reverses all the political relations of the United States, and will form a new epoch in our political course. . . . There is on this globe one single spot, the possessor of which is our natural and habitual enemy. It is New Orleans, through which the produce of three-eighths of our territory must pass to market. . . . The day that France takes possession of New Orleans . . . we must marry ourselves to the British fleet and nation."

2. WESTERN EXPANSION

War between Britain and France was once more on the horizon, and Napoleon did not want to have the extra and heavy burden of defending distant Louisiana, which he felt the British would undoubtedly try to seize. To everyone's surprise he offered to sell all of Louisiana to the United States for fifteen million dollars. The two American ambassadors hastily concluded a treaty with Napoleon. Jefferson now faced a serious problem. He had argued for a strict interpretation of the Constitution; was he now to use a power of acquiring new territory which was not mentioned in the Constitution? Jefferson would have preferred to have waited for an amendment to be added to the Constitution giving the President this power. But he knew that the amending process was very slow and he feared that Napoleon might change his mind in the interim. Supported by his closest advisers he decided to throw caution to the winds and placed the treaty before the Senate for ratification. Ironically, in the debate that ensued the Federalists, in opposing the treaty, argued that the Constitution did not give the executive the power to buy new territory, while the Republicans argued that the joint treaty-making power of President and Senate covered the situation. The fact that the West was predominantly Republican in politics and that the acquisition of Louisiana would greatly increase the Republican party's future political strength, plus the Eastern Federalists' innate distrust of the West, helps to explain why the Federalists opposed the treaty. Nevertheless, the Senate ratified the treaty and on December 20, 1803 Louisiana was formally transferred to the United States.

Behind the obvious temptation of the offer lay another reason for Jefferson's decision to accept the treaty immediately. Jefferson believed deeply in what succeeding generations of Americans were to call "Manifest Destiny," a belief that United States influence must be felt in every part of the North American continent. Two years before the Louisiana Purchase he had written:

> However our present interests may restrain us upon our own limits, it is impossible not to look forward to distant times, when our rapid multiplication will expand beyond those limits and cover the whole northern, if not the southern, continent with a people speaking the same language, governed in similar forms and by similar laws.

The Republican Congress had already eased the terms on which settlers could buy lands in the public domain and the population of the Northwest Territory grew so rapidly that Ohio was admitted as a state in 1803. Similar growth occurred in the Southwest. But it was the trans-Mississippi West that really fired the imaginations of Jefferson, his advisers and the settlers of the mid-continental valley. The negotiations with France for New Orleans had just begun when Jefferson obtained from Congress a secret vote of money for an expedition to collect information on the Far West. Under Jefferson's secretary, Meriwether Lewis, and Lieutenant William Clark, the expedition finally set out in May 1804. Crossing prairies, foothills and mountains the explorers reached the Pacific at the mouth of the Columbia River. The journey established a tenuous claim by the United States to the huge Oregon country which, at that time, was largely the preserve of the British Hudson's Bay Company but was claimed also by Spain and Russia. While the expedition's report underestimated the worth of the intervening prairies, which it thought were mostly desert, the information about the fur trade, lumber, and mining possibilities of the Rocky Mountains gathered by the explorers greatly stimulated the Easterners' ambitions to acquire the whole continent and gave impetus to the idea of "Manifest Destiny." This American sense of nationalism was further strengthened by the course of the Napoleonic Wars.

3. FOREIGN AFFAIRS AND THE WAR OF 1812

In 1803 the war between Britain and France that Napoleon had anticipated when he offered to sell all of Louisiana to the United States had begun. Napoleon's power was supreme in Europe. To strike a blow at Britain's trade, he issued a series of decrees, called the Berlin and Milan decrees, forbidding neutral ships to visit British ports. In retaliation Britain issued orders-in-council forbidding neutral ships to trade in French-controlled European ports. Since British sea-power was dominant, she was able to enforce her orders-in-council. The principal group to suffer from this double blockade was the booming American merchant marine. From 1804 to 1807 the British confiscated hundreds of American ships and searched nearly all United States merchantmen for deserters from the British navy. Over-eager British captains often "impressed" Americans, who they claimed were British deserters. In 1807 a British warship, the *Leopard,* halted an American frigate, the *Chesapeake.* After inflicting several American casualties, the captain of the *Leopard* removed from the American ship a British deserter and three Americans who had served in the British navy. A loud cry for retaliation echoed throughout the American press and Congress.

Jefferson responded to the *Chesapeake* affair by obtaining from Congress an Embargo Act in 1807 which in effect prohibited American trade with Europe. Although Jefferson hoped thus to keep the United States out of a costly war, his policy had two major economic results. It created a widespread commercial depression along the American seaboard, which spread quickly to farm areas, and it stimulated American domestic manufacturing to replace the loss of imports from Europe.

The Louisiana Purchase

Despite a growing uneasiness along the eastern seaboard the Republican candidate, James Madison, won the Presidential election of 1808. Madison, although he was both learned and respected, lacked the human managerial skills by which Jefferson had controlled Congress. This weakening of the executive influence was compounded when the congressional elections of 1810 returned a group of fire-eating Republican expansionists from the South and West. Soon known as the War Hawks these men, led by Henry Clay of Kentucky and John C. Calhoun of South Carolina, pressed for war with Britain. In their bellicose speeches they tempted many people with dreams of the easy acquisition of

Canada, and Florida, the property of Britain's Spanish ally. At one time
Calhoun boasted: "In four weeks from the time that a declaration of war is
heard on our frontier the whole of Upper Canada and a part of Lower
Canada will be in our possession."

In the years before the War of 1812 the War Hawks both responded
to and exploited the strong sense of American nationalism which deeply
resented Britain's control of the United States economic life. The continuing British interference with American shipping began to swing some
Eastern businessmen towards support of the tough War Hawk line. In
1810 Congress enacted the Macon Bill, which ended the embargo, and
added the proviso that if either France or Britain lifted its commercial
decrees, the United States would stop trade with the other. Napoleon

A Scene on the FRONTIERS as Practiced by the HUMANE BRITISH and their WORTHY ALLIES —

Bring me the Scalps
and the King our master
will reward you —

Reward for
Sixteen Scalps

Arise Columbia's Sons and forward press,
Your Country's wrongs call loudly for redress;
The Savage Indian with his Scalping knife,
Or Tomahawk, may seek to take your life,

By bravery aw'd they'll in a dreadful Fright
Shrink back for Refuge to the Woods in Flight;
Their British leaders then will quickly shake,
And for those wrongs shall restitution make.

This cartoon reflects the American view of British-Indian relations on the frontier. President Madison declared, in his suitably inflammatory war message to Congress on June 1, 1812: "In reviewing the conduct of Great Britain toward the United States our attention is necessarily drawn to the warfare just renewed by the savages on one of our extensive frontiers—a warfare which is known to spare neither age nor sex and to be distinguished by features peculiarly shocking to humanity."

seized the opportunity and announced the revocation of his decrees against neutral shipping. Madison at once gave Britain three months' notice; at the end of that time Congress prohibited trade with Britain. The action was a double trap for the President. France did not really change her policy, and yet had induced the United States to join the French blockade against British trade. It also strengthened the War Hawk position by stirring up support for war with Britain.

Westerners were not averse to war with Britain on other grounds also. They wanted to clear the Indians from the path of westward settlement. Already there had been a series of bloody battles and forced treaty-concessions between the Indians and the American frontiersmen. In 1811 an Indian confederacy under the Shawnee chief, Tecumseh, was engaged in a very indecisive armed struggle at Tippecanoe in which no one was quite sure who was winning. Yet in one way Tippecanoe *was* decisive. The War Hawks claimed that the British weapons used by the Indians in this battle and others were proof that Britain would have to be driven from

North America. In addition, many Westerners felt that their exports out of New Orleans were imperilled by Britain's orders-in-council.

Responding to all these pressures, President Madison asked Congress to declare war on Great Britain in June 1812. The best summary of the reasons for the war was given in a private letter by Andrew Jackson, who was later to be President of the United States, written three months before the congressional declaration of war:

> We are going to fight for the re-establishment of our national character . . . for the protection of our maritime citizens impressed on board British ships of war . . . to vindicate our right to a free trade . . . in fine to seek some indemnity for past injuries, some security against future aggression, by the conquest of all British domains upon the continent of North America.

The War of 1812 had grown out of a welter of bungled diplomacy and strident nationalistic ambition. Perversely, while it was a supreme example of nationalism it greatly intensified sectional feeling. Although many Americans saw the war as a second war of independence, many others firmly opposed the war with Britain. While some Eastern businessmen agreed that it was necessary for the United States to assert her rights against British "domination," others felt that the war was principally an expression of anti-British republicanism and radical frontier democracy. Still others feared further disruption of their trade. Most of New England opposed the war, and the region continued to trade with British North America throughout the hostilities. New England Federalist leaders in December 1814 met in Hartford to declare the right of any state to nullify federal legislation. Using language oddly similar to that of the Virginia and Kentucky Resolves of 1798, they proposed seven amendments to the Constitution, all aimed at strengthening the Northeast at the expense of the Southern and Western expansionists.

The actual conduct of the war was tragic and farcical. Both the government and the armed forces were totally unprepared for war and remained in that condition throughout most of the hostilities. Enlistments lagged far behind requirements and several states refused to let their militia serve outside the state. During an attack on Queenston Heights in Upper Canada in October 1812, this policy was embarrassing for the United States and fortunate for Canada, as New York militiamen remained firmly on the American side of the Niagara River. Loans were undersubscribed, generals were incompetent and the navy often inadequate. By the end of the war much of Maine and Illinois territory was in British hands and most of the Atlantic coast was under effective blockade by the Royal Navy. Nevertheless, while the British hemmed in the Atlantic seaboard and burned Washington, individual American ships performed brilliantly and captured thirteen hundred British craft of different types. In January 1815, just before news of the peace treaty arrived, General Andrew Jackson decisively beat a British invasion force at New Orleans. Such events tremendously reinforced American nationalism. Furthermore, although American commerce had suffered heavily, the scarcity of imported European goods had stimulated American manufacturing.

The Treaty of Ghent, signed after lengthy negotiations on December 24, 1814, ended the war, but changed nothing. It provided for the return "of all territory, places and possessions whatsoever taken by either party from the other during the war." The British government had decided that the European situation at the end of the Napoleonic Wars was too unstable to permit longer, heavier efforts in North America. The American negotiators, because of the steadily deteriorating military situation in the United States, were unable to gain any assurances about neutral rights at sea and failed also to secure their other objectives of territorial gains in Canada and Florida. Definition of the Canadian-American boundary was left to future negotiations while nothing at all was said about the future of Florida. As a later President, John Quincy Adams, who helped to negotiate the Treaty, put it, "We have obtained nothing but peace."

4. ECONOMIC NATIONALISM AND
THE "AMERICAN SYSTEM"

One intangible gain for the United States was a new sense of national purpose. With the Federalists discredited by their foot-dragging wartime attitude, the National Republican party absorbed the leading national politicians and all eyes turned to problems of economic growth and westward expansion. The vibrant post-war nationalism was reflected in vigorous economic policy, territorial expansion and diplomacy.

The chief architect of economic policy in these years, Henry Clay, an ex-War Hawk Senator from Kentucky, liked to talk of the "American System." Clay's "System" meant the very positive use of government to encourage the growth of industry and trade as well as to extend American political control over the western hemisphere. Supported by another ex-War Hawk Senator, John Calhoun of South Carolina, Clay carried forward his pre-1812 expansionist ideas. But now expansionism was endorsed by most businessmen, attracted not only by dreams of American-controlled hemispheric trade but by plans to use the government to protect them against foreign competition and furnish them with a stable banking system and "internal improvements" such as better roads, bridges, canals and harbours and, by the 1830's, railways. To guard against the tendency of local banks to over-issue both credit and paper currency Clay and Calhoun secured an act of Congress in 1816 to charter a second Bank of the United States to replace the first National Bank whose charter had not been renewed in 1811. Four-fifths of its stock was bought by private business-men and one-fifth by the government. The policy of the Bank of the United States was to compel state banks to limit their issues of paper money in an attempt to stabilize the nation's finances.

In the same year Congress passed another Hamiltonian measure, a

Before the steamboat came into use, keelboats carried large cargoes from Louisville to New Orleans. Freight rates were high — $5 per hundredweight — but steamboats reduced these steadily until, by 1840, they were little more than 25c per hundredweight.

new tariff act. Even Southerners, following Calhoun, put aside their free trade convictions to vote for the 1816 tariff which was designed to protect infant American industries. Some Southerners and most Westerners hoped to see factories built in their own localities as a result of protection such as the new act afforded against cheap English goods, which had begun to swamp the American market in 1815 once the war was over.

With these foundations of the "American System" laid, and with the National Republicans again winning the Presidency in 1816, Clay's aims seemed well advanced. Booming prosperity in the United States after 1814 created opportunities which lured thousands to the trans-Allegheny West. In the decade from 1810 to 1820 the population west of the Appalachians more than doubled to reach a total of 2,200,000, which was greater than that of New England. Through the tortuous river valleys piercing the Appalachian barrier flowed unbroken streams of settlers, merchants and land speculators. The most heavily travelled route was along the federally built National Road which by 1818 reached from Cumberland in Maryland to Wheeling on the Ohio River. William Cobbett, an English observer in 1817, was amazed by this western spectacle: "The rugged road, the dirty hovels, the fire in the woods to sleep by, the pathless ways through the wilderness, the dangerous crossings of the rivers"; all this he wrote in order "to boil their pot in gypsy fashion, to have a mere board to eat on, to drink whiskey or pure water, to sit and sleep under a shed far inferior to English cowpens, to have a mill at twenty miles distance, an apothecary's shop at a hundred, and a doctor nowhere."

Yet it was done; and both the demands of the West and the profits to be made produced a frenzied economic growth. More roads were built with federal assistance and many were added by private companies which charged tolls for their use, and were frequently subsidized by state legislatures. Even so, transportation costs for importing and exporting from the West were high, either by road or by the hundreds of keelboats which had to be rowed when travelling upstream. Steamboats and canals helped to reduce costs. The first successful steamboat, the *Clermont*, was built by Robert Fulton, and in 1807 this formidable little vessel, spewing forth sparks and dense smoke from the black column of its single funnel, made the one-hundred-and-fifty-mile trip up the Hudson River from New York to Albany in thirty hours. One trembling witness observed: "Fishermen became terrified and they saw nothing but destruction devastating their fishing grounds, whilst the wreaths of black vapour and rushing noise of the paddle wheels, foaming with the stirred-up water, produced great excitement." By 1830 over two hundred steamboats were plying trans-Appalachian rivers, and upstream freight rates had been more than halved.

To supplement the river systems came the canals in the 1820's and 1830's. The greatest of these was the Erie Canal, finished in 1825 and linking Albany with Buffalo three hundred and sixty miles away. This startling achievement gave the Americans a continuous navigable water route from New York City to Toledo at the Western end of Lake Erie. It cut the cost of east-west freight by nine-tenths and the time consumed in travel by more than one-half. The new commercial tie with the West made New York City the greatest trade centre on the seaboard and stimulated a tremendous export of grain, lumber and other produce from the West. It also encouraged Eastern manufacturers to produce for the mushrooming Western market. From the Canadian point of view completion of the Erie Canal was a critical blow to Montreal merchants in their long competition with New York to be the centre of trade between Europe and the American mid-continent.

5. JUDICIAL NATIONALISM

The new post-1812 nationalism was also reflected in the judgements of the Supreme Court where Chief Justice John Marshall firmly upheld the powers of the federal government against the claims of the states. The most important statement of judicial nationalism came in 1819 in the case of *McCulloch versus Maryland*. This legal dispute involved the validity of an act passed by the state of Maryland taxing a branch of the Bank of the United States. Since the Bank was founded upon a charter granted by the federal government, Marshall regarded the Maryland action as an attempt to limit or even to destroy the federal power. In effect, the question before the Court was once again whether the federal government had the power to charter the Bank. Marshall, repeating the arguments used by Alexander Hamilton in 1791, declared the Maryland statute unconstitutional. The federal government, he claimed, had "implied powers" which could be used to achieve legitimate national

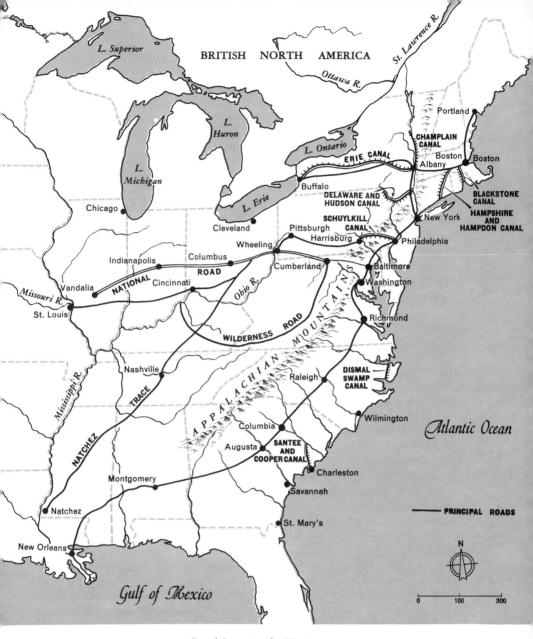

Travel Routes to the West

objectives. Speaking of the elastic clause of the Constitution, Marshall maintained:

> Let the end be legitimate, let it be within the scope of the Constitution, and all means which are appropriate, which are plainly adapted to that end, which are not prohibited, but consist with the letter and spirit of the Constitution, are constitutional.

Other decisions prohibited the states from interfering with interstate commerce, regulation of which Marshall declared rested exclusively in the hands of the federal authority. By 1835 when Chief Justice Marshall died, he had given added dignity and judicial support to the Hamiltonian view of the federal government's authority.

6. THE GROWTH OF SECTIONALISM

By 1820, however, the prosperity of the "era of good feelings" ended and an economic recession set in. With it sectional tensions revived. The South was not sharing equally with the North in the growth of industry and Southerners grew suspicious of the "American System." Many Westerners blamed the depression of 1819-24 on the Eastern businessmen who controlled credit and currency through the Bank of the United States.

By 1820, also, slavery had emerged as the most ominous focus of sectional disagreements. Since the end of the seventeenth century the proportion of Negro slaves in the Southern plantation labour force had been steadily increasing. At the end of the eighteenth century, just as liberal feeling had seemed ready to accept a gradual termination of the slave system, a single mechanical invention produced a cataclysmic economic development, which quickly smothered pro-emancipation opinion in the South. The invention was that of the cotton gin by Eli Whitney, in 1793, which increased a slave's output of cleaned cotton from one to fifty pounds a day. When it was harnessed to water power or steam a cotton gin could turn out a thousand pounds daily. Almost at once the farmers of Georgia and South Carolina deserted the cultivation of indigo and rice, Virginians restricted their tobacco acres and, together with Tennessee and North Carolina planters, turned to cotton. Within a very few years cotton had become King in the South.

But cotton-growing is hard on the soil and the search for fresh land was intense as Southerners poured across the territory north of the Gulf of Mexico. By 1820, advocates of slave emancipation in the South were few and far between. To have asked a large Southern planter to emancipate his slaves would have been almost the same as asking a New England businessman to turn over half his factory for some worthy public purpose.

In these same years, Southerners' suspicions of the Northeast grew rapidly. Because of greater employment opportunities in the growing industry of the Northeastern states, immigrants from the British Isles and Europe flowed into the North and threatened to give that section a majority in the Senate. This would have mattered little had it not been that Northern business was pressing for greater tariff protection while the South, as it became increasingly a staple-producing region, disliked even the existing tariff. In addition, many Northerners wished to eliminate slavery from the Union, as an institution contrary to the spirit of the Declaration of Independence. Moreover, the Northern majority in the House of Repre-

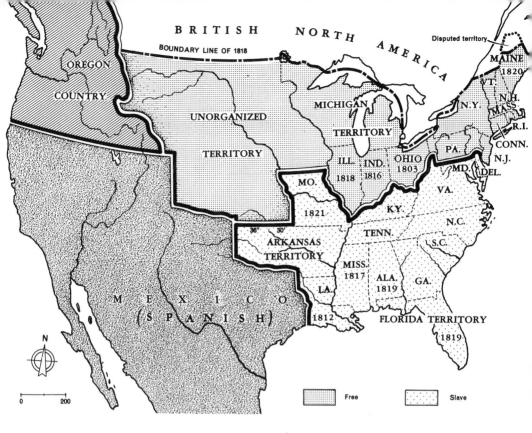

The Missouri Compromise

sentatives was growing steadily, especially since only three-fifths of the large slave population in the South counted for purposes of representation in the House of Representatives. Since the South could not hold its own in the lower house it became more important to maintain its voting power in the Senate. Each state possessed two Senate seats regardless of state population, and if the South were to control the Senate it had to keep pace with the North, state by state, in westward expansion, ensuring that as many slave as non-slave states were admitted to the Union.

In 1819, when there were eleven slave and eleven non-slave states, the people of Missouri applied for admission to the Union as a slaveholding state. Lying beyond the Mississippi, Missouri was not covered by the slavery prohibition clause of the old Northwest Ordinance. In the North, public meetings and legislatures passed resolutions opposing the admission of Missouri as a slave state. Southerners argued that all states had equal rights and that it was unconstitutional to place a condition upon one of them. One Southerner wrote: "We have kindled a fire which all the waters of the ocean cannot put out, which seas of blood can only extinguish."

As the clash of opinion reached the danger point several congressional leaders, of whom the most prominent was Henry Clay, sought a compromise. In 1820, North and South finally agreed to several measures, known collectively as the Missouri Compromise, designed to maintain equal balance of slave and non-slave states in the Senate. By the Compromise, Missouri was admitted as a slave state; Maine, hitherto a part of Massachusetts, was granted a longstanding wish for statehood, as a free state; slavery was prohibited "forever" in all federal territory north of latitude 36° 30′, the southern boundary of Missouri. Although the Missouri Compromise solved the problem temporarily, the crisis had deepened sectional feeling. Future difficulties arising from the slavery problem were foreshadowed when the last Virginian President, James Monroe, elected in 1816, nearly refused to sign the legislation of 1820 because the Constitution did not specifically empower Congress to exclude slavery, a form of property rights, from the territories.

7. NATIONALISM AND DIPLOMACY

While growing sectional differences threatened the domestic unity of the United States, the country continued to expand westward. Nearly unanimous support was given to that aspect of the "American System" which proclaimed that the destiny of the United States was to incorporate the whole of the continent within the American political system. To a large extent this was an economic ambition. But many Americans also believed that the proper role of the world's greatest republic was to liberate "subject areas" such as the Spanish and British colonies from the corrupt control of monarchical Europe. While economic motives have always loomed large in the history of American expansion so too has the conviction that the "Great Experiment" in democracy is a genuinely superior form of society and government.

In the years immediately following the War of 1812 there was general agreement both about the need for expansion and for a more permanent political settlement with Britain, the dominant maritime power in the world. Thus in 1817 the United States and Britain signed the pact known as the Rush-Bagot Agreement which grew out of the "unfinished business" of the Treaty of Ghent. This agreement provided that neither nation would ever maintain more than four small armed vessels on the Great Lakes. Although the pact did not exclude the later construction of such defensive military works as the Rideau Canal and Fort Henry in Upper Canada it did cut down the cost of naval defence for both nations and it helped to establish a tradition of settlement by negotiation rather than by war. This tradition was further developed in 1818 when the United States and Britain accepted the conclusions of the four commissions provided for by the Treaty of Ghent to settle problems of boundaries and fisheries. The 1818 agreements granted limited fishing rights to Americans in the inshore waters of Labrador, Newfoundland and Nova Scotia. They also fixed the western boundary between the United States and British North America at the forty-ninth parallel from the Lake of the Woods to the

Rocky Mountains, and settled some disputed parts of the boundary line from the St. Croix River to the St. Lawrence. The Oregon country was left "free and open" to Americans and British subjects.

In the south Spain, its power declining, was unable to resist American expansionist pressure. Between 1810 and 1813 the United States occupied West Florida. In 1818 General Andrew Jackson invaded East Florida to subdue Seminole Indians who had been raiding across the border. Despite a violent Spanish protest, the Secretary of State, John Quincy Adams, persuaded President Monroe to be firm in attempting to secure East Florida. The result, after long negotiations, was the Transcontinental Treaty of 1819, by which Spain ceded Florida to the United States and withdrew her claims to Oregon and the Pacific Coast north of the forty-second parallel. In return the United States relinquished its claim to the huge Spanish province of Texas.

Another indication of Spain's declining power in the Americas was the development of a movement for independence in the Spanish American colonies. Inspired by French revolutionary ideas, the Spanish colonies in America took advantage of Spain's troubles during the Napoleonic Wars and staged a series of revolts beginning in 1810. The new republics so formed immediately sought diplomatic recognition from Britain and the United States. Since one-fifth of United States external trade was already with the Latin American region, Henry Clay pressed for quick recognition in 1818, but Congress delayed doing so. By 1823, however, the scene had changed. A revolution in Spain had overthrown the Spanish monarchy and the Holy Alliance of Russia, France, Austria and Prussia had sent a French army into Spain, re-established the monarchy and was contemplating recovery of the lost Spanish American empire. Since Britain had dissociated herself from the European alliance and her commerce with Latin America was booming with the ending of Spanish imperial restrictions, there was no real danger that the Royal Navy would permit European intervention. Nevertheless, George Canning, the British Foreign Secretary, sought from the American minister to Britain, Richard Rush, a joint Anglo-American declaration against the Alliance's intervention in Latin America, adding to his proposed joint statement: "We could not see any portion [of Latin America] transferred to any other power, with indifference." John Quincy Adams believed that this was a British device to prevent the United States from acquiring areas such as Cuba or Texas in the future. Convinced that Britain would safeguard the independence of the American republics in any case, Adams thought that recognition of the republics by the United States should be accompanied by a separate American declaration against intervention. Further, he had a particular reason for wishing to assert United States' claims right across the continent to the Pacific. Russian fur-traders were active along the Pacific coast and claimed to own not only Alaska but the Pacific coast as far south as the fifty-first parallel.

In addition to these material and territorial considerations, Monroe and his Cabinet thought that the United States, on principle, should assert strong support for republican régimes. All these reasons together moved the President to include in his December 1823 address to Congress a number of statements which later became known as the Monroe Doctrine:

> The political system of the allied powers [the Holy Alliance] is essentially different . . . from that of America. . . . We owe it, therefore . . . to candour and to the amicable relations existing between the United States and those powers . . . to declare that we should consider any attempt on their part to extend their system to any portion of this hemisphere as dangerous to our peace and safety. . . . With the governments who have declared their independence and maintained it, and whose independence we have . . . acknowledged, we could not view any interposition . . . by any European power in any other light than as the manifestation of an unfriendly disposition toward the United States.

The President also asserted with obvious reference to Russia that the United States could not tolerate any new colonization in the Americas and in turn that the United States would not concern itself in wars which related only to Europe. Since American power was relatively slight, the Monroe Doctrine was little more than a pretentious and rather annoying statement in 1823. It was, however, significant for the future, a future in which the United States was to move steadily towards the position of a world power.

CHAPTER 4

Andrew Jackson's America

Andrew Jackson was called many things in his time: King Veto, Andrew I, and a demagogic tyrant by his enemies; "Old Hickory," anti-monopolist and friend of the "common man" by his supporters. Jackson was an unsophisticated product of the Indian-fighting frontier, with little formal education. Born in the back country of South Carolina, he served in the Revolutionary War and then studied law and settled in Tennessee. He later represented Tennessee in Congress. He was described at this time as "a tall, lank, uncouth-looking personage, with long locks hanging over his face, and a cue down his back tied in an eel skin; his dress singular, his manners and deportment that of a rough backwoodsman." In office his native abilities seemed to grow and he appeared to take on considerable personal dignity.

Jackson began his term of office with the Southerner's traditional concern for states' rights, but he ended by greatly strengthening the power of the Presidency. He had failed in business as a land speculator, and this strengthened his belief that money should have a fixed value to prevent banks from cheating small businessmen and farmers; yet his own bank policy intensified the effects of a major depression and caused widespread misery among the common people. In spite of all his contradictions, however, "Old Hickory" stood for democracy, and in general the Age of Jackson was an age of reform.

1. POLITICAL BACKGROUND

Before Jackson's election there had been turbulent changes in the political alignment of sections and leaders. During their long tenure of office the Republicans had become increasingly conservative. Beginning as an alliance of Southern planters, New York merchants and farmers, with small businessmen and settlers in the West, the Republicans drew increasing support from Eastern business interests, and in the end their version of economic nationalism, with its growing emphasis on government assistance to business, was challenged by the very people whose interests they had originally championed.

Rifts in the National Republican party in the early 1820's produced four "favourite sons," or regional candidates, one of whom was Jackson, to contest the Presidential election of 1824. While each was nominally a Republican, none could rightly claim to have the endorsement of the whole party. None of them secured a majority in the electoral college and the choice between Jackson and his three opponents had therefore to be decided by the House of Representatives. Henry Clay, Jackson's rival as a Western candidate, threw his support in the House to John Quincy Adams, the nominee of the Northeast, who was thus named President. It had been a very bitter struggle and when Adams immediately appointed Clay Secretary of State, Jackson's supporters cried "corrupt bargain." This charge hung over the entire Adams administration and Jackson's supporters used it to draw more people into what they were already calling the Democratic party. As the remaining National Republicans became increasingly identified with Eastern business interests, a number of their leaders deserted and joined the Jacksonian Democrats.

Jackson especially made much of the "corrupt bargain" charges against the Adams-Clay administration and managed to convey to his followers his personal bitterness at being "cheated" out of the Presidency. Stump speakers and Jacksonian editors carried the message effectively to the people. A four-year campaign of vicious vilification of the honest, if conservative, John Adams produced an overwhelming electoral victory for Jackson and the Democrats in 1828. Although the Jacksonians won few votes in New England they drew strong support in every other region of the country. The South and the West supported Jackson because he was identified with both those sections and because he was a "democrat." The middle class and artisans of the middle Atlantic states voted for him in opposition to control of the government by "aristocrats." Jackson thus succeeded in being all things to most people, and in this laid down an enduring pattern for Presidential aspirants.

Leadership changes and personal politics alone, however, do not explain the rise of the Democratic party. More important were state constitutional reforms which increased the political importance of the "common man." By the 1820's Westerners, Eastern farmers, wage-earners and small businessmen violently resented the dominant position occupied in the republic by the "aristocratic" men of wealth. Such resentment was reflected in the adoption of manhood suffrage in a large number of states. By 1825 the general adoption of white manhood suffrage had produced many changes in American politics. The need to attract support among the newly enfranchised voters of town and country led to more emotional appeals and to what the austere old families of Boston and Philadelphia called the rule of demagogues. To the working class and small farmers the franchise meant a chance to influence government more directly. They used their new power to establish the rule that party candidates should be named by elected party conventions rather than by legislative caucuses (meetings of party representatives in Congress). They also shifted the power of naming Presidential electors from the state legislatures to the qualified voters of the state.

The flurry of political reform had its counterpart in the tenor of excitement which existed in American society throughout the Jacksonian era. Experimentation in social relationships, and demands for economic reform filled the air. Groups of liberals campaigned for repeal of closed-Sunday laws, while others joined with more radical "utopians" to experiment with ideal communities in which property would be owned in common and the results of labour equally divided. An early but futile experiment in desegregation was made at a plantation in Nashoba, Tennessee, where whites and Negroes lived on terms of equality. Small organized groups of skilled workmen in the North pressed vigorously for free education, the end of imprisonment for debt, the protection of workers against irresponsible contractors, and recognition of the right to strike and bargain collectively. Writers proclaimed that American democracy was on the march in every area of life.

Symbolizing the "arrival" of the common man, or the triumph of King Mob as the anti-Jackson people called it, was the Presidential inauguration in 1829. Rather than hold a staid and formal reception, Jackson staged a wide-open party at the White House, with everybody welcome. The result was a scene of incredible confusion with costly crystal smashed and trampled into Brussels carpets, and elegant brocades ripped and stained beyond repair. Eventually the crowds were drawn out of the White House by the ingenious device of placing huge vats of spiked punch on the lawns. Respectable Washington was horrified.

2. POLICIES AND PROBLEMS

Jackson's belief in social equality and equality of opportunity led to other controversial policies, one being the expansion of what was known as the "spoils system." He dismissed a thousand of the ten thousand federal civil servants and replaced them with Democratic supporters. Previous administrations had also acted upon the assumption that "to the victor go the spoils," but they had been rather more circumspect in their methods. Jackson acted quickly and openly. Worse, he defended the system, calling it "rotation in office," and declaring that it was necessary in a democratic country. Like contemporary advocates of complete democracy in England, he argued that this "reform" would prevent any group from developing a vested interest in office. Jackson's supporters argued that while their wealthy opponents, who came to be known as Whigs, could reward their election workers in other ways, the Democrats could only offer the rewards of public office. Jackson's statement in praise of the system also reveals a striking difference between the complex government of today and that of his time:

The duties of all public offices are, or at least admit of being made, so plain and simple that men of intelligence can readily qualify themselves for their performance; and I cannot but believe that more is lost by the long continuance of men in office than is generally to be gained by their experience.

Jackson regarded himself as the tribune of the people and did not hesitate to use the executive power with vigour if he thought special interests inside or outside Congress were ignoring the general welfare. In his two terms he vetoed more legislation than had all his predecessors together—hence the nickname, King Veto. His concern for the general welfare, however, did not extend to the welfare of the Indians. He gave full support to the policy of forcing all Indians to move beyond the Mississippi. When the Cherokees and Seminoles presented evidence in the Supreme Court that the state of Georgia was treating them with extreme injustice, including corruption, force and fraudulent treaties, the President refused to order troops to support the court order restraining the state in its Indian policy. "Chief Justice Marshall has made his decision," Jackson declared, "let him enforce it!" Land-hungry Westerners were overjoyed by this open flaunting of the executive over the judicial power.

In other ways Jackson showed his nationalism both negatively and positively. In May 1830 he vetoed a bill to provide federal aid in the construction of an important road from Maysville to Lexington in Kentucky. He argued that since the road would be entirely within one state it did not qualify for federal funds. This negative use of the executive power pleased the people of New York, Pennsylvania and other Eastern states who had financed most of their own transportation routes. On other occasions, Jackson showed less concern both for states' rights and for economical government and, with positive use of executive influence, secured more funds for internal improvements than had his conservative predecessor, Adams.

Such issues caused a growing turmoil inside the Jackson cabinet, in Congress, and in the nation. The political and social changes which had brought Jackson to the White House were also increasing the suspicion and rivalry among the geographic sections of the republic. While Southerners were delighted to have a man from Tennessee in the Presidency, they were also alarmed by the growing influence of the North in Congress. In particular they feared the steady increase in the tariff. In 1816 the South had approved a protective tariff, but the years had shown that such protection not only failed to foster Southern industry, but forced Southerners to pay more for manufactured goods. When the tariff was raised once again in 1828, the South Carolina legislature approved a document known as the South Carolina Exposition and Protest which maintained that the 1828 tariff was unconstitutional because it had for its purpose not the raising of revenue, but the protection of one section of the country at the expense of another. The anonymous author of the Exposition was John C. Calhoun, then Vice-President of the United States. Sensing that the

Andrew Jackson was a firm believer in the principle of rotation in office—of giving as many of his supporters as possible a share in public office. In his first message to Congress he warned of the dangers of allowing a few men to enjoy office and power for a long time. "Office is considered as a species of property, and government rather as a means of promoting individual interests than as an instrument created solely for the service of the people. Corruption in some, and in others a perversion of correct feelings and principles, divert government from its legitimate ends and make it an engine for the support of the few at the expense of the many." He went on to justify the removal of many officials. "In a country where offices are created solely for the benefit of the people, no one man has any more intrinsic right to official station than another. Offices were not established to give support to particular men at the public expense. No individual wrong is, therefore, done by removal, since neither appointment to, nor continuance in, office is a matter of right."

South could never again out-vote the North in Congress, Calhoun advocated the Doctrine of Nullification, which reiterated the "compact theory" of the Virginia and Kentucky Resolves, but also went much further. If a state believed that the compact had been broken by an act of the federal government, announced Calhoun, a state convention could declare such act to be null and void within its borders. South Carolina's Doctrine of Nullification plainly spelled trouble for the future.

Conservative New Englanders such as John Quincy Adams and Daniel Webster, Senator for Massachusetts, whose followers were coming to be known as Whigs, also expressed sectional grievances. Above all they feared a too rapid western expansion both because it might involve heavy federal expenditures and because Westerners tended to support Democrats who proposed lowering the price of one dollar and twenty-five cents an acre for public lands. Whigs favoured sale of western public lands at reasonable prices and distribution of the resulting funds to the states. Such a policy was designed to slow down emigration from the East and thus, by retaining a plentiful labour supply, to keep wages low in Eastern towns; also, by distributing the proceeds to the states the federal treasury would not accumulate so much money from land sales. This, in turn, would strengthen Whig arguments for high tariffs as a source of federal revenues.

Southern leaders detected political possibilities in the reluctance of the East to grant Western demands for cheap public lands. The people of the Southeast were suffering hard times. Their soil was exhausted from prodigal use and they had to pay tariff-inflated prices for imported British

With his eyes fixed steadily on John C. Calhoun who, as Vice-President, presided in the Senate, Daniel Webster stated, during the Webster-Hayne debate: "When my eyes shall be turned to behold for the last time the sun in heaven, may I not see him shining on the broken and dishonoured fragments of a once glorious Union: on States dissevered, discordant, belligerent; on a land rent with civil feuds, or drenched, it may be, in fraternal blood! Let their last feeble and lingering glance rather behold the glorious ensign of the republic, now known and honoured throughout the earth, still full high advanced, its arms and trophies streaming in their original lustre, not a stripe erased or polluted, not a single star obscured, bearing for its motto no such miserable interrogatory as 'What is all this worth?' nor those other words of delusion and folly, 'Liberty first and Union afterwards'; but everywhere, spread all over in characters of living light, blazing on all its ample folds, as they float over the sea and over the land, and in every wind under the whole heavens, that other sentiment, dear to every true American heart, 'Liberty **and** Union, now and forever, one and inseparable'."

manufactures. Calhoun and other Southerners hoped to align the South and the West politically against the North and with this alliance pull down the obnoxious tariff wall.

Out of this sectional friction came one of the greatest debates in American history. In January, 1830 Senator Robert Hayne of South Carolina delivered a speech charging that the Eastern Senators were working to keep both tariff and land prices high in order to discourage the working class from westward migration. He was answered the following day by Daniel Webster. In flowery but powerful oratory the Massachusetts Senator denounced Hayne as threatening nullification and secession. He called upon the Senate to rally to the Union, with all that was implied by obedience to federal law, including tariff law.

Inside Jackson's cabinet the conflict of sectional opinion was further complicated by personal animosity, particularly between Jackson and Calhoun. In 1831 the President reorganized his administration, bringing Calhoun's influence to an end, and shortly thereafter Calhoun resigned as Vice-President. He was immediately elected to the Senate to represent South Carolina and lead the growing Southern resistance to Jackson's leadership. With the passage of another high tariff law in 1832 South Carolina was convinced that protection had become a permanent feature of American policy; the state accordingly decided to experiment with the Doctrine of Nullification.

Following the procedure suggested by the Exposition and Protest in 1828, a special state convention declared that the tariff law of 1832 and all other protective legislation were null and void in South Carolina. It forbade federal and state officers to collect duties in the state. The convention showed its teeth by threatening secession from the Union should the federal government try "to reduce this State to obedience" by force. Faced with actual nullification, Jackson acted decisively. He announced publicly that the State Ordinance was "incompatible with the existence of the Union" and privately referred to its promoters as "wicked demagogues" who deserved the gallows. The Congress passed a Force Act authorizing the President to use the army and navy to uphold federal law, and Jackson dispatched warships to Charleston harbour, artillery units to Fort Moultrie, and ordered troops to be ready for service.

In 1833 a compromise solution averted the immediate danger of civil war. A compromise tariff was arranged by Henry Clay and John Calhoun, who wished to avoid armed conflict, which provided that over a ten-year period all customs duties would be substantially lowered. Conflict was avoided, both sides declared victory, and South Carolina got in the last word by nullifying the Force Act. The split in the nation, however, was deepening.

In addition to the nullification struggle Jackson launched open war against the Bank of the United States. Under the management of Nicholas Biddle of Philadelphia the Bank had become a careful regulator of credit and the value of money. By granting or refusing loans to smaller, independent banks, the Bank of the United States controlled the amount of loans and credit that could be extended to businessmen. Throughout the nation, dozens of state-chartered bank owners and small businessmen, looking for easier credit, resented the power of the National Bank. Small bankers and businessmen charged that the Bank was a privileged Eastern monopoly because while one-fifth of its stock was owned by the government, the rest was owned by private Eastern investors. They asserted that the profit on its loans, made mostly in the South and West, went to enrich the Eastern bankers and those Europeans who owned some of its shares. What the Bank's opponents sought was a loose banking system under which they could gamble in land and money values without regard for the actual welfare of the farmer or worker.

Sensing in the rising Democratic criticism of the Bank an issue on which Jackson might be defeated in the 1832 election, Henry Clay induced Nicholas Biddle to apply for renewal of the Bank's charter, although the existing charter would not expire until 1836. This was a calculated gamble which proved to be a major political blunder. When the Bank Bill passed both houses of Congress, Jackson at once vetoed it and accompanied his

In the election of 1832 Biddle's Bank fought openly for the defeat of Jackson, hoping thus to retrieve the Bank veto. It poured money into the Whig campaign chest and bought up newspaper editors with handsome "loans." After the election Jackson ordered the removal of government funds from the B.U.S., hoping to prevent its further political activity and to cushion the shock of the Bank's demise in 1836. Public funds were deposited in what the Whigs called "pet banks." Democratic cartoonists had a field day.

veto with a strongly-worded summary of all the arguments against "the Monster," as the Bank was sometimes nicknamed:

> Distinctions in society will always exist under every just government. . . . But when the laws undertake to add to these natural and just advantages artificial distinctions, to grant titles, gratuities and exclusive privileges, to make the rich richer and the potent more powerful, the humble members of the society—the farmers, mechanics and labourers—who have neither the time nor the means of securing like favours for themselves, have a right to complain of the injustice of their government.

Biddle and Clay so misread popular feeling that they actually reprinted the veto message and used it as part of their own election campaign in 1832. The message, however, inspired fears among frontiersmen, Eastern workers and small businessmen, and actually helped Jackson to be re-elected with a handsome majority.

In turn, Jackson committed a grave error. He decided to kill "the Monster" without waiting for its natural death in 1836, and wrote: "Until I can strangle the hydra of corruption, the Bank, I will not shrink from my duty." He instructed Roger B. Taney, his Secretary of the Treasury, to withdraw all government deposits from the Bank of the United States and to distribute them among a large number of state banks, which were quickly dubbed "pet banks." This curtailed the ability of the Bank of the United States to control credit. Without the restraining power of the Bank of the United States, local banks expanded their credit and loans. Speculative fever produced a boom in land sales and other "investments." In 1836, western land sales were ten times greater than the average of the preceding ten years. As bank notes became less stable in value, even the Jacksonians began to worry and in 1836 Jackson issued a Specie Circular which required government land offices to accept only gold or silver in their sales. Since local banks had issued much more paper money than they could redeem in specie, credit collapsed at once, and state bank notes fell sharply in value. Thus the prosperity of Jackson's second term was pricked, and soon after "Old Hickory" left office in 1837 the country was deep in depression.

3. DECLINE OF THE DEMOCRATS

Yet Jackson was at the peak of his popularity in 1836 and was able to name Martin Van Buren as his successor. The Democratic convention confirmed his decision and the electorate endorsed it in November. But Van Buren soon aroused widespread opposition. Suave, elegant, and an ardent lover of fashionable horse-racing, he lacked the common touch of his rough-hewn predecessor. Within a short time there were accusations that Van Buren had transformed the White House into a veritable Versailles with extravagent silver decorations and gold service for the table. Stories of the Democratic President delicately sipping champagne from the dainty shoe of a female guest did little to increase his popularity.

But the President's personal unpopularity was only one reason for the declining fortunes of the Democrats. More important was the onset of world-wide depression in 1837, which struck the United States with particular severity. American banks had borrowed heavily from British banks to finance the economic expansion of the 1830's. Faced with financial ruin, the British banks began to recall their loans from American banks. Without credit factories shut down, unemployment soared, and many workers suffered semi-starvation. Thousands of farmers, unable to meet interest payments, lost their lands as banks foreclosed on mortgages. For three years America looked little like the land of opportunity. Bread riots broke out in New York City, and political agitation reached a fever pitch. For these grave national ills Van Buren had no effective remedy.

Under the circumstances, the new Whig party easily won the election of 1840. The Whigs astutely refrained from producing a platform, contenting themselves with blaming the depression on the Democrats. In choosing a Presidential candidate the Whigs ignored Henry Clay who, despite his brilliance, had made too many enemies, and selected a political

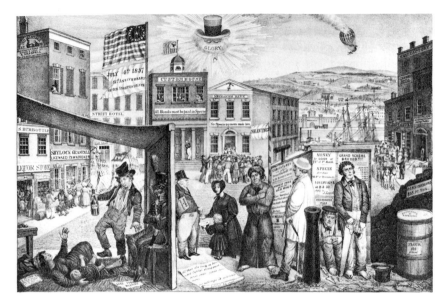

This cartoon illustrates the impact of the panic of 1837: high prices (flour rose from $5.62 to $7.77 a barrel and coal from $6.00 to $10.50); business depression (the banks refused to redeem their notes in specie or hard money); and "loco foco" agitation. Many Americans believed that the nation was on the verge of another revolution, as flour and bread riots recalled the beginning of the French Revolution. One February morning in 1837 New Yorkers awoke to find angry posters on the street corners, "Bread, Meat, Rent and Fuel! Their prices must come down! The Voice of the People shall be heard and will Prevail!"

unknown, General William Henry Harrison. The "victor" in the inde-cisive battle of Tippecanoe, Harrison would appeal to the frontier, while Vice-Presidential candidate John Tyler of Virginia would attract Southern states' righters. The Whigs organized hundreds of torchlite processions highlighted by floats bearing model log cabins to symbolize Harrison's humble birth as opposed to Van Buren's "aristocracy." Prominent in the processions were kegs of hard cider, whose purpose was more practical than symbolic. Slogans such as "Tippecanoe and Tyler too," or "Harrison, two dollars a day and roast beef" replaced more serious campaigning. Such appeals proved irresistible and the conservative Whig party swept the country.

Inauguration day, 1841, was so cold and wet that the new President caught pneumonia. Within five weeks he was dead and the Virginian, Tyler, was President. Almost at once the Whig party split as the Southern President vetoed two bills pressed by Northern Whigs to recharter a Bank of the United States, and strongly opposed bills to increase the tariff. The followers of Henry Clay resigned from the Cabinet and were replaced by Tyler-men. Yet in spite of these divisions the country resumed its extraordinary industrial and agricultural expansion as the Age of Jackson gave way to that of the industrial revolution.

CHAPTER 5

America and the Industrial Revolution

The split in the Whig party revealed the growing strain placed upon national institutions by the basic economic and social differences among the three major sections of the United States. The Northeast passed through an industrial revolution which transformed it into an urban industrial society. The South, also prosperous and expanding, retained its agricultural base in a cotton economy. The Northwest, like the South, was agricultural, but it developed an economy radically different from the Southern plantation economy. Not only were the products of the two sections different, but the independent farmer of the Northwest did not need and had no sympathy for the South's slave system. Thus, while all parts of the American economy expanded in the 1840's, this growth intensified rather than reduced the sectional differences within the nation. In politics the basic conflict was between Northeast and Southeast, each of which hoped to establish an alliance with, or control over, the expanding trans-Allegheny West. During the 'forties the North gradually won out in this competition because the canals and railways constructed by Northern finance bound the West economically and politically to the Northeast. As this development progressed, the South became more fearful of losing its control of the federal government and more insistent upon protecting its rights and maintaining the slave system.

Perhaps the most striking difference between North and South in the 1840's lay in the social organization of the two sections. The South was a rigidly structured society with plantation masters at the top of a social pyramid which broadened down through small farmers, poor whites and, at the bottom, Negro slaves. Classes in Northern society were much more fluid. Although there were striking economic distinctions between the rich mill-owner and the poverty-stricken immigrant labourer, the spirit of Northern society was egalitarian. European visitors to the United States often saw the combination of the egalitarian and commercial spirit as the most pronounced characteristic of society in the Northeastern states.

1. THE RISE OF INDUSTRIALISM

The period was marked by revolutionary changes in farming and industry that would one day transform the United States into the most powerful nation in the world. Like the earlier political revolution, the basic patterns of the industrial revolution in the Northeastern states were imported from Britain. One incident may symbolize this relationship. An English textile worker named Samuel Slater accepted the offer of Moses Brown, a wealthy Rhode Island merchant, to smuggle to the United States the plan of an English factory loom, in spite of laws forbidding emigration of Britain's skilled factory workers, and so became the father of the American factory system.

Factory production of textiles expanded rapidly in New England during and after the War of 1812. By the 1830's there were textile factories on nearly every stream in the region. In 1846, the sewing machine invented by Howe revolutionized the making of shoes, clothing and leather articles. They, too, could now be made most profitably in factories rather than home workshops. The resulting expansion of the Eastern factory system meant markets for the growing stream of raw materials—wool, timber, coal, iron—flowing back from the new West. By 1850, with the development of steam power and the discovery of new midwestern coal and iron deposits, the middle states were beginning to catch up with the East in factory growth. And everywhere in the North the cities and towns grew like mushrooms.

The factory system required better forms of business and financial organization. Since individual businessmen usually lacked sufficient capital to establish factories, organizers formed an increasing number of public companies and corporations to bring together investors who bought shares in the enterprises. The new type of business organization produced a distinct capitalist class. It also meant changes in the life of the working class. Employees began to have fewer contacts with the factory managers, who in turn simply carried out the decisions of remote owners and stockholders. With the increasing use of the principle of "limited liability" whereby stockholders were responsible for company debts only up to the value of their stock, businessmen felt secure in investing widely in a variety of industrial undertakings. The limited company with large numbers of stockholders also made it possible for small groups of men, in combination, to control several companies while actually owning only a fraction of the total stock. Such groups were the forerunners of the huge trusts that have come to dominate North American business in our own day.

Impersonal industrial relations of this kind seemed to intensify the investors' itch for profits. The result was the lengthening of the work day, the decline of real wages, the growth of child labour, and the spread of slums in many Northern cities. The United States, in short, reproduced many of the same evils which attended the industrial revolution in England. During the 1840's there were protests against these conditions but they were

Charles Dickens' Martin Chuzzlewit, disembarking in New York from the packet-ship **The Screw**, recorded the first sights and sounds: " 'Here's this morning's **New York Sewer!**' cried one newsboy. 'Here's this morning's **New York Stabber!** Here's the **New York Family Spy!** . . . Here's full particulars of the patriotic loco-foco meeting yesterday, in which the Whigs was so chewed up; and the last Alabama gouging case . . . and a full account of the Ball at Mrs. White's last night, where all the beauty and fashion of New York was assembled; with the **Sewer's** own particulars of the private lives of all the ladies that was there!' "

America· had become a brash, unsophisticated and commercial society whose values were assessed mainly in commercial terms. The "loco-foco" meeting reported by the **New York Peeper** was a meeting of working men to protest against their poverty and miserable working conditions. Conversely, Mrs. White's ball indicated the growth of a social hierarchy based upon the wealth accumulated by Eastern merchants and bankers.

usually futile. Workers in some highly skilled trades managed to form unions, which conducted several long and bitter strikes in the 1850's. But the mass of industrial workers had no unions, and the employees who tried to organize soon found themselves unemployed. The courts and middle-class opinion strongly supported the employers in their suppression of attempts to unionize. In 1815 Judge Roberts in Pittsburgh had handed down a typical decision. Roberts refused to recognize the legality of labour unions and declared that any organization of labour was a conspiracy, a threat to both employers and employees. In 1842, however, in the case of *Commonwealth versus Hunt*, the Massachusetts Supreme Court declared that while trade unionism might diminish an employer's profits, it might also be "highly meritorious and public spirited." This decision entertained the possibility of legality for trade unions, but it had very little effect at this time, for most courts continued to decide in favour of employers. In such circumstances was the urban wealth of the North forged.

Principal Railways, 1860

The industrial growth was accompanied by the spread of railways to link the markets of North and West. Railways used the corporate form of organization and soon became the chief means of transportation. For some time after the fourteen-mile Baltimore and Ohio Railway opened in 1830, however, the lower costs of water transport enabled canals to compete effectively with railways. Passengers on the early woodburning trains saw other advantages in canal or sea travel. On the Albany and Schenectady Railway:

> They used dry pitch for fuel, and there being no smoke or spark catcher to the chimney or smoke stack, a volume of black smoke

strongly impregnated with sparks, coals and cinders came pouring back the whole length of the train. Each of the passengers who had an umbrella raised it as a protection against the smoke and fire. They were found to be but momentary protection, for I think in the first mile the last umbrella went overboard, all having their covers burnt off from the frames, when a general mêlée took place among the deck passengers, each whipping his neighbour to put out the fire.

But with such improvements as iron rails, covered passenger and freight cars, and standard gauges, the railways were soon carrying the great bulk both of freight and passengers. By 1860 there were 30,000 miles of track, much of which was interconnected for through freight. Governments assumed much of the financial risk involved in building the American railway network. States made loans to railway companies, bought equipment for them and guaranteed their bonds. The federal government gave them free grants of land. However, promoters and construction companies, often controlled by American or British bankers, retained the profits from building and operating the railways. Thus the railways, too, played a part in the transformation of the industrial and corporation pattern that was sharply changing the class structure of the United States.

There were comparable advances in other forms of transportation and communication. Within six years of the building of Samuel Morse's first telegraph line in Maryland in 1844, the major American cities could communicate by wire. By 1860 all cities east of the Rockies were linked by telegraph, and in 1861 the network was extended to San Francisco. American shipbuilding reached its peak in the 1850's when the New England clipper ships were the swiftest sailing-ships afloat. Although Britain's development of propeller-driven steamers with iron hulls established British supremacy in ocean transport, American vessels plied a vigorous trade in the world's ports. And it was the American Commodore Matthew Perry who in 1854 first secured a treaty from Japan opening Japanese trade to Americans.

The opportunities presented by American industrial expansion attracted not only European capital but a steady stream of eager immigrants. In 1840 the United States population stood at seventeen million; by 1860 it was thirty-one million because of immigration and a high birth-rate. The United States was also moving toward urbanization. In 1840 one-twelfth of the people lived in cities of eight thousand or more; by 1860 the percentage of urban dwellers had almost doubled. At the same time the United States was becoming a more continental nation; by 1850 nearly fifty per cent of all Americans lived west of the Appalachian Mountains.

Most immigrants in the first half of the nineteenth century came from the United Kingdom and northwestern Europe. The majority of them found work in factories or on railways, canals or farms where they provided much of the labour required for America's economic expansion. Although Americans generally liked to think of their nation as a refuge for oppressed Europeans, thousands of native-born citizens deeply resented the influx

An American cartoon shows John Bull worried about the emigration of hundreds of thousands of the "lower orders" to the United States. Nativists in America did not share the optimism of this artist.

of immigrants.   Eastern workers feared that the abundance of cheap labour would result in lower wages.   Conservative Whigs deplored the tendency of immigrants to vote for the Democrats, particularly in the big cities where Democratic political machines like New York's Tammany Hall often found jobs for the newcomers.   Protestants were distressed because many of the Irish and German immigrants were Roman Catholic. The native-born expressed their opposition to immigration by emphasizing their "Americanism" and by forming associations designed to prevent Roman Catholics and foreigners from holding public office.   In 1845 agitation of this kind culminated in the formation of the Native American party whose platform called for sweeping changes in the naturalization laws.   The party was later referred to as the Know-Nothing party because its members were sworn to secrecy about its purposes and answered all questions with a curt "I know nothing."

Between 1825 and 1850 new methods and inventions made farming more efficient and more profitable.   Wooden ploughs gave way to metal ones, and in the 1830's McCormick's mechanical reaper took much of the backbreaking labour out of harvesting.   New interest in livestock breeding, crop rotation, and fertilizing the soil, increased productivity just as vast new farming areas were coming under cultivation. Much of the produce from the farms of the old Northwest, especially pork and wheat flour, found a market in the one-crop areas of the South.

This commerce was largely carried on the Ohio and Mississippi river systems and created an economic bond between the South and the West. In politics this intersectional commerce often led Southerners and Westerners into an alliance to protect their mutual interests, especially with respect to the tariff which both farm sections wished to keep low.

2. THE GROWTH OF SECTIONALISM

Northern leaders were very much aware of the importance of sectional economic interests. One of their main concerns in building canals and then railways was to establish closer economic ties by providing easy export routes for Western farmers into the Northeast. In what amounted to a race between Northeast and Southeast for economic control of the West, the Northeast had several important advantages. Its financial institutions were stronger and it had more businessmen who were interested in railways both as investment opportunities and as marketing systems. Also, while the South purchased considerable quantities of Western farm produce, the Northeast was rapidly becoming the commercial centre for shipping Western grain and flour to transatlantic markets. As Western grain production increased, so did the importance to the West of Northern railways, commercial services and shipping lines. Moreover, it was from Northern manufacturers and importers that Westerners bought the equipment necessary to develop their thriving farm economy.

Helping to cement the economic bond between the Northeast and the West was an increasingly tense conflict between Western farmers and Southern planters over the question of land settlement in the West. The farmers, frequently supported by Northeastern factory workers and newspaper editors, demanded a policy of free land grants to anyone who would undertake to establish a homestead in the West. Southerners were bitterly opposed to such a policy, fearing that it would simply encourage the flow of small "free" farmers to the Mississippi valley and thus impede the spread of the Southern plantation economy which was based on slave labour. Behind their fears lay a complex pattern of social and economic facts.

While King Factory established his sway in the North, King Cotton held triumphant court in the South. Eli Whitney's cotton gin had ensured the expansion of cotton culture into Virginia, North Carolina and Tennessee. By 1840 the Southern states were producing seven-eighths of the world's supply of cotton, and cotton exports accounted for fifty-one per cent of the value of the total American export trade. As cotton planters relentlessly moved across the Deep South, through Georgia, Alabama and Mississippi, their demand for slaves, as well as for new lands, became voracious. In the 1840's and '50's Southern prosperity was augmented by bumper crops of tobacco, hemp, sugar and indigo. Producers of these commodities gave full support to the claims of the Cotton Kingdom for a generous share in westward expansion.

Although the South provided considerably more than half the total exports of the United States and was thus extremely important to the nation's economic life, its social structure, politics and customs were so different from those of the other sections as to make it almost a nation within a nation. Southerners despised the way of life that was developing in the North almost as much as did the English travellers who visited the United States in these years. Claiming to be democratic, the South really reserved political and social leadership to an aristocracy of the great planters. Some planters revelled in a romantic dream in which they saw themselves recreating an almost medieval society where the aristocratic values of chivalry, military valour and leadership would live again. Favourite reading for the Southern aristocrat, sitting with a mint julep under his white-pillared portico, was Sir Walter Scott.

But such romantic dreaming could be enjoyed only by a few. The social structure in the South was as sharply divided as in the North. There were about seventeen hundred planters who owned over one hundred slaves each. Ten times as many, however, owned less than half a dozen. And of the total population of seven million, six million whites belonged to non-slaveholding families. Many of these "poor whites" lived on small farms and dreamed of the day when they could enlarge their holdings and buy slaves. Others were simply degraded hangers-on of the plantation system. Yet virtually all of the lower-class whites supported the institution of slavery, hoping either to become slave-owners or fearful that emancipation of the Negro would depress their own social and economic position.

Southerners believed that slavery was essential to the Cotton Kingdom. Although importation of slaves from Africa had been legally ended in 1808 under the Constitution, many were smuggled in after that date, and in some states slave-breeding became a business in itself. Competition in the slave market forced the price of a first-class field worker up to eighteen hundred dollars, a large sum in the early nineteenth century. By 1860 there were four million Negro slaves in the South, representing an immense capital investment. To keep the slaves "in their place" the Southern whites constructed a complex system of laws forbidding anyone to teach Negroes to read and write or for whites and Negroes to intermarry. Planters encouraged their slaves to attend Negro religious services on the plantations where all teaching was focused on the rewards of the after-life. Stringent punishment was meted out to anyone assisting an escaped slave. Although many Southerners must have been secretly conscience-stricken if they reflected upon the glowing words of the Declaration of Independence, "all men are created equal," they felt obliged in public to defend their "peculiar institution" of slavery. Southern slaves, they declared, with some justification, were better cared for than Northern factory workers. The slave huts on the great plantations were scarcely

The result of slave trading was graphically described in a letter written by a woman slave in 1852. "Dear Husband: I write you a letter to let you know my distress. My master has sold Albert to a trader on Monday court day and myself and other child is for sale also and I want you to let [me] hear from you very soon before next cort [sic] if you can. . . . I don't want a trader to get me. . . . I am quite heartsick."

luxurious, but the Negro knew that his master would look after him in sickness and old age, and many Negroes appeared happy under the system. On the other hand, no Negro family was secure from the possibility of being broken up by the sale of one or more of its members. As the soil in the Southeast became exhausted and many planters moved to the rich black soil of the Gulf states more and more slaves were "sold down the river" to overseers who frequently manacled the unfortunate Negroes in gangs as they marched to the fields. Furthermore, the slave system encouraged immorality by making light of marriage and by brutally corrupting white owners who came to accept whipping and branding without personal qualms.

With more and more deeply etched distinctions between the Cotton Kingdom and the North, sectionalism became an increasingly perilous feature of the American political scene. While many Northerners considered the South to be a morally decadent society the "slavocracy" in these years was by no means lethargic. Enjoying highly disciplined political leadership in its race with the North for control of the West, the South also maintained a very strong position in the total economic life of the nation. Perhaps the chief competitive failures of the Cotton Kingdom were its refusal to diversify its farming, and its reluctance to invest in industrial development, commercial services, or shipping. As a result the planters not only saw more and more of their profits eaten up by Northerners and Europeans, but also became increasingly dependent on the cotton economy.

3. CULTURAL DEVELOPMENT

While this period of unprecedented growth produced tension and conflict between sections and classes within the nation, it also produced a vigorous American literature. American writing in this period had its roots in England, but it was influenced by American problems and had a distinctive American flavour. James Fenimore Cooper, Edgar Allan Poe and Washington Irving were deeply romantic in feeling, and wrote about American subjects, but frequently in a European style and with European audiences in mind. Poe, in particular, castigated Americans for their provincialism and often experimented with novel rhythms and strange themes in his poetry and short stories. Cooper celebrated in popular style the romance of the frontier, while Walt Whitman wrote boisterously of the strident American democracy. Herman Melville's great novel *Moby Dick* grew out of an essentially American experience. Some writers like James Russell Lowell reflected the nationalist feeling of expansion, while others like Emerson and Thoreau were highly critical of the loss of individuality in the urban, democratic developments of their day.

The growth of democracy also produced great changes in American journalism. The 1830's saw the beginning of such penny newspapers as the New York *Sun,* the New York *Herald* and Horace Greeley's New York *Tribune.* Although these dailies catered to the tastes of the masses, they also contained much more serious political comment and reporting than is usual today and their editors played a prominent part in American political life.

The rise of literacy which made such newspapers possible was the result of the spread of free public schooling. By 1850 most children in non-frontier areas of the North could attend public schools, although many were deprived of an education because of the necessity to work. Even in the South public education for whites advanced rapidly. As early as 1821 Massachusetts established the first public high school. There was often widespread opposition to these developments, especially by the wealthy who regarded tax-supported education as an unwarranted interference with individual rights by the government.

On this complex basis of class fears and ambitions, sectional suspicions, economic growth, beckoning opportunity and unexampled natural resources, the young American giant moved forward to gain control of its western empire. In doing so it brought the nation to the greatest crisis in its history.

CHAPTER 6

The Failure of Compromise

The westward course of empire in America not only provided exciting opportunities for individual Americans but brought great questions of public policy more clearly into focus. Would expansion be gradual and guided by patient diplomacy or would it be urgent and forceful? Would Northerners or Southerners control the trans-Mississippi West? Would the "peculiar institution" of slavery move inexorably across the continent? Failure to find permanent answers to these questions eventually precipitated the nation into a great civil war. Historians still debate the causes of the American Civil War. Some feel that the conflict was "irrepressible" while others blame a "blundering generation" that failed to produce adequate leadership. Whatever its causes, the war was a mixture of high ideals, great ambition, and stark tragedy.

1. MANIFEST DESTINY AND TERRITORIAL EXPANSION

By the 1840's the American conviction that it was their "manifest destiny" to expand across the entire North American continent was deeply rooted. A vociferous delegate to the Democratic Convention in 1844 expressed a widespread sentiment when he exclaimed:

Land enough—land enough! Make way, I say, for the young American Buffalo—he has not yet got land enough. . . . I tell you, we will give him Oregon for his summer shade, and the region of Texas as his winter pasture. [Applause.] Like all his race he wants salt, too. Well, he shall have the use of the two oceans—the mighty Pacific and the turbulent Atlantic shall be his. . . . He shall not stop his career until he slakes his thirst in the frozen ocean. [Cheers.]

Continental expansion was regarded as part of God's plan for the American Republic. The New York *Morning News* confessed: "Our own idea is that the American idea or impulse, is fit and just, in harmony with the fair and bountiful orders of nature and with the manifest designs of the Creator." Economic motives, however, were more obvious and

89

important stimulants to expansion. Businessmen and politicians regarded the West as a market for the growing industries of the East, as a rich source of raw materials, and as a base from which to extend American commerce across the Pacific to the teeming markets of the Far East.

American continental expansion inevitably brought her into conflict with Great Britain. Yet the possession of a common language and culture and Britain's desire not to lose the splendid opportunity of investing in the United States proved stronger than the legacy of suspicion from the American Revolution and the War of 1812. Thus, despite the crises that emerged in the 1840's it was in this period that Anglo-American friendship began, as both countries made great efforts to settle their differences amicably.

The Maine-New Brunswick Border Dispute

The first problem to be resolved concerned the border between New Brunswick and Maine. The boundary had not been clearly established after the American Revolution, and in 1839, rival lumbermen clashed over disputed timber rights in the Aroostook Valley. A truce was arranged, but a final settlement of the boundary was urgently needed. In 1841 Lord Ashburton was sent to the United States to negotiate a settlement with Daniel Webster, the Secretary of State. Lord Ashburton was a member of the Baring family which controlled a large British financial house, with very substantial sums invested both in the United States and in British North America, and war did not appeal to him as a method of settlement. Eventually, the Webster-Ashburton Treaty of 1842 granted the United States most of its boundary claims. Britain's concession was, clearly dictated by Imperial interests rather than by those of the British North American colonies. Yet the Treaty was widely criticized in the United States, and many expansionist Democrats felt that Webster had been bought by an Anglo-American "money interest" and a smooth-talking British diplomat.

Far more troublesome and important than the Maine-New Brunswick boundary was the problem of Texas. The United States had renounced its claim to Texas in the treaty of 1819 but during the 1820's twenty thousand settlers with two thousand slaves from the Southern United States moved into Texas, with the approval of the Mexican government. The Mexicans, however, soon realized that the new population of Texas would encourage American annexationism. In 1836 when General Santa Anna's government attempted to curb further immigration and to enforce Mexican tariff and anti-slavery laws, the Americans in Texas revolted. Led by experienced Indian fighters from the southern frontier, the Americans fought desperately against the Mexican forces led by Santa Anna. The most famous battle was at the Alamo Mission in San Antonio where one hundred and eighty-five Americans were killed, including such folk-heroes as Davy Crockett and James Bowie. After several further battles, Americans under General Sam Houston captured Santa Anna in a surprise attack and forced from him a treaty conceding the independence of Texas. In 1837, just before he left office, Andrew Jackson issued diplomatic recognition to Texas as an independent republic.

Recognition was the first step necessary to securing entry into the American Union. The great majority of Texans favoured annexation to the Union but in the United States many people had doubts. Anti-slavery elements were strongly opposed, because they feared that the South wanted Texas admitted so that it could create several new slave states and thus control the Senate. The mood of the country, however, was so clearly expansionist that the outcome was predictable. After her brief career as the Lone Star Republic, Texas entered the Union in December 1845. Annexation, however, had been complicated by demands from the North for the outright acquisition of Oregon, whose ownership had been left undetermined by the Convention of 1818, to balance the annexation of Texas. The problems of both Texas and Oregon were central to the Presidential election campaign of 1844.

The Whigs nominated, as their candidate for President, Henry Clay who sought to remove the Texas issue from politics, while the Democrats nominated James K. Polk, an uninhibited expansionist. In a hard-fought election, Polk and the Democrats argued vigorously for expansion and the campaign gave rise to the cry "fifty-four forty or fight," implying that if Britain did not concede all of the Oregon country up to the southern border of Alaska to the United States there would be war. To appease Northern opponents of Texas annexation, the Polk Democrats successfully associated it with general expansion to the Pacific, calling for "the reoccupation of Oregon and the reannexation of Texas." Polk won the election by a slim margin. A colourless Tennessee politician of little imagination, Polk was nevertheless tenacious and hard-working, and after his election he pressed his expansionist plans with no little skill. Recognizing the dangers of openly breaking with Britain at the same time as he courted war with Mexico, Polk decided to settle the Oregon question first.

Before 1830, Oregon had been of interest mainly to fur-traders, but in the following two decades, hundreds of settlers had made their way to it by wagon-train thereby blazing the Oregon Trail. Despite the American claims of effective occupation, British historical claims to the country, as well as the presence of the Hudson's Bay Company in it, gave England the stronger case. Thus, in the negotiations to end the joint British-

The extreme expansionists thought they saw, in Polk's inaugural address, evidence that he intended to insist on all of Oregon up to 54° 40'. Others, however, began to suspect that he was entertaining the thought of compromise. The British ambassador, within a few weeks of Polk's inauguration, reported the latter impression to London, adding: "Fortunately for the country, the party in the Senate who think with the extremists is so insignificant . . . that Mr. Polk need have no fear that he will not be supported amply, both in and out of the Senate, if he should wisely determine to adopt a moderate and pacific course of policy. . . ." This English cartoon suggests that English opinion did not take "fifty-four forty, or fight" very seriously.

"WHAT? YOU YOUNG YANKEE-NOODLE, STRIKE YOUR OWN FATHER!"

American occupation, Polk was willing to compromise. However, in abandoning his outrageous claim to the whole of Oregon, he gave up much less than did the British who were anxious for peace between Britain and the United States. The treaty of 1846 extended the boundary between British North America and the United States westward from the Rockies along the forty-ninth parallel to Puget Sound, and thence through the Straits of Juan de Fuca to the ocean. Although disappointed Northern Democrats protested vehemently, most Americans seemed happy in the knowledge that they had peacefully gained the richest part of the Columbia valley and valuable Pacific coast harbours.

While the Oregon settlement was being arranged, Polk prepared to acquire the southwestern empire of Texas, New Mexico and California. In November 1845 he sent a special envoy, John Slidell, to Mexico, with an offer to purchase New Mexico and California for thirty million dollars if Mexico would recognize the American annexation of Texas. When Slidell was not even received by the Mexican government, Polk ordered General Zachary Taylor to occupy the territory between the Nueces and Rio Grande rivers, claiming that the Rio Grande was the southern boundary of Texas. The Mexicans defended the territory, and President Polk sent a message to Congress declaring that "war exists, and, notwithstanding all our efforts to avoid it, exists by the act of Mexico herself." Congress accepted this diplomatic double-talk and immediately declared war on Mexico in May, 1846. The Mexican War was popular with everyone except the Northeast and anti-slavery people who saw it as another

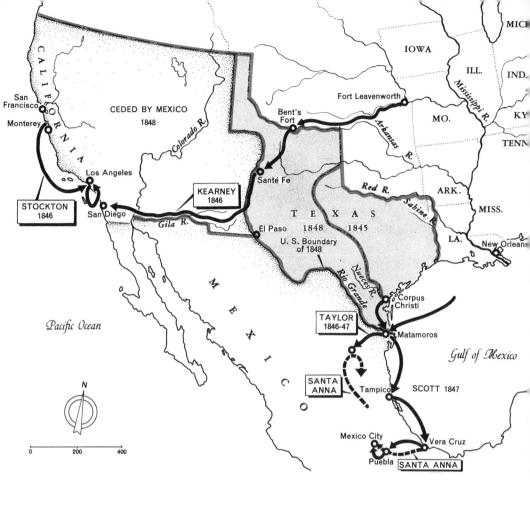

The Mexican War, 1846 - 1848

manœuvre of the Southern slaveholders to extend their territory and increase their power. Whigs such as a Congressman named Abraham Lincoln declared that Taylor was not on American soil when the first "incident" occurred, and voted against the declaration of war.

The chief results of the widely scattered warfare were the defeat of Mexico, the Treaty of Guadeloupe-Hidalgo, 1848, and the enhancement of General Taylor's reputation as a military hero. Mexico gave up her claims to Texas and ceded the whole of New Mexico and California to the United States for fifteen million dollars. Five hundred thousand square miles were thus added to the enormous continental domain of the United States. This western empire not only contributed immense wealth and excellent commercial ports on the Pacific; it intensified the mounting suspicion between North and South.

The Forty-Niners who poured into California in the thousands found a ramshackle capital in San Francisco. A city even then, with more than a little glamour, it also teemed with lawless adventurers from the East. These conditions produced many songs such as this:

> Oh what was your name in the States?
> Was it Thompson or Johnson or Bates?
> Did you murder your wife,
> And fly for your life?
> Say, what was your name in the States?

2. EXPANSION AND SLAVERY

The election of 1848 revealed the concern felt by the major parties about the relationship of westward expansion and the slavery question. Despite their previous opposition to the war, the Whigs, hoping to capitalize on expansionist sentiment, nominated the hero of the Mexican War, General Taylor, as their candidate for President. The Democrats nominated Lewis Cass, a Michigan Senator, who ran on a platform which purposely evaded all issues. A group of disaffected Democrats put forward a third candidate, former President Van Buren. The latter group received support from many former Whigs and Democrats who called themselves Free Soilers and who believed that slavery should be kept out of the West so that the land could be taken up by free farmers. The division in Democratic ranks ensured the election of General Taylor.

The pace of events sharpened the mounting political crisis. In 1849 gold was discovered in the Sacramento Valley of California. The gold rush of '49 gave California a population of eighty thousand by the end of that year. From all over the United States, from Europe and from Latin

America adventurers raced to the new Eldorado. Overland across the plains and the Rockies, through the steaming jungle of Panama or by the long, dangerous voyage around Cape Horn, came thousands in search of "easy" wealth. Gambling, drinking and fighting in a lawless society, the Forty-Niners nevertheless managed to produce a constitution for the territory which prohibited slavery and authorized the government, elected under its authority, to seek the admission of California to the Union.

In the face of Southern opposition to California's entry, Taylor endeavoured to emulate the vigorous executive role of Jackson. He invited California, New Mexico and Deseret (Utah), where a Mormon community had sprung up on the edge of the desert, to formulate constitutions for submission to Congress. Each of the constitutions forbade slavery. The South was furious as it saw the prospect of free states outnumbering slave states. As Senators and Congressmen turned up in Washington armed with knives and revolvers, it became evident that only compromise could avoid civil war.

Attempts at compromise had, of course, to take account of past American experience and of changing attitudes. There had always been Americans who disapproved of slavery, but it was not until the 1820's that the abolitionist or anti-slavery forces began to gain prominence. By 1831, when William Lloyd Garrison founded an abolitionist newspaper, the abolitionist crusade began to assume major significance. Many Northerners became convinced that human bondage was an intolerable evil which denied all the principles upon which the United States had been founded. More moderate Northerners argued that Congress should at least use its authority to prohibit the expansion of slavery into the territories.

This "free soil" argument annoyed the Southerners not only because they were anxious to preserve their "peculiar institution." They were also convinced that they had to maintain power in the Senate to prevent the federal government from adopting such measures as a high tariff which would endanger their economic interests. Southern spokesmen answered Northern attacks on the slave system by arguing that it was essential to the cotton economy and denying that it was a moral evil. Such eloquent defenders of the slave system as John C. Calhoun passionately insisted that slavery was justified by scripture and by usage in history. "I hold that in the present state of civilization," he argued, "where two races of different origin, and distinguished by colour, and other physical differences, as well as intellectual, are brought together, the relation now existing in the slaveholding states between the two is, instead of an evil, a good — a positive good."

According to Southerners, moreover, slavery was an essential foundation for a democratic society and they pointed to ancient Athens to support their case. By having the menial economic and domestic tasks performed by slave labour the more intelligent, white classes were allowed the leisure to develop strong political and cultural traditions. Slavery

So ill that he had to be helped up the Capitol steps on February 5, 1850, Henry Clay delivered one of the most significant speeches of American history. Supporting the various resolutions of the 1850 Compromise, the physically exhausted statesman spoke for three hours and on the following day spoke nearly as long again. His theme was clear and to it he returned repeatedly: "Mr. President, it is passion, passion; party, party; and intemperance — that is all I dread in the adjustment of the great questions which unhappily at this time divide our distracted country."

became, in these terms, a prerequisite of freedom and democracy. Finally, Southern politicians argued, Congress could not regulate slavery in the territories since the federal government was only the agent of the states in administering the territories; in addition the Constitution actually guaranteed property and recognized slaves as property. Thus, they argued, only a *state* government could prohibit slavery. Bitterness mounted rapidly as the abolitionist campaign gained impetus, flooded the South with propaganda and pressed Congress for action.

The argument reached a critical juncture in 1849 when California applied for admission as a state. A further complication was added when some Westerners, like Senator Stephen A. Douglas of Illinois, suggested that in the territories to be established in the land ceded by Mexico the inhabitants should be allowed to choose whether or not to prohibit slavery. This idea was called "popular sovereignty" or "squatter sovereignty." Southerners remained very suspicious of this proposal and suggested instead the extension of the Missouri Compromise line, 36° 30', to the Pacific.

By late 1849 this critical issue demanded solution.. Henry Clay, the seventy-three-year-old author of the Missouri Compromise and the 1833 Tariff Compromise, was now given a final opportunity to play a great role in mediating between the sections. In January 1850 he presented a series of compromise resolutions to Congress, which provided that: California was to be admitted to the Union as a free state; territorial governments of Utah and New Mexico were to be established in the rest of the Mexican cession, which could determine the status of slavery themselves; the slave trade, but not slavery, was to be abolished in the District of Columbia; Congress was to enact a stringent fugitive slave law; the Texan public debt was to be assumed by the United States to compensate Texas for giving up claims to part of New Mexico.

Debate on these proposals was bitter and prolonged. Southern extremists wanted definite congressional support of slavery in the new territories. Northern extremists, like Senators William H. Seward of New York and Charles Sumner of Massachusetts, declaring that slavery was a sin in the eyes of God, said it should be prohibited in all the territories. Despite the revulsion of even moderate Free Soilers at the proposal to tighten up the fugitive slave laws, Daniel Webster persuaded many to support the Clay formula. A Southern convention at Nashville, Tennessee, failed to support a proposal that the Southern states should secede from the Union, and in the end national unity was temporarily preserved.

The Compromise of 1850 saved the Union for ten years. But Calhoun's last speech in the Senate revealed how difficult those ten years would be. Dying, and unable to speak because of his perpetual coughing, Calhoun had his speech read for him to a crowded Senate. His central point was that the "great and primary cause" of the controversy was "that the equilibrium between the two sections has been destroyed." Arguing that the South was virtually denied access to the new territories, he declared that the ties that bound the states together were slowly but surely breaking. Northern opposition to slavery was splitting even the churches and political parties. Only a complete guarantee to the South of security for her institutions and of a low tariff could prevent dissolution of the Union.

3. THE FAILURE OF COMPROMISE

While the 1850 Compromise "worked," it silenced none of the forces that were opposed to it. Already, the temper of the North in its contest with the South was beginning to harden. This was seen particularly in the passage by many Northern state legislatures of the Wilmot Proviso, which was originally an amendment to a congressional act of 1846. President Polk described it in his diary:

Late in the evening of Saturday, the 8th [of August, 1846], I learned that after an exciting debate in the house a bill passed that body, but with a mischievous and foolish amendment to the effect that no territory which might be acquired by treaty from Mexico should ever be a

135,000 SETS, 270,000 VOLUMES SOLD.

UNCLE TOM'S CABIN

FOR SALE HERE.

AN EDITION FOR THE MILLION, COMPLETE IN 1 Vol., PRICE 37 1-2 CENTS.
" " IN GERMAN, IN 1 Vol., PRICE 50 CENTS.
" " IN 2 Vols,. CLOTH, 6 PLATES, PRICE $1.50.
SUPERB ILLUSTRATED EDITION, IN 1 Vol., WITH 153 ENGRAVINGS,
PRICES FROM $2.50 TO $5.00.

The Greatest Book of the Age.

When Harriet Beecher Stowe was introduced to Lincoln in 1862 the President observed: "So you're the little woman who wrote the book that made this great war." Considering the book's impact upon both North and South, Lincoln's exaggeration was pardonable.

slaveholding country. What connection slavery had with making peace with Mexico is difficult to conceive.

The amendment was defeated in the Senate, but its effect remained. David Wilmot, the Pennsylvania Democrat who moved the amendment, had seen the connection between slavery and peace with Mexico, and by 1852 his "Proviso" had virtually become a political platform for Northern opponents of slavery. However, the Democratic candidate for President, Franklin Pierce, won the election of 1852 on a platform which endorsed the 1850 settlement. By that time many Whigs had left their party, either to join the Free Soil party or the Southern wing of the Democratic party, and the Whig party was close to its death.

Not all the provisions of the 1850 Compromise were honoured. In the North, mass meetings of abolitionists and Free Soilers agreed to ignore the new Fugitive Slave Law, and Northern legislatures passed "personal liberty laws" which forbade the holding of fugitive Negroes in state jails. The publication of Harriet Beecher Stowe's *Uncle Tom's Cabin* added fuel to the spreading fire of Northern anti-slavery sentiment.

As abolitionist pressure mounted, the South became more aggressive in its own defense. With the silent approval of the New Yorker, William L. Marcy, who was Secretary of State, Southerners concocted a plan to purchase or seize Cuba as an outlet for Southern expansion. When the plan became too well known it had to be repudiated by Marcy because of the furious Northern opposition to it. Such opposition was the more outspoken because of the previous passage in 1854 of the extremely controversial Kansas-Nebraska Act.

That Act was designed to give territorial government to the vast area between the Missouri River and the Rocky Mountains. In its final form it drew a line across the region at the fortieth parallel of latitude, naming the northern section Nebraska and the southern Kansas. The provisions of the Act repudiated the 1850 Compromise by specifically repealing the Missouri Compromise of 1820. The assumption behind the Act seemed to be that Nebraska would eventually become a free state and Kansas a slave state. The principle of "popular sovereignty," introduced first in the 1850 Compromise, was employed again in the provision of the Kansas-Nebraska Act that settlers in the new territories were to be "perfectly free to form and regulate their domestic institutions in their own way."

The chief author of the Act was Stephen A. Douglas, the Little Giant of Illinois, a diminutive but powerful politician who represented expansionist railway and real estate interests of the North. A transcontinental railway supported by federal land grants was planned which would pass through Nebraska. The Southerners wanted to have a southern route, the Northerners a northern route, with Chicago as terminus. The proposed southern route from New Orleans to the Pacific had the advantage of passing through territory which was already largely settled. The Northerners were anxious to overcome this advantage by hastening settlement on the northern plains. To surmount Southern opposition to voting for a northern route, Douglas had to offer a substantial inducement, namely, repeal of the Missouri Compromise and the consequent opening of the plains to slavery. To Northerners he argued that this was only a nominal concession since, "in that climate, with its production, it is worse than folly to think of its being a slaveholding country." More important, thought Douglas, repeal of the Compromise would solve the Kansas-Nebraska problem, retain the unity of the Democratic party, and possibly hoist Douglas himself into the Presidency. But Douglas badly miscalculated the effect of the Act which was finally passed on May 25, 1854. The North suspected him of selling out to the slave interests and imperilling the agrarian future of the plains. The South began to suspect him of double dealing when they heard him say slavery could not survive in the new territory.

The vote in Congress on the Kansas-Nebraska Act split both the Whig and Democratic parties. In the summer of 1854, largely at the instigation of the Free Soil leaders, local conventions were held throughout the Northwest to establish a new Republican party, which held its first national convention in 1856. The Republican party expressed both Northern ambitions to control the West and the mounting Northern resentment against Southern attempts to dominate the Senate and Cabinet. Many Republicans were morally outraged by slavery and many others felt that, while the "peculiar institution" might be tolerated in the South, its advance into the West would block off that great region from settlement by free Northern farmers. A majority of Northerners believed that a strong

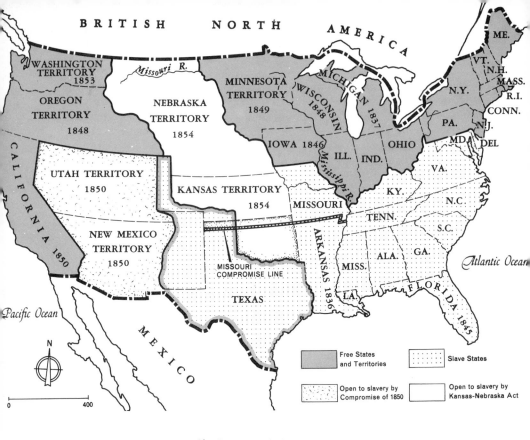

The Extension of Slavery, 1850 - 1854

new party was necessary in order to obtain congressional action to maintain or increase tariff protection, to keep slavery out of the West and to subsidize transcontinental railways and other internal improvements. Thus, although the Republicans were strictly a sectional party, they appealed to very many Northern Democrats who disapproved of the Kansas-Nebraska Act, most Conscience Whigs (the name given to those opposed to slavery), and all the Free Soilers.

Meanwhile, events in Kansas moved the Union closer to disintegration. Pro-slavery and anti-slavery migrants streamed into Kansas. Missourians, described as border ruffians by Northerners, poured across the border on the first election day and succeeded in fraudulently electing a pro-slavery territorial legislature. In January 1856 Free Soilers elected their own legislature and governor. Open violence soon erupted. Rifles supplied to free-state supporters through the efforts of a Brooklyn abolitionist preacher, Henry Ward Beecher, were known as "Beecher's Bibles." The *Squatter Sovereign*, a pro-slavery newspaper, said Southerners would "lynch and hang, tar, feather and drown, every white-livered abolitionist who dares to pollute our soil." The attacks and counter-attacks took over two hundred lives. The area was termed Bleeding Kansas in the national press and the struggle was not finally settled until 1861, in the first year

In the years preceding the Civil War, Northern abolitionists, with some Southern sympathizers, organized the Underground Railroad to assist escaping slaves. Over 100,000 slaves valued at some $30,000,000 are supposed to have escaped to the North and to Canada. One valiant Negress, Harriet Tubman, went back many times to the South and led more than three hundred slaves to freedom along the intricate network of the "Railroad." This is a tunnel in Cleveland presumed to have been used by fugitive slaves.

of the Civil War, when Kansas was admitted to the Union as a free state.

With Kansas a burning issue in 1856, the Democrats nominated James Buchanan of Pennsylvania rather than Stephen Douglas as their candidate for President. Although he won the election, Buchanan was too cautious, too anxious to evade rather than settle issues, to be a successful leader in a time of crisis. The deepening crisis, moreover, was emphasized when the Republican candidate took thirty-three per cent of the popular vote, all of it from states north of the Mason-Dixon line, the traditional dividing line between North and South.

Within a week of Buchanan's inauguration sectional fevers were heightened by the Supreme Court decision in the Dred Scott case. Dred Scott was a Negro slave in Missouri who had previously travelled with his owner in the free state of Illinois and in Louisiana Purchase territory which had been declared free by the Missouri Compromise. He was persuaded to sue for his liberty on the grounds that he gained his freedom by living in a free state and in a free territory. The majority decision, written by the Southerner, Chief Justice Roger B. Taney, stated that no Negro could be a citizen of the United States. In addition, Taney wrote that by the Fifth Amendment the Constitution required the federal government to protect property in all the territories. Therefore, he concluded, the Missouri Compromise was unconstitutional since it deprived masters of their property in slaves. The implication of this decision was that slavery could not be prohibited by territorial legislatures, and that it could therefore be extended indefinitely in the territories. To Northerners, this meant that Douglas' "popular sovereignty" doctrine was a sham which could not prevent the spread of slavery.

A serious financial crisis in 1857 further aroused the North. As prosperity continued to decline in 1858-59 there was serious unemployment and distress in the North. This had two significant political results. Since Southerners escaped the worst effects of the depression, they clung more stubbornly to their faith in their agricultural economy, particularly in cotton, which boomed through these years. In the North the Republican party responded to the depression by pressing for a higher protective tariff and free homesteads in the West. This platform helped to consolidate Republican strength in many Northern areas.

At this time there began to emerge from relative obscurity the towering and tragic figure of the man upon whom would be laid the responsibility for the ultimate "solution" of the sectional strife. Abraham Lincoln wrote of himself in 1858: "It may be said I am, in height, six feet four inches, nearly; lean in flesh, weighing on an average one hundred and eighty pounds; dark complexion, with coarse black hair and gray eyes." He might have added that his face was gaunt, his nose prominent, his eyes unusually deep-set, all of which suggested his somber, brooding character. He educated himself by reading the Bible, biographies, and books on history and law. As a young lawyer in Illinois, Lincoln became a Whig, with distinctly conservative attitudes to politics and society. On its formation, he became associated with the Republican party. He was elected four times to the Illinois state legislature, and served for one term in the House of Representatives at Washington. While generally popular in his own district, "Honest Abe" leapt to no one's mind as Presidential material. He liked and often told amusing stories but his most marked characteristics were those of melancholy and quietness. Beneath all this, however, lay a cool accuracy in the assessment of political problems, a chess-like approach which sometimes seemed to lack scruple.

Lincoln never believed that the Negro was equal in capacity to the white man, although he did believe that he should, by gradual emancipation from slavery, be given equal *rights*. As he saw the nation falling apart, with the slavery issue aggravating all the other points of difference, Lincoln came to believe that the fundamental issue was nothing less than maintenance of the Union itself. In 1858 he made this clear in a speech to a Republican Convention:

> In my opinion, the agitation against slavery will not cease until a crisis shall have been reached and passed. "A house divided against itself cannot stand." I believe this government cannot endure permanently half slave and half free. I do not expect the Union to be dissolved; I do not expect the house to fall; but I do expect it will cease to be divided.

"In four years—four years of battle-days—his endurance, his fertility of resources, his magnanimity, were sorely tried and never found wanting. There, by his courage, his justice, his even temper, his fertile counsel, his humanity, he stood a heroic figure in the centre of an heroic epoch. He is the true history of the American people in his time. Step by step he walked before them; slow with their slowness, quickening his march with theirs, the true representative of this continent; an entirely public man; father of his country, the pulse of twenty millions throbbing in his heart, the thought of their minds articulated by his tongue." Such was the eulogy of Lincoln written by Ralph Waldo Emerson in 1865.

At that convention the Illinois Republicans nominated Lincoln to contest the Senate seat held by the famous Democratic orator, Stephen A. Douglas. Douglas accepted Lincoln's challenge to a series of public debates. He read Lincoln's past speeches carefully and decided to pillory his opponent as the advocate of a "war of extermination." Lincoln replied that he did not propose war, but advocated constitutional means of excluding slavery from those territories where it did not already exist. During one debate at Freeport, Illinois, Lincoln asked Douglas, in the light of the Dred Scott decision: "Can the people of a United States territory, in any lawful way, against the wish of any citizen of the United States, exclude slavery from its limits prior to the formation of a state constitution?" Lincoln hoped to trap Douglas into either abandoning his popular sovereignty doctrine or repudiating the Dred Scott decision. Douglas replied with a statement that quickly became known as the Freeport Doctrine: "The people have the lawful means to exclude it or include it as they please, for the reason that slavery cannot exist a day or an hour anywhere, unless it is supported by local police regulations." The declaration gratified Democratic supporters of popular sovereignty, but it also showed Southern Democrats that Douglas did not believe that the territories were really open to slavery. Thus, while Douglas won the Senate election, he was to lose the support of more than half his party when he was nominated for President in 1860.

The Lincoln-Douglas debates boosted Lincoln's political reputation, but they did little to calm sectional feelings. The crisis deepened in October, 1859 when a band of fiercely evangelical abolitionists, led by a fiery fanatic named John Brown, seized a federal arsenal at Harper's Ferry. They intended to seize weapons, retire to the Virginia mountains and from there conduct other raids to free the slaves. Undoubtedly, Brown planned to spread his operations throughout the South and free all the slaves, possibly by mass insurrection. His coup failed; he was captured, tried, and convicted of treason in a Virginia court, and hanged. Extremists in both sections seized upon the event to advance their cause. Southern "fire eaters" said Brown's raid was the product of a widespread plot in the North. Northern writers practically deified Brown: Emerson called him "the rarest of heroes, a pure idealist," while Thoreau declared ominously after the execution that Brown had become "more alive than ever he was." This idea was popularized in the song "John Brown's Body," which later became the marching song of Northern troops during the Civil War.

By the summer of 1860, with relations between North and South at low ebb, it was clear that the Democratic party was mortally divided. Its national convention which met at Charleston, South Carolina, to nominate a Presidential candidate rejected a plank endorsing slavery and its territorial extension. On this the delegates from eight Southern states withdrew from the convention, thus depriving Stephen Douglas of the two-thirds majority necessary for nomination as the party's candidate. A second convention at Baltimore nominated Douglas, but only after the Southerners had again departed. The Southern Democrats then nominated a separate candidate, John C. Breckenridge of Kentucky, on a defence-of-slavery platform. Since most of the Protestant churches and many other institutions had already broken into two sections over the issue of slavery, the disruption of national parties severed the last intersectional bond in the country.

Unlike the Democrats, the Republicans were in basic agreement as they met in Chicago to nominate their candidate and write his platform. The main planks of the platform included federal aid for a transcontinental railroad, no extension of slavery in the territories, a protective tariff and free homestead grants in the West. Each of the last three planks was a direct challenge to the Democrats. In 1857, under Southern leadership, a Democratic Congress had enacted the lowest tariff since 1816, and the same forces had blocked successive bills to provide free grants of territorial land to farmer-settlers.

Because some of the best known Republicans were either too radical in their abolitionism or too obviously the representatives of special interests, the delegates passed them by in choosing a Presidential candidate. On the third ballot the careful planning of Lincoln's convention managers paid off, and Lincoln won the nomination as the compromise candidate most acceptable to Eastern and Western Republicans. A reporter at the crucial convention observed: "There was a moment's silence . . . and as deep breaths of relief were taken there was a noise . . . like the rush of a great wind, in the van of a storm — and in another breath, the storm was there. There were thousands cheering with the energy of insanity."

The Chicago Lincoln-boosters were right in their predictions of sectional voting strength. The Republicans won every Northern state, including California and Oregon. Breckenridge won the Deep South plus Maryland and Delaware, while Douglas, with nearly as many popular votes as Lincoln, carried only Missouri. Only twenty-six thousand votes were cast for Lincoln in the entire South. The sectional cleavage appeared to be complete; Lincoln was elected President by the North and with a minority of the total votes cast.

4. THE ROAD TO WAR

What followed was the most disastrous "lame duck" period in American history, the period between the election of a President in November and his inauguration in March. For four months Buchanan remained President but he was unwilling to take strong action, while Lincoln did not have power until March and refused till then even to give clear recommendations to the Republicans in Congress. In these circumstances, no one exercised leadership and the nation drifted into war by what appeared on the surface to be inevitable steps.

With the announcement of Lincoln's election, Southern extremists at once declared that the South must secede from the Union. It could not, they declared, remain safe under a "Black Republican" President. Distorting the facts, these leaders vigorously spread the idea that the Republicans wished to abolish slavery everywhere in the Union and to crush the South economically. Since the Republicans controlled neither the House of Representatives nor the Senate, and possibly never would have gained such control if the South had not pursued the course it did, the logic of the Southern extremists was obscure. But this did not prevent it from being effective. Many Southerners were unable to discern the real facts, as they read and heard daily the most terrifying predictions, and saw the President-elect cartooned as a coarse baboon with the abolitionist William Lloyd Garrison coiled about his body like a serpent. They were told that the South was a nation in its own right and was economically healthier than the North which depended upon the "white slave labour" of the factory system bolstered by a tariff which strangled Southern commerce. Southerners also conjured up a vision of a Southern nation, expanding into Cuba, Mexico and even further.

As in 1832, radical Southern opinion was led by South Carolina, where a convention on December 17, 1860 unanimously passed an Ordinance of Secession from the Union. Although moderate spokesmen in the South opposed South Carolina's action, the extremists prevailed, and by February 1, 1861, Florida, Georgia, Mississippi, Alabama, Louisiana and Texas had

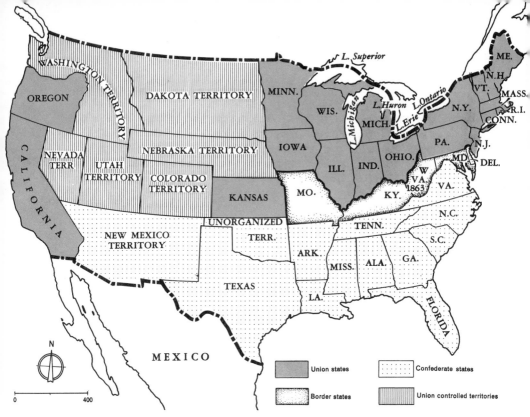

The Alignment of the States in 1861

all joined South Carolina to form the Confederate States of America. Confronted by the accomplished fact, many moderates then gave up their opposition. Jefferson Davis, Senator from Mississippi and former Secretary of War, was chosen President, and Alexander H. Stephens of Georgia, Vice-President of the Confederacy. By March 4, 1861, when Lincoln was inaugurated, a strong Southern government already existed. Many Southerners had been persuaded that secession could be accomplished peacefully, and emissaries were sent to Washington to arrange for the division of federal property in the South. Nevertheless, a substantial army was also being recruited.

In his inaugural address Lincoln was both conciliatory and firm. He promised to enforce all United States laws and to retain possession of all Union property. Hoping to influence anti-secessionist opinion in the South, he declared: "In your hands, my dissatisfied fellow-countrymen, and not in mine, is the momentous issue of civil war. The government will not assail you. You can have no conflict without being yourselves the aggressors." His opinion was not shared by all Northerners.

Many businessmen of New York and New England, particularly textile manufacturers, bankers and shippers, whose prosperity was closely connected with the cotton industry and with financing the Southern economy, believed that if the South really wanted to leave the Union it should be allowed to do so in peace. At the same time there were a number of serious attempts at compromise. The most significant was a set of resolutions proposed in the Senate by John J. Crittenden of Kentucky. These were in the form of proposed amendments to the Constitution which would ban slavery in the territories north of 36° 30′, but would establish it by law south of that line; whenever Northerners frustrated the Fugitive Slave Law, the slave owner was to be compensated; and there should be a special denial of the right of Congress ever to prohibit slavery within a state. Extremists in both sections opposed the Crittenden proposals. While refusing to give official advice to Republicans in Congress, since he had not yet been inaugurated, Lincoln wrote to one Congressman: "Entertain no proposition for a compromise in regard to the extension of slavery. The instant you do they have us under again: all our labour is lost, and sooner or later must be done over." Here Lincoln was explaining his fundamental position: if slavery were permitted to move into the territories the Republican party would fall apart. The agreement to oppose the extension of slavery lay at the very centre of Free Soil-Republican political organization. In Lincoln's view, political unity in the North, on a platform that *should* appeal to moderate opinion in the South, was the only hope of holding the American Union together. His most basic political belief was in the sanctity of that Union; a Union which he was convinced was organic and antedated the Constitution itself. This philosophy he made clear at his inauguration when he declared:

> No State upon its own volition can lawfully get out of the Union; that resolves and ordinances to that effect are legally void; and that acts of violence, within any State or States, against the authority of the United States, are insurrectionary or revolutionary, according to circumstance.

The circumstance occurred almost at once. During Buchanan's last weeks in office the Confederacy had seized most federal property in their states. Intent upon acquiring Fort Sumter in Charleston harbour, the chief remaining federal military post in South Carolina, the Confederate government ordered General Beauregard to demand the surrender of the fort. The fort's commander, Major Anderson, refused to surrender and the Confederate batteries opened fire on the fort at 4:30 a.m. on April 12, 1861, half an hour after the deadline set by Beauregard. After thirty-four hours of steady bombardment, and with his fort a flaming pile of rubble, Anderson lowered the Union flag, to the intense excitement of the society of Charleston which had been watching from their grandstand seats on the harbour front. The warning of Robert Toombs, Confederate Secretary of State, who had advised against attacking the fort, was about to be realized: "The firing upon that fort will inaugurate a civil war greater than any the world has yet seen."

CHAPTER 7

Civil War

The American Civil War illustrated two major forces in the mid-nineteenth-century western world: nationalism and democracy. Nationalism was most perfectly expressed in Lincoln's belief that maintenance of the Union was the highest principle for Americans to follow. In this sense the war was for the reunification of the American nation-state, just as Bismarck's wars and the Italian wars of reunification, fought at about the same time, were for the establishment of comprehensive national states. The war also hammered home, by the ultimate appeal to force, the doctrine of majority rule, which underlies all forms of democracy. But the action of the North in rejecting the right of the South to secede, even after popular conventions in the Southern states had elected that course, confirmed the fears expressed by a French visitor, de Tocqueville, early in the century, that majority rule must ultimately weaken American liberalism and the respect for minority rights.

1. ISSUES AND DIVISIONS

Perhaps the principal irony of the Civil War was that the slaveholding South, denying liberty to millions of human beings within its borders, fought for the liberty of its white population to refuse dictation from the Northern majority. It was on issues of this sort, more than on the apparently uppermost question of slavery, that families were divided and the nation torn asunder. And behind all of the great moral-political questions lay a multitude of economic ambitions. Southern cotton planters sought unlimited expansion of their agrarian-commercial society based on slavery; Northern manufacturers, railway promoters and land speculators wanted to integrate the West into a huge business complex, not only to provide markets for Eastern manufacturers and a field for investment, but to counterbalance Southern votes in Congress in order to assure the maintenance of a protective tariff and other legislation favourable to Northern business. The economic ambitions of the North increased as the demands of war revealed the strength of the Northern economy, and approaching military victory made political and economic domination of the entire nation by the North possible.

Following the bombardment of Fort Sumter, Lincoln waited to see what course the uncommitted border states, like Virginia, which formed a buffer between the Confederacy and the North, would take. After a few days of futile negotiations between the Union government and representatives of the border states, however, he called up seventy-five thousand men from the state militias. As a result, Virginia decided to join the Confederacy rather than contribute troops for the invasion of the South. Not all the people of Virginia favoured secession, however. The people in the northwestern part broke away from the state and drew up a constitution; and in 1863 the district was admitted to the Union as the state of West Virginia. Despite sharp divisions of opinion among the people, Arkansas, Tennessee and North Carolina followed Virginia out of the Union almost immediately. Division of loyalties was deep also in the slave states of Missouri, Kentucky, Maryland and Delaware, which, after considerable debate, decided to stay inside the Union.

Equally tragic were the personal decisions which had to be made. In North and South, families divided as brother fought brother, and son fought father. The Lincoln family had close relatives in the Confederate armies, while the family of Jefferson Davis, President of the Confederate States, had relatives fighting for the North. A civil war is always the most bitter kind of conflict and the scars of the American Civil War have yet to heal completely. In an effort to smooth over some of the legacy of hard feeling, modern historians have renamed the struggle "The War Between the States," or "The War for Southern Independence." Whatever it is called, it remains one of history's most tragic conflicts, involving greater numbers of casualties than either Napoleon's long campaigns, or those of Bismark to unify the German Empire.

2. THE MILITARY CAMPAIGNS

At the outset, most European observers believed that the Confederacy would win its independence. While the twenty-three Union states had a population of twenty-two million and the Confederacy only nine million (of whom nearly four million were Negro slaves) the South had the advantage of interior lines of communication and supply, and a much higher morale. Hundreds of thousands of people living in the "loyal" border states, as well as in the southern districts of Indiana, Ohio and Illinois were pro-Southern. Moreover, the training of Southern soldiers and the ability of Southern commanders were far superior to that of their Northern counterparts. But, in spite of these positive advantages, the only real hope of the South lay in achieving an early victory.

Northern armies outnumbered the Southern by three to two at the beginning of the war; by the end of the fighting the proportion was two

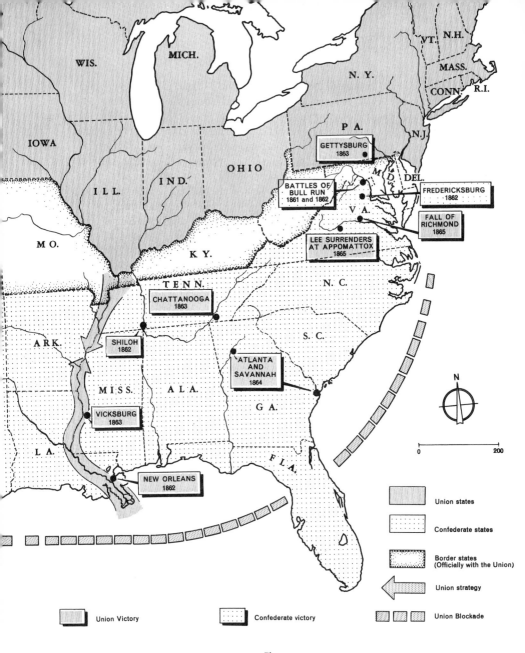

The Civil War

to one. Virtually all of the textile, iron, steel and munition factories were in the North, as were the major banking institutions. Moreover, the North produced much more foodstuffs and provisions than the South. Since most of the merchant marine and navy were in Union hands, a Northern blockade of Southern ports went into operation at once and became increasingly effective as the war progressed, despite the daring exploits of Southern blockade runners.

For two years a quick Southern victory appeared possible. To break the Confederacy, the blue-clad Northern armies were forced to take the offensive. Their strategy was to move directly against Richmond, Virginia, the Confederate capital, only a hundred miles from Washington, and simultaneously secure command of the Mississippi River in order to encircle and strangle the South. At Bull Run in the summer of 1861 the first attempt on Richmond ended in the rout of General McDowell's Union Army. By the spring of 1862, the Union General, George B. McClellan, had reorganized the Army of the Potomac and prepared again to move on Richmond. Taking the peninsular route between the York and James rivers, McClellan reached Fair Oaks from which he could see Richmond. A too cautious man, he waited for reinforcements and when General Robert E. Lee, the Confederate commander, launched a counter-attack, McClellan retired. Lee was perhaps the most brilliant soldier on either side and he was surrounded by able commanders. A few months after Fair Oaks he routed the Northern forces at the second Battle of Bull Run. What had started as a Union drive on Richmond was turning into a Southern invasion of the North, with Washington in continuous danger. McClellan and Lee met at Antietam in mid-September, 1862. The Confederate army was forced to retreat, but McClellan did not pursue his advantage. Following victories at Fredericksburg in December and Chancellorsville in May 1863, Lee once more invaded the North through Maryland and Pennsylvania, again threatening the cities of Washington, Baltimore and Philadelphia.

To stop the Southern advance Lincoln placed General George C. Meade in command of the Northern forces. On July 1 Meade's ninety thousand men met Lee's seventy thousand grey-clad Confederate soldiers at Gettysburg, a small Pennsylvania town. For three blood-stained days the battle raged in the valleys, on the ridges and across the town. On the third day Lee ordered General G. E. Pickett with fifteen thousand of the best Confederate troops to make a desperate attempt on the key Northern position at Cemetery Ridge. The assault was made and a few men actually gained the ridge, but the main body had been slaughtered by murderous Union artillery and rifle fire. The following day Lee withdrew across the Potomac. Once more a Union General, this time Meade, was slow in pursuit, and allowed Lee to escape. President Lincoln was frustrated by the Union's constant inept generalship. "We had them within our grasp; we had only to stretch forth our hands and they were ours," he wrote. "Still, I am very grateful to Meade for the great service he did at Gettysburg," he added. Gratitude was in order, for Gettysburg was perhaps the most decisive battle of the war.

Meanwhile, the steady tightening of the naval blockade was slowly but inexorably smothering the South. In a desperate effort to break the blockade, the South invented a novel device. Naval engineers covered the hull of an old frigate, the *Merrimac*, with iron plate and sent her into Hampton

Roads where she easily demolished three wooden blockade ships. The
North had prepared for such a vessel, however, and when the *Merrimac*
returned on the following day she encountered the *Monitor*, a heavily-
armoured pill-box with powerful cannon mounted on a hollow raft. The
two iron-clads fought to a draw, neither being able to sink the other. The
effort to break the blockade failed, but a new era in naval warfare had
begun.

The first sign of a Northern victory appeared in the West, where a
brilliant American general had been serving his apprenticeship. General
Ulysses S. Grant was one of a number of Northern graduates of West
Point who had failed to obtain preferment in the army before the war,
due partly to Southern domination of the War Department and the higher
military offices. He had resigned his commission and in private life had
failed both in farming and in business. Re-entering the army at the beginning of the war he was assigned to the western campaign under General
Halleck. Here he distinguished himself by cracking the Confederate de-

The greatest battle of the Civil War was fought at Gettysburg July 1-3, 1863. Lincoln's
disappointment when, as he said, "our army held the war in the hollow of its hand and
would not close it," can be seen in the letter he wrote (but did not send) to General Meade.
"I am sorry to be the author of the slightest pain to you. You fought and beat the enemy
at Gettysburg, and of course, to say the least, his loss was as great as ours. He retreated,
and you did not, it seems to me, pressingly pursue him. You had at least 20,000 veteran
troops with you and as many more raw ones within supporting distance, all in addition
to those who fought with you at Gettysburg; while it was not possible that he had received
a single recruit, and yet you stood and let the river run down, bridges be built, and the
enemy move away at his leisure without attacking him. Again, my dear General, I do not
believe you appreciate the magnitude of the disaster involved in Lee's escape."

fenses in Kentucky and Tennessee and withstanding an all-out counter-attack at Shiloh. By July 4, 1863, with the capture of Vicksburg, Northern forces controlled the Mississippi and had thus cut off Louisiana, Arkansas, Mississippi and Texas from the rest of the Confederacy.

In March 1864 Lincoln placed Grant in command of all Union armies and the new commander prepared the final strategy of the war. General Meade was to continue pressing Lee back upon Richmond; a land and sea attack was to be made on Mobile, Alabama; and the western armies were to move eastward as rapidly as possible. Grant himself moved to the Richmond front, while Generals Sheridan and Sherman wreaked havoc in Virginia's Shenandoah Valley and in Georgia. Grant ordered Sheridan: "In pushing up the Shenandoah Valley it is desirable that nothing should be left to invite the enemy to return. Take all provision, forage and stock wanted for the use of your command. . . . Do all the damage to railroads and crops you can. Carry off stock of all descriptions and Negroes, so as to prevent further planting. If the war is to last another year we want the Shenandoah Valley to remain a barren waste." The orders were carried out faithfully. Sherman was even more thorough. He captured and burned Atlanta, Georgia in September 1864, and from there cut a swathe of total devastation across Georgia to the sea, where he arrived at Savannah in December. His exploit is commemorated in the song "Marching through Georgia."

The stage was now set for the final pincer movement of the war. Sherman moved north through the Carolinas, laying waste everything in his path including the important cities of Columbia and Charleston. On April 25, 1865, his Southern opponent, General Johnston, surrendered outside Durham, North Carolina. Meanwhile, Grant had pushed southward on the road to Richmond. In the spring of 1864, he had started moving through the Wilderness, a massive marshy forest, where he was stoutly opposed by Lee. Already criticized in the North for his willingness to lose large numbers of men in costly, if victorious manœuvres, Grant declared: "We have now ended the sixth day of very heavy fighting. . . . I propose to fight it out on this line if it takes all summer." Fifty-five thousand Northern soldiers died in the Wilderness campaign. The battles which followed were equally wasteful of life, but the war of attrition succeeded and Richmond fell early in April, 1865. Lee tried desperately to escape southward but, cut off from supplies and blocked by Union forces moving north, he finally met Grant at Appomattox Court House on April 9, 1865, to seek terms of surrender. For the South it was unconditional surrender, relieved only by the personal military generosity of Grant. Grant undertook to provide rations for twenty-five thousand Southern troops; officers and men of the Confederate army were paroled; officers were allowed to keep their side arms; and all were permitted to keep their own horses, since these would be necessary to work the farms to which most of the Confederate soldiers would now return.

3. THE WAR ON THE HOME FRONT

The greater resources of the North had turned the tide in the final year of the war, but not before many serious crises had been weathered. Both sides had resorted to conscription and to bounties for enlistment. The North provided that exemption from military service could be purchased for three hundred dollars. Opposition to this concept of "a rich man's war and a poor man's fight" led to several riots, the worst of which lasted three days in New York in the summer of 1863. The South found its power to meet the immense financial needs of war severely restricted and tried to solve its problems by printing vast amounts of paper money. The North resorted to the printing of paper money also, but had superior resources to back it. In the North, an income tax, levied for the first time, and tariff increases, which reached an average rate of forty-seven per cent, provided increased revenue to finance the war. Despite this, most of the cost of the war was raised by huge loans, government war bonds which were sold by private firms on a commission basis. The chief bond salesman was Jay Cooke of New York, who became the richest banker in the country. To encourage the sale of bonds the National Banking Act of 1863 permitted any group of businessmen who had certain specified resources to secure a charter for a "National Bank," provided their bank then subscribed at least one-third of its capital to government bonds. This borrowing provided about four-fifths of the Northern war costs and the bonds became a handsome business investment by the end of the war. It was a Hamiltonian process which tended to increase business interest in the operations of the federal government.

The war made possible the realization of several planks in the Republican platform. In 1862 the Homestead Act provided one hundred and sixty acres of land in the public domain free to any *bona fide* settler, a measure which had long been blocked by Southern planters in Congress. In 1864 an Immigration Act permitted businessmen to import industrial labourers. Furthermore, in 1862 Congress had chartered a railway system to be paid for largely out of public resources to connect Chicago with San Francisco. These various measures, passed during the course of the war, represented the achievement of a generation of Whig-Republican demands. Another demand, however, became particularly crucial as the war progressed: emancipation of the slaves. Lincoln had never regarded emancipation of the slaves as the major issue in the war. Indeed, he wrote in August 1862:

> My paramount object in this struggle is to save the Union, and is not either to save or destroy slavery. If I could save the Union without freeing any slave, I would do it; and if I could save it by freeing all the slaves I would do it; and if I could do it by freeing some and leaving others alone I would also do that.

But as the war dragged on, more and more Northerners agreed with the abolitionist wing of the party that the war could be justified only if it resulted in freedom for the Negro slaves. To this body of opinion was added that of many businessmen who had at first been either lukewarm or opposed to the war. They now foresaw the economic opportunities that could be opened for themselves by destroying the political and economic power of the Southern planters. The representatives of this group within the Republican party became known as the Radicals. In the spring of 1862 Congress emancipated the slaves in the District of Columbia and in the territories. But led by Thaddeus Stevens in the House and by Charles Sumner in the Senate the Radicals demanded total and immediate emancipation of all slaves as well as a tough post-war policy to prevent the resurrection of a Southern-dominated Democratic party.

In addition to mounting pressure within his own party, Lincoln faced serious difficulties which might be solved by emancipation. Britain and France both favoured the South, and English policy was of crucial importance. The English textile manufacturers depended on Southern cotton, and the upper class sympathized with the more aristocratic Southerners. Relations between England and the North worsened rapidly, and war nearly broke out late in 1861 when a Union cruiser stopped a British mail steamer, the *Trent*, on the high seas and removed from it two Confederate diplomats who were travelling to England and France. The British government protested vigorously, sent nine thousand troops to Canada in preparation for a possible war, and alerted the Atlantic naval squadrons. Lincoln disavowed the action and released Mason and Slidell, the two diplomats. While this avoided an open break, the Northern blockade continued to create critical difficulties between the two countries. Cotton shipments were reduced which annoyed the British; and the British government winked at the building of Southern commerce raiders in British ports which angered the North. These raiders, of which the best known was the *Alabama*, did great damage to Northern shipping and led to further diplomatic friction between Britain and the United States.

Lincoln decided in the summer of 1862 that he must weaken his Radical critics and also allay anti-Northern opinion in England, particularly since the war was then going very badly for the North. Under the authority of his wartime powers as Commander-in-Chief he issued an Emancipation Proclamation on January 1, 1863. The President noted that emancipation had become "a military necessity absolutely essential for the salvation of the Union." Since this was its purpose, the Proclamation "freed" only those slaves in any state which was then in arms against the Union, leaving slaves in the loyal border states untouched. Many people in the North thought this hypocritical and while the Proclamation weakened abolitionist attacks, it also strengthened the political opposition of Northern anti-war Democrats. However, the Proclamation was useful as a symbol. English anti-slavery opinion was impressed by it. Moreover, English businessmen began to feel that Northern grain to make bread for the textile workers was as important as Southern cotton with which to feed the machines, particularly as alternative sources of cotton were developed.

A Southern sympathizer pictures a satanic Lincoln signing the Emancipation Proclamation under a picture of Negro riots in Santo Domingo. Lincoln's home-town paper, however, declared: "True Patriots of every name rally around the President, determined that the Union shall be preserved and the laws enforced." In England the Proclamation swung opinion to the side of the North. Richard Cobden wrote: "The great rush of the public to all the public meetings called on the subject shows how wide and deep the sympathy for personal freedom still is in the hearts of our people."

In short, the danger that Britain might give aid to the Confederacy was avoided and time was given for the superior strength of the North to have its effect.

Skepticism in the North about ever defeating the South helped to prolong the war. In 1862, a year of dismal military reverses, Democrats gained seats in the House of Representatives; and before the Presidential elections of 1864 even Lincoln believed that he would be defeated by the Democratic nominee, General McClellan. However, the Democratic claim that the war was a failure and that peace should be negotiated was disproved by Union victories in the autumn. Lincoln was re-elected, with Andrew Johnson, an ex-Democrat from Tennessee, as Vice-President.

Much of the opposition to Lincoln stemmed from dislike of his heavy-handed methods on the domestic front. He tolerated no open opposition to the Union war effort, enforced conscription as rigidly as was possible, imprisoned opponents and set military courts in border states to suppress opposition. Personally concerned about the extent to which he was using the executive power, Lincoln was anxious to have constitutional authority for the final emancipation of the slaves. Thus an amendment to the Constitution was put before Congress early in 1864. It required almost a year and a good deal of sharp political pressure to get the necessary two-thirds vote in each House, but by December, 1865, Congress had passed the measure and the necessary three-quarters of the states had ratified the Thirteenth Amendment, which declared:

> Neither slavery nor involuntary servitude, except as a punishment for a crime whereof the party shall have been duly convicted, shall exist within the United States, or any place subject to their jurisdiction.

Economically, the North prospered in the final two years of the war. Capital was actually accumulated faster than it was consumed. On the farms and in the factories new machinery was extensively introduced, production of coal, metals and timber soared, and the railway systems were extended and improved. These developments, together with the financial, tariff and land legislation mentioned earlier, laid the basis on which Northern business organizations could become completely national in extent. The boom also meant high prices, profiteering in war production, and low wages. The fortunes which grew out of the war catapulted a group of Northern businessmen into positions from which they could control the nation's post-war economic life.

The war thus laid the basis for reunification, but it was an expensive basis by any measurement. Six hundred thousand men had died and an equal number had been wounded. Huge areas of the South lay devastated and on the verge of famine. Over five billion dollars had been spent, and the costs of recovery and pensions doubled that amount. But the great question was on what basis a conquered South would resume its place within the Union. The Radical Republicans urged exclusion from government of all former Confederate leaders until such time as the Republican party was organized throughout the South and in a position of permanent control. Others saw the inhumanity of such a policy of vengeance. The leader of the moderates was the President himself. Tempered by the burden of wartime responsibility, Lincoln was acutely aware of the extent of the tragedy through which his nation had passed. As he told his Cabinet he hoped that "there would be no persecution, no bloody work, after the war was over. None need expect [he would] take

any part in hanging or killing these men, even the worst of them. . . .
Enough lives have been sacrificed. We must extinguish our resentments
if we expect harmony and union." To the end he clung to his purpose of
maintaining the Union. The end came too soon.

On April 14, 1865, eleven days after the fall of Richmond, and while
Washington was still in a state of jubilant celebration, Lincoln attended
a stage performance at Ford's Theatre in the capital. As he sat in his box
he was shot and killed by a demented actor, John Wilkes Booth, as part
of a plot to avenge the South. The murder of the President removed the
principal force that might have restrained the Radical demand for recrimi-
natory policies against the South. Herman Melville, one of the country's
greatest writers, summed up the meaning of the President's death:

He lieth in his blood—
The father in his face;
They have killed him, the Forgiver—
The Avenger takes his place.

CHAPTER **8**

Radical Peace and Bourbon Triumph

In the spring of 1865 the South lay in ruins. The economic, social, political and moral destruction of the area can hardly be exaggerated. Most of its railway system had been torn up and the rolling stock burned. In wide regions nearly all livestock had been slaughtered or driven away, houses looted, towns and cities burned to the ground. Scarcely a factory was left standing. With so many men in the army, the plantation structure had crumbled. The organization of churches, schools and universities had, in many districts, withered away. With all available funds, private and public, absorbed by the war, relief agencies established by the Confederacy disappeared. In the near absence of a transportation system the few available stocks of food and other supplies could not be properly distributed. Famine stalked the Southern land, turning thousands of recently wealthy planters' families into hungry beggars and visiting death by starvation upon thousands of liberated slaves.

Faced with the results of such deliberate annihilation and wartime pressures, the spirit of Southern white leaders was not likely to be conciliatory. That spirit, which was to govern white politics in the South for generations after the war, is best seen in the revised will of a ruined planter, written in 1866:

> I give and bequeath to my . . . descendants throughout all generations, that bitter hatred and everlasting malignity of my heart and soul against all the people north of Mason and Dixon's line, and I do hereby exhort and entreat my children and grandchildren . . . to instill in the hearts of . . . all their future descendants from their childhood, this bitter hatred and these malignant feelings. . . .

Faced with the problem of reconstructing their crumbled society, Southern white political leaders thought of restoring a plantation economy as similar as possible to what had existed before the war. This purpose was frustrated by two powerful factors: Northern insistence on completely subjugating the South, and the Thirteenth Amendment to the Constitution

119

which gave immediate legal freedom to four million slaves. The problem of what to do with the "freedmen" was extremely pressing. The South had deliberately kept the Negroes illiterate and they had no appreciation of political questions. They naively believed that emancipation meant a permanent holiday. Furthermore, unlike most peasants of Europe, when they were freed from serfdom, the American freedmen received no land. They became a vast wandering and propertyless population. Such a situation was an open invitation to chaos, riot and chronic lawlessness. Moreover, abolition of slavery meant that planters were deprived of their labour and if not quickly solved, the lack of labour would prevent even the beginnings of Southern economic recovery. These, then, were some of the problems with which white Southerners had somehow to grapple and with which Washington had to deal legislatively.

1. RADICAL RECONSTRUCTION

In the midst of the war, Lincoln had prepared his answer to the problem of reconstructing the post-war Union. He declared that since secession was not legally possible the Confederate states had never been

This is how Richmond appeared to a Northern war artist as the Union Army entered it on April 3, 1865. Whitelaw Reid, a New York journalist, toured the South a few weeks later and described in detail the pauperization of the South which made even less bearable the military devastation: "Window glass has given way to thin boards in railway coaches and in the cities. . . . A complete set of crockery is never seen, and in very few families is there enough to set a table. . . . At the tables of those who were once esteemed luxurious providers you will find neither tea, coffee, sugar, nor spices of any kind. Even candles, in some cases, have been replaced by a cup of grease in which a piece of cloth is plunged for a wick."

outside the Union. At the end of 1863, using his executive power of pardon, Lincoln granted pardon to any Southerners who swore allegiance to the Union, excluding only the leaders of the Southern army and governments. He proclaimed that when ten per cent of the 1860 voters of any Confederate state had sworn to support the Constitution and emancipation, they could re-establish a normal state government. By the spring of 1865 Arkansas, Louisiana and Tennessee had reconstructed state governments on this basis. The Radicals in Congress, however, refused to accept the conciliatory policy of Lincoln. They argued that the Confederate states *had* left the Union, had waged war upon the United States, and were thus "conquered provinces" at the end of the war. Moreover, they declared, the power of admitting such "new" states to the Union was vested by the Constitution in Congress and not in the executive. By this argument, Congress, not the President, had the exclusive power to plan "reconstruction."

This claim led to the passage through Congress of the Wade-Davis Bill in 1864, which asserted congressional control of the South, and provided that a *majority* of voting citizens must swear allegiance before a Confederate state could be readmitted to the Union. Lincoln refused to sign the Bill and it died because the session ended before Congress could again pass it. Such was the situation at the time of Lincoln's assassination.

As Vice-President, Andrew Johnson automatically became chief executive on Lincoln's death. Johnson was a "poor white" Tennessee farmer who had been a Jacksonian Democrat before the war. Without any formal education he had risen through politics to become a Senator and had served as military governor of Tennessee after Union troops occupied the state. He was a sincere man of considerable ability, but possessed little tact or diplomatic skill. Like most poor whites of the South, he had an abiding dislike of big planters. He was, therefore, expected to side with the Radicals in their policy of destroying the political and economic power of the Bourbons, as the conservative Democrats of the Southern states were sometimes called by their opponents because of their autocratic ways. After his first few weeks in office, however, he adopted Lincoln's conciliatory policy. In doing so, he invited an open struggle with the Radicals in Congress.

By the autumn of 1865 all of the seceded states except Texas had accepted the Presidential conditions for reconstruction and had functioning state governments. To deal with the problem of economic recovery and of the freedmen, the new Southern governments passed black codes, which required freedmen to accept work, to live in designated districts, and to become "apprentices" if they were children. Negroes were also excluded from trades in which they might compete with white workers. In other ways, too, the black codes severely limited the civil rights of Negroes, and none of the codes gave Negroes the right to vote. A great many freedmen, lacking skills or property, had little alternative but to return to their former owners, either as servants or as sharecroppers, where

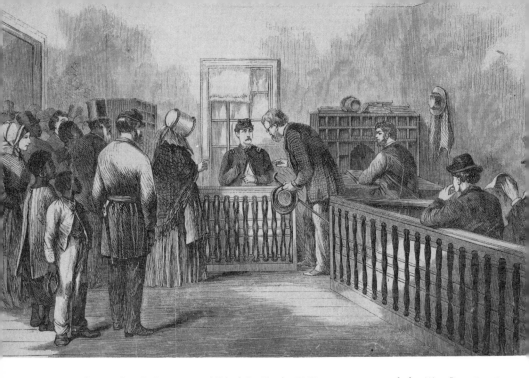

The Freedmen's Bureau, established in March, 1865 as an agency of the War Department to assist freed Negroes, mediated between white people and Negroes in relation to work contracts, reported cruelty and injustice to the Northern military commanders, and helped establish Negro schools. Despite President Johnson's opposition to the good work of the Bureau, Congress extended its authority in 1866. Ex-Confederates loathed the Bureau and were additionally incensed when it actively assisted the Republican party to secure Negro votes. Above is a scene from the Bureau's Richmond office.

they could farm small plots owned by a planter and receive a small share of the resulting crops. Usually the local storekeeper charged more for the goods the Negroes bought than the Negroes were able to pay for from their share of the crops, and the latter were soon sunk in perpetual debt and disabled from ever owning land of their own. These conditions, which were to endure in the South for many years, led to severe racial friction. Race riots and lynchings scarred the South, especially in Mississippi in 1866, and produced a growing conviction in the North that the Democrats were trying to re-establish slavery under different names. Conversely, as Southern planters and merchants, lacking capital of their own, went deeply into debt to Northern commercial houses, they felt that they were being mercilessly exploited by avaricious Northern businessmen and their political henchmen.

In the congressional elections of 1866, Northern suspicion of Southern anti-Negro feelings, President Johnson's refusal to compromise with the Radicals, and the determination of Northern businessmen to exploit the South gave the Radicals a majority in both Houses of Congress. As a result they were in a position to override Johnson's veto of their legislation. They refused to seat Southern Congressmen and Senators who had been

The establishment by the Radicals of military rule and then "carpet bag" government in the South reflected the views of Thaddeus Stevens who declared in September, 1865: "We hold it to be the duty of the Government to inflict condign punishment on the rebel belligerents, and so weaken their hands that they can never again endanger the Union." Southern whites resented bitterly their "subjection" to Northern reconstruction policy.

elected under the Presidential reconstruction terms and instead established their own conditions on which the ex-Confederate states might again enter the Union. These conditions were defined in the Reconstruction Act of 1867 which placed the South under Union military rule. Only when a seceded state adopted a new constitution, which disfranchised a large proportion of white political leaders, enfranchised adult male Negroes, and ratified the Fourteenth Amendment could it re-enter the Union.

The Fourteenth Amendment provided full citizenship to the freedmen and sought to protect their civil rights by declaring that no state might enact "any law which shall abridge the privileges or immunities of citizens of the United States," or which shall "deprive any person of life, liberty or property, without due process of law," or which would "deny to any person within its jurisdiction the equal protection of the laws." The Amendment declared that "all persons born or naturalized in the United States, and subject to the jurisdiction thereof, are citizens of the United States and of the State wherein they reside," thus denying the contention of Chief Justice Roger Taney in the Dred Scott case that Negroes were not citizens. Finally, it debarred from public office any Confederate leader who had not been specifically pardoned by Congress and refused to honour debts contracted by the Southern states during the period of Confederacy.

Under the congressional reconstruction policy, state governments were established throughout the South, based upon Negro suffrage and restricted white suffrage. As a result the new legislatures were composed of illiterate freedmen, scalawags and carpetbaggers. Carpetbaggers were Northern opportunists who invaded the South looking for commercial opportunities and who organized branches of the Republican party, while scalawags were opportunistic white Southerners who threw in their lot with the Republicans.

Although these legislatures passed some constructive legislation, particularly in educational matters, many of them suffered from a large degree of corruption. Furthermore, because of their composition and the military supervision under which they were established, they also stimulated mounting racial friction.

In Washington, the Radicals sensed complete victory. When Johnson tried to block their attempt to destroy permanently white Southern political influence, the Radicals passed the Tenure of Office Act and the Command of the Army Act. The first prohibited the President from removing any member of the Cabinet without the consent of two-thirds of the Senate, thus depriving him of control of the Cabinet. The second transferred control of the army from the President to Congress. When Johnson dismissed Edward Stanton, his Secretary of War, because Stanton betrayed Cabinet information to Radical congressional leaders, the House of Representatives voted to impeach Johnson. On trumped-up charges the House alleged that the President had committed "high crimes and misdemeanours" in trying to block the Radical policy. At the impeachment trial in the Senate, the House prosecutors failed by one vote to convict the President on the charges. It was a very close call for the doctrine of separation of powers. Had the Radicals succeeded, a precedent would have been established which, if repeated, might have destroyed the independence of the Presidency.

2. THE GRANT ADMINISTRATION

By the time of the election of 1868 most of the Southern states had ratified the Fourteenth Amendment and had been readmitted to the Union. As their candidate for President, the Republicans nominated the Civil War hero, General Ulysses Grant. Waving "the bloody shirt" (which meant playing up the Civil War and Northern losses) and crying "Vote the Way You Shot" the Republicans sought approval of the Radical reconstruction policy. The Democrats tried to make the issue "cheap money" and appealed to the debt-ridden farmers by proposing to re-issue greenbacks, or paper money, which the government had been withdrawing from circulation under business pressure. The real issue, however, remained that of the Radical reconstruction policy.

While Grant won by two hundred and fourteen to eighty votes in the electoral college, in the popular vote of 5,700,000 his majority was a mere 300,000. Without the Negro vote the Democratic candidate would undoubtedly have been elected. The election not only testified to the growing disenchantment with the Radical Republicans but confirmed the Radicals in their view that the Negro vote was essential to their hold on power. The Radicals immediately proposed and obtained ratification of the Fifteenth Amendment to the Constitution in 1870 which guaranteed more specifically than had the Fourteenth the freedman's right to vote.

White political leaders in the South also realized that it was the Negro

A Radical Republican artist shows what many Northerners thought Southern Redemptionists were doing to the Fourteenth and Fifteenth Amendments. The passage of Force Acts was heavily influenced by such opinion.

vote which deprived them of their accustomed role of dominance. They decided that the only means of retaliation left open to them was intimidation and violence. They formed secret societies with such mysterious names as Knights of the White Camellia and Ku Klux Klan. Hooded in white sheets, the Ku Klux Klan members rode forth at night issuing spectral warnings against voting to the defenceless Negroes. By day the Klansmen visited their wrath upon carpetbaggers, scalawags and Negroes, shooting, flogging, burning and generally terrorizing all who disregarded their warnings. Against this kind of secret organization neither the Radical Congress nor carpetbag governors prevailed. Attempts to enforce the reconstruction legislation were ineffective and under the sway of the "Redeemers" of Southern white power one state after another returned to the Democratic political fold in state and federal politics. Meanwhile, Northern businessmen had begun to doubt the wisdom of the Radical policy. By the Amnesty Act of 1872 Congress removed the political limitations of the Fourteenth Amendment for all but five hundred Southerners. At the same time, the Freedmen's Bureau, established by Congress in 1865 to protect Negro rights, was allowed to die.

Meanwhile, in the North, corruption was as widespread under the Grant administration as it was under the Southern reconstruction governments. Honest but dull, Grant stood as the symbol of official Republican respectability, behind which financial speculators and railway promoters like Jay Gould and "Jubilee Jim" Fisk manipulated prices and took huge profits from publicly protected or subsidized enterprises. Grant, who supported the most extreme Radical policy in the South, was an expansionist in foreign policy. He was barely restrained by his able Secretary of State, Hamilton Fish, from helping rebels to throw the Spaniards out of Cuba, and he supported an abortive plan to annex Santo Domingo. Grant was also cool toward attempts to lower the tariff or to reform the civil service, which was a chief centre of governmental corruption. In short, he seemed to represent the worst spirit of acquisitive materialism in the victorious North, just as he had represented the high human costs of winning the war.

Nevertheless, Grant and the Republicans won the election of 1872. In his second term Grant softened his policy toward the South, but this merely had the effect of hastening the return of white supremacy. Even scalawags were returning to the Democratic party, and by 1876 only three Southern states remained uncertainly in Republican hands. Meanwhile, other events weakened the Republican party elsewhere in the nation. Late in 1872 the Credit Mobilier scandal burst upon the nation. Credit Mobilier was a construction company organized by promoters of the Union Pacific Railway. The construction company was given building contracts at huge profit rates by Union Pacific directors and then the same men, as controllers of Credit Mobilier, pocketed the proceeds. In order to fend off legislative interference with this process, considerable sums were spent in bribing both Congressmen and state legislators, including many leading Republicans. Then, early in 1873, a fierce depression which was to last for five years hit the nation. Despite popular cries that more paper money should be issued to restore the sources of credit, the Republicans stuck to the conservative policy of withdrawing paper money, and making payments in specie or coin, a policy which only helped to lengthen and deepen the depression.

3. THE END OF RECONSTRUCTION

While businessmen supported the general tariff, monetary and railway policies of the Republicans, many of them began to think the cost of corruption too high. The cost was symbolized not only in the Credit Mobilier scandal but also in the activities of such men as Senator Roscoe Conkling. This enterprising lawyer was the Republican political boss of New York State and had complete control of the patronage connected with the Customs House at the Port of New York. Millions of dollars were extracted annually by Conkling and his Customs appointees from importers and other merchants for facilitating their business at the Customs House. The money was then distributed in such a way as to support Republican political power and enrich insiders like Conkling himself.

Facing the election of 1876, Republicans sought to avoid the taint of corruption by refusing to nominate for President James G. Blaine of Maine, who was closely associated with legislative bribery, and by nominating instead Rutherford B. Hayes, an honest and undistinguished politician from Ohio. After sixteen years out of office, the Democrats were more than anxious to return. Although they were divided on some matters like the tariff, they were united in support of their candidate, Samuel J. Tilden, a wealthy corporation lawyer and Governor of New York. Tilden was widely known for having dealt a heavy blow to the notorious Democratic machine of Tammany Hall by sending its boss, William Marcy Tweed, to the penitentiary for his long record of municipal graft.

The nomination of Tilden revealed that the parties were becoming more and more similar. Each was now a great intersectional alliance endeavouring to appeal to all the chief interest groups in the country, and each was increasingly dominated by Eastern business. The pattern of politics for the ensuing two decades was becoming clearly established.

The election itself was very close. When the popular vote was counted, Tilden appeared to be the victor, with a plurality of 250,000. However, there were conflicting returns from three Southern states which were still under military supervision, and from Oregon which had entered the Union in 1859. The task of selecting the victor was given to a special congressional commission whose members, voting on party lines, gave all the disputed states to Hayes. Although the Democrats knew that they could hold up the decision by strong opposition in the House, they suddenly ended their opposition and Hayes was declared President.

The Democratic capitulation was due to extremely important behind-scenes bargaining. Business interests with both Northern and Southern connections persuaded Democratic leaders in the South to accept Hayes as President in return for an unwritten promise by Hayes and the Republicans to withdraw troops from the South, appoint Southerners to the Cabinet and, not least important, grant subsidies for Southern railways. This alliance of Southern Democrats with Northern Republican businessmen brought about the formal end of Radical reconstruction in the South. Despite passing frictions, it has also continued to be the most consistently powerful political alliance in the United States. Because the South voted almost solidly Democratic until 1928, and has voted predominantly so ever since then, the Democrats have enjoyed an unbroken influence in the congressional committees which possess an almost life-or-death power over proposed legislation. The chairmanship of Senate and House committees is decided by seniority, and the Southern Democrats have thus held disproportionate power in Congress. They have usually voted with conservative Republicans to block "progressive" legislation.

The end of reconstruction also opened the door to the triumph of "Jim Crow" or segregationist legislation throughout the South. By the end of the 1880's terrorism as a means of eliminating Negro political activity gave way to special laws. These laws provided that no one could vote unless he had paid a poll tax or, in some cases, unless he could pass special literacy tests. Since many white people could fail both of these tests, some states enacted "grandfather clauses" which allowed any adult male to vote if his father or grandfather had been enfranchised on January 1, 1867, a date prior to the First Reconstruction Act and the Fourteenth Amendment. Other laws prohibited Negroes from using the same railway cars as white people and segregated the races completely in schools and other public places. These laws were clearly a violation of the Fourteenth

Amendment, but for the time being at least the Supreme Court concurred in the return of white supremacy in the South.

It is not difficult to condemn the use of force to compel the South to remain in the Union; the use of force to carry through total and immediate emancipation of four million slaves, without at the same time accepting responsibility for establishing them in freedom; and the failure to curb corrupt exploitation of the Northern victory. Much of subsequent American history has been deeply and often adversely affected by the aftermath of the Civil War and reconstruction.

CHAPTER 9

The Businessman's Revolution

At the end of the Civil War the United States was still principally a farming country. While capital was being accumulated with which to finance large scale industry, most business firms were relatively small and most of their business was carried on locally. But, by 1900 business organization was nation-wide and controlled by giant industrial and financial companies. Governments underwrote the privileges of wealth, and helped to promote the rapid growth of class differences, with tariff legislation, distribution of natural resources either free or at a fraction of their real worth, by clearing western Indians off the most valuable western land, and by using force to suppress labour unrest. As early as 1873 Mark Twain helped to write a book entitled *The Gilded Age* which described contemporary life. So effective was his description of the way in which men were making and spending money at that period that historians have borrowed his title to designate the years from the end of the Civil War to 1900. Another writer called the period "The Great Barbecue" because during those years it was so easy for political camp-followers to get a share of the public wealth in lands, timber-rights, mineral deposits, or franchises to operate public utilities.

1. REVOLUTION ON THE RAILWAYS

United States economic growth was stimulated by the completion of the western railway network. In 1873 there were about 70,000 miles of railroad in the country. Twenty years later there were 170,000 miles. This railway network made possible the economic integration of West and East. Railway-building also employed hundreds of thousands of labourers and attracted millions of dollars of investment from European and American financiers. Along each of the western lines dozens of towns sprang up, each expecting to be a great mercantile or industrial centre, each attracting land speculators, small businessmen and farmers,

129

and each requiring heavy financial credit from Eastern sources at high rates of interest.

The resource used to finance railways was public land, a pattern later copied by Canadian governments. From 1862 to 1871 Congress granted to railroads, either directly or through state legislatures, one hundred and sixty million acres of public land whose value was in excess of four hundred million dollars. The pattern was set in 1862 by legislation chartering the Central Pacific and Union Pacific railways, the former to build eastward from Sacramento and the latter to build westward from Omaha. Each was given free right of way and, along the right of way, ten square miles of land, in alternate sections, for each mile of track constructed. In addition, the roads could import steel rails free of duty and could obtain interest-free government loans ranging from $16,000 for each mile built in level country to $48,000 per mile in the mountains. Thus the company which laid the most track received the largest measure of public support. In the race to reap these rewards, the Central Pacific Railway imported ten thousand Chinese labourers while the Union Pacific employed similar numbers of Irish immigrants. The construction camps of both companies were scenes of violence as the labourers drank, gambled and fought. In addition, much time was spent fighting off the desperate assaults of Cheyenne, Shawnee and Arapaho Indians who realized that the railways spelled an end to their way of life. Nevertheless, in May 1869, the two lines met at Promontory Point, Utah, and a golden spike was driven to symbolize the wealth that would flow from the immense achievement.

The meeting of the Central Pacific and the Union Pacific railways in 1869 marked an epoch in the economic development of the United States.

So huge were the fortunes to be made as an insider of "The Great Barbecue" from the distribution of public resources, that the men who shared in the spoils soon wielded great economic and political power. Outstanding among the "Robber Barons," as such men have been called, was Jay Gould who rose to eminence through railway and associated financial operations. Gould's financial transactions are instructive. He sold his holdings in the Erie Railroad at a huge profit just before a financial crash in 1873, and then began to purchase the shares of the Union Pacific whose value had been depreciated by the depression. By 1878 he controlled the Union Pacific and was buying stock in other western railways. As soon as he had gained control of the Kansas Pacific he was in a position to threaten ruinous competition with the Union Pacific which he also controlled. To avoid this the Union Pacific was compelled to buy his Kansas Pacific shares at nine times what he had originally paid for them. Transactions of this kind weakened the financial condition of Union Pacific. When Gould saw the shaky condition of Union Pacific he secretly sold all his stock in the company, but not before he had had the railway issue ten million dollars in new stock to raise money for the construction of branch lines. Much of this money went to a contracting company which Gould largely owned. Gould played a similar game with the Southern Pacific Railway. By gaining control of competing roads in Texas, Gould forced Southern Pacific into joint manipulation of rates and traffic.

Similar financial battles occurred among the men who controlled other large railway systems, battles in which the banking houses of New York became more and more involved as the total investment in railroads increased rapidly. Since all economic activity was ultimately linked with banking and transportation, the railroad financiers became increasingly important on the national scene. Men like Gould, Collis P. Huntington, Leland Stanford, J. J. Hill, Commodore Cornelius Vanderbilt or Edward J. Harriman emerged from the financial battles richer than the medieval barons or oriental potentates of history. While they stand as symbols of "self-made" men and the principle of competition, their wealth really came from public resources. Their goal was the elimination of competition by forming ever larger rail networks under unified control or by "sharing" arrangements between competitors. By the end of the century six men owned or controlled 100,000 miles of American railways, and these six were closely associated with either the House of Morgan, or Kuhn, Loeb and Company, two gigantic banking firms in New York.

2. THE REVOLUTION IN BUSINESS ORGANIZATION

Technological changes, such as the Bessemer process in steel making, and the development of labour-saving machinery offered unlimited opportunities of expansion in industry. But they also encouraged the growth of large corporations because amounts of capital larger than were usually available through individual ownership or simple partnership

This cartoon by Keppler, entitled "Bosses of the Senate," appeared in **Puck** in 1889.

were required if the opportunities for development were to be seized. Thus the corporation, which had taken some root before the Civil War, came into full flower after 1865. In the post-war period of cut-throat competition the well-financed corporation was in a position of great advantage. It could survive price-wars and buy out its smaller competitors; it could spread branches across the country, organize "pools" with others to share the markets and maintain high prices; and it could, on occasion, even bargain with the railroads for favourable rates.

However, American law provided penalties for "conspiracies in restraint of trade," that is, for practices whereby competitors secretly agreed to fix prices and lessen competition. To get around the law, groups of investors combined their resources to purchase controlling blocks of stock in a number of companies. They then formed a board of trustees, or a trust, which could manage all the companies they controlled as a single organization. By this trust method, competition was cut down or eliminated entirely in a wide range of manufacturing industries and in transportation, communications and utilities. The goal of business organization became the establishment of a monopoly, which is the exclusive right to operate in a certain field. Defenders of the system argued that monopolies were the most efficient and cheapest form of business enterprise. They pointed out that the monopoly, or trust, controlled the raw materials, had lower administrative costs, used modern and expensive mechanical inventions, and eliminated competitive production and distribution. However, the undoubted savings of the monopolies or trusts were seldom passed on to the consumer in the form of lower prices, while the costs of labour-saving machinery were frequently met by increasing the employees' hours of work or reducing wages. As the national economy grew more wealthy in these years the actual number of firms decreased; at the same time the operations of the beef trust, the sugar trust, the whisky trust, the oil trust and others, grew in volume.

The growth and nature of the trusts is well illustrated by the career of Andrew Carnegie and the growth of the steel industry. The son of Scottish immigrants, Carnegie had started work as bobbin boy in a cotton factory at a dollar twenty a week. At thirty, he was able to quit his job as a district superintendent for a railroad and start his own construction business which specialized in building iron bridges. This led him to investigate the problems of iron and steel production. After a trip to England he decided that the new Bessemer process of steel manufacture was the key to the future. Forming the firm of Carnegie, McCandless and Company he built a huge steel mill near Pittsburgh. His connection with railway operators brought him a steady flow of large orders, and by 1879 Carnegie's factory was producing most of the nation's steel.

In 1882, Carnegie combined his operations with those of Henry C. Frick who controlled most of the coking industry. This was a first big step in the creation of a "vertical" monopoly in steel, that is, a trust controlling all the stages and materials that enter into the production of steel. He went on to buy vast areas of the great Mesabi iron range of Minnesota, extensive coal fields in Pennsylvania, limestone quarries, a fleet of iron ore ships and scores of railway cars. By the end of the century, when he had bought out many competitors and established a virtual empire of steel production, profits on his undertakings amounted to forty million dollars each year. In 1901 he decided to retire. So great were his assets that it required the largest investment banking house in the country, J. P. Morgan and Company, to arrange a whole new trust, the United States Steel Corporation, to acquire the Carnegie interests. United States Steel was capitalized at $1,400,000,000 and controlled more than half of all American steel production. By that time the total steel production in the United States was more than that of England and Germany combined.

Carnegie himself was part of the spirit of his times. He was ruthless in eliminating his competitors, hired private armies to suppress workers who organized strikes in his mills, and used his full financial power to influence government and courts in his favour. Unlike many of his brother financiers he professed no religious faith, unless it was a gospel of wealth and competition. As he wrote:

> The contrast between the palace of the millionaire and the cottage of the labourer with us today measures the change which has come with civilization. This change, however, is not to be deplored, but welcomed as highly beneficial. It is well, nay essential, for the progress of the race, that the houses of some should be homes for all that is highest and best in literature and the arts, and for all the refinements

of civilization, rather than that none should be so. . . . We might as well urge the destruction of the highest existing type of man because he failed to reach our ideal as to favour the destruction of individualism, Private Property, the Law of Accumulation of Wealth, and the Law of Competition; for these are the highest results of human experience.

In retirement he spent a portion of his fortune endowing public libraries and art galleries.

John D. Rockefeller was to oil what Carnegie was to steel. Starting with nothing, Rockefeller worked his way up in the wholesale produce business and through incredible thrift saved enough to establish an oil-refining firm. Having made his original profits from Civil War demands for produce, Rockefeller went ahead rapidly after 1865. His methods of forcing companies to sell out to or join with him were utterly ruthless and included disruption of competitors' operations by strong-arm squads as well as continuous threats of economic destruction. By the end of the century, his company, Standard Oil, was one of the most notorious monopoly trusts. Nevertheless, it was able to survive all attempts by judges and legislators to break it up. Rockefeller gave a slightly different view of the process of industrial combination than did Carnegie:

> This movement was the origin of the whole system of modern economic administration. It has revolutionized the way of doing business all over the world. The time was ripe for it. It had to come, though all we saw at the moment was the need to save ourselves from wasteful conditions of competition. . . . The day of combination is here to stay. Individualism has gone, never to return.

The pattern of combinations, monopolies and trusts spread to all sections of the United States economy and constituted a second industrial revolution which affected every aspect of American life. It vastly increased the national wealth and made the owners of big business the most influential men in the country. As more and more Americans went to work in industry, cities and towns grew in size and began to challenge the farm regions in political importance. Most of American political and social history in the years 1865 to 1917 is a record of attempts to adjust the forms of American life to the facts of the industrial age. The concluding stages of western settlement, the conduct and goals of foreign policy, the nature of the party system, and social policy were all affected by the businessman's revolution.

3. THE LAST FRONTIER

The last American land frontier in the Far West was different in many ways from the pre-war frontiers east of the Mississippi. Railways, telegraphs and business organization caught up quickly with the frontiers of the post-Civil War years. In 1860, the only state organized in the Great Plains was Texas. But by 1890, on the basis of population density figures, the census bureau declared that there was no longer a frontier of settlement.

The western mining frontier was also fast-moving. Everywhere in the mining communities the lure of sudden wealth, combined with the absence of federal law and order, produced conditions of anarchy in which murder, gambling and prostitution were glorified as "freedom," suspicion of the police was rampant, and the most widely accepted faith was in the six-shooter. To remedy these conditions, temporary governing committees, often, at least to begin with, vigilante committees, were formed. Eventually territorial status was granted to the area and with it came federal marshals to maintain law and order. Territorial status was followed by the territory's admission to the Union as a state.

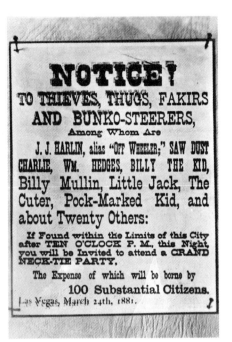

This policy was repeated again and again in the West, bringing into existence the states of Nevada, Colorado, Wyoming, Arizona, Idaho, Montana and North and South Dakota.

As territorial government was established, and as mining gave way to farming and ranching, the Plains Indians knew that their original fear of railways had been well justified. In 1860 the Indian population of the plains and mountains numbered about 250,000, about 75,000 more than the number of white men in the same region. Their way of life was simple. They lived off the huge herds of buffalo estimated as high as twelve million head in the early 1860's. Tough buffalo-hunting tribes such as the Apaches, Navajos and Sioux captured and trained wild horses both for hunting and warfare. Superbly skilled as cavalry, the warriors of the plains could ride slung beside or under the bellies of their horses at full gallop, and at the same time deliver a stream of deadly arrows. A single skilled bowman could have as many as eight arrows in the air at one time.

As the westward thrust of population pushed the eastern Indians past the Mississippi, Indian wars became more frequent and more vicious, and the defending plainsmen became more deadly as warriors. Gradually, railways were driven into the area, and wagon trains brought miners and settlers. Pony express riders established communications and army posts were established to police the country. A long war of attrition was begun with the grim aim of eliminating the last Indian barrier to settlement.

In 1875 the government allowed thousands of prospectors into the Black Hills reserve of the Sioux. The enraged Indians resisted courageously. At the Battle of the Little Big Horn in 1876 General George Custer and 265 soldiers were wiped out in an attack led by Chief Sitting Bull. The chief and many of the Sioux warriors escaped to Canada and, although the warfare continued sporadically, the tribe sued for peace in 1881.

The first stage of the war was the decimation of the buffalo population by rifles. The most famous of the buffalo-hunting white men was Buffalo Bill Cody who is reputed to have shot more than four thousand buffaloes in a year and a half, for sale as meat to the construction camps of the Kansas Pacific Railway. Other hunters, organized by Eastern business-men, slaughtered millions of the prairie herds for the Eastern market in hides and fur. Thus by the end of the 1880's there were only a few hundred buffaloes left in the entire West. Since the Plains Indians had depended upon the herds for everything from shields and clothing to teepees and food, the destruction of the buffalo helped to destroy their way of life. It remained only to subdue, in a series of bloody and often merciless battles, the last fierce show of Indian spirit.

The policy of the federal government was to force the Indians into tribal reservations, usually in the regions of the country thought to be least valuable. Indians fought this policy the more bitterly since the Bureau of the Interior, which was responsible for Indian affairs, and its Western agencies, were riddled with corruption. Agents cheated the Indian even when he did enter a reservation by depriving him of what good land had been within the reservation's boundaries, over-charging him for goods, and demoralizing him with liquor. The most valiant of the last Indian rebellions were fought by the Sioux under such famous chiefs as

Crazy Horse, Little Crow and Red Cloud. The region reserved for the Sioux had been penetrated by the Northern Pacific Railway and then violated by white miners after a gold strike had been made there. In 1876 the federal government sent a large military force to subdue the Sioux. The force was commanded by General George Custer, a famous Civil War leader. When Custer's force and the Sioux met in the Little Big Horn River region in the Dakota badlands, the Indians under Sitting Bull wiped out Custer's cavalry detachment. But such victories could not prevent the steady, irresistible flow of white settlement and the remorseless imposition of the white man's rule.

Following protests against the brutality of the federal government's Indian policy, Congress passed the Dawes Act in 1887. This legislation broke up the tribal reservations and granted small sections of land to each family. This policy, however, was not successful. The Indians found the transition from nomadic life to farming in a permanent settlement extremely difficult. Moreover, under the terms of the Homestead Act white men frequently got the best land. Some Indians did leave their local communities and succeeded in the white world, but their success was the exception that proved the rule. By 1934, although all Indians had been granted citizenship ten years earlier, the steady decline and pauperization of the Indian population prompted a reversal of policy. The Wheeler-Howard Act established tribal landholding on reservations, and endeavoured to encourage self-government within reservations as well as preservation of Indian crafts and customs.

With the elimination of the Indian barrier, the way was opened for the establishment on the plains of the Cattle Kingdom, whose origins lie in the Texas of the 1820's. American immigrants in the Mexican province rounded up herds of wild cattle and wandering horses and branded them. They adopted the range equipment developed by Mexican cowherds— lasso, chaps, "five-gallon hats," and specially adapted saddles, spurs and bits. Until the end of the Civil War, Texan long-horn cattle were sold mainly for their hides. After 1865, however, with the completion of the railway network, Eastern demands for beef could be met from the West, and the Cattle Kingdom entered its golden age. A steer which could be bought in Texas for three dollars was worth as much as forty dollars in an Eastern market. The problem was to move the cattle from the range to the railhead. This was solved by the cattle drive which was made possible by the existence of the huge stretch of unfenced grassy plains reaching from Texas to Canada and from the farms of the midwest to the Rockies.

Each spring marketable cattle were rounded up and under a cattle boss and a team of cowboys were driven slowly north across the plains, fattening on the lush grasses as they went. The direction taken by these long annual drives was determined by water and grass supplies along the way, but eventually they ended at a railroad. A typical railhead was one developed by Joseph McCoy, a Chicago meat wholesaler, who arranged with the Kansas Pacific Railroad for special freight rates on cattle shipments. At

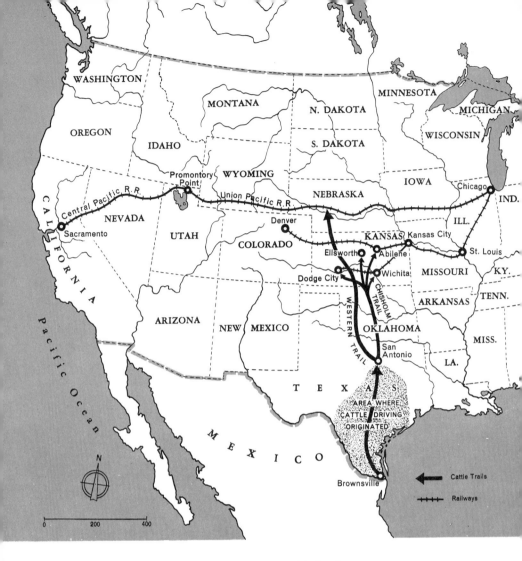

Cattle Trails and Railroads

Abilene, Kansas, McCoy built huge stabling and loading facilities, and constructed a hotel where the cattle bosses could do business with the agents of Eastern abattoirs. Abilene, the first of a series of "cow-towns," handled seventy-five thousand head of cattle in 1868, and at its peak activity in 1871, seven hundred thousand longhorns were herded through the town's pens.

Other railroads were quick to follow the lead of the Kansas Pacific. Along the prairie lines there sprang up a whole series of cow towns similar in their violent character to the mining towns. In Dodge City, for example, twenty-five men were murdered in the town's first year, and the inhabitants are credited with converting the word "stiff" into a noun. Social chaos stemmed partly from the relatively slow growth of local institutions of law and order and partly from the intense boredom, as well as constant danger, of the cowboy's life. Nor did the cowboy, unless lucky at gambling, have the prospect of an easy fortune that lured the miner. His pay was usually between twenty and forty dollars a month, and all of it could be lost in one night at the gaming tables of Wichita or Sedalia. The money in the Cattle Kingdom was made by the big herd-owners, the service towns and railways, and the meat-packing industry. As profits grew, more and more Eastern money, and even European money, was invested in the herds of the open range.

The cattle industry, too, was transformed by inventions. The refrigerated railway car made it possible for the meat-packing industry to move closer to the range, and Kansas City and Chicago became the chief centres. Refrigeration on ocean ships extended the markets for American meat to Europe. These developments led to the growth of huge trusts which dominated the meat-packing industry.

The Cattle Kingdom's period of prosperity was brief, lasting little more than the twenty years between 1865 and 1885. In 1862, the Homestead Act gave one hundred and sixty acres of free public land to any settler who would pay a small recording fee, live on the land and cultivate it for five years. Settlement of the forbidding plains under the Homestead Act was slow, for the plains were generally believed to be a region of desert, while the tough prairie grass, the absence of water, and the threat of roving cattle and horses constituted other problems. The invention of the steel plough provided an implement to deal with the tough prairie sod, and in the 1850's a simple framework windmill was devised which, mass-produced by the Fairbanks-Morse company, by the late 1860's, solved the water problem. Factory production of barbed-wire fencing in the 1870's enabled farmers on the treeless plains to build effective fences. By 1880 this bane of the cattlemen was being sold at the rate of eighty million pounds a year. Five years later the open range was nearly at an end as overstocking, criss-crossing by the fences of wheat and sheep farmers, and quarantine laws limiting regional movement of cattle all led the heavily financed cattle industry to adopt fenced-in ranches. The cowboy of the open range became the much less romantic ranch-hand.

The West was hostile to the first farmers. In the early period of settlement thousands of them lived in sod houses and faced the rigours of sub-zero blizzards with a bare minimum of protection. Always they faced the enmity of cattle barons and their henchmen, who fought the farmers' advance every inch of the way. Nevertheless, by 1900 eighty million acres had been granted to settlers under the Homestead Act. The rapid growth of western settlement owed much to the railroads, which spent millions of dollars advertising their lands in the eastern states and in Europe. To Minnesota, Wisconsin and the Dakotas came hundreds of thousands of Germans and Scandinavians and to the rest of the Western states went a mixed but unbroken stream of ambitious Easterners and Europeans. Occupied farming land in the United States more than doubled between 1860 and 1900, rising to 841,000,000 acres in the latter year. With this inflow of population, the last territorial governments disappeared. In 1912 the admission of Arizona and New Mexico brought the number of states to forty-eight where it remained until the admission of Alaska and Hawaii in 1959.

4. ECONOMIC AND SOCIAL TENSION

Economically, the new West restored agricultural production to its former place in the balance of total American production. The wheat farms of the prairies, using the steadily improved farm machinery turned out by the McCormick and other Eastern implement factories, quadrupled American grain production between 1860 and 1900. But western farmers had mortgaged their land to Eastern banks and trust companies in order to buy improved machinery and more land. Toward the

Led by Frederick Jackson Turner, many American historians have declared that the westward movement of the frontier is the most important theme in American history and explains the development of American character and institutions. In 1893, just as the frontier was coming to an end, Turner wrote: "To the frontier the American intellect owes its striking characteristics. That coarseness and strength combined with acuteness and inquisitiveness; that practical, inventive turn of mind, quick to find expedients; that masterful grasp of material things, lacking in the artistic but powerful to effect great ends; that restless nervous energy; that dominant individualism, working for good and evil, and withal that buoyancy and exuberance which comes with freedom—these are the traits of the frontier, or traits called out elsewhere because of the existence of the frontier."

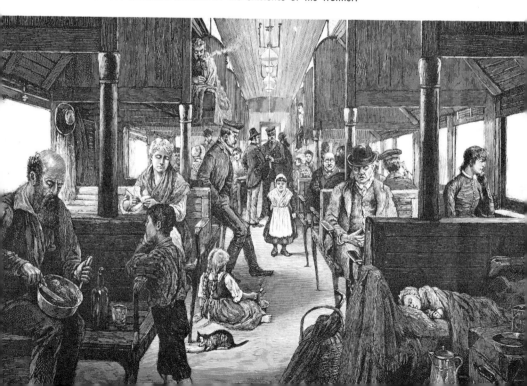

end of the 1880's the price of wheat began to fall with the entry of Australia into the world market and the revival of wheat production in Russia and even Germany. At the same time, a period of continuous good rainfall ended on the plains, and in 1893 a sharp depression hit the country. All of this brought the farmers lowered incomes and mortgage foreclosures. These troubles brought about the formation of a number of farmers' protest organizations.

Trouble was also brewing in the booming East where workers had failed to share in the business prosperity and were the first to feel the economies introduced during a depression. In the growing industrial cities the contrast between abject poverty and unprecedented riches, which fascinated so many contemporary writers and cartoonists, was difficult to exaggerate. In 1893 government census bureau figures indicated that over seventy per cent of the national wealth was owned by less than nine per cent of American families. The wealth of the new millionaires was conspicuously consumed. Their immense houses were the setting for opulent entertainments attended by platoons of servants. Luxury hotels were the scenes of dinners and balls at which guests were offered favours such as cigarettes rolled in one hundred dollar bills. At one party the financier, August Belmont, appeared in a suit of armour inlaid with gold; at another, given by Randolph Guggenheim, at a cost of two hundred and fifty dollars a place, the meal was eaten to the accompaniment of the singing of nightingales perched in transplanted rose trees. The Guggenheim evening was topped off by gifts to guests of jewelled match-box souvenirs. In New York and other industrial cities, the wealthy filled their mansions indiscriminately with statuary and paintings gathered on European tours. Each summer they made pilgrimages to famous seaside towns, like Newport, Rhode Island, where the Vanderbilt marble house cost more than $9,000,000 to build. The social Four Hundred of New York entertained senatorial political bosses at glittering restaurants such as Delmonico's, and deftly ensured, by financing the major party campaigns, that legislative, executive and judicial policy would interfere with their interests as little as possible. Such extravagant display by the "Robber Barons" aroused a mixture of envy and hatred in those who witnessed but did not share in it.

By the end of the century it was apparent that the process of consolidating the control of capital through trusts and interlocking membership on boards of directors had resulted in virtual control of American economic life by the great financial houses. As one candid member of the moneyed class put it:

> We own America; we got it, God knows how, but we intend to keep it if we can by throwing all the tremendous weight of our support, our influence, our money, our political influence, our political connections, our purchased senators, our hungry congressmen, and our public-speaking demagogues into the scale against any legislation, any political platform, any Presidential campaign, that threatens the integrity of our estate.

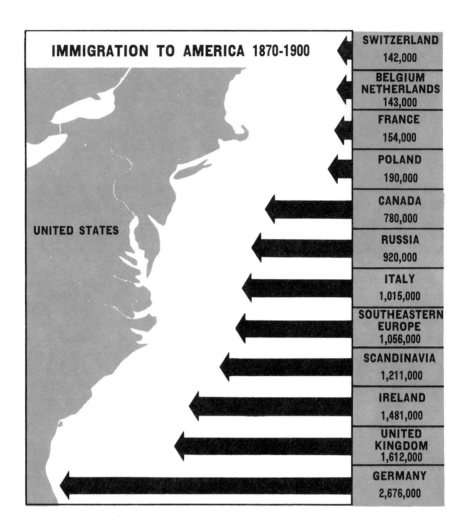

IMMIGRATION TO AMERICA 1870-1900

UNITED STATES

SWITZERLAND	142,000
BELGIUM NETHERLANDS	143,000
FRANCE	154,000
POLAND	190,000
CANADA	780,000
RUSSIA	920,000
ITALY	1,015,000
SOUTHEASTERN EUROPE	1,056,000
SCANDINAVIA	1,211,000
IRELAND	1,481,000
UNITED KINGDOM	1,612,000
GERMANY	2,676,000

Complicating the structure of American society was a sharp increase in immigration and a more rapid growth of urban as compared to rural population. Between 1860 and 1890 more than nine million people came to the United States from Europe, particularly from the British Isles and Germany. The Scandinavian countries also sent many immigrants in the 1870's and 1880's, who settled mainly in the midwest and northern prairies. Late in the 1890's a fresh influx came from southern and eastern Europe, Italy, Russia, the Balkans and Poland. This was the last big surge of immigration to the United States, and it reached its peak in the first decade of this century when nearly nine million people moved through the reception station at Ellis Island in New York Harbour. While many of the German and Scandinavian immigrants went west, most of the later immigrants settled in the cities.

Once again "nativism" assumed dangerous proportions, as native-born

Americans irrationally blamed the new arrivals for depressions and anything else of which they disapproved. Even industrial leaders, who generally favoured an increase in the supply of labour, because it made lower wages possible, supported the mounting demand for restrictions on immigration. Some of the new Americans brought with them European radical ideas, from anarchism to socialism, and since this was a time of intense industrial strife, it was an easy step to blame all unrest on "foreign agitators." As the railroad lawyer, Chauncey M. Depew, remarked: "The ranks of anarchy and riots number no Americans. The leaders boldly proclaim that they come here not to enjoy the blessings of our liberty and to sustain our institutions but to destroy our government, cut our throats, and divide our property." The labour unions became the most vociferous opponents of immigration not only because it was very difficult to organize immigrants who were unaccustomed to American problems and habits, but because the newly arrived were often willing to accept lower wages and poorer working conditions than those accepted by the native-born. Pressure for restriction of immigration eventually produced a series of very effective laws. In 1882 Chinese immigration was prohibited; in the 1890's regulations prohibited entry of diseased persons; in 1907, by a "gentleman's agreement," Japan undertook to refuse passports to its citizens who wished to go to the United States to seek work; between 1921 and 1924 the United States adopted a quota system which limited immigration from any European country to two per cent of the number of that country's nationals living in the United States in 1890. Despite special legislation after 1945 favouring persons displaced by war and revolution, immigration since 1921 has remained slight.

However, immigration greatly stimulated industry and population growth. Western and midwestern farm areas grew so rapidly that the centre-point of population moved from Ohio in 1860 to Columbus, Indiana by 1890. At the same time, urban population grew much more quickly than rural, and Eastern farm regions actually declined in population as people moved to industrial jobs in towns or to fertile lands farther west. Many new midwestern towns and cities, whose industry was based on iron and steel, or on the processing of agricultural commodities, grew fantastically. By 1880 Chicago, with a population of nearly a million, had replaced Philadelphia as the country's second largest city.

In both Eastern and Western industrial cities, sprawling tenements and slums stood in marked contrast to the great mansions of the wealthy. Almost without property, urban industrial workers depended entirely on wages which were usually at bare subsistence level. While the total "national wealth" was growing at unprecedented rates, and the cities boasted such new amenities as gaslight, sewer systems and in the 1880's even electric arc-lamps and tram lines, the great majority of urban dwellers lived in conditions that rivalled the filth of medieval towns and bred both vice and violence.

Amidst the teeming growth and unrest of these years there were sub-

The photograph at the left was taken by the Danish immigrant, Jacob Riis, during his compassionate study of New York slums in 1890. Describing a similar wretched scene, he wrote: "Come over here. Step carefully over this baby—it is a baby, in spite of its rags and dirt—under these iron bridges called fire-escapes but loaded down, despite the incessant watchfulness of the firemen, with broken household goods, with washtubs and barrels, over which no man could climb from a fire. This gap between dingy brick walls is the yard. That strip of smoke-coloured sky up there is the heaven of these people. Do you wonder the name does not attract them to the churches?"

In contrast with this scene there existed, in the same city, another world of elegance and opulence in which rooms like the hall in Mrs. A. J. Stewart's mansion were not uncommon.

stantial advances in education and literature. One of the most startling developments was the appearance of mass-circulation daily newspapers. Newspapers such as Joseph Pulitzer's St. Louis *Post Despatch* and the New York *World* introduced the use of cheap wood-pulp paper, typewriters and linotype machines. Publishers like William Randolph Hearst and E. W. Scripps, seeking new ways to increase production, improved their news services, introduced coloured comics, and printed sensational exposés of corruption in politics. Circulation rose from three million in 1870 to twenty-four million in 1899, and with mounting revenue from advertising, newspapers became big business. Popular magazines recorded similar circulation increases. "Crusades" to reform municipal political machinery were mixed indiscriminately with jingoistic condemnation of foreign nations and demands for assertion of American rights and power. Such journalism stimulated the outburst of expansionism of the late 1890's and a widespread reform sentiment in the early twentieth century.

As businesses mainly concerned with profit and loss, the newspapers seldom challenged the basic assumptions of middle-class American society. They constantly elaborated the theme of "rags to riches" and seldom missed an opportunity to explain that failure was the result of sloth and lack of initiative. The stories of Horatio Alger, with their reiteration of the success which invariably attended honest endeavour in an America of limitless opportunity, became symbols of the age. Thousands of aspiring middle-class Americans took up the cult of "self-improvement" of which the outstanding expression was the Chautauqua lectures given by travelling speakers who brought "culture" to ordinary men and women throughout the nation.

More serious efforts to improve the cultural level of the nation resulted in rapid expansion of all levels of public education. By 1900 most states had compulsory school attendance laws for primary grades, and between 1880 and 1900 high school enrollment rose from 100,000 to 500,000. State governments founded universities to supplement the facilities of the older private universities. Under the Morrill Act of 1862 the federal government granted land to the states for the purpose of improving agriculture and scientific education. In the older universities, graduate studies began to develop and to reflect the influence of research scholars trained in British and European, particularly German, universities.

Thus, despite the uneven growth and the increasing class distinctions, the early years of the "businessman's revolution" were a time of very real opportunity. The excitement of a nation on its way to world power, the adventurous avenues that led to the West or to mastery in business, the insistent urge in sensitive minds to portray in literature the nature and meaning of America—to become a Mark Twain, a Stephen Crane, a Henry James—all of this was a part of the post-Civil War years. When some of the avenues were closed by spreading monopoly or by economic depression many Americans turned their energies to fighting for rights and opportunities in a land of natural plenty.

CHAPTER 10

Parties and Protests

The years following 1865 saw revolutionary social and economic changes in American society but these were not reflected in the nation's major political parties. On the contrary, the parties remained the instruments by which the privileged and wealthy controlled American life. In 1888 the party system in the United States was closely examined by an astute British diplomat, Lord James Bryce, in a notable book, *The American Commonwealth.* Bryce wrote:

> Neither party [Republican or Democratic] has any clear-cut principles, any distinctive tenets. Both have certainly war cries, organizations, interests, enlisted in their support. But those interests are in the main the interests of getting or keeping the patronage of the government. Tenets and policies, points of political doctrine and points of political practice, have all but vanished.

1. PARTY POLITICS 1876-1896

By the end of the 1870's the Republicans had fulfilled the purposes for which the party had been founded. They had eliminated "the slavery threat" to western expansion, gained free land in the West, and encouraged industrial development with a high tariff and federally endowed railways. During the same period the Democrats had defended as best they could the rights of the white South. In 1876-77 the political compromise between Southern Democrats and Northern Republican businessmen had brought about a new alignment of forces and with it a disappearance of party principles. The result was a long seesaw battle in which the voting strength of the major parties was remarkably even. The Democrats did not win the Presidency from 1860 to 1912, except for Grover Cleveland's two terms (1885-89; 1893-97), but they enjoyed majorities in Congress more often than the Republicans. On the other hand, in the elections of 1876 and 1888 a Republican President won in the electoral college, though he had only a minority of the popular vote.

The real debates on policy took place within rather than between the parties. Both the Democratic and Republican parties were controlled by conservatives who accepted, broadly, a political philosophy to which the name "Social Darwinism" has been given. Briefly, this philosophy applied the ideas developed in Charles Darwin's *The Origin of Species* (1859) to the problems of social and economic policy. Darwin believed the species had evolved over a period of millions of years through a process of "natural selection," in which the weaker members died off and the stronger survived. The corollary of this doctrine of the "survival of the fittest" was that one should not interfere with the supposed natural law governing the process. As expounded by the English writer, Herbert Spencer, Social Darwinism held that millionaires were the fittest to survive because they had obviously adapted best to the natural laws of economics. Conversely, slum-dwellers were the least fit. Attempts to overcome social inequality by such means as unemployment relief, regulations governing wages, hours of work and other economic activity, or even by providing free education, were harmful because they interfered with "natural processes" of survival and progress.

Spencer's books were read by millions of Americans, and he had many outspoken disciples among writers, scholars, judges, politicians, editors, clergymen and businessmen. As used in general discussion, Social Darwinism was simply an argument for keeping government out of business and social relationships. Yet the very people who used the argument to oppose government regulation of business saw nothing incongruous in demanding that government should maintain a high protective tariff, assist businessmen by grants of natural resources, or by suppressing strikers. The doctrine of Social Darwinism was also convenient for those who were extending Jim Crow laws in the Southern states or endeavouring to pre-

Writing of the anti-Chinese riots in the West in the late 1870's, Mary R. Coolidge observed: "They [the Chinese] were so many, so thrifty, so uncomplaining, so glad to work at any price, and above all so alien, so strange—so 'heathenish.' To the followers of the Workingmen's Party they seemed such a facile tool for the greedy capitalist that it was only natural to suppose that they were the chief cause both of his riches, and of their own [the workingmen's] hardship. Yet the Chinese had not caused drought, nor decline of mineral production, nor speculation and panic in stocks and real estate, nor land monopoly. . . ." The anti-Chinese feeling was another manifestation of nativism or Social Darwinism.

serve a privileged status for native-born Americans. In order to defend white supremacy in the South, nativism in the North, and later, overseas expansion, the argument was put forward that the "Anglo-Saxon race," by its dominant position in the world, was obviously fittest to survive.

R. B. Hayes, who had become President as a result of the compromise of 1876-77, fulfilled the bargain by which his election had been secured in Congress. The government withdrew troops from the South, appointed a Southern conservative to the Cabinet and secured minor measures of reform in the civil service. Congressmen gave Hayes little support for that kind of honest reform, but they applauded his tough handling of the bitter railway strikes of 1877, which resulted from heavy wage cuts. When rioting occurred in Pittsburgh and West Virginia Hayes sent federal troops to suppress the strikers.

In 1880 the Republican General James A. Garfield of Ohio was elected President. Garfield had been a compromise between General Grant, who sought to return to the Presidency, and the openly corrupt J. G. Blaine. Chester A. Arthur, who had been Customs Collector of the Port of New York under the régime of the corrupt Roscoe Conkling, the political boss of the city, became Vice-President as a concession to the party stalwarts. The depth of political corruption in the period was illustrated when Garfield was shot four months after his inauguration by a disappointed office-seeker. To the surprise of the Conkling gang, Arthur, who as Vice-President succeeded Garfield, showed signs of independence, and sympathy for reform. He supported the Pendleton Act of 1883, which prohibited party assessment of civil servants for political contributions and which proposed the practice of appointing civil servants on the basis of competitive examinations. The later growth of the Pendleton system was spasmodic and, although the Civil Service Commission now administers appointments to most positions, the majority of the really important posts still remain outside its jurisdiction. One unforeseen result of the Pendleton Act was that the party bosses turned increasingly to big business for contributions to political funds.

As the federal elections of 1884 approached, the Republicans were badly split. The old guard, who disliked Arthur for his sympathy to reform, succeeded in denying him a second term, and nominated Blaine as their candidate for the Presidency. As a result, many Republicans supported the Democratic nominee, Grover Cleveland. Cleveland was Governor of New York State and had been Mayor of Buffalo. In both offices he had earned a reputation for honesty and independence. Cleveland was elected President, but Republicans retained control of the Senate and effectively blocked much of the administration's legislative programme.

Cleveland stood for upright if unimaginative administration. He made himself unpopular with Democratic party leaders by vetoing many private bills for increased Civil War pensions. He also took back over eighty million acres of land from railroads that had not fulfilled the conditions of their grants. More and more strongly he supported lowering the tariff

In the desperate 1892 strike against Carnegie's great steel works at Homestead, Pennsylvania, the Company imported bands of armed Pinkerton detectives. Amidst flowing blood these men crushed the strike. Grover Cleveland, no radical himself, commented on "the tender mercy the workingman receives from those made selfish and sordid by unjust governmental favouritism."

on the ground that it was unjust taxation, often due to political pressure from certain powerful manufacturers. As the belief began to spread in the West and among Eastern reformers that the tariff was the "father of trusts," in that it gave unreasonable protection against British competition, Cleveland openly supported tariff reduction in 1887.

His tariff proposals were defeated in the Senate, and in the 1888 elections the Republicans elected their candidate Benjamin Harrison on a platform that included an unequivocal protectionist plank. Harrison believed in high tariffs, hard money, and in general, in the right of business to control government. He was content to have his Cabinet selected by Republican party leaders. Under the leadership of William McKinley, a Senator from Ohio, the Republicans framed a new tariff law. Enacted in 1890, the McKinley tariff satisfied even the most extreme protectionists. Higher tariffs, however, meant a higher cost of living, and this, in turn, brought political discontent. In an attempt to stem this discontent in the agrarian West and South, the government passed the Sherman Silver Purchase Act in 1890, providing for government purchase of the estimated output of the western silver mines. The silver was to be used as specie against which the government could issue more banknotes, thereby putting more money into circulation and aiding debt-ridden farmers. Unfortunately, too little silver was purchased and too little paper money was issued for the Act to be really effective.

Serious labour unrest from 1890 to 1892 added to the disenchantment with the Republicans. The labour discontent culminated in a strike in 1892 against the Carnegie Steel Company in Homestead, Pennsylvania. A vicious industrial war followed. Although Harrison supported the employers, the party managers realized that a combination of Western farm resentment and Eastern labour unrest could be fatal at election time, and Andrew Carnegie was asked to make concessions to labour. But Carnegie was determined to defeat the union at all costs, and refused. As Henry Frick, his partner and manager of the steel company, wrote to Carnegie: "I feel sorry for President Harrison, but I cannot see that our interests are going to be affected one way or another by the change in administration."

Many business leaders put their faith in Cleveland in 1892 and their support won him the Democratic nomination for President. They knew that he was "sound" on gold, that is, opposed to the issue of paper money and consequent inflation, and that his attitude to the tariff had been much modified during the four years he spent in New York business circles after his defeat in 1888. The Republicans nervously put forward Harrison for re-election. In a comparatively quiet election the Democrats won by a very narrow margin.

Cleveland's second administration was marked by depression, industrial warfare and social upheaval. Even before inauguration day, 1893, a panic on the New York stock market had set the stage for a depression which lasted until 1896. Cleveland employed his full powers as chief executive to use military force and the courts in suppressing strikes. He resisted attempts to increase credit for hard-pressed Western farmers, and refused to veto the act which imposed the very high tariff of 1894. By 1896, although incapacitated much of the time by attacks of gout, Cleveland had managed to offend every major group in the nation, save the most powerful businessmen. Just before the nominating convention of that year, a prominent Southern Democratic newspaper observed: "Grover Cleveland will go out under a greater burden of popular contempt than has ever been excited by a public man since the formation of the government."

The people's dissatisfaction with Cleveland as President, and with their inability under the existing party system to share in the choice of candidates for government office, was reflected in growing demands for reform.

2. THE DEMAND FOR REFORM

In the 1880's and 1890's not all Americans accepted the ideas of Social Darwinism. Men of letters constantly criticized the materialism of the age. Mark Twain's *The Gilded Age* was only one of many books which reflected deep discontent with social injustice and merely material progress. Perhaps the most widely read book of the period was Edward Bellamy's *Looking Backward*. Bellamy pictured the United States as it would be in the year 2,000 when the problems of the 1880's had been solved. He forecast that during the twentieth century, the American people would recognize the efficiency of the monopolistic system in industry but, to eliminate social injustice, would place all big business under government ownership. Bellamy wrote that under this new "nationalist" ownership, the more rational application of scientific methods would enable men to move constantly towards a "nobler, happier plane of existence." In cities all over the United States "nationalist" clubs and maga-

In his moving book **The Bitter Cry of the Children**, the socialist muckraker, John Spargo, describes the plight of children working in the coal mines: "Work in the coal breakers is exceedingly hard and dangerous. Crouched over the chutes, the boys sit hour after hour, picking out the pieces of slate and other refuse from the coal as it rushes past to the washers. From the cramped position they have to assume, most of them become more or less deformed and bent-backed like old men. . . . The coal is hard, and accidents to the hands, such as cut, broken, or crushed fingers, are common among the boys. Sometimes there is a worse accident: a terrified shriek is heard, and a boy is mangled and torn in the machinery, or disappears in the chute to be picked out later smothered and dead."

zines sprang up to promote various aspects of Bellamy's version of socialism. Americans increasingly discussed the merits of public ownership of utilities and railways, telegraphs, banks, and more extensive aid to education.

Other writers analyzed American industrial society and often deplored the control exercised by private corporations over the nation's destiny. Henry Demarest Lloyd led a group of writers who presented carefully documented studies of the actual operation of particular monopolies. His major book, *Wealth Against Commonwealth* (1894), was a detailed history of Rockefeller's Standard Oil trust, and an indictment of the "Robber Barons."

> Our barbarians come from above. Our great money-makers have sprung in one generation into seats of power kings do not know. . . . Without restraints of culture, experience, the pride, or even the inherited caution of class or rank, these men, intoxicated, think they are the wave instead of the float, and that they have created the business

which has created them. . . . They claim a power without control, exercised through forms which make it secret, anonymous, and perpetual.

Other social scientists in the 1880's and 1890's rejected the idea that uncontrolled private enterprise produced the best kind of life and maintained that "the doctrine of *laisser-faire* is unsafe in politics and unsound in morals." Some Protestant clergymen pointed out that the Christian gospel had a social message as well as an individual one, and that the state should regulate business to ensure everyone equality of opportunity. The Social Gospel Movement declared that love and co-operation were better Christian principles than competition and "survival of the fittest."

This movement in the Protestant churches, and the concern of the Roman Catholic church, led to an increase in charitable work. Some individuals founded "settlement houses," which, like Jane Addams' Hull House in Chicago, were attempts to help the poor by providing day nurseries, discussion clubs and gymnasiums. From the workers in private charities and the settlement houses, came a growing pressure for reform which forced reluctant city governments to provide playgrounds, parks and kindergartens for the poor. Some reformers went further and demanded the elimination of corruption at city hall, strict regulation of housing standards, and public ownership of municipal utilities.

Associated with the mounting reform spirit in the 1890's was a movement for equal rights for women which gained momentum as more and more women entered colleges and business. The movement finally culminated in 1919 in ratification of the Nineteenth Amendment by which women won the right to vote.

From the ranks of labour came further stimulus to the spirit of reform. After the Civil War, labour tried to improve its position by extending and broadening its basis of organization. If labour were to bargain effectively with the nation-wide organization of capital, it too would have to organize on a national basis. It would have to represent not just the "aristocracy" of skilled workers but also the great masses of unskilled and semi-skilled labourers. It was to be a long, hard fight, however, before such an organization would be achieved. Ranged against labour were not only the powerful industrial leaders, but usually the state and national governments, the press and the courts as well. Moreover, there were divisions within the ranks of the labour movement itself.

The first attempt to establish a national union of all workers ended in failure when the National Labour Union, founded in 1866, collapsed in the depression of 1873. A second union, the Noble Order of the Knights of Labour, was organized in 1869 and enjoyed much greater success. The Knights' immediate goals were the traditional ones of most unions: "to secure to the toilers a proper share of the wealth that they create," an eight-hour day, prohibition of child labour, equal pay for both sexes and legislation to safeguard the workers' safety and health. Their long-term aims were more radical, for the Knights sought to reform the whole industrial structure by establishing a kind of guild socialism in which all industry would be co-operatively owned and run. They actually launched thirty co-operative undertakings, but most of these failed because of business hostility and inexperienced management.

In 1885 the Knights of Labour reached its peak of influence, when it staged a successful strike against the mighty railway empire of Jay Gould. In the following year its membership increased seven-fold to 700,000 and its success seemed assured. But in that very year disaster struck the movement. On May 1, the Knights led a widespread strike in support of the eight-hour day. During one of the great outdoor meetings, in Haymarket Square, Chicago, someone threw a bomb which killed one policeman and injured several others. The guilty person was never found, but business and government leaders used the occasion to attack the successful national union. Eight anarchists were falsely accused of murder, and seven were sentenced to death.

Some definite conclusions were drawn from these events by a cigarmaker named Sam Gompers. Gompers' family had come to New York as immigrants in 1863 and Sam had gone to work at the age of ten in a cigar-making factory. Gompers' observations persuaded him that labour should fight for limited aims only and that it should use economic weapons exclusively. In 1886 Gompers became one of the founders of the

During a miners' strike in Ohio in 1884 miners and their wives attacked "blackleg" workmen who were guarded by a detachment of Pinkerton's detectives.

American Federation of Labour, and was to be A.F. of L. President from then until his death in 1924.

The A.F. of L. was a federation of craft unions, each of which retained a large degree of autonomy. A craft union was one in which members of the same trade, printers, railwaymen etc., were grouped together. Since many of these unions had branches in Canada, they became "internationals." A.F. of L. unions, and the Federation itself, had little interest in organizing any but skilled workers. Believing in "business unionism" they concentrated on making industry bargain with A.F. of L. unions. They also worked to ensure that industry should hire only union members, improve wages, hours and working conditions, and enter into contracts with labour on all such matters. They decided to avoid partisan politics and to gain their ends by bringing pressure to bear on individual legislators and executives. As Gompers said, he was "partisan for a policy rather than for a party." By the early 1890's the A.F. of L. unions had a membership of 250,000 skilled workers. But strikes in 1892 and 1894 further increased middle-class hostility to unionism of any kind, and growth was very slow for another decade. By 1900 the A.F. of L. had achieved a membership of 500,000.

Except in railways, mines and the lumbering industry, unskilled and semi-skilled workers remained largely unorganized until the 1930's. This meant that labour did not, until that period, achieve a degree of strength that could even begin to match that of capital. For this failure "Gomperism" was the principal reason; nevertheless, for skilled workers, the A.F. of L. secured many gains. But while Gompers' policy remained dominant, there also developed a body of opinion in American labour which favoured direct political action for socialist goals, and organization on an industrial rather than a craft basis. An industrial union is one which includes all workers in a single industry, such as steel production or mining, rather than a single craft such as carpentering or plumbing.

Eugene V. Debs was the most influential advocate of combining socialist political action with industrial unionism. In 1893 before he was converted to socialism he had organized the American Railway Union which, unlike the major Railroad "Brotherhoods," was open to all railway workers regardless of trade or skill. Within a year the A.R.U. had 150,000 members. In 1894 Debs demonstrated the principle of labour unity by giving support to workers who had gone on strike against the Pullman Palace Car Company in a suburb of Chicago.

Following the financial depression of 1893, George Pullman, the great railway car manufacturer, had discharged a third of his workers and lowered wages for the remainder by forty per cent. In the company-owned town of Pullman, store prices and rents were kept at their previous levels. When the Pullman workers struck, Debs gave the strikers help from A.R.U. funds, while A.R.U. members boycotted all trains carrying Pullman cars. Fearful that the strike might succeed and industrial unionism spread, the railroads asked the federal government to support them with federal troops.

President Cleveland and Attorney-General Olney responded quickly, despite the constitutional provision that federal troops should be used internally only at the request of the state governor or legislature.   When Governor Altgeld of Illinois argued that there was no necessity for the intervention, the President evaded the Constitution by ordering the troops to protect the mails, a federal responsibility.   At the same time Attorney-General Olney obtained from a Chicago federal court an injunction, or court order, to prohibit the strike.   Troops were used to break the strike, despite Altgeld's protests to Cleveland, while Debs and other strike leaders were arrested and jailed for violating the court injunction.

The Pullman strike had significant results.   The violence which accompanied it strengthened middle-class hostility towards trade unionism and the successful use of the court injunction showed employers how to break future strikes.   The authority for issuing the injunction was the Sherman Anti-Trust Act which had been passed in 1890, ostensibly for the purpose of preventing "conspiracies in restraint of trade," that is, business monopolies and trusts.   Its use as a weapon against labour disillusioned many working-class people.

Debs' experiences converted him to socialism and he was Presidential candidate for the newly-formed Socialist party in elections from 1900 to 1920.   But despite deplorable social conditions and inequalities, American workers did not give majority support to parties or unions which advocated anything more radical than minor modifications of the capitalist system. Although radical movements like the Industrial Workers of the World (disrespectfully known as the "Wobblies") gained considerable strength in the Western forest and mining industries in the first two decades of the twentieth century, the conservative A.F. of L. remained the dominant voice of labour.

3. THE FARMERS' PROTEST

The history of farmers' organizations and labour unions is similar in many ways, but the farmers faced several problems peculiar to agriculture.   On the great plains of Nebraska, western Kansas and the Dakotas, drought and locusts often left a trail of complete desolation and doomed whole communities to chronic indebtedness.   Moreover, farmers had no control over prices on the world agricultural market.   A large wheat crop would bring prosperity to a Western farm only if the market price of wheat were high; bumper crops in the Ukraine or Argentina might cause wheat prices to tumble.   Moreover, wheat prices were at the mercy of speculators who bought and sold on the commodity exchanges in Chicago and New York.   United States farmers protested vigorously against high tariffs and trust control of railways and bank credit.   They argued that such policies kept farm costs so high that it was often cheaper for a Western farmer to burn his corn or wheat than to pay the cost of marketing it. Although Southern farmers did not need as much expensive farm machin-

In the depression year of 1873 the protesting Grangers issued a "Farmers' Declaration of Independence" couched in terms which suggested a sense of historical precedent: "When in the course of human events, it becomes necessary for a class of people, suffering from long continued systems of oppression and abuse, to rouse themselves from an apathetic indifference to their own interests, which has become habitual; to assume among their fellow citizens that equal station, and demand from the government they support, those equal rights to which the laws of nature, and of nature's God entitle them; a decent respect for the opinions of mankind requires that they should declare the causes that impel them to a course so necessary to their own protection."

One of their main complaints was against the railway companies: "The history of the present railway monopoly is a history of repeated injuries and oppressions, all having in direct object the establishment of an absolute tyranny over the people of these states un-equalled in any monarchy of the Old World, and having its only parallel in the history of the Medieval Ages, when the strong hand was the only law, and the highways of commerce were taxed by the Feudal Barons, who from their strongholds, surrounded by their armies of vassals, could levy such tribute upon the traveller as their own wills alone should dictate."

ery as the Westerners, they, too, often paid more for necessary equipment and fertilizer than they received from the sale of their crops.

As prices fell, more and more farmers were forced to take out new mortgages or increase old ones. When prices failed to revive and costs remained high, farmers could not meet their high interest payments and many lost their farms. By 1900, more than one-third of all American farm families did not own their farms.

Western and Southern farmers determined to band together to exert more influence on government and business policies. The first major farmers' organization was the Patrons of Husbandry, organized in 1866.

Known also as the Grange, the Patrons—more commonly called Grangers —soon had local Granges in all "farm states" and by 1875 boasted of 800,000 members. The Grangers sought to overcome the loneliness of isolated Western farm life by organizing social and educational activities. They also established co-operatives for buying farm machinery and other equipment, in order to get wholesale prices. Many of these co-operatives, like those established by the Knights of Labour, were deliberately under-sold by merchants and bankers who foresaw a serious loss of profit if the co-operative movement succeeded. The Grange also brought pressure to bear on local legislatures and Congress for such measures as currency inflation to ease the repayment of debts, tariff reductions and railway rate regulation. In the early 1870's, beginning in Illinois, the Grangers suc-ceeded in getting state laws to regulate railway and warehouse rates.

Railroads and other businesses reacted violently to rate regulation, afraid that if it were to succeed government control might be further ex-tended to business methods and profits. Thus railway lawyers challenged the "Granger Laws" in the courts. But in 1877 the Supreme Court decided that state governments did possess the right to regulate many kinds of business. Chief Justice Waite gave his opinion that "When private prop-erty is devoted to public use, it is subject to public regulation." Despite this victory, the Grangers failed to influence monetary or tariff policy or to promote government regulation of the trusts. By the 1880's the Grangers had become a purely social organization and their political activity was taken over by Farmers' Alliances and independent political parties in many states.

One factor which had stimulated the farmers to take political action and, as one of the Western Alliance women said, "to raise less corn and more Hell," was a Supreme Court decision in 1886. A Supreme Court Judge, Mr. Justice Field, gave it as his opinion that to limit profit was, in effect, to deprive the business owner of some of his property: "All that is beneficial in property arises from its use, and the fruits of that use," he wrote, "and whatever deprives a person of them deprives him of all that is desirable or valuable in the title and possession." Now, the Fourteenth Amendment, originally passed to help the freedmen after the Civil War, declared that no state shall "deprive any person of life, liberty, or *property*, without due process of law," and the Fifth Amendment placed a like restriction upon Congress; the implications of Field's decision, then, were that government could not regulate business. Specifically, however, Field's decision declared that state regulation of railways was unconstitutional because it infringed upon the congressional power to regulate "interstate commerce." Since practically all railways were parts of systems which crossed state lines, Field's decision seriously undermined any attempts at state regulation.

As protests against the monopolies and the trusts, and demands for their regulation continued to mount, some measure of reform was gained. Congress gave in to the demand from farmers and some businessmen who objected to discriminatory freight rates, and passed the Interstate Commerce Act. This Act attempted to establish a federal commission to regulate freight rates. Conservative business interests, however, challenged the legislation and the Supreme Court acted quickly. In 1890, and again in 1897, it ruled that fixing railway rates by government action meant depriving the railways of "property" without "due process of law," that is, court action. The implication of these and other court decisions was that a corporation was a "person" in the eyes of the law, and thus was entitled to all the protections of personal rights provided in federal and state constitutions.

The other main result of political protests against monopolies had been the Sherman Anti-Trust Act passed in 1890. After a congressional investigating commission had revealed details of trust operations, the Act was passed through both Houses with only one opposing vote. The Sherman Act made illegal "every contract, combination in the form of trust or otherwise, or conspiracy in restraint of trade or commerce among the several states or with foreign nations." It empowered the government to prosecute violators of the Act. But since many of its terms were not clearly defined, the Sherman Act was not very effective.

The failure of most attempts to bring the giant trusts under public control left many doubts about the success of the democratic process, and promoted another round of efforts to achieve political reform. For such a political reform movement there were many precedents reaching back to the days of Jefferson and Jackson. One of the most recent had occurred in the 1870's and was known as the Greenback movement, "greenback" being the popular name for government-printed currency. The Greenback party advocated the printing of more paper money as a means of easing financial credit for farmers. A ringing declaration in the platform revealed its basic attitude:

> We demand a government of the people, by the people and for the people, instead of a government of the bondholders, by the bondholders and for the bondholders.

Greenbackers elected fourteen Congressmen in 1878 and enjoyed considerable electoral success in the 1880's. At the same time farmers throughout the West and South formed Farmers' Alliances to press state and federal legislatures to pass laws favourable to agriculture. By 1890 the Southern Alliance had three million white members while the Coloured Farmers' Alliance had another 700,000. Combined Alliance membership in the West was about 650,000.

By 1889 a united farmers' party seemed possible. In a convention at St. Louis the leaders of the various Farmers' Alliances found many points of agreement for what might be a national "farmers' platform": government control of railways and public utilities; tariff reform; easier farm credit; monetary inflation; and government warehouses for farm produce. But there were also points of disagreement. Northerners resisted the Southern Alliance's refusal to admit Negroes to its membership, which meant that the Coloured Alliance had to remain a separate organization. Southerners, on the other hand, were reluctant to undertake the formation of a separate national political party. They were accustomed to working inside the Democratic party, which was the only effective party in the South, and they did not want to form a third party, because it might weaken the anti-Negro Democrats in the South and lead to increased Negro rights.

Most Southern farm leaders, however, set their third party doubts aside temporarily to help in establishing the National People's party. The new organization was generally known as the Populist party and its platform included all of the essential Alliance planks: a flexible national currency issued solely by the central government; unlimited minting of silver coins; a graduated income tax to replace revenue lost by lowering the tariff; a government sub-treasury which would pay farmers eighty per cent of the value of crops stored for sale in government-operated warehouses; public ownership and operation of telegraph and telephone systems as well as of all railways; and elimination of corporate land speculation in the West. The general point of view of the Populists was clearly shown in a few bitter sentences:

> Corruption dominates the ballot-box, the Legislatures, the Congress, and touches even the ermine of the bench. The people are demoralized. . . . The newspapers are largely subsidized or muzzled, public opinion silenced, business prostrated, homes covered with mortgages, labour impoverished, and the land concentrated in the hands of capitalists. . . . The fruits of the toil of millions are boldly stolen to build up colossal fortunes for a few, unprecedented in the history of mankind; and the possessors of these, in turn, despise the republic and endanger liberty.

In the 1892 Presidential election the Populist candidate, James B. Weaver, won more than eight per cent of the popular vote. The Populists also elected seven Senators and a considerable group of Representatives as well as several state governors and numerous state legislators. No third party had done as well since the birth of the Republican party in the 1850's, and Populist hopes ran high. But the Populist vote was very weak in the older agricultural states such as Iowa, Illinois and Wisconsin and negligible in the populous Eastern states. Moreover, white Southern Populists remained skeptical of the third-party idea and continued to devote most of their energy to capturing state branches of the Democratic party. Even in the West, the idea of capturing the Democratic party and using it to achieve Populist reforms was spreading.

4. THE ELECTION OF 1896

By 1896, some Populist leaders were ready to return to the Democratic party in an effort to capture the federal Democratic convention. They were aided in this plan by President Cleveland's extreme

William Jennings Bryan greatly irritated Republicans by the power of his spell-binding oratory. They called him a "Baby Demosthenes" and even "a slobbering demagogue." Despite three defeats as Democratic Presidential candidate, he continued to fight what he called "the gold interests."

unpopularity and the continuance of the depression which inclined many Democrats to be sympathetic towards reform ideas. Some Democratic leaders felt that the central Populist idea of inflation and "free silver" would be a very popular election issue. The Democrats, therefore, decided to "steal the Populists' thunder," and the chief proponent of this strategy was William Jennings Bryan of Nebraska.

The 1896 Democratic convention was divided sharply on the issue of a gold standard versus a silver standard (or hard money versus inflation) but it was clear that the supporters of gold, who would have nominated Cleveland, were in a minority. The Democratic platform repudiated all of Cleveland's policies, from the gold standard and hard money to anti-labour measures. Although Bryan was supported by wealthy Western silver interests, he persuaded the delegates he was a reformer and carried the convention with one of the most famous speeches in American history:

> If they ask us why it is that we say more on the money question than we say upon the tariff question, I reply that, if protection has slain its thousands the gold standard has slain its tens of thousands . . . when we have restored the money of the Constitution, all other reforms will be possible. . . .
> You come to us and tell us that the great cities are in favour of the gold standard; we reply that the great cities rest upon our broad and fertile prairies. Burn down your cities and leave our farms, and your cities will spring up again as if by magic; but destroy our farms and the grass will grow in the streets of every city in the country. . . .
> Having behind us the producing masses of this nation and the world,

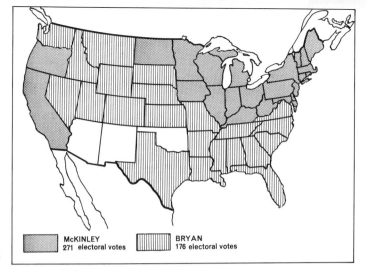

McKINLEY
271 electoral votes

BRYAN
176 electoral votes

The Election of 1896

supported by the commercial interests, the labouring interests and
the toilers everywhere, we will answer their demand for a gold standard
by saying to them: you shall not press down upon the brow of labour
this crown of thorns, you shall not crucify mankind upon a cross
of gold.

Bryan's silver tongue brought the convention to its feet in a frenzy of
emotion. But although he repeated his "cross of gold" speech in various
forms across the country and the Populist party endorsed his candidacy,
he did not win the election. The Democrats in urban centres refused to
support him, and this more than offset the support he gained from the Populists. More important, Bryan's campaign for inflation had little appeal
for the worker who, with more-or-less fixed wages, did not see how he
could benefit from inflation. Divisions within the Democratic party proved
disastrous. Very astute Republican tactics and an increase in the price
of wheat two months before the election together proved disastrous to
Democratic hopes and the Populist movement.

The Republican party in 1896 was largely managed by Marcus A.
Hanna, a wealthy businessman from Cleveland, Ohio. Hanna had groomed
William McKinley, a Senator from Ohio, for the Presidency, as a man
of no ideas who would do what he was told. Billing McKinley as "the
advance agent of prosperity" and author of the 1890 high tariff, Hanna
easily secured for him the Republican nomination. During the election
McKinley delivered a few ghost-written and non-committal speeches from
his verandah in Canton, Ohio, while Bryan covered 18,000 miles in an
exhausting speaking tour. Businessmen contributed over $10,000,000
to the Republican war chest, while Democrats fought the campaign with
$425,000. Farmers were threatened with foreclosure of mortgages, and
factory hands with unemployment should Bryan be elected and "free
silver" triumph. The election of 1896 came close to being a class struggle
and was described by a "conservative" observer as:

A rising of miserable bankrupt farmers, and day labourers who have
made the greatest fight against organized capital of the world that has

ever been made in this country—or perhaps ever. No money, no press, no leaders, no organization. Amidst abuse, ridicule, intimidation, bribery—against forces so powerful and so subtle that they reach the bravest and most honest men in the country.

Although McKinley won 271 electoral college votes to Bryan's 176, the Republican plurality was only 600,000. But in other ways it was a decisive election. The Populist party died with Bryan's defeat, killed by rising farm prices, and by the decision to co-operate with the Democratic party. Conservatism took on a new lease of life. The way was prepared for expansion overseas. The result also reflected basic changes in American society, particularly the steady progress of urbanization. Many reformers and liberals who were concerned about city and industrial problems were not enthusiastic about Bryan with his stress on Western farm interests. To some extent the Bryan "crusade" was the last political explosion of agrarianism. While many reform planks from Western protest movements were to appear in later party programmes, after 1896 the initiative for reform was to come primarily from the cities and towns of the East and Midwest.

CHAPTER 11

"A Splendid Little War"

The American spirit of "Manifest Destiny" which had remained unbroken since the founding of the Republic reached one of its periodic peaks of enthusiasm at the end of the nineteenth century. The years following the Civil War had seen a steady preparation for this. In 1867, for example, William H. Seward, Secretary of State under Lincoln and Johnson, was quite confident that his purchase of Alaska from Russia was a prelude to the peaceful annexation of Canada. His successors used the new American foothold in the north to declare that the Bering Sea was *mare clausum*, that is, a closed sea in which American authority was absolute. In other areas of the Pacific, as well as in Latin America, the growing assertiveness of the United States became more and more evident as the century drew to its close.

1. "MANIFEST DESTINY" ABROAD

One spectacular illustration of the American sense of destiny was occasioned by a border dispute which arose between Venezuela and the colony of British Guiana. The dispute was a long-standing one, but it came to a head when gold was discovered in the area. Britain repeatedly refused to submit the dispute to arbitration. In 1895 Secretary of State Olney wrote a note to the British Prime Minister in which he reasserted the Monroe Doctrine, and claimed that no European power had the right to interfere in "American" affairs. Olney denounced European imperialism, and proclaimed that the Americas lay within the United States "sphere of influence." "Today," he wrote, "the United States is practically sovereign on this continent, and its fiat is law upon the subjects to which it confines its interposition."

To support Olney's position, President Cleveland obtained funds from Congress for a commission to determine the boundary between Venezuela and British Guiana. He declared that it was the duty of the United States to enforce the findings of this commission "by every means in its power," which meant war if Britain remained adamant. At this time, however, various alliances were being formed on the continent of Europe, all of which excluded Britain. As a result, Britain was most anxious to have the friendship of the United States and she therefore refrained from forcing the issue and using her vastly superior naval power. The boundary question was resolved when Britain agreed to accept the decision of an arbitration tribunal which in the end upheld the British case.

Another aspect of the "sphere of influence" interpretation of the Monroe Doctrine was revealed in 1889, when delegates from the Latin American republics met with representatives of the United States in the first of what was to be a regular series of conferences. The delegates established the International Bureau of American Republics which later became the Pan-American Union, with its headquarters in Washington. Although the Union set up many useful committees for the purpose of exchanging information, the Latin American nations regarded it as an instrument of American influence, or even domination. Their conviction that they were not equals with the United States in the Union was strengthened when the American government directly interfered with a revolution in Chile in 1891, and a trade dispute in Brazil in 1893. More and more, it became apparent that the main concern of the United States in Latin America was to exclude European influence and to support politicians there who were favourable to the expansion of American trade and investment.

In Chile, Peru, Costa Rica and other Latin countries, Americans invested heavily in railways, copper, silver and tin mines and grew increasingly influential in the politics of these countries. In 1899 the owners of American banana plantations formed the United Fruit Company, an American corporation which soon dominated the economic life of small states like Costa Rica, Nicaragua, Santo Domingo and Guatemala. The company, which also had large interests in Cuba and Colombia, came to exert great influence upon the policies of the American government towards the so-called "banana republics" in Latin America.

The expansion of the United States into the Pacific was also vigorous, if less firmly supported by public opinion. Ever since Commodore Matthew C. Perry opened Japan to American trade in 1854, American businessmen had taken an increasing interest in the commerce of the Pacific. Supported by farm-state representatives, Congress in 1856 passed a law enabling the President to annex any island which was rich in guano, a natural fertilizer. As a result, the United States acquired a considerable number of tiny islands in the Pacific. Other islands such as Samoa, with its fine harbour of Pago Pago, were desired as coaling stations for the United States Pacific trading ships. In 1878 a treaty with the ruling Samoan monarch gave the United States the harbour rights sought by American businessmen. But in 1889, the Germans, who also had economic interests in the islands, sought to undo this agreement by overthrowing the Samoan government. The matter was temporarily settled in that same year when Britain, Germany and the United States established a joint

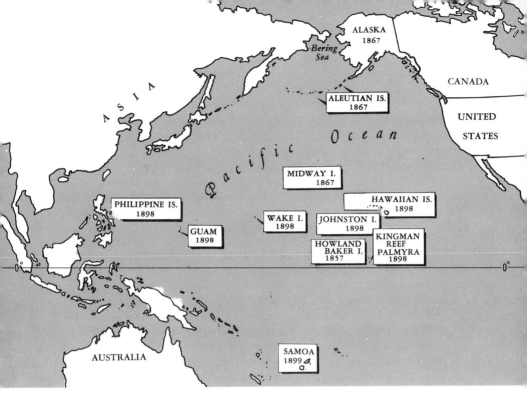

The United States in the Pacific

"protectorate" over Samoa. Ten years later a new agreement gave Pago Pago to the United States and the rest of Samoa to Germany.

Far more important to the United States in its expansionist mood was the acquisition of the Hawaiian Islands, first visited by American missionaries in the 1820's. Economic ties soon strengthened the religious connection. American immigrants produced sugar and pineapples there for the home market, and sailed their whalers into Hawaiian ports. Increasingly concerned about the dangers presented by imperialist rivalries in the Pacific, the Americans strengthened their naval power by securing from the Hawaiian government in 1887 the exclusive right to use Pearl Harbor. In the same year, seeking still greater control, American businessmen engineered the overthrow of the corrupt government of King Kalakaua of Hawaii and forced him to accept a new form of government—called the "Bayonet Constitution" by the Hawaiians—which gave white foreigners the vote and disfranchised the bulk of the native population. Six years later, when the Hawaiians under Queen Liliuokalani tried to regain power, the American community rose against them and set up a republic. Although the American minister in Hawaii supported the rising and authorized the use of American troops, the Cleveland administration in Washington was not enthusiastic about the means adopted and refused to annex the islands at that time.

2. THE NEW IMPERIALISM

By 1898 the United States, like the nations of Europe, was caught up in a wave of imperialism. During the nineteenth century, the United States had filled out her continental domain and reached tentatively into Latin America, Alaska and the Pacific. The new American imperialism of the twentieth century was a different matter, involving the annexation of far-flung islands in the Caribbean and the Pacific and the use of financial influence and naval power to secure control over the policies of other states.

Imperialism in the United States had roots similar to European imperialism. American capitalists sought new areas in which to invest their surplus money, new sources of raw materials to feed American industry, and new markets for industrial products. Since the achievement of these goals was felt to require the co-operation of government through appropriate foreign diplomatic policies and the use of armed forces, there developed an intimate relationship between business policy and American foreign policy. At the same time, as the economic depression lifted after 1896, a more confident national spirit began to assert itself in the United States. Americans wished to turn away from the painful years of civil war, industrial strife and political bitterness, and to immerse themselves in some kind of unifying national achievement. Given these strong motives, other arguments for entry into the world of imperial competition fell quickly into place. The application of Social Darwinism to international relations led easily to the conclusion that the United States must increase in size and power in order to survive. The American dream required that the United States should use its new economic and military power to protect what the British poet Rudyard Kipling called "the lesser breeds without the law" and show them the road to republican democracy. Finally, it was confidently asserted that the United States must seize and safeguard the approaches to the New World or else its national security would be precarious in a world of grasping imperial powers and military alliances.

In the 1880's and 1890's many powerful advocates of imperialism appeared. The most literate imperialist was Captain A. T. Mahan of the United States navy. In his book *The Influence of Sea Power Upon History* and in many other articles and books, Mahan argued that British power had always depended upon her naval superiority which enabled her not only to act decisively in war, but to build the sinews of economic and military strength by controlling colonies, naval stations and even world commerce. As the proper inheritor of this British power, Mahan continued, the United States must act quickly to build a large navy and emulate earlier British imperial policies. It was therefore imperative that the United States control the Caribbean and construct a canal through the Central American isthmus. Mahan also expanded the current doctrine of Social Darwinism. The white Anglo-Saxons, he declared, had proved their exceptional power to survive in the evolutionary race and should face up to the challenge of the future, the principal feature of which would be an epic struggle between Eastern and Western civilizations.

A powerful group of young Republicans supported Mahan's arguments for a great navy and an imperialist foreign policy. Among the most prominent of these were Senators Henry Cabot Lodge of Massachusetts, Albert Beveridge of Indiana and William McKinley of Ohio. Theodore Roosevelt, who became Assistant Secretary of the Navy in 1897, and John Hay, who became Ambassador to London in 1897 and Secretary of State in 1898, were other prominent Republican imperialists. Their ranks were strengthened by the support of a number of Democrats outside Congress and several influential editors, clergymen and businessmen. One of the most voluble spokesmen of American imperialism was Josiah Strong, a minister who crusaded for reform in the cities but who also believed firmly in the superiority and "Manifest Destiny" of the American branch of the "Anglo-Saxon" people. In a widely read book, *Our Country*, he proclaimed that the "peculiarly aggressive traits" developed by Americans were calculated to spread reform, social justice and "spiritual Christianity" across the face of the earth.

Bowing to this imperialist persuasion, Congress passed a Naval Act in 1890, which appropriated money to construct ships of every class. By 1900 the United States navy, with an official policy of being "second to none," had become the world's third largest sea force. The navy was more than ready for the crisis that developed in 1898 in the affairs of Spanish Cuba.

3. THE SPANISH-AMERICAN WAR

American interest in Cuba was almost as old as the Republic itself. Before the Civil War, that interest had been mostly on the part of slaveholders who viewed Cuba as a possible new slave state. After the war, American investment in Cuban sugar plantations, processing plants and railways had grown steadily and by 1898 amounted to more than fifty million dollars. At the same time, the United States had become the major market for the sugar upon which the economy of Cuba rested. In 1894, however, the American duty on foreign sugar was increased, a move which brought economic ruin to Cuba. The Cubans, who with the Puerto Ricans were the last of Spain's subjects in the New World, were driven to desperation by this aggravation of their perennial poverty. Although the Cubans had been in chronic revolt against Spain since the 1860's, the fresh outbreak of rebellion in 1895 led some Americans to fear that success for the rebels might mean occupation of the island by another European power, possibly France which, through its project to build a Panama Canal, already had interests in that area.

Other factors combined to tempt American imperialists to think of intervening in the Cuban revolt. Cubans purposely damaged American property on the island, in the hope that the United States would intervene

MAINE EXPLOSION CAUSED BY BOMB OR TORPEDO?

Capt. Sigsbee and Consul-General Lee Are in Doubt---The World Has Sent a Special Tug, With Submarine Divers, to Havana to Find Out---Lee Asks for an Immediate Court of Inquiry---Capt. Sigsbee's Suspicions.

CAPT. SIGSBEE, IN A SUPPRESSED DESPATCH TO THE STATE DEPARTMENT, SAYS THE ACCIDENT WAS MADE POSSIBLE BY AN ENEMY.

Dr. E. C. Pendleton, Just Arrived from Havana, Says He Overheard Talk There of a Plot to Blow Up the Ship---Capt Zalinski, the Dynamite Expert, and Other Experts Report to The World that the Wreck Was Not Accidental---Washington Officials Ready for Vigorous Action if Spanish Responsibility Can Be Shown---Divers to Be Sent Down to Make Careful Examinations.

Although the cause of the Maine's destruction was completely undetermined, the yellow press added the Maine to the atrocity stories of Spanish concentration camps in Cuba to whip up war feeling in the United States. The Spanish press replied in kind: "Scoundrels by nature, the American jingoes believe that all men are made like themselves . . . they are not even worth our contempt, or the saliva with which we might honour them in spitting at their faces."

to protect its interests and ultimately help overthrow Spanish rule. Some American businessmen thought it would be well worth-while to impress the Latin American countries with the new power of the United States. The idea of acquiring Cuba, or a naval station there, also fitted admirably into the ideas of Mahan's followers. Finally, in attempting to put down the revolt the Spanish government resorted to a ruthless policy of repression. General "Butcher" Weyler and his 200,000 troops showed no mercy as they herded thousands of Cuban rebels into concentration camps. The sensational press in the United States covered the Cuban revolt in lurid detail, printing highly coloured stories and drawings of Spanish atrocities. As newspaper circulation soared, an increasing number of Americans demanded that their government take action to liberate the Cuban people.

For a time there seemed some chance of a peaceful solution of Cuba's problems: the Spanish government in Madrid recalled Weyler and abandoned the concentration camp policy. Then, in February 1898, came a new crisis which made war with the United States almost inevitable. The great battleship, the U.S.S. *Maine*, pride of the new American fleet, blew up in Havana harbour. She had been sent there at the request of the American consul-general to "protect American lives and property." Although no one ever determined the cause of the explosion, the Hearst press and other sensationalist papers at once reported that the *Maine* had been blown up by "enemy" action. The big-navy men in the government, and the popular press clamoured for war with Spain. A flood of letters and personal appeals urged President McKinley to send a war message to Congress.

The President was reluctant to yield to this pressure, for the American

Teddy Roosevelt, as Assistant Secretary of the Navy, helped organize direct pressure on Mc-Kinley to intervene in Cuba. On April 5, 1898 Roosevelt reported to a friend: "I have preached the doctrine to [the President] in such plain language that he will no longer see me! If we will not fight for the blowing up of the **Maine** . . . we are no longer fit to hold up our heads among the nations of the world." At San Juan Hill Colonel Roosevelt led the Rough Rider troop which he had personally raised, but he was highly critical of American military operations. As he wrote to his friend Senator Lodge: "We have won so far at a heavy cost; but the Spaniards fight very hard and charging their entrenchments a-gainst modern rifles is terrible. We are within measurable distance of a terrible military disaster; we **must** have 'help—thousands of men, batteries and **food** and ammunition. . . . I have no blanket or coat; I have not taken off my shoes even; I sleep in the drenching rain, I drink putrid water."

ambassador in Madrid had just informed him that the Spanish government had agreed to meet every American demand, including an immediate armistice with the rebels. Spain was willing to accept independence, autonomy or American annexation as a future for Cuba. But the weak McKinley could not resist the popular clamour for war and finally accepted the arguments of close advisers like "Teddy" Roosevelt who maintained that the "blood of the murdered men of the *Maine* calls for the full measure of atonement." Roosevelt's real meaning was made clear in a hundred speeches and letters: the United States, he argued, needed a war to keep it from getting "flabby" and to advance its world mission. Other Republican leaders believed that a war would unite the nation, and reduce the mounting demand for political reform as well as the demand for government regulation of business that had been stimulated by the economic depression of the 1890's. On April 11, 1898, McKinley sent a message to Congress in which he said nothing of the latest reports of Spanish concessions and urged Congress to declare war against Spain.

The "splendid little war," as Secretary of State John Hay described the Spanish-American War, found the United States generally ill prepared. The navy, however, was ready. Roosevelt, the Assistant Secretary of the

Navy, had anticipated the war and had ordered Commodore George Dewey who was in charge of the Pacific fleet to stand ready to seize Manila, the capital of the Spanish colony of the Philippines. Aided by the benevolent neutrality of the British naval force in the area, Dewey succeeded in his mission. In Cuba American military success owed more to Spanish incompetence than to United States skill. The Secretary of War was a Michigan politician who had been more interested in patronage than in proper maintenance of the army. Thus American troops fought in heavy winter uniforms in the Cuban heat and far more died of disease than from enemy action. Nevertheless, several reputations were made in the Spanish-American war. The outstanding hero to emerge from the war was Teddy Roosevelt who organized a troop of cavalry, known as the Rough Riders, and was present at the principal battle of the war, the capture of San Juan Hill. In reality, the dangerous positions on the hill had been taken by American Negro troops before Roosevelt's famous charge was executed; but the charge caught the fancy of the people of the United States, and did much to aid Roosevelt's later political career.

The treaty with Spain, which ended the war in 1898, reflected the expansionist enthusiasm stimulated by the war itself. The United States took from Spain Puerto Rico in the Caribbean, and Guam and the Philippines in the Pacific. Cuba was given "independence" as an American protectorate. The United States paid twenty million dollars compensation to Spain for these acquisitions, and spent many more millions as well as hundreds of lives subduing a fierce three-year rebellion against American rule in the Philippines. An amendment to the congressional declaration of war had specified that Cuba should not be annexed, and it was not; but a measure passed in 1901 seriously limited Cuban sovereignty by leaving control of Cuban foreign and financial policy in United States hands.

The Spanish-American War had achieved much of the programme advocated by the imperialists, who immediately began to consolidate and expand their gains. One of the peace negotiators remarked that the acquisition of the Philippines made the Pacific an American lake, into which much commerce and investment was expected to flow. The success of the war, and general business prosperity, helped to bring about another Republican victory in 1900, in which McKinley was re-elected, with Theodore Roosevelt, the hero of the Rough Rider charge at San Juan Hill, as his Vice-President. Despite the founding of an Anti-Imperialist League, which gained the adherence of men in both parties, popular opinion supported the new aggressiveness of United States policy and, for good or ill, the United States was launched on an imperial course which would sweep her ever more surely into world politics.

4. THE COURSE OF IMPERIALISM

John Hay, McKinley's Secretary of State, followed up the new American gains in the Pacific by active intervention in Chinese affairs.

In 1899, in diplomatic notes to Russia, England and Germany, he enunciated an "Open Door" policy to be followed by Western powers in their relations with the Chinese empire. Each of the three recipients of the notes already had territorial concessions and special trading rights in China. By these means they discriminated against other foreign traders and ignored the Chinese customs laws. The Chinese government was weak and corrupt and could not prevent the foreign powers from acting as they wished. In his note Hay declared that European powers active in China should give equal treatment to all nations, and should support the Chinese tariff collectors. This policy would be of advantage to the United States because the Chinese had already granted concessions on duties to American imports. The other powers accepted Hay's position in principle, especially since it did not involve any restriction on their acquisition of territory in China. In 1900 a rebellion, known as the Boxer Rebellion, broke out against foreign control of China. The United States participated with the other European powers and Japan in suppressing it and in forcing the payment of an indemnity by the Chinese government. The Americans agreed, however, that their share of the indemnity should be used to promote Chinese education.

In 1901 President McKinley was assassinated. Theodore Roosevelt became President and under him the imperial movement quickened. In 1904-05, Japan and Russia fought a war in which Japan was speedily victorious. Afraid that Japan might move to exclude the United States from the China Sea trade, Roosevelt accepted a Japanese request to mediate between the belligerents. Thus the treaty ending the Russo-Japanese War was concluded by negotiators meeting in Portsmouth, New Hampshire. The Treaty of Portsmouth seemed to symbolize America's advance into world politics. It also heralded the expansion of Japanese power in the Pacific. This ominous development induced Roosevelt to send the American navy on a "training cruise" around the world, as an exhibition of power. Nevertheless, the President arranged an agreement in 1908 in which Japan and the United States agreed to uphold the Open Door principle in China and recognize the integrity of China and each other's interests in the Pacific.

At home, Roosevelt moved quickly to consolidate United States control of the Caribbean and to construct a canal through the Isthmus of Panama. In 1901 Secretary of State John Hay turned to good use the growing willingness of Britain to co-operate with the United States by concluding a treaty by which Britain accepted the American plan to build and police a canal under United States authority. The route selected by the United States lay through the province of Panama, part of the Republic of Colombia.

Hay negotiated a treaty with Colombia by which that country granted to the United States a strip of land across the isthmus in return for ten million dollars and an annual payment of two hundred and fifty thousand dollars. The Colombian Senate, however, refused to ratify the treaty. Rather than

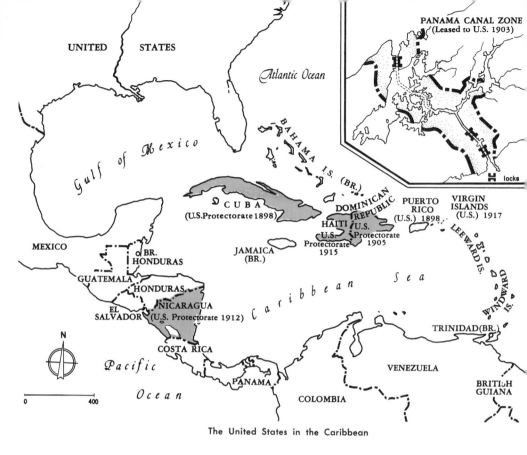

The United States in the Caribbean

be held up by this obstruction, Roosevelt gave clandestine support to several groups who wished to foment a rebellion in Panama and to detach that province from Colombia. On November 3, 1903 the U.S.S. *Nashville* anchored off Panama and on the following day a "spontaneous" rebellion began. Other American ships joined the *Nashville* and prevented Colombia from suppressing the revolt. On November 6 the State Department recognized the rebel government and within a week Roosevelt received the chief organizer of the revolt as Ambassador of the new Republic of Panama. At once a treaty was arranged by which Panama granted the United States a permanent zone across the isthmus in return for the ten million dollars and two hundred and fifty thousand dollars annuity proposed to Colombia. In later years Roosevelt reminisced:

> If I had followed traditional conservative methods, I should have submitted a dignified state paper of probably two hundred pages to the Congress and the debate would be going on yet, but I took the Canal Zone and then left Congress—not to debate the canal, but to debate me, and while the debate goes on, the canal does also.

The Panama Canal, completed in 1914 after heroic engineering efforts, added greatly to the naval capability of the United States, and stimulated the economy of the entire west coast. But the method of its acquisition

Anti-imperialists disliked Teddy Roosevelt's "big stick" methods in the Americas. Self-righteously, Roosevelt produced his corollary to the Monroe Doctrine in 1905: "Chronic wrongdoing, or an impotence which results in a general loosening of the ties of civilized society, may in America, as elsewhere, ultimately require intervention by some civilized nation, and in the Western Hemisphere the adherence of the United States to the Monroe Doctrine may force the United States, however reluctantly, in flagrant cases of such wrongdoing or impotence, to the exercise of an international police power."

strained relations between the United States and Latin America for a long period of time. Although the United States made a compensatory payment of twenty-five million dollars to Colombia in 1921, the payment did little to soothe outraged Latin American opinion.

Roosevelt's motto was that in diplomacy one should "speak softly and carry a big stick." The "big stick" was again in evidence in a dispute with Canada over the Alaska boundary in 1903. By making it perfectly clear that failure by Britain to support the American claims would mean the use of force, Roosevelt made a mockery of the "impartial tribunal," set up to settle the boundary. The whole controversy produced tensions in Canadian-American relations similar to the effects produced in Latin America by the Panama adventure.

In 1905, asserting the right of the United States to intervene in the affairs of the Dominican Republic, Roosevelt proclaimed a corollary to the Monroe Doctrine. When the Latin republic defaulted in its foreign debt payments Roosevelt intervened in order to prevent a European creditor nation from employing forcible debt collecting.   In cases of "chronic wrong-doing" by an American nation, said Roosevelt, the United States must itself act as policeman since, by the Monroe Doctrine it denied to European nations the right of intervention in the Americas.   Following this doctrine under Roosevelt and the next two Presidents, Taft and Wilson, the United States intervened with her armed forces in the Dominican Republic, Haiti, Honduras, Nicaragua and other nations.   Indeed, between 1900 and 1930, most of the Caribbean republics were little more than American protectorates.   The period from 1909 to 1913 saw a particularly emphatic phase of imperialism, sometimes described by the term "dollar diplomacy."   Philander Knox, President Taft's Secretary of State, induced American banking houses to extend their investments in Latin America and then to act as virtual government agencies.   President Wilson professed aversion to "big stick" methods, but such procedures continued to be used after he became President in 1913.   In Mexico, where American investment in railways, oil wells, mines and cattle had reached the impressive figure of over a billion dollars by 1913, Wilson intervened both indirectly and directly in support of the opponents of the "strong man" Huerta who was a threat to the stability required by United States investors.   While Wilson insisted that his motives were liberal, the argument failed to impress Latin Americans.

By the time the First World War broke out in Europe, the United States had become a major world power.   Its imperial interests reached across the Americas and to the Orient.   Americans had even participated in the important European conferences at the Hague (1899) and Algeciras (1906).   While many Americans were increasingly critical of imperialism and of any diplomatic connection with European powers, the involvement of the United States in world trade and politics was to make it more and more difficult for America to remain aloof from world affairs.

CHAPTER 12

The Politics of Progressivism

The years after 1896 saw the collapse of the Populist programme and the triumph of imperialism in foreign policy, but they also witnessed a surge of reform zeal which spread from the cities to state and federal politics. The men and women who urged a wide variety of reforms in these years were called Progressives. Many of them had been inspired by the Populist programme, while others were attracted by the critical writings of men like Edward Bellamy and H. D. Lloyd. Most of them were middle-class, professional people and small businessmen who felt that the "businessman's revolution" with its trusts and "kept politicians" had deprived them of their traditional status in American society. Business decisions, they felt, were made at the board meetings of the great trusts, while political policy was made in smoke-filled rooms presided over by powerful political bosses. The Progressives asked the question: under such conditions, where was the equality of opportunity supposedly guaranteed by the American way of life?

1. THE DEMAND FOR REFORM

Like the Jacksonians of an earlier age, the Progressives believed that most social ills could be cured by ensuring that the control of government was at all times directly in the hands of a majority of the people; and that monopoly or special privileges of any kind were destructive of American ideals. Many of them were alarmed by the growing inequality between classes in America, and felt that the powers of government must be used to guarantee minimum standards of welfare and to prevent unlimited control of economic life by a few great trusts. Such beliefs plainly ran counter to the ideas of Social Darwinism, for they required government intervention in what Social Darwinists held was the "process of natural selection." Progressives argued that it was "natural" for men to seek social justice and to use a democratic government to achieve the desires of a majority of the people. Some Progressive writers

175

pointed to examples of social economic legislation in Britain, Germany and France as worthy of imitation. They maintained that effective factory inspection laws, various forms of social insurance, workmen's compensation acts, and laws against child labour were necessary if democracy were to survive the triumph of large scale industrial organization and urbanization. In his inaugural address in 1913, President Woodrow Wilson summed up this aspect of Progressive thought:

> There can be no equality of opportunity, the first essential of justice in the body politic, if men and women and children be not shielded in their lives, their very vitality, from the consequences of great industrial and social processes which they cannot alter, or control, or singly cope with.

The demand for political and economic reform was reinforced by the spread of "social gospel" thought in the churches. Religious leaders argued that sin was encouraged by environment, and that Christians had a moral obligation to remove the social and economic evils in society. A host of journalists wrote articles for magazines exposing the facts about monopoly in banking, meat-packing, oil, steel and indeed every branch of industry and finance. These journalists, whose articles were based on the most careful research, probed all aspects of American life, from the appalling exploitation of children in industry to corruption in the Senate, from malpractice in municipal administration to the methods by which great wealth had been garnered by the few. Dozens of magazines devoted themselves to "muckraking," as this kind of journalism came to be known. While some of the muckrakers became socialists and supported extensive public ownership and economic planning, the majority concluded that less drastic political, social and economic reforms could make the American system work satisfactorily.

Progressivism as a political movement originated in a multitude of demands for municipal reform. At the turn of the century, disgusted with the widespread graft of urban political governments, the people elected reform candidates to office in one city after another. Frequently the reformers met with violence and intimidation, but often, too, they were supported by substantial businessmen who disliked both the inefficiency and the dishonesty of rule by political bosses. In the 1890's New York's Tammany Hall machine was defeated and a reform mayor was elected in Chicago. In neither case was the change permanent, but the idea spread. In 1901 a prominent businessman, Tom Johnson, was elected mayor of Cleveland and held the post until 1910. Under Johnson the city's tax system was reformed and Cleveland became a model of good municipal government. Municipal reformers elsewhere developed the idea of "commission government," or civic government conducted by a commission of men without party affiliation. A number of cities carried this idea one step farther by having the elected commission appoint a single person as "city manager." Reform governments in many cities

"Fighting Bob" LaFollette explains the virtues of the "Wisconsin Idea." Governor of the state from 1900 to 1906, he achieved the direct primary, improved labour legislation, a progressive tax system, strict laws to conserve natural resources, and non-partisan commissions to regulate business. Entering the United States Senate in 1906 LaFollette gave impetus to the Progressive movement in national politics.

improved the quality of life by programmes of beautification, slum clearance and social welfare. Frequently, however, both the reform administrations and their reforms were short-lived, often because the ousted party politicians sought the help of their associates in the state government which had power to limit the activities of city governments. As a result, Progressives began to turn their attention to the reform of state politics.

Progressive movements appeared in most of the states during the first decade of the twentieth century, and affected the policies of both political parties. The outstanding Progressive state governor was Robert M. LaFollette of Wisconsin. First elected in 1900, LaFollette took over the Republican organization and cleaned out its machine politicians. Using ideas produced by a "brains trust" of professors in the University of Wisconsin, the Governor launched a major reform programme. With the help of Progressive Republicans in the legislature he secured stricter regulation of railways and public utilities by the state government and a more equitable tax system. Progressives in many other states implemented similar if less extensive reforms.

In devising ways of ensuring popular control of governments at all levels, the Progressives borrowed ideas publicized earlier by Populists, and added several new ones of their own. As a means of preventing political parties or governments from being controlled by machines or corporations, the Progressives advocated "direct democracy," particularly the use of "initiative," "referendum," and "recall." Initiative allowed voters themselves to initiate legislation by providing that any bill which got the signature of a given percentage of the electorate (usually five to eight per cent) had to be introduced in the state legislature. If the legislature then turned such a bill down, it could be referred to the voters in a referendum. A referendum might also be requested for any bill which was before the legislature in the normal manner. Recall provided that any elected official could be removed from office before his term expired if twenty-five per cent of the electorate signed a petition for another election. In 1921 the Governor of North Dakota and some other administrative officers were removed from their positions by the use of recall. However, although many states adopted these procedures, none of them made any serious impact upon American democracy, and only in a few states are they still on the statute books.

Another Progressive plank was the "direct primary," which was first introduced by LaFollette in Wisconsin. By this procedure party candidates were to be selected not by caucuses or conventions but by "primary" elections in which all registered party members could vote. Designed to reduce the control of party bosses over candidates, it was adopted by all but three states by 1916, and soon applied to federal, state and even in some cases Presidential candidates. While the method permitted reform candidates to win party nominations over the opposition of party bosses it also increased the expenses of candidates by making two election campaigns necessary. Whether the direct primary actually made democracy more "direct" by increasing the voters' control of candidates and representatives is debatable. Some observers feel that it has merely made control of the major parties more complicated without making it more democratic. Similar doubts have been entertained about the direct election of federal Senators. Progressive agitation for this reform resulted in ratification of the Seventeenth Amendment to the Constitution in 1913, which provided that Senators were to be elected by the voters rather than by the state legislatures.

The political philosophy of the American Progressives exhibited a traditional aspect of American thought dating back to Tom Paine and Thomas Jefferson: the conviction that all government is suspect, in that it tends to breed vested interests and restrict individual liberty. Yet, the Progressives' suspicion of all government was continually in conflict with their other principal purpose of using government positively to ensure both equality of opportunity and social welfare. As a result, when the influence of the Progressives came to be felt in federal politics, there was lack of agreement on several basic ideas, and despite a widespread support for reform the outstanding Progressive Presidents, Theodore Roosevelt and Woodrow Wilson, were essentially conservative in temperament and policy.

2. THE ADMINISTRATIONS OF ROOSEVELT
AND TAFT

Two curious political developments accounted for Theodore Roosevelt's accession to the Presidency. In 1900 Thomas Platt, the political boss of New York, had secured the Vice-Presidential nomination for Roosevelt, in order to "kick Teddy upstairs," because as Governor of New York Roosevelt had refused to co-operate with Platt's Republican machine. Not only had he opposed the appointment of Platt's nominees to public offices and the granting of legislative favours to Platt supporters, he had also indicated support of Progressive political ideas. Platt was not deterred from arranging the Vice-Presidential nomination by the warning of another party boss, Mark Hanna, who observed: "Don't any of you realize that there's only one life between this madman and the White House?" In Hanna's eyes Roosevelt as President would be a disaster because Roosevelt believed that the government should be as active in domestic affairs as it had been in foreign affairs. In September 1901 Hanna's worst fears were realized when President McKinley was assassinated by a half-crazed anarchist and Roosevelt became President. The party bosses received skeptically Roosevelt's assurance that as President he would "continue, absolutely unbroken, the policy of President McKinley."

Theodore Roosevelt was incapable of following anyone's policy unbroken. He became one of the most colourful of American Presidents. Born into a well-to-do middle-class family he had been a rancher in the West and advocated the "red-blooded" life for everybody. While he believed that large corporations were necessary to the continued economic growth of the country, he distrusted men of great wealth, particularly "vulgar" *nouveaux riches*, and thought that in the public interest trusts should be regulated by government. He also thought that the government should hold the balance between such contending interests in society as labour, farmers and industrialists.

In 1902 Roosevelt directed his Attorney-General to launch a suit under the Sherman Anti-Trust Act to dissolve a monster amalgamation of banking-railway interests known as the Northern Securities Company. This company held a controlling interest in several major railways. It had been formed after a battle in the New York Stock Exchange between two great financial groups, each of which was striving for control of the railways involved. As the price of the railway shares fluctuated, many small investors were ruined, and in the end the principal competitors came together to form the Northern Securities Company which would control all of the lines over which the battle had raged. In attacking this huge new trust Roosevelt knew that he was pursuing a popular Progressive line. Many Progressives believed that he was going to break up *all* the trusts and become a genuine "trust-buster." In fact, Roosevelt believed in using government power only to prevent glaring injustices resulting from the misuse of trust organizations. When the Supreme Court in the Northern Securities Case (1904) ordered the trust dissolved Roosevelt declared: "The most powerful men in this country were held to accountability before the law." Roosevelt's reputation for positive executive leadership had also been enhanced by his intervention in a coal strike in 1902. In this

As this cartoon suggests, Roosevelt gained a widespread reputation as tamer of all the trusts. In fact, his purpose was a very limited one of regulating the "bad trusts." In 1908 he said: "The attempt [in the Sherman Anti-Trust Act] to provide in sweeping terms against all combinations of whatever character, if technically in restraint of trade . . . must necessarily be either futile or mischievous, and sometimes both."

crisis he compelled the mine-owners to accept arbitration of the dispute by threatening to have the army take over operation of the mines.

By 1904 the President's popularity easily won him the Republican nomination. Disillusioned by two defeats under Bryan's leadership, the Democrats nominated as their candidate the conservative Judge Alton B. Parker of New York. Although many Progressive votes went to the Republican Roosevelt, he also retained the confidence of big business, which contributed heavily to his campaign in the belief that Roosevelt's brand of trust-busting was not a major threat to their interests. Winning every state outside the Democratic South, Roosevelt announced, after the election, with characteristic lack of caution: "Under no circumstances will I be a candidate for, or accept another nomination."

In his second term, Roosevelt continued to be Progressivism's best propagandist and supported a number of significant Progressive measures. Government regulation of railways was made more effective by the Hepburn Act in 1906, which increased the powers of the Interstate Commerce Commission and gave it some control over freight rates. "Muckraking" books on the dangers of patent medicines and meat-packing processes led to public demand for government action in these fields. As a result, Roosevelt supported congressional leaders in passing the Pure Food and Drugs Act of 1906 which outlawed some of the worst abuses in these industries. The President also led in the Progressive drive for conservation of natural resources, which were being savagely depleted by mining and lumber

This photograph shows Teddy Roosevelt in a typical, two-fisted campaign posture.

corporations. Roosevelt set aside nearly a hundred and fifty million acres of unsold timber land as forest reserves, and supported the appointment of Gifford Pinchot, a dedicated conservationist, to the Department of Agriculture, to supervise conservation. While the policy of conservation touched only the fringes of the problem, it was at least a long-delayed beginning.

Despite a financial panic in 1907, Roosevelt's popularity was at its peak when the Republican Convention met in 1908. The outgoing President used his influence to secure nomination of his close friend, William H. Taft. Although the Democrats turned again to W. J. Bryan, they failed to exploit effectively the Progressive mood of the country. Taft was elected and almost at once showed himself to be much less in sympathy with Progressive measures than Roosevelt had appeared to be. He failed to control the Republicans in the Senate and they took the party steadily toward conservatism. In 1909 Taft signed the Payne-Aldrich tariff bill, which favoured special interests and repudiated the Republicans' campaign plank of tariff reform. He also allowed the Roosevelt conservation policy to be jettisoned in favour of large corporations that wished to exploit reserved coal lands.

In 1911 Taft supported a movement to sign a reciprocity agreement with Canada. This alienated the Republican farm belt especially, while his apparent lack of interest in Progressivism offended many of Roosevelt's supporters. Led by G. W. Norris in the House, and Robert LaFollette and Albert Beveridge in the Senate, a group of Republicans organized

William Howard Taft, a genial conservative, rides to the inauguration ceremony of 1913 with an ascetic idealist, Woodrow Wilson.

the Progressive Republican League in 1911. The League endorsed LaFollette as its Presidential candidate. At this critical juncture Roosevelt returned from an African game-hunting holiday and explosively re-entered politics. Convinced that Taft had run the party on the shoals, and that he, Roosevelt, was the only one who could recapture Progressive voting strength, he announced that he was a candidate for the Republican nomination as President. This not only ruined LaFollette's chances but split the Progressive group, and in June 1912 the Republican Convention, under conservative control, renominated Taft.

Roosevelt's supporters withdrew to form the Progressive party with "T.R." as their candidate. The Progressive platform of 1912, described as the New Nationalism, included all the planks concerned with direct democracy and gave heavy emphasis to the need for closer regulation of big business, tariff reform and conservation. In addition, it specified a wide range of social reforms; minimum wage legislation, the eight-hour day, prohibition of child labour and "the protection of home life against the hazards of sickness, irregular employment and old age through the adoption of a system of social insurance adapted to American use." In a speech announcing his candidacy, Roosevelt had proclaimed that he felt just like a bull-moose entering the fray; the Progressive party was at once dubbed the Bull-Moose party.

3. WOODROW WILSON AND THE NEW FREEDOM

In 1912 Bryan's influence helped to swing the Democrats towards reform and win the nomination for Woodrow Wilson, who had gained a reputation as a reformer and honest politician when he was Governor of New Jersey. Before entering politics in 1910, the quiet and studious Wilson had been a professor of political science and, later, President of Princeton University. Of Virginia Presbyterian stock, Wilson possessed not only a stern piety, but also a distinctly conservative Southern outlook on such matters as the position of Negroes and women in society. He explained his ambition for power by arguing that power should be willingly accepted by men whose intelligence was matched by their sense of public responsibility. As a political scientist he had argued that the American congressional system, with its sometimes paralyzing separation of powers, should be held together by strong and conscientious executive leadership. To many Americans, Wilson appeared as a cold and unbending figure;

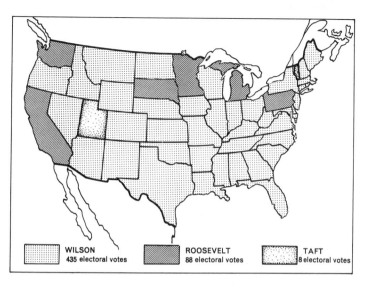

The Election of 1912

to others he embodied the triumph of idealism in politics.

The Democratic platform, termed the New Freedom, advocated more vigorous anti-trust action, lower tariffs, conservation, and banking and currency reform. The Democrats placed less emphasis on social reform, however, than did the Bull-Moosers. In actual practice, the differences between the New Freedom and the New Nationalism of the Progressives were slight. Louis D. Brandeis, a friend of Wilson's and one of the greatest American judges, said that Wilson was for regulated competition while Roosevelt was for regulated monopoly. Few people saw the distinction clearly if, indeed, there was much distinction. In practice, Roosevelt was more willing to accept as natural the increasing size of business units, as long as government remained strong too, while Wilson was more doubtful about the very existence of trusts. In any event, the measures later supported by Wilson and passed by Congress from 1913 to 1916 were to add perceptibly to the positive role of government in the United States, while not lessening the tendency of economic power to be concentrated in fewer and fewer hands.

In the election of 1912 the deep split in the Republican ranks told heavily against them, while businessmen in the Democratic party did not feel that Wilson's brand of Progressivism was a real threat to them. The result reflected the Progressive mood of the nation. Wilson received 41.86 per cent of the popular vote; Roosevelt, 27.40 per cent; Taft, 23.18 per cent; and Debs, the Socialist candidate, 5.99 per cent. Since Wilson's majorities had been in the most populous Northern states, as well as in the South, his electoral college vote was a clear majority. The Democrats also won both Houses of Congress.

Like Roosevelt, Wilson used his executive powers with vigour. Calling a special session of Congress in 1913, he supported a tariff bill which cut the average duty from about thirty-eight per cent to twenty-nine per cent. When special interests lobbied strenuously against the bill the President openly denounced them, and intervened personally to secure its passage. The Sixteenth Amendment giving Congress specific power to levy income taxes was adopted in the same year. Indeed, the tariff of 1913 included such a tax, long demanded by Progressives, partly to provide revenue lost by the reduced duties, partly as a more equitable method of raising public money. In December 1913 Congress also passed banking legislation which went some way towards meeting the Populist-Progressive demands for an expandable currency and easier credit. The Federal Reserve Act established a Federal Reserve Board to supervise banking. In 1916 Congress also created a Federal Farm Loan Board which provided credit on favourable terms to farmers.

The Democrats implemented their anti-trust plank in 1914 by passing the Federal Trade Commission Act which forbade "unfair" business practices, without defining them, and by the Clayton Act, which attempted to define and outlaw the procedures by which giant trusts were formed and competition was lessened. Having received the support of the A. F. of L. and Sam Gompers in 1912, Wilson agreed to a clause in the Clayton Act excluding labour unions from prosecution as "combinations in restraint of trade." Gompers hailed this as a great victory but the Supreme Court later decided that such exclusion was impossible. On some occasions, however, Wilson showed decidedly conservative inclinations by failing to give his support to federal legislation against child labour until it became politically necessary to endorse the Keating-Owen Act of 1916, which attempted unsuccessfully to outlaw child labour in industry.

Much of the President's apparent purpose of regulating business was nullified by the appointment of anti-regulation businessmen to administrative positions, and the Clayton Act itself was suspended when war broke out in Europe in 1914. Deeply disillusioned, LaFollette observed that neither Roosevelt nor Wilson was a profoundly committed Progressive. Both Roosevelt and Wilson saw the necessity of catering to the Progressive mood, and both distrusted irresponsible economic power; but both also drew back before the prospect of a determined and sustained conflict with the nation's major economic leaders.

The Progressive period established precedents for positive government and placed on the statute books some salutary laws of a protective nature, but it did not seem to modify the basic direction of economic and political development. At the end of the period the Morgan and Rockefeller financial and industrial interests between them controlled corporations whose value was greater than the assessed worth of all property in all the states west of the Mississippi. The process of concentration of wealth was to be hastened by the First World War and by the conservative period that followed in the 1920's. On the other hand, Progressivism deepened the American faith that a democracy, given determined leadership, could control its own destiny. Thus, while many Progressives were disappointed by the relatively superficial reforms of the period, others were heartened by the evidence it provided of political vitality.

CHAPTER 13

Wilson's Dilemma

When Woodrow Wilson became President he had little interest in foreign affairs, yet they were to dominate the greater part of his public life. Although wedded to the ways of peace, he took his country into its first major overseas war and became deeply involved in the very European diplomacy which he decried.

1. THE BACKGROUND OF INTERVENTION

When, in 1914, war broke out in Europe between Britain, France and Russia on one side, and the empires of Germany and Austria on the other, Wilson issued a proclamation of neutrality in which he asked the American people to be "neutral in fact as well as in name." Strict neutrality, however, was not easy, for the majority of Americans, including the President, were sympathetic to Britain and France. At the same time there were large minorities who felt differently. In 1914 almost thirty-three million Americans were either naturalized citizens born outside the United States or were the children of such citizens. Of these, about eight million had a German background and over four million an Irish one. Unlike the native-born, the foreign-born were not swayed by the ties of language, custom and political tradition, or by Britain's pro-American diplomacy which had been the rule since the Civil War. The Irish, and many other foreign-born Americans, saw Britain as "perfidious." Some native-born Americans felt the European war was an imperialist conflict, just one more symptom of the sickness of European diplomacy. Progressives felt that participation in such a war would destroy American liberal ideals. Faced with this kind of division in public opinion, the President decided the United States should remain neutral and should try to exercise a determining influence upon the post-war settlement, and perhaps even to mediate between the contenders in order to end the war more quickly. The events of the war and changing public opinion in the country, however, were to make this increasingly difficult.

Woodrow Wilson is seen here in a genial mood during a speech in 1915. Events were soon to darken his mood and his dilemma deepened when Germany announced that all the waters "surrounding Great Britain and Ireland . . . are hereby declared to be within the seat of war and that all enemy merchant vessels found in those waters . . . will be destroyed."

A significant factor in changing public opinion was British control of the transatlantic cables. The heavily pro-Allied news that came by this route was supplemented by the skilful work of a Canadian writer, Sir Gilbert Parker, who became chief of British propaganda in the United States. Supplying speakers, information and editorial comment to newspapers, Parker effectively established the image of brutal and despotic Huns holding Belgian babies aloft on their bayonets and ready to crush all that was best in western civilization. For a while this process of opinion-forming was partly counterbalanced by American irritation with Britain's blockade of German ports, her supervision of all neutral shipping, and the long list of goods she declared contraband.

But Americans resented even more bitterly Germany's resort to submarine warfare. In February 1915 Germany declared that enemy merchant vessels in the seas around the British Isles would be sunk without warning and that neutral ships entering that zone would do so at their peril. In May 1915 a German submarine sank the Cunard liner *Lusitania* off the Irish coast, and a hundred Americans were drowned. The ship was carrying munitions and other contraband. Nevertheless, the sinking of the *Lusitania* made the agitation for American intervention in the war mount rapidly. Wilson sent extremely stiff notes to the German government, and Bryan, who was not in sympathy with this policy, resigned. (Bryan had tried to persuade Wilson to prohibit Americans from travel in the war zone.) He was replaced as Secretary of State by Robert Lansing, whose sympathies were strongly pro-British. In addition, the American ambassador in London, Walter Hines Page, and Wilson's personal friend and roving ambassador, Colonel Edward House, were urging the President to give more active support to the Allies.

For nine months after the *Lusitania* episode Germany refrained from extensive submarine attacks on merchant shipping, and even promised not to resume them. Meanwhile, through Colonel House, Wilson vainly attempted to mediate between the Allied and the Central Powers. By the end of 1915 the President was convinced both that the United States could not stay out of the war should it continue much longer, and that the prospects of an early end to hostilities were faint. As he said to Congress in December: "I assure you that there is not a day to be lost. There may be at any moment a time when I cannot preserve both the honour and peace of the United States." He gave full support to a preparedness campaign which rapidly expanded the armed services and established a Council of National Defence to co-ordinate industry for war production. Nevertheless, Wilson won the election of 1916 primarily with the slogan "He kept us out of war." An important factor in the 1916 election, however, was the adoption of several social reform planks by the Democrats, which persuaded a number of Republican Progressives, who had voted for the Bull-Moose party and the New Nationalism in 1912, to support Wilson in 1916.

In January 1917 a desperate Germany decided to risk driving the United States into war by resuming unrestricted submarine warfare in the hope of strangling France and Britain before American troops could reach Europe. Diplomatic relations with Germany were terminated immediately. During February German submarines sank more than two hundred merchant ships, many of which flew neutral flags. By early March the prospect of a German victory was very real. British morale was faltering, French troops had mutinied, and Russia was crippled by the March Revolution which overthrew the Czar's government. The last factor was doubly significant, for, as a leading Progressive noted, the Revolution seemed to "cast the influence of a great nation in favour of true democratization of the war against merely imperialistic use of victory." The collapse of the Czarist régime seemed to make more possible the realization of Wilson's plea for a peace without victory and a League of Nations to maintain an international peace.

At the same time, there were forces at work which were less idealistic than the aims of Wilson and his supporters. In the early months of the war most American securities owned by British and French investors had been sold to Americans in order to finance purchases in the United States. For the first time the United States became a creditor nation and, in a sense, formally ceased to be a European economic colony. Of more immediate importance was the fact that the United States had increasingly financed the Allied war effort. A German victory would wipe out much of this investment. Moreover, many American businessmen were interested in the economic opportunities offered by the preparedness campaign and even more in the prospects for expansion which would inevitably follow American entry into the war. More specific events, however, were to become the immediate causes of war.

Early in March 1917 the British intercepted and decoded a message from Alfred Zimmermann, the German Foreign Secretary, to the German ambassador in Mexico, which revealed a German attempt to arrange an alliance with Japan and Mexico should the United States enter the war. Mexico was promised that Texas, Arizona and New Mexico should be restored to her as a reward. After a week's hesitation, Wilson gave the Zimmermann note to the press as a means of securing greater public support for his decision to arm American merchant ships. When American ships fell prey to the submarine campaign in March, Wilson finally felt justified in asking Congress to declare war on the side of the Allies. He had resisted longer than many statesmen would have felt able to, and although by April he had little choice, he was still painfully aware of the implications of his decision. A prominent New York journalist gave this report of an interview with the President the day before Wilson asked Congress to declare war:

> "We couldn't fight Germany and maintain the ideals of Government that all thinking men share. . . . Once lead this people into war," he said, "and they'll forget there ever was such a thing as tolerance. To fight you must be brutal and ruthless, and the spirit of ruthless brutality will enter into the very fibre of our national life, infecting Congress, the courts, the policeman on the beat, the man on the street." Conformity would be the only virtue, said the President, and every man who refused to conform would have to pay the penalty.
>
> He thought the Constitution would not survive it; that free speech and the right of assembly would go. . . .

On the following morning Wilson delivered his message to the Congress:

> With a profound sense of the solemn and even tragical character of the step I am taking . . . I advise that the Congress declare the recent course of the Imperial German Government to be in fact nothing less than war against the government and people of the United States; that it formally accept the status of belligerent which has thus been thrust upon it. . . . The world must be made safe for democracy.

On April 4, 1917 the Senate passed the declaration of war.

2. THE RESULTS OF INTERVENTION

Wilson's fears about the effects of the war upon America were only slightly exaggerated. At once the spirit of Progressivism was cast aside. Despite the President's statement that the war was not against the German people, the Committee on Public Information mobilized scholars, speakers, editors, clergymen to pound home the idea that the whole of German history showed the depravity of the Hun. The Committee's work strengthened the bigotry that lies dormant in every nation, with the result that hundreds of thousands of German-Americans went in fear, hundreds of foreigners, pacifists, socialists and liberals were maltreated, and not a few were killed by violent outbursts of "patriotism." In June 1917 the Espionage Act provided severe penalties for opposition to conscription for military service and in May 1918 the Sedition Act went much further.

HALT the HUN!

BUY U.S. GOVERNMENT BONDS
THIRD LIBERTY LOAN

George Creel who headed the Committee on Public Information which was established in 1917 to counter "subversive ideas" later regretted the excesses of the patriotic campaign, writing: "The chauvinists, however, managed to figure largely in the Liberty Loan drives . . . and flooded the country with posters showing 'bloody boots,' trampled children and mutilated women."

It decreed fines of $10,000 and imprisonment for twenty years for anyone hindering the sale of Liberty Bonds, discouraging recruiting, commenting adversely on the American form of government, or advocating "any curtailment of production in this country of anything necessary or essential to the prosecution of the war."

One of the most striking features of life on the domestic front was the economic boom fostered by war orders, which was accompanied by uncontrolled profiteering. Vast fortunes were made, despite higher income and corporation taxes. The War Industries Board and other government bodies, established to stimulate production, lacked the power to prevent fraudulent contracts, hoarding of scarce commodities or inflation. Property values and prices rose more rapidly than wages and salaries, which caused severe hardship for many classes. The American Federation of Labour consented to a no-strike pledge in 1918 and Samuel Gompers was appointed to the War Labour Conference Board which was established to advise the government on labour matters. The increased acreage under cultivation and a rise in prices led farm income to increase nearly thirty per cent from 1915 to 1918, although much of this gain was offset by inflation. Higher levels of direct taxation and the sale of bonds financed the war.

The United States made a major contribution to the Allied war effort.

American doughboys leave New York harbour for "over there" early in 1918.

At the outset, the navy was of crucial importance. Anglo-American convoys reduced shipping losses by two-thirds between April and November 1917 and the two navies effectively countered the submarine menace by mining the North Sea route by which the submarines escaped. This reversal of German undersea fortunes came at the crucial moment for Britain and France, since the former rate of loss in merchant shipping if sustained might well have given Germany the quick victory on which she had gambled when she decided to resume unrestricted sea warfare. Curbing the submarines also meant that when the main stream of the American Expeditionary Force began to cross the Atlantic early in 1918 it did so in relative safety. Two million American soldiers eventually reached Europe, and no troop transport was sunk.

The military result was decisive. With the psychological encouragement of the American declaration of war, reduction of losses at sea, and speeding up of supplies, the Allies withstood the major offensive launched by the Germans on the Western Front in the spring of 1918, although Germany had 300,000 more soldiers than the Allies. The advantage in men was cancelled by summer, and at the end of the war in November the presence in Europe of a million and a half Americans gave the Allies a marked superiority in manpower. To raise its manpower the United States relied on the Selective Service Act of May 1917 which compelled all men between twenty-one and thirty (later between eighteen and forty-five) years of age to register for service. Conscripts were chosen by lottery from among the five classes defined in the Act. There were cases of irregularity in this method of raising an army, but there was no serious complaint about the principle of the legislation, apart from those who opposed the war itself.

By the time of the Armistice of November 11, 1918 American losses stood at 48,000 killed in action, 2,900 missing and 56,000 dead from disease. Compared to the British war dead of 947,000, the French of 1,385,000 or even the Canadian of 60,000, these losses were relatively slight. On the other hand, the experience was bitter and the cost high enough to raise a post-war isolationist feeling equal in intensity to wartime patriotic fervour.

3. WILSON AND THE PEACE SETTLEMENT

This isolationist feeling impeded and ultimately destroyed Wilson's magnificent attempt to secure a lasting peace. Before the United States entered the war he had appealed for "peace without victory," and after 1917 he had repeated that the Allies fought neither for revenge nor for territorial gain, but only to destroy autocratic government. In January 1918 he placed before Congress a programme for peace that embodied his famous Fourteen Points, which included the following: "open covenants of peace, openly arrived at"; freedom of the seas, in peace and war; the removal of economic barriers among nations; the reduction of armaments "to the lowest point consistent with domestic safety"; the adjustment of European boundaries to conform with lines of nationality; the free and autonomous development of subject peoples in Europe; an impartial adjustment of colonial claims which would take into account the interests of the peoples concerned; and a general association of nations to guarantee and protect the political independence and territorial integrity of its members. Wilson became the hero of millions of war-weary Europeans, for in his programme, it seemed, was the promise of genuine liberal democracy and peaceful internationalism.

It was, however, infinitely more difficult to implement such high aspirations than it was to state them. Acting both as a stimulant for a Wilsonian peace and as an obstacle to it was the Bolshevik revolution in Russia in November 1917, which was headed by Lenin. The triumph of Bolshevism, with its idea of International Communism, warned the Allies that western democracy and capitalism might be destroyed if a genuine peace were not made on a lasting basis. Yet the fear of Communism led the Allied powers to launch an unsuccessful military campaign in Russia in 1918 to unseat Lenin and the Bolsheviks, even though the White Russians, whom the Allies supported, represented the kind of autocracy that Wilson had pledged himself to destroy. Moreover, while other Allied leaders applauded Wilson's sentiments, they were by no means willing to forego the fruits

France welcomes Woodrow Wilson arriving for the Paris Peace Conference, December, 1918. He is followed by his Fourteen Points which he wishes to make the basis of negotiation. Teddy Roosevelt was furious, and wrote: "Let us dictate peace by the hammering guns and not chat about peace to the accompaniment of the clicking of typewriters."

of victory. The desire for revenge, the demand for territorial gains, the concern for security and the promises made to each other in secret treaties all stood in the way of the implementation of the Fourteen Points.

At Paris, where representatives of the victorious Allies gathered to draw up a peace treaty, Wilson's high idealism clashed with the hard-headed realism of Lloyd George of Britain, Georges Clemenceau of France and Vittorio Orlando of Italy. Faced with their insistence on revenge, security, and territorial gains, Wilson had to compromise on one principle after another. National self-determination was sometimes sacrificed on the altar of security and compensation for the victors, as agreed earlier in a variety of secret treaties. The German empire disappeared. The German people were so humiliated by occupation of their territory and so weakened by the imposition of enormous reparations for the damage their armies had caused in Europe that the basis was laid for another German appeal to arms, less than a generation later, which almost destroyed western civilization. Freedom of trade and freedom of the seas were virtually ignored. Wilson fully realized how great were the concessions he had made, and in an attempt to console himself he wrote in September 1919: "It is a very severe settlement with Germany, but there is not anything in it that she did not earn."

The price of all Wilson's concessions was the agreement of the Allies to establish a League of Nations and include it as an essential part of the peace settlement. Wilson pinned his hopes for "a just and lasting peace" on the League. "It is a definite guarantee by word against aggression," he told his colleagues at Paris. "It is a definite guarantee against the things which have just come near bringing the whole structure of civilization into ruin." A Covenant defining the League's functions was drawn up. Under Article X, the heart of the Covenant according to Wilson, members of the League promised "to respect and preserve as against external aggression the territorial integrity and existing political independence" of its members. The member nations were pledged to bring matters that threatened war before the League and submit them to inquiry and arbitration. Article XVI created machinery to stop an aggressor by providing for the imposition of economic and military sanctions against it. A Permanent Court of International Justice was established at The Hague under the Covenant of the League.

Although the Europeans may have been less convinced than Wilson that the League would solve all the problems of diplomacy and war, the chief opposition to the League came not from Europe but in the United States. This was due partly to political blunders by the President and partly to traditional factors in American foreign policy. In the congressional elections of October 1918, the Republicans won control of Congress, despite Wilson's appeal to the electorate to give him a mandate by electing Democrats. The appeal served only to alienate those Republicans who had supported the President's military and foreign policy, however, and Wilson's subsequent failure to take any Republicans to Paris further outraged his opponents. This last blunder was tragic, for there were many outstanding Republicans who shared his views and who would have been of great value at Paris and later in the political struggle at home.

The traditional American fear of European diplomacy further strengthened Republican opposition to Wilson. Despite an amendment to the Covenant which conceded that the Monroe Doctrine should be beyond League jurisdiction and another that permitted a member to withdraw from the League, many Americans viewed the League as an instrument of European diplomacy which would involve the United States in every European war. The principles of collective security and American isolationism were thus starkly opposed. Led by Henry Cabot Lodge, chairman of the powerful Senate Committee on Foreign Relations and a personal enemy of Wilson, a group of isolationist "irreconcilables" gathered their forces in the Senate to oppose any connection with the League. Not only did the League destroy American freedom of action, cried Senator William Borah, but as an association based on force it threatened American democracy:

> You cannot yoke a government whose fundamental maxim is liberty to a young government whose first law is force and hope to preserve the

RATIFICATION RAPIDS

When Wilson returned from Paris with his Fourteen Points mangled in the Versailles Treaty and his League of Nations an integral part of the same treaty, Americans knew that a rough passage lay ahead.

former. . . . We may become one of the four dictators of the world, but we shall no longer be master of our own spirit. And shall it profit us as a nation if we shall go forth to the domination of the earth and share with others the glory of world control and lose that fine sense of confidence in the people, the soul of democracy?

Not only the Republican isolationists were opposed to the League and the peace treaty. German-Americans felt that Wilson had too readily accepted a harsh and vindictive peace. Irish-Americans were incensed that he had not supported the movement for Irish independence. Many Democrats themselves wanted to see American obligations under the Covenant defined and reduced, while some liberals and Progressives although supporting ratification, were reluctant to endorse the harsh terms of the peace treaty.

Nevertheless, Wilson rightly believed that a majority of the people and even of the Senate favoured American membership in the League. What Wilson needed at this critical juncture was patience, flexibility, diplomacy, and above all that astute political sense which could see when small concessions would bring major gains. But these fine arts the President lacked. He refused to accept any amendments or reservations which might have conciliated enough of his opponents in the Senate to give him the necessary two-thirds majority. When the anxious French ambassador assured him that the Allies would willingly accept the amendments to secure American entry to the League, Wilson was adamant: "I shall consent to nothing. The Senate must take its medicine." Wilson felt that he had compromised too much at Paris to get the League established; now he would begin to save his soul. The days of compromise and concession were over; it would be total victory or absolute defeat.

It was absolute defeat. As the Senate debated fourteen reservations proposed by Senator Lodge, supposedly designed to limit American obligations but in fact drawn up to make American membership in the League impossible, President Wilson took his case to the people. For a month in the fall of 1919 he toured the country, as if in an election campaign, denouncing his opponents and pleading with his people to endorse the principles of collective security which might prevent another world war. Already weakened by wartime strains and the influenza he had contracted in Paris, the frail President suffered a complete physical collapse. From his bedside he appealed successfully to the Senate to reject the treaty with the Lodge reservations.

Wilson and Lodge were asked from all sides to find a basis of compromise, but both refused. In March 1920 when the treaty again came before the Senate with reservations, many Democrats disobeyed the President and supported the treaty, in an attempt to find a way out of the deadlock. But the vote of forty-nine to thirty-five was still seven short of the necessary two-thirds majority. Wilson had gambled and lost. The United States rejected the treaty and the League. Not until July 1921 did the United States formally declare that hostilities were over. Not until the bleak days of the Second World War did the United States assume that position in the world which Woodrow Wilson had fought for in 1919 and 1920 at the cost of his life.

The period of imperialism, Progressivism and war came to an end in general disillusionment: disillusionment of idealistic Progressives at the results of a war supposedly fought to make the world safe for democracy; and disillusionment of a President who believed that his justification for taking his nation into war had been stolen from him. On the other hand, the United States was entering another period of rapid economic growth, and the election of 1920 symbolized the dual mood of disillusionment and expectancy. In that election the totally undistinguished Republican Senator Warren Gamaliel Harding of Ohio defeated the Democratic candidate James M. Cox of Ohio to become President of the United States. Cox was a Wilson supporter and his defeat seemed to endorse Harding's electoral method of standing on both sides of every question, including the treaty and the League, and allowing the party machine to provide the few speeches he delivered. Harding's own analysis of the election provided the name by which the period from 1919 to 1929 would be known: "America's present need is not heroics but healing," he said, "not nostrums but normalcy; not revolution but restoration." It was both Harding's weakness and his political strength as an "average man" that he should unwittingly employ a word unknown to the English language. The United States was about to enter a period of "normalcy."

CHAPTER 14

Farewell to Reform

Warren G. Harding's ideal of "normalcy" dominated the 1920's and marked the triumph of political conservatism and *laissez-faire*. Most influential Americans now accepted the ideals of the business community without question. The government abandoned the wartime policies of economic planning and gave unrestricted free enterprise a green light. Successive Republican administrations refused to resume the prosecution of the trusts, and instead extended lavish aid to private business. Businessmen supplemented these public policies by organizing extensive and effective anti-union campaigns. Judicial decisions also reflected the triumph of "normalcy" as the courts declared unconstitutional the former Progressive measures in the field of social welfare and industrial regulation. The philosophy of "normalcy" was best expressed by Herbert Hoover, who became Republican President in 1928:

> When the war closed, the most vital of all issues . . . was whether governments should continue their wartime ownership and operation of many instrumentalities of production and distribution. We were challenged with a peacetime choice between the American system of rugged individualism and a European philosophy of diametrically opposed doctrines—doctrines of paternalism and state socialism. The acceptance of these ideas would have meant the destruction of self-government through centralization of government. It would have meant the undermining of the individual intitiative and enterprise through which our people have grown to unparalleled greatness.

Ironically, Mr. Hoover delivered his "rugged individualism" speech during the election campaign of 1928, just one year before the stock-market crash touched off the Great Depression of the 1930's.

1. RADICALISM AND CONFORMITY

The " 'Twenties" have attracted the attention of an army of novelists, historians, and dramatists who have given the decade such names as the Roaring 'Twenties, The A'spirin Age, The Jazz Age, and Prosperity Decade. However, despite their profusion, none of these titles reveals the potent combination of vitality and frustration that characterized the United States in the years that followed the First World War.

A series of disturbing events heralded the new period of "normalcy." The very high cost of living at the end of the war produced serious unrest among farmers and workers. Following the Armistice of 1918, criticism of government policy mounted sharply. A wave of strikes rocked the nation's economy and thoroughly alarmed leaders in government and business. More significant were demands by mine and railway unions that the government assume the ownership and operation of their industries (as it had done with the railways during the war). To many people, such demands had an unpleasant "Bolshevist" ring that recalled the successful Russian Revolution of 1917, and the attempted Communist revolutions in eastern Europe in 1919. Linking unions, strikes, and demands for public ownership with Bolshevism, the press, business, and government used propaganda techniques developed during the war to create public fears of imminent revolution. Isolated acts of violence, exaggerated out of all proportion, were portrayed as part of a monstrous Bolshevist or anarchist plot to overthrow the government by disrupting industry. Soon known as the "Red Scare," these charges had such a profound influence on public opinion that civil liberties became as insecure during the early 1920's as they had been during the war.

In 1919 and 1920, individual anarchists committed acts of outrage which helped to bolster the Red Scare campaign. Parcels in the mails, addressed to prominent persons, were found to contain bombs. One bomb exploded on the front lawn of Attorney-General Mitchell Palmer's home. In September 1920 a bomb exploded on Wall Street in New York killing thirty-eight people and injuring many more. Some politicians and newspapers used the tragedy to demand the eradication of radicalism from American life. Five socialist members of the New York Legislative Assembly were expelled on the ground that they could not properly swear to uphold the American Constitution. A man who shot and killed a foreign-born American citizen for saying "to hell with the United States" was swiftly exonerated in court. A kind of vigilante action by conservatives caused liberals and dissenters to live in fear of bitter criticism or actual molestation.

Thousands of people who had previously supported Progressive candidates now accepted without question the Red Scare news stories and editorials. Wilson's Attorney-General Palmer, a former Progressive, moved swiftly from Progressive principles. After issuing an injunction forbidding union leaders to organize a coal strike, Palmer ordered a nation-wide roundup of foreign-born radicals. Of the more than six thousand people who were arrested, over five hundred were eventually deported. Many of those arrested were neither Communist nor foreign-born. The most notorious case of the period was that of Niccolo Sacco and Bartolomeo

Vanzetti, both Italian-born philosophical anarchists, who were arrested following the hold-up and murder of two men carrying a factory payroll. Accused of the crime, Sacco and Vanzetti were found guilty in a Massachusetts court, and sentenced to death.   Liberals within and outside the United States charged that the court had been influenced by the poisonous atmosphere engendered by the Red Scare and that the trial and verdict had been a gross miscarriage of justice.   On the basis of new evidence, the liberals launched a campaign to obtain a retrial.   The execution of Sacco and Vanzetti was delayed, but in 1927 both went to the electric chair.   Many Americans were firmly convinced of their innocence, and believed they had really been executed because they were anarchists.

In the South, the Ku Klux Klan revived with terrifying vigour and broadened purpose, and soon became an important and vicious instrument for the enforcement of conformity to the Klan's idea of Americanism. Reorganized in 1915, the Klan announced as its aim the protection of a Protestant and Anglo-Saxon United States from the multiple threat of foreign political ideas, Negroes, Jews and Roman Catholics.   Fiery crosses aflame on dark Southern hilltops announced an assault on some unfortunate "un-Americans."   The Klan remained an important power in Southern

In the 1920's many new members were initiated into the Ku Klux Klan.   The revived Klan was not only anti-Negro; it stood for nativism and conformity and was a symbol of "normalcy."   Employing the lash, tar and feathers, and even branding, it attempted to pillory anyone who questioned its own narrow-minded concept of Protestant, "Anglo-Saxon," white, fundamentalist domination of the United States.

and Midwestern politics until revelations of widespread corruption in the late 1920's seriously damaged its already unsavoury reputation.

The pressure for religious conformity was strong in the South where Protestant fundamentalists secured state legislation to prohibit the teaching of anything that contradicted a literal interpretation of the Bible. In Tennessee, a high school teacher named John T. Scopes determined to test a state law by purposely teaching the Darwinian theory of evolution, although the law forbade mention of anything that denied "the story of the Divine creation of man as taught in the Bible."

Scopes' trial was a national event. Widely publicized as the "monkey trial" it involved some very prominent contestants. William Jennings Bryan led the state's case, and Clarence Darrow, the nation's most famous liberal lawyer, led the defence of Scopes. In the steaming Tennessee summer, with the entire court in shirtsleeves and swarming with reporters, the trial was a knock-down battle. At first Bryan insisted that it was necessary for every Christian to believe that the world was created in six days in the year 4004 B.C., because this was the accepted fundamentalist interpretation of the Bible. Since this was believed to be true, Bryan argued, the state had a duty to enforce such teaching in its public schools. Darrow reviewed the literature which questioned many of the traditional translations of Biblical sources. Then he trapped Bryan in a net of logic. In reply to Darrow's question, "Do you think the earth was made in six days?," Bryan replied, "Not six days of twenty-four hours." From this crack in the argument, Darrow forced Bryan to admit that creation might have extended over millions of years. Bryan's point about literal meaning was thus destroyed. Although the court found Scopes guilty and imposed a nominal fine, the Scopes-Darrow argument in defence of freedom of opinion and unfettered education helped to reduce pressures of conformity.

Indeed, during the most intense years of the Red Scare, liberal opinion was never silenced. Individual members of the Supreme Court, for example, dissented vigorously from majority decisions against political freedom. In a 1919 case before the Supreme Court, the noted Justice Oliver Wendell Holmes enunciated one of the most famous American definitions of civil liberties. In every case of alleged disloyalty, he declared, the question is "whether the words used are used in such circumstances and are of such nature as to create a clear and present danger that they will bring about the substantive evils that Congress has a right to prevent." The "clear and present danger" doctrine was specifically intended to limit the rights both of legislatures and of courts to restrict freedom of speech and political association.

2. THE POLITICS OF "NORMALCY"

Politically, the 1920's opened with an orgy of corruption. President Harding, the former editor of a small-town Ohio newspaper and a machine politician, was completely uninterested in moral questions.

His private life was a mixture of poker and promiscuity, and his administration was riddled with dishonesty. Although he appointed some capable men to his Cabinet, he recruited most of his advisers from his old cronies of the "Ohio Gang." The most shocking of many grave scandals was the "give-away" of the Teapot Dome and Elk Hills naval oil reserve lands in Wyoming and California. The Secretary of the Navy, Edwin Denby, and Secretary of the Interior, A. B. Fall, arranged the transfer of the oil reserve lands from the Navy Department to the Department of the Interior. Fall then leased the lands to two business groups, in return for which he received $400,000. Harding himself escaped the worst of the revelations when he died of a paralytic stroke in August, 1923. Like a predecessor in the Presidency, Ulysses S. Grant, he had fallen prey to the wiles of evil friends.

Calvin Coolidge who, as Vice-President, succeeded Harding on the latter's death combined the New England virtues of thrift and business acumen. He had slowly climbed the rungs of the Massachusetts political ladder, and at the time of his nomination to the Vice-Presidency was Governor of the state. As President, Coolidge maintained Harding's *laissez-faire* policies, and is supposed to have declared that "the business of the United States is business." He refused to intervene in a major coal strike and replaced the advocates of business regulation in agencies such as the Interstate Commerce Commission with men who believed that business should be given an entirely free hand. Coolidge believed that the government should confine itself to maintaining law and order and administering essential services as inexpensively as possible.

By 1924, Progressive influence was largely eliminated from both major parties. A hastily-contrived new electoral alliance took up the name in an effort to carry on Progressive principles. This 1924 Progressive party nominated Robert LaFollette for President and Senator Burton K. Wheeler of Montana for Vice-President. Unlike the major party platforms which were non-committal on most points, the Progressive programme called for public ownership of railways, farm relief, a referendum before a declaration of war, abolition of court injunctions in labour disputes and other familiar Progressive policies. In the campaign, LaFollette received sixteen per cent of the popular vote, but since his opponents identified him with the radicalism which was so much feared at this time, he was no match for the incumbent "prosperity President" whose campaign slogan was "keep cool with Coolidge."

Four more years of prosperity left the Republicans in an equally favourable position to fight the 1928 election. Having accepted Coolidge's blunt remark that he did not "choose to run," the Republican Convention nominated Herbert Hoover, a candidate who was popular in the business world. A former Roosevelt Progressive, Hoover had served as administrator of post-war Belgian relief and later as Secretary of Commerce. In these fields he had proved himself a humane and efficient administrator. In addition, he conformed to the image of the successful businessman. Born on an Iowa farm, he had gained an engineering degree from Leland Stanford University. From engineering he moved to business promotion and soon became a wealthy man. To oppose Hoover the Democrats nominated Alfred E. Smith, the Governor of New York. A rather unpolished politician, Smith had risen from the slums of New York and had gained a reputation as a liberal.

The party platforms in 1928 did not differ significantly, and with no serious third-party threat the contest was one of personalities and interests. Hoover was billed as the "engineer in politics," the able administrator who would resist radical change and preside over unending prosperity. Smith campaigned as a man of the people, but was handicapped by "Republican prosperity," and the facts that he was a Roman Catholic and that he favoured the abolition of Prohibition. In 1918 the sale and manufacture of liquor had been prohibited in the United States. Smith stood for the repeal of the Eighteenth Amendment which had made this Prohibition a part of the Constitution. In wide areas of the South and West which were normally Democratic, Smith's opposition to Prohibition, together with deep-seated Protestant feelings on the part of the electorate, reduced his vote considerably. On the other hand, he appealed to the rising political consciousness of urban immigrants and their descendants, for Smith's own grandparents had been Irish immigrants. Nevertheless, Hoover won all but eight states in the electoral college and received 21,-391,000 popular votes to Smith's 15,016,000.

3. THE ECONOMICS OF "NORMALCY"

Economic policy and social attitudes provide further clues to the nature of the 1920's. Encouraged by the absence of anti-trust suits, and with the active assistance of Herbert Hoover as Secretary of Commerce, businessmen worked effectively to minimize competition. In all fields of commerce and industry, mergers of firms swallowed up thousands of small competitors and consolidated the control of economic activity in fewer and fewer hands. In a variety of ways, government actively subsidized business. Trade missions to foreign countries multiplied. The large merchant marine created by the government during the war was sold off to private companies at nominal prices. Private shipping lines were encouraged by high mail subsidies and changes in the tariff which favoured goods imported in American ships. And although the government gave the Interstate Commerce Commission additional power to supervise railway financing, it also encouraged the railroad companies to form combinations for greater efficiency. Tax reductions for business increased the amount of money available for investment, which in turn helped to inflate stock values above their real value and thus left the market weak in the face of any decline in confidence which would lead people to sell their stocks.

Republican tariff policy further assisted the major industrialists. In 1923 the Fordney-McCumber Act restored the levels of protection that had existed prior to the tariff of 1912. The return to high tariffs hindered European recovery from the ravages of war, and other nations raised their tariffs in retaliation. Even after the stock market collapse, and despite mounting public protest, Hoover signed the Hawley-Smoot Tariff Bill which raised duties still higher, and retarded economic recovery during the Great Depression.

The Supreme Court co-operated wholeheartedly in the general trend to reduce government intervention in the economy. In 1919 Progressives in Congress had secured passage of a Child Labour Act which placed a special tax on any firm employing children under fourteen years of age. In 1922 this use of the federal taxing power was declared invalid by the Court.

The Court furthermore declared unconstitutional a law fixing minimum wages for women and children in the District of Columbia. At the same time, federal courts issued frequent injunctions against striking unions and refused to outlaw company labour spies whose job it was to discover the identity of union organizers and to try to gather incriminating evidence against them. With this judicial assistance, business launched a full-scale attack on labour unions. The National Association of Manufacturers and other business organizations sponsored advertisements promoting the "open shop" and company unions. Almost every strike was portrayed as the work of alien radicals. Although the labour force expanded steadily during the 1920's, membership in the American Federation of Labour declined by more than a million workers.

Despite the tension in industrial relations, American productivity increased rapidly. The assembly line technique, developed first by Henry Ford, spread to other industries, but nowhere was it more successful than in the automobile industry. The first conveyor belt was used in the Ford factory in Michigan in 1914, and it reduced the time taken to assemble a "Model T" from fourteen hours to an hour and a half. As production and profits rose proportionately, other manufacturers followed Ford's lead. Automobile production soared throughout the 1920's and government expenditures on highways kept pace. Other industrial developments created a whole new range of household equipment and appliances, as well as new means of entertainment. Whether as cause or result, such production materials became a part of the turning away from idealism to a

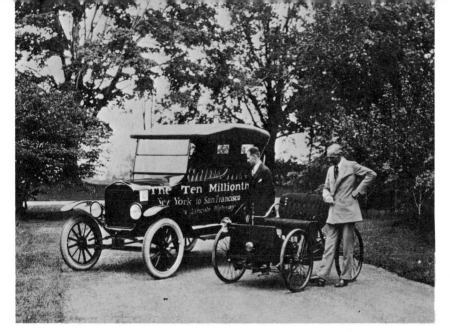

Henry Ford was one of the first manufacturers to develop the mass-production system. By 1926, employing electrically-operated assembly lines and wide-reaching agreements with other industries, he reduced to thirty-three hours the time between the removal of iron ore from a lake freighter and the appearance of a new Ford at his factory doors.

scramble for excitement and material comfort. The day of the coonskin-coated college boy, of the short-skirted, boyish flapper, of the Charleston and "bathtub gin" was also the day when the gangster Al Capone and many like him could erect empires based on bootlegging, gambling and prostitution; empires which could and did corrupt hundreds of businessmen and policemen.

The Eighteenth Amendment, prohibiting the manufacture or sale of alcoholic beverages, had been ratified in 1919 almost in a fit of absent-mindedness; yet it was to create national lawlessness on a quite unprecedented scale. The Volstead Act, drafted to enforce Prohibition, was passed with only scattered protests. It was not until enforcement machinery was ready that most Americans woke up to all the implications of the Amendment. There were some eighteen thousand seven hundred miles of sea and land frontiers to be guarded against smugglers. With fast automobiles and motor-boats, war-surplus machine-guns and a huge potential market, it was not difficult for criminals to organize virtual empires based on the illicit production, smuggling and distribution of all kinds of alcohol. Providing liquor and "protection" to thousands of "speakeasies," as the illegal bars came to be called, underworld gangs competed for larger and larger shares of the market. Reputable citizens patronized the trade in all its forms, until much respect for law disappeared. In Chicago, the centre of the industry, where controllers of the trade took in many millions of dollars annually, gang warfare reached its peak as Al Capone consolidated his power by such methods as the elaborately planned "massacre" of St. Valentine's Day, 1929, when his men machine-gunned seven members of the gang of his chief opposition. Touring his Chicago empire in an armoured car, Capone was as well known as any of the nation's political figures. And every city of any size had its Al Capone. Not until the Amendment and the Volstead Act were repealed was the rapidly-growing Federal Bureau of Investigation able to restore a semblance of order. Moreover, generations later, many protection rackets outside the liquor trade remained as a monument to the age.

The murderous gang warfare of Chicago and other large cities was a reflection of the public's lack of concern with the kind of political idealism for which Progressives had stood. Many people found escape in the thousands of pseudo-plush movie palaces which replaced the pre-war nickleodeons of early motion-picture days. By 1919 Mary Pickford, Charlie Chaplin and other famous screen stars were household names, and Hollywood was the seat of a heavily financed, over-glamourized industry. In 1928 *The Jazz Singer* with Al Jolson introduced "talkies" and further stimulated the film industry, which was already one of the largest industries in the country.

In the same decade, radio became a mass-communication medium and a major form of entertainment. The first commercial station opened in 1920 and by the end of the decade nearly half the American population owned radio sets. As with newspapers earlier, radio played an important role in advertising and tended to increase the acceptance of commercial values in the entertainment and cultural fields. For broadcasting political conventions, and for campaigning, the use of radio compensated to some extent for decreasing attendance at political meetings. After he became President, radio was one of the most effective devices of communication employed by Franklin Roosevelt, particularly in his famous "fireside chats."

As with earlier phases of American industrial development, much that was new in the 1920's was derived from earlier British and European inventions, which American organizers developed in mass-production factories. At the end of the war a number of important German chemical patents were appropriated by the American government and given to American companies. From this beginning, companies like DuPont and Union Carbide vastly expanded their production of plastics, explosives and other chemical-based commodities. The same years also saw a vast increase in the generation of electricity and the discovery of new means to transmit it both to and within large factories. These developments resulted in more efficient factory organization and made possible the spread of factories into areas which had hitherto been short of power. With such improvements in production came a vast expansion in the manufacture and consumption of domestic labour-saving and entertainment equipment, such as vacuum cleaners, washing machines, phonographs and radios.

The growth of aviation, stimulated by the First World War, also accelerated the pace of life in the 1920's. As with shipping, the federal government heavily subsidized the aviation industry. Tentative airmail and passenger services began in 1920, and in 1926 the Air Commerce Act

When Charles A. Lindbergh flew the Atlantic alone in 1927 he captured the imaginations of people all over the world.

granted mail subsidies to private airlines. In 1927 enthusiasm reached a peak when Charles A. Lindbergh, in the tiny monoplane, *Spirit of St. Louis,* made the pioneer solo transatlantic flight in thirty-three and a half hours.

4. THE END OF "NORMALCY"

Despite the widespread material progress and political complacency, many people were disturbed during the torrid 'twenties. They noted that "good times" were not shared equally by all regions and classes. The urban middle class was the chief beneficiary, while average working-class "real wages" rose very little. High American tariffs made it difficult for foreign nations to sell enough in the United States to enable them to purchase American surplus farm products, and this resulted in a steady decline in farm income, which was not halted until after 1933. In Congress, a farm bloc of both Republican and Democratic Senators and Representatives from Western and Southern states pressed hard for easier farm credit. The McNary-Haugen Bill, which would have enabled the government to purchase surplus farm products to be sold below market prices to other nations, was twice vetoed by President Coolidge, despite the substantial assistance given to industry in the same period. In 1929, at President Hoover's instigation, Congress passed an Agricultural Marketing Act which gave limited assistance to farmers, but neither the President nor Congress took further significant action on the farm problem until after the election of 1932.

In addition to the worsening plight of the farmers, large areas of industry failed to recover from a minor depression which had followed the end of the war. Coal-mining, leather and textile manufacturing and other basic industries were hit by changing patterns of consumption or by price-wage policies which kept the real wages of workers very low. In short, while "national income" rose spectacularly, it was unevenly distributed. In 1929, forty-two per cent of American families received less than $1,500 a year, while more than 24,000 families received more than $100,000 a year. Corporations also built up huge profits, much of which went into further investment. Many Americans came to believe that prosperity would be unending, and hundreds of thousands of people poured every dollar they had saved or could borrow into the stock market and speculation reached astronomic proportions. The boom became a bubble and the bubble burst.

Late in October 1929, stock prices dipped. People who had been buying stock "on margin," that is, without enough cash to back up their orders, began to sell. Within two weeks stocks had fallen twenty-five billion dollars in price. Despite the explanation of the most prominent bankers, businessmen and the President that there was only a failure of confidence, the declines continued. Between September 1929 and July 1932 the value of stocks listed in New York dropped from ninety billion dollars to fifteen and a half billion. By then it was evident to many people that the real reasons for the crash lay deeper than the investors' loss of faith in the market.

Many people lost their savings immediately in the stock market crash. Millions more were crushed as the shock waves reached out through banking and industry. Hundreds of businesses closed and unemployment spread rapidly. Mounting unemployment meant decreasing purchasing power

Hundreds of thousands of unemployed Americans lived in shacks during the depression. Communities of these makeshift dwellings—like this one in New York City—came to be known as "hobo camps" or "Hoovervilles."

and this in turn brought more unemployment. By 1932 there were more than twelve million Americans unemployed, which meant that thirty million people were without a regular source of income. Many thousands of people, no longer able to pay rent, moved into wood-and-tin shanty towns on the scarred fringes of great cities, frequently called "Hoovervilles," in derisive tribute to the President. Hundreds of thousands of men joined the straggling breadlines or "hopped freights" or "rode the rods" in a futile search for jobs. By far the most terrifying economic collapse ever to hit the nation, the Great Depression continued to be minimized in the statements of the President and those businessmen who managed to survive it.

The American people became increasingly critical of Hoover's apparently callous aloofness, but despite rising opposition, Hoover told reporters: "Nobody is actually starving. The hoboes, for example, are better fed than they have ever been. One hobo in New York got ten meals in one day." Despite his bad public relations, Hoover did try to curb the depression, but each of his measures was partial and none seemed to attack the root trouble. Hoover's most positive act was to obtain from Congress a law establishing the Reconstruction Finance Corporation which could "prime the economic pump" by lending money to businesses to keep them afloat when private credit had dried up. One and a half billion dollars were lent by this agency in 1932. The Reconstruction Finance Corporation was to be a potent factor in the economic recovery programme of Franklin D. Roosevelt.

Perhaps Hoover's most serious error was to refuse to allow the federal government to enter the field of unemployment relief. With millions of Americans dependent for their survival upon public relief, the inability of states and municipalities to finance relief payments brought the most dangerous kind of despair, frequently raising the question whether the American economic and political system itself was valid. By 1932 many state and city governments were virtually bankrupt and the spectre of widespread starvation began to materialize. But with his deep faith in the responsibility of the individual for his own welfare, Hoover steadfastly refused to press for federal assistance in relief payments. He argued that relief was "unearned income" which would demean its recipients, while to use federal funds for an essentially "local" problem would threaten the federal structure of the United States. By the autumn of 1932 he seemed like a man in a trance, unwilling to believe the stark evidence of mass destitution.

It was in such dark and dangerous circumstances that the election of 1932 took place. In opposition to Hoover the Democrats nominated Franklin Delano Roosevelt, a man who had been vaguely associated with the Progressive wing of the party as Wilson's Assistant Secretary of the Navy and Vice-Presidential candidate in the 1920 election. While "F.D.R." has become almost a legendary figure in American history, he was a relatively unknown quantity at the time of his election in 1932. He had won the New York State Governorship in 1928, a year of low fortunes for

Bread lines, like this one on Broadway, were a common occurrence in 1932 when America went to the polls. In a land of plenty millions stood in line for charity. A Senate committee heard this evidence: "One woman went along the docks and picked up vegetables that fell from wagons. Sometimes the fish vendors gave her fish at the end of the day. On two different occasions this family was without food for a day and a half. . . . Another family did not have food for two days. Then the husband went out and gathered dandelions and the family lived on them."

the Democrats, and had been re-elected handsomely in 1930. At the Democratic Convention in 1932 he was nominated over Al Smith, who bore the stigma of defeat from the last campaign. Observing his wealthy Hudson Valley background and country squire manner, left-wing Democrats were dubious about Roosevelt's qualifications. One psychological factor in his favour, however, was the triumphant struggle he had waged during the early 1920's against a crippling attack of poliomyelitis, a disease which had left him dependent upon steel braces on both legs. Related to this was a buoyant personality which radiated confidence and good cheer, symbolized by a jauntiness of attire and a broad smile. In the later days of his long Presidency, these characteristics became almost trade-marks, as did the dramatic black naval cloak he wore to wartime conferences.

In 1932 the Democratic platform was a mixture of caution and promises: a balanced budget, repeal of prohibition, lowering of tariffs on a reciprocal basis with other nations, unemployment insurance and old age pensions, reinforcement of anti-trust legislation, federal aid for state unemployment relief, planned public works, and other direct assistance to economic recovery. Emphasizing those planks which savoured of the Progressive tradition, Roosevelt promised a New Deal for the American people, vigorous executive action, and continuing concern for the "forgotten man." Without preaching a radical solution, he convinced most voters that he would bring vigour to the White House to replace the drift and hesitancy of Hoover, who confined his campaign to warning of the dire results of a Democratic victory.

The election was decisive. Carrying all but six states, Roosevelt received 22,821,000 popular votes to Hoover's 15,761,000. The Democrats also won large majorities in both House and Senate. Coolidge Prosperity had ended in Hoover Depression, and the Republicans were given credit for both false prosperity and fatal depression.

CHAPTER 15

F.D.R. and the New Deal

As Franklin Roosevelt took the oath of office as President he looked out from the steps of the Capitol upon a nation in ruins. In his inaugural speech, he declared his intention to restore to the United States what he considered to be its original goals, the maintenance of human dignity and equality of opportunity. The new President left no doubt of his determination to act strongly:

> The money-changers have fled from their high seats in the temple of our civilization. We may now restore that temple to the ancient truths . . . there must be an end to a conduct in banking and in business which too often has given to a sacred trust the likeness of callous and selfish wrongdoing. . . . In the event that the Congress shall fail [to enact the necessary measures of recovery] I shall ask the Congress for the one remaining instrument to meet the crisis—broad executive power that would be given me if we were in fact invaded by a foreign foe. . . . [The people] have asked for discipline and direction under leadership. They have made me the present instrument of their wishes. In the spirit of the gift I take it.

1. ROOSEVELT AND HIS CABINET

Some observers feared that this speech heralded a move by the United States in the direction of dictatorship in the manner of Hitler in Germany and Mussolini in Italy, while others recalled the dark days of Andrew Jackson and the rule of King Mob. Even the President's observant and politically active wife, Eleanor Roosevelt, recorded her anxiety at the huge demonstration accorded her husband's reference to powers ordinarily granted in wartime. Yet, despite his determination to use the executive power to its full extent, Roosevelt was equally resolved to work within American political traditions and to preserve the capitalist system. Like earlier Progressives, he believed in reforming existing institutions rather than replacing them. His own favourite description of his political

Franklin D. Roosevelt converses here with Raymond Moley, chief economic adviser in the early days of the New Deal. Describing the policy of Roosevelt's Brain Trust, Moley wrote: "We believe that any attempt to atomize big business must destroy America's greatest contribution to a higher standard of living . . . the development of mass production. . . . We recognized that competition, as such, was not inherently virtuous."

method was to say that he was like a football quarterback: he called a play and if it worked he followed it up; if it did not work, he tried another. Experimentation became his watchword. He spoke from conviction when he said in his first inaugural address: "The only thing we have to fear is fear itself—nameless, unreasoning, unjustified terror which paralyzes needed efforts to convert retreat into advance."

Roosevelt's greatest asset was his liking for people. He was not of an original turn of mind, but he had the ability to dramatize ideas which he had picked up from others. He had, too, an innate understanding of politics which enabled him to work with some of the least respectable Democratic party machines, while at the same time retaining the loyalty of many friends in more idealistic circles. His Cabinet reflected this. James A. Farley, his Postmaster-General, was a professional politician who knew every nook and cranny of the party, and who dispensed patronage. Frances Perkins, Secretary of Labour was the first woman Cabinet member in the United States; her sympathies were Progressive. The Secretary of State was Cordell Hull, a conservative Democrat from Tennessee with a Southerner's belief in low tariffs. Henry A. Wallace of Iowa, whose father had been in Republican Cabinets, became Secretary of Agriculture and proved to be one of the most radical members of the Roosevelt team. The Secretary of Commerce was Harold Ickes.

In addition to his Cabinet, Roosevelt gathered about him a group of very close advisers, which soon came to be called the Brain Trust. Some of these he appointed to special administrative posts; others he simply consulted. Harry Hopkins, a former social worker, was influential in framing unemployment relief and rehabilitation policies. Several professors from Columbia University supplied the basic ideas for new policies in banking and agriculture. Indeed, the Brain Trust produced so many ideas that Roosevelt's main task was to choose among them. Such use of academic advisers was then a novelty and provoked sharp criticism from pro-

Of the New Deal work programmes the Civilian Conservation Corps had the longest life; it was not terminated until 1941. Single unemployed men between 17 and 23 years of age worked at road building and reforestation. Here a group is lined up for canteens, having just been issued clothing at Camp Dix, New Jersey.

fessional politicians who resented the intervention of the amateurs into what they regarded as their special field.

2. THE HUNDRED DAYS

The new President moved with unprecedented speed to redeem his campaign promise of a "new deal for the forgotten man." Immediately after his inauguration on March 4, Roosevelt called a special session of Congress to meet on March 9, 1933. In the hundred days that followed, he set a record for both legislative and executive accomplishment.

An acute banking crisis faced the President on his first day in office. Roosevelt ordered all banks closed for four days until Congress could meet and on its first day of sitting Congress passed an Emergency Banking Act which provided the conditions within which the banks could safely be reopened. Under this act, the government insured deposits in approved banks and the Reconstruction Finance Corporation extended credit to enable thousands of banks to resume business on a sound basis. The Banking Act of 1935 later increased federal supervision of the banking system and gave the Federal Reserve Board power to regulate rates of interest.

On March 21, 1933, Roosevelt recommended to Congress three approaches to the crucial question of relief of the unemployed: federal grants to the states for financing direct relief payments to the unemployed; a bigger programme for such traditional federal projects as roads and public buildings in order to provide more jobs; and the creation of what came to be called the Civilian Conservation Corps. The last was quickly brought into being and enrolled 300,000 single men for conservation work. Each received free board and thirty dollars a month in pay. The C.C.C. remained in being until 1941 and assisted more than two and a half million young men who accomplished impressive feats of reforestation and allied conservation work. Roosevelt's other two recommendations were likewise acted upon in that first hundred days. As time went on, however, and unemployment stubbornly persisted, the government, influenced especially by Harry Hopkins, placed more and more emphasis upon providing jobs for the unemployed as opposed to simple relief. Millions of men were put to work on projects ranging from the building of roads, airports, schools, bridges and dams to the construction of aircraft carriers. A new agency, the Works Progress Administration (W.P.A.), was set up in 1935 to co-ordinate this many-sided effort and Hopkins became its head. Stressing the importance of saving both the dignity and the skills of trained people, the W.P.A. sponsored projects in the fine arts, theatre, music and historical research as well as others of the kinds already mentioned. The W.P.A. spent over eleven billion dollars in the next six years and found work for more than eight million people. In addition, the federal government spent over four billion dollars in underwriting direct relief up to 1941.

Many tax-payers deplored the billions of dollars spent in relief and there can be no doubt that the relief measures did not solve the unemployment problem, since in 1939 there were still nine million people out of work. They did add a vast amount of public property and equipment to the nation, however, and, as one observer put it, "they placed a lift under the wings of the people's spirit." A prominent banker, answering the many harsh attacks on the New Deal made by his colleagues, remarked: "Well, if the country was willing to spend thirty billion dollars in a year's time to lick the Germans, I don't see why people should complain about its spending five or six billions to keep people from starving."

The government's emergency plan for revitalizing industry was launched with the establishment of the National Recovery Administration (N.R.A.) which was brought into being by the National Industrial Recovery Act. Designed to provide "the machinery necessary for a great co-operative movement throughout all industry," N.R.A. actually adopted much the same policy towards industry as had been followed by Herbert Hoover when he was Secretary of Commerce under Coolidge. Anti-trust laws were suspended, and industrial leaders drew up "codes of fair competition," endorsed by N.R.A. All "co-operating" firms displayed posters and window stickers bearing the device of a blue eagle under the N.R.A. initials. Although both industry and labour welcomed the plan at first, it soon became apparent that N.R.A. benefited the largest firms most

In the drive of the C. I. O. to organize industrial unions to match the organization of industry itself, a new strike method known as the "sit-down" was used. In 1936 workers refused either to work or to leave General Motors factories. The Governor of Michigan intervened when the company replied with propaganda and violence. Although General Motors recognized the United Auto Workers union, in 1939 the Supreme Court declared the sit-down strike to be illegal. Here a Labour-day parade in Detroit commemorates the 1936 battle.

because its policy fostered monopoly, price maintenance, production cutbacks and division of the market.

In the summer of 1934 a Review Board reported that N.R.A. was doing more harm than good, even to the point of hindering recovery. Consumers disliked it because one of its purposes was to keep prices up, and even Roosevelt, who had pinned high hopes on N.R.A., breathed a sigh of relief when the Supreme Court ruled N.R.A. unconstitutional in May of 1935. In the opinion of the Court, the National Industrial Recovery Act delegated legislative powers improperly to the executive branch and infringed states' rights by regulating trade within, as well as between, states.

Section 7a of the National Industrial Recovery Act had required that every code should guarantee the right of collective bargaining, and had also established maximum hours of work and minimum wages, and condemned "sweatshops" and child labour. Under the terms of this section, it was possible for labour to organize a new drive for members, and union membership rose from 2,800,000 to 3,700,000 in two years. As labour strength grew, Congress became more responsive to its interests and requests. In 1935 Congress passed the Wagner Act, creating a National

Labour Relations Board (N.L.R.B.). The new Act restated the rights of collective bargaining and established tight rules against employers' coercion of employees. The N.L.R.B. was empowered to certify unions as bargaining agents whenever the union enrolled a majority of workers in a firm or industry. Despite fierce opposition by management, the N.L.R.B. was extremely effective, and the number of "company unions" declined sharply. By 1941 the Board had settled amicably seventy-five per cent of the strikes dealt with, and by that year union membership had risen to 10,480,000.

The new security given to the unions by the New Deal facilitated the organizing of industrial unions. Led by the fiery John L. Lewis, President of the United Mine Workers of America, a group of A.F. of L. unions founded a Committee for Industrial Organization (C.I.O.). The C.I.O. set itself the task of organizing all the mass-production firms on an industry-wide basis, beginning in 1937 with automobile and steel companies. Employing the drastic method of "sit-down" strikes (strikes in which the men refuse to leave a plant until their union is recognized) and mass demonstrations, the C.I.O. drive in 1937 was forcibly opposed by employers and led to widespread violence. Opposed by the craft union leadership of the A.F. of L., the C.I.O. was suspended from the American Federation of Labour in 1938 and became the Congress of Industrial Organizations. The two were finally reunited in 1955.

Despite Roosevelt's own doubts about some of the methods employed by the unions, the rising strength of labour was extremely important to him politically. The C.I.O. in particular worked hard for the "Roosevelt coalition." This coalition consisted of organized labour; Southern Democrats who supported most New Deal measures; big-city Democratic machines; and Western farmers, who were increasingly won away from the Republicans.

At the time of Roosevelt's inauguration, the western "farm-belt" was in a depressed condition which was accompanied by scenes of violence. On the Great Plains, farmers organized to prevent mortgage foreclosures, while physical assaults on sheriffs' deputies and finance-company agents were commonplace. Reduced to penury, and in daily fear of losing their homes, many farmers demanded that the government correct the market forces over which the farmers themselves had no control. Thus, at the same time as the National Industrial Recovery Act was passed, Congress enacted the Agricultural Adjustment Act, creating yet another "Administration," the A.A.A. The purpose of A.A.A. was to establish "parity" farm prices, that is, to make the prices of farm products rise until they were as high compared with other prices as they had been in 1909 to 1914. Farmers made agreements with A.A.A. to cut down the acreage sown to particular crops, in return for cash payments. The idea was to increase farm income by reducing the size of the crop and thus raising prices. It was financed by special taxes levied on firms processing farm products, such as meat-packers and flour millers. As part of the first year's production cut-back, thousands of acres already seeded were plowed under and millions of young pigs killed. This aspect of A.A.A. horrified consumers generally, and political liberals in particular, since it meant both higher prices for food and destruction of food which was desperately needed both at home and abroad. While prices of farm products rose appreciably, it was found that A.A.A. benefited large producers much more than small, especially in the South where crop reduction losses were frequently passed on to tenants and share-croppers. In January 1936, the Supreme Court declared A.A.A. unconstitutional on the ground that the controls exercised and the taxes imposed violated state jurisdiction. However, later New Deal acts firmly established the principle that farmers were entitled to government assistance and planning, to counterbalance the many kinds of help given to industry and commerce. Yet, despite the fact that widespread drought and devastating dust storms had deepened the lengthy farm depression, the New Deal farm programme was bitterly criticized by urban conservatives for its cost and because it created scarcity as a solution to the farm problem rather than expanding exports.

In this remarkable hundred days, Congress passed yet another act that broke new ground. In May 1933 the Tennessee Valley Authority (T.V.A.) was created and given power to embark on the New Deal's greatest experiment in planning. With authority to build dams, generate and sell electric power, undertake conservation and flood control measures and "to provide for the general welfare of the citizens" of the area, T.V.A. was really a regional experiment in socialism. It represented the triumph of years of campaigning by the notable Western Progressive, Senator George W. Norris. In an area of 40,000 square miles which touched seven states T.V.A. brought a section of the United States which had been in a chronic condition of economic depression into thriving activity. Huge control dams produced electric power, which was distributed through the Authority to provide rural electrification. The dams formed the basis for much new industry, saved vast areas from destruction by flood, and irrigated many more. Low-cost housing was built in many adjoining communities, co-operatives were organized, new agricultural methods developed, public health agencies established and large recreational areas created on the new lakes. David Lilienthal, one of the first T.V.A. directors, wrote:

> This is the story . . . of how waters once wasted and destructive have been controlled and now work, night and day, creating electric energy to lighten the burden of human drudgery. Here is a tale of fields grown old and barren with the years, which now are vigorous with new fertility, lying green to the sun; of forests that were hacked and despoiled, now protected and refreshed with strong young trees just starting on their slow road to maturity. It is a story of the people and how they have worked to create a new valley.

Partly because of T.V.A.'s success, private power companies led a well-financed campaign to have it declared unconstitutional. Compelled

The Norris Dam in Tennessee was named for the Nebraska Senator who was the strongest supporter of the T. V. A. and public power development. Despite the opposition of private power companies, the Supreme Court upheld this New Deal Act and T. V. A. created a prosperous community in what had been a chronically depressed region.

to reduce their power rates, as T.V.A. showed how cheaply electricity could be distributed, the power companies supported Wendell Willkie, President of the Commonwealth and Southern Corporation, in challenging T.V.A. However, in 1936 the Supreme Court decided that T.V.A.'s powers as an interstate authority were entirely constitutional.

3. CONSOLIDATING THE NEW DEAL

The year 1935 marked a turning-point in the development of the New Deal. The plays called in 1933 had had time to show their worth. On the one hand there were distinct signs of recovery; on the other, unemployment continued to be high. Where from here? The social stress of five years of depression had by this time raised up a strange variety of prophets, each of whom believed himself possessed of the answer. Three won followings large enough to pose serious threats to Roosevelt's leadership and the Democratic hold on power. One was Father Charles Coughlin, a Michigan priest with a wide radio following, who preached a radical doctrine of semi-fascism. Although he supported Roosevelt at first, he opposed him violently after 1935. Another was Dr. Francis Townsend, an elderly California physician, who gained wide support from old people with a plan to provide everyone over sixty with an income of two hundred dollars a month. The object was to boost purchasing power and so speed recovery. Money to finance the plan was to be raised by levying a sales tax. Millions of people voiced support for Townsend despite the fact that his scheme would have cost the impossible sum of twenty billion dollars a year. The most serious threat came from the third, Senator Huey Long

A Republican newspaper lampoons the New Deal as a hopeless mixture of conflicting policies and agencies and paralyzing bureaucracy.

of Louisiana. Known in Louisiana as the "Kingfish," Senator Long controlled the state as though he owned it. Although his régime was as corrupt as any in American history, he introduced a number of popular reforms. By 1935 he had become a national figure and was securing considerable national support by a vague plan to "share the wealth." His career came to an abrupt end when he was shot by a personal enemy.

The Great Depression produced a Socialist political party in Canada which opposed the major parties and demanded fundamental changes in the economic system. No similar party arose in the United States. American Socialists did not believe that the New Deal was a permanent answer to the problem of the depression but they were not able to cope with the political appeal of the President. Norman Thomas, who had succeeded Eugene Debs as the Socialist candidate for President, explained the decline in Socialist voting strength in one word: "Roosevelt." At the same time, however, Roosevelt and Congress were aware of radical pressure from left-wing political elements, and took steps to offset it. In the summer of 1935, Congress passed a series of new laws that introduced permanent reforms and moved the New Deal leftward.

One such measure was the National Labour Relations Act, already noted as the Wagner Act. A Wealth Tax Act raised tax levels steeply on large personal and corporation incomes. The Public Utilities Holding Company Act provided for the break-up of trusts in public utilities if they could not prove that they passed on the savings of monopoly to consumers. However, the most significant legislation of 1935 was the Social Security Act which provided old age pensions, unemployment insurance, and aid for dependent mothers and children. Funds for unemployment and old age insurance were raised by a payroll levy on employees, with equal contributions from employers. The cost of the other benefits was shared by the federal and state governments.

As the elections of 1936 approached, opposition to Roosevelt among Republicans, and even on the part of some Democrats, reached fever pitch. To them, the legislation just described constituted "creeping socialism." Through an organization known as the Liberty League the Republicans built up a huge anti-Roosevelt election fund. Most of the nation's newspapers were also against the President. But the economic upturn, and the undoubted benefits enjoyed by millions of Americans from New Deal legislation left no doubt about Roosevelt's renomination and little about his re-election. The Republicans nominated Governor Alfred Landon of Kansas and took as their platform the need to defend the Constitution. Roosevelt conducted a free-swinging, moderately left-wing campaign in which he castigated the country's "economic royalists" who, he declared, knew they were losing their monopoly of power and wealth. "They are," he said, "unanimous in their *hate* for *me—and I welcome their hatred.*" The election result was a landslide for Roosevelt.

Roosevelt's second inaugural address, delivered in January 1937, was perhaps bolder and more challenging than his first, and presaged a programme of further reform. "In this nation," he declared, "I see tens of millions of its citizens—a substantial part of its whole population—who at this very moment are denied the greater part of what the very lowest standards of today call the necessities of life." Ironically, the very size of the Democratic majority in Congress might tempt his followers, as Roosevelt shrewdly realized, to be freer in criticizing and opposing his proposals. A second possible stumbling-block lay in the Supreme Court which had already invalidated the N.R.A. and the A.A.A. To rally his supporters and at the same time to defeat the opposition of the Supreme Court, Roosevelt proposed to Congress a Court Reform bill which he and his Attorney-General had quietly prepared. The bill gave the President power to appoint a Supreme Court justice for each justice who failed to retire at the age of seventy. Arguing that the majority of the "nine old men" who constituted the Court were allowing conservative social views to interfere with their judgment on laws made necessary by new problems, Roosevelt said he needed power to appoint liberal men to the Court. At once conservative opinion raised a storm of protest. The Court bill was denounced as a court-packing scheme which destroyed the concept of judicial independence. A number of leading Democrats opposed the bill, some because they were irked by Roosevelt's failure to consult them in advance, some because they believed it would destroy the constitutional separation of powers. Debate in Congress and the country was long and bitter. The President's case was weakened when one justice who had frequently voted against New Deal measures suddenly changed his stand in several critical cases. The result was that the Court reversed the decision it had made in 1923 that the federal government could not outlaw child labour and then went on to uphold the constitutionality of basic New Deal legislation such as the Wagner Act, the Farm Mortgage Act of 1935, and the Social Security Act. In July the Court bill was finally shelved.

In 1935 and '36 the Supreme Court declared many key acts of the New Deal to be unconstitutional, on the grounds that they gave too much power to the executive, invaded states' rights, and transferred property from one person to another without "due process of law." Roosevelt's Court Reform Bill was designed to enable him to appoint younger, liberal judges to the Court. "Little by little," he said, "new facts become blurred through old glasses fitted, as it were, for the needs of another generation."

Later, several conservative justices retired, enabling Roosevelt to appoint in their place liberals such as William Douglas and Felix Frankfurter. While both sides claimed victory in the Court fight, it was clear that the outcome was a "reformed" Court. On the other hand, the Democratic party had been seriously divided over the issue and Roosevelt never recovered the degree of political strength he enjoyed from 1934 to 1936.

In his second term Roosevelt obtained reforms which rounded out the New Deal. There were further measures to help farmers and to regulate business. Two acts were of outstanding importance. In 1937 the Wagner-Steagall Act established a United States Housing Authority which began a long-term programme of easy loans to state and municipal low-rental housing and slum-clearance agencies. Despite conservative Democratic opposition, Roosevelt also obtained passage of the Fair Labour Standards Act in June of 1938, under which interstate industry was required to adopt, over a four-year period, a maximum work week of forty hours and a minimum wage of forty cents an hour.

By 1939 the New Deal had lost its impetus; foreign affairs began to demand the President's primary attention. What had it accomplished? The Roosevelt programme had failed to cure the business depression or solve the unemployment problem. It had added some twenty-three billion dollars to the national debt. Federal power had been sharply increased over that of the states, and a complicated bureaucracy which administered the many new agencies appeared to have become a permanent feature of American life. On the other hand, the New Deal had demonstrated that democratic government was not helpless in the face of a supreme social crisis, and it had avoided extreme measures such as the communistic programme of Russia, or the Fascist régime in Germany. The opportunity for self-help afforded labour by the New Deal, together with the aid it gave to farmers, created what the Harvard economist J. K. Galbraith has called "countervailing powers" in the American economy. That is, organized labour and agriculture achieved sufficient power to enforce a more just distribution of incomes and this in turn helped to modify the pattern of alternating booms and depressions, so characteristic of American experience up to this time.

Like all American Presidents who may be accounted great, Roosevelt left the powers of the Presidency considerably increased. Certainly he gained the undying enmity of major sections of the business world and the middle class, but the final American judgement upon him was perhaps expressed by the fact that as the world slid more and more deeply into the Second World War, and despite sharp domestic criticism, Roosevelt was re-elected when he ran for an unprecedented third term in 1940.

Approaching that election, the Republicans hoped to capitalize on the increasingly conservative temper of the country. They nominated Wendell Willkie who, although he had been a leading opponent of T.V.A., was supported by liberals, and chose as his running mate the Progressive Senator Charles McNary of Oregon. Roosevelt broke precedent by accepting the nomination for a third time, with Henry Wallace as his nominee for Vice-President. Emphasizing the need for continuity in leadership and defending the New Deal reform record, the Democrats won thirty-eight states and retained control in Congress though with reduced majorities.

By the time of Roosevelt's third inauguration, war had broken out again in Europe and problems of neutrality and preparedness were already concerning the administration. Foreign and war policies were to be the chief concern of the President and the nation from 1941 until Roosevelt's death in the spring of 1945.

CHAPTER 16

From Versailles to San Francisco

Strong expressions of isolationism were common in the two decades following the end of the First World War. A large majority of Americans returned strongly to the old faith that the United States should hold aloof from the diplomacy and wars of Europe. The inaugural address of President Harding in 1921 reflected the popular disillusionment with "European diplomacy":

> I have no unseemly comment to offer on the League [he said]. If it is serving the Old World helpfully, more power to it. But it is not for us. The Senate has so declared, the executive has so declared, the people have so declared. Nothing could be more decisively stamped with finality.

While isolationist feelings were dominant in the United States, complete detachment from Europe was to prove impossible. By 1920 the United States was the world's wealthiest nation, and ever-widening economic interests as well as older political and cultural forces drew her inescapably into world affairs.

1. THE POLICY OF ISOLATION

America never joined the League of Nations, but the State Department which was charged with the conduct of foreign affairs, quickly realized that it could not safely ignore the League's work in many fields which were of concern to the United States. Thus the United States sent observers to sessions of the League's non-political committee in Geneva and, as some critics declared, "moved into the League through the back door."

In 1928 the policy of isolationism was further modified when Secretary of State Kellogg drew up a treaty with the French Foreign Minister, Aristide Briand. Eventually signed by sixty-two countries, the Kellogg-Briand pact contained a specific renunciation of war "as an instrument of national policy" among the signatories. The treaty included no machinery for enforcement; but the very fact that the United States participated in such diplomacy modified its isolationist position.

A more pronounced modification of American isolationism occurred in 1921. The United States, as we have seen, had a very practical interest in the Pacific; Americans began to watch with deepening suspicion the expansion of Japanese power in that area. To cut short fears that a naval race among the United States, Britain and Japan might again lead to war, President Harding invited Britain, France, Italy and Japan to confer in Washington on a plan to limit armaments. Later, other powers who had interests in the Pacific were added to the Washington Conference. A treaty among the four principal powers—the United States, Britain, Japan and France—was drawn up which agreed on a "ten-year holiday" in the construction of capital ships, and on limits on the size of capital ships which could be built. The four nations also agreed to respect each other's interests and possessions in the Pacific and to settle any disputes by conference. Another treaty signed by all nine members of the enlarged Conference in February 1922 accepted the principle of the Open Door for China.

In the late 1920's and early 1930's the United States took part in other disarmament conferences. None of these met with any success. In 1933 Germany withdrew from such discussions, protesting the injustice of retaining the limitations of arms imposed upon her in 1919; and in 1935 Japan withdrew when the United States and Britain refused to concede her demands for equality in naval tonnage. Although the disarmament conferences failed, the United States had intimately involved itself in this world problem.

Problems in the Pacific continued to concern the United States, and in this area the members of the cabinet differed on American policy. When the Japanese seized Manchuria from China in 1931, Secretary of State Henry Stimson sent a sharp note to Japan pointing out the violation of its treaty obligations. Stimson also suggested to President Hoover that the United States co-operate with the League of Nations to impose economic sanctions on Japan. Hoover refused, on the ground that sanctions might mean war. As a result, Japan suffered no serious opposition at the outset of her campaign for conquests.

In Latin America in the 1920's, the United States continued to intervene to protect American investments. Public dislike of this policy increased steadily till in 1928 the United States signed arbitration treaties with the Latin American republics. In the following year President Hoover made a goodwill tour of Latin America, and in 1930 he lent his support to a State Department announcement which officially revoked the Roosevelt corollary to the Monroe Doctrine. When he became President, Franklin Roosevelt continued the policy of military withdrawal and made popular a phrase first used by Hoover to describe the new trend: the Good

When the Japanese attacked China in their push for Manchuria, they left behind grim tasks for Chinese Red Cross workers.

Neighbour Policy. In 1933 a Conference of American States at Montevideo drew up a pact, which was signed by the United States, declaring that "no state has the right to intervene in the internal affairs of another." In May 1934, after a revolution and the installation of a President likely to favour American business interests, Cuba was freed from the terms of the Platt Amendment, which had virtually given control of her foreign policy to the United States. But in Cuba, as in the other Latin American republics, American investments continued to grow so rapidly that, while officially the United States withdrew, unofficially, through embassies and corporation offices, Latin America remained subject to heavy American influence.

During the 1930's American isolationist feeling became even more intense. This espousal of isolationism was the result not just of post-war escapism but also of revelations made by a Congressional Committee headed by Senator Gerald P. Nye of North Dakota. In 1934 the Nye Committee investigated relations between munitions-makers and financiers on the one hand, and government departments on the other. The Committee produced considerable evidence which seemed to prove that the desire to protect investments abroad had been a principal cause of American entry into the First World War. It was also alleged that manufacturers of munitions and naval supplies and equipment still exerted considerable influence at disarmament conferences in Washington and other major capital cities. Nye himself spoke of the makers of munitions as "merchants of death" and argued that the United States could hope to stay out of the next war only if she made it illegal for American businessmen to trade with any belligerent country.

Yet, generally unnoted at the time, the United States economic relations with the rest of the world were developing in a way which would make it difficult to adhere to such a policy. The great bulk of American foreign trade came to be conducted with Britain, France, and their empires, and with China, rather than with Germany, Italy and Japan. This trade pattern materially influenced the outlook of American government and business as war loomed between the first group and the second.

The isolationist movement reached its climax in the passage of a series of Neutrality Acts between 1935 and 1937. This legislation forbade American arms shipments to any belligerent state, prohibited loans or credits to such states, and provided that any trade with a belligerent must be on a "cash and carry" basis, that is, paid for on delivery and carried in ships provided by the belligerent nation. Events in Asia, Europe and Africa intensified the drive to maintain American neutrality, as Italy seized Ethiopia, Germany re-occupied the Rhineland and began to build up new armed forces, Japan renewed her assault on China, and an armed revolt led by General Franco overthrew democratic government in Spain.

2. THE ROAD TO WAR

Although there was a growing concern in the United States about the implications of these events, most Americans endorsed a policy of neutrality for their country. Cautiously in 1937 Roosevelt began to lead public opinion away from extreme forms of isolationism. In October he delivered a speech in Chicago, quickly dubbed the "quarantine speech," in which he declared:

> When an epidemic of physical disease starts to spread, the community approves and joins in a quarantine of the patients in order to protect the health of the community. . . . War is a contagion, whether it be declared or undeclared. . . . We are adopting such measures as will minimize our risk of involvement, but we cannot have complete protection in a world of disorder in which confidence and security have broken down.

The speech was sharply criticized, yet it left little doubt about where Roosevelt's sympathies lay, as Europe moved again towards war. In April 1939 the President sent a personal appeal to Hitler and Mussolini, the dictators of Germany and Italy, to cease their aggressions. But though Americans began gradually to comprehend the nature of Nazi-Fascist inhumanity, isolationist feeling remained high in the United States. Roose-

This cartoon from the Philadelphia **Inquirer** in 1939 reveals the dilemma of American foreign policy. After September 1939 most Americans wished to avoid involvement but they also feared for their own security if they did not bolster the democracies. The Neutrality Acts of 1935 and 1937 made no distinction between aggressors, and many wished to have them repealed. In September, Roosevelt asked Congress for repeal, so that the United States could aid the democracies, and was supported 55-24 in the Senate and 243-72 in the House of Representatives. Opposition was led by Senator Arthur Vandenberg who declared: "The proponents of the change vehemently insist that their steadfast purpose, like ours, is to keep America out of the war, and their sincere assurances are presented to our people. But the motive is obvious, and the inevitable interpretation of the change . . . will be that we have officially taken sides."

velt had to keep assuring the people that his intention to avoid involvement in any European war remained firm. An America First movement, led by such popular figures as Senator Nye and the Lone Eagle, Colonel Charles Lindbergh, the first man to fly solo across the Atlantic, was formed from a strange mixture of Irish and German Americans, midwestern Progressives, Fascist sympathizers and, until Hitler attacked Russia in June 1941, Communists.

Gradually, but to outsiders far too slowly, American public opinion moved away from isolationism. In November 1939, after war had broken out in Europe, the Neutrality Acts were amended to permit the sale of weapons to Britain and France. After the fall of France before the onslaught of the Germans, Roosevelt showed that he would assist the British Commonwealth, then standing almost alone. In August 1940 he met the Canadian Prime Minister, Mackenzie King, and agreed to form a Permanent Joint Board on Defence, between the two countries. In September of the same year, he transferred fifty old destroyers to the United Kingdom in return for long-term leases on bases in Newfoundland, Bermuda and the West Indies.

To secure support for his pro-Allied policy, Roosevelt appealed to the American people in his third inaugural address in January 1941, when he declared that America's faith in the Four Freedoms justified all aid to the Allies short of war. The Four Freedoms he defined as freedom of speech everywhere in the world, freedom of worship, freedom from want, and freedom from fear of aggression. Two months later he devised a formula for aid to the Allies to which the name of Lend-Lease was given. Using the argument that if a neighbour's house caught fire one would not hesitate to lend a garden hose to put out the fire and stop it from spreading, he asked Congress to make America an "arsenal of democracy" by "lending" arms and equipment to Britain to protect the United States. Bitter opposition to the Lend-Lease Bill in Congress revealed the lingering strength of isolationism. Senator Wheeler of Montana exclaimed that it was "the New Deal's triple A foreign policy [a reference to the Agricultural Adjustment Administration]; it will plow under every fourth American boy," a comment the President described as "the most untruthful, as well as the most dastardly, unpatriotic thing that has ever been said."

But the adoption of Lend-Lease committed the United States formally to massive aid in the struggle against Germany, Italy, and Japan. Isolationist opinion declined, as more and more Americans came to see the true nature of the Fascist menace. Yet the isolationists were still too powerful to make it possible for Roosevelt to order the United States navy to convoy Lend-Lease goods through the submarine-infested North Atlantic to Britain. Instead, he adopted the doctrine of "hemispheric defence," and proclaimed the North Atlantic a neutral zone as far as Iceland. The Americans occupied Greenland, and established a base in Iceland, and United States navy vessels escorted convoys that far. Germany's answer to this policy was a promise to sink "every ship with contraband for Britain, whatever its name" and in the fall of 1941 several American ships were shot at or sunk. Roosevelt issued orders to the United States navy to retaliate should American convoys be attacked and in October Congress approved the arming of merchantmen and permitted them to sail to belligerent ports. In effect, the naval war with Germany had begun.

Meanwhile, in June 1941 American and British officers had held secret meetings to discuss strategy if the United States were to enter the war. In August came a public demonstration of Roosevelt's position when he met Winston Churchill, by then Prime Minister of Great Britain, on board ship in the misty reaches of Argentia Bay, Newfoundland. While the President refused to make any military promises at this meeting, the two statesmen signed an Atlantic Charter which called for self-determination of nations, freedom from fear and want for all peoples, freedom of the seas, disarmament, and the "destruction of the Nazi tyranny." Thus by the fall of 1941 President Roosevelt had taken his country to the brink of war, largely by executive decision and without the knowledge of the public until well after the event. Roosevelt justified this procedure on the

This photo shows but a small part of the damage resulting from the Japanese attack on Pearl Harbor, December 7, 1941. All planes were on the ground and only skeleton crews were on watch at the docks. Yet on November 27 the Navy Department, after breaking the Japanese message code, had sent the following to its Pacific commanders: "This despatch is to be considered a war warning. Negotiations with Japan . . . have ceased, and an aggressive move by Japan is expected within the next few days. The number and equipment of Japanese troops, and the organization of naval task forces indicates an amphibious expedition against either the Philippines, Thai or Kra peninsula, or possibly Borneo."

ground that public opinion, and especially congressional opinion, was not moving as quickly as the course of events required. If this were true, events in the Far East soon transformed the situation, and produced nearly unanimous public support for war.

Japan's resumption of war against China in 1937 had heralded the beginning of a programme to establish a huge Japanese empire which would dominate all of East Asia. While American interests, policies, and even treaty obligations were all directly threatened by Japanese expansion, the United States was even slower to act in the East than in Europe. Frequent American protests about Japanese aggression were as futile as American loans to China. Even after Japan openly allied itself with Italy and Germany in September 1940, the United States hesitated to place an embargo on American trade with Japan. By mid-1941 Japanese troops were slashing their way through the jungles and rice-paddies of French Indo-China, and appeared to be well on their way to Malaya, the Dutch East Indies and Australasia. That autumn, United States negotiations with Japan revealed that Japan wanted from the United States complete cessation of American aid to China and non-interference with further Japanese expansion. These negotiations were still going on when Japan assaulted the United States' great Pacific naval base of Pearl Harbor in Hawaii.

On December 8, 1941 President Roosevelt announced to Congress that a state of war existed between Japan and the United States: "In the past few years and most violently in the past few days, we have learned a terrible lesson. . . . We must begin the great task that is before us by abandoning once and for all the illusion that we can ever again isolate ourselves from the rest of humanity. We are going to win the war, and we are going to win the peace that follows."

3. AMERICA AT WAR

Although the American commanders in Hawaii had received unmistakable warnings that war might come at any moment, the warnings were disregarded. American officers, in Washington and in the Pacific, expected that the next Japanese aggression would be against the Philippines or in the East Indies. Thus, when United States intelligence reports showed suspicious Japanese ship movements early in December, and even the presence of unidentified planes near Hawaii, the reactions in Washington and at Pearl Harbor were incredibly casual. On Sunday December 7, 1941, most of the senior officers at Pearl Harbor were spending a quiet day ashore, relaxing with friends, content in the knowledge that skeleton crews were keeping watch aboard the ships at the base. In Washington the government and military strategists were away from their offices. In the early afternoon of that day Japanese planes taking off from carriers at sea moved on Hawaii and caught the base completely off-guard. Nearly all the American defensive planes were destroyed before they could leave the ground, five battleships were either sunk or shattered, and several thousand men were killed. One historian of Roosevelt's diplomacy summed up the result of Pearl Harbor thus:

> There was just one thing that [the Japanese] could do to get Roosevelt completely off the horns of the dilemma, and that is precisely what

they did, at one stroke, in a manner so challenging, so insulting and enraging, that the divided and confused American people were instantly rendered unanimous and certain.

On December 8, President Roosevelt read to a stunned Congress his message asking for a declaration of war against Japan:

Yesterday, December 7, 1941—a date which will live in infamy—the United States of America was suddenly and deliberately attacked by naval and air forces of the Empire of Japan. . . .

I believe I interpret the will of the Congress and of the people when I assert that we will not only defend ourselves to the uttermost but will make very certain that this form of treachery shall never endanger us again.

Within an hour, Congress had responded to the President's message by declaring a state of war to exist by act of Japan. Only one dissenting vote was recorded. On December 11, Germany and Italy formally declared war upon the United States in accordance with a treaty they had signed with Japan in 1940.

Japan quickly exploited the advantage gained by her surprise attack. Her troops captured the Malay peninsula without delay, and in February 1942 the British naval base of Singapore fell to their assault. Other Japanese forces broke through to the north, cutting off the supply line from India to China and, soon after, Japanese amphibious forces overwhelmed the Dutch East Indies. While these rapid conquests were occurring, the powerful Japanese fleet carried invasion and occupation forces throughout the South Pacific, taking positions on the supply routes to New Zealand and Australia. In the north they seized Kiska and Attu on the western tip of the Aleutian Islands, thus posing a direct threat to North America itself. This disastrous phase of the war in the Pacific was climaxed by the defeat of the American forces in the Philippines, and their surrender in June 1942 of the last heroically defended fortress of Corregidor in Manila Bay. The American commander in the Philippines, General Douglas MacArthur escaped to Australia to organize the long campaign for regaining the South Pacific.

For Europe 1942 was a year of dread. With all of Western Europe in German control, Nazi armies advanced rapidly on two fronts to capture the Near East. Marshal Rommel, Germany's Desert Fox, approached the Suez Canal through Egypt. In 1941 Germany had launched an assault on the Soviet Union which had met with initial success. In this year of Axis triumph, a German army rushed towards the Baku oil fields in southern Russia, while a heavily armoured German assault moved in on Stalingrad to the north. Around the globe the Allies, or as the term now emerged, the United Nations, faced rapid loss of territory and increasingly precarious communications and supply routes. In addition the Soviet Union, fighting for its very existence, was calling for the opening of a second front by invasion of Western Europe. Latin America, which,

"FLYING TIGERS"
and Winged Dollars

FROM almost every State of the Union they come . . . from little country villages you have difficulty finding on the map . . . square-chinned, adventure-loving, wide-grinned boys, with a flair for danger.

They call it "adventure," but, actually, as events have shown, it is the truest patriotism any man ever knew. China looks upon them with awe—and deep affection—as they sweep over enemy lines in battered old planes that are called "dive bombers" out of a sporting spirit of sarcasm. But they've made an unforgettable record . . . over Burma . . . across the jagged peaks of Burma's peril-beset road . . . into the maelstrom of a rice-field land that is now hissing with challenge.

The entire world watches their exploits with prayerful respect . . . our own fighting forces call them back into the fold. Squadron leaders or keen-eyed pilots, they are willing to take any chance to DO THE JOB.

Sit beside these "Flying Tigers" as they roar out to new fame i . . be a living part of the planes they pilot, old or new . . . look down on death, and smile. Your Bond Dollars give you this great privilege. They become *flying dollars* . . . every God-inspired penny . . . for a cause that is as spiritual as the glory of those who make a so much greater sacrifice than *money*.

SPONSOR

This World War II bond drive advertisement appealed to the sense of high drama stimulated by stories of the dangerous endeavour to keep open the Burma Road supply line to China.

with the exception of Argentina, accepted a recommendation to break diplomatic relations with the Axis countries, provided little assistance. Half of the republics declared war, but their main contribution was the provision of raw materials.

In the United States the unity created by Pearl Harbor rendered mobilization of men and industry relatively easy. As in the First World War, a selective service draft was used to raise men for the armed services and its task was made more effective by the enrolment of women in the army, navy and coast guard to release enlisted men for combat duty. Thanks to lessons remembered from the First World War, and ready popular acceptance of governmental regulation brought about by the New Deal, the government handled problems of production and distribution effectively. Price control and rationing of commodities in short supply held inflation in check, and ensured a more equitable sharing of hardships than had been the case in 1917-18. Both wages and profits rose steadily as production grew. Overtime work became commonplace and many billions of dollars were poured voluntarily into war bonds. The War Production Board, armed with extensive powers, rapidly converted industry to production of war materials. Congress gave even greater power in 1943 to the Office of War Mobilization, which exercised virtually total authority to plan the national economy. Despite the new controls, much industry remained outside war production. In such areas profits also rose rapidly, and numerous private fortunes were founded. Labour unions confined their right to strike to non-war industries, and demanded closer control of the firms concerned. One result of such planning was a national income of a hundred and eighty billion dollars by 1944, as compared to forty billion dollars in 1932. In association with Canadian war production, which was also climbing to undreamed-of heights, the United States produced war *matériel* in sufficient quantity to keep Britain and Russia in the battle at the height of Nazi successes.

It was the successful organization of American production and manpower that justified the major strategy worked out in January 1942 at British-American military talks. Here the leaders of the United Nations laid the foundation for much closer co-operation than was ever achieved by the Axis powers. Despite the political risks it involved, Roosevelt accepted a strategy which meant restricting the war against Japan to a holding operation while concentrating the major effort against Germany. Fortunately, this decision was made possible by an American-Australian naval victory over a Japanese fleet in the Coral Sea in the spring of 1942; and by the successful repulse of a major Japanese naval-air assault on Midway Island, the loss of which would have endangered the Pearl Harbor base.

By late 1942 the Allies had begun a new phase of the war against Germany. The invasion of North Africa provided an alternative to the opening of a second front in Western Europe which Russia was still demanding. It was Churchill's scheme to strike at the "soft underbelly of

Europe" by way of the Mediterranean. At the battle of El Alamein, General Montgomery defeated Rommel's desert troops, who began their flight back toward Tunisia. In November American troops landed in North Africa and all of French North Africa fell to the Allies. The last enemy resistance in Tunisia collapsed in May 1943. In July Allied forces invaded Sicily under General Dwight D. Eisenhower as Allied Commander-in-Chief. The invasion of Italy and the fall of Mussolini's government followed rapidly. However, it took long months of hard fighting to complete the conquest of Italy. The best that can be said for the Italian campaign is that a considerable Nazi force was pinned down in Italy by the need to impede the Allied advance northward.

At the same time, in the summer of 1943, the Nazi tide was turned in Russia. In the most bloody battles of the war, Russian armies rolled back the German thrust to the Dnieper River. Reeling from these reverses, the Germans suffered even more by assaults from the air. Having gained control of the air, Allied bomber fleets raked German industrial cities in a merciless attempt to weaken morale, diminish production, and disrupt communications. Remembering the aerial Battle of Britain, the attack on Pearl Harbor, and the massive loss of life in Russian cities, Allied commanders, governments and peoples were less concerned than they might otherwise have been with the morality of attacking civilian populations. The very survival of individual and national freedom seemed to be at issue; the stakes seemed great enough to justify fighting barbarism by barbaric methods.

Behind the scenes in the United States, Britain and Canada, scientists were already working out the military application of one of science's most dramatic and lethal discoveries. Indeed, at the beginning of the war, three refugee scientists from Europe, led by Albert Einstein, had told President Roosevelt that German physicists were working on the principle of atomic fission with a view to producing a revolutionary mass-destruction bomb. Allied researchers began to work on the same problem. Throughout the war, experiments were carried out at three universities, and in a laboratory at Los Alamos, New Mexico.

In the meantime, the Allies had sufficiently pummelled the Nazis to permit launching of the final stage of the war in Europe. The American General, Dwight D. Eisenhower, was appointed Supreme Allied Commander, and after long and detailed planning at Eisenhower's headquarters in England, June 6, 1944 was chosen as the day on which an assault would be launched from England across the Channel to Europe. The Allies invaded Western Europe from a beach-head in Normandy. At the same time, the Russians threw all their effort into a drive through Romania. Despite some temporary reverses and continuing loss of life, the Allies relentlessly pressed the Nazi divisions back upon their homeland. On May 8, 1945 Germany surrendered unconditionally.

The impending collapse of the Nazis was quickly reflected in the war in the Pacific. By early 1945 General MacArthur was finishing the reconquest of the Philippines, while the island of Iwo Jima, even closer to Japan, had fallen to American forces. Okinawa, only four hundred miles from the Japanese home islands, fell to the United States in July after the costliest of the Pacific battles. By this time, the Allied scientists had solved the problem of splitting the atom, and had begun the manufacture of atomic bombs. The Allied leaders, after conferring together at Potsdam, issued an ultimatum calling upon Japan to surrender unconditionally and warning of "utter devastation of the Japanese homeland" if she did not. When Japan rejected the ultimatum it was decided to use the new bomb.

In 1944 Franklin Roosevelt had been re-elected to the Presidency for an unheard-of fourth term. His principal appeal to the electorate was that the conduct of the war, the impending victory and the problem of a post-war settlement all required that there should be no break in United States leadership at that time. His candidate for the Vice-Presidency was an obscure Missouri Senator named Harry S. Truman. But Roosevelt's superhuman exertions through the years of depression and war had taken their toll of his frail body, and he died suddenly at White Springs, Georgia, on April 12, 1945. His successor was faced immediately with an appalling decision. President Truman obtained the concurrence of Winston Churchill in the decision to drop atomic bombs on Japan. Arguing that the unknown horror to be released would be justified by the saving of American lives, Truman showed no qualms about using the new weapon. The

Only women, children and aged men were found by the assault forces of Marines as they pushed across Okinawa immediately after their landing. Here two Marines help an aged man to the safety of the rear lines.

United States Chief of Staff, General George Marshall, warned that it might cost 500,000 lives to force a Japanese surrender by conventional methods of attack. The scientists advising Truman's special committee recommended using the bomb. Mr. Truman has recorded in his memoirs:

> They recommended further that it should be used without specific warning, against a target that would clearly show its devastating strength. I had realized, of course, that an atomic bomb explosion would inflict damage and casualties beyond imagination. . . . It was their conclusion that no technical demonstration they might propose, such as over a deserted island, would be likely to bring the war to an end. It had to be used against an enemy target.
>
> The final decision of where and when to use the atomic bomb was up to me. Let there be no mistake about it. I regarded the bomb as a military weapon and never had any doubt that it should be used.

Such are the reflections of the President who assumed a responsibility

Hiroshima, August 6, 1945. The first atom bomb levelled the entire city and killed or injured nearly every one of the 343,000 inhabitants. Bombs of the same explosive power are now considered "tactical battlefield weapons," dwarfed as they are by the almost unlimited power of hydrogen or thermonuclear weapons.

greater than that ever assumed by another human being: the unleashing for military purposes of the very cohesive force of the universe itself.

On August 6, 1945 a single American plane dropped an atomic bomb over the Japanese city of Hiroshima. The destruction was appalling. The entire city was levelled and eighty thousand people were killed out-right. Many more thousands died soon after of radiation burns, and each year since 1945 other people have died of the lingering results of the first atomic attack. Two days later Nagasaki was obliterated with a slightly more powerful bomb. On August 14 Japan surrendered, stipulating only that the Emperor should continue to rule.

4. THE END OF ISOLATION

The United States experienced the Second World War much more deeply than it had the First. Thirteen million citizens had been enlisted, compared to the first war's three million, and more than two hundred thousand were killed in battle. The cost was ten times greater than that of the war of 1917-18, and the action had been on a global scale. These facts, perhaps, explain the willingness of the country to accept membership in an international organization after the war. The united response to the Japanese attack of December 1941, and the United States entry into the war, had taken some of the vigour out of domestic political battles. Although Republicans made some gains in the 1942 mid-term congressional elections, by 1944 the war was being won, and a number of leading Republicans had been appointed to administrative posts. Even the incredible nomination of Franklin Roosevelt for a fourth term was accomplished without much fuss. Harry S. Truman, the candidate for the Vice-Presidency, who was to succeed to the Presidency on Roosevelt's death, was selected to placate the conservatives and city political bosses. His nomination followed a bitter struggle in the Convention. Truman had begun his career as a small businessman in Independence, Missouri, and had made slow progress through local politics to the Senate. He had, however, co-operated with the most powerful Democratic bosses and had gained some public attention as Chairman of a Senate committee investigating war contracts.

The Republicans nominated the urbane and ambitious Thomas E. Dewey, Governor of New York. Since Dewey had acquiesced in most of the Roosevelt policies, he had little to attack in his campaign, and Roosevelt won again with a substantial electoral college majority, but a reduced majority of the popular vote. The victory of the conservative Democrats in the Convention struggle over the Vice-Presidency assumed great importance, for Roosevelt was to survive less than three months of his fourth term. Harry S. Truman took the oath of office less than two hours after Roosevelt's death. In the cabinet meeting which followed he had to decide whether to go ahead with a conference which had been called to meet at San Francisco on April 25 for the purpose of founding the organization which came to be known as the United Nations. In his memoirs he noted:

> I did not hesitate a second. I told press secretary Early that the conference would be held as President Roosevelt had directed. There was no question in my mind that the conference had to take place. It was of supreme importance that we build an organization to help keep the future peace of the world. It was the first decision I made as President.

In 1945 any other decision would have frustrated the majority opinion of the country. This opinion had been expressed as early as September 1943. In a congressional resolution supporting the creation of an effective international organization to keep the peace, the United States had pledged active membership in such an organization. At a conference of the Allies held in Moscow in November of 1943 this policy had been accepted, and in the summer of 1944 at Dumbarton Oaks in Washington a United Nations Charter was drafted. At Yalta in February 1945, Roosevelt, Churchill, and Stalin had agreed to call a United Nations founding conference at San Francisco in April. Recalling the fate of the League of Nations at the hands of the Senate in 1919-20, Roosevelt decided that the United Nations Organization should not be connected with any peace treaty. Also, profiting by Wilson's errors, he arranged that both Republicans and Democrats should be represented in the delegation.

After eight weeks of debate at San Francisco, a Charter was adopted for the United Nations. A General Assembly provided equal representation for each member nation. The Assembly could debate any matter within the terms of the Charter. The Security Council of eleven members was given executive power to investigate disputes, plan peaceful adjustments and take any kind of agreed action against declared aggressors. The permanent members were the United States, Russia, Great Britain, France and China. The six non-permanent members were to be elected by the Assembly. The United States, Russia and Britain all agreed that Security Council decisions on disputes and similar "substantive" matters must be approved by seven members, including all of the five permanent members; thus each permanent member of the Security Council exercised a veto in such matters. An Economic and Social Council (U.N.E.S.C.O.), with other special agencies and commissions, was made responsible to the Assembly and was to gather information and to work for the removal of economic and social conditions which might be the roots of war. The Charter also provided for an International Court of Justice to which disputes might be submitted voluntarily, and a Trusteeship Council to keep check on conditions in territories held in trust by United Nations members.

The American Senate in July 1945 ratified the United Nations Charter with only two negative votes. At the same time it ratified the Bretton Woods Agreement which provided for an International Bank for Reconstruction and Development, and an International Monetary Fund. These latter institutions were designed to keep national currencies stable and to help post-war economic recovery.

Clearly the United States, as well as the other founding nations, hoped by such measures to avoid the consequences that had followed the peace settlement of 1919 in Europe. On the other hand, post-war co-operation was by no means perfect, nor were the problems of negotiating peace treaties to be easily solved. The military alliance with Russia had never been free of mutual suspicion, despite the feeling of understanding that had grown between Roosevelt and Stalin. Britain and the United States were not prepared to share the secret of atomic energy with their wartime ally and this, together with sharp competition for the control of central and eastern Europe, dissipated the basis of wartime co-operation. Even at the San Francisco Conference there were disturbing signs that the great nations were jockeying for control of the new organization. The American delegation, realizing that Latin America would normally vote with the western powers, supported the application for membership made by Argentina although Argentina had been a centre of enemy intrigue throughout the war. The United States won its point against Russian opposition, and also succeeded in barring Poland from immediate membership because Poland's government was friendly to the Soviet Union.

Nevertheless, the selection of New York City as site of the splendid new United Nations headquarters symbolized American acceptance of the unavoidable responsibilities of the immense power the United States had achieved. In the post-war world, as in previous American history, the United States gave evidence of a sense of destiny. Now its sense of mission was to become a dominant factor in international affairs.

CHAPTER 17

From Fair Deal to
New Frontier

1. PROSPERITY AND URBANIZATION

The atomic age which opened in 1945 saw the United States pass through a series of crises, both domestic and foreign. It was a time of tension and quickly changing patterns of life in which the nation became, according to some, an Affluent Society, according to others, a Garrison State. Although unemployment persisted and an average of four million workers still lacked jobs, more Americans were prosperous than ever before in their history. Politics reflected this affluence by resuming a generally conservative tone. Urbanization continued and by 1960 more than sixty-five per cent of the one hundred and eighty million Americans lived in urban centres, compared with forty per cent in 1900. By creating more varied economic interests in each region the spread of industry and urbanization modified the sectionalism of American politics. As a result, Republicans increased their normal voting strength in the South, while Democrats found new support in the midwestern "corn belt."

Prosperity and urbanization also brought significant cultural changes, and these affected Canada as well as the United States. Wide areas of life became more nearly standardized across the nation, from houses and motels to clothing and manners of speech. In business, the large corporation became even more dominant. Young men training for managerial positions in such firms commanded much larger salaries than their fathers could have hoped for at the same age. They seemed more willing than earlier generations had been to accept a prospect of slow but sure and well-paid advancement as opposed to the riskier course of launching their own small businesses. More and more, too, they adjusted their habits, the size and make of their cars, and the location of their homes to the corporation's assessment of what was appropriate to their business status. A new premium was placed upon loyalty to the corporation itself. Sociologists began to distinguish a new American type which they dubbed the Organization

238

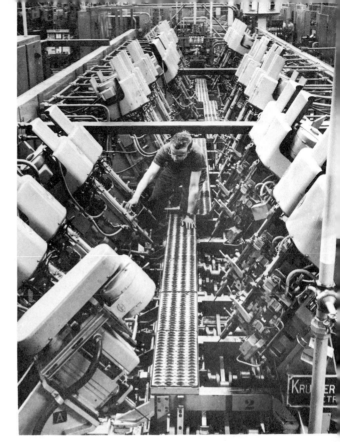

Automation in industry, as illustrated by this machine which drills the entire oil system in a Ford crankshaft in one continuous operation, is a factor in unemployment, as well as a progressive step in production methods. Similar machinery on farms can, for example, enable one man in ten minutes to feed an automatically blended mixture to five hundred hogs and four hundred cows. Previously the same job required half a day's work by five men.

Man. Living in split-level suburban houses millions of such men basked in the steady accumulation of their mass-produced luxuries, only occasionally reflecting upon the pre-packaged and unadventurous patterns of life to which they and their families conformed.

In post-war America national productivity increased rapidly, while the average working day in industry was shortened to eight hours or less. As trade unions grew in size and strength real wages rose steadily. Yet the distribution of wealth was still markedly unequal. In the mid-1950's about seventeen per cent of American families still lived on earnings of less than $1,500 a year. As in other modern western democracies, the advance of automation created a need for more workers with technical training and the numbers enrolled in high schools, technical schools, colleges and universities rose rapidly. Moreover, the number of office or "white collar" employees increased sharply in relation to the number of production or "blue collar" workers. The growth of this new middle class concerned with sales, distribution, advertising, office records, office management, and laboratories has been significant politically, because, as a group, such workers have shown themselves to be conservative. Moreover, since few of them belonged to unions, they failed as a class to win proportionately as great an increase in income as did unionized labour or the executive class.

The growth of automation in industry also meant that less varied and skilled work was required of production workers, and employees tended to derive less satisfaction from their work than formerly. In addition, a very large proportion of the urban population lived in highly standardized suburbs. One result was that the increased leisure available to most people was sometimes as much a problem as a blessing. The way of life was reflected in an unwillingness to make leisure hours creative. Thus television, which burst upon the market in the late 1940's, concentrated on light entertainment. There was, too, an increasing dominance of spectator rather than participation sports.

At the same time, however, the dawning age of "mass culture," as it has been rather disdainfully called, also brought with it phenomenal sales of paperback books, both literary and academic, growing attendance at symphony concerts and increased sales of art reproductions and recorded classical music. Equally important was the preoccupation of America's intellectuals, artists and writers with self-analysis, criticism and social research. From well-endowed university faculties of graduate studies poured a stream of historical, sociological and scientific studies of the highest order. In contemporary English letters some of the greatest names are those of Americans.

Creative thought and criticism were also stirring in the churches. Total church membership rose from about forty-five per cent of the population in the 1920's to over sixty per cent in 1962. While churchmen and non-churchmen agreed that this extremely high incidence of church affiliation reflected in part mere unwillingness to be different in a society that emphasized conformity, in part it bespoke discontent with a materialistic mass society. ·At its best this revival of religion meant a return to an earlier American emphasis upon the dignity of the individual and upon loyalties higher than those of state, section or nation. Individual churchmen and church groups took a prominent part in many kinds of social action. Many led in the movement for nuclear disarmament, and some courageous ones faced extreme personal risks in agitating for desegregation of the races in the South.

2. THE POLITICS OF PROSPERITY

Post-war politics reflected the complexity and prosperity of American life as well as the terrifying realities of a world power struggle in which Americans were deeply involved. President Truman, in close co-operation with Congress, permitted a rapid dismantling of the American war machine. Demobilization of the huge military forces was so swift that America's ability to occupy Axis countries was imperilled. Once home, the millions of ex-servicemen were treated with enlightened generosity. Under a series of acts popularly called the "G.I. Bill of Rights," ex-soldiers were entitled to a variety of re-establishment benefits. These included completion of education at all levels, technical training, low-rate loans for buying houses or setting up businesses, and inexpensive insur-

The G.I. Bill of Rights provided free vocational and university training for hundreds of thousands of discharged veterans. Here a class studies methods of contour farming.

ance. The purchasing power so provided gave a quick stimulus to domestic production. Business got a further boost when most of the sixteen billion dollars' worth of industrial plants constructed by the government during the war were turned over to private purchasers on nearly give-away terms. Finally, the pent-up demand of consumers for goods of all kinds unobtainable during the war—no domestic automobiles had been produced since 1942 for example—led business to invest in new plants and housing at a rate three times that of the 1920 boom years.

In these circumstances business profits, already high in war production, climbed even more steeply. Labour became restless as wages failed to keep pace with prices and profits. In late 1945 and in 1946 labour disputes became serious, with over a million and a half workers on strike in January 1946. The terms on which strikes in the automotive and electrical industries and in the coal mines were settled led to a general rise in wage rates. These increases in costs were passed on by management to the public in higher prices. Rising prices (inflation) destroyed the real value, or buying power, of the wage increases. Thus the unions fought for second and third rounds of wage increases in 1946 and 1947. Labour leaders argued for continuance of wartime price controls through the Office of Price Administration (O.P.A.), and the President himself favoured this course. But the bill to continue O.P.A. for one year was so watered down in Congress in response to business pressure that the President vetoed it and price controls ended in July, 1946. Struggling with the bitter chaos of industrial relations, President Truman was compelled to put both the mines and the railways under temporary government ownership pending settlement of the most serious strikes of these two years.

In the 1946 mid-term elections Republicans won control of both houses in the Eightieth Congress. A direct result of this resurgence of conservatism was the passage of the Taft-Hartley Act in June, 1947 over President Truman's veto. The Act restricted the right to strike by requiring a sixty-day "cooling off" period before a strike could be called, allowed management to sue unions both for breach of contract and for damages resulting from jurisdictional disputes, and made illegal the "closed shop," that is to say, any provision in a labour contract requiring management to hire only men who were already union members. The Act also outlawed the practice of having employers collect dues for the union by deducting them from pay cheques of all employees whether union members or not. Unions were forbidden to make contributions to political parties and union officials were forced to swear that they were not Communists, on pain of withdrawal of recognition of the union as a properly constituted bargaining agent. Nevertheless, unions increased their membership by some two and a half million in the decade after the war. During these years, unions negotiated a growing number of contracts which included such fringe benefits as company provision of recreational facilities, longer holidays, and health insurance and retirement pension plans. The unions also circumvented the veto on their contributing to political parties out of union funds by establishing their own political education committees and placing considerable funds at their disposal. Through these committees unions continued to give important support to the Democratic party.

The Eightieth Congress made certain that no President could again serve more than two terms by sponsoring the Twenty-Second Amendment which was ratified in March, 1951. Then, over the President's veto, Congress reduced taxation by nearly five billion dollars, and rejected executive-sponsored reform legislation.

By 1948, the Democratic party appeared to be severely disrupted. Conservative Southern Democrats, repelled by Truman's pro-labour attitude and by his defence of equal civil rights for Negroes, refused to support the President's renomination in the Democratic Convention. Instead they founded a States' Rights Democratic party, which was quickly dubbed the Dixiecrat party, and nominated Governor Strom Thurmond of South Carolina as their candidate for President. By this move they hoped to prevent any candidate winning a majority of electoral votes. If that happened, then (as in 1824) the House of Representatives would choose between the contenders and in the House their power as a united bloc might be decisive. At the same time many liberal and left-wing Democrats were dissatisfied with Truman's foreign policy and skeptical about his domestic policy. These dissidents formed a Progressive party and nominated Henry Wallace. Wallace had been Secretary of Agriculture under Roosevelt, and had resigned from Truman's Cabinet in 1946 in protest against what he considered to be the government's excessively hard-bitten attitude towards the Soviet Union. The Republicans nominated Governor Dewey of New York for a second time, with a stand-pat domestic platform and a foreign policy which differed little from that of the Democrats.

Eyeing the serious three-way Democratic split, all observers predicted a big Dewey victory. But Truman, in an almost single-handed whistle-stop campaign, castigated the Eightieth Congress for its reactionary policies

and effectively preached a "fair deal" to the Negroes, labour unions and
farmers in language reminiscent of the heyday of the New Deal. Refusing
to believe anything but the predictions, and before the Western returns
were in, the Chicago *Tribune* printed a special election-night issue head-
lined: "Dewey Defeats Truman." There were red faces the next morning
when it was discovered that the unassuming but tough little man from
Independence had staged the nation's most startling political surprise.
Truman's popular vote was 24,105,000 to Dewey's 21,969,000. The
Dixiecrats carried only South Carolina, Mississippi, Alabama and Louisiana. Wallace carried no state.

Since the Democrats had also recaptured a majority in both Houses
of Congress, Truman immediately launched his Fair Deal programme,
which he presented as an extension of New Deal policies. After bitter
debate, and despite the opposition of Southern Democrats, the President's
supporters in Congress secured legislation to raise the legal minimum wage,
to subsidize low-rental housing and slum clearance, to extend rent-control,
to increase by ten million the number of employees covered by the Social
Security Act and to provide aid to Europe in its struggle to recover from
the ravages of war. Much of this legislation, however, was hobbled by
amendments and inadequate provision for its financing and Congress completely rejected civil rights measures, repeal of the Taft-Hartley Act, and
a bill designed to keep up farm prices.

3. THE CONSERVATIVE REACTION

In spite of the support given Truman's Fair Deal, the
climate of opinion remained conservative. Tension between the United
States and Russia and the knowledge after 1949 that Russia possessed the
atomic bomb provided fertile soil for a new witch-hunt. In 1948, a former Communist agent named Whittaker Chambers declared that one Alger
Hiss, a State Department employee, had turned over classified, or secret

President Truman speaks to a rural audience in Wyoming during his remarkable whistle-
stop campaign of 1948. He is telling them he will not be frightened away from his programme by cries of "socialism."

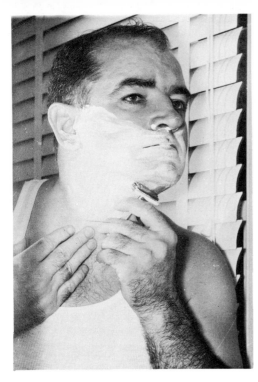

Senator Joseph McCarthy, who symbolized the early Cold War frenzy of fear about the largely mythical threat of Communist subversion, welcomed all the publicity he could get—even while shaving! Ultimately he went too far and cut his own throat politically.

documents, to him. In a congressional hearing, Hiss denied the charges and later sued Chambers for slander. Chambers produced fresh evidence to support his charges, and in 1950 Hiss was finally convicted of perjury and sentenced to five years in jail. Many people felt that the trials were inconclusive, but while the outcome was pending, government agents uncovered several other Communists in administrative posts. Congress speedily passed a bill requiring all Communist action organizations and all organizations controlled by Communists ("Communist front" organizations) to register with the Attorney-General and place on file the names and addresses of their officers. The President vetoed this measure as dangerous to freedom of thought. Congress repassed it over his veto. The courts went even further. Heretofore they had held that an overt act must be proved before a person could be convicted of treason. Now the Supreme Court in 1951 upheld an act of 1940 which made it illegal even to teach doctrines of forcible revolution or to be a member of a group which taught such doctrine. As a result, the government's prosecution of eleven leading Communists succeeded and they received jail terms averaging four years each.

Seizing upon the uneasiness in the public mind, Senator Joseph McCarthy of Wisconsin delivered a sensational speech in the spring of 1950 in which he declared that the State Department was riddled with Communists and that he had a list naming two hundred and five of them. When pressed for the names, he whittled the list down to eighty-one, then to fifty-seven, and finally could not produce a single name. Falsehood and slander nevertheless carried McCarthy far. In the mid-term elections of 1950, he helped defeat Senator Tydings of Maryland, who had been chairman of a Senate committee which declared McCarthy's charges to be "a nefarious campaign of half-truths and untruths." As part of his campaign against Tydings he produced a retouched photograph which falsely suggested that Tydings was friendly with a leading Communist. McCarthy continued to produce charges that Communism was rampant in the government and to reduce Senate investigating procedures to the level of the gutter. Demagogic attacks upon the Secretary of State, General George C. Marshall, and many other distinguished Americans, alleging them to be "soft on Communism" and disloyal, culminating in a particularly irresponsible assault upon the army, finally led to the censuring of McCarthy by his fellow Senators in 1954.

Remarkably few people chose to fight McCarthy openly in his day of power. Even Dwight Eisenhower, who as Republican Presidential candidate in 1952 was the head of McCarthy's party, failed to repudiate him. McCarthyism thus spread across the nation in the form of a vast witchhunt. Local demagogues took up the cry and were able to force loyalty oaths on school teachers and university professors. They succeeded in removing from public and private positions thousands of people thought to be too radical in their views, and in censoring library holdings. In the end, the State Department itself suffered severely as potential public servants refused to join it and run the risk of public smearing by congressional committees, or private slander. Though McCarthy himself died in 1957 the fever had still to run its course.

As the 1952 elections approached, President Truman decided not to run again, and the Democrats nominated Governor Adlai Stevenson of Illinois. A suave and cultured politician, Stevenson appealed to literate Americans without attracting strong support from liberals, some of whom suspected him of compromising on such questions as civil rights. His outstanding wit and apt turns of phrase may even have been a disadvantage to him in appealing to the ordinary voter. The Republicans chose General Eisenhower. Popular with the army, unassuming, yet inspiring confidence with his fatherly manner, Eisenhower's political inexperience was no apparent disadvantage to him. Promising to end the Korean War, to weed out the corruption which had been revealed in Washington and to tighten internal security, Eisenhower gave conservative feeling a rallying point. Election night showed a startling Republican ability to cut deeply into the traditionally Democratic South. With Eisenhower's victory twenty years of Democratic rule came to an end.

Although Eisenhower's dramatic visit to Korea, in fulfilment of a campaign promise, did not alter the course of peace negotiations, the Korean War came to an end six months after his inauguration. In domestic affairs, programmes Truman had initiated were scaled down or reversed. The housing programme was curtailed, the budget trimmed, taxes cut and supports to farm prices lowered. Though private hydro-electric power development was favoured at the expense of further public power develop-

ments, nevertheless the Eisenhower government gained congressional consent to proceed with the long-debated project for joint Canadian-American
construction of the St. Lawrence Seaway and its related power plants.

In the conservative 1950's there remained one group actively dissatisfied with things as they were, namely the Negroes. From 1914 to the
1950's, hundreds of thousands of Negroes had migrated to northern cities
and others had served in the armed forces. They discovered that while
migration brought them greater economic advantages they still faced substantial prejudice and modified segregation. In cities like Chicago and
Detroit, vast districts of Negro housing and business grew up quite separate
from white districts, and race riots were the usual result where a Negro
family endeavoured to break the pattern of residential segregation. Jobs
invariably went first to white applicants, and Negroes found it very difficult
to rise very far in the professions or business. During the Second World
War, Congress established a Fair Employment Practices Committee to
investigate and curb open discrimination on grounds of colour, race or
creed. Although Southerners prevented this legislation from being renewed
at the end of the war, many state governments in the North and West created similar committees. Truman forced some advance towards desegregation in the armed services, and the President's Committee on Civil Rights
in 1946 recommended sweeping federal action against all forms of discrimination in schools, transportation, public services, housing and employment. Legislation to implement the recommendations was killed by a
strong opposition from Southern Senators.

It was against this background of halting achievement, bitterness and
stalemate that the Supreme Court handed down a crucial decision in 1954
which rejected the view that the Fourteenth Amendment was honoured if
Negroes were provided with "separate but equal" facilities. In 1954, Chief
Justice Warren declared that separate school facilities for Negroes were
"inherently unequal." Clearly, this implied that segregation in other social
situations was also contrary to the Fourteenth Amendment. The Court
thereupon issued orders calling for desegregation in education wherever
separate schools were the rule. Declaring that this should be accomplished with "all deliberate speed," the Court recognized that its instructions
demanded nothing less than a social revolution in the South, and possibly
in the North also.

While some progress towards desegregation was made in Missouri,
Tennessee, Maryland and Kentucky, violent resistance came in the Deep
South. A notable test came in Little Rock, Arkansas, in the autumn of
1957, where Governor Orval Faubus used state troops to prevent Negro
children from enrolling in a city high school. President Eisenhower, while
avoiding a clear statement in support of the principle of desegregation,
argued that the Court's decision was the law of the land and must be upheld;
he ordered federal troops to escort the Negro children to school. The point
was won, but Faubus was overwhelmingly re-elected as Governor. In the
following autumn further trouble arose when the Little Rock School Board

demanded more time to give effect to the Court's order. The Court, in a unanimous decision, refused, declaring that "the constitutional rights of children not to be discriminated against in school admission on grounds of race or colour declared by this Court can neither be nullified openly and directly by state legislators or state executives or judicial officers, nor nullified by them through any evasive scheme for segregation."

"Evasive schemes" were prepared in several of the Southern states, but proved too expensive to operate on a permanent basis. Resistance remained in the open. President Eisenhower appealed to all to co-operate in achieving the goal of equality between the races, but progress remained painfully slow. Meanwhile, lawyers for the National Association for the Advancement of Coloured People continued the long struggle in the courts to break down the system of segregation in all areas of life. In addition, Negroes in Southern cities such as Montgomery, Alabama, organized boycotts of segregated public services and "sit-ins" at public places such as lunch-bars. Such protests often led to violence and jail terms for the demonstrators. By 1961, groups of liberals from the North, comprising both Negroes and whites, were staging "freedom rides" by travelling in desegregated buses through the South and endeavouring to use segregated waiting rooms and restaurants. While all Americans recognized that the barriers which shored up white supremacy were crumbling around the periphery of the South, and would fall eventually, the battle still raged bitterly. In the autumn of 1962 Governor Ross Barnett of Mississippi challenged federal authority by refusing to admit a Negro to the State university. In the storm that followed, the Communist world was not slow to make the most of this serious blot on democratic practice.

President Eisenhower, although critically ill in 1955 and June of 1956

Following the crucial Supreme Court decision on desegregation in 1954, Southern schools began reluctantly to open their doors to Negro children. Here National Guardsmen at Sturgis, Kentucky, hold off a hostile crowd after the first Negro is admitted to the high school in September, 1956.

When desegregation, under court orders, penetrated the Deep South, the result was a serious crisis. In the autumn of 1962 a Negro, James Meredith, was finally enrolled at "Ole Miss" (University of Mississippi) over the last-ditch protests of Governor Barnett and threats of armed resistance by local white supremacists. Here Meredith is hanged in effigy from a dormitory window while the town of Oxford was under virtual military occupation.

was nevertheless renominated enthusiastically by the Republicans in the summer of 1956. Once again, his personal popularity proved politically superior to the sophisticated sentences of Adlai Stevenson, and he won the 1956 election. The second Eisenhower administration was dominated even more than the first had been by problems of foreign policy. Furthermore, an economic recession began in 1957 which threatened both domestic prosperity and the economic strength which most Americans believed necessary in any kind of competition with the Soviet Union for world influence.

4. THE REVIVAL OF LIBERALISM

While the country passed safely through the recession, the pace of economic growth was markedly reduced and the number of unemployed remained high. The Democrats concentrated public attention on the lagging economy as they prepared for what they believed was inevitable victory in 1960. The Democratic Convention in that year gave the nomination to Senator John F. Kennedy of Massachusetts. Son of a very wealthy Irish Roman Catholic family of Boston, Senator Kennedy had campaigned vigorously for some months prior to the Convention and appealed to a broader section of the party than any of his leading competitors. Liberals in the party were dismayed by Kennedy's choice of the ultra-conservative Lyndon Johnson of Texas as his running-mate. Others feared that religious feelings might jeopardize Kennedy's chances of election. On the Republican side, President Eisenhower gave his blessing to

Richard Nixon, the Vice-President, who was duly nominated. It had been Eisenhower's policy to increase the responsibilities of the Vice-Presidency and accordingly Nixon's name had been much before the public. Yet he was not wholeheartedly endorsed either by the old guard of the party or by liberal Republicans who would have preferred a candidate less closely associated with right-wing opinion.

Thus both candidates represented the middle sections of their respective parties. Both were young and both campaigned tirelessly. A special feature of the election was the first television debate between Presidential candidates, an event which many commentators believe influenced the outcome markedly. The programmes set forth by Nixon and Kennedy did not diverge sharply either in domestic or foreign policy and the contenders discussed mostly the question of how best to "get America moving in the '60's." The outcome was the closest in American history; so close that the final victory of Kennedy was not certain for several weeks after the first counting of the ballots.

In his first months in office, President Kennedy prepared to advance towards what he called the New Frontier. His legislative programme included a large extension of federally-subsidized housing, federal aid to education, federally-sponsored medical care for the aged, a broad programme of urban redevelopment and considerable tariff reduction. By 1963 some cautious progress had been made in these directions, but serious opposition from the long-standing congressional alliance of Southern Democrats and right-wing Republicans blocked much of the legislation Kennedy wanted. On the other hand, Kennedy succeeded in getting congressional support for some important parts of his programme, such as a trade bill in 1962 which gave the President greater power than ever before to reduce tariffs. In Kennedy's view, lower tariffs, increased foreign trade and keen competition provided one key to greater productivity at home and closer and more mutually beneficial ties with America's allies in Western Europe.

CHAPTER 18

Foreign Policy in the Cold War

Two great questions confronted the United States as the Second World War moved to its close. The first was the question of what America should do to help her desperately war-battered Allies recover health and strength. The second was the problem of future relations with the Soviet Union. In 1945 American leaders approached these questions with a mixture of caution and confidence, but as time passed confidence diminished and the concern for world economic recovery gave way to an obsession with problems of security.

1. RECOVERY AND SECURITY

The basis of post-war diplomacy was laid at the wartime conferences held at Yalta and Potsdam in February and July of 1945. At Yalta, Roosevelt, Churchill and Stalin agreed to divide Germany into four occupation zones—British, American, Russian and French—and to exact reparations from Germany in work and equipment. But the western leaders could secure no guarantees from Stalin concerning the future of the Russian-occupied nations of eastern Europe except that they should have governments "broadly representative" of their people. Churchill argued for a "hard-headed" bargain with Stalin which would have divided Europe and Asia into Russian and western spheres of influence and advocated that Japan and Germany be rebuilt rapidly as strong industrial states to act as barriers against Russian expansion. Roosevelt disagreed; he preferred to think that Russia and the western Allies could co-operate through the United Nations and avoid the traditional device of military alliances that had brought on a holocaust twice in his lifetime.

By the time the Potsdam Conference met, Truman had succeeded Roosevelt as President of the United States and Clement Attlee had replaced Churchill as Prime Minister of Britain. The two new leaders agreed to administer Germany through an Allied Control Council until a peace treaty had been arranged, and to establish a Council of Foreign Ministers to draw up peace treaties with former enemy states. By the time treaties had been hammered out for Romania, Bulgaria, Hungary, Finland and Italy and signed early in 1947 so much friction had developed between the United States and Russia that, for the time being at least, there seemed no possibility of their reaching agreement on a settlement with Austria or Germany.

The kinds of situation which generated this friction are well illustrated by the cases of Greece and Turkey. In Greece a shaky but pro-western government was under attack by the Greek Communist party which, with Russian aid, was exploiting the misery of the people and their discontent with monarchy in a bid to win power. A similar situation existed in Turkey. In 1947 the British government advised the American State Department that Britain could no longer afford the burden of shoring up these two governments. Yet Greece and Turkey were key states; if they were to join the Communist camp Russia would gain control of all the Balkans and the Dardanelles. This President Truman was determined to prevent. He laid it down that "it must be the policy of the United States to support free peoples who are resisting attempted subjugation by armed minorities or by outside pressures." This was at once dubbed the Truman Doctrine, and in its support the United States had, by 1950, spent $659,000,000 in stemming the advance of Communism in the eastern Mediterranean.

That same spring of 1947 the United States also came fully to grips with the question of Europe's economic recovery. Truman's Secretary of State, George C. Marshall, outlined a massive programme for lending American assistance to European programmes for recovery. The Marshall Plan, as it was called, began with an annual budget of five billion dollars. These funds were distributed by an Economic Co-operation Administration (E.C.A.) upon a plan worked out by representatives of the western European governments themselves through the newly formed Organization for European Economic Co-operation (O.E.E.C.). Technically membership in the Organization was also open to the states of eastern Europe within the Communist sphere of influence. As George Marshall declared, in announcing the plan:

> Our policy is directed not against any country or doctrine but against hunger, poverty, desperation, and chaos. Its purpose should be the revival of a working economy in the world so as to permit the emergence of political and social conditions in which free institutions can exist.

In practice, the countries within the Soviet sphere boycotted the Marshall Plan and the Soviet Union set up its own "Molotov Plan" for the economic reorganization of the eastern European states. Nevertheless, by 1951 the O.E.E.C. had spent twelve billion dollars in American aid, and the programme is usually credited with having prevented the Communists from winning power in France and Italy.

Yet, despite the evident success of the Marshall Plan in stemming Communism in western Europe, distrust of Russia led the United States to give her foreign policy an increasing military emphasis. A straw in the wind was an article in *Foreign Affairs* by George Kennan, published in the summer of 1947. Kennan was an official of the State Department who had seen service in Moscow and had concluded that the most effective policy for the United States would be one of "containment" of Russia and her Communist satellite's. The United States, he argued, should support and strengthen non-Communist states around the periphery of the Communist world so as to be able to bring immediate counter-pressure to bear against any threat of Communist expansion. This would mean the acquiring and manning of suitable military bases in a kind of encirclement of the Soviet bloc.

Events in Czechoslovakia powerfully influenced public opinion to adopt this view of what American policy should be. Since 1946, Czechoslovakia had been ruled by a coalition of Communists and non-Communists. Now, in February 1948, with fresh elections impending, the Communist minority seized power. A chill ran through the West. Although Communist strength in Czechoslovakia reflected Czech fears that a revived German power might again threaten her, the West regarded the Czech coup as loss of a "Western" state. Communist success there seemed to many Western leaders to cast a long shadow westward. They began more definitely to look upon their relations with the Soviet states as a struggle for power in the nature of a war—a "Cold War" as the phrase went.

Germany inevitably became a major battle ground of the Cold War. In 1946 the United States stopped the sending, as reparations, of German factory equipment to Russia from the American occupation zone. To Russia reparations in kind seemed essential to repair the devastation visited upon her industrial cities by German armies. The Western powers claimed that Russia was taking more than had been agreed upon and that the exaction of reparations on this scale would imperil German recovery. On her side, Russia saw the Western policy of rapid re-industrialization of Germany as an attempt to re-establish the power of a state particularly likely to menace Russian security.

To enforce her case Russia, in June of 1948, clamped a tight economic blockade on Berlin. Although deep inside the Soviet occupation zone Berlin was jointly occupied by the former Allies. By blocking the city's supply routes from West Germany, Russia hoped to force the British and Americans to leave the city and modify their German policy. The Western powers responded by mounting a huge airlift to supply their zones of the city. Blockade and airlift lasted nearly a year and were ended when the Council of Foreign Ministers agreed to review the entire German question. They reached no agreement, however, and in September 1949 the West took the decisive step of creating a separate state in their zones, namely, the German Federal Republic (West Germany). The Soviet government responded by creating the German Democratic Republic (East Germany) in October. The fact of a permanently divided Germany and a truceless Cold War had emerged.

2. THE PROBLEM OF DISARMAMENT

Another fact, ominously mushroom-shaped, heightened apprehension in the West. By 1949, Russia was known to have the secret of producing atomic bombs. A nuclear arms race had been foreseen as early as 1945 and revulsion against it had prompted a long but fruitless search for agreement on arms control and disarmament. On this problem, the United States, for obvious reasons, was the chief spokesman of the West. Even before the testing of the first atomic bomb, Secretary of War Henry L. Stimson raised with President Roosevelt the problem of the future:

> I went over with him the two schools of thought that exist in respect to the future control after the war of this project, in case it is successful, one of them being the secret close-in attempted control of the project by those who control it now, and the other being the international control based upon freedom both of science and access.

By the autumn of 1945 Stimson strongly favoured the second alternative and thought the United States should agree to cease bomb production and to impound existing stocks of bombs. Concerned about future Russian-American relations, he remarked:

> Those relations may be perhaps irretrievably embittered by the way in which we approach the solution of the bomb with Russia . . . if we fail to approach them now and merely continue to negotiate with them, having this weapon rather ostentatiously on our hip, their suspicions and their distrust of our purposes and motives will increase.

A Communist youth rally marching down Berlin's historic Unter Den Linden in 1950 reflected the deepening split between the two Germanys.

Secretary of the Navy James Forrestal, on the other hand, argued that the United States should exercise a United Nations "trusteeship" over the new weapon, and declared that "until we have a longer record of experience with the Russians on the validity of engagements . . . it seems doubtful that we should try to buy their understanding and sympathy."

In its Atomic Energy Act, Congress accepted Forrestal's reasoning and placed tight safeguards on atomic energy information. The first American proposal on disarmament, the Baruch Plan, followed the same line in 1946. It proposed the establishment of an international agency under the United Nations which would own and operate every aspect of atomic energy production and which would have power to inspect atomic installations in any country. Once the system of close inspection was working, the United States would agree to destroy its stock of atomic weapons, ban their future production, and provide for punishment of any nation that broke the agreement. The Soviet Union turned down the Baruch Plan and offered an alternative based upon immediate ending of bomb production and destruction of existing bombs. Noting that the United States could count upon a clear majority in any United Nations body, and that the time for giving up the monopoly of the bomb was left to the discretion of the United States, Soviet spokesmen declared that Russia could not feel secure under Western control of atomic weapons. In succeeding meetings in the United Nations Disarmament Commission, the General Assembly and special disarmament committees, Russia and the United States by and large kept to the positions taken up in 1946. The United States insisted that a system of international inspection be worked out in full detail before any stage of disarmament or arms control was initiated. The Soviet Union reiterated its demand for immediate general disarmament but refused to subject itself to the type of control system deemed necessary by the West. So the arms race went on. In the United States it absorbed a growing percentage of the annual national income every year after 1945. It meant too a sharp increase in the influence of military men upon foreign policy.

It is a peculiarity of nuclear weapons that they are not usable in the sort of warfare which has, in fact, occurred in one hot spot after another since 1945. It followed that the deepening mutual fears and suspicions between East and West led each side to have recourse to the traditional device of a system of military alliances at the same time as they poured billions into the development of new nuclear weapons. The first step towards a Western alliance was taken in the spring of 1948 when, with American encouragement, a military and economic alliance was signed by Britain, France and the Benelux countries (Holland, Belgium and Luxembourg). A further step was taken in 1949 when Senator Arthur H. Vandenberg, a one-time isolationist moved that the United States should seek security through a series of regional military pacts. This initiative, which was strongly supported by Canada, led to the signing of the North Atlantic Treaty later in the same year, which established the North Atlantic Treaty Organization (N.A.T.O.). The original members were the United States,

Shown at the U.S.-N.A.T.O. air base at Adana, Turkey are F100 Sabre fighters. This was the home base of Francis G. Powers whose U-2 "spy plane" was shot down over Russian territory in 1960, creating a major international crisis.

Britain, Canada, France, Belgium, the Netherlands, Luxembourg, Italy, Portugal, Denmark, Iceland and Norway. Joint training schemes and a N.A.T.O. army in Europe were established and each member agreed that an armed attack against one N.A.T.O. member "shall be considered an attack against them all." Pursuing the policy of containment, the United States secured the admission to N.A.T.O. of Greece and Turkey in 1951 and of a rearmed West Germany in 1955. The Soviet Union responded by bringing the East European states into the Warsaw Treaty of 1955 and uniting their military forces under a single Russian command.

3. THE COLD WAR IN ASIA

Europe was not the only region to witness a deepening conflict between the interests of East and West. In the long run, if it were poverty, misgovernment and frustrated hopes that gave Communists their following, the greatest challenge would arise in the vast, underdeveloped and poverty-stricken continents of Asia, Africa and South America. The challenge touched the United States most nearly, of course, in Latin America. In 1947 the United States and all the Latin American countries signed the Treaty of Rio under which they agreed that an attack on any of them should be considered an attack on all, and the following year set up the Organization of American States (O.A.S.) to give body to this undertaking. Further, members reaffirmed the pledge not to interfere in one another's domestic affairs.

Military alliance was supplemented with economic aid. In his inaugural address of 1949 President Truman outlined a four-point programme for his new term of office. His fourth point was the provision of technical assistance to underdeveloped countries. The "Point Four Programme," as it came to be called, was launched with a vote of $400,000,-000 and similar sums were appropriated by Congress in succeeding years. After 1950 the United States also contributed substantially to the programme of mutual assistance launched by the members of the Commonwealth and known as the Colombo Plan. Yet neither in Latin America nor elsewhere has the technical and economic aid so far provided solved the immense economic problems of the peoples concerned.

In Asia, the confrontation between the Western world and Communism occurred even more abruptly and starkly than it had in Europe. During the Second World War, the Chinese government of General Chiang Kaishek had received continuous, if limited, aid from the United States. It was, however, not the only government in China. In the northwest province of Shensi the Chinese Communist party had established a separate soviet state. Even the crisis of the Japanese war had not brought these two governments to work together, and in 1945, with that war ending, overt civil war seemed likely to break out again between them. Most State Department officials distrusted Chiang's régime as corrupt; the chief American representative in China considered Chiang both reactionary and unreliable and wrote that the party he headed, the Kuomintang, was "a structure based on fear and favour, in the hands of an ignorant, arbitrary, stubborn man." Yet the United States decided that the long struggle between the Kuomintang and the Communist party might best be ended and China's unity restored by heavily subsidizing Chiang's government. But the Kuomintang continued to withhold overdue reforms and to make a system of corruption; civil war recommenced and the Communists grew in strength. A crisis was reached in 1949. Thousands of Chiang's troops deserted and many provincial governors went over to the Communists. Rapidly driven southward, what remained of Chiang's forces withdrew to Taiwan (Formosa). By the end of 1949 the Chinese Communists, under Mao Tse-tung, controlled all of China.

The conclusion was inescapable that the United States' China policy had failed. A powerful China Lobby, composed of businessmen with Far Eastern interests and a number of Republican Congressmen, preached that Mao Tse-tung must be ousted by force and Chiang reinstated as ruler of China. Their vilification of the State Department, coupled with that of Senator McCarthy, intensified anti-Communist feeling in the United States. As a result, the United Sates refused to follow the British lead of recognizing the Communist government of China, a refusal which became more adamant as a result of the Korean War.

The general worsening in East-West relations led to tragic consequences in the Korean peninsula. In 1945 Korea had been freed from Japanese control and, pending the establishment of an independent government, the United States and the Soviet Union occupied the country, dividing it between them at the thirty-eighth parallel of latitude. In the north, a Communist régime was established, while in the south a pro-Western government was organized. Declaring that the South Koreans were contemplating a forceful reunification of the peninsula, a North Korean army invaded South Korea in June, 1950. President Truman immediately sent American naval and air support to South Korea and the Security Council requested United Nations members to assist the South Korean government, an act that was possible only because Russia was temporarily boycotting the Security Council and failed to exercise its veto. While the Commonwealth of Nations and several other Western and pro-Western states contributed to the United Nations army, the United States provided four-fifths of the forces required during the ensuing three years of war, and the American, General MacArthur, became commander of the U.N. forces.

The Korean War exacted a bitter price, but established firmly the principle that any United Nations military action should aim to repel aggression without altering the original political position of the contending states. Thus in October 1950 when General MacArthur succeeded in crossing the thirty-eighth parallel and began to move towards the Yalu River which forms the border between North Korea and China, he was forbidden to bomb sites in Manchuria from which Chinese men and supplies were being sent to the North Koreans. When MacArthur publicly criticized this decision President Truman dismissed him from his command. The resulting military stalemate in Korea led to truce negotiations which dragged on until 1953 when an agreement was signed which restored approximately the *status quo ante bellum*. The war cost the United States more than fifteen billion dollars and thousands of lives. Even more important, it increased American determination not to recognize the government of China.

A tightening of lines followed these events in China and Korea. In 1951 the United States signed a treaty of peace with the Japanese government. Japan immediately made a defence agreement with the United States which permitted the Americans to maintain bases on the islands. In 1954 John Foster Dulles, President Eisenhower's Secretary of State, negotiated a treaty creating the South East Asia Treaty Organization (S.E.A.T.O.). It was signed by the United States, Britain, France, Australia, New Zealand, the Philippines, Pakistan and Thailand. Since important East Asian states such as India, Burma, Ceylon and Indonesia did not join it, S.E.A.T.O. was not as closely knit or as powerful as N.A.T.O. but it became an important agency of American policy. Another important link in the system of interlocking regional defence alliances was the Middle East Treaty Organization made up of Britain, Turkey, Pakistan, Iran and Iraq and created during 1955. Although the United States did not formally join the Middle East Organization it was largely inspired by the Secretary of State, John Foster Dulles, and was heavily endowed with American funds. The containment of the Soviet bloc had been carried far—on paper, at least.

While still President of Columbia University, Dwight D. Eisenhower was photographed chatting, in June 1952, with his friend, the lawyer-diplomat John Foster Dulles. Eisenhower named Dulles Secretary of State after the November elections, and relied heavily upon him until ill-health forced Dulles from office in 1959. On several occasions, however, the President had to restrain the hot-tempered Dulles from risking war in such delicate areas as the China Sea. Willing to go to the brink of war in diplomacy, Dulles was sometimes accused of "brinksmanship."

4. THE "BALANCE OF TERROR"

As the system of alliances grew, it became more and more difficult to define what the "free world" was which it was the purpose of American policy to defend. The Cold War made some strange bedfellows. Spain and Portugal, both dictatorships, received assistance without which their governments probably could not have survived. The governments of Greece and Turkey, while technically democratic, were constantly opposed to social reform. Pakistan, Iraq and Iran all had totalitarian governments of varying sorts. In Asia, Chiang Kai-shek's régime in Formosa, which the United States continued to recognize as the government of China and which could not have survived without American support, was an outright dictatorship. In South Korea and in the states that gained their independence from France in Indo-China (Laos, Cambodia and Viet-Nam), American aid was given to the most right-wing governments. Successive American administrations feared that left-wing governments in underdeveloped nations might elect a policy of neutrality in the Cold War, as, in fact, many states in Africa and Asia did. What then would become of the carefully constructed system of military alliances and the goal of containment?

It was possible to think of containing the Soviet bloc so far as concerned its expansion by force of conventional arms. What could not be con-

One link in the U.S. nuclear deterrent system is a British base at North Luffenham. Here are poised three Thor missiles capable of obliterating huge areas inside Russia. While American officers would actually direct the launching of the Thor missiles, permission to do so would have to be given by the British government. Each of these keys opens the lock of a missile control system. They can only be used by a British officer.

AIR MINISTRY PROPERTY
THIS IS A
PROHIBITED PLACE
UNDER THE OFFICIAL SECRETS ACT

tained was its nuclear capability. By 1953 it became clear that both the United States and Russia possessed hydrogen bombs of infinitely greater power than the first atomic bombs. No important military, scientific or political observer doubted that a major war would bring a holocaust of destruction so great as to stagger the imagination. In the absence of controlled disarmament, official American opinion held that a "balance of terror" provided the surest guarantee against such a war. The Soviet governments under Stalin, Malenkov and Khrushchev, and American governments under Truman, Eisenhower and Kennedy all placed on record their intention of using nuclear weapons in the event of an assault upon any of their respective territories or major interests. Each nation endeavoured to establish the "credibility" of this policy, that is, its ability and willingness to use nuclear weapons. Each declared that it would not use such weapons in aggression and each kept its nuclear knowledge secret from the other. Both Russia and the United States supported a policy of restricting the number of nations which possessed nuclear weapons in the hope that control would thereby be made easier. Nevertheless, Britain, which co-operated in wartime atomic research, achieved its own nuclear bomb production in 1955; France tested her first atomic bomb in 1959; and it was predicted that China would acquire similar capacity by the late 'sixties.

Critics of the policy of a "balance of terror" argued that such a balance was inherently unstable since the two sides were never likely to agree as to when a desirable balance had been reached. More specifically, the evidence available seemed clearly to show that the United States continued to possess a much greater nuclear striking power than did the Soviet Union. This led to heavy military pressure inside Russia to expand the Communist nuclear armoury and its system of launching sites to match the world-wide system developed by the United States. But if American nuclear weapons were more numerous than Russian, a chill of fear touched American imaginations when the first Russian Sputnik was launched in 1957. This leap into space added a whole new dimension to the military problem, and in the conquest of space Russia evidently had stolen a march on the United States. Congress at once voted large additional appropriations for the American programme of space exploration.

As an ever larger portion of the American economy came to live by contracts related to military and space exploration requirements, the relationship between industrial corporations and government departments concerned with defence became more extensive and more intimate than ever before. This was noted by Dwight Eisenhower in his farewell address as outgoing President when he warned of the danger of a huge "military-industrial complex." Such a complex, he intimated, might make it very difficult to arrive at governmental decisions based upon the general interest as opposed to the special interests of the industrial-military leaders.

In international relations, the belief that survival hung upon a balance of terror seemed to have two effects. Each new crisis inescapably raised the question: might *this* bring on nuclear war? It arose in the continuing struggle to maintain a Western sector of Berlin deep inside East Germany; the Russian clamp-down on the revolt in Hungary in 1956-57; the ebb and flow of Communist and American influence in Indo-China, with its chronic guerilla warfare; the announcement of the Eisenhower Doctrine in 1957 that the United States would intervene to support any Middle Eastern state threatened by foreign-supported internal subversion; the shooting-down of an American U-2 spy plane over Russia in 1960. However, it also brought home to both the United States and the Soviet Union the imperative need for co-existence. In the early 1950's Secretary of

State John Foster Dulles had spoken of an "agonizing reappraisal" of American policy which might lead to "utilizing the deterrence of massive retaliation at times and places of America's choosing." In 1954 President Eisenhower shifted ground when he declared that East and West "must find ways of living together."

Events in Cuba showed with searing clarity the nature of the problems involved in waging the Cold War under the conditions imposed by the balance of terror. Before 1959 Cuba had been ruled by a dictator, Fulgencio Batista. When a determined guerilla fighter, Fidel Castro, led a successful revolt against this régime most Americans applauded. However, when Castro announced that as part of his reform programme he would nationalize, with or without compensation, a number of key industries and services owned mostly by American investors, and would redistribute the land owned by the big American-owned sugar plantations, conservative opinion in the United States turned against him. American firms cut off oil supplies to Cuban refineries, and when Castro accepted crude oil from Russia, the United States put an embargo on Cuban sugar, the island's main export. Behind the scenes and unknown to the American public or Congress, the State Department and the Central Intelligence Agency planned an invasion of Cuba with a force of pro-Batista Cubans and mercenaries. Shortly after President Kennedy came to office, he gave his consent to this pre-arranged plan. The resulting attempt at invasion in 1961 was a fiasco. The successful Cuban resistance strengthened the Castro government, sharply increasing its anti-American attitude, and cemented Cuba's ties with Russia more closely. As Cuba clearly emerged as the first Communist state in the Americas, President Kennedy and his Secretary of State, Dean Rusk, asserted the right of the United States to intervene with armed force anywhere in the Americas if such action was deemed necessary to prevent the establishment of a government incompatible with "the American system." This Kennedy Doctrine was, in fact, a greater expansion of the Monroe Doctrine than the Roosevelt Corollary had been. It also contravened the Treaty of Rio and the Charter of the O.A.S., both of which outlawed armed intervention in the affairs of any American state by any other American government. On the other hand, it was consonant with the principle of containment, and thus revealed the complexity of the problems created by emphasis on the military aspect of containment.

After the 1961 invasion, the United States began to put pressure on her allies to join the economic blockade of Cuba, but with little success. For the rest of Latin America President Kennedy announced an "Alliance for Progress" which would involve a massive increase in American financial aid to those Latin American states that showed political stability and a forthright resistance to Communism. By 1963 some progress had been made with the new assistance plan, though a number of Latin American states were reluctant to endorse the tough policy against Cuba.

In October 1962, Cuba suddenly found herself the centre of the most serious international storm since the end of the Second World War. When

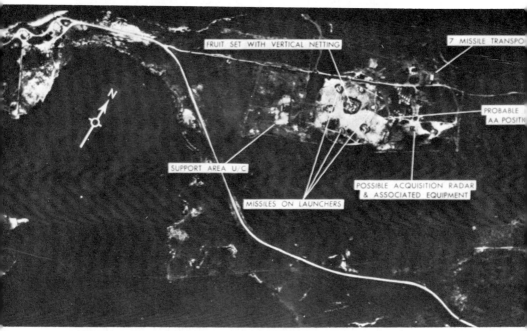

FRUIT SET WITH VERTICAL NETTING

7 MISSILE TRANSPO

PROBABLE
AA POSITI

SUPPORT AREA U/C

POSSIBLE ACQUISITION RADAR
& ASSOCIATED EQUIPMENT

MISSILES ON LAUNCHERS

In October, 1962, the world shuddered at the edge of war as President Kennedy announced an American blockade of Cuba. While the crisis was still unresolved, the United States issued an aerial view of one of the Russian-built missile sites which the U. S. said must be removed. On October 28 the immediate war threat receded as Chairman Khrushchev directed the removal of nuclear missiles from Cuba.

American Intelligence planes revealed that Russia, despite her denials, had installed launching bases for nuclear missiles in Cuba, President Kennedy ordered a tight naval blockade of Cuba and announced that any ship approaching the island would be stopped and searched. Moreover, he clearly intimated that if the missile bases were not quickly dismantled, the United States would take whatever military steps were necessary. Since the Soviet Union had publicly undertaken to defend Cuba against any act of war and since a naval blockade is usually considered an act of war, the world waited breathlessly upon the outcome. Through the mediation of U Thant, the Acting Secretary-General of the United Nations, President Kennedy agreed to lift the blockade if the Soviet Union would remove the nuclear missiles and dismantle the bases. The world passed safely through the crisis, but the experience revealed with painful clarity what little voice the allies of the United States and the Soviet Union actually had in decisions which took them all to the very brink of nuclear war. It also reminded people everywhere of the real meaning of the spectre with which they had been forced to walk since 1945.

The dangers through which President Kennedy's government had to steer its course are clear enough. Fortunately it could draw on sources of strength equally real: a profound respect for law and the procedures of law on the part of most Americans which survived even the assaults of a Joseph McCarthy and a Governor Barnett; an enduring belief that foreign policy must have a moral justification; and a long tradition of vigorous democratic action.

PART TWO: CANADA

CHAPTER 19

The Question of Survival

1. BRITAIN'S FRENCH COLONY

Britain's conquest of Canada created serious problems for both victors and vanquished. For the French Canadians the conquest was a tragedy and the central event in their history. British governors replaced French, while English-speaking merchants from Britain and the thirteen colonies quickly assumed control of the colony's economic affairs. A small number of wealthy French Canadians returned to France, but most of the habitants and small businessmen had no alternative but to remain in Canada under the conqueror and hope for the best.

The Roman Catholic Church also remained and continued to play a central role in the life of the colony. Indeed, since the Church was the only important institution in the colony that was not taken over by the Protestant conquerors, its importance actually increased after the British conquest. It not only ministered to the religious needs of its flock but it inspired in French Canada a continuing sense of mission. Cut off from their mother country and deprived of much of their secular leadership, the French Canadians turned for leadership to the Church and particularly to the parish priest. Ever since the conquest, the Roman Catholic Church has remained one of the main sources of strength in the defence of the French-Canadian way of life.

Britain's new colony was primarily agricultural although there was a small merchant class engaged in the fur trade and in importing manufactured goods. A Swedish traveller has left the following description of New France at the time of the conquest:

All the farms in Canada stand separate from one another, so that each farmer has his possessions entirely separate from those of his neighbour. Each church, it is true, has a little village near it; but that consists chiefly of the parsonage, a school for boys and girls of the place, and the houses of tradesmen, but rarely of farmhouses. . . . The farmhouses hereabouts are generally all built along the rising banks of the river. . . . The country on both sides was very delightful. . . . The fine state of its cultivation added greatly to the beauty of the scene. It could really be called a village, beginning at Montreal and ending at Quebec, which is a distance of more than one hundred and eighty miles.

The people in general were a gay and hardy lot, faithful to their Church but enjoying boisterous good times. Years of adversity in the colony had made them strong and tough. One French observer, describing their mixed characteristics, wrote: "The Canadians are tall, well made, and well set on their legs, robust, vigorous, and accustomed in time of need to live on little. They have intelligence, and vivacity, but are wayward, light-minded and inclined to debauchery." This was the land and the people that came under British rule in 1759.

The British government's first problem was to frame a policy for the government of the new subjects. Its solution was the Proclamation of 1763, designed to transform Quebec into an English-speaking colony. The Proclamation prohibited settlement west of the Appalachians pending some solution of the Indian problem, and so determined that the American colonists would not be able to expand westward. The British hoped that this situation would produce a movement of English-speaking settlers from the thirteen colonies into Quebec in sufficient numbers to submerge the existing French-speaking population. To strengthen the attraction of Quebec for immigrants from the thirteen colonies and England, the Proclamation of 1763 promised the early establishment of English law and representative institutions in the colony.

But the policy of assimilating the French Canadians was doomed to failure. The expected stream of immigrants never became more than a trickle. With its cold climate and foreign culture, Quebec had few attractions for American colonists when the rich lands of the Ohio valley lay beckoning. When immigration from the British colonies failed to materialize, successive governors concluded that the policy of anglicizing Quebec was not realistic. Moreover, many British officials developed a sympathy and respect for the French Canadians. General James Murray, the first British Governor, described them as "perhaps the bravest and best race upon the Globe." Murray refused to establish the assembly that had been promised by the Proclamation of 1763. He felt that such an assembly would become the tool of an English-speaking minority since the French Canadians would be excluded from the assembly, because British law still denied Roman Catholics the rights of full citizenship. One government official wrote: "An assembly so constituted might pretend to be a representative of the people there, but it would be a representative of only the 600 new English settlers, and an instrument in their hands of dominating over the 90,000 French."

Murray's refusal to introduce an assembly aroused the anger of the English-speaking minority in the colony, and in 1765 the British government appointed Sir Guy Carleton to replace him. Carleton at first disliked

Governor Murray's benevolent attitude towards the French Canadians angered the Anglo-American merchants who had felt that the new colony would be their economic and political preserve.

the French Canadians and intended to grant the wishes of the English-speaking minority. But the aristocratic British Governor soon discovered that he had little in common with the pushing and troublesome group of British merchants. The French Canadians, on the other hand, he found increasingly attractive. In 1772, Carleton informed the British government of his firm conclusion that "barring a catastrophe shocking to think of this country must, to the end of time, be peopled by the Canadian race." Since Canada would remain a colony with a French-speaking majority, Carleton believed that Britain should establish a new set of governing principles to replace the Proclamation of 1763.

The Governor had other reasons for recommending a new policy. In view of the growing discontent in the thirteen colonies to the south, Carleton felt that the British government should take steps to ensure the loyalty of Quebec. If the colony could be made firmly loyal to Britain, it could be used as a strategic base in the event of trouble in the American colonies. As a military man and an aristocrat, Carleton felt that the real power in Quebec lay with the seigniors and the higher clergy. If Britain could win the loyalty of these two groups, all would be well for, he felt, the habitants, the largest group in the colony, would naturally follow the lead of their superiors. Carleton believed that the British merchants, while difficult and troublesome, were not numerous enough to cause any serious problem. For these reasons he advised the British government to work out a new system of government that would appeal mainly to the seigniors and the clergy. The result was the Quebec Act passed in 1774.

The Quebec Act recognized and guaranteed the position of the Roman Catholic Church in the colony and legalized its right to collect tithes from its members. The Act also recognized French law insofar as it applied to such civil matters as landholding, seigniorial dues and marriage rites. By these guarantees the British government hoped to weld the leaders of the French-Canadian community to the British Crown and to ensure their loyalty in any future crisis.

The Quebec Act, however, denied the new colony an elective assembly, one of the traditional features of British colonial government. In spite of the repeated demands of the English-speaking merchants, Carleton and the British authorities felt that there were good reasons for refusing an assembly. Since the French Canadians had never had elective institutions, they would not want them now. Moreover, since any assembly would inevitably be dominated by the British minority, its establishment would only undermine the confidence in Britain that Carleton was so anxious to establish. In addition, assemblies in the thirteen colonies had been a chronic source of friction between Britain and her American subjects, for they were constantly demanding more powers than the British government was prepared to grant. Thus, in Quebec, Britain established a system of non-representative government. Power rested with an appointed governor and an appointed advisory council composed of both English, and French-speaking members, including Roman Catholics.

The denial of representative government infuriated the merchant class who protested that the mother country had deprived them of a basic right of all Englishmen. However, two important provisions of the Quebec Act took some of the edge off their discontent. The more humane English criminal law replaced the relatively savage French penal code. The old French civil law was kept, however, and its retention remained a grievance because the merchants believed that it was not suited to the needs of a developing commerce. But, to the merchants, by far the most attractive features of the Quebec Act were the territorial changes. The Act extended the boundaries of the colony to include the rich fur-trading territory between the Ohio and upper Mississippi rivers which had formerly been part of the French empire. The new boundaries meant that the merchants in Canada would now be able to exploit the fur trade in this area without fear of competition from the merchants of Albany and New York. The developing commercial system of the St. Lawrence region needed a rich hinterland.

As a whole, the Quebec Act satisfied fully only the upper-class French Canadians. Neither the merchants nor the lower classes found in it much to cheer about. Its most serious effect, perhaps, was the anger it aroused among the people in the thirteen colonies. One observer wrote of the Quebec Act: "It not only offended the inhabitants of the province itself, in a degree that could hardly be conceived, but alarmed all the English

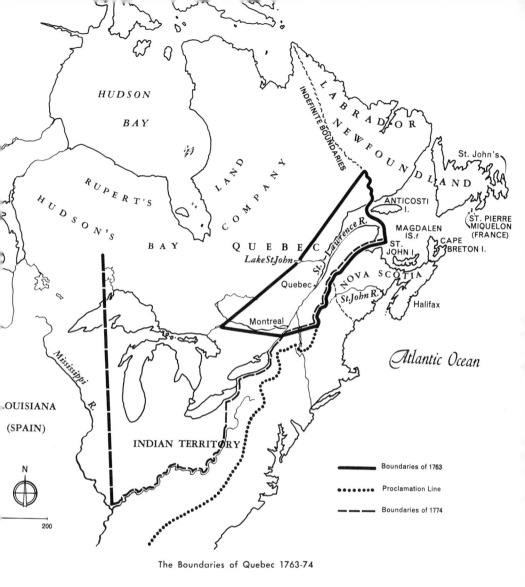

The Boundaries of Quebec 1763-74

provinces in America, and contributed more perhaps, than any other measure whatsoever, to drive them into rebellion against their sovereign." By 1774, rebellion in the thirteen colonies was developing rapidly.

2. CANADA AND THE AMERICAN REVOLUTION

Sir Guy Carleton had been right in anticipating trouble in the American colonies. One of his main reasons for suggesting the extension of Quebec's boundaries to include the Ohio valley region had been to ensure the safety of this area if the colonists revolted. As it happened, this territorial transfer was one of several features of the Quebec Act which actually accelerated the movement towards rebellion. With the Ohio valley within the jurisdiction of Quebec the route to western settlement was closed, and the thirteen colonies were hemmed in on the seaboard. New England merchants and would-be land speculators and settlers would have to abandon their plans for exploiting the fertile western lands. In other ways, too, the Act of 1774 seemed to threaten colonial liberties, for it established on their very doorstep, and in defiance of established British tradition, a form of government that denied the people representation. Just as offensive to zealous New England Protestants was the legal recognition that the Act extended to the Roman Catholic Church. For these reasons the American colonists included the Quebec Act among the "Intolerable Acts" which helped move them farther along the road to revolution.

When the American Revolution did break out, the people of the thirteen colonies looked north hoping that Nova Scotia and Quebec would join them in the fight against the mother country. In a letter to the inhabitants of Quebec, the Continental Congress condemned the system of government in the northern colony. "We defy you, casting your view upon every side, to discover a single circumstance, promising from any quarter the faintest hope of liberty to you or your posterity, but from an entire adoption into the union of these colonies." But neither Nova Scotia nor Quebec believed that its best interests would be served by joining the rebels to the south.

Many Nova Scotians had originally come from New England and they had a deep sympathy with the revolutionaries. There was a minor attempt to start a revolution in Cumberland County in 1776, but the ease with which it was squelched indicated the hopelessness of the revolutionary cause. Faced with large numbers of British troops and the ever-present British navy, most Maritime colonists adopted a neutral outlook. "The neutral Yankees of Nova Scotia," as they have been called, would fight neither for the British against their kinsmen, nor against the British for the cause of independence. The basic reason for this attitude was simply that most Nova Scotians did not share the grievances of their southern cousins. They had no serious complaints about the operation of the mercantilist economic regulations by which Britain bound her Empire together. In fact, Nova Scotia benefited greatly through her access to the protected British market that the system guaranteed. More immediate economic considerations also suggested the wisdom of neutrality. The American War of Independence brought prosperity to Nova Scotia as Halifax became the centre for naval and military supplies for the British forces fighting the revolutionaries. But perhaps the most important reason that Nova Scotia did not join the revolution was that it simply could not have done so if it had wanted to. Its population was very small, and scattered about the coast in isolated communities. Under these circumstances, decisive and united action by the colonists was so difficult as to be impossible.

In Quebec, too, there was an attitude of near-neutrality which surprised and dismayed Carleton, who had expected that his benevolent rule

The original caption for this drawing of the American attack on Quebec read: Le 31 décembre 1775, les Américains dirigent deux attaques contre Québec, l'une par le faubourg St. Roch et l'autre par les Foulons: c'est à ce dernier endroit que leur général Montgomery fût tué par la décharge d'une pièce de canon servie par des volontaires. Peu après le siège fût levé.

would produce widespread popular support. The Church leaders and seigniors did remain loyal, as the Governor had anticipated, but the Quebec Act had not satisfied either of the most important groups in the colony. The British merchants were still irritated because they had not been granted a voice in government through an elected assembly. The habitants, the largest group in the colony, were unhappy because the Quebec Act provided for the legal enforcement of the tithes of the Church and the feudal rents of the seigniors. To these two groups the American Revolution might well have had some appeal. Although the Roman Catholic Bishop, Briand, told his flock, "Your oaths, your religion, lay upon you the unavoidable duty of defending your country and your king with all the strength you possess," the habitants remained unenthusiastic. They were neither anxious to fight for their British conquerors nor were they willing to fight against them on the side of the traditional enemy from New England, the *Bostonais*, as they were called.

The leaders of the rebellion in the British colonies tried to win support for their cause in Canada. In October 1774, they called upon the French Canadians to "seize the opportunity presented by Providence itself." On behalf of the Continental Congress, John Brown travelled to Quebec where he aroused modest support among French Canadians and British merchants, but generally speaking the American appeal fell on deaf ears. In May 1775, some rebellious spirits covered a bust of George III with black paint and hung a garland of potatoes around its neck. An inscription left beneath the mutilated statue read: "Behold the People of Canada, or the English idiot." But more than pranks were needed to overthrow British authority. When the American armies under Richard Montgomery and Benedict Arnold invaded Canada in 1775, the habitant did little either to defend his country or to assist the invaders.

Quebec's failure to join the thirteen colonies was, then, due mainly to the attitude of the mass of the population. The sympathy which the habitant might have felt for his self-styled liberators soon dissolved when he received worthless currency for the goods which he sold to the army of the Continental Congress. Furthermore, despite their lukewarm attitude towards the British, the French Canadians could see no real advantage in joining the Americans. After all, the British were only a minority in Quebec; united with the more populous thirteen colonies, the French Canadians would be in a minority. And few French Canadians could forget that for more than a century they had fought and competed with the same Americans to the south who were now claiming to be their friends. Thus, throughout the period of hostilities, the habitants preserved an attitude of neutrality and carefully assessed their own interests. Carleton realized this truth when he wrote: "I think there is nothing to fear from them while we are in a state of prosperity, and nothing to hope for while in distress." In all probability no more than five hundred French Canadians joined the invading armies.

The English-speaking merchants in Quebec generally remained passively loyal to the Empire which was the source of their economic strength and prosperity. A few, like Thomas Walker of Montreal, joined the Americans. But most of them realized that the British Empire gave them a protected market and provided the capital they needed to extend their business activities. Moreover, the British merchants, like the French merchants before them, had come to realize that their trading system based on the St. Lawrence was in competition with the economy of the thirteen colonies, especially New York. If they were to join the rebellious colonies, they would have to share their profitable western hinterland with their southern competitors. Thus, whatever political attractions the American Revolution may have had for the inhabitants of Canada, French-speaking or British, other interests of an economic and cultural kind held them to their British allegiance.

A final and decisive factor which kept Quebec from joining the rebellion was the failure of the American invasion. For although the American army captured a poorly defended Montreal in 1775, their winter-long siege of Quebec, punctuated by a futile New Year's Eve assault on the city, was a dismal failure. When spring opened the St. Lawrence to navigation, the arrival of a British naval force compelled the Americans to give up the battle and retreat to New York. With their retreat went all hope of support for the revolutionary cause.

Yet, while neither Quebec nor Nova Scotia joined the thirteen colonies in their fight for freedom from the control of the British government, the

This artist's conception of the arrival of the Loyalists suggests that the people who departed from the revolting American colonies in search of new homes in the Maritimes were elegantly dressed aristocrats. Yet this class represented only a minority of the exiles. An official in Halifax described the majority when he wrote: "I cannot better describe the wretched condition of these people than by enclosing your Lordship a list of those just arrived in the Clinton transport, destitute of almost everything, chiefly women and children, all still on board, as I have not yet been able to find any sort of place for them, and the cold setting in severe."

American Revolution had an enormous effect on the history of Canada. Indeed, it helped to create Canada. After a brief two decades of North American unity under British authority, the continent was again divided in 1783, with the independent Americans masters of the southern half and the British colonies, with their French and English populations, in possession in the north.

The Treaty of Versailles, 1783, defined the new division of North America. On the seaboard, the St. Croix River became the dividing line, while in the West the British gave up all the lands south of the Great Lakes. This latter decision brought cries of dismay from the merchants in Quebec for this territory seemed to them to be essential to their fur-trading empire. Since their loyalty to Britain had stemmed in large measure from their unwillingness to share this rich hinterland with New England and New York traders, they were enraged that British diplomats, by a stroke of the pen, should now give their patrimony to the rebels. One result, however, was to force the British merchants in Canada to seek future opportunities in the British territories north of the Great Lakes.

But it was not just in the drawing of boundaries that the American Revolution helped to create Canada. Equally important were the rapid changes in the composition of the population that occurred during the

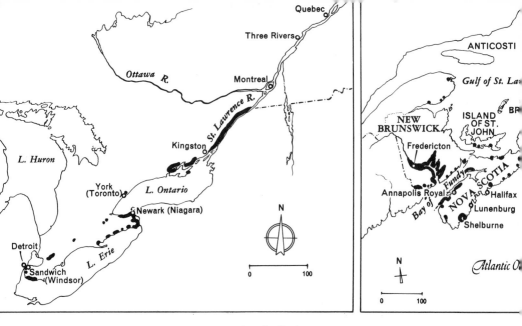

Loyalist Settlements

last years of the war and the first years of peace. The American Revolution produced the first large-scale British immigration to Canada, and thereby helped to determine its bi-cultural nature, one of Canada's fundamental characteristics.

3. THE LOYALIST MIGRATIONS

The people of the thirteen colonies had not been unanimous in their opposition to British rule. One-third of the population opposed the revolution. Life in the thirteen colonies became increasingly difficult for those who refused to support the rebellion, and by the end of the war about 100,000 Americans demonstrated their loyalty to the motherland by leaving their homes to start a new life elsewhere. They came from all classes of colonial society, and included farmers and lawyers, clergymen and government employees, teachers and soldiers. Often they paid a very high price for their loyalty to Britain. Many had to abandon all their material possessions and endure long periods of intense suffering before finding new and secure homes. As late as 1786, a Loyalist petition for assistance from the British government painted this vivid picture of their hardships:

> It is impossible to describe the poignant distress under which many of these persons now labour, and which must daily increase should the justice of Parliament be delayed until all the claims are liquidated and reported . . . ten years have elapsed since many of them have been deprived of their fortunes, and with their helpless families reduced from independent affluence to poverty and want; some of them now languishing in British jails; others indebted to their creditors, who have lent them money enough barely to support their existence, and who

unless speedily relieved, must sink more than the value of their claims when received, and be in worse condition than if they had never made them; others have sunk under the pressure and severity of their misfortunes; and others must, in all probability, soon meet the same melancholy fate, should the justice due them be longer postponed.

Obviously, the British authorities faced a serious human problem.

At the peace negotiations in 1783, Britain tried to gain some protection and compensation for the Loyalists, but the weak government of the newly independent thirteen colonies was neither willing nor able to ease their plight. As a result, thousands of Loyalists sought new homes in other British colonies. Because of its proximity, Canada was an obvious place to settle and eventually about 40,000 found new homes in Nova Scotia and Quebec.

The largest group of Loyalists, about 30,000, went by sea from New York to Nova Scotia. Many of these, particularly those with upper class backgrounds, found life in the struggling little colony of Nova Scotia too difficult. Despite such governmental assistance as food, land, and tools, some drifted back to the United States and others moved on to Great Britain. But the majority, forced by necessity to make the best of their

This encampment of Loyalists on the St. Lawrence was formed by people who had fled overland from the rebelling thirteen colonies. Moving up from New York, the group first settled near Sorel, later obtaining lands along the Upper St. Lawrence west to the Bay of Quinte, including such settlements as Cornwall and Kingston. Many of these Loyalists were members of the armed services, such as the King's Royal Regiment of New York, while others were farmers and small-scale tradesmen.

grim situation, gradually won the battle for survival, and laid the foundations of the Maritime provinces. Before the American Revolution, the
population of Nova Scotia had been only about 17,000, mainly clustered
around Halifax. Some of the newcomers joined this well established
group, but most settled on the north shore of the Bay of Fundy. To
solve the administrative problem created by this division of the population,
as well as to meet the demands of the new settlers, the British government in 1784 established a new colony, New Brunswick, with its capital
at Fredericton on the St. John River.

Another 10,000 Loyalists travelled overland to Quebec. Some came
up the Richelieu route to the upper St. Lawrence and Lake Ontario while
others pushed farther west into the Niagara peninsula. Since many of these
people had fought for the British in the revolutionary war, or were land-
hungry frontier farmers from the back country, they were much better
equipped to cope with the rigours of Canadian pioneer life than their
counterparts in the Maritimes, many of whom were drawn from seaport
towns where they had enjoyed wealth and position. These hardy Loyalist
settlers were the vanguard of an army of immigrants from the United
States that was to continue its northward trek long after the last of the
Loyalists had trickled across the border.

As in Nova Scotia, the large-scale English-speaking immigration into
Quebec dictated changes in the organization of the colony. The proportion of French to British and the accompanying political situation which
had led to the Quebec Act were now radically altered. The English-
speaking Loyalists strenuously objected to living under French laws which
restricted land tenure to a seigniorial system. Nor were they willing to
accept a form of government which lacked representative institutions.
While the Loyalists had refused to sever their ties with Britain, they were
generally just as firm in their belief in the virtues of representative government as were the American rebels. As a Loyalist petition in 1785 stated:
"They were born British subjects, and have ever been accustomed to the
government and laws of England."

In demanding a new form of government for the British colony on
the St. Lawrence and the Great Lakes the Loyalists had the support of
the British merchants in Montreal, who had never been satisfied with the
settlement of 1774. In 1791, the British government acceded to their
demands and passed the Constitutional Act which replaced the old province
of Quebec with the province of Upper Canada in the west and Lower
Canada in the east. In the western, English-speaking province, the new
Act established British laws and institutions. Lower Canada, with its
French-speaking and Roman Catholic majority, retained French civil law,
seigniorial tenure and the rights granted to the Roman Catholic Church
in 1774. The major innovation of the Constitutional Act was the introduction of elective assemblies in both Upper and Lower Canada.

In the western colony, the Loyalists had long demanded an assembly.
In Lower Canada, however, the demand had come mainly from the British

merchants and settlers; the French-speaking inhabitants were initially uninterested in the idea and some British officials were openly opposed. One British official in Lower Canada wrote: "The Canadian Habitants are I really believe an industrious, peaceable, and well-disposed people; but they are, from their want of education and extreme simplicity, liable to be misled by designing and artful men, and were they once made fully sensible of their own independence, the worst consequences might ensue." However, the British government ignored these objections and granted each colony an elective assembly. The assembly was the weakest part of the colonial government as its decisions were subject to the veto of an appointed upper house, the legislative council, and an appointed governor and executive council. Nevertheless, the assemblies soon became the centres of political activity and controversy in the colonies.

Carleton's "catastrophe shocking to think of," the American Revolution, drastically altered the character of Quebec. In the thirteen colonies, an independent republic had replaced the first British Empire in North America. North America was permanently divided. All that remained to Britain were the four provinces that had been formed out of the territory of the old French Empire. But the coming of the Loyalists had immensely strengthened the loyalty of these territories to Britain. In fact, the Loyalists placed their attachment to the Empire above everything else, and often expected others to do the same. This loyalism with its emotional attachment to the Empire and its strong anti-American flavour became one of the chief characteristics of English-speaking Canada in its formative years. But this characteristic was complicated by the bi-cultural nature of Canada which became increasingly evident after the American Revolution. It remained to be seen whether these two elements could be combined successfully in what was left of Britain's Empire in North America.

CHAPTER 20

The Growth and Defence of British North America

The political settlement and geographical division of 1791 marked a fresh beginning for British North America and the British Empire. But the success of the venture depended heavily upon the growth of population, especially in Upper Canada, and the development of a sound economy. Without a growing population the colonies would remain weak, economically stagnant and in danger of absorption into the thriving American republic. The unfriendly relations between Great Britain and the United States which bred the War of 1812 were a threatening reminder that the struggle for the survival of British North America was by no means over.

1. PEOPLING THE NEW BRITISH AMERICAN COLONIES

Each colony developed in its own way in the generation after 1791. Land-hungry settlers moved into the fertile lands of the Canadas but largely by-passed the Maritimes where much of the terrain and soil were not well suited to agriculture. Nevertheless, a few hundred settlers from Scotland arrived in the Maritimes during these years. Under the direction of the Scottish philanthropist, Lord Selkirk, a group of eight hundred was settled in Prince Edward Island in 1803. By 1812, the population of the Atlantic colonies was still less than 100,000; but the population of these colonies formed a tightly-knit little society. Except in Prince Edward Island, the major industries were fishing and lumbering, neither of which supports large populations. While Nova Scotians had long been engaged in fishing, their craftsmen soon became excellent builders, not only of fishing-boats, but of large sailing-ships for the oceanic trade. The great Bluenose schooners that sailed out of Halifax for Atlantic and Pacific ports were among the finest ships in the world during the age of sail. The people of forest-covered New Brunswick depended chiefly on the lumbering trade for their livelihood. Every year great rafts of white pine logs floated down the St. John and Miramichi rivers to the coast.

This is a view of Halifax in the last quarter of the eighteenth century, showing the harbour which provided such a perfect landing place for the British fleet during the wars against the American colonies and the French. Manpower for the British ships was often recruited in the town and one advertisement, which appeared in the Nova Scotia **Gazette** in 1779 read: "Seamen and able-bodied landsmen who wish to acquire riches and honour are invited to repair on board the **Revenge**, private ship of war, now lying in Halifax Harbour, mounting 30 carriage guns, with cohorns, swivels, etc., bound for a cruise to the southward for four months, vs. the French and all H. M. enemies, and then to return to this Harbour."

New Brunswick lumber fed the shipbuilding industry and was sold to Great Britain and the West Indies. During the Napoleonic Wars, when Britain was cut off from her European sources of supply, the Royal Navy relied on New Brunswick for the masts and spars of its warships.

The Maritime colonies traded extensively with the West Indian islands. Lumber and dried codfish were carried to the Caribbean where they were exchanged for sugar, molasses and rum. The Maritimes hoped to take the place of New England in the old triangular trade, among North America, the West Indies and Britain, which had existed before the American Revolution. Unhappily, New Brunswick and Nova Scotia were unable to produce enough foodstuffs to feed the sugar plantations, and despite the Navigation Acts which protected Empire markets for goods produced within the Empire, the Maritimes were unable to overcome American competition. Yet the system of imperial preferences, or mercantilism, was a fundamental source of strength for all the North American colonies. It gave the colonies a protected market for their products, and the Napoleonic Wars gave the colonial economies another push forward by forcing Britain to turn to North America for food, shipbuilding materials and ships.

In the Canadas, rapid economic progress was accompanied by a spectacular increase in population. A steady stream of pioneers poured across the Canadian-American frontier in search of fertile new lands. Some of the first settlers came from Vermont to farm in the Eastern Townships. But 9,000 English-speaking immigrants did little to alter the essentially

French character of Lower Canada, for the French-Canadian population was quickly multiplying as a result of one of the highest birth rates in recorded history and a considerably reduced death rate. By 1812, there were about 330,000 people in Lower Canada, nearly three times the number in the same area at the close of the American Revolution.

While most French Canadians lived on small farms and produced food for the home market, the dynamic centre of British North America was Montreal, which, by 1812, had a population of 30,000. Here was the focal point of the fur trade, lumbering and finance in Canada. The men who controlled the economy were almost all English-speaking, for the French Canadians had been displaced by the English-speaking merchants during and immediately following the conquest and were destined thereafter to hold only secondary positions in the economic life of the colony.

Even more striking changes took place in Upper Canada. In 1791 its population was only 14,000, but twenty years later 90,000 settlers were clearing land and sowing crops. Most of these new Canadians came from the United States, restlessly following the frontier of free land regardless of political boundaries. Much of the credit for the foundation of Upper Canada belongs to John Graves Simcoe, the first Governor of the colony. Simcoe was a soldier, and a man of intense loyalty to the British connection. His main aim as Governor of Upper Canada was to develop a society that would be the "image and transcript" of Great Britain. He had grandiose but impractical plans for the development of the colony, plans which included the manufacture of hats, mining schemes, meat curing and shipbuilding. "A thousand details crowd upon my mind," he once wrote enthusiastically, "that would be productive of the most salutary consequences." While many of his projects failed, he never lost sight of the prime necessity of the colony: population. If Upper Canada were to become the "Bulwark of the British Empire in North America" as he hoped, it needed a vast increase in settlement. Since settlers from Great Britain were slow in coming, he turned his attention to attracting farmers from the United States. He was fearful that the Americans might bring republican sentiments with them, but he hoped that generous land grants would convert "the repentant sinners of the revolted colonies." These "late loyalists" represented a new element in the Upper Canadian colony, and one which the original Loyalists did not readily accept. As relations between Britain and the United States worsened in the years before the War of 1812, the American immigrants were often, and usually unjustly, suspected of disloyalty.

Nevertheless, it was these settlers who carved a rough, pioneering society out of the forests of Upper Canada. Soon dwellings and prosperous farms stretched from Kingston to the Bay of Quinte, up to the Ottawa valley and along the fertile Niagara peninsula. In the 1790's German and French-speaking settlers began moving from the United States into Markham and Waterloo townships and Scottish settlers, sponsored by Lord Selkirk, established themselves around Lake St. Clair.

The wife of the Lieutenant-Governor of Upper Canada, John Graves Simcoe, did this sketch of Kingston in the 1790's. Mrs. Simcoe's diary is a major source of information about early Upper Canada, while her sketches and water colours provide important visual representations of the colony in the formative years.

It was in the area around York on Lake Ontario that the most important developments were evident. When Governor Simcoe arrived in Upper Canada in 1792, the seat of government of the colony was at Newark, the modern Niagara-on-the-Lake. But since this settlement was too exposed to American attack, the capital was moved to York in 1793, although Simcoe himself preferred the inland site of London. While Kingston remained the largest urban centre until the 1820's, the choice of York as capital encouraged a gradual shift of population to the south central section of the colony. For the first few years the military garrison of two hundred men was the largest single element in the population of York. Not until 1797 were facilities ready for the first meeting of the government at the new capital.

Once York became the capital, roads and settlement began to branch out from it. Simcoe formed a military corps, the Queen's Rangers, whose main purpose was to clear land and construct roads such as Yonge Street, which linked York and Lake Simcoe, and Dundas Street, which ran across the Niagara peninsula from Burlington to the Thames River. By 1800 a road from York to Kingston joined an already completed road to Montreal. These roads had a dual purpose: to permit mobility of troops and to open up new lands for settlement.

A generous system of land grants was practised in Upper Canada. Loyalists and those later arrivals, who were often called "late loyalists," could obtain lands ranging in size from one hundred to a thousand or more acres in return for an oath of allegiance to the Crown. The system of course was open to abuses. Speculators frequently acquired large tracts of the most fertile lands, thus forcing settlers to move out to the frontier. But occasionally, men who acquired large holdings worked energetically to fill them with settlers. One of the most remarkable of the early settlements was organized by the eccentric Colonel Thomas Talbot. After serving as Simcoe's secretary and then in the Napoleonic Wars, Talbot retired from the army and returned to Upper Canada. In 1803 he obtained a land grant of 5,000 acres on the shore of Lake Erie. For each settler he placed on a farm, Talbot received another two hundred acres of land. Before 1850 Talbot's holdings had increased to 65,000 acres. Here, near the present-day St. Thomas, Colonel Talbot ruled his domain like a feudal baron, spurring his tenants on, entertaining in a gay fashion, and loudly denouncing Methodists because, he claimed, no total abstainer could be loyal to the Crown.

Socially, Upper Canada remained backward and underdeveloped. The provincial capital at York was slow to emerge from the position of a muddy little village to an important centre. One inhabitant wrote in 1801: "York contains about 100 houses and upwards and where about 7 years ago there was an entire wilderness there are several very handsome buildings two in particular the Chief Justice's house and Mr. Jarvis secy of the province. . . ." Social and intellectual life in the province was also slow to develop. In 1799 one foreign observer wrote: "Throughout all of Canada, there is no public library, except in Quebec and this is small and consists mostly of

The new capital of Upper Canada, the port of York on the Bay of Toronto, Lake Ontario, was still a very modest settlement in 1804.

French books." Yet at social affairs such as dinners, receptions and balls, the local population could turn itself out colourfully, though the fashion, at least according to one commentator on Kingston society in 1804, seemed somewhat out of date. He wrote:

> Among the ladies, that is, the young ones, the present exaggerated Grecian costume was further exaggerated, with the addition of cropped heads, the waists between the shoulders. Some of their elders . . . rejoicing in imitating court dresses of a half century before; long waisted, stiff silk gowns, with lace . . . aprons; high-heeled shoes and their powdered hair rolled over huge toupées stuffed with wool. . . . Some of the younger men were cropped, and wore no powder; some of the leaders wore bob-wigs, most of them had their hair tied in long queues.

But styles and fashions were less important to Upper Canadians at the beginning of the nineteenth century than roads and schools and churches.

While some of the towns gradually acquired schools, the farming communities usually depended on the travelling schoolmaster whose arrival was frequently as uncertain as his qualifications. Nor was life easy for the schoolmaster. One traveller noted that she had passed "some school houses built by the wayside; of these, several were shut up for want of schoolmasters: and who that could earn a subsistence in any other way would be a schoolmaster in the wilds of Upper Canada? Ill fed, ill clothed, ill paid—or not paid at all—boarded at the houses of the different farmers in turn."

The religious life of the colony was, perhaps, better developed. While Presbyterians and Baptists were strong on the frontier, it was the travelling Methodist ministers who attracted the widest following. Many of these preachers followed the settlers north from the United States and were prepared to carry their message into the roughest parts of the colony. Typical of these men was Nathan Bangs, who was born in Connecticut, and by 1801 had become a Methodist circuit rider in Canada. He recalled later:

> I believe that I was the first Methodist preacher that ever attempted to preach in Little York . . . and I preached in a miserable half-finished house, on a week-evening, to a few people . . . and slept on the floor under a blanket. This was in 1801. I was then attempting to form a circuit on Yonge Street . . . and I was induced to make a trial in this new little village, the settlers of which were as thoughtless and wicked as the Canaanites of old.

Jealous of the success of the Methodists, other religious groups often condemned the circuit riders as American sympathizers, a dangerous charge during the early years of the nineteenth century when relations with the United States were very unsettled.

2. FRICTION ON THE BORDER
AND THE WAR OF 1812

The peace settlement of 1783, which gave the thirteen colonies their independence, did not completely satisfy either the Americans or the British. British merchants in Canada refused to leave the fur-trading posts that lay south of the Great Lakes, on the pretext that the Americans had failed to compensate the Loyalists for property losses. After much friction the Americans sent John Jay to London in 1794 to negotiate a settlement. The British finally agreed to surrender the disputed posts, especially as the Americans had driven the Indians farther west and the eastern posts were no longer very important as centres for the fur trade.

Despite this agreement, border problems remained an unsettling influence in Anglo-American relations. British traders continued to work closely with the Indians in the American west. American settlers who suffered from Indian raids believed that the British traders encouraged the Indians and knew that the Indians got guns and ammunition from British traders in return for furs. Moreover, they suspected that the British were encouraging the Indian leader, Tecumseh, to resist American authority and to attack unguarded American settlements in the Ohio valley. Despite Tecumseh's defeat at the battle of Tippecanoe in 1811, the Americans remained convinced that only the defeat of the British in North America could satisfactorily end the Indian menace. This conviction, combined with widespread anger over the question of maritime rights, led President Madison to declare war on Britain in June 1812.

Obviously the war was a most serious threat to Canada, since it was only in North America that the United States could hope to defeat Britain. The population of the United States in 1812 was about ten times that of Canada, while Britain's European military engagements greatly restricted her ability to defend her North American colony. Since there were fewer than 5,000 British regular troops in Canada when the war broke out, it was fortunate for Canada that President Madison was never able to get his country united behind him in the war. Moreover, American conduct of the war was hopelessly ineffective.

The major battles in the War of 1812 were fought on a wide front in Upper Canada, the area most open to attack and most coveted by the "war hawks" in the western United States. As they had in 1775, the invading American armies expected that the local population in Canada would welcome this opportunity to free themselves from British rule. General Hull, who crossed the river from Detroit into Canada, issued a long manifesto to the Canadians, outlining the American view on the causes of the war and promising respect for Canadians and their property. "The United States offers you peace, liberty and security," the manifesto concluded. "Your choice lies between these and war, slavery and destruction."

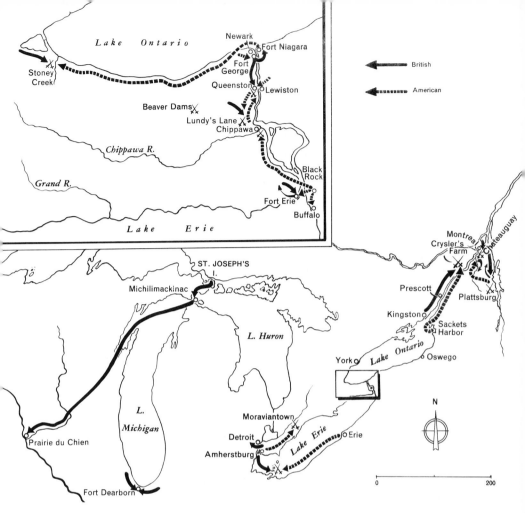

The War of 1812

Because of the large number of American settlers in the colony, there was good reason to fear that Hull's manifesto might receive a sympathetic response in Upper Canada. In July, 1812, General Brock, the commander of the British army, wrote from Fort George: "There can be no doubt that a large portion of the population of this neighbourhood are sincere in their professions to defend the country, but it appears likewise evident to me that the greater part are either indifferent to what is passing, or so completely American as to rejoice in the prospects of a change in Governments." The defection of two members of the Upper Canadian legislature to the Americans and the real or suspected disloyalty of many American settlers caused the government serious concern. To illustrate vividly the price of treason, the authorities ordered the "Bloody Assize" at Ancaster in 1814. Fifteen men were found guilty of treason and eight of these plunged to their death from the gallows on Burlington Heights.

More important than open treason was the apparent lack of popular enthusiasm for the war. In November 1812 Brock wrote: "My situation is most critical, not from anything the enemy can do, but from the disposition of the people—The population, believe me, is essentially bad—A full belief possesses them that all this Province must inevitably succumb." Brock realized that a defensive war would not save Upper Canada. An immediate victory was necessary to shake the people from their apathy. Attack was the obvious tactic for Brock to follow, and he sent his armies into the American territory. The British forces took Michilimackinac and their Indian allies captured Fort Dearborn, while a small army under Brock boldly crossed the St. Clair River and captured Detroit. Brock then hastily returned to defend the Niagara peninsula where American troops were massed for an attack on Queenston Heights. The attack was repulsed in October, but the gallant Brock gave his life in the Battle of Queenston Heights. Yet his brief period of command had done much to determine the final outcome of the war, for he had prevented the Americans from gaining the quick victory which they had anticipated and his decisive leadership had restored confidence among the people.

In 1813 the Americans advanced as far as Stoney Creek on the Niagara peninsula and Moraviantown in the west, where Tecumseh was killed, before they were stopped or defeated. They gained control of Lake Ontario and captured and burned the muddy capital of York. In 1814 they once again marched across the peninsula, before being routed at Lundy's Lane.

While the major campaigns in the war were in Upper Canada, Lower Canada was not entirely spared. Here, too, the political situation was dangerous and the loyalty of the French Canadians doubted. For four years before the war the colony had been administered by a governor who was bitterly antagonistic to the French Canadians. Sir James Craig was a hot-tempered military man who believed that the French Canadians were disloyal and should be assimilated. He tried to rule with an iron hand, fighting bitterly with the leaders of the French party in the assembly, and jailing the editors of the popular French-Canadian newspaper, *Le Canadien.*

It was fortunate, therefore, that just before the war with the United States Craig was replaced by Sir George Prevost, who adopted a conciliatory attitude towards the French Canadians. Soon after his arrival Prevost reported that "several circumstances have occurred since I have assumed the administration of the Government to induce me to believe that there are persons disaffected towards His Majesty's Government amongst the Canadians as Agents of France and America." Prevost set about removing the causes of discontent by co-operating with the French Canadians, establishing better relations with the Roman Catholic Church than had existed during Craig's régime, and appointing French Canadians to the army and civil service. Thus, when the war began, Prevost was able to rely upon the services of the local militia. Under a French-Canadian com-

An artist named Akerman sketched this view of Fort George in Upper Canada as it appeared in 1812. Brock believed that the major American assault on the Niagara front would be against Fort George not Queenston and looked upon the first American attempt to cross the river at Queenston as a feint. But on the night of October 13, the firing was so heavy up the river that he realized his error. Ordering all troops to follow him, he mounted his horse and raced to Queenston to find that the Americans had taken the heights and the British battery at the top. In a foolhardy manner he charged up the hill—an easy target for American marksmen. Later on General Sheaffe, who had followed him to Queenston, reorganized the British forces and with the aid of the Indians moved carefully through the woods to attack the Americans on the heights. Having suffered heavy casualties, lacking reinforcements because the New York state militia refused to cross the river and fight on foreign soil, and terrified by the prospect of being scalped, the Americans surrendered. The battle ended the first critical phase of the Niagara campaign.

mander, Lieutenant-Colonel Charles de Salaberry, a French-Canadian regiment fought bravely throughout the war. In 1812 an attempted American attack on Montreal was easily repulsed. The next year de Salaberry's troops played an important part in the defeat of the American army at Chateauguay, and two weeks later the Americans suffered a second defeat at Crysler's Farm.

In the spring of 1814 Napoleon's defeat released some battle-tested British veterans for service in North America. The British burned Washington in retaliation for the burning of York. In the far West fur-traders, Indians and a few British troops captured Prairie du Chien, while the British successfully defended Michilimackinac, and Prevost led a powerful army along Lake Champlain as far as Plattsburg before he was forced to withdraw.

The Maritime colonies suffered none of the disadvantages of the war that were felt in the Canadas. No American invasion took place there. The British navy easily guaranteed the security of the colonies on the eastern seaboard. Here the war was limited to privateering, an activity in which many Nova Scotian captains proved themselves masters. Moreover, shipbuilders and merchants in the Maritimes seized the opportunity presented by the British blockade against American shipping to move into former American markets and capture some of the carrying trade. A period of prosperity thus marked the years of the War of 1812 in Nova Scotia and New Brunswick.

By the end of 1814 the war had dragged to a conclusion. Clearly, neither side had won. But even a draw was an impressive achievement for Canada, for despite the odds against her, Canadian independence from the United States had been preserved.

The peace settlement of 1814, the Treaty of Ghent, ended the fighting, reaffirmed the pre-war boundaries, and laid the basis for the settlement of the western boundary between the two countries. Three years later, in 1817, the Rush-Bagot Treaty between Britain and the United States prohibited large-scale naval armaments on the Great Lakes, and a Convention in the following year accepted the forty-ninth parallel of latitude as the boundary between Canada and the United States in the territory between the Lake of the Woods and the Rocky Mountains. The Convention of 1818 temporarily settled the troublesome problem of American fishing rights on the east coast of British North America, by permitting American fishermen to enter harbours for supplies, though denying them the right to fish within three miles of shore.

The peace settlement did not dispose of all the disputes between the two North American neighbours, but it removed some of the major sources of friction. For Canada, the war gave proof of the country's will to exist apart from the United States. Both English- and French-speaking Canadians had fought to resist the American invaders, and the two groups were drawn together in a common bond of anti-Americanism. This was the sentiment which underlay the remark of Egerton Ryerson, the great Upper Canadian Methodist leader, who wrote: "British and Canadian loyalty, patriotism and courage, defeated their [the Americans'] dark designs against the liberty of mankind." Once more, the loyalism that characterized early Canada was strengthened by the events of the years 1812-15. The men who had proven their loyalty were among the men who were going to rise to positions of power and influence in the colony in the post-war years. They were often men who were prepared to use their reputation for loyalty as a political weapon, branding their critics as sympathetic to the Americans and promoters of treason.

CHAPTER 21

Post-war Expansion

The successful defence of British North America in the War of 1812 brightened the future prospects of the British North American colonies. Moreover, the war once more confirmed the direction that the economic and commercial development of the area would follow. The Treaty of Versailles in 1783 had cut Canada off from the rich lands of the Ohio valley. While fur-trading posts had been retained in the area south of the Great Lakes for more than ten years after that, the merchants of Montreal were beginning to look more carefully at the lands north of the Lakes. Then Jay's Treaty in 1794 and, more emphatically still, the hostilities of 1812-14 made it clear that the United States had no intention of allowing British and Canadian traders to ply their trade south of the Lakes. It was to the west and north that the merchants of Canada, who were mostly based in Montreal, now had to look.

1. THE STRUGGLE FOR THE NORTHWEST

As early as 1778 a semi-illiterate American trader, Peter Pond, had crossed the prairies as French explorers had done before him and pushed north of Lake Athabaska towards Great Slave Lake. Soon his path was being pursued, and new trails blazed, by a number of trader-explorers. In 1789 Alexander Mackenzie, following Pond's lead, discovered the great river, later called the Mackenzie, which he followed to the shores of the Arctic Ocean. In 1793 Mackenzie and a small party fought turbulent waters and hazardous cliffs to become the first Europeans to reach the Pacific by the overland route. He wrote in his diary: "I now mixed up some vermilion in melted grease, and inscribed in large characters, on the south-east face of the rock on which we had slept last night, this brief memorial—'Alexander Mackenzie, from Canada, by land, the twenty-second of July, one thousand seven hundred and ninety-three'." After Mackenzie's important journey, a host of adventurous explorers fol-

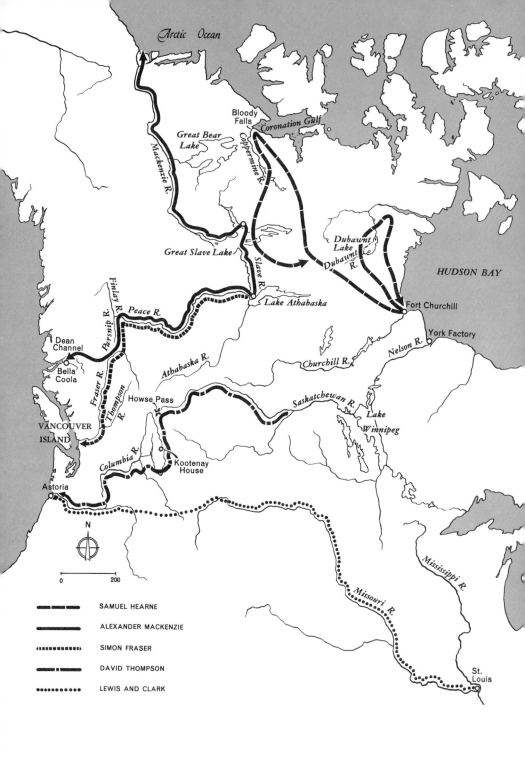

Arctic Ocean

Bloody
Falls
Coronation Gulf

*Great Bear
Lake*

Coppermine R.

Mackenzie R.

*Dubawnt
Lake*

*Dubawnt
R.*

HUDSON BAY

Great Slave Lake

Slave R.

Lake Athabaska

Fort Churchill

Finlay R.

Peace R.

Parsnip R.

Dean
Channel

Bella
Coola

Athabaska R.

Fraser R.

Churchill R.

Nelson R.

York Factory

*Thompson
R.*

Howse Pass

Saskatchewan R.

Lake
Winnipeg

VANCOUVER
ISLAND

Columbia R.

Kootenay
House

Astoria

N

0   200

Mississippi R.

Missouri R.

St.
Louis

▬ ▬ ▬ ▬   SAMUEL HEARNE

▬▬▬▬▬   ALEXANDER MACKENZIE

▬▬▬▬▬   SIMON FRASER

▬ ▬■▬ ▬   DAVID THOMPSON

●●●●●●●●●   LEWIS AND CLARK

Western Expansion

The broad-bottomed canoe provided the perfect means of transportation for fur traders of the North West Company. It was fast, light, and capable of carrying heavy loads of men and furs. A further advantage was noted by a Montreal merchant when he wrote: "The inland navigation from Montreal, by which the North West trade is carried on, is perhaps the most extensive in the known world, but is only practicable for canoes on account of the great number of carrying places . . . upwards of ninety from Montreal to Lake du Bois, and many of them long ones."

lowed his path, with men like David Thompson and Simon Fraser attaching their names to two of the great rivers of the Rockies.

As the fur trade moved west, the Montreal merchants began to worry seriously about the pressure of competition from the Hudson's Bay Company. The advantages of the Hudson's Bay Company in this competition resulted from unified organization, large financial resources, and, most important, access to cheap transportation by water through the Hudson Bay. Since the Montreal merchants could do little to reduce the growing cost of transporting furs overland from points farther and farther west to Montreal, they concluded that competition among themselves must be removed. In this way they would be able to pool their resources for a combined struggle against the powerful merchants stationed on Hudson Bay. In 1788 the major Montreal groups banded together to form the North West Company. In 1804 a further step towards a completely unified organization was taken when the last substantial group of independent Montreal traders, the XY Company, was brought into the North West partnership. But in the long run, this union of forces and the enterprising spirit of the Nor'Westers was not enough to overcome the superior financial resources and cheaper transportation route of the Hudson's Bay Company.

The rivalry between the two corporations often broke into what was little less than open warfare. A major crisis arose in 1812 when Lord Selkirk, who owned much of the Hudson's Bay Company, decided to plant a colony of Scottish settlers in the Red River valley near the present site of Winnipeg. The colony was to provide food and serve as a base for the operation of the Bay men throughout the West. To the Nor'Westers the Red River settlement was a threat to their survival, for it lay across their chain of trading-posts which stretched from the Great Lakes to the Rockies. The Montrealers stirred up their half-breed allies against the colonists and, after a series of provocations which included the destruction of the crops at Red River, the colonists decided to take measures to defend themselves. But the colony was poorly armed and, when open warfare broke out at Seven Oaks in 1816, twenty-one colonists were killed and the colony fell into the hands of the North West Company.

Lord Selkirk was not prepared to give up without a fight. Bent on revenge, he hired a group of Swiss mercenaries who seized the main North West post at Fort William. This action was quite illegal, but it made Selkirk's determination to open up the Canadian West to settlement very clear to the fur-traders. Once more settlers were brought back to Red River to begin the arduous task of carving out a livelihood, that would be more permanent and secure than the nomadic existence of the fur-traders or trappers.

The massacre at Seven Oaks with its aftermath was only one sign that the Nor'Westers were fighting a losing battle against the powerful Hudson's Bay Company. The older company was too strong, too experienced, too firmly entrenched and too well financed to be defeated by the Montreal men. As the arrival of traders and settlers pushed the fur-bearing animals farther north and west, the costs of the North West Company increased and profits fell. By 1821 the battle was over. In that year the two companies arranged a merger which, while certainly giving the Montreal merchants a fair settlement, marked the victory of the Bay over the River. For many years to follow, the connection between the St. Lawrence and the West, which had begun in the days of La Vérendrye, was broken.

2. THE NEW ECONOMY

With the fur trade dying, Canada had to find something to serve as the basis for a new and profitable commercial empire. The economy that developed from this search was in many ways the result of a sagging economy and heavy unemployment in Great Britain following the Napoleonic Wars, which forced hundreds of thousands of Britons to emigrate. Many of these came to Canada. To some the long sea voyage to their new homes was a nightmare:

> Before the emigrant has been a week at sea he is an altered man. How can it be otherwise? Hundreds of poor people, men, women, and children of all ages, from the drivelling idiot of ninety to the babe just born, huddled together without light, without air . . . sick in body, dispirited in heart . . . without food or medicine . . . dying without the voice of spiritual consolation, and buried in the deep without the rites of the Church.

The above sketch shows a work party clearing the land in October 1834, for the establishment of Stanley, New Brunswick. (The surveying party for the New Brunswick and Nova Scotia Land Company had arrived in July). To the left in the picture is the Nashwick River, with the frame of a mill visible. Toward the right is an almost completed tavern, apparently considered of primary importance to the pioneers. In the extreme right a surveying party is preparing to leave and a team of oxen is bringing up supplies. By the end of the year the new town was sprinkled with modest homes.

But once ashore, the immigrants settled down to the work of clearing new farms and planting crops. In the 1820's the population grew and the area of land under cultivation expanded rapidly. One successful method of promoting settlement was the granting of large areas of land to individuals or companies. Talbot's tract was an early successful example of this practice. Another such venture was the Canada Land Company, established in 1826, which was largely responsible for settling the areas around Goderich and Guelph. A similar company in the Eastern Townships of Lower Canada, the British American Land Company, held more than 800,000 acres of land. Organizations like the Canada Land Company and the British American Land Company not only brought out settlers, they also provided such local necessities as saw mills, grist mills, brick kilns, school-houses and roads. Such developments eased the lot of the settlers and bettered their chances of success in their new occupations.

Despite the large inflow of immigrants from Britain, and the work of the land companies, there remained several serious obstacles to settlement in Canada. Some settlers expected to make a quick, easy fortune in the new land. When they found that this dream could not be realized, many moved on to the apparently greener pastures of the United States. One reason for disillusionment was the land-grant system. In Lower Canada, where the seigniorial system was still in use, most of the large seigniories had passed into the hands of land speculators, and it was difficult for immigrants without capital to acquire good lands. Sometimes settlers found that the lands they were offered were nearly useless. The experience of one unfortunate settler was described by a traveller who met "a Scotch family returning from Canada to Columbus, Ohio, who had been decoyed away . . . with the offer of a lot of *land* for nothing—but which was found to be a complete *swamp*. When they got there the wife and children were nearly tormented to death with mosquitoes—no roads to their shanty —no friends within a considerable distance—nothing to be bought, and many other miseries we have not repeated."

In Upper Canada the orderly progress of settlement was complicated by a confusion of land policies which gave free lands to Loyalists and militia veterans of the War of 1812, and thus excluded later immigrants from some of the best lands. Moreover, large tracts, both of Crown lands and clergy reserves (lands set aside for the use of the Protestant Church), lay uncultivated, while other tracts were held by businessmen, and even public officials, for speculative purposes. As late as 1838 a British investigator reported that, although nearly all the available land had been granted, "a very small proportion, perhaps less than a tenth, of the lands thus granted, had been occupied by settlers, and much less reclaimed and cultivated."

Much of the work of clearing and building bush farms in the 1830's was done by group effort, or working bees. Susannah Moodie, who settled in the Peterborough area, doubted the value of such pioneer bees: "A logging bee followed the burning of the fallow as a matter of course. In the bush, where hands are few and labour commands an enormous rate of wages, these gatherings are considered indispensable and much has been written in their praise, but to me they present the most disgusting picture of a bush life. They are noisy, riotous, drunken meetings, often terminating in violent quarrels, sometimes even in bloodshed." Yet Mrs. Moodie also realized that they were an important social event: "People in the woods have a craze for giving and going to bees, and run to them with as much eagerness as a peasant runs to a racecourse or a fair, plenty of strong drink and excitement making the chief attraction of the bee."

This rudimentary school, sketched in 1845 in Adelaide Township, was characteristic of the pioneer conditions in the outlying sections of Upper Canada throughout the first part of the nineteenth century. It was these circumstances that caused discontent among settlers who believed that their needs were not properly attended to by the governing authorities. "The lack of schools and other privileges . . . was felt most keenly . . . as their children were of an age to require both schooling and society," one observer whose family had come to Upper Canada from New England maintained. Another pioneer wrote bitterly: "My children are without education and must remain so unless I shift my quarters. . . . The aristocracy dread the common people getting an education, well knowing that knowledge is power, and that power always destroys Toryism."

By 1838 Upper Canada had a population of nearly 400,000. But population growth alone was not enough to produce a contented, flourishing society. The land system, inadequate provision of roads and schools, trade slumps such as the one which hit the colony in the mid-thirties, and, not least of all, the bleak contrast between Canadian backwardness and the progress of the neighbouring United States multiplied the discontent in the colony. In 1829 a petition sent from Upper Canada to the British parliament declared: "The people of Upper Canada are in the view of the United States, in daily intercourse with its citizens; they are of the same race of men, speaking one language; they see the people on their adjoining frontier thriving and contented under domestic governments instituted for the common benefit and protection. . . ." The burden of this petition was that something was seriously wrong with the governmental system of the British colonies. Others thought that the people themselves

A letter to the Commissioners of the Canada Company, dated March 1, 1830, enclosed copies of the contracts for two roads from Goderich to Wilmot and London: "For the two roads the outlay this year will be in cash about £670 and land £1340. One article in these agreements may require some explanation to the Court—'sowing the roads with grass seed.' This although expensive at the first is of very great consequence and in the end proves an important saving. By this means fodder is provided for the cattle during the winter which prevents them wandering into the woods and in the spring and summer as they eat the grass they at the same time destroy the young wood which will always spring up in a new clearance when there is not sufficient travelling to prevent it and this is certainly not likely to be the case on these roads for some time. When either this precaution or others not less expensive and far less beneficial are not taken, the road in a year or two becomes choked with young trees. The one cut through the clergy reserves by Mr. Robinson's between the township of Beverley and Guelph is an exemplification of this. Although it was only cut in the year 1828 it has been absolutely impassable for the last eight months, the wood being upwards of 7 or 8 feet high."

showed a lack of industry and therefore lagged behind their energetic American neighbours. One of the most vocal and witty exponents of this view was Thomas Chandler Haliburton of Nova Scotia. Haliburton's criticisms were expressed through his brilliant literary creation, Sam Slick, the "gen-u-ine Yankee" clockmaker and pedlar, who was constantly drawing an unfavourable contrast between American progress and Canadian backwardness.

Yet, despite difficulties and criticism, conditions were not as bad as they were often painted. The basis at least of a sound economy was being laid. The centre of that economy was Montreal, the traditional capital of Canadian commercial life. After the Hudson's Bay Company had defeated the Montreal merchants in the struggle for the fur trade in the northwest, Montreal businessmen turned their minds and their financial resources to new plans for commercial development. These plans were based on the rivers and lakes of the Canadian Shield, for this natural transportation system still provided the cheapest means of carrying the products of the North American hinterland to Europe. By the 1830's new staples, such as timber and grain, were replacing furs as the main exports to European markets. As the pioneers of the Canadas cleared their new lands, they had lumber and potash to sell abroad. Later the grain from their new farmlands was available for export. In return the settlers imported such European manufactured products as farm implements and clothing. Here, then, was the opportunity to create a new and prosperous trade to take the place of the fur trade.

It was not only the hinterland of Canada that the Montreal merchants were anxious to serve. The Ohio valley and the growing American West represented even more lucrative fields of activity. The Montreal merchants dreamed of nothing less than making their city the economic capital of a North American commercial empire, the focal point in the trade between inland North America and Europe.

Two conditions had to be met if the Montreal merchants were to succeed in this new venture. First, the natural water-ways they used would have to be made more efficient at critical points by the building of roads and canals, for once more, as in the early days of the fur trade, Montreal and New York became keen rivals for control of the North American products that could be sold profitably on the international market. Already, in 1825, New York merchants had completed the Erie Canal linking Buffalo on Lake Erie with the port of New York. If Canadian merchants were to meet the threat of this cheap transportation system, they too needed an efficient canal system. The first improvement in the Canadian water-ways system was the short canal at the Lachine rapids upstream from the Island of Montreal. The Lachine Canal was built largely with public funds provided by the government of Lower Canada, and it was opened to traffic in the autumn of 1824. But this small canal barely touched the essential problem of tying the St. Lawrence system to the rich grain lands in the interior. This latter task was to be fulfilled by the Welland Canal. Plans for such a canal had already begun in 1818 under the direction of an energetic St. Catharines businessman, William Hamilton Merritt; but Merritt's plan was as expensive as it was ambitious, and it was not until 1824 that he had collected sufficient funds to make it practical to have his company chartered. Before the canal was completed in 1829, heavy government assistance was required, and in the end the canal became the property of the government. Once it was opened, traffic could move from Lake Erie to the Welland River, then through the Niagara River to Lake Ontario. The first condition for the new empire had been fulfilled, but it had not solved all of the merchants' problems.

The second condition essential for success was that the Montrealers should enjoy a protected market in Great Britain and free access to the farming communities in the United States. The protected British market gave the Montreal merchants an important advantage over their American competitors. Since Britain classified United States wheat that was shipped through or milled in Canada as Imperial produce, Canadian merchants could ship both American and Canadian grain to Britain without paying the heavy duties faced by United States merchants. Moreover, if Canadian merchants could retain free access to the United States, they could sell the manufactured products imported from Britain in the American West.

It was a grand scheme. It was also a great gamble, for the objectives of the Canadian merchants actually ran counter to the trend of events in both the United States and Great Britain. In Britain the triumph of the industrial revolution was gradually pressing the country towards a policy of free trade, which would end the colonial preferences so important to the Canadian merchants. The United States, on the other hand, was just beginning to feel the first effects of industrialization, and American manufacturers were pressing for a tariff that would protect their home market from overseas competition, especially British. Thus, the Canadian merchants' hopes of selling British manufactured products in the United States were threatened, while at the same time the preferential tariff treatment that Canadian merchants enjoyed in Britain was gradually being whittled away. Nor were these the only obstacles in the way of the commercial community's ambitions.

A major problem for the Canadian merchants was the political division of Canada. While the St. Lawrence system was a geographic and economic unit, it was divided politically into Upper and Lower Canada by the Constitutional Act of 1791. This division made it extremely difficult to co-ordinate plans for economic development. English-speaking Montreal merchants found themselves stranded in an ocean of French Canadians who were not sympathetic to costly economic development programmes. After all, the French Canadians argued, canals and roads would have to be paid for with funds collected from the farmers of Lower

The plan to construct a canal between Kingston on Lake Ontario and Ottawa on the Rideau River grew out of a fear, after the War of 1812, that a future American attack on Canada might cut off the St. Lawrence water-way. The earliest surveys for the Rideau Canal were carried out in 1816, but it was not until 1826 that the British government authorized Colonel By and the Royal Engineers to begin construction. The canal was completed in 1834.

Canada, who would not share the profits the businessmen hoped to make. As *Le Canadien* observed in 1806: "Some people wish to create a mercantile aristocracy, the most abominable, the most pernicious of governments, equally detrimental to the authority of the Crown, to the interests of the landowners and to the liberties of the people." This quarrel between the English-speaking merchants and the spokesmen for the French-Canadian farmers was one of the root causes of the political difficulties of Lower Canada.

Even in Upper Canada, where there was no cultural division, there were deep suspicions among the pioneer farmers that the business community was little concerned about the needs of rural areas. Upper Canada was financially weak and to most struggling farmers local improvements such as roads, land surveys and schools were far more important than canals and other facilities which seemed designed only for the benefit of the commercial class. Thus, in Upper Canada, too, political discontent was closely connected with the struggle over economic policy. These disputes and struggles were made far more bitter by the form of government that had been established in the colonies in 1791.

CHAPTER 22

Reaction, Reform and Rebellion in the Canadas

Surveying the events of the American Revolution after 1783, the British government concluded that Britain had lost the thirteen colonies not because she had exercised too firm an authority over them, but because she had given them too much popular control over local governments, and allowed them too much independence from Imperial control. If the same mistake were not to be made in the remaining colonies in North America, a system of government would have to be devised that would keep any assembly firmly in check. This was the intention behind the form of government that was established under the Constitutional Act of 1791.

1. THE CONSTITUTIONAL ACT, 1791

The Constitutional Act provided for an executive consisting of a governor appointed by the British government and an executive council appointed by the governor to act as his advisers. The legislature was made up of an appointed legislative council and an elected legislative assembly. The legislative council and assembly were to be the colonial counterparts of the House of Lords and the House of Commons in the British parliamentary system. However, the elected assembly was similar to the British House of Commons in appearance only, for its legislative power was subject to a double check. Either the governor or the legislative council could refuse to approve the acts passed by the assembly. Executive control over the representative assembly was further strengthened by the fact that the members of the executive council and the members of the legislative council came to be either the same people, as in the Maritimes, or to overlap, as in the Canadas.

The executive branch of government was important not merely because of the power it was granted, but because of the men who were appointed to positions of influence. In all the colonies, the governor gathered around him men who held, and wished to protect, positions of power and influence in the community. In Upper Canada, for example, John Strachan, a leader of the Anglican Church, was a member of both the Executive Council (1818 - 1836), and of the Legislative Council (1820 - 1841). He used his position to defend the privileges of his Church against the growing criticism of other Protestant groups such as the Methodists. Another powerful member of the group was John Beverley Robinson. A former pupil of Strachan, Robinson served under Brock in 1812 and was the prosecutor at the Bloody Assize at Ancaster. After the war, he rose rapidly in the public service of Upper Canada, winning for himself the position of Attorney-General, Solicitor-General, and finally Chief Justice of the colony. Associated with these powerful men of the church and the judiciary were businessmen like William Hamilton Merritt who planned and built the Welland Canal. These men and their supporters composed a tight oligarchy, which controlled the patronage and favours that the government could dispose of as part of its offices.

In 1839, a British government report noted: "The bench, the magistracy, the high offices of the Episcopal Church, and a great part of the legal profession, are filled by the adherents of this party; by grant or purchase, they have acquired nearly the whole of the waste lands of the Province; they are all-powerful in the chartered banks." It was these men who, with the governor, ran the affairs of the colony, without regard to the wishes of the people's elected representatives. Only the governor or the British government could remove them from office.

In Upper Canada this oligarchy was known as the "Family Compact"; its counterpart in Lower Canada was the "Chateau Clique." While the governmental system under the Constitutional Act superficially resembled the parliamentary system in Britain, it was in practice very different, and it was intended to be so. As one British minister wrote: "We pretend to give Canada the same constitution as we ourselves live under. All we can do is lay the foundation for the same constitution when increased population and time shall have made the Canadians ripe to receive it."

2. THE REFORMERS AND DISCONTENT
IN THE CANADAS

The differences of interests between the appointed executive, which exercised the real power, and the assembly, which represented the people, made political quarrels in the colonies almost inevitable. In each of the colonies there gradually developed two parties that we may describe loosely as conservative and reforming. The conservative or Tory element was led by the people who held positions on the executive and legislative councils and were anxious to preserve the status quo. Their opponents were the Reformers, radicals whose objective was to gain control of the government and make it more democratic and responsive to the popular will. The Tories were quick to charge the Reformers with attempting to introduce the American form of government into Canada, and therefore with disloyalty. The Reformers answered that it was the Tories whose attitude represented a real danger to the continuance of the British connection. By their selfish refusal to yield any of their authority to the elected representatives of the people, and by their mis-management of the colony's affairs, the Tories were following a course that would eventually lead to violence as it had done in the thirteen colonies. As the rebellions of 1837 were to show, the Reformers were not entirely mistaken.

The Reformers' criticisms were directed against the colonial authorities, rather than against Great Britain. One Reformer in Upper Canada wrote in 1824: "We like American liberty well, but greatly prefer British liberty. British subjects, born in Britain, we have sworn allegiance to a constitu-tional monarchy, and we will die before we violate that oath." Certainly, most Reformers saw clearly enough that membership in the British Empire was an advantage to colonies still much in need of British investment, and of the trade preferences Britain gave to colonial products. But the Reformers wanted the government of the colonies to conform more closely to the British parliamentary system. In the British system, the elected House of Commons had far more control over the actions of their execu-tive than did the colonial assemblies.

There were also widespread grievances among the Reformers because of the privileged position of the Church of England. The Presbyterians, Methodists and Baptists deeply resented the privileges granted to the Anglicans. In Upper Canada, under the Constitutional Act, one-seventh of the land was specifically set aside for the support of a "Protestant clergy." . The Anglicans claimed the right to all the land thus reserved, and, under the vigorous leadership of Bishop Strachan, their claim was upheld. The other Protestant groups wanted to see the clergy reserves either divided among the various denominations, or sold to support edu-cation. In Egerton Ryerson, the fiery Methodist leader, these groups found a leader who was just as determined as Strachan. But despite the strong opposition of the Reformers, the struggle over what should be done with the clergy reserves was not finally resolved until the 1850's.

Yet another grievance was the fixed belief of the pioneer farmers that the members of the Family Compact were more interested in promoting their own welfare than in providing the local improvements that would make pioneer life easier. A government which allowed the clergy reserves to lie uncultivated, and which could not find money to build roads and schools for the frontier settlements, could nevertheless find public funds to support such enterprises as the Welland Canal and the Bank of Upper Canada. To the farmer and workingman it seemed clear that the political monopoly of the minority was being used to build up an economic monopoly.

In Lower Canada, similar social and economic grievances were aggra-vated by cultural conflict, for the ruling oligarchy was largely English-speaking while the great majority of the people and their representatives

The farmers of both Upper and Lower Canada frequently complained about the expenditure of public funds on commercial improvements such as the harbour developments at Cobourg. One radical gave expression to the widespread suspicion of the commercial classes when he wrote: "We entered another room which was occupied by 11 Lower Canada merchants and their runners. They were busily employed writing mortgages and cognovits in the hope of getting some of those in their debt to sign them! They reminded us of the artifice and activity of spiders preparing their murderous web in the silent hour of night, in order to enable them to allure, capture and prey upon their innocent and unsuspecting victims!" Nevertheless the whole country benefited from the improved transportation system. As one member of the Lower Canadian assembly insisted: "Was it nothing to open a free communication with the great internal seas of our continent, those seas which providence has bestowed upon us as a source of inexhaustible wealth. . . . The waters of this continent had but two great outlets, the St. Lawrence and the Mississippi, and Montreal and New Orleans must be the greatest marts of trade on the continent."

in the assembly were French Canadians. In 1814, Sir George Prevost, the Governor-General, sent to the British government the following description of the situation in Lower Canada: "The divisions in the House of Assembly have become national in character; on one side the English minority, with whom the official class is allied, on the other side the Canadian majority backed by the mass of the people. The heat engendered by this party strife passes from the House of Assembly to its constituents. The whole country is by now divided into two parties, one the party of the administration, the other that of the people."

This racial division between French and English in Lower Canada had not been expected by the framers of the Constitutional Act. Indeed, it had been hoped that the grant of representative institutions to the French Canadians would help transform them into English Canadians. Instead the leaders of the French-Canadian majority rapidly learned to use the assembly to protect their nationality and block the plans of the English-speaking businessmen to change Quebec into a commercial society. In the first assembly of 1792, the French-Canadian members won recognition of French as an official language on a footing equal with English. Soon their rallying cry and the motto of the first French-Canadian newspaper, *Le Canadien,* established in 1806, became "Our Language, Our Institutions, Our Laws."

The opposition of the French-Canadian leaders to the English-speaking commercial class showed itself in an insistence that taxes be levied on trade rather than on land. Moreover, they fought for the preservation of the traditional system of seigniorial land tenure in the face of the desire of the British to introduce freehold tenure, a form of landholding which would make land sales and speculation easier. When the Canada Tenures Act, passed by the British parliament in 1825, permitted proprietors to change from seigniorial to freehold tenure, the French Canadians set up every possible obstacle to its application.

Gradually the leaders of the reform movements in both the colonies began to demand that the executive branch of the government be brought under popular control. They disagreed on whether this could better be achieved by adopting the United States republican system, under which the President is directly responsible to the electorate, or the British cabinet system, which makes the executive responsible to the elected legislature. This debate divided the Reformers into two groups: the moderates, who favoured the British solution, and the radicals, who looked with increasing sympathy to the United States example.

By 1815 the French Canadians had found a leader in the brilliant, eloquent, and emotional young lawyer and seignior, Louis-Joseph Papineau. As Speaker of the assembly, Papineau became the outspoken defender of his people. Although he was liberal in his desire to increase popular control over the government of Lower Canada, he was also greatly motivated by the knowledge that popular control over government in Lower Canada meant French-Canadian control. In 1834 he declared: "One nation should never govern another." But in Lower Canada, Papineau saw that under the Constitutional Act one nation, the English, did govern another, the French-Canadian. Nevertheless, the struggle in Lower Canada was not simply one of French against English, for John Neilson, the Scottish editor of the Quebec *Gazette,* and other English-speaking Canadians, strongly supported Papineau, at least until he began to move from demands for reform to acts of rebellion. Similarly the Chateau Clique had supporters among the French-Canadian seigniors and the higher clergy who distrusted Papineau because of his "free thinking" religious views and his advanced democratic ideas.

The conflict in Lower Canada centred mainly on the question of the control of the revenue. Because it received the revenues from land sales and fees as well as the customs duties collected under the Quebec Revenue Act of 1774, the executive branch had its own source of income and was,

Early in his career Papineau was an outspoken champion of British institutions and the British connection. As his many attempts to secure reforms failed, however, he became bitter and disillusioned. In 1828 he wrote to his close friend and ally, John Neilson: "The injustice done to my country destroys me and agitates me to such a degree that I am not always capable of taking counsel of an enlightened patriotism, but rather of anger and hatred against its oppressors. . . . The descendants of the French have no equal rights with their masters of British origin. . . . The history of no other colony presents a similar spectacle of immorality."

as a result, largely independent of the elected assembly in matters of ordinary finance. Papineau and his followers soon realized that until they gained control of all revenue they could not hope to control the actions of the Chateau Clique. The executive was willing to allow the assembly control of revenues, but only on the condition that the assembly in turn would grant a permanent civil list, that is a permanent guarantee of the salaries of government officials. Papineau refused, for obviously such an agreement would curtail the control which the assembly could exercise over these officials once their salaries were guaranteed.

One of the major reasons that the Chateau Clique in Lower Canada wanted to prevent the French Canadians from winning complete control of government was their fear that the English-speaking minority would then be at the mercy of the French. This fear was strongest among the members of the English-speaking merchant class, who realized that once the French Canadians were in control there would be little hope of levying taxes for the kind of improvements necessary to promote commerce.

In one attempt to overcome these difficulties, the British government in 1822 proposed that Upper and Lower Canada be reunited. If this were done, the English-speaking population in the Canadas would be able to work together without fear of French-Canadian domination. But the proposal so threatened the existence of the French Canadians as a cultural group, and they opposed it with such great vigour, that the British dropped the idea.

This concession to the French Canadians did nothing to weaken their desire for control over the executive. Indeed, the victory spurred them on to fight harder for recognition of the assembly's right to control the entire revenue of the colony. In 1831 the British authorities tried to conciliate Papineau and his party by granting the assembly control of the revenue, even without the guarantee of a permanent civil list. Although the assembly, led by Papineau, had won this notable victory, the Reformers were still not satisfied. Their appetite for power whetted, the French-Canadian leaders pressed for popular election of the legislative council. However, as Papineau's demands became more radical, some of his followers, notably John Neilson, drifted away from him.

In 1834, a climax came when Papineau rose in the assembly to outline a long list of real and alleged grievances. The famous Ninety-Two Resolutions contained flamboyant admiration for United States institutions and struck a new note: the threat of open rebellion. Resolution Fourteen stated what was now the heart of Papineau's demands:

> Resolved, that this House is nowise disposed to admit the excellence of the present Constitution of Canada, although His Majesty's Secretary of State for the Colonies has unseasonably and erroneously asserted, that it has conferred on the two Canadas the institutions of Great Britain; not to reject the principle of extending of frequent elections much further than it is at present carried; and that this system ought especially to be extended to the Legislative Council, although it may be considered by the Colonial Secretary incompatible with the British government, which he calls a monarchical government, and too analogous to the institutions which the several States, composing the industrious, moral and prosperous confederation of the United States of America, have adopted for themselves.

Until these demands were met, Papineau defiantly declared that his party would refuse to grant funds to carry on the government. Clearly, Papineau and his more radical followers were now moving down the road to rebellion.

In Upper Canada, despite the absence of bitter cultural conflict, similar events were taking place. Shortly after the War of 1812, an intemperate young Scotsman, Robert Gourlay, raised a furore in the colony with his criticism of the land-tenure system and the lack of internal improvements. The government quickly threw him into jail and later expelled him from the colony. Soon two American settlers, Barnabas Bidwell and his son Marshall Spring Bidwell, were in trouble with the ruling authorities for criticizing government policy and the Family Compact. When Barnabas was ejected from the assembly because of his American birth, the voters returned his son. Ejection of the younger Bidwell raised the question of the rights of thousands of American settlers, many of whom were suspected by the Compact of holding radical views. Not until 1828 did the government finally agree to allow naturalized Americans the same privileges of citizenship as others in the colony.

Meanwhile, by the 1820's, the Reformers in Upper Canada had found a fighting leader in the firebrand journalist-politician, William Lyon Mackenzie. In 1824, this redheaded Scotsman, whose passion for justice knew no discretion, began attacking the established authorities in his paper,

This somewhat amateurish portrayal of an Upper Canadian hustings in the election of 1828 gives some idea of the excitement and vigour of the open elections of the time. This meeting at Perth had William Morris, a moderate Liberal and champion of the Presbyterian Church, pitted against Alex Thom. An account of an election at Durham eight years later gives some picture of the spirit of the day: "There was astonishingly little fighting considering the number of wild Irishmen we brought down . . . so for want of better game our Patlanders occasionally got up a snug fight amongst themselves, but though there were three or four "kilt" I did not hear of any serious damage." Another man wrote from Napanee of the contest in Lennox and Addington: "There was only one polling-place in the country and that was at Bath. It was a little booth on the edge of the village. . . . The taverns at Bath were crowded with men wrangling about votes. Whiskey was flowing freely, and there were plenty of drunken men and brawls in the streets." (A later generation wisely closed the bars on election day!)

The Colonial Advocate. In 1826, Tory roughnecks threw his printing-press into Toronto harbour. Mackenzie's supporters replied by triumphantly electing him to the assembly where he immediately seized on the revenue issue, just as Papineau had done in Lower Canada. Unfortunately for the Reform cause, Mackenzie was less successful than Papineau in solving it. In 1831, the Tories won a majority in the assembly and agreed to provide a permanent civil list in return for control of the revenue. Mackenzie was furious for he realized that this concession left the executive independent of the assembly. "Our representative body," he wrote, "has degenerated into a sycophantic office for registering the decrees for as mean and mercenary an executive as was ever given as a punishment for the sins of any part of North America in the nineteenth century."

Such invective was too much for the Family Compact and the Governor. An obedient assembly expelled Mackenzie for libel, and although he was re-elected four times, he was expelled on each occasion. In 1835 he was elected as the first mayor of Toronto, and, following a Reform victory in 1834, later took his seat in the assembly as well. By this time, however, Mackenzie's growing radicalism had disturbed his more moderate followers. Egerton Ryerson, the Methodist leader, had deserted the Reform cause in 1833, describing its leaders as atheists and republicans. Led by the quietly effective Toronto lawyer, Robert Baldwin, moderate Reformers were unwilling to accept what appeared to be the radical American programme that Mackenzie was beginning to advocate. In 1835, Mackenzie's radicalism became plain for all to see in his Seventh Report on Grievances, which was a scathing attack on land policy, patronage and corruption, the power of the Family Compact, and the iniquities of oligarchical government and appointed councils. As one of Mackenzie's letters reveals, he too was moving down the road to rebellion: "The crisis is fast approaching in the affairs of Canada which will terminate in independence and freedom from the baneful domination of the mother country, and the tyrannical conduct of a small and despicable faction in the colony."

Into this troubled situation stepped Sir Francis Bond Head. Bond Head's knighthood had been granted by William IV for his adeptness with a lasso, an art he had learned in South America, but of colonial government he knew nothing, and his Tory temperament made conflict with the Reformers inevitable. At first, however, he acted moderately, appointing Baldwin and two other moderate Reformers to the Executive Council. But Baldwin soon realized that his new position gave him no real power since Bond Head felt free to ignore the advice of his Council. When the Governor's position became clear, the entire Council, Tory and Reformer alike, resigned and the assembly passed a resolution supporting their action. At this point, the assembly of Upper Canada for the first time refused to vote funds for the use of the Executive. The elected members also demanded that the Executive Council be formed of men who had the confidence and support of the assembly. What was necessary, a resolution of the assembly declared, was "a responsible executive council to advise the lieutenant-governor on the affairs of the province."

Like the old soldier he was, Governor Bond Head took the initiative. Dissolving the assembly, he made a personal appeal to the electorate. It was a furious and bitter election campaign in which Bond Head branded his critics as traitors scheming to destroy the British connection. He called upon "every noble-minded Englishman, Irishman, and United Empire Loyalist" to support him. To a friend in England he wrote: "I am playing a game here in which I am king, and all the rest of the cards knaves; and yet I believe I have at last managed to trump them, but it is hard work. . . . This is a fine country, if we could but get it quiet, in which I have nearly succeeded by upsetting the radicals." Where emotional appeals were inadequate, Bond Head successfully used bribery and intimidation to ensure the return of government supporters. The result was an assembly which could be relied upon to support him. With this successful election behind him, Bond Head threw moderation to the winds and refused to make any concession even to the moderate Reformers. As for

Mackenzie's radical followers, they now lost all hope of change by constitutional means.

In Lower Canada, Papineau had reached almost the same conclusion. Following the assembly's refusal to grant funds in 1834, the British had sent Lord Gosford, as Governor-General, to Quebec with orders to investigate the deadlock and adopt some conciliatory measures. Gosford offered to appoint some of Papineau's followers to the Legislative Council, but refused to recommend that it be elected. Papineau rejected the compromise. The deadlock continued and the assembly refused to grant funds for the salaries of government officials. In March 1837, Lord John Russell, the British Colonial Secretary, intervened. In his famous Ten Resolutions he bluntly rejected the appeal for an elected legislative council and an executive in any way responsible to the assembly. Russell felt that to grant responsible government would be nothing less than to make the colonies independent. If the Empire were to be maintained, the governor and his council had to be responsible to the British government, not to the local assembly. Moreover, one of Russell's Resolutions declared that if the assembly refused to grant funds for the carrying on of government, the governor could legally spend money without the approval of the assembly. In short, taxation without representation, the situation which had helped to bring on the American Revolution, could be practised in Canada.

The radicals in Canada concluded that nothing was to be gained by further appeals to the British government. William Lyon Mackenzie wrote angrily in his newspaper:

> The secret is told at last—The screeds and councils and constitutions, the pledges and kingly declarations, the proclamations and acts of parliament and ministerial statements, to which the judge on the bench, the representative in the legislature, and the loyalist in his family circle referred as proofs that colonists were freemen are swept away in one instant by an almost unanimous resolution of the House of Commons in England, agreeing to rob, plunder, steal and defraud the people of Lower Canada of their money, the produce of taxation, to apply that money to purposes the people by their representatives would not consent to apply it, and to refuse them all substantial redress of the grievances under which they have so long and so patiently laboured.

Mackenzie's vigorous and rousing attack found a ready audience, for by the summer of 1837 a depression had hit the Canadian colonies. A financial panic in the United States, a trade depression in England, poor crops and low prices, bankruptcies and unemployment provided fertile ground for the seeds of political revolt that Mackenzie and Papineau had been sowing.

3. THE REBELLIONS OF 1837

The rebellion came first in Lower Canada. Although Papineau and his supporters had certainly been talking the language of revolutionaries, its outbreak was accidental. E. B. O'Callaghan, a hot-headed Irish supporter of Papineau, wrote that the reply to Russell's Resolutions should be resistance. He declared: "HENCEFORTH, THERE MUST BE NO PEACE IN THE PROVINCE—*no quarter for the plunderers.* Agitate! *Agitate!!* Destroy the revenue; denounce the oppressors. Everything is lawful when the fundamental liberties are in danger." This loud talk had not been backed up by any serious preparations for a rebellion. Yet, the mass meetings organized by "les Patriotes," as the Reform party was called in Lower Canada, resulted in rioting in Montreal on November 7, 1837. Believing that his presence in the city might lead to further trouble, Papineau decided to leave Montreal. Ironically, the government interpreted this move as an attempt by the Patriote leader to gather support among the country people. Attempts to arrest the leaders of the Reform party led to a series of armed clashes at St. Eustache, St. Denis, and St. Charles. At St. Eustache, hastily gathered rebel forces took cover in a church. A British officer described the scene as British troops moved in: "The rebels were found stationed in the gallery still defending themselves, and having cut away the staircase, every attempt to dislodge them for awhile proved utterly fruitless, but on a sudden the church was in flames and on the part of the rebels all was lost. These unfortunate and misguided people were then to be seen dispersing in every direction; few escaped. One hundred and twenty were made prisoners, but the estimated loss in killed and wounded was great." The rebels in Lower Canada were easily defeated

The Patriote forces lacked leadership and were poorly armed. Nevertheless they fought bravely and made use of their knowledge of the country north of Montreal. At St. Charles on November 25, bridges across the Richelieu were destroyed, forcing the advancing British troops to construct temporary bridges from trees. Even when the government forces did succeed in crossing the river they were faced with a hard fight before driving the rebels out of the fortifications that had been constructed on the outskirts of St. Charles.

Prisoners taken during the 1837 rebellions were thrown into prison to await summary trial. "The democratic Blood has poured irresistibly down the flood of time and, growing faster and faster, will topple the unavailing barriers which may be erected against it. In these circumstances must we take to slaughter or might we not better wear down a bad government through constitutional opposition which may, and which must, be shown in Parliament?" This was Louis-Joseph Papineau's position in May, 1837. By November, however, the dispute had moved, unintentionally, from the assembly to the battlefield. There British troops defeated the Patriote forces, imprisoning those leaders who did not escape to the security of the United States.

by the better equipped and trained troops that the government had at its command. Papineau and his chief lieutenants escaped to the United States where they hoped to regroup their forces and gain American assistance.

The rebellion in Upper Canada was precipitated by events in the lower province. When Mackenzie heard the news of the battle in French Canada, he began to organize his forces. A handbill entitled "Independence," which was circulated among Mackenzie's sympathizers, illustrated the revolutionary spirit that had captured the radicals. It read: "MARK MY WORDS, CANADIANS! The struggle has begun—it might end in freedom; but timidity, cowardice, or tampering on our part, will only delay its course. We cannot be reconciled to Britain. . . . We are determined never to rest until independence is ours. . . . Up then brave Canadians! Get ready your rifles, and make short work of it." But despite revolutionary enthusiasm among the leaders, the revolt was a hopeless, mis-

Samuel Lount and Peter Matthews, two Reform party members, were hanged during the period of repression that followed the collapse of Mackenzie's rebellion in Upper Canada. John Ryerson wrote to his brother Egerton Ryerson in April 1838, shortly before Lount and Matthews were hanged: "Monday I was down in town and met Lount's brother. The Brother told me that he had not been allowed to see his brother since he was committed to prison although he had made frequent applications. . . . A good deal of feeling seems to be excited respecting the execution of these unfortunate men; the petition which came down from Newmarket was signed by five thousand persons; a number are now being circulated throughout the city. . . . There seems to be a determination on the part of certain persons connected with the executive to carry things to extremes."

managed affair from the beginning. Mackenzie gathered his disorganized force of ill-armed farmers and workingmen at Montgomery's Tavern, which stood near the present intersection of Yonge and Eglinton in Toronto. Sir Francis Bond Head proved almost as incapable of organizing his forces as Mackenzie was of leading the rebels. The major clash occurred on December 7, and the rebels were quickly dispersed. After the "battle," Mackenzie wrote: "And never did men fight more courageously. In the face of a heavy fire of grape and cannister, with broadside following broadside of musketry in steady and rapid succession, they stood their ground firmly, and killed and wounded a large number of the enemy, but were at length compelled to retreat."

Defeated, Mackenzie followed Papineau across the border into the United States. There the exiles from both provinces attempted to reorganize their men and win support from the Americans for a new attempt to overthrow the government in Canada. Apart from a few minor raids and border skirmishes, nothing came of their efforts. While some Americans along the border gave private aid to the exiled rebels, the American government had no desire to provoke war with Great Britain. The chief result of the border raids was to encourage repressive measures by the ruling authorities in the Canadas, who took the opportunity to make arrests on very slight suspicion of disloyalty. Only two men were executed but many others were exiled to such penal colonies as Van Diemen's Land and Australia.

Despite the widespread discontent in both Upper and Lower Canada, the majority of the population refused to believe that rebellion was the only solution. The radical views of Mackenzie and Papineau, which implied both republicanism and independence, alienated many of those who shared their dissatisfaction with the existing order. In Upper Canada both Loyalists and more recent British immigrants were unwilling to jeopardize the British connection, while in Lower Canada the Roman Catholic Church and many of the habitants distrusted the democratic, anti-clerical and, to some, revolutionary views of Papineau and his followers. Yet, while the rebellions had failed, they had also succeeded; for the British government, abruptly reminded of the disastrous consequences of 1776, decided that a thorough-going investigation of the British North American problem was necessary.

CHAPTER 23

Durham's Report and the Triumph of Responsible Government

No better man than John Lambton, first Earl of Durham, could have been selected to investigate the crisis in the Canadas. Durham was an extremely wealthy man, fully in sympathy with the nineteenth-century industrial and commercial revolution. Yet he was also a convinced reformer, who had won the title "Radical Jack" for his prominent role in the struggle for the Reform Bill of 1832. Well-read and highly intelligent, he had learned the finer arts of diplomacy as British ambassador to Russia. Although he was charming and tactful when the occasion demanded, he had a haughty and arrogant temperament, often accentuated by the severe headaches which were a symptom of the disease that was to kill him at forty-nine. Durham was reluctant to accept the assignment to British North America. "The undertaking is a fearfully arduous one," he wrote, "and nothing but the extreme emergency of the case could induce me to make such a sacrifice."

1. DURHAM'S REPORT

The "extreme emergency" was not just the problem of the Canadian uprisings. At stake, too, was the continued existence of the British Empire. By 1837 many people in Britain believed that the time had come to emancipate the colonies, particularly those like the British North American colonies, which were a problem to govern and an expense to defend. The sentiment was strengthened by the growing belief that Imperial trade preferences were a liability and that Britain should adopt free trade. Of what use was an empire if it were not profitable?

Durham did not share these sentiments and staunchly maintained his belief in the value of the Empire. He belonged to the group of colonial reformers who argued that a liberal grant of self-government, an enlightened administration, free trade and large-scale British emigration to the colonies would promote the welfare of both Britain and the colonies and strengthen the bonds between them.

Fear that Canadian rebels, who had fled to the United States after the failure of the Rebellion in 1837, would find sympathy and support for an invasion of Canada, deeply distressed the authorities in the Canadas. Sir George Arthur, Lieutenant-Governor of Upper Canada, wrote: "I have the greatest difficulty to bring myself to believe that the American Sympathisers would make another crusade to this territory: but I have received from such various quarters reports of the collection of arms, ammunition, and the cannon which General Scott could not recover in February last, that it would be wrong in me any longer to delay soliciting your interference with the Government of the United States.

"There are, so far as I can ascertain, about two thousand persons who have left this Province and have taken up their residence in the frontier taverns on the American Side. These people, of course, will continue to excite and agitate the lawless characters that are to be met with at Lockport, Rochester, Lewistown, Buffalo—and in the neighbourhood of these places."

PATRIOT MEETING.

W.E.H.U.N.T.T.O.O.

Spirit of '76!

"Liberty and Equality thro'out the World."

AT a special Meeting of a portion of the members of THE PATRIOT LODGE OF THE CITY OF BUFFALO, held this morning, March 2, SCHUYLER ROSS was appointed Chairman, and H. D. HUFF, Secretary. On Motion, the following gentlemen were appointed a committee to draft resolutions expressive of the views of the meeting:

Geo. W. Bull,	Elias Doty,	Joseph Shepard,
A. M. Clapp,	John Pierce,	Wm. Kennedy,
John C. Haggerty,	J. P. Davison.	D. Lockwood,
James Lawson,	Wm. Butterworth,	Pearl L. Sternberg,
F. W. Emmons,	Geo. B. Gates,	F. S. Wheeler,
Wm. Lewis,	A. M. Grosvenor,	Thos. H. Quinn,
Wm. Wells,	John W. Stewart,	Nathan Norton,
Horace H. Hungerford,	Wm. S. Waters,	Stephen C. Clark,
Geo. McKnight,	C. F. Butler,	Loomis Lyman,
V. R. Strickland,	F. Cowing,	J. Houston.

The committee, through their Chairman reported the following resolutions, which were UNANIMOUSLY ADOPTED—
Resolved, That as PATRIOTS, we totally disclaim all connection with a RESOLUTION published in a hand bill, purporting to have been passed at a meeting of our Lodge on Saturday evening, in which George P. Barker is recommended for Mayor—and do not consider said resolution BINDING on ANY PATRIOT.

Resolved, That while we cherish the principles of LIBERTY, EQUALITY, and '76 we cannot consent that a portion of ANY POLITICAL PARTY shall get together and pledge us to the support of their cause and candidate, under the sacred name of PATRIOTS!!!

Resolved, That as we have never taken any obligation by which we are to relinquish our rights as citizens, and as GEORGE P. BARKER DID REFUSE to attend the last meeting in commemoration of the Burning of the Caroline, when requested so to do, and as he has said that if elected Mayor he should consider it a LOCO FOCO VICTORY we cannot as PATRIOTS give him our support.
Resolved, That the proceedings be signed by the Chairman and Secretary, and published.

SCHUYLER ROSS, Chairman.

HENRY D. HUFF, Secretary.

To assist him in British North America, Durham enlisted the support of two prominent and able colonial reformers, Edward Gibbon Wakefield and Charles Buller. A powerful advocate of a freer system of colonial government, the charming and witty Buller was a valuable addition to Durham's staff. The imaginative Wakefield was well known for his ideas and achievements in the field of large-scale emigration to the colonies. More widely publicized was his ill-fated attempt to abduct an heiress, for which escapade he had spent two years in jail.

As Durham descended the gangplank at Quebec late in May 1838, the guns roared in salute and the guard of honour in their scarlet tunics stood rigidly at attention. In a magnificent uniform, heavily embroidered with silver and decorated with the Order of the Bath, Durham rode up the rocky streets of Quebec on a prancing white horse. The crowds cheered, sensing that perhaps upon the shoulders of the new Governor-General rested not only their future but that of the Empire as well.

Yet even as the crowds cheered, there were sporadic outbursts of violence and threats of new uprisings in Lower Canada. To pacify the colonies and restore order would require determination and humanity. Durham revealed both qualities when he pardoned most of the rebels and exiled eight to Bermuda. Complete pacification of the Canadas, however, was impossible while there remained the danger of an attack from the United States. In Buffalo, William Lyon Mackenzie had received an enthusiastic welcome, and soon a thousand men, armed with guns removed from the United States arsenal, were waiting for the signal to march. All along the border—at Troy, Burlington, Rochester, Ogdensburg and Montpelier—Americans voted money and supplies for the "patriots" and formed Hunters' Lodges whose members swore "never to rest until all tyrants of Great Britain cease to have any Dominion or footing whatever in North America."

Shortly after his arrival Durham travelled to Niagara Falls where he ostentatiously reviewed British and Canadian troops. Crossing the border he attended lavish dinner parties and held sociable conversations in which he convinced the Americans that whatever British policy in the Canadas had been in the past, under him it would be liberal, democratic, and just. Durham's charm was irresistible and, while the border remained unsettled, the immediate threat of invasion disappeared. As Charles Buller wrote:

> A million of money would have been a cheap price for the single glass of wine which Lord Durham drank to the health of the American President. . . . It is only the man of statesmanlike mind who can produce a great result out of things so small as an invitation to dinner, or the drinking of a glass of wine.

Durham and his staff had also been carefully studying the causes of the 1837 rebellions. As Durham's Report later revealed, they saw at once that the economic and social problems of the colonies centred on the conflicts between the Family Compact or Chateau Clique and the elected assembly. They also accepted the argument of Robert Baldwin, the Upper Canadian Reformer, that the solution of these problems was a system of government under which the governor would choose his advisers in the executive council from men who had the confidence of the legislative assembly. As Durham wrote in the majestic prose that graced his entire Report:

> We are not now to consider the policy of establishing representative government in the North American Colonies. That has been irrevocably done. . . . To conduct their Government, harmoniously, in accordance with its established principles, is now the business of its rulers; and I know not how it is possible to secure that harmony in any other way, than by administering the Government on those principles which have been found perfectly efficacious in Great Britain. . . . [The Crown must] submit to the necessary consequences of representative institutions; and if it has to carry on the Government in unison with a representative body, it must consent to carry it on by means of those in whom that representative body has confidence. Every purpose of popular control might be combined with every advantage of vesting the immediate choice of advisers in the Crown, were the Colonial Governor to be instructed to secure the co-operation of the Assembly in his policy, by entrusting the administration to such men as could command a majority.

The governor would still have an important role to play, but it would be in working with the assembly rather than supporting the executive and legislative councils in opposition to it. Government would thus spring from the popular will, and, said Durham, "If the colonists make bad laws and select improper persons to conduct their affairs, they will generally be the only, always the greatest sufferers; and, like the People of other countries, they must bear the ills which they bring on themselves, until they choose to apply the remedy." The alternative to responsible government, he warned, was an army strong enough to prevent further rebellions against the oligarchic rule of the Compact and Clique.

Durham attempted to reassure his readers that responsible government did not mean complete self-government and separation from Britain. On the contrary, Britain would retain control of these matters of Imperial interest: the management of public lands, in deference to Wakefield's hope for large scale emigration to the colonies; the regulation of external trade and foreign affairs; the form of the constitution itself; and relations with the Indians. But in all ordinary questions of domestic policy the colony would govern itself.

Although he fervently believed in responsible government, Lord Durham refused to recommend its introduction in Lower Canada, for it would mean placing the English-speaking minority under the French-Canadian majority. He had seen that the constitutional conflict in Upper Canada had economic and social roots, but he attributed the Lower-Canadian crisis almost exclusively to a conflict of races. As he wrote in one celebrated passage: "I expected to find a contest between a government and a people; I found two nations warring in the bosom of a single state: I found a struggle not of principles but of races." There was no doubt in his mind that, however gracious and hospitable the French Canadians were, the future lay with the British. It could hardly be otherwise. Like the English-speaking merchants in Montreal, he believed in industry and commerce, in the development of transportation facilities and the encouragement of a business-like and progressive spirit. He shared their views of the commercial possibilities of the St. Lawrence system, and deplored the unprogressive and stubborn nature of the French Canadians who blocked its development.

Union of the two colonies appeared to be the ideal solution to both the economic and the political problem. Union would end the fatal division of the St. Lawrence water-way system. It would also solve the constitutional dilemma. With Upper Canada's rapid increase in population, the English-speaking Canadians would soon be the majority. They would then not only dominate political life in the united colony, but by sheer superiority of numbers, Durham thought, they would assimilate the French Canadians.

Durham had come to these conclusions, which he later embodied in his Report, within six months of his arrival in Canada. His investigations were cut short in September when the British government refused to support his banishment of the exiles. Outraged by this lack of confidence,

In September 1838 Lord Durham learned that his ordinance banishing political prisoners to Bermuda had been disallowed by the British government. Immediately he decided to resign from his post and return to England. Before departing, Durham wrote heatedly to the British Colonial Secretary: "I am bound to tell you privately that I could never have anticipated the possibility of such treatment as I have received. Having succeeded far beyond my most sanguine hopes, in restoring tranquillity and inspiring confidence, all over the continent of North America, I little expected the reward I have received from home—disavowal and condemnation." Expressions of regret at Durham's decision came from all over the colony, **Le Canadien** remarking that the attack on Durham could "compromise the peace and integrity of the Empire."

Durham returned home to write his Report at breakneck speed and face his enemies in the last few months of life remaining to him. The publication of the Report in 1839 aroused a storm of protest. Upper Canadian Tories charged that his analysis of Compact rule was inaccurate and biased, and denounced responsible government as a reward for disloyalty and rebellion. The English-speaking minority in Lower Canada applauded the idea of union, but suspected that responsible government would give power to the French. The French Canadians, understandably, were enraged. Only the Upper Canadian Reformers greeted the Report with enthusiastic approval. On the evils of oligarchy and the need for responsible government Durham had completely vindicated the position they had held for ten years. But more important than the mixed cries of joy and anger in the Canadas was the official reaction of the British government.

2. RUSSELL'S COMPROMISE

The Imperial government readily accepted the arguments for union of the two Canadas, and in 1840 passed the Act of Union to come into effect a year later.   Like Durham, the British ministers maintained that the French Canadians should not be placed in a position to dominate the legislature of the Canadas.   Since English-speaking Canadians were then in a slight minority in the two colonies the British ministers gave equal representation to Upper and Lower Canada, or Canada West and Canada East as they now became known, failing to realize that the rapid immigration to Upper Canada would soon place English-speaking Canadians in a commanding majority.

Despite the power and logic of Durham's arguments for responsible government, the British ministers remained unconvinced.   As long as the colony remained a colony, the governor must be responsible to the British government and not to an executive council chosen from the legislative assembly.   As Lord John Russell, the Colonial Secretary, wrote:

> It may happen . . . that the Governor receives at one and the same time instructions from the Queen and advice from his Executive Council, totally at variance with each other.   If he is to obey his instructions from England, the parallel of constitutional responsibility entirely fails: if, on the other hand, he is to follow the advice of his Council, he is no longer a subordinate officer, but an independent sovereign.

Responsible government, then, was synonymous with independence.   Durham's argument that this conflict would not arise because matters of Imperial concern would remain in Britain's hands was considered to be unrealistic and impossible.   Russell wrote:

> There are some cases of internal government, in which the honour of the Crown or the faith of Parliament, or the safety of the State, are so seriously involved that it would not be possible for Her Majesty to delegate her authority to a Ministry in a colony.

Nevertheless, the Liberal government* in Great Britain, of which Russell was a member, had no desire to return to the system of oligarchic government that had caused the rebellions of 1837.   In the future the people of Canada were to have a greater voice in their own government, and the governor was to select his advisers from "men whose principles and feelings were in accordance with the majority" and administer the colony in co-operation with the legislative assembly.   However, the governor was not to be bound to follow the advice of his council, which was still responsible to him and not to the assembly.   What remained to be seen was whether this compromise, so easily stated on paper, could be worked out in practice.

---

* It was also known as the Whig or Reform government.

A grateful Canadian government has erected a monument for Baldwin and LaFontaine on Parliament Hill in Ottawa. Not only did these two men co-operate in the achievement of responsible government but they also began that tradition of French-English co-operation which lies at the foundation of the bi-cultural experiment in Canada.

3. THE CRITICAL YEARS 1840-1846

The man selected for the difficult task of initiating the Russell compromise was Charles Poulett Thompson, who was elevated to the peerage as Lord Sydenham. Sydenham was a man of considerable experience in business and politics. He realized that to succeed he had to persuade a majority in the assembly to follow him instead of any other combination of political leaders. In short, the Governor had to be his own Prime Minister and party leader. With an Imperial loan to provide the necessary means he reduced the provincial debt and undertook an ambitious programme of public works. As Sydenham suspected, most Canadians were more concerned with obtaining material improvements than with solving their constitutional problems. Even the restless members in the assembly were seldom a match for the shrewd Governor whose parliamentary skill was highly regarded even in England. There were two men, however, who did not fall under the Sydenham spell. Louis LaFontaine held the ranks of the Lower Canadian Reformers solid in opposition to the new Governor. Sydenham shared Durham's views of the French-Canadian problem, and refused to invite the "disloyal" French to serve on the council. Robert Baldwin, who had supported Sydenham until he realized that he would not accept the full implications of responsible government and intended to govern himself, continued to press in the assembly for full responsible government. Baldwin's stubborn and insistent pressure and the increasing strength of the Baldwin-LaFontaine alliance on the principle of responsible government forced the Governor to seek the assembly's approval for a set of resolutions introduced by Harrison, one of his ministers. The resolutions stated that the governor was responsible "to the Imperial authority alone" but:

> That in order to preserve between the different branches of the Provincial Parliament that harmony which is essential to the peace, welfare and good government of the Province the chief advisers of the representative of the Sovereign, constituting a Provincial administration under him, ought to be men possessed of the confidence of the representatives of the people. . . .

The Harrison resolutions were little more than a restatement of Russell's policy, but they were sufficient to appease men less determined than Baldwin and LaFontaine. What would happen if the Governor could not find men "possessed of the confidence of the representatives of the people" remained to be seen. Sydenham had avoided such a crisis by governing himself and building up his own party in the assembly, but Sydenham fell from his horse the day after the Harrison resolutions were passed and died two weeks later.

As his successor, Sir Robert Peel's Conservative government, which had defeated the Liberals in 1841, appointed Sir Charles Bagot. Unlike Sydenham, Bagot had no parliamentary experience, but his charm, tact and impartiality had helped him to build an extremely successful diplomatic career. Peel instructed him to follow the general policies of Sydenham, but suggested that the blanket rejection of all the French Canadians might be reconsidered. This conciliatory policy towards the French had been urged upon Peel by Charles Buller:

> We have put down their rebellion, destroyed their nationality, and in doing this reduced them to a miserable state of social subjection. The Governor that would raise them up to a social equality by mere justice and kindness would make them the instruments instead of the enemies of Government. The French Canadians if rightly managed are the natural instruments, by which the Government could keep in check the democratic and American tendencies of Upper Canada.

Upon his arrival in Canada, Bagot immediately decided that he neither could nor would adopt Sydenham's techniques. As he informed his superiors in London: "It was only by dint of the greatest energy, and I must add the unscrupulous personal interference of Lord Sydenham, combined with practices which I would not use, and your Lordship would not recommend, in addition to the promise of the Loan and the bribe of Public Works, that Lord Sydenham managed to get through the Session." Moreover, Bagot soon realized that the precarious personal party that Sydenham had built up had disintegrated, and the defeat of the executive in the assembly was almost certain. To Bagot the solution was equally clear. Since Baldwin and LaFontaine jointly possessed a majority in the assembly, they should form a new executive council. Bagot knew only too well that Baldwin and LaFontaine were committed to the principle of responsible government, which he had been instructed to reject. He knew also that opinion in England, at the Colonial Office, and in influential circles in Canada was utterly opposed to giving any power to the French-Canadian Reformers, so many of whom, like LaFontaine, had supported Papineau. Yet in Bagot's opinion both political necessity and a generous humanity pointed to the same end. In September 1842 he persuaded the Reform leaders to take office.

Bagot's "Great Measure," as it was called, was really an admission that responsible government existed. As he wrote to the Colonial Secretary, Baldwin was "the actual and deservedly acknowledged leader of the strongest party in the House, and in the Country. . . . Whether the doctrine of responsible government is openly acknowledged, or is only tacitly acquiesced in, virtually it exists." While the Montreal *Gazette* charged that Bagot had handed over "the British party . . . to the vindictive disposition of a French mob," the Governor patiently explained the significance of his action to the outraged Colonial Secretary, who had advised conciliation of the French but no more.

> I have removed the main ground of discontent and distrust among the French Canadian population; I have satisfied them that the Union is capable of being administered for their happiness and advantage, and have consequently disarmed opposition to it. I have excited among them the strongest feelings of gratitude to the Provincial Government; and if my policy be approved by Her Majesty's Government, I shall have removed their chief cause of hostility to British institutions, and have added another security for their devotion to the British Crown.

Unfortunately, illness soon forced Bagot to resign and the British government seized the opportunity to send a new governor to Canada who would at least stop the clock, if not turn it back. Sir Charles Metcalfe was an experienced administrator and a man of liberal views, but his experience in India and Jamaica had not given him much faith in colonial assemblies nor had it led him to look kindly upon men whose profession of loyalty to the British connection he regarded as "utterly worthless." His own position was clear: "Whether my contest be with a malignant minority, or with a majority of the House of Assembly, or with the whole colony run mad, my duty must be the same. I cannot surrender Her Majesty's authority, or the supremacy of the Mother Country."

Inevitably, Metcalfe differed with his Canadian advisers, and, in November 1843, Baldwin and LaFontaine resigned. For a year the Governor vainly attempted to find a majority in the assembly. Finally, in November 1844 he appealed directly to the people to elect a more sympathetic assembly. Led by Metcalfe, who campaigned personally in the election, the Conservatives denounced the Reformers as petty office-seekers interested only in patronage, as traitors and republicans, who would break the British connection. This appeal to loyalty and patriotism won the support of Egerton Ryerson and the Methodists and gave Metcalfe

Joseph Howe was born in Halifax in 1804, the son of a United Empire Loyalist from Boston. Howe left school at thirteen to become a printer's apprentice and later a journalist. In 1835 he published an article attacking the magistrates on the grounds of maladministration. When sued for criminal libel he defended himself brilliantly and did much to establish the freedom of the press in the colony. Elected to the legislature, he became the champion of reform and responsible government.

and the Conservatives a precarious majority. As in 1837 there were murmurings of revolt, and in 1845, when Metcalfe went home to die, it remained to be seen whether Canada was to have responsible government or government by bayonet.

4. THE VICTORY GAINED, 1846

The issue was largely determined by events in England. In 1846 the British government, secure in its industrial and commercial supremacy, swept away the old policy of mercantilism and adopted free trade. With the abandonment of the old economic base of the Empire, it no longer seemed as important to retain firm political control over the colonies. An even more decisive factor was the victory of the Liberals in the 1846 election. Since their defeat in 1841 the English Liberals had been reconsidering their attitude towards responsible government for the colonies. As they observed the course of events in Canada and studied the arguments of Durham and Buller, and of Baldwin in Upper Canada and Joseph Howe in Nova Scotia, the logic of responsible government appeared irresistible. When the new government took office, Lord Grey, a brother-in-law of Lord Durham, became Colonial Secretary, and among his staff was Charles Buller. Grey immediately made it clear that responsible government would be granted to the North American colonies.

The first colony to benefit was Nova Scotia. Under the leadership of the brilliant journalist, Joseph Howe, the Reformers in Nova Scotia had struggled for responsible government as vigorously as the Canadians, although they had never resorted to rebellion. Joseph Howe's *Letters to*

Lord John Russell in 1839 had been as eloquent a statement of the need for constitutional change as was Durham's Report. In one sentence the fiery "tribune of Nova Scotia" had summed up his case: "We seek for nothing more than British subjects are entitled to; but we will be content with nothing less."

No sooner was he installed in office than Lord Grey informed Sir John Harvey, the Lieutenant-Governor of Nova Scotia, that a new policy had been adopted in colonial affairs. Grey's dispatch was one of the most important that had ever crossed the Atlantic to British North America.

> I have . . . to instruct you to abstain from changing your Executive Council until it shall have become perfectly clear that they are unable, with such fair support from yourself as they have a right to expect, to carry on the government of the province satisfactorily, and command the confidence of the Legislature. . . . In giving, therefore, all fair and proper support to your Council for the time being, you will carefully avoid any acts which can possibly be supposed to imply the slightest personal objection to their opponents. . . . A refusal to accept advice tendered to you by your Council is a legitimate ground for its members to tender to you their resignation, a course they would doubtless adopt should they feel that the subject on which a difference had arisen between you and themselves was one upon which public opinion would be in their favour. Should it prove to be so, concession to their views must, sooner or later, become inevitable, since it cannot be too distinctly acknowledged that it is neither possible nor desirable to carry on the government of any of the British provinces in North America in opposition to the opinion of the inhabitants.

When the Nova Scotia election of 1847 returned a majority of Reformers and the government lost a non-confidence motion early in 1848, Sir John Harvey accepted the resignation of his ministers and called upon Howe and the Reform party to form a new administration. Responsible government in Nova Scotia had become a fact.

A year earlier Lord Grey had sent Lord Elgin, Durham's son-in-law, to Canada as Governor-General. Before Elgin's departure, he too had been given a copy of the dispatch quoted above with instructions to "act in conformity with the principles there laid down . . . and to withdraw from the position into which Lord Metcalfe had, by unfortunate circumstances been brought . . . and to make it generally understood that, if public opinion required it, he was equally ready to accept [the Reformers] as his advisers, uninfluenced by any personal preferences or objections." When the Canadian electorate returned a Reform majority in the 1847 elections, Elgin immediately asked Baldwin and LaFontaine to form a new government.

Although this decision caused grumbling among the Conservatives, the real test did not come until 1849, when the assembly passed the Rebellion Losses Bill to compensate those people in Canada East who had suffered property damages during the 1837 rebellion. To the English-speaking community in Canada East the Bill was nothing more than a reward for treason and rebellion, and an act of revenge by LaFontaine and his friends, many of whom had been rebels. Lord Elgin and the British government had misgivings about the justice of the Bill. But Elgin realized that responsible government meant following the advice of his ministers on matters of local concern, and assented to the Bill.

The reaction was violent. The Tories who opposed responsible government hurled a stream of insult and abuse at the Reform leaders, who actually feared for their lives. Elgin's carriage was pelted with stones as it passed through the streets of Montreal. On April 7, 1849, opponents of the Bill stirred a street mob to rioting which ended only after the skies over Montreal were lit up by the flames of the burning Parliament buildings. But the flames were really the death of the old order, for responsible government had triumphed. Lord Durham had also triumphed, but only in part. For responsible government was won not by the assimilation of the French but by the co-operation of both communities in Canada. Baldwin and LaFontaine had proved Durham right while also proving him wrong.

Mob violence followed Lord Elgin's decision to sign the Rebellion Losses Bill in 1849. The English-speaking element in Montreal interpreted the action as a betrayal of the Empire and an acceptance of French domination. "Anglo-Saxons! You must live for the future; your blood and your race will be henceforward your supreme law if you are faithful to yourselves. You will be English if you no longer may be British," stormed the Montreal **Gazette**. After stoning Lord Elgin's carriage, the mob fired the Parliament buildings which burned as the crowd cheered.

CHAPTER 24

The Uneasy Union

1. REORGANIZING THE ECONOMY

The number and magnitude of the evils that afflict our country, and the universal and increasing depression of its material interests call upon all persons animated by a sincere desire for its welfare to combine for the purposes of enquiry and preparation with a view to the adoption of such remedies as mature and dispassionate investigation may suggest. . . . THIS REMEDY CONSISTS IN A FRIENDLY AND PEACEFUL SEPARATION FROM [THE] BRITISH CONNECTION AND A UNION UPON EQUITABLE TERMS WITH THE GREAT NORTH AMERICAN CONFEDERACY OF SOVEREIGN STATES.

This manifesto appeared in the Montreal *Gazette* on October 11, 1849. It was not drafted by fanatical crackpots but represented the considered opinion of the most prominent, respectable and powerful businessmen in Canada East. The three hundred and twenty-five men who signed it were the "solid" citizens of the community, men who instinctively voted Conservative. Their proposed solution, however, was the most radical one imaginable for Canada's problems for it meant the end of Canada as a community separate from the United States. Priding themselves above all on their loyalty to the British connection, the English-speaking merchants were driven to this desperate extreme by the conviction that the mother country had abandoned them. Britain had not only supported responsible government, which seemed to put control of the colony in the hands of the "disloyal" French Canadians; even more serious, between 1846 and 1849 the British government had established free trade and abolished the Navigation Acts, thus ending the old colonial system. The tariff privileges enjoyed by the Canadian merchants in the Imperial market disappeared and they lost their important advantage over American merchants. Their vision of a great commercial empire, based on the St. Lawrence water-way system, and stretching into the rich lands of the West, was now just a mirage. Disillusioned, fearful and angry the

Montreal businessmen concluded that if they could not defeat their competitors in the United States, they had better join them.

The Annexation Manifesto found little support among most Canadians. The economic problems were undoubtedly serious, but as in 1837 most people in 1849 were unwilling to accept the political consequences of the Manifesto. Even the Tories in Canada West turned deaf ears to the proposal. Rejecting annexation as a solution, they proposed a federation of all the British North American colonies, an adventurous suggestion that foreshadowed the later creation of the Dominion of Canada.

A more practicable solution for the present was the attempt to develop freer trade with the United States. Lord Elgin was an enthusiastic supporter of this idea of reciprocity with the United States and pressed his views on the British government: "You have a great opportunity before you—obtain reciprocity for us and I venture to predict that you will be able shortly to point to this hitherto turbulent colony with satisfaction in illustration of the tendency of self-government and freedom of trade to beget contentment and material progress."

The lever that might be used to pry open the American market for Canadian natural products was the American desire to use the rich Canadian inshore fisheries denied to them by the Convention of 1818. Despite the prohibition, New England fishermen attempted to fish in British North American waters. By 1850, squadrons of the American and British navies sailed off the coasts of Nova Scotia and Newfoundland to protect their citizens, and the danger of an armed clash was imminent. Since the British were anxious to resolve this troublesome problem, Lord Elgin was authorized to negotiate a settlement which would include trade questions with the United States. Despite the American desire to have access to the fisheries, Lord Elgin needed all his personal charm and diplomatic skill in Washington to secure acceptance of a treaty. Over cigars and champagne, Southern Senators were persuaded that reciprocity would keep Canada out of the Union, while their Northern colleagues were not discouraged from seeing reciprocity as a way of obtaining new markets and as a prelude to annexation. Elgin took Washington society by storm, but, as his secretary observed, he "never loses sight for a moment of his object, and while he is chaffing Yankees and slapping them on the back, he is systematically pursuing that object. The consequence is, he is the most popular Englishman that ever visited the United States." In the end Elgin was successful. The reciprocity treaty of 1854 provided for free exchange of natural products between the United States and the British North American colonies, free navigation of the St. Lawrence and Great Lakes water-ways, and mutual access to the inshore fisheries.

The reciprocity agreement strengthened the Canadian economy. Natural products such as grain and timber from the Canadas, and fish and timber from the Maritimes, found wide markets in the United States. One-half of the trade of the Canadas and two-thirds of the trade of the Maritimes remained with Great Britain despite reciprocity, but the newly

In the Canadas the production of square timber for the British market remained, until the 1860's, the most important single commercial activity. In 1863 some fifteen hundred men were engaged in cutting timber in the Ottawa region alone, while some ten thousand men were employed in Canadian saw mills. By the 1860's the production of deals, boards and planks was beginning to exceed that of the old square timber. Logs floated out of the bush were sawn at local mills before being floated in rafts down the St. Lawrence to Quebec where they were loaded on ocean-going vessels for the export market.

opened market in the United States provided a very necessary addition. Perhaps more important, by decreasing the dependence of the colonies on Britain, the reciprocity agreement helped to encourage a growing sense of maturity in British North America.

One practical sign of this new maturity was the decision of the Canadian government in 1859 to impose a customs tariff which protected Canadian manufacturers against British imports. When Britain protested against this measure, Canada argued that responsible government meant full Canadian control over the colony's economic life. A. T. Galt, the Canadian Minister of Finance, bluntly informed the British that "the Government of Canada acting for its Legislature and people cannot, through those feelings of deference which they owe to the Imperial authorities, in any manner waive or diminish the right of the people of Canada to decide for themselves both as to the mode and extent to which taxation shall be imposed." The British reluctantly accepted the Canadian argument, and self-government was thus recognized in another area of the colony's life.

The reciprocity agreement of 1854 was also significant in a more general way. The fact that the treaty had been negotiated for all the British North American colonies suggested that the area could be treated as a unit rather than as a group of totally separate colonies. Did this not suggest the possibility of a political union of all British North America?

If the colonies could be linked together by new means of communication, and if their populations grew large enough to provide a prosperous home market, political union would become feasible.

2. RAILWAYS AND WESTWARD EXPANSION

The population of the British North American colonies grew rapidly in the 1850's. The number of people in Canada West jumped from 445,000 in 1841 to 952,000 in 1851, when for the first time it exceeded that of Canada East. While growth in the Maritime colonies was slower, by 1861 they contained 662,000 people compared with 2,500,000 in the Canadas. This population growth was the result of economic changes important enough to justify the title of a revolution. At the core of the commercial revolution was the coming of the railway and, with it, a spirit of buoyant optimism. The St. Thomas *Weekly Despatch* declared in 1853:

> It is exceedingly gratifying to witness the spirit of enterprise and progress which has of late sprung up as it were simultaneously in every section of Upper Canada. We hear nothing but Railways, Steamers and Telegraph lines. A few years since it was not so. It seems but yesterday when the projection of a costly line of Railway such as the Grand Trunk or even Great Western would have been considered a mere chimera, an idle fancy of speculative imagination. This state of things has disappeared, the spirit of improvement is abroad, the march of Canada from end to end is onward, its prosperity is astounding the dormant settlers who were content to live in peaceful retirement enjoying the comforts derived from hard toil and incessant plodding.

Railways were needed or demanded everywhere in British North America. Many local lines were built by enterprising companies in all the colonies, but it was the more grandiose projects in the Canadas that caught the imagination of both politician and businessman. A. T. Galt, who was both, underlined the importance of railways to Canada when he remarked: "Unless Canada can combine with her unrivalled system of inland navigation a railroad system connected therewith and mutually sustaining each other, the whole of her large outlay must remain forever unproductive." What Galt and others realized was that the old St. Lawrence commercial system could only be revived if British North America was bound together and extended by rails of steel. A network of railways running north and west from Toronto was built to tie the western and northern hinterlands to the centres of trade and commerce. Among these was the Northern Railway, running north from Toronto to Lake Simcoe and thence to Georgian Bay, which was designed to reach into new areas of settlement north of Toronto and draw farm products to the city's markets. A second project was the Great Western, developed to link Hamilton with American railways which ran to Buffalo and Detroit. A third was the

The Great Western Railroad was one of several roads that were designed to draw traffic from the northern and western hinterlands into the Toronto and Hamilton areas. The Great Western, which began construction in 1847, was to provide a connection between the New York railroads running into Buffalo and the Canada West centres of Hamilton and Windsor. By 1855 the line was completed, and for several years proved a highly profitable enterprise, probably because it formed a section of the only direct railway route from Chicago to New York.

St. Lawrence and Atlantic from Montreal to Portland, Maine, which gave the Canadians a winter port when the St. Lawrence was ice-bound.

But what British North America needed most was a single line that would join British North American terminals rather than run to American ports. The greatest of such projects was the Grand Trunk, which was to run from Sarnia to Halifax. Much of the money and engineering skill needed to begin this vast enterprise came from Britain. Construction had scarcely started when it was realized that the project would require more capital than was originally anticipated, and local governments were repeatedly called upon to provide funds to save the railway from bankruptcy. By 1860 the Grand Trunk was completed in the Canadas, but its eastern outlet was provided by the line running to Portland, Maine.

There still remained the major problem of building an all-Canadian line to link the Maritimes with the Canadas. In 1858, A. T. Galt summed up the dangers which this situation created: "The position of Canada is both peculiar and exceptional. A population now numbering three millions of British-born subjects resides in the interior of America and during the winter season are absolutely proscribed from any intercourse with either Great Britain or the other colonies except through a foreign country [the United States] jealous of the power of England upon the continent. . . ." The Grand Trunk lacked the resources to build the line itself; indeed, each

The growth of industry, such as the Great Western railway works at Hamilton, accompanied the economic boom of the railway age and reciprocity.

year it sank more deeply into debt. The British government refused to provide the capital. And as long as the colonies remained politically divided they, too, lacked the necessary concerted effort and financial resources.

The financial problems of the railways produced many headaches for Canadian politicians in the 1850's. The heavy costs of construction and operation meant that railway promoters had to appeal repeatedly for public funds, with the result that railway development and politics became closely interwoven. This situation was not always good for either the railways or the politicians since it opened the door to extravagance and corruption. One Grand Trunk representative wrote:

> My work was almost exclusively "lobbying" to get a Grand Trunk Bill through. . . . The Canadian Ministers were willing but weak—the majority a doubtful quantity. Although up to the last minute I felt that there was a chance of getting the bill through I was always doubtful, since it was clear that some twenty-five members, contractors, etc., were simply waiting to be squared either by promise of contracts or money. As I had no authority to bribe, they simply abstained from voting and the bill was thrown out. £25,000 would have bought the lot. . . .

In an underdeveloped country like Canada, the government was the only institution rich enough to provide the railway builders with the capital they needed. And one thing was certain: if the country were to thrive it had to have railways.

By the end of the 1850's much had been achieved in the field of railway building. In 1850 only sixty-six miles of railroad existed in all of British North America. Ten years later the mileage had increased to 2,065. From the strictly financial point of view, the railways never achieved the success expected, but they did contribute a great deal to the growth of such industries as foundries, rolling mills and locomotive shops. The major industrial centres were Toronto and Hamilton, though smaller industries such as the manufacture of boots and shoes, the fabrication of cotton goods and the production of agricultural implements developed in other towns.

More important than these economic changes were the social and political changes that came with the railways. Railways broke down the isolation of pioneer communities. It was obvious that in the same way railways could tie together the whole of British North America into one vast economic unit; and economic union might bring political union with it. Thus, political and business objectives for the building of railways were tied together. As one newspaper noted in 1854: "Railway operations are calling into existence new wants and new enterprises, creating new markets and filling men with bigger thoughts."

Many of these "bigger thoughts" were directed towards the northwest, which seemed to provide the key for the further growth and prosperity of British North America. The Grand Trunk had failed to win control of the traffic from the American West, but the great expanse of the Canadian northwest above the forty-ninth parallel lay open and virtually untapped. By the 1850's, businessmen and politicians were beginning to examine the possibility of transforming this area into the kind of settlement that would fill an important role in building a prosperous economy. This was the dream of many easterners and it was summed up by the Toronto *Globe*, one of the first eastern newspapers to recognize the potential of the West.

> If Canada acquires this territory, it will rise in a few years from a position of a small and weak province to be the greatest colony any country has ever possessed, able to take its place among the empires of the earth.

If the West could be acquired and settled, it would not only provide farm products for eastern cities and for export, it would also furnish a market for the new manufactured products being developed in the Canadas.

In 1850 all of the British lands in the West were owned by the Hudson's Bay Company, which continued to carry on its lucrative fur-trading enterprise. As always the Company discouraged settlement, for settlers drove out the fur-bearing animals. But to the south the westward movement of settlers in the United States was growing so great that some of them began to look enviously at the fertile, unpopulated lands of the Hudson's Bay Company. The Oregon boundary dispute in 1846 illustrated what could happen in such a situation.

The Convention of 1818 had made the forty-ninth parallel the Canadian-American boundary as far west as the Rockies. Beyond that the border was undefined. Until the 1840's the Hudson's Bay Company remained in undisputed control of the lower Columbia River valley and had its headquarters near the southern end of the river, at Fort Vancouver.

Oregon Boundary Dispute

In the 1840's, however, American settlers were flooding into the Oregon territory and soon demanded its formal annexation to the United States. Their appeal found a ready response in the United States and James Polk, the Democratic candidate for the Presidency in 1844, won the election on the campaign cry of "Fifty-four Forty or Fight," which was a claim not just to the Oregon territory, but to all of the Pacific coast south of Alaska. Britain refused this extravagant demand, but finally agreed to relinquish the territory south of the forty-ninth parallel.

The Oregon compromise set Canadians thinking more seriously about the future of the West. Fear of American expansion was heightened when the discovery of gold on the Fraser River in 1858 brought thousands of American prospectors to British Columbia from the exhausted gold fields of California. Firm action by Governor James Douglas kept the tumultuous gold seekers under control, but the danger remained that the Americans might once again demand annexation to the United States. Isolated from Britain's other North American colonies, British Columbia and Vancouver Island were likely areas for American expansion unless, somehow, these areas could be drawn closer to the rest of British North America.

Between British Columbia and the Canadas lay the large open spaces of the prairies and the Rockies. Here, the only important settlement was Fort Garry on the Red River, where Selkirk's Scottish settlers had been joined by those offspring of the fur trade, the half-breeds. As one Hudson's Bay Company officer wrote, Red River became:

The favourite retreat of the Company's servants. . . . Here they find

The connection between the little colony at Red River and the settlement at St. Paul in Minnesota was a natural one, for the expansive, calm Red River provided an easy means of transportation. This connection was drawn closer in 1859 with the introduction of steamers on the Red. From Canada's point of view, this close relationship between Red River and the United States represented a danger, for it could easily lead to annexation of the western colony to the State of Minnesota. An American observer reported in December 1861: "The Americanization of this important section of British North America is rapidly progressing. Unless the British parliament acts promptly . . . I shall confidently expect a popular movement looking to independence or annexation to the United States."

themselves with the companions of their youth, their fellow adventurers; those with whom they tugged at the oar, and shared the toil of the winter march; and when they meet together to smoke the social pipe, and talk of the scenes of earlier days, "nor prince nor prelate" can enjoy more happiness.

Long isolated in the centre of the continent, the settlers at Red River were first drawn into the mainstream of North American life by pioneers passing westward across the United States. By 1850, three hundred Red River carts rumbled along the prairie trail from Minneapolis to Fort Garry carrying supplies and mail, and by the end of the decade steamboats on the Red River had cemented the north-south bond. Minnesota had become a state in 1858 and ambitious local politicians cast envious eyes on the unoccupied territory to the north. By 1860 it was clear that unless Canada established communications with Red River, the fertile western colony would fall prey to the expansionist ambitions of the United States. Land-hungry farmers in Canada West, who saw their sons emigrating to the United States, supported the western expansion of Canada. So did eastern manufacturers, who dreamed of a settled West as a market for their goods. But as long as the Canadas were unable to solve their own political problems, territorial expansion was impossible.

George Brown stated the heart of his own political programme very clearly in writing to John Sandfield Macdonald in 1854: "I tell you frankly, then, that far from having any ambition, to be the head of the party—I **would not take office under any circumstances were it offered to me.** All I desire is the success of the principles to which I have attached myself, and if you can form a government pledged to separation of church and state—representation by population—and non-sectarian schools—I will not only aid you in doing so but will support your government with all my heart and vigour."

3. POLITICAL TROUBLES

In the 1850's Canadian politics entered a new and unsettled period. The source of the trouble lay in the Union Act of 1841. The Act had never really united the two sections of Canada, for, by granting equal representation to Canada East and Canada West, it perpetuated a division based primarily on race. For ten years the system worked well enough because the Reform supporters of Baldwin in Canada West and LaFontaine in Canada East shared a common objective: responsible government. Once responsible government was achieved, however, in 1849, the interests of French- and English-speaking Canadians began to diverge. And it was the nature of the constitution itself that caused the most serious dissension.

Until the early 1850's Canada West had the smaller population and was satisfied with equal representation. But as soon as the population of Canada West exceeded that of Canada East, some English-speaking Canadians began to demand that representation in the legislature should be based on population. Since this would mean an increase in the number of English-speaking members, the French Canadians firmly opposed the idea, fearing that an English-speaking majority might interfere with the language, religion and schools of the people in Quebec.

In Canada West the advocates of "rep-by-pop" found a vigorous leader in George Brown, editor of the Toronto *Globe*. Brown's demand for a reform of the system of representation was popular in Canada West, and after Baldwin retired in 1851 Brown soon became the real leader of the Reform party. The French Canadians distrusted and feared Brown, an ardent Presbyterian who opposed state support for Roman Catholic separate schools and attacked what he called "French domination" of the union.

Since the French Canadians were no longer willing to co-operate with the Reformers from Canada West, they gradually moved closer to the English-speaking Tories. Like the French Canadians, the Tories from Canada West were opposed to constitutional changes. Their main interest was economic development and many of their leaders were associated with the Grand Trunk Railway and the businessmen who were developing the commerce of the St. Lawrence. By 1854 the alliance of French Canadians and English-speaking Canadian Tories had been moulded into the Conservative party by the capable hands of John A. Macdonald and Georges Etienne Cartier.

Macdonald was a young Kingston lawyer whose wit, attractive personality and ability to work with others gradually won him the leadership of his party. He was a practical man who believed that the union as it existed could work if the government promoted a favourable climate of economic development. Moreover, he realized that his party could only win a working majority if French- and English-speaking Canadians co-operated. As he told a friend: "If a Lower Canadian Britisher desires to conquer, he must stoop to conquer. He must make friends with the French. Without sacrificing the principle of his race or lineage, he must respect their nationality. Treat them as a nation and they will act as a free people generally do—generously. Treat them as a faction and they become factious."

Georges Etienne Cartier, a French Canadian, was, like Macdonald, anxious to promote a new alliance of the moderates from Canada East and Canada West. Like LaFontaine before him, Cartier believed that the cultural rights of French Canada, as well as the interests of the Montreal business community with which he was closely connected, could be protected and promoted by co-operation of English and French political leaders. Although the Macdonald-Cartier party became the strongest alliance in the union, its cohesion was precarious and it was threatened with disintegration whenever sectional issues arose.

Nevertheless, the Macdonald-Cartier government, formed in 1854, did manage to enact a number of important measures without stirring up sectional divisions. For example, in 1854, after years of heated controversy, both the clergy reserves and seigniorial system were abolished. Moreover, the government actively supported the construction of the Grand Trunk Railway. But the sectional problem persisted, and Macdonald's support in Canada West declined because he refused to accept "rep-by-pop." Macdonald and Cartier even found it impossible to select a permanent capital, for the French Canadians favoured Quebec or Montreal, while English-speaking Canadians insisted on Toronto or Kingston. When the matter was referred to Queen Victoria, the backward lumbering town of Ottawa was selected as a compromise. But the legislature refused to accept the decision, and the Macdonald-Cartier ministry was driven from office. It was soon back in power, however, for George Brown's Reformers had no success in finding a majority that would keep them in office. Their only possible supporters were members of the *parti rouge* in Canada East, whose French-Canadian nationalism made them difficult allies and whose radicalism and anti-clericalism alienated them from the conservative rural voters and the powerful leaders of the Roman Catholic Church.

Brown's failure to retain office increased the discontent of his followers in Canada West. Some of the more radical Reformers, who were known as "Clear Grits," demanded that the union should be dissolved completely. Brown was not prepared to go so far. Instead he proposed that the existing legislative union should be replaced by a federal union which would place most power in the hands of local legislatures, with the central government controlling only a few matters of common interest to both sections, such as tariff and defence.

Brown was not the only Canadian politician who, by the 1860's, was convinced that the union was no longer workable. Although Macdonald and Cartier preferred to work within the union, they were willing to consider the possibility of a federal scheme that would include not just the Canadas, but also the Maritimes. In 1858 A. T. Galt, the Montreal railway man, had joined the Macdonald-Cartier ministry as Minister of Finance on the condition that the government seriously consider the creation of a federal state. Galt believed that only under a federation of all the colonies could the railroad problem be met, and the West brought into closer association with the rest of British North America. Moreover, by the 1860's sectional disagreement within the union had become so acrimonious that the colony could not even agree on measures to strengthen the militia at a time when relations with the United States threatened to lead to war. Despite two elections and three separate governments between 1861 and 1864, it proved impossible to reach an agreement even on this question of defence.

In 1864 George Brown pronounced the failure of the union when he declared: "We have two races, two languages, two systems of religious belief, two systems of everything, so that it has become almost impossible that, without sacrificing their principles, the public men of both sections could come together in the same government. The difficulties have gone on increasing every year." A constitutional renovation was obviously necessary.

CHAPTER 25

Founding a New Nation

Political paralysis in the Canadas in the 1860's made the idea of a union of all the British North American colonies an attractive prospect. With all the colonies brought under a single roof, the economy of the entire area could be united and the means provided for a solution to the problem of railways and western expansion. But it was not only the internal political and economic difficulties of the colonies that emphasized the need for a new political arrangement. Developments outside British North America pointed towards the same conclusion. In the 1860's, as so often happens in Canadian history, events in Great Britain and the United States gave impetus, and even definition, to developments that were taking place within British North America itself.

1. AMERICAN THREATS AND BRITISH CONCERN

From the middle of the nineteenth century, Great Britain had been following a policy of free trade, and colonies were no longer regarded as being of economic advantage to the mother country. Sometimes they were even looked upon as "millstones around the Mother Country's neck," as Benjamin Disraeli put it in 1852. Canada's decision in 1859 to erect tariff barriers to protect Canadian manufactured goods against competition from British as well as other foreign imports increased British doubts about the colonies as markets.

If the Empire was no longer of economic benefit to Britain, some of the more extreme British anti-Imperialists (or "little Englanders" as they were called) questioned the value of having colonies at all. An English Liberal was thinking particularly about Canada when he remarked that if colonies "are to be constantly applying to us for guarantees for railways, and for grants for fortresses, and for works of defence, then I think it would be far better for them and for us—cheaper for us and less demoralizing for them—that they should become an independent state, and maintain their own fortresses, fight their own cause, and build up their own future without relying upon us." While such extreme views never won full acceptance, they did influence the development of Britain's colonial policy. Their effect was indicated in the growing desire of the British government in the 1860's to have colonies, such as those in North America, assume financial responsibility for such matters as defence in order to reduce the tax burden on British electors. The British were sympathetic therefore to plans for larger unions, like the federation plan suggested in British North America, for such unions would be better able to stand on their own feet without continued financial and military support from the mother country. The London *Times* was expressing this view when it commented on the federal scheme in 1864: "Conscious as we are of our inability to protect these colonies by land in case of war, we must naturally rejoice at any event which seems to place them in a position in which they would be better able to protect themselves." Britain's desire to cut costs was particularly important to Canada in the 1860's, and not only because the British were reluctant to provide financial support for such colonial projects as railway building. What concerned the colonial politicians much more was Britain's apparent indifference to British North America's fate when trouble with the United States began to develop during the American Civil War.

While neither Britain nor the North American colonies were directly involved in the bloody war which began in April 1861 in the United States, the four years that followed were times of serious crises in Anglo-American relations. As always in such crises, Canada found herself in the centre of the storm. The resulting fear of American aggression was a powerful factor in bringing federation to completion. In fact, in 1865, Cartier went so far as to suggest that the British colonies had either "to obtain British North American Confederation or be absorbed in an American Confederation."

The bad relations between Britain and the United States grew out of the North's conviction that Britain's sympathies were with the Confederacy. Many upper-class Englishmen undoubtedly favoured what they thought of as the aristocratic South, and some British politicians went so far as to express publicly their hope that the South would win freedom from Northern domination. In the United States there were Northerners who felt that the country's attention could be turned from the Civil War to the annexation of Canada. Although President Lincoln had no interest in this wild plan, it was enthusiastically advocated by his Secretary of State, William Seward. Seward's plan was even popularized in a little song, which was sung to the tune of "Yankee Doodle":

> *Secession first he would put down*
> *Wholly and forever,*
> *And afterwards from Britain's crown*
> *He Canada would sever.*

Clearly, if there were a threat to Canada, the colony's defences would have to be greatly strengthened. While this need was, or should have been, obvious from the beginning of the Civil War, it became urgent after a series of incidents brought Anglo-American relations close to the breaking-point. In November 1861, two envoys who had been sent to Britain by the Southern Confederacy were removed from the British steamer *Trent* by sailors from a Northern warship. Britain's vigorous protest at this interference with a British ship aroused tempers on both sides of the Atlantic. Nevertheless, restraint prevailed on both sides and the incident was not allowed to explode into war. But Anglo-American relations remained tense. The North had good reason to complain when the warship *Alabama,* built in a British shipyard, was sold to the Confederacy. Used as marauders, the *Alabama* and other ships plied American coastal waters bombarding Northern posts and sinking Northern shipping. Northerners felt that the sale of the *Alabama* was definite proof of the British government's hostility to their cause. Southern conspirators also used

Following the **Trent** affair, the British government, as partial preparation for a possible war with the United States, dispatched nearly fifteen thousand troops to Canada. In the end the **Trent** dispute was settled peacefully, though the incident left many Canadians fearful of American aggressive intentions towards Canada. Good relations with the United States were only slowly restored. In December, 1861 the Buffalo **Express** stated: "Out of this **Trent** affair has come one permanent good. The old, natural, instinctive and wise distrust and dislike for England is revived again in the American heart, and will outlive all the soft words and snivelling cant about international brotherhood and reciprocity."

British territory as a base from which to plan attacks on the North. Confederate agents in Canada had little difficulty obtaining supplies, gathering information about Northern troop movements, and raising men for border raids. All of these incidents, threats and rumours made Canada's position precarious. Britain, recognizing the seriousness of the situation, sent 15,000 reinforcements to Canada late in 1861. Since winter had already set in when the troops arrived at Halifax, their trip to Quebec by sleigh was agonizingly cold and slow. Nothing could have emphasized more forcefully the need for the much discussed intercolonial railway from Halifax to the Canadas. But railway building had to wait until the colonies' political difficulties could be solved.

2. THE POLITICS OF CONFEDERATION

The idea of a federal union of all British North America had been under discussion in the Canadas, at least, since Galt had made his proposal in 1858. But it was not until 1864 that a ministry was formed which was definitely pledged to place federation before all other policies. The man chiefly responsible for this action was the Reform leader, George Brown. In June 1864, a committee to consider federation, which had been appointed at Brown's urging, reported in favour either of a local federation of the two Canadas, or a larger scheme to include all the British colonies. On the same day that this report was presented to the Legislature, the Macdonald-Cartier ministry was defeated.

George Brown decided that the time for decisive action had arrived. Swallowing his personal dislike of Macdonald, the Reform leader announced that he was prepared to enter into a coalition government with any Conservative who was willing to support the idea of federation. In a speech he delivered explaining his position, Brown expressed his strong desire to end the political troubles of Canada. He declared: "I do frankly confess, Mr. Speaker, that if I never have any other parliamentary success than that which I have achieved this day in having brought about the formation of a Government more powerful than any Canadian Government that ever existed before, pledged to settle, and to settle forever, the alarming sectional difficulties of my country, I would have desired no greater honour for my children to keep years hence in their remembrance than that I had a hand, however humble, in the accomplishment of that great work. . . ." Although Macdonald had opposed the federal proposals earlier in committee, he immediately saw that Brown's conciliatory gesture offered a real opportunity for settling the problems of the union. He accepted Brown's offer and years of bitter political feuding between the two men were temporarily put aside by a common resolve to establish a new nation.

But whether Brown and Macdonald were to succeed in achieving their common goal depended on the decision of another well known figure, Georges Etienne Cartier. Without the agreement of the French Canadians, no alteration of the existing union would be possible. The French Canadians had always been the strongest opponents of any change in the existing political arrangements, but in 1864 Cartier realized that the time for negative opposition to such changes had passed. French-Canadian rights could be made even more secure in a federal union. Cartier also shared with Macdonald and Brown the desire to see the economic promise of a wider union fulfilled. He therefore joined the coalition of Conservatives and Reformers and brought with him a crucial bloc of French-Canadian votes. Macdonald, Brown and Cartier formed the core of the new government but they were ably supported by men like A. T. Galt, E. P. Taché, William McDougall and the stirring orator, Thomas D'Arcy McGee.

The formation of the "Great Coalition" was merely the beginning of a strenuous search for a new constitution for British North America. The coalition represented only Canada, and, before their aims could be achieved, allies would have to be found in the Maritimes. In 1864 the time was ripe to approach the politicians in the Atlantic colonies, for these men were slowly moving towards the consideration of a Maritime union. Such a union could either be the first step towards the union of all British North America, or an obstacle to that larger union. The Canadian politicians determined to take the initiative and forestall talk of Maritime union by placing the idea of a union with the Canadas before the Maritimers. The Maritime leaders had made plans for a meeting among themselves in September 1864, at Charlottetown. The Canadian government asked if it could send delegates to this conference to present a plan for federation. The Maritimers agreed that they might.

In September all the important Canadian leaders attended this first conference at Charlottetown. Brown, Macdonald, Cartier and Galt had their arguments well prepared, and the delegates from the Maritimes listened to them attentively. The Maritimers had never been very enthusiastic about a local union, but perhaps this wider federation that the Canadians presented so persuasively would be advantageous. At any rate it would be well worth discussing further. Therefore it was agreed that a second meeting should be held at Quebec in October. The most impor-

Delegates from the legislatures of Canada, New Brunswick, Nova Scotia and Prince Edward Island met at Charlottetown on September 1, 1864 to "take into consideration the union of the British North American colonies."

When the Confederate agents who slipped across the border and attacked St. Albans in Vermont were allowed to escape unpunished by a Canadian court, talk of war was heard in the United States. "It may be said that this will lead to war with England," the New York **Times** declared, "But if it must come, let it come. Not ours, the guilt. . . . We were never in better condition for war with England." As the war scare grew, Canadian troops were made ready for defence; by January, 1865 two thousand Canadian militiamen had been placed along the American border.

tant result of the Charlottetown meeting was that the leaders of Canada and the Maritimes, in coming together to discuss common problems, had realized that common solutions might be found for those problems. The Halifax *Witness* remarked after the meeting: "There is less aversion to Canada. Indeed, there seems to be a positive desire for union . . . the distinguished men whom Canada has sent . . . have succeeded in removing some prejudices, and greatly modifying some real obstacles to union. As things look at present we must have a Colonial Union of some kind with the least possible delay." This was a substantial achievement. The paper might have added that the Charlottetown conference had also produced some very effective Maritime leaders for the cause of federation. One was the hard-working and somewhat long-winded Dr. Charles Tupper, the Conservative Premier of Nova Scotia. The other was the capable Reform Premier of New Brunswick, Leonard Tilley.

On October 10, the federation discussions were resumed at Quebec City. There was now great impatience to get on with the work. "We can't wait," George Brown wrote, "we are *not going to be tied to Lower Canada for twelve months more.*" The ever present fear of attack from the United States created an even greater sense of urgency. In the middle of the Quebec conference a new incident focused the attention of the delegates on the American danger. On October 19 a small group of Confederates slipped across the border from Canada into Vermont and attacked the village of St. Albans. Fears of Northern retaliation against Canada increased when the Americans protested against the failure of a Montreal court to punish the St. Albans' raiders.

The threat of American action was close to the thoughts of the delegates at Quebec as they discussed the Macdonald-Tilley motion "that the best interests and present and future prosperity of British North America will be promoted by a federal union under the Crown of Great Britain, provided such union can be effected on principles just to the several provinces." The discussion centred on the division of powers between central and local governments, and the debate recalled many of the arguments that were heard at Philadelphia in 1787 when the American constitution was being drawn up. Macdonald hoped that the gathering would approve a legislative union in which there would be a single government, because he was convinced that the American Civil War had revealed the fatal weakness of a federal system. But delegates from Quebec and the Maritimes were anxious to preserve local autonomy, and it became clear, as Brown noted, "there was but one choice open to us—federal union or nothing." Nevertheless, most of the delegates agreed on the need for a union with a strong central government. One delegate described the discussions:

> For the first few days the leading delegates of the Lower [Maritime] Provinces exhibited caution and vigilance upon every question affecting the interests of these provinces. . . . As the business proceeded and the details of the federal union were from day to day laid down, parties evinced a visible elasticity of judgment, and were observed gradually to harmonize with those whose opinions they had previously met in a style more polemical in character. The current seemed to set with the Canadians. The Maritime delegates, one after the other, were observed to drop into the stream; and, with few exceptions, the members appeared to float along with it, scarcely producing a ripple on its now gentle surface.

Eventually the persuasiveness of the Canadians won over all the Maritime delegates except those from Prince Edward Island and Newfoundland.

The conference adjourned on October 29, and the delegates returned to their provinces to begin the hard fight to win popular approval of the Quebec Resolutions. "Will the people follow the example and rise to the level of the occasion—to settle now the destiny of this northern country and the people that dwell here?" asked the Montreal *Gazette*. The question was now more pressing than ever, for relations with the United States were so unsettled that the possibility of war hung darkly over the British North American colonies. The Civil War was moving into its final stages, and the powerful Northern armies would soon be free to threaten Canada. But a more immediate danger than an organized American attack was the threat of border raids by the fanatical Irish-American Fenian Brotherhood. By late 1864 Irishmen in the United States of America were devising plans to free Ireland from British rule by embroiling the United

Speaking in the Confederation Debates in 1865, Macdonald appealed for immediate acceptance of the Quebec Resolutions. "If we do not take advantage of the time," he declared, "if we show ourselves unequal to the occasion, it may never return and we shall hereafter bitterly and unavailingly regret having failed to embrace the happy opportunity now offered of founding a great nation under the fostering care of Great Britain and our Sovereign Lady Queen Victoria."

States in a war with Britain. This they proposed to do by attacking Canada. Macdonald learned from a secret agent, shortly after the Quebec conference, that the Fenians were training in New Jersey in preparation for a drive across the border in mid-January, 1865.

Canada could easily deal with the Fenians as long as the American government remained friendly. But by the end of 1864 another American action brought new fears to British North America. Since 1860 pressure had been mounting in the United States for the abrogation of the reciprocity treaty of 1854. In January 1865 the United States Senate passed a resolution calling for the termination of the treaty in 1866. While this action was in keeping with the provisions of the treaty, it was interpreted as a sign of American unfriendliness, and gave further point to the arguments that the economy of British North America could only survive and expand if it were directed by a single political authority.

When the Canadian Legislature met in February 1865, most members were conscious of the critical stage that had been reached in the affairs of British North America. In the lengthy debate on the resolutions drawn up at Quebec, the leading Canadian politicians and many of their followers had an opportunity to express themselves on the federation proposals. Macdonald defended the scheme against those who felt it was too weak to succeed and warned of the dangers that faced the colonies if they remained disunited. Cartier tried to quiet the misgivings of those in French Canada who feared that the federal plan would threaten French-Canadian rights. "In our Confederation there will be Catholics and Protestants, English, French, Irish and Scotch, and each by its own efforts and success will add to the prosperity, to the might and to the glory of the new federation. We are of different races, not to wage war among ourselves, but to work together for our common welfare," Cartier argued. Galt explained the economic advantages of the scheme, and assured the English minority in Canada East that its rights, too, would be protected.

As the debate continued through many days, it was George Brown, speaking for the Reformers in the coalition, who voiced the thought that was weighing heavily on the minds of many members. "There is one consideration," he said, "that cannot be banished from this discussion, and that ought, I think, to be remembered in every word we utter; it is that the constitutional system of Canada cannot remain as it is now [loud cries of hear, hear]. Something must be done. We cannot stand still. We cannot go back to chronic sectional hostility and discord—to a state of perpetual Ministerial crises." When the vote was finally taken, the Quebec Resolutions won the approval of the Canadian Legislature by a solid ninety-one to thirty-three vote, with twenty-two of the opposing votes coming from representatives of Canada East, who believed that French Canada would suffer a loss of its rights in a federation in which English-speaking Canadians would make up the great majority. This vote in the Canadian Legislature was the only occasion on which the plan of federation was submitted to even this limited form of popular approval in the Canadas.

In the Maritimes the struggle between the supporters and opponents of the Quebec Resolutions was bitter and its outcome long remained in doubt. Enthusiasm for the scheme had never been great in the Atlantic colonies and even the promised intercolonial railway failed to overcome the Maritimers' deep suspicion of the Canadians. Although Prince Edward Island and Newfoundland rejected the plan immediately, it could still succeed if the two larger colonies, Nova Scotia and New Brunswick, gave it their approval. But in Nova Scotia Joseph Howe, the popular leader of the Reform forces since the 1840's, turned his powerful influence against Confederation. Howe had not been a member of his colony's delegation at Quebec, and a combination of personal jealousy of Tupper and a genuine belief that Nova Scotia's interests were being sacrificed turned him against the federal plan. He used his effective pen to attack what he sarcastically called "the Botheration Scheme." The effect of Howe's attack was so great that Tupper decided not to place the Quebec Resolutions before the Nova Scotia assembly, lest they be defeated.

In New Brunswick, matters were even worse. In March 1865, Tilley called an election and the anti-Confederation forces defeated him. But the new government had no positive policies, or any workable scheme to meet the obvious need for a railway linking New Brunswick with the Canadas. A complete stalemate seemed to have been reached in the Maritimes when outside events again intervened. The British government, anxious for the success of Confederation, instructed the Governor of New Brunswick, who had previously shown no enthusiasm for Confederation, "to further the cause of union by every means within his powers." As the anti-Confederation government was already falling apart, the Governor was able to carry out his orders by forcing a new election early in

1866. In the midst of the campaign Tilley's argument for union with the Canadas received forceful support by threatened Fenian raids on the New Brunswick border. With the support of the Governor, fear of the Fenians, and lavish financial aid from Canada to assist him, Tilley swept back into office. The Confederation scheme was on the move again. Tupper in Nova Scotia now took heart. He issued a call to arms: "If we remain disunited . . . the time may come when we shall have the British flag lowered beneath the Stars and Stripes, and the last gun fired from the Citadel as a British fort." The Legislature harkened to the appeal, and authorized delegates to attend a further conference in London to discuss Confederation.

At the Westminster conference in London in December 1866, the Quebec Resolutions remained the basis for the new constitution, though some final touches were added. In London, a British official wrote: "Macdonald was the ruling genius and spokesman and I was greatly struck with his powers of management and adroitness. The French delegates were keenly on the watch for anything which weakened their securities; on the contrary, the Nova Scotia and New Brunswick delegates were jealous of concession to the *arrière* province." The only major changes that were made provided larger financial grants to the Maritimes and a constitutional guarantee that an intercolonial railway would be built.

In March 1867, the British parliament passed the British North America Act. "We are laying the foundation of a great state," the British Colonial Secretary declared, "perhaps one which at a future day may even overshadow this country." At last the scheme was complete. The delegates, filled with elation at their success but wearied from the long discussions and the round of social activities, were anxious to get home and begin preparations for July 1, the day on which Confederation would become a fact.

3. THE NATURE OF THE NEW GOVERNMENT

The intention of the men who wrote the British North America Act was to adapt the traditional British parliamentary system to the needs of the new North American nation. The most obvious and necessary modification arose from the fact that British North America's regional and cultural diversities made a unitary system of government impossible. Therefore, like the United States, the new country was given a federal constitution. At the same time, Canadian leaders were well acquainted with the American system of government and were determined to avoid the features of the American system which they believed had helped to provoke the bloody Civil War.

They believed that the main weakness of the American system lay in a division of powers between the states and the federal government which had left the states too strong. To guard against this weakness, the framers

"Fenians mounted two deep upon horses; Fenians in lumber wagons, carrying boxes of ammunition; Fenians on foot, whistling bayonets about their heads, frantically leaping mudpuddles and shouting 'Come on'," was the way the New York **World** described the movement of Fenian invaders on Fort Erie on June 1, 1866. The next day these Canadian volunteers met the invaders at Ridgeway and were driven back, having suffered six dead and more than thirty wounded. War fever swept the western part of the province and the militia made ready to fight. By June 4, the Fenian raiders, some fifteen hundred strong, retreated across the Niagara River. The next week, a similar raid took place in Canada East, raising a further temporary scare. But by the end of the first week in June, the threat had passed as the American government began to take action to halt the raids.

of the Canadian constitution tried to establish a central government so powerful that it would be impossible for any local government to challenge its authority. They carefully divided authority between the federal and provincial governments, giving to the provincial authorities only certain specifically enumerated powers that were clearly local in their application. These included direct taxation within the province, authority over municipal institutions, construction of roads, the passage of laws concerning "property and civil rights" within the province, and many other powers of a purely provincial nature. In addition, the control of education was placed within the jurisdiction of the provinces, but the federal government was given the right to act in educational matters to protect the rights of minorities. This latter provision was designed to protect both French-Canadian minorities in English-speaking Canada, and the English-speaking minority in Quebec.

The federal government, under the British North America Act, was empowered to make laws for the "peace, order and good government" of Canada in *all areas not specifically granted to the provincial legislatures.* In giving this general residual power to the federal government the Fathers of Confederation hoped to avoid the problem of states' rights, which had caused such serious friction in the United States. In 1866 Macdonald explained the Canadian solution to the states' rights difficulty: "Ever since the [American union] was formed the difficulty of what is called 'State Rights' has existed, and this had much to do with bringing on the present

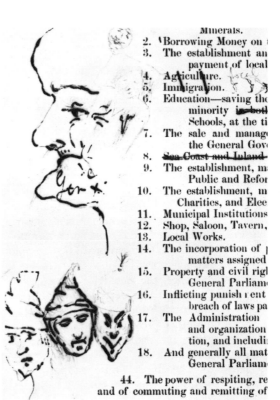

Minerals.
2. 'Borrowing Money on
3. The establishment an
   payment of local
4. Agriculture.
5. Immigration.
6. Education—saving the
   minority
   Schools, at the ti
7. The sale and manag
   the General Gov
8. ~~Sea-Coast and Inland~~
9. The establishment, m
   Public and Refor
10. The establishment, m
    Charities, and Elee
11. Municipal Institutions
12. Shop, Saloon, Tavern,
13. Local Works.
14. The incorporation of
    matters assigned
15. Property and civil rig
    General Parliam
16. Inflicting punish ent
    breach of laws pa
17. The Administration
    and organization
    tion, and includi
18. And generally all mat
    General Parliam

44. The power of respiting, re
and of commuting and remitting of

As the form of the new federal system was being debated at Quebec in 1864, an unknown member of the group drew caricatures of his colleagues. This set of resolutions was found in the Macdonald Papers but is not John A's work and is on the page where the provincial powers, which ultimately became Section 92, were being outlined.

unhappy war in the United States. They commenced, in fact, at the wrong end. . . . Here we have adopted a different system. We have strengthened the General Government. We have given the central legislature all the great subjects of legislation. . . . We have thus avoided that great source of weakness which has been the cause of the disruption of the United States." Some of the main powers of the federal government were listed in Section 91 of the British North America Act. These included the regulation of trade and commerce, defence, the power to raise money by any form of taxation, banking and currency laws, and criminal law. But the list of powers set out in the Act was not intended to be exhaustive. It was given merely to illustrate some of the powers that were included in the general authority of the central government.

The wide authority of the federal government was also made clear in a number of other ways. The central government was given the power to appoint the lieutenant-governors of the provinces. This meant that the lieutenant-governor was to act as an officer of the federal government. An even more important example of the authority of the federal government was the federal power of disallowance which gave the central government the right to veto acts of the provincial legislatures which it judged not to be in the national interest. So strong was the federal government that Macdonald, its chief architect, claimed that it had "all the advantages of a legislative union," that is, a unitary rather than a federal union.

The structure of the new Canadian government followed closely the British practices that had always guided the colonies. An executive officer, or governor-general, was placed at the head of the governmental pyramid. The governor-general was not only to play the role of monarch in the Canadian system, but was also to represent the British Colonial Office in Canada. The governor-general was not to be completely powerless. In certain limited circumstances he could refuse to grant a dissolution of parliament to a prime minister. But in most matters the governor-general was expected to follow the advice of his cabinet according to the well established principles of responsible government.

Under the British North America Act the Canadian parliament, like its British model, was to be composed of two houses, the Senate and the House of Commons. The Commons was the more important of these two chambers because its members were elected, while those of the second chamber, the Senate, were appointed. Representation in the House of Commons was determined upon the principle of representation by population, with Quebec granted sixty-five members and the representation of the other provinces determined in proportion. It was assumed that most of the important members of the cabinet would be drawn from the House of Commons.

The upper house of parliament, or Senate, like the British House of Lords, was non-elective. But since Canada lacked an hereditary aristocracy, the appointed house of parliament could not be called a House of Lords. Therefore the American name, Senate, was adopted. In theory the powers of the Senate were equal to those of the Commons, except that money bills could originate only in the elected house. In practice, the House of Commons, as in England, exercised far more power, for it was to this house that the cabinet was responsible.

Members of the Senate were to be appointed by the federal government. They had to be at least thirty years old and own property valued at $4000. The Senate was expected to serve two special purposes. First, it was to be a check on any hasty action taken by the House of Commons. As Macdonald noted in 1865, the Senate "must be an independent House, having a free action of its own, for it is only valuable as being a regulating body, calmly considering the legislation initiated by the popular branch, and preventing any hasty or ill-considered legislation which may come before that body, but it will never set itself in opposition against the deliberate and understood wishes of the people." The Senate's second important function was to protect provincial rights and represent sections. This feature was emphasized by the stipulation that Ontario and Quebec would each have twenty-four Senators and the Maritimes another twenty-four. But since the Senators are appointed by the federal government and not the provinces, the Senate has not in practice been a very adequate reflection of provincial interests. Indeed, apart from preventing hasty and imprudent legislation, the Senate's chief purpose today is to provide a means of rewarding political services rendered to the governing party.

These, then, were the main features of the new government established in 1867: a federal system with a strong central government, a bicameral legislature with the House of Commons exercising the primary authority, and a governor-general advised by a cabinet which acted as a body collectively responsible to parliament. It was, in short, Britain's traditional system of government modified to meet the needs of Canada.

In the new constitution, Macdonald thought he had won acceptance for a form of government that would undermine local loyalties and defeat the sectional forces that had destroyed the earlier union. It was his hope that the whole scheme would be capped by a name that would announce to the world the establishment of a new nation. The name he wanted was the Kingdom of Canada. But the British government, concerned that this title might irritate the republican United States and convinced that the colony was seeking too elevated a status, rejected Macdonald's suggestion and substituted the title of Dominion. This title did not alter Macdonald's view that Confederation marked the appearance of a new nation on the world's stage. He had defined his view in 1865 when he told the Canadian assembly that under the new scheme Canada would be "able from our union, our strength, our population, and the development of our resources, to take our position among the nations of the world. . . . Instead of looking upon us as a merely dependent colony, England will have us as a friendly nation—a subordinate but still a powerful people— to stand by her in North America in peace or in war."

On July 1, 1867, the first step was taken towards fulfilling Macdonald's vision when the federation of the four British colonies came into effect. The Toronto *Globe* exulted on that first Dominion Day: "With the first dawn of this gladsome summer morn we hail this birthday of a new nationality." But realistic politicians like the country's first Prime Minister, now Sir John A. Macdonald, realized that despite the great step that had been taken, some of the hardest work still lay ahead. It remained to be seen whether policies could be found that would transform and expand the federation into a prosperous nation.

CHAPTER 26

The Uncertain Nation

"We don't know each other. We have no trade with each other. We have no facilities or resources or incentives, to mingle with each other. We are shut off from each other by a wilderness, geographically, commercially, politically and socially. We always cross the United States to shake hands." This description of the "New Nation" by the *Acadian Recorder* was pessimistic, but it did indicate the enormous difficulties that Canada faced. The new nation needed imaginative leaders if these divisions were ever to be overcome.

The man on whom the heaviest responsibility fell was Sir John A. Macdonald, the Dominion's first Prime Minister. The first quarter-century of Canada's history was to be almost completely dominated by this gay and shrewd politician. While Macdonald's first government still contained some representatives of the Liberal party, it rapidly became a purely Conservative administration. Brown had left the coalition almost as soon as Confederation had become a certainty. Indeed, it was somewhat amazing that the puritanical Scot from Toronto had been able to co-operate for so long with his debonair countryman from Kingston. In forming his first Dominion government, Macdonald had to bring in men from the Maritimes. Charles Tupper from Nova Scotia, who was later to become Macdonald's most faithful colleague, had to be left out of the first cabinet but Leonard Tilley from New Brunswick was given a portfolio. A. T. Galt and G. E. Cartier remained as the two chief pillars of strength in central Canada, which now became Ontario and Quebec. It was on these men that the greatest onus fell for making the experiment in nation-building a success.

1. ROUNDING OUT THE UNION

The first task of Macdonald's new government was to complete the physical structure of Confederation. Newfoundland and Prince Edward Island had remained aloof in 1867, while Nova Scotia had been absorbed reluctantly. To the West lay the territories of the

The Expansion of Confederation

Hudson's Bay Company, which, if not united to Canada, might fall into the hands of the United States. Beyond the Rockies lay Vancouver Island and British Columbia, united in 1866, whose population was overwhelmingly American. Each of these colonies would require different bait if they were to be attracted into the net of Canada's Manifest Destiny. In the end Macdonald caught all but Newfoundland, though none came without resistance.

In the East, Nova Scotia was the immediate problem. Out of the nineteen federal members of parliament from Nova Scotia, only one, Charles Tupper, was elected as a supporter of the new union. At the same time a provincial government with an anti-Confederation majority of thirty-six to two won power at Halifax. The leader of the forces which preached secession from Confederation was the powerful Joseph Howe. When his efforts to have the British government annul the union failed, and the United States turned a deaf ear to requests for a trading agreement, a compromise with the federal government became inevitable. In 1869 Macdonald used all his charm and persuasiveness to convince the Nova Scotians that a new financial arrangement involving "better terms" would redress their grievances. The price paid for an end to the secession movement was a cabinet post for Joseph Howe and an increase of $140,000 in the federal subsidy to Nova Scotia. Macdonald in his usual realistic way remarked: "Nova Scotia is about to take the shilling and enlist, though I am afraid it will consider itself for some time, a conscript rather than a volunteer."

It was another four years before Macdonald could overcome the sturdy independence of the little colony of Prince Edward Island. However, as the colony slipped further and further into debt in its efforts to build a railway, the prospect of assistance from the Canadian treasury grew more and more appealing. Moreover it became increasingly clear that large tracts of land owned by absentee landlords could never be purchased by Prince Edward Island without outside financial assistance. Assumption of its railway obligations, and a promise to buy out the absentee land-holders were the main features of the agreement which, in 1873, brought Prince Edward Island into the Canadian union. In addition, however, the federal government agreed to pay a generous annual subsidy to the Island government and to provide a means of communication with the mainland. The advantages to Canada of this union were both strategic and economic, for Prince Edward Island was desirable for the defence of Canada and for the control of the valuable Atlantic fisheries. For the same reasons, Canada wooed the colony of Newfoundland. Separated geographically from Canada and supported by the fisheries and commerce of the North Atlantic, the Newfoundlanders repeatedly resisted union with Canada until 1949.

The federal government faced even greater difficulties in extending its authority to the West. The western area presented four immediate difficulties: it was owned by the Hudson's Bay Company which was most reluctant to give up its valuable fur-trading territories without compensation; there was no established means of communication between Canada and the Red River colony; the settlers at Red River, most of whom were French and British half-breeds or Métis, showed no interest in becoming Canadians; and finally the United States, which had the most direct communications with Red River, was suspected of harbouring ambitions to annex the area. These factors, combined with the blunders of the federal government and the tactlessness of a small but noisy group of recent settlers from Ontario, help to explain the outbreak of the Red River Rebellion in 1869.

In November 1869, after a long series of negotiations, the Hudson's Bay Company gave up its claim to the Canadian West in return for a million and a half dollars in cash, 45,000 acres of land around its posts, and large tracts of land elsewhere. The purchased territory was transferred to the British government, which was to turn it over to Canada when the Dominion was ready for it. All of these negotiations had taken place without any consultation with the people in the Red River colony, who suspected that their property and cultural rights were in jeopardy. These suspicions were confirmed both by Canadian government land surveys in Red River, and by the boasts of many Canadians who had recently moved into the colony that they would soon be in command.

Under the leadership of Louis Riel, an eloquent and intelligent young Métis of unstable temperament, the half-breeds decided to defend their rights by force. Riel had no desire to make the colony an independent country, but only to make sure that the people had some voice in determining their own fate. "If we rebel against the country which wishes to buy us, we are not rebelling against the supremacy of England, which has not yet given its approval for the final transfer of this country. . . . We wish only that the people of Red River be a free people." The first step that Riel's followers took to protect their rights was to prevent the entry of William McDougall, the man appointed by Macdonald to assume authority in Red River on behalf of Canada following the transfer of that territory to the Canadian government. Riel then set up a provisional government to negotiate an agreement with Macdonald on the future of the colony. Unfortunately, the continued opposition of the Canadian minority in the colony enraged Riel, and, in March 1870, he undertook to show the Canadians that he meant business by executing a young Ontario troublemaker, Thomas Scott, on grounds of insubordination and striking his guards.

The execution of Scott brought a sudden calm to Red River, but it complicated the problem of reaching an agreement with Macdonald's government. Ontario demanded the head of Riel, and warned the government not to negotiate with "men who come here with their hands red with blood." Quebec, on the other hand, sympathized with Riel and his followers in their attempt to preserve their cultural identity. Thus Macdonald faced not only a rebellion in the West, but also a racial crisis in central Canada and within his own party, which demanded all the political agility he could muster.

To appease the Red River colony and Quebec, he agreed to negotiate with delegates from Red River on terms of entry into Confederation. The result was the Manitoba Act of 1870, which created the small province of Manitoba with the same institutions and powers as the older provinces. The Act guaranteed French language rights, Roman Catholic schools, and Métis land titles. The federal government gave the new province a generous financial subsidy but maintained control over unsettled lands in order to use them for the promotion of immigration and railway construction.

While these negotiations were under way, Macdonald's government tried to appease Ontario by sending a force of British regulars and Canadian militia to Red River to subdue the Métis, and also to show the United States that Canada meant to increase her authority in the West. But Riel had achieved his object and, not wishing to tempt fate, disappeared before the army reached Red River. Gradually relations between British and French in Canada returned to normal. But while Canada's political structure had survived a severe test, Sir John Macdonald had not heard the last of Louis Riel.

The final step in pushing the sovereignty of Canada to the Pacific was the incorporation of British Columbia. The Pacific colony was sparsely settled and heavily in debt after the gold rush had subsided in the 1860's. Before it lay the alternatives of union with Canada or annexation to the United States. The fear that the coastal colony would join the United States was enough to convince Macdonald and his colleagues that a generous offer should be made to British Columbia to attract it into the Confederation.

The Imperial authorities also believed that union with Canada offered the best solution to British Columbia's difficulties. In 1871, led by a colourful politician, who had changed his name from Smith to Amor de Cosmos (Lover of the World), the unionists in British Columbia triumphed and a delegation journeyed to Ottawa. The terms of union included not only a generous subsidy but, more important, the promise of a railway to the Pacific to be started in 1873 and completed in ten

The difficulties of Colonel Wolseley's troops, dispatched to the Red River colony in 1870, resulted not only from natural hazards. There was no possibility of sending troops through the United States, which would have afforded a quieter route; indeed the United States government even denied the Canadians the use of the canal at Sault Ste Marie for the transportation of military equipment. Moreover there was the fear that the Indians might cause trouble for, as one officer noted, "There is no doubt that a hundred determined men might have inflicted tremendous loss on the troops with comparative impunity; for, thoroughly acquainted with the vast network of lakes, they could have fired the boats as they passed through narrow channels, or blocked up the portages, and done much mischief in a variety of ways, while to have attempted to pursue them through the woods and lakes would have been madness." At Fort Frances, a group of Indians did threaten the troops, but were pacified with presents of pork and flour.

years. Macdonald wrote: "The terms can, I think, be fully justified on their own merits; but we may expect considerable opposition in our parliament on the ground that they are burdensome to the Dominion and too liberal to British Columbia." The Prime Minister was right. There was heavy criticism of the terms both in 1871 when they were accepted, and later when economic depression made them difficult to fulfil.

Thus by 1873, with both Prince Edward Island and British Columbia in the union, Canada stretched from sea to sea. It was a substantial achievement in five short years, but Canada remained a fragile union whose brittle skeleton had still to bé clothed in the flesh of economic and social development.

2. DIPLOMACY, RAILWAYS AND SCANDAL

Macdonald's plans for the development of Canada were strongly influenced by the fear that the United States had unfriendly intentions towards the new Dominion. At the same time he was fully aware of the importance of the large United States market for Canadian goods. Indeed, he never entirely gave up the hope that a new reciprocity agreement could be negotiated between the two countries. Unsettled relations between Britain and the United States, and also the strength of the protectionist interests in the United States, made it impossible to restore reciprocity in the first years after Confederation. But in 1871, when a conference was called in Washington to consider a variety of Anglo-American problems, Macdonald thought that the opportunity had arrived to begin discussions of the trade question.

Many of the questions considered at Washington directly affected Canada. The United States claim against Britain for damages caused by the British-built Confederate raider, *Alabama*, was the most important problem from the American point of view, but several disputes touched Canada more closely. There was a disagreement over the boundary between Canada and the United States in the Straits of Juan de Fuca off Vancouver Island; there was the question of damages claimed by Canada for the Fenian raids; and above all, there was the problem of the rights of American fishermen to fish in eastern Canada coastal waters. These latter rights had been granted to the United States by the 1854 reciprocity treaty, but that treaty had now been terminated. Nevertheless, American fishermen were naturally reluctant to abandon these rich fishing-grounds.

Since all these questions related to Canada, Macdonald himself was made a member of the British delegation, an appointment which represented recognition of Canada's new status. Unfortunately for Canada, Macdonald was caught in a very awkward situation at Washington, for the British were prepared to pay a fairly high price to win the friendship of the Americans. Macdonald described his difficulties in a letter to Charles Tupper in Ottawa:

MOTHER BRITANNIA: "Take care, my child!"
UNCLE SAM: "Oh! never mind, if she falls, I'll catch her!"

In 1870, as the Washington Conference approached, many Canadians feared that Britain might desert Canada, allowing the new nation to fall into the hands of the United States. And there were certainly Americans who looked forward to the destruction of British influence in North America. Senator Charles Sumner insisted in January, 1871: "The greatest trouble, if not peril, being a constant source of anxiety and disturbance, is from Fenianism, which is excited by the proximity of the British flag in Canada. Therefore the withdrawal of the British flag cannot be abandoned as a condition or preliminary of such a settlement as is now proposed. To make the settlement complete the withdrawal should be from this hemisphere, including provinces and islands."

If a majority of my colleagues should at any time conclude to accept terms that I do not approve of, I must, of course, either protest and withdraw, or remain on the Commission and trust to non-ratification of the treaty by Canada. If I take the first course it will disclose to the Americans the fact of a difference of opinion, a conflict, in fact, between Canada and England. This the Americans are anxious to establish, in order to get up a sort of quarrel between the two, and strengthen that party in England which desires to get rid of the colonies as a burden. If I continue to act on the Commission, I will be attacked for making an unworthy sacrifice of Canada's rights. . . .

Macdonald could not stand alone against the Americans and the British, and it soon became clear that Canada was going to make several sacrifices for the cause of better Anglo-American relations. After a period of hard bargaining, during which the Canadian Prime Minister put up a stiff but futile fight for reciprocity, the Treaty of Washington was signed. Under that agreement the Juan de Fuca boundary and the *Alabama* claims were referred to an arbitration board. Moreover, United States fishermen were to be allowed access to Canadian fisheries for a price which was also to be settled by arbitration. The British privately agreed to compensate Canada for Fenian damages. Macdonald knew that the treaty would not be popular at home; for while he had failed to get reciprocity the Americans had secured access to the Canadian fisheries.

Shortly after the acceptance of the Washington Treaty, the Canadian voters were given another reason to be dissatisfied with the Macdonald government. While it had been assumed since the first discussions of Confederation that a transcontinental railway would eventually bind the whole country together, the method of carrying out this expensive project had remained unsettled. The first railway to be built was the Intercolonial, which had been promised to the Maritimes in the British North America Act. In return for a British loan the Canadian government agreed to build the line to Halifax through the uninhabited forests of northern New Brunswick so that in the event of war with the United States it could not easily be destroyed by the Americans. Militarily the route made sense, but commercially it was a poor choice and politically it alienated the inhabitants of southern New Brunswick.

"WE IN CANADA SEEM TO HAVE LOST ALL IDEA OF JUSTICE, HONOR AND INTEGRITY."—THE MAIL, 26TH SEPTEMBER.

Building a railway to the Pacific coast also presented difficulties. The government decided that the railway could best be constructed by a private company with substantial government assistance of thirty million dollars and fifty million acres of choice land. So attractive were the terms that two companies were anxious to obtain the contract. One company, led by Senator D. L. Macpherson, was largely a Toronto organization. The other, headed by Sir Hugh Allan of Montreal, had the financial support of a group of American capitalists. Allan used all of his great influence with Macdonald and Cartier to win the contract. Not only did he exclude some of the Americans from the company on the request of Macdonald but he also contributed heavily to the Conservative campaign fund in 1872. A telegram from Macdonald during the campaign which read, "I must have another ten thousand; will be the last time of calling; do not fail me; answer today" was only one of the pieces of evidence which later brought about the Conservatives' downfall.

Macdonald was re-elected in 1872 and shortly afterwards gave Allan the contract. But a diligent Liberal Opposition soon uncovered the unsavoury details of Allan's $300,000 donation to the Conservative election fund. While Macdonald and Allan indignantly denied that the $300,000 had anything to do with the granting of the contract, even Macdonald's followers were disillusioned by what came to be called the "Pacific Scandal" and the Prime Minister was forced to resign in November 1873.

3. THE HESITANT LIBERALS AND CONSERVATIVE REVIVAL

The Liberals, who replaced the Macdonald government, were led by Alexander Mackenzie, a Sarnia stone-mason. Mackenzie was honest and a good administrator, but he lacked imagination and a capacity for leadership at a time when his party needed both. In 1873 the Liberal party was strongest in Ontario, but even there Mackenzie's grip on the party was not secure. His staunchest supporter was the sharp-tongued Richard Cartwright; but Cartwright was a free trader and was not very popular with business leaders in Canada who were anxious for tariff protection. Another Ontario minister was the brilliant but unpredictable Edward Blake who moved in and out of the cabinet at will and refused to bow to Mackenzie's leadership.

In Quebec the party was much weaker. The chief cause of this weakness was the strong opposition to the Liberals by a wing of the Roman Catholic Church, very powerful in Europe at that time, which held that the Church was superior to the state, and that a Catholic's first loyalty should be not to the state but rather to the Papacy which was "beyond the mountains." Thus the term "ultramontane" was applied to them. In Canada, by the middle of the nineteenth century, the ultramontane party in the Quebec Church was led by the strong-willed Bishop of Montreal, Monseigneur Bourget.

Bishop Bourget watched his diocese carefully in order to detect and stamp out any signs of anti-clericalism. Since European liberals were clearly anti-clerical, and even anti-religious, Bishop Bourget suspected that Liberals in Canada were guilty of the same sins. This suspicion was based not only on similarity of names, but also because he found in the Institut Canadien signs of the views he hated most. The Institut Canadien had been established in Montreal in 1844 with the purpose of organizing discussions and providing a library for its members. Before this apparently innocent institution was very old, however, Bishop Bourget discovered some facts about it that deeply disturbed him. In the first place, speeches were being made at the Institut's meetings which contained sentiments very like the anti-clerical doctrines frequently expressed by European liberals. One speaker had gone so far as to state that "the government of Pope Pius IX is the most despotic which exists in the world." Other members, including the old revolutionary, Louis-Joseph Papineau, who had returned to Canada from his long exile in France, maintained that the Church had no right to meddle in secular affairs. These anti-clerical speeches were bad enough, but the Bishop also learned that the Institut's library contained books that Roman Catholics were forbidden to read without the approval of the Church. The Bishop therefore decided to take firm action against the offending organization.

When Bishop Bourget insisted that the interdicted books be removed from the Institut's library, the members replied that, since their organization was secular and had a civil charter, the Church had no control over it. This was an open challenge to the authority of the Bishop. The war between the Bishop and the Institut raged for several years until finally, in 1869, Monseigneur Bourget, with Papal support, issued a pastoral letter forbidding Roman Catholics to belong to the Institut. Anyone who refused to follow the Bishop's instructions was to be denied the sacraments of the Church.

The matter might have ended there, for membership in the Institut was already declining, but shortly after the issuing of the Bishop's pastoral letter an obscure member of the Institut named Joseph Guibord died. Since Guibord had refused to renounce his membership in the Institut the Church refused to allow his body to be buried in that part of the cemetery reserved for Roman Catholics. Guibord's friends took the case to the courts in an attempt to force the Church to allow the body to be buried in the Roman Catholic cemetery. The essential issue in this case was whether the matter was to be governed by civil or Church law and, in effect, whether the Church was subordinate to the state. It was not until 1874 that the legal question was finally settled when the Judicial Committee of the Privy Council, the final court of appeal, ruled that Guibord had a right to be buried in a Roman Catholic cemetery.

Thus, nearly six years after his death, Guibord was to be buried properly. The first attempt to move his body to the Roman Catholic cemetery was a failure, for his funeral cortège was halted by a mob of irate citizens. A few days later, under the protection of a thousand armed soldiers, Guibord was finally buried and his grave covered with cement to prevent any attempt to remove the body. But Bishop Bourget was not yet defeated. The day after the funeral, he announced that the ground which contained Guibord's body was not to be considered consecrated ground!

In itself the Guibord case was not important, but it threw into relief the strength of the hostility that some leaders of the powerful Roman Catholic Church in Quebec felt towards anti-clerical organizations. The Liberal party, some of whose supporters had belonged to the Institut, was looked upon with deep suspicion by clerics like Bishop Bourget. Thus the party found itself seriously handicapped in Quebec. "Our great weakness," Wilfrid Laurier, a young Quebec Liberal, told a friend in 1874, "is the everlasting one: the hostility of the priests."

The young Laurier took it upon himself to try to bring the running battle between the clergy and the Liberal party to an end. To do this he believed that he had to convince the Roman Catholic Church that Canadian Liberals had nothing in common with the revolutionary, anti-clerical liberals of Europe. In June 1877, he put forward his views in a brilliant speech on "Political Liberalism" in which he denied the charges made by the Church against his party. He claimed that Canadian Liberals accepted the evolutionary, reformist views of British liberals rather than the radicalism of European liberalism. He added that the Roman Catholic Church had nothing to fear from his party, though he made it clear that he did not believe that priests had any right to use the spiritual power of the Church to influence the political opinions of their parishioners.

A second point in Laurier's famous speech was a warning that it was dangerous for Quebec to listen to those politicians and priests who wanted to form a Roman Catholic party:

> You wish to organize all Catholics into one party, without other bond, without other basis than a common religion; but have you not reflected that by that very fact you will organize the Protestant population as a single party, and that then, instead of the peace and harmony now prevailing between the different elements of the Canadian population, you will throw open the doors to a war, a religious war, the most terrible of all wars?

Laurier's opposition to a Roman Catholic party, or a French-Canadian party was a view he continued to hold throughout his long political career.

Laurier made his speech at an opportune moment, for Bishop Conroy had been sent by Pope Leo XIII, a far more liberal prelate than Pius IX, to examine the Church-state problem in Quebec. Conroy accepted Laurier's definition of liberalism in Canada and agreed that clerical intervention in politics was unwise. In future, the Quebec bishops were forbidden "to teach from the pulpit or elsewhere that it is a sin to vote for any particular candidate or party; even more it is forbidden to announce that you will refuse the sacraments for this cause. You are never to give your personal opinions from the pulpit." It was a striking triumph for the young Laurier.

The Mackenzie administration secured a number of important reforms in the political system. Under the direction of Edward Blake, the Minister of Justice, several important steps were taken to widen Canadian powers of self-government. In 1875 a Canadian Supreme Court was established which limited the number of appeals taken to the Privy Council in England, though it did not end them. In addition, Blake succeeded in having the powers of the governor-general clarified in order to limit further his right to act without the advice of the cabinet. Other reforms included the introduction of the secret ballot, a Corrupt Practices Act to prevent bribery of public officials, and legislation to control election expenses, all of which helped to reduce corruption and raise the level of Canadian political life.

When the Liberals moved from constitutional and political reforms to plans for economic development, however, their record was much less impressive. No sooner was the Mackenzie government in office than a world-wide trade depression slowed down the growth of the Canadian economy and caused a serious decline in government revenues. While the Intercolonial railway was pushed ahead and completed in 1876, the Pacific railway problem was more difficult to solve. The Mackenzie government constructed seven hundred miles of line through northern Ontario, largely to connect existing water-ways, and surveyed much of the route. But the pace was much too slow for Manitoba and British

To the Liberals who had often heard the Conservatives trumpet the values of reciprocity and free trade, the National Policy looked suspiciously like a ruse to secure office. The Grit Prime Minister, Alexander Mackenzie, was blunt in his denunciation of protection: "The very idea of protection is embodied in Robinson Crusoe building his own house with a knife made out of bone, whittling a weed out of which he made cloth with needles of bone and stitching it into articles of clothing. . . . Undoubtedly Robinson Crusoe was the leader of the protectionist party on the Island of Juan Fernandez at that time. Let any of our protectionist friends . . . go and live as Mr. Robinson did and thus practise what they so adroitly teach."

Columbia, while Ontario complained of the heavy taxes necessary to build a railway across a sea of muskeg and mountain. To bolster the country's sagging economy, Mackenzie's government made another attempt to secure reciprocity with the United States in 1874, only to see an indifferent American Senate reject the bill without any serious discussion.

The rumblings of economic discontent mounted and as the 1878 election approached the electoral pendulum was clearly swinging back towards the Conservatives. The people were beginning to believe the Conservative posters that proclaimed: "The weevil came in with the Grits [Liberals] and prosperity with John A." Shrewd Sir John and his able colleague, Tupper, were convinced that they knew the desires of the country when they began campaigning for a "National Policy." In its most elementary form, the National Policy meant a protective tariff for Canadian industry; but it meant more than just a tariff. It also meant a return to vigorous government support for railway building, immigration, and overall economic development. In the election of 1878 the voters forgot past Tory sins and voted for the National Policy. Macdonald was to be given another chance.

CHAPTER 27

Railways, Riel and Sectionalism

Sir John A. Macdonald had already announced his plans for the economic development of the country when he and the Conservatives returned to office in 1878. He intended to replace the hesitant Liberal programme of railway building with a vigorous new scheme. During the election campaign he had also promised to raise the tariff to protect Canadian industry and to stimulate new economic growth within a transcontinental economy. Finally, more people were needed to build up the home market for Canadian products. When the empty plains were filled, they would become the breadbasket of the nation. Western wheat would be shipped along the new railway line to be exchanged for eastern manufactured goods. But as Macdonald was to learn, it was far easier to plan the National Policy than it was to guarantee its success.

1. IMPLEMENTING THE NATIONAL POLICY

In 1879 the first of the new policies was implemented when the tariff was increased on both agricultural and manufactured products entering Canada. The new duties on manufactured products, amounting to twenty-five per cent and higher, were the most important features of the tariff, for Canadian farmers had little to fear from foreign competition. The high protection thus given to industry later caused farmers and Maritimers to criticize the tariff as a policy designed to meet only the needs of central Canada. But Macdonald and his Finance Minister, Leonard Tilley, argued, and expected, that the tariff would benefit all sections of the country by helping to encourage a diversified and prosperous economy. Perhaps the importance of Macdonald's tariff policy is best illustrated by the fact that few governments after 1879 have seriously attempted to change it.

Rapid completion of the Canadian Pacific Railway was vital to the Conservative prescription for a prosperous economy. Liberal policy had been for the government to build the railway on a "pay-as-you-go" plan,

In this cartoon entitled "On the Fence" Officer Macdonald is saying, "No more jumping over the fence, Jonathan. You must go around by the gate and pay your toll."

In advocating the National Policy of tariff protection, Sir John Macdonald had said: "Not only is this country made a slaughter market by being overwhelmed by the sweepings of the United States, but it has sometimes been made a sacrifice market by ruinous proposals for the purpose of suppressing any given trade. We all remember what the salt manufacturers of the United States did when the salt manufacturers first opened work in Goderich. The salt manufacturers of Syracuse and Salena sent in their salt with instructions to undersell Canadian salt on the Canadian market, to crush this infant industry. The shoe trade was dealt with in the same way by the leather manufacturers of the United States." Canadian manufacturers, he said, could not compete; plants would close and the people move to the United States.

in order to keep taxes and government expenditure low. Once back in office Macdonald returned to his original policy of appealing to private contractors to build the line by offering lavish government assistance. In 1880 a new Canadian Pacific Railway syndicate was formed under George Stephen of the Bank of Montreal, and Donald Smith of the Hudson's Bay Company. The government offered these businessmen twenty-five million dollars, twenty-five million acres of the best land in the West, seven hundred miles of completed railway, permanent tax exemptions on railway property, duty-free importation of necessary building materials, and a promise to prohibit the construction of competing lines to the south or southwest of the Canadian Pacific Railway line for twenty years. The railway was to be completed by 1891. The generosity of these terms demonstrated Macdonald's determination to get the railway built. In February 1881, the Prime Minister wrote to A. T. Galt: "At last the C.P.R. is a fixed fact. Royal assent given, Royal charter under the act issued, company organized, and it now remains for Stephen and Company to show what mettle they are made of."

But Macdonald's troubles were just beginning, for the generous assistance given to the builders of the C.P.R. in the original contract was not enough to ensure completion of the railway. By 1883 the company was at the government's door with a request for a loan almost as large as the original cash grant. Macdonald's first impulse was to reject the request, but he was quickly reminded by one of his advisers that "the day the

Canadian Pacific busts, the Conservative party busts the day after." Macdonald knew that the fate of the government and perhaps even the fate of the country depended on finishing the railway. He granted the loan. Two years later, another loan was requested and granted, this time with less hesitancy, for the railway had just proven its worth by transporting troops to the Northwest during the second Riel rebellion.

Although building a transcontinental railway was a very expensive project for a young country, Macdonald insisted that it was imperative for Canada's survival. Only with a railway to provide the basis for economic development could the widely separated sections of the country be welded into a single nation. As he explained in 1878: "Until this great work is completed our Dominion is little more than a 'geographical expression.' We have as much interest in British Columbia as in Australia, and no more. The railway once finished, we become one great united country with a large interprovincial trade and a common interest."

On November 7, 1885 Macdonald received a long-awaited telegram. "The first train from Montreal is approaching Yale, within a few hours of the Pacific Coast. The last spike was driven this morning by Honourable Donald Smith at Craigellachie, in Eagle Pass, some 340 miles from Port Moody. On reaching the coast our running time from Montreal, exclusive of stoppages, will be five days, averaging twenty-four miles per hour." It was a great day for Canada, rivalling in importance July 1 itself.

The completion of the Canadian Pacific Railway was perhaps the major achievement of the Macdonald government. The results of the government's immigration policies were much less impressive. Immigration, too, was of major importance to Canada, for the railway would be of little value if it passed through a sparsely populated country. The government hoped that, once the railway made the prairies accessible, immigrants, especially from Great Britain, would flock to Canada. "The most important subject which can engage the attention of the High Commissioner in England," Macdonald told A. T. Galt, Canada's first High Commissioner, "is the development of the North-West Territory." But only a few settlers came. A world depression lowered prices and dried up trade throughout North America. Canada was particularly hard hit because as an underdeveloped country she depended heavily on outside sources for capital investment. Moreover, as a producer of grain and raw materials, Canada prospered only when there was an expanding foreign market for these products. Since there was no expanding foreign market in the late eighties and early nineties, Canada's economy stagnated and it was very difficult to attract new settlers. Many of those who came soon found life too hard and moved on south to the United States. By the 1890's even natural increase failed to enlarge the population, as many native-born Canadians gave up hope of better times and moved to the United States.

Thus, by the 1890's the hopes upon which Macdonald's National Policy were built remained largely unfulfilled. The government was not entirely

As part of its immigration programme, the government of Canada encouraged group settlement and set aside blocks of land in Manitoba for Swiss, German, Scottish and other settlers. The most successful settlement was the Mennonite colony established in 1874. The first group is shown here as they arrived in Winnipeg.

Determined to leave Russia when their right to exemption from military service was cancelled, the Mennonites searched far and wide before selecting Manitoba as their future home. The Canadian government promised them freedom of worship, freedom from military service, and the right to their own schools. By 1879 there were six thousand Mennonites in Manitoba.

to blame, for it had no control over the external economic forces which had such a profound effect on Canadian development. Even more serious than Canada's economic difficulties, however, were the cultural and sectional clashes that threatened the very existence of the new Dominion.

2. RIEL AGAIN

Macdonald had naturally designed his immigration policies to people western Canada. In the early 1880's the pace of settlement had increased and the West was experiencing its first real boom. When the Canadian Pacific Railway reached Winnipeg in 1881, a stream of settlers and fortune seekers poured into Manitoba. Between 1871 and 1883, the population of the province grew from 25,000 to 150,000. As land prices soared, new settlers moved on to the Northwest Territories where the population expanded from a few hundred in 1871 to 50,000 twenty years later.

But by 1883, this short-lived bubble of western prosperity had burst. As world grain prices fell, western farmers felt the pinch of economic depression and attacked the federal government's economic policies. The farmers resented the high rates charged by the Canadian Pacific Railway for carrying grain to market. They criticized the tariff as a device to force them to pay high prices for goods produced by eastern manufacturers. By 1884 many western farmers were convinced that the federal government was completely ignoring their needs. A few agrarian leaders talked of open rebellion. One organizer of the Manitoba "Farmers Union" wrote in 1884 that the time had come for direct action. "The fact of the matter is, we have nothing to resist us, the military here is nothing but a pack of boys, and we have easy access to the store rooms." Farther west the British and European settlers were equally unrestrained. An editorial in the Edmonton *Bulletin* asked:

> If it was not by—not threatening, but actual rebellion and appeals to the British government for justice that the people of Ontario gained the rights they enjoy today and freed themselves from a condition precisely similar to that into which the Northwest is being rapidly forced, how was it? Was it not by armed rebellion coupled with murder, that Manitoba attained the rights she enjoys today from the very men who now hold the reins of power at Ottawa? If history is to be taken as a guide, what could be plainer than that without rebellion the people of the Northwest need expect nothing, while with rebellion, successful or otherwise, they may reasonably expect to get their rights.

The Prince Albert *Times* agreed with this view: "There is a ring of true metal about it which indicates pretty plainly the temper of the Nor'Wester."

But despite dissatisfaction and even rebellious muttering among these settlers, the most serious discontent in the West was among the Indians and the Métis. Both groups felt that the pressure of the expanding European population threatened their lands and their nomadic way of life. The Dominion government's Indian policy aimed at gradually settling the wandering tribes on reservations. Though not a very generous policy, it was fairer in its treatment of the Indians and was more successfully carried out than the policy of the United States, where settlement of the West had cost a good many lives—mainly Indian. But not all the Indians in western Canada were prepared to exchange their freedom and independence for a quiet life on a reservation. A few tribes remained sullenly suspicious of the threat implicit in advancing settlement. In 1884 a government agent wrote: "I never saw the Indians mean business before, the thing has got to be looked at seriously and precautions taken before it is too late." In Ottawa the warning was largely ignored.

The claims of the Métis received no more attention than those of the Indians. Many Métis had moved to the Northwest Territories from Manitoba after 1870 to establish their own independent community free from the influences and controls of a dominant Anglo-European civilization. By the 1880's a new crisis jeopardized their dream of freedom, for once again the vanguard of a new wave of surveyors and settlers threatened their landholdings, to which they had never legally established claims. No doubt the Métis had been careless about legal technicalities but the Macdonald government casually and consistently ignored all their pleas for a settlement of their land claims. The new advance of settlement was particularly serious for the Métis because there remained no new attractive uninhabited areas into which they could move.

In Ottawa Macdonald's government seemed to have too many other problems to consider the grievances of the westerners. Although the warnings of approaching disaster became more and more urgent, Macdonald, the Minister responsible for the West, continued to ignore petitions which demanded generous treatment for the Indians and Métis, settlement of land titles, lower tariffs and local self-government. In the fall of 1884 the government agent in the West wrote to the Prime Minister: "If the half-breed question is arranged this winter it will settle the whole business; if not a good force in the North will be necessary." But Macdonald took the light-hearted and cynical view that "no amount of concession will prevent people from grumbling and agitating." By the beginning of 1885, the troubles in the Northwest were far more serious than Macdonald realized.

In March 1884, the Métis had invited Louis Riel to return from Montana, where he was teaching, to lead them once again. Their invitation mentioned some of their grievances:

> We may say that the part of the North-West in which we are living is Manitoba before the troubles with the difference that there are more people, they understand things better, and that they are more determined; you will form an idea as to the conditions upon which the people base their claims, for the reason that there are many people in the North-West whom the government has recognized less than Indians; and yet it is these poor half-breeds who have always defended the North-West at the price of their blood and their sacrifices for a country which is stirring up the whole world today.

The letter concluded: "The whole race is calling you!" Riel returned reluctantly. He was now fifteen years older and his mental instability had increased. For a time, after the 1870 uprising, he had undergone treatment in an asylum and suffered from religious delusions. The Riel who arrived in Prince Albert in the spring of 1885 was a man suffering from religious and political delusions which made him entirely unfit for the task he had assumed.

With Riel's return the Métis' discontent rose to fever pitch. The situation was even more explosive than in 1869, for this time it also involved several Indian tribes led by two powerful warriors, Poundmaker and Big Bear. Fighting broke out in March at Duck Lake when a North West Mounted Police detachment, sent to investigate a Métis gathering, was driven off by force. Immediately after this victory, Poundmaker seized Battleford, and Big Bear's Indian followers massacred settlers in the little village of Frog Lake.

These bloody events finally roused Ottawa. Macdonald dispatched a force of 8,000 men, under General Middleton. The swift arrival of this force, made possible by the newly completed Canadian Pacific Railway,

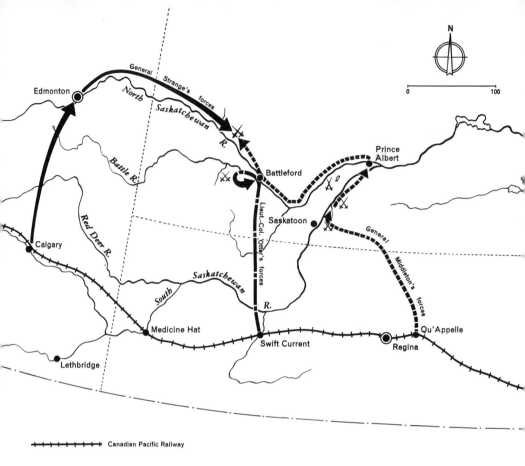

The Northwest Rebellion

ended the threat of a general Indian uprising. But complete pacification was not gained without further bloodshed. At Fish Creek the Métis forces won a last victory, before the superior number of government troops forced the rebels to surrender at Batoche. On May 15, 1885 Louis Riel surrendered and was taken to Regina to stand trial.

The fate of Louis Riel had raised a furore in central Canada in 1870. Once more in 1885 English-speaking Canadians demanded Riel's life as a revolutionary and as the murderer (in 1870) of Thomas Scott. In Quebec French Canadians, overlooking Riel's religious heresy, sang the praises of the Métis leader as the defender of French-Canadian minority rights. Even the moderate Laurier declared: "Had I been born on the banks of the Saskatchewan I would myself have shouldered a musket to fight against the neglect of governments and the shameless greed of speculators."

Riel stood trial in Regina in the summer of 1885. His defence lawyers argued that he was insane and therefore not responsible for his acts. Riel denied that he was unbalanced. An English-speaking Protestant jury found him guilty and sentenced him to hang, although his English-speaking

"I know that through the grace of God, I am the founder of Manitoba. I know that though I have no open road for my influence, I have big influence—concentrated as a big amount of vapour in an engine. I believe by what I have suffered for fifteen years, by what I have done for Manitoba and the people of the Northwest, that my words are worth something," Louis Riel declared before the crowded little court room in Regina. The jury found him guilty of treason and recommended clemency. The judge sentenced him to hang.

lieutenant, William Jackson, was quickly found innocent because of insanity. Macdonald now had to face the difficult question of whether to grant the Métis leader a reprieve. Subjected to pressure from all sides, the Prime Minister finally decided to let Riel die, thinking that Quebec would stand by him anyway. "We will have lively times in Quebec," he wrote, "but I feel pretty confident that the excitement will die out."

On November 16, 1885, Louis Riel was hanged. In death he became a martyr to the cause of French-Canadian rights. "Riel, our brother, is dead, victim of his devotion to the cause of the Métis of whom he was the leader, victim of fanaticism and treason," declared Honoré Mercier, who would soon be premier of Quebec. Riel's execution opened a Pandora's box of sectional and cultural discontents which plagued Macdonald until his death and eventually destroyed his Conservative party.

3. CONSTITUTIONAL AND SECTIONAL TROUBLES

Riel's execution caused Quebec to turn in on herself and re-examine the position of a cultural minority within Confederation. Macdonald's decision to allow Riel to die, despite Quebec's opposition, was the first warning to French Canadians after 1867 that on issues which united English-speaking Canada the minority would have to accept defeat. Fortunately for Quebec, English-speaking Canadians were united on few public questions.

The immediate result of Riel's execution on the political level was to weaken the Conservative party's hold on Quebec, a hold which had been loosening since Cartier's death in 1873. In federal politics this weakening was not immediately apparent. Macdonald's French-Canadian colleagues stood by him because they feared their resignations would start a racial war. But on the provincial level the Conservatives were driven from office by a coalition of Liberals and French-Canadian nationalists led by the passionate orator, Honoré Mercier. Now the Liberals had a strong foothold in Quebec, which, combined with their strength in Ontario, could be used to launch an attack on the Conservatives in Ottawa. Macdonald recognized the danger at once. "The triumph of the Liberals over the corpse of Riel," he told Charles Tupper, "changes the aspect of affairs *quoad* [with respect to] the Dominion government completely. It will encourage the Grits and opposition generally; will dispirit our friends, and will, I fear, carry the country against us at the general election." Macdonald's prediction was not entirely accurate, for the Conservatives did win the election of 1887.

Mercier in Quebec was not the only thorn in Macdonald's flesh. By the late 1880's the premiers of both Ontario and Manitoba were attacking his conception of the Canadian federal system. Sir John A. Macdonald believed in the necessity of strong central government, with the provinces holding minor positions. One way in which the Conservative leader had restricted the activities of the provinces was by exercising the federal power of disallowance. Under the British North America Act the federal government could veto provincial laws which it considered were unconstitutional or which seemed to conflict with the national interest. Between 1867 and 1896, the federal government disallowed sixty-eight provincial laws. Among them were laws passed by the Manitoba government to charter railways to run to the United States boundary and destroy the Canadian Pacific Railway's monopoly, which Manitoba farmers blamed for high freight rates and inadequate branch lines and elevators. Since these acts were in conflict with the monopoly that the railway had been granted in

LET THE BIG CHIEF BEWARE!

A cartoon by Bengough shows Manitoba borne down by the C.P.R. monopoly. Macdonald's response to the complaints from the West was revealed in a confidential letter written to a supporter: "When the North West is filled with people—**they may agitate as they please against it**—but it is not for the present population of Canada or the provinces east of Manitoba to exclaim against a monopoly (if it be one) created for their special benefit. Manufacturers might as well complain of a Protective Tariff especially made for their advantage."

1880, Macdonald had them disallowed, even though they had been passed by a Conservative government in Manitoba. The result was serious discontent in Manitoba, and the defeat of the provincial government by one pledging itself to an anti-Macdonald crusade. Ontario, too, felt that it had suffered unjustly from Macdonald's free use of the power of disallowance, especially in the matter of control of navigation on rivers and streams.

Discontent also developed in the Maritimes during the 1880's. Confederation had not brought prosperity to the Maritimes and the depression of the 1870's and 1880's had hit them badly. While their economic problems were due largely to changes in the world economy and transportation systems (such as the widespread use of the iron ship which destroyed their shipbuilding industry) they laid the blame squarely on the doorstep of the federal government. The chief criticism was levelled at the tariff, which not only increased the cost of manufactured goods, but also, by reducing imports, made it more difficult for foreign countries to buy Canadian exports. To the Maritimer the tariff looked like an instrument of the devil, the latter only faintly disguised as an Ontario or Quebec manufacturer. By 1886 discontent in Nova Scotia had reached such a pitch that Premier W. S. Fielding's Liberal government passed a motion upholding the province's right to secede from Confederation.

These conflicts between the federal government and the provinces came to a head in 1887, when the premiers of Ontario and Quebec summoned an Interprovincial Conference to discuss the grievances of the provinces. British Columbia and Prince Edward Island, which had Conservative governments, refused to send delegates, and Macdonald, who had been invited to send representatives, chose to ignore the meeting and condemned it as a Liberal party rally. Nevertheless, the representatives of five provinces met, and passed a series of resolutions which were designed to alter the constitution and weaken the federal government. The dissident provinces called for increased subsidies, a voice for the provinces in choosing senators, and the transfer of the federal power of disallowance to the Imperial government. Far more important than the resolutions passed by the Interprovincial Conference was its illustration of the opposition that had developed to Macdonald's policies.

Although the provincial premiers failed to weaken the powers of the federal government, Macdonald faced another kind of attack that was not as easy to withstand. He could fight the provinces to a standstill at home, but when they carried their cases to the Judicial Committee of the Privy Council in England, the last court of appeal, he was less successful. As early as 1883 the Privy Council had begun to hand down decisions whose effect was to emphasize the legislative powers of the provincial governments and restrict the federal authority. Though Macdonald believed that the constitution was being misinterpreted by the Judicial Committee, he had no way of fighting the decisions. By 1896 the provinces, with the aid of the English judges, had won for themselves a breadth of power that Macdonald thought had been effectively denied to them in 1867.

4. THE OLD MAN, THE OLD FLAG, THE OLD POLICY

In the last years of Macdonald's life the country that he had led for so long suffered under strains that seemed to threaten its very existence. After the hanging of Louis Riel in 1885, relations between English-speaking and French-speaking Canadians moved slowly towards a crisis. But the "Old Chieftain's" most serious problem was the depressed economic condition of the country. By the late 1880's it was evident that the National Policy had not produced a prosperous and united Canada. The main difficulty was the world-wide economic depression, but as conditions grew worse, many people became convinced that the basic cause of Canada's economic difficulties was the high tariff. This view found strong support among farmers, and people living in the Maritimes, who believed that the high tariff benefited only the manufacturers of central Canada. What Canada needed was not protection, but free trade with the United States, which would not only allow Canadians to sell their products on the huge American market, but would reduce the cost of goods imported from the United States.

As conditions in the country became more serious, the Liberals, who had always fought for freer trade, intensified their attack on the Conservative tariff policy. In 1887, the Liberal party advocated complete free trade with the United States, or "unrestricted reciprocity." In the federal election campaign of 1891, the chief issue was the National Policy versus unrestricted reciprocity.

The Liberals argued that unrestricted reciprocity would mean the removal of all tariffs between Canada and the United States, but each country would maintain its own tariff against the rest of the world. Macdonald and the Conservatives claimed that unrestricted reciprocity was impossible unless Canada and the United States adopted a single, uniform tariff against other countries. If this were not done, products imported into the United States could move freely into Canada without being subject to Canadian tariff laws. The Conservatives believed that a common tariff would mean commercial union between Canada and the United States. The inevitable consequence of commercial union, they argued, would be the political union of the two countries and the disappearance of Canada.

Macdonald was not opposed to a limited trade agreement with the United States, provided that it did not threaten the basis of the national economy that he was attempting to establish. Indeed, in 1891 his government attempted to negotiate a new trade treaty with the Americans. But the effort failed. Therefore, in order to counter the growing popularity of the Liberal proposal, Macdonald condemned unrestricted reciprocity as disloyal and a threat to Canadian independence. In the election campaign, the Conservative slogan was "the old man, the old flag, the old policy." Macdonald set the tone of his campaign with his famous declaration:

> The question which you will shortly be called upon to determine resolves itself into this: Shall we endanger our possession of the great

In this cartoon on Macdonald's 1891 campaign, Sir John is saying: "What, traitor! Deal with a Yankee, and thus betray the Old Flag! Never, Never! What's that—you must trade or die? Then die, a thousand times! What can be more glorious than to die for the Old Flag?!" (In a footnote "Old Flag" is defined as a euphemism for Protected Monopolists who contribute liberally to election funds.)

TROOLY LOIL!

heritage bequeathed to us by our fathers . . . with the prospect of ultimately becoming a portion of the American Union? As for myself, my course is clear. A British subject I was born, a British subject I will die. With my utmost effort, with my latest breath, will I oppose the "veiled treason" which attempts by sordid means and mercenary offers to lure our people from their allegiance.

The emotions stirred up by Macdonald's plea, the support of the businessmen whose interests were protected by the high tariff, and the fear of many people that the Liberal policy would lead to political union with the United States, enabled the Conservatives to limp back into office by the narrowest possible margin. Macdonald had once more succeeded in winning his countrymen to his concept of Canada as an independent British nation in North America. Even the Liberals concluded that unrestricted reciprocity was not a policy that the electorate would support, and in 1893 it was dropped from the party's platform.

Nevertheless, the result of the election of 1891 was as much a personal victory for old Sir John as it was for his party or his policy. For more than thirty years he had been at the centre of events in British North America. The shaping of the new nation, both its successes and its failures, had taken place under Macdonald's guidance. Even his opponent, Laurier, admitted that Macdonald's "actions displayed unbounded fertility of resource, a high level of intellectual conception, and, above all, a far reaching vision beyond the event of the day, and still higher, permeating the whole, a broad patriotism, a devotion to Canada's welfare, Canada's advancement, Canada's glory."

Even as Macdonald formed his new cabinet in 1891, there were frightening signs of new cultural conflicts that would be difficult to settle. But Macdonald did not have to face these problems. Tired out from the hard winter of campaigning, the old man died on June 6, 1891. Goldwin Smith, an English historian living in Canada, wrote: "When this man is gone who will there be to take his place? Who else is there who knows the sheep or whose voice the sheep know? Who else could make Orangemen vote for Papists, or induce half the members for Ontario to help in levying on their own province the necessary blackmail for Quebec? Yet this is the work that will have to be done if a general break-up is to be averted." During the five years that followed Macdonald's death, no one was found in the Conservative ranks who had the master magician's touch.

CHAPTER 28

Race, Religion and Victory for Laurier

While Macdonald had successfully countered the major challenge to his National Policy by defeating reciprocity, he had not conjured away other threats to the national unity. Above all, he had been unable to soothe the increasing bitterness of the relations between French- and English-speaking Canadians. After his death, the Conservative party was unable to find a leader of similar stature and ability. For five unhappy years a succession of Conservative leaders wrestled with problems of race and religion, as their party was torn apart by internal divisions and external pressures.

1. MOUNTING CONFLICT

After the hanging of Louis Riel, the relations between French- and English-speaking Canadians grew increasingly strained and acrimonious. In Quebec, the martyred Riel became a symbol of the injustice and tyranny of the English-speaking majority. As one French-Canadian leader remarked: "In killing Riel, Sir John has not only struck a blow at the heart of our race, but above all he struck at the cause of justice and humanity, which represented in all languages and sanctified by all religious beliefs, begged mercy for the prisoner of Regina, our poor brother of the North West." Conscious as never before of their minority position in Canada and their weakness in the face of a united English-speaking community, the French Canadians became increasingly nationalistic and sensitive to any assaults on their culture.

In English-speaking Canada, Riel also became a symbol, a symbol of the British nature of the new Canadian nation. By the late 1880's, many English-speaking Canadians were loud in their assertions that Canada was an English and Protestant country and vigorous in echoing Lord Durham's contention that the nation could not survive as a country of two cultures. While most realized that the people of Quebec could never be assimilated, they were adamant in opposing the spread of French culture beyond the

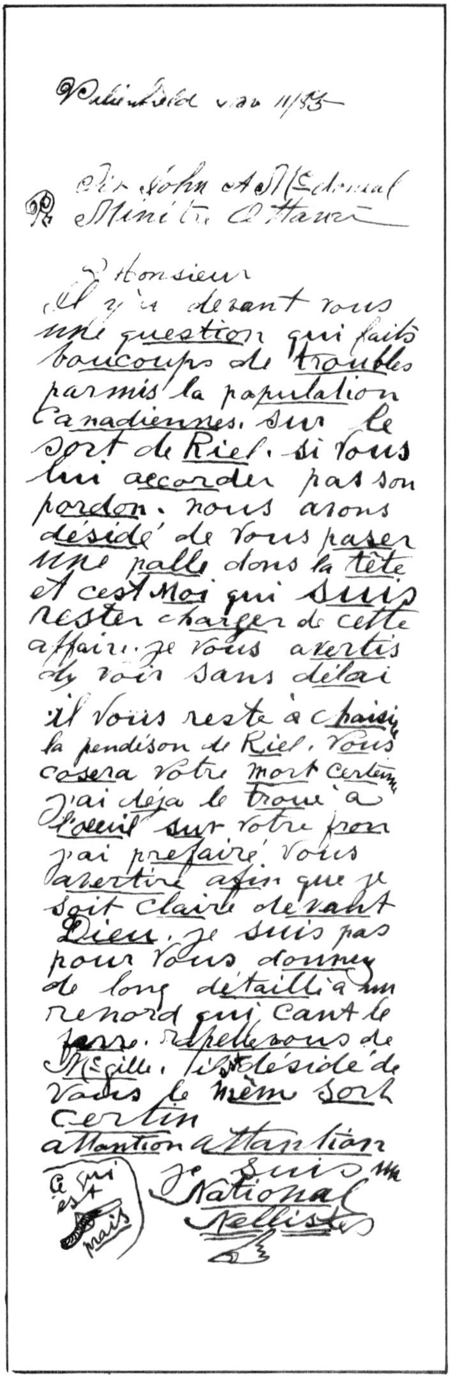

[Handwritten letter, in French:]

Prairieside v 20 11/85

Sir John A McDonald
Ministre Ottawa

J'Monsieur

Il y a devant vous une question qui fait boucoups de troubles parmis la papulation Canadiennes. sur le sort de Riel. si vous lui accorder pas son pordon. nous avons deside de vous paser une palle dans la tête Et cest Moi qui suis rester charger de cette affaire. je vous avertis de voir sans delai

Il Vous reste à chaisir la pendison de Riel. Vous cosera votre mort certain j'ai deja le trou à l'oeuil sur votre front j'ai prefaire vous avertir afin que je soit claire devant Dieu. je suis pas pour vous donner de long detaillé à un renord qui cant le jarre. rapellevous de McGill. l'Isleside de Vades le mêm sort certin a Mantion attantion

je suis National Vellist

[Handwritten letter, in English:]

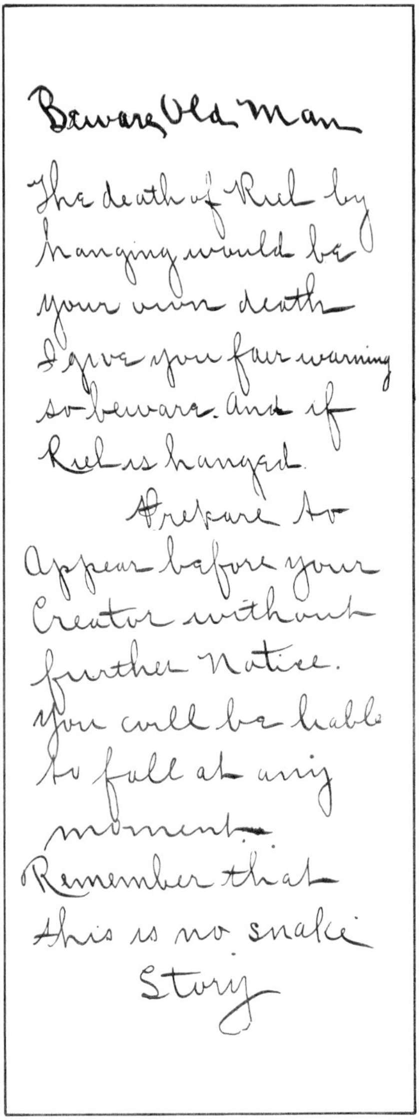

Beware Old Man

The death of Riel by hanging would be your own death I give you fair warning so beware. And if Riel is hanged.

Prepare to Appear before your Creator without further Notice. You will be liable to fall at any moment. Remember that this is no snake Story

An illustration of the tragic divisions over the fate of Louis Riel and the racial passions that his death aroused can be seen in the letters to Sir John Macdonald in the Public Archives of Canada. Macdonald was warned not only that the life of the party would be determined by Riel's fate but even that his own life was at stake.

borders of that province. Claims of the French Canadians for recognition of their minority rights and respect for their culture outside of Quebec were treated with contempt by English-Canadian extremists. As the *Orange Sentinel*, spokesman for the anti-Catholic Orange Order and other like-minded English-speaking Canadians, declared in 1886: "Must it be said that the rights and liberties of English people, this English colony, depend upon a foreign race? The day is near when an appeal to arms will be heard in all parts of Canada. Then, certainly, our soldiers, benefiting by the lessons of the past, will have to complete the work they have begun in the North West." The basic question facing Canada, exclaimed D'Alton McCarthy, a prominent Conservative, was "whether this country is to be English or French." The Liberal John Charlton observed that "the sentiment that received the greatest applause was when I asserted that a successful French nationality in the North American Continent was a hopeless dream, for that question had been settled upon the Plains of Abraham." The *Orange Sentinel*, McCarthy and Charlton represented the extreme view, but the extremists seemed often to drown out the moderates who, like Sir John Macdonald, believed that "there is no paramount race in this country, there is no conquered race in this country; we are all British subjects and those who are not English are none the less British subjects on that account."

The racial and religious conflict became even more intense in 1888 when Honoré Mercier passed the Jesuit Estates Act. In 1773 the Society of Jesus had been abolished by the Papacy and its property in Canada

To many English-speaking Canadians the emotional Honoré Mercier, who had won power in Quebec in the aftermath of the Riel crisis, represented a threat to Anglo-Saxon Protestant supremacy in Canada. The Toronto *Mail* declared, "The French priest, it is true, cannot formally import into Ontario his Church Establishment and his system of Tithes. But this matters little, if he can thrust out the British population and plant in its room a population which will be under his sway, and from which he can swing practically any payments which he thinks fit. . . . He will, to all intents and purposes, detach Eastern Ontario from the British and Protestant civilization of which it now forms a part, and annex it to the territory of the French race, which is also the dominion of the priest." The fear that the French population was spreading throughout Canada was one of the reasons which led D'Alton McCarthy to begin his campaign for the abolition of the French language in the Northwest Territories and in Manitoba.

MERCIER'S DREAM
OF THE FUTURE MAP OF THE DOMINION.

had reverted to the Crown. When the Society was re-established in 1842, the Jesuits naturally requested either the restoration of their property or compensation. After forty years of disputes and negotiations, Mercier sought to settle the long-standing and contentious problem by valuing the estates at $400,000. Of this sum, $60,000 was to go to Protestant schools in Quebec, while the remainder was to be divided among the Jesuits and other Roman Catholic bodies as the Pope saw fit. The bill passed the Quebec Legislature unanimously.

But in Ontario the Jesuit Estates Act aroused a storm of protest, although the province was in no way affected by the measure. Outraged by the appeal to the Pope, many English-speaking Canadians echoed the fears and threats of the Toronto *Mail*: "If the British and Protestant element in Quebec [which supported the Bill!] will not save itself, we must try to save it for our own sakes. That the abandonment of Quebec to the ultramontane and the Jesuit will be the death of Canadian nationality is clear enough. But Ontario will not be safe." In the House of Commons militant Protestant and Francophobes demanded the disallowance of the Act. Macdonald bluntly refused and reprimanded his supporters, as did the leaders of the Liberal party. Nevertheless, thirteen English-speaking Canadians, variously described as the "Noble Thirteen" or the "Devil's Dozen," broke party lines to vote for disallowance. By this time the leading spokesman for the anti-French and anti-Catholic element was D'Alton McCarthy, who split with Macdonald on the issue.

Thwarted in his demand to secure disallowance of the Jesuit Estates Act, which would serve as a symbol of English and Protestant supremacy in Canada, McCarthy announced his intention of carrying on a crusade for the abolition of French language rights and Roman Catholic separate schools outside Quebec. "Now is the time," he informed the Orange Lodge at Stayner, Ontario, "when the ballot box will decide the great question before the people, and if that does not supply the remedy in this generation bayonets will in the next." In the fall of 1889, he carried his campaign into Manitoba and the Northwest Territories, where the English-speaking majority gave him a more than sympathetic hearing and ultimately adopted his views.

In 1890 the province of Manitoba abolished French as an official language and virtually abolished separate schools, guaranteed in the Manitoba Act of 1870, by withdrawing all public funds from their support. The question was immediately taken before the courts to test the constitutionality of the legislation and, as a result, was not an issue in the election of 1891. As the old chieftain knew only too well, however, here was an issue that could divide the nation as it had never been divided before, and it was an issue that he had not been able to destroy at birth.

2. CONSERVATIVE FAILURE

As the Manitoba School Question wound its way through

the courts, the Conservative party disintegrated in the face of conflicting views about the racial and religious conflict. Its lack of leadership both contributed to this and reflected the divisions within the party. When Macdonald died there were three logical candidates for the succession: Sir Hector Langevin, Sir Charles Tupper, and Sir John Thompson. But Langevin was then deeply implicated in a scandal that was to end his career; Tupper had no desire to leave the pleasant and apparently lucrative office of the Canadian High Commissioner in London; and Thompson was rejected by the McCarthy wing of the party because he was a convert to Roman Catholicism. The mantle therefore fell on old Sir John Abbott who rightly declared: "I am here because I am not particularly obnoxious to anyone." Eighteen months later Abbott resigned because of ill-health and Thompson, clearly the ablest man in the party, was selected to succeed him, despite rumblings of discontent from anti-Catholic elements in the party. Two years later, with the Manitoba School Question still before the courts, Thompson died at fifty, at Windsor Castle. With Tupper, Macdonald's old war-horse, still preferring the sidelines, the party seemed bereft of leadership. Responsibility for selecting a new Prime Minister fell on the Governor-General, Lord Aberdeen, whose wife summarized their views of the contenders in the following manner:

> This has come so suddenly that there has been no preparing for any successor & Mackenzie Bowell was only appointed acting premier in Sir John's absence quite in a temporary way. Mr. Foster the Minister of Finance is an able man, a good speaker and a good man, but he has no power over other men and showed no power for leading in the House once before when Sir John was away. And then that clique against him and his wife because they married in the United States, after she had divorced her husband makes a difficulty. And Mr. Haggart who is the strongest man is admittedly a Bohemian & also idle. . . . Mr. Mackenzie Bowell himself is 75, rather fussy, & decidedly common place, also an Orangeman, at one time Grand Master of the Orangemen of N. America & also presided at one of the tip-top grand Orange affairs at Belfast—but he is good & straight man & he has great ideas about the drawing together of the colonies & the Empire. . . .

A LIVE SHELL

On the deck of the good ship **Dominion.**
Who will tackle it first?

In the end Bowell, as the senior cabinet minister, was chosen, but he lacked the qualities of strength and judgement needed by his party in a time of crisis.

Bowell was hardly settled in his new office when the crisis over the Manitoba schools came to a head. As early as 1892 the courts had decided that Manitoba was within her constitutional rights to abolish separate schools. But the further question remained whether the federal government had the power to take remedial action. Section 93 of the British North America Act provided that if a province interfered with the educational rights that a minority possessed at the time of union, an appeal could be made to the federal government to remedy the grievance. Once it was decided that the Manitoba legislation was constitutional, the minority therefore, fully supported by the Roman Catholic Church and the people of Quebec, petitioned the federal government for remedial legislation. And in January 1895 the Judicial Committee of the Privy Council declared that the federal government had the power to act. The legal question was solved; the political question remained. Could or should the Conservative government pass remedial legislation?

For a year the Conservatives drifted. There were repeated threats of resignations in the cabinet and in January 1896 seven men actually did resign, only to return later. With one hand the government begged Manitoba to amend its legislation and with the other threatened and blustered. Cabinet meetings were orgies of dissension and argument, and ministers attacked and counter-attacked each other in the Commons and in the press. Sir Joseph Pope, Macdonald's former secretary, wrote that these were days "I never recall without a blush, days of a weak and incompetent administration by a cabinet presided over by a man whose sudden and unlooked-for elevation had visibly turned his head, a ministry without unity or cohesion of any kind, a prey to internal dissensions until they became a spectacle to the world, to angels, and to men."

Finally in February 1896 the government decided to introduce remedial legislation to force the government of Manitoba to restore separate schools. But with the natural five-year life of parliament due to expire in the spring, the opposition saw an ideal opportunity for obstruction. For weeks the bill was before the House of Commons. Liberals and anti-remedialist Conservatives debated each of the one hundred and twelve clauses at length. Members slept in committee rooms, at their desks, and in the corridors as the debate continued day and night. The more boisterous filibusters provided their own entertainment as they waited their turn to speak, with Nicholas Flood Davin, the colourful bard from Regina in the Northwest Territories, delighting the members with a Blackfoot dance which he ended by springing onto the long table in the smoking room and "jigging down the centre, kicking over bottles and tumblers and plates at every step." After a solid month of debate, only fifteen of the one hundred and twelve clauses had been passed, and the government withdrew the bill. Soon afterwards the House of Commons was dissolved and an election called for June 11, 1896. Before the campaign got under way, Bowell was replaced by the aging Tupper who had finally returned from England in a last desperate attempt to save the party he had helped Macdonald create.

The Conservative party entered the election divided. Some candidates openly denounced remedial legislation, while Tupper and his colleagues argued that it was an act of justice to the minority. Realizing that their appeal would fall on stony ground in Ontario, the Conservatives counted on the support of the Roman Catholic Church in Quebec to bring them an overwhelming victory there. They hoped too that while Laurier would be denounced as a French-Canadian Roman Catholic in the English-speaking provinces, he would be denounced by the Roman Catholic Church in Quebec for opposing the remedial bill.

Laurier, who had become leader of the Liberal party in 1887, found himself in a very difficult position. He opposed the remedial bill, but he did not object to the restoration of separate schools; indeed, he promised that if elected he would secure justice for the minority in Manitoba. The answer, he said, was not threats and the coercion of a province, but a policy of "sunny ways," of peaceful and amicable negotiations with the government of Manitoba. The Conservatives, he claimed, have "blown and raged and threatened and the more they have raged and blown, the more that man Greenway [the Premier of Manitoba] has stuck to his coat. If I were in power I would try the sunny way. I would approach this man Greenway with the sunny way of patriotism, asking him to be just and to be fair, asking him to be generous to the minority, in order that we may have peace among all the creeds and races which it has pleased God to bring upon this corner of our common country."

Laurier's objection to the coercion of a province and his policy of sunny ways won favour in English-speaking Canada. But in Quebec the leaders of the Roman Catholic Church grimly supported the Conservatives. One influential priest publicly warned Laurier that "the episcopacy, like one man, united with the clergy, will rise up to support those who have fallen in defending us." But with the spectre of a religious war before him, Laurier clung steadfastly to the principles he had enunciated in 1877 when he had denied the Church's right to interfere in politics and appealed for politics free from religious strife. "So long as I have a seat in the House," he said in March 1896, "so long as I occupy the position I do now whenever it shall become my duty to take a stand upon any question whatever, that stand I will take not upon grounds of Roman Catholicism, not upon grounds of Protestantism, but upon grounds which can appeal to the consciences of men, irrespective of their particular faith, upon grounds which can be occupied by all men who love justice, freedom and toleration."

With religious education and French culture at stake, the bishops regarded Laurier's statement as little short of heresy and cultural betrayal. Remedial legislation appeared to be the only action guaranteed to restore

QUEBEC GETS A SHOW.

SIR ADOLPHE CARON—" Me and Joe Ouimet will now exhibit Sare Mackenzie. Bowell in the act of forming his heroic resolve to protect ze rights of ze menoritee."

Most people suspected, in many ways un-fairly, that Bowell, the Orangeman, had no intention of passing remedial legisla-tion. The unfortunate Prime Minister was under strong pressure from both sides. This contemporary cartoon shows two of his Quebec cabinet ministers gently persuading Sir Mackenzie to go ahead with remedial action.

separate schools and, after much discussion and argument, the bishops issued a *mandement* or statement to guide the electorate of Quebec:

All Catholics ought to give their votes only to candidates who swear formally and solemnly to vote in Parliament in favour of legislation giving the Catholic minority in Manitoba the school rights which are recognized as theirs by the British Privy Council. This solemn duty is necessary for every good Catholic, and you would not be justified either before your spiritual guides or before God himself if you fail to fulfil this obligation.

One of the greatest political cartoonists in Canada sixty years ago was the French Canadian, Henri Julien. His satirical sketches of Laurier's cabinet depicted each Liberal minister as a Negro minstrel. Sir Wilfrid himself conducted the performance while various ministers played their virtuoso parts. This cartoon of Joseph-Israel Tarte, Laurier's most important lieutenant in Quebec, reveals the highly emotional and frenzied part played by Tarte in the political life of Quebec. Beginning his career as an ultramontane, he then became an ally of Sir Hector Langevin and Sir John Mac-donald. Early in the 1890's, however, he uncovered scandals in the party and with his usual flair for headlines exposed them. This led him into the arms of Laurier and the Liberal party. During the Manitoba Schools crisis and the campaign of 1896 Tarte helped to organize the Liberal party and has often been given credit for Laurier's victory in Quebec.

Although the *mandement* was not explicit, it was clear that the bishops endorsed Conservative candidates. Equally emphatic clerical statements were issued from the other side. The Protestant Churches were opposed to remedial action and separate schools. One Methodist minister informed his congregation that support of remedial action "would stare the voter in the face at the Judgement Day, and condemn him to eternal perdition."

When the ballots were counted, Laurier and the Liberals had emerged with a clear majority. Five years of Conservative bungling, economic distress, and lack of leadership had destroyed Macdonald's old party. In Quebec, the electors rejected the appeal of the Roman Catholic Church, and gave Laurier a resounding victory, while in Ontario he won half the seats despite the attacks on his race and religion.

In office, Canada's first French-Canadian Prime Minister at once adopted the policy of sunny ways. Laurier's emissaries persuaded the government of Manitoba to grant concessions to the minority, such as provisions for instruction in French where ten students spoke the language, and religious instruction at the end of the day. Like most compromises, this satisfied no one, but it did, for the moment at least, end the cultural strife that had threatened to destroy the nation. With this question out of the way, Laurier was able to turn to the tasks of national development that Macdonald had left unfinished.

CHAPTER 29

Laurier and National Development

The Liberal ministry that Laurier formed in 1896 has been called the "government of all talents." Its greatest strength was the Prime Minister himself. Like Sir John A., Laurier was a master of the art of party management and could direct the efforts of men with strong and sometimes diverse opinions towards a common goal. His immense personal charm and his oratorical power in both English and French made him very popular in all sections of the country. Though determined and steady of purpose, he was willing to compromise when the nation's welfare demanded it. He enjoyed politics and the exercise of power and, like Macdonald before him, he was determined to build a stronger, more united Canada.

Macdonald had laid the framework for the Canadian nation. Laurier knew that to complete the structure he would have to heal the sectional and racial conflicts that had divided and weakened the country. His main aim was always to bind French- and English-speaking Canadians together in a common nationality, by following a path that was neither narrowly English nor French, Roman Catholic nor Protestant, but broad enough to win the acceptance of all groups. As he told a friend:

> My object is to consolidate Confederation and to bring our people, long estranged from each other, gradually to become a nation. This is the supreme issue. Everything else is subordinate to that idea.

In his first cabinet, Laurier included the men he thought were best qualified to assist in the tasks of uniting and developing the country. To the important post of Minister of Finance he appointed W. S. Fielding, the former Premier of Nova Scotia. Here was a clear indication that the Liberals had abandoned unrestricted reciprocity, for Fielding, unlike Richard Cartwright who had expected to become Finance Minister, was not a free trader. Oliver Mowat, who gave up his position as Premier of Ontario to become Minister of Justice, was also regarded as a "safe" man by central-Canadian businessmen. From the Manitoba government came the experienced politician and businessman, Clifford Sifton, the western representative in Laurier's cabinet. As Minister of the Interior, Sifton's main task was to fill the western plains with prosperous farmers. In Quebec, Laurier turned away from the old *parti rouge* elements in the party who were still suspected by the Church and chose Joseph-Israel Tarte, at one time a staunch Conservative, as Minister of Public Works. Tarte, who had once remarked that "elections are not won by prayers," had helped Laurier to win his victory over the Roman Catholic Church in Quebec in the 1896 election.

The new administration clearly indicated the changes which had taken place in Liberal thinking since 1878. Instead of Mackenzie's caution, there was now a confident acceptance of policies of national development very similar to those of Macdonald. But one very important circumstance had changed. Soon after Laurier took office in 1896 world prosperity returned. New markets opened up, money for investment flowed more freely, and immigrants looked to Canada as a land of promise. Thus, the Liberals had the opportunity to make their national economic developments a success, whereas depression had prevented Macdonald from achieving his goals.

1. LIBERAL ECONOMIC POLICY

The first indication of Laurier's willingness to accept the basic elements in Macdonald's National Policies was the Fielding tariff of 1897. In opposition, the Liberals had always been critical of the protective tariff, and in 1891 had proposed unrestricted reciprocity with the United States. But under the guidance of W. S. Fielding the Liberals in 1897

In the field of economic policy, Laurier's chief lieutenant was W. S. Fielding, Minister of Finance. From 1884 to 1896 he had served as Premier of Nova Scotia, but he accepted a call to Ottawa in 1896 to become a member of Laurier's "Ministry of All Talents." In 1897 his first budget included the Imperial preference and in 1911 it was Fielding who negotiated the reciprocity agreement with the United States—the agreement which played such a large part in the defeat of the Liberals in 1911. When the Liberals returned to office a decade later, the new Prime Minister, Mackenzie King, once more chose Fielding as Minister of Finance, a post he held until 1925. (Cartoon by Henri Julien)

In 1897 Clifford Sifton joined Laurier's cabinet after assisting in the settlement of the Manitoba School Question. For eight years he served as one of the most vigorous and powerful members of the Liberal administration, energetically directing the immigration policies which finally opened up the West. In 1905, however, when Saskatchewan and Alberta, two areas which Sifton had done so much to create, were given provincial status, Sifton left the Laurier government because he believed that the Prime Minister had attempted to establish separate schools in the new provinces. "You may rely upon it," Sifton wrote to a friend, "that nothing but an overwhelming sense of the importance of the issue led to what I fear may be regarded as a final severance of my relations with the Prime Minister, at a period when he seemed to have reached the zenith of his power and influence, and when apparently nothing but success was in store for the Liberal party." (Cartoon by Henri Julien.)

accepted the principle of protection, though with some reductions in duties on such items as binder twine, wire fencing and farm implements to meet the demands of their western supporters. Sifton summed up the Liberal government's view when he wrote: "The people decided some eighteen years ago to have the protective policy, and got it and have stood by it ever since. And the business of the country . . . has adapted itself to the tariff; and the introduction of a tariff from which the principle of protection would be entirely eliminated would be fraught with results that would be most disastrous to the whole Canadian people."

The Liberals did make one important change in the country's tariff policy: they introduced a preferential tariff which offered lower rates to countries which reduced their tariffs against Canada. Since Britain practised free trade, she was most affected by this policy. The result was that the Canadian tariff on British imports was reduced first by one-eighth and later by one-third. But even this measure did not seriously alter the basically protective character of the Canadian tariff. Although the Liberals made some minor alterations in the tariff before 1911, it was probably only pressure from the growing number of western agrarian voters that prevented them from adopting even higher tariffs.

Tariffs alone could not ensure prosperity and expansion for Canadian industry. W. S. Fielding found a more satisfactory method when he noted: "The best way you can help the manufacturers of Canada is to fill up the prairie regions of Manitoba and the Northwest with a prosperous and contented people, who will be consumers of the manufactured goods of the east." The filling up of the West was an object pursued vigorously by the Laurier government, and especially by Clifford Sifton.

In immigration as in most other respects, changed world economic conditions greatly aided the Liberal programme. The revival of prosperity and the growth of industry in Europe increased, just as transportation costs began to decline on the transatlantic steamships. This prosperity also lured settlers to western Canada from both eastern Canada and Europe, settlers who in earlier years might have gone to the United States. But by 1896 the American frontier was closed and many people who had left Canada for the United States in the earlier period now began to find their way back across the border, as did Americans themselves. With the good farmlands of the United States taken up, the Canadian prairies became "the last, best west," the last frontier of North American agriculture.

Railways and steamship lines assisted the government's immigration programme. The Canadian Pacific Railway had received large tracts of land from the government and hoped to sell it to settlers. But the government played the leading role in encouraging people to settle in Canada. The North Atlantic Trading Company, created by Sifton, spread information about Canada throughout Europe and arranged for immigrants to travel to new homes in the Canadian West.

This effort to attract European settlers, in addition to those from Britain and the United States, was one way in which Sifton's immigration policy differed from that of the Macdonald government. Sifton believed that the best pioneers for the Canadian West were not urban industrial workers, but hardy farmers. As he put it himself: "I think a stalwart peasant in a sheep-skin coat, born on the soil, whose forefathers have been farmers for ten generations, with a stout wife and a half-dozen children,

The Standard
Weekly Supplement of Empire.

LONDON, THURSDAY, AUGUST 27, 1908.

CANADA OFFERS

1. 160 acres of excellent farm land to every male over 18 years of age who is able and willing to take upon himself the duties of settlement—millions of acres still available.

2. A home in the land of sunshine and contented people where are to be found the best land on earth, low taxes, good markets, free schools, churches, etc.

3. An opportunity to grow up with the country where development along every line is constantly offering chances for the man with push and principle.

CANADA WANTS

1. Experienced farm labourers to till her vast fertile fields.

2. Farmers financially able to take homesteads or purchase land.

3. Domestic servants, for whom there are splendid openings and prospects.

Illustrated Pamphlets, giving full particulars, may be obtained from

Mr. J. OBED SMITH,
Assistant Superintendent of Emigration,
11-12, Charing Cross, London, S.W., England.

Or from **Mr. W. D. SCOTT,**
Superintendent of Immigration, Ottawa, Canada.

is good quality." Between 1897 and 1912 some 594,000 people came to Canada from Europe. Another 961,000 came from the British Isles, while 784,000 crossed into Canada from the United States. But it was immigrants from Europe, with their new languages and cultures, that began to change the character of Canada. Although Mennonites and Icelanders had settled in Canada in the 1870's and 1880's, it was the new national and religious groups, the Germans, Ukrainians, Poles, Doukhobors and others, who gave the Canadian West a character similar to that of the "melting pot" of the United States. But because of Canada's smaller population, these groups were more slowly and less completely absorbed into the older English-Canadian culture.

Although many went to the urban factories, most of the new immigrants took up farming in the West. Soon new methods of cultivation and new types of grain transformed the dry, flat prairies into one of the greatest grain-growing areas in the world. Since rainfall was limited on the prairies, only large farms could produce enough grain to make farming profitable. To cultivate these large farms, machinery was necessary as well as numerous additional hands at harvest time. By the turn of the century, the

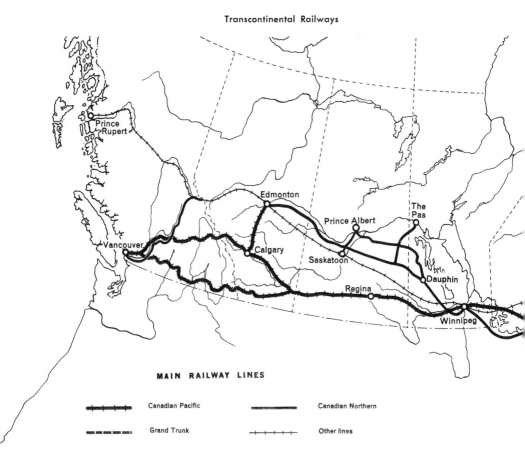

Transcontinental Railways

MAIN RAILWAY LINES

Canadian Pacific

Canadian Northern

Grand Trunk

Other lines

development of new mechanized ploughs, binders and threshers made farming easier and more efficient. Each autumn thousands of young men from eastern Canada went West to find temporary employment in harvesting the crop. Many remained to establish their own homesteads.

Science was not only applied to machinery; it was also applied to developing new varieties of wheat. Because of the short growing season in the West it was essential to produce new types of grain that would mature between the late spring and the early autumn frosts. To promote the science of agriculture the government established several experimental stations. In 1904, Charles Saunders and his team of scientists produced the quick-maturing, rust-resistant Marquis wheat, which in due time extended the farming frontier north into the fertile Peace River country. Soon Canadian Number One Northern wheat was in demand throughout the world. New people, new lands and new varieties of grain, these were the elements which produced the "Wheat Boom" during the first decade of the twentieth century. This western boom spread prosperity throughout most of the country.

In 1895 only 66,000 people lived in the vast Northwest Territories

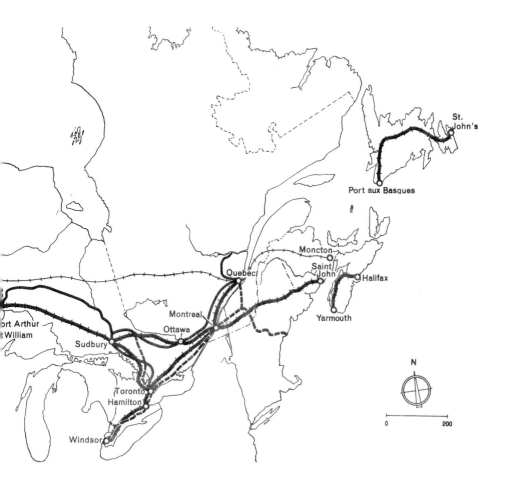

between Manitoba and British Columbia. Ten years later the number leaped to 400,000, ample testimony to the vigour of Sifton's immigration policy. Although the Territories had had responsible government since 1897 the powers of their government were limited, but their growth in population inevitably brought demands for provincial status. By 1905 the Laurier government bowed to the views of the people and created two new provinces, Saskatchewan and Alberta.

Drawing the boundaries proved to be a far less difficult task than designing the new provincial constitutions. The most serious difficulty arose over the provisions to be made for education in the new constitutions, or Autonomy Bills. Roman Catholic and French schools had been established in the Territories in 1875, but these minority privileges had gradually been whittled down. In drawing up the Autonomy Bills, Laurier hoped to satisfy his Church and his people by including a clause which restored the school system that had existed in the Northwest in 1875. A storm of protest arose in the West and Ontario. The Toronto *Telegram* condemned Laurier's action as "fastening the dead hand of denominational control" on the western schools. The dispute split Laurier's cabinet and Clifford Sifton, who had been absent when the Bills were drawn up, submitted his resignation in protest. Sifton's resignation, and the obvious strength of English-speaking Canadian opposition to separate schools, forced Laurier to reverse his course and leave the western schools as he had found them.

The growth of the West placed heavy demands on the country's railway facilities. At harvest time there were never enough railway freight cars to carry western grain to the seaports, and the prairie farmers soon began to demand more railways. Several groups of railway promoters, desiring to gain a share of the profitable traffic of the Canadian Pacific Railway, were eager to meet their demands. In 1902 the Grand Trunk petitioned the government for assistance in building a line from North Bay to the Pacific coast. This petition was followed by a counter-proposal from two western promoters, William Mackenzie and Donald Mann, who were laying plans for a transcontinental railway, the Canadian Northern. When efforts to persuade the two groups to combine in a single venture failed, Laurier agreed to charter both companies. "We cannot wait," Laurier claimed, "because at this moment there is a transformation going on in the conditions of our national life which it would be folly to ignore and a crime to overlook." That transformation was the enormous increase in the output of the western farmer.

The scheme adopted to aid the Grand Trunk Pacific and the Canadian Northern in 1903 was very similar to Macdonald's earlier combination of public and private enterprise. Both the Grand Trunk, which was to be built from Winnipeg to Prince Rupert, and the Canadian Northern, which planned a third transcontinental line, were granted large scale government assistance. To Conservative criticism of the government's generosity, Sifton replied: "My own view is that twenty years ought to see at least twelve million people in Canada, but if this result is to be accomplished, small ideas of trying to cut off expenditures on railways and public works will have to be dropped. For myself, I am altogether in favour of going ahead." This was the same argument that Macdonald had used against his Liberal critics in the 1880's.

Laurier's optimism about the future of Canada, and his inability to resist the pressure from powerful railroad promoters, resulted in the construction of two new transcontinentals to compete with the Canadian Pacific Railway. The cost of each of the new systems exceeded expectations, while mismanagement and corruption brought further financial burdens. When the lines were completed they were forced into ruinous competition for traffic in areas like northwestern Ontario where one efficiently run railway would have been enough. Chronic financial problems time and again forced the promoters to seek further governmental assistance. Finally, at the end of the First World War, and at great expense to the Canadian taxpayer, the government was forced to take over the railways and unite them into a single, publicly-owned corporation, the Canadian National Railways.

But this result lay in the future. During Laurier's term of office the future of Canada seemed unbounded. The success of Sifton's immigration policy, the growth of business behind the protective tariff, and the massive capital investment represented by the new railway schemes, brought prosperity to all of Canada. With prosperity came a new, glowing optimism about the prospects of the country. This new confidence was well summed up by Laurier's famous remark: "The nineteenth century was the century of the United States, the twentieth century will be the century of Canada."

2. TRADE AND INDUSTRY

Laurier's optimism about Canada's future was, at least in part, based on solid achievements. The growth of population, of primary importance to the rapid development of the country, was remarkable. In the years between 1891 and the outbreak of the First World War, the number of Canadians grew from four million eight hundred thousand to nearly eight million. Production and trade also increased substantially. In 1891 exports of Canadian wheat amounted to about two million bushels a year; within twenty-five years this figure had risen to over one hundred and fifty million bushels. In the same period the export trade as a whole rose in value from eighty-eight million dollars to seven hundred and forty-one million dollars, while the value of manufactured products showed more than a fourfold increase.

Important factors in this growth were the opening up of new areas of wealth and the diversification of the economy. The most spectacular development was in the northern Yukon Territory, where the discovery of the Klondike gold field brought a vast and colourful influx of fortune seekers in the years 1898-1903. But elsewhere there were more stable and

substantial economic advances.   In northern Ontario, the discovery of
gold, silver, copper and nickel produced a mining boom.   Similar developments were taking place in the interior of British Columbia.   In addition,
British Columbia, Ontario and Quebec were rapidly increasing their production of timber and wood pulp.   To meet the needs of these new primary
industries, as well as to add comfort to everyday living, the hydro-electric
resources of Canada's great rivers were gradually being harnessed for use.
The establishment of the Ontario Hydro-Electric Power Commission was
only one example of the exploitation of natural resources for the public's
benefit.

3. THE PROBLEM OF EXPANSION

The rapid growth brought problems in its wake.   Unregulated business expansion brought about large concentrations of wealth
and power which did not always place the public interest before private
gain.   The development of large corporations and monopolies, which was
a distinctive feature of the business development of the United States
during the last decades of the nineteenth century, was duplicated on a
smaller scale in Canada.   Between 1909 and 1911, one hundred and ninety-
six firms were combined into forty-one corporations.   Since 1889 there had
been laws in Canada prohibiting monopolies which restrained free competition, but they had rarely been applied.   Even the new Combines Investigation Act which the Liberals enacted in 1910 proved too weak to prevent
the growth of monopoly.   Apparently few people were worried about the
dangers in this situation that were pointed out by a young Conservative
Member of Parliament from Manitoba in 1911.   This young man, Arthur
Meighen, remarked: "At present our great industries are coming together,
and more and more we are being brought industrially under the power of
mergers and combines.   If matters go on as they are, absolutely unhindered,
absolutely uncontrolled, the powers of the corporations will be more absolute, more despotic than will be the powers of Parliament itself."
Most seriously affected by the growth of big business was the urban
working class which turned increasingly to trade unions to protect their
interests.   The first labour unions in Canada dated back to the mid-
nineteenth century, but these had been chiefly organizations of skilled
craftsmen like printers and typographers.   In 1885 the Knights of Labour
spread into Canada from the United States, and for a few years succeeded
in organizing unskilled workers.   But the hard times of the 1890's made
the extension of unionism difficult because labour was cheap and readily
available.   Nevertheless, the central organ of Canadian unionism, the
Trades and Labour Congress of Canada, which had been established in
1886, grew in strength and laid the foundations for a great expansion of
labour organization after the turn of the century.
In 1901 there were only 1,078 union locals in the country, but within
ten years the number had nearly doubled and membership exceeded
175,000.   For the most part the union leaders worked quietly to increase

Paying with Gold Dust. Fall 1899.

One of the favourite routes to the Yukon gold fields ran from Skagway and Dyea across Lake Bennett, then through the Chilkoot Pass. One official at Lake Bennett described the scene as the ice began to break up at the end of March, 1898: "I went up the hill behind the office to see the start and at one time counted over eight hundred boats under sail on the 11½ miles of Lake Bennett. . . . More than thirty thousand persons, every one of whom had received assistance or advice, had passed down the Yukon. Over $150,000 in duty and fees had been collected, more than thirty million pounds of solid food, sufficient to feed an army corps for a year, had been inspected and checked over by us." The size, rapidity, and colour of the Yukon Gold Rush has probably never been equalled in any frontier economic expansion. The Yearbook of British Columbia noted in 1899: "Perhaps no other event or combination of events occurring outside the area of the battlefield has, during the present century, so profoundly affected the English-speaking people and generally has had so wide an influence in so short a space of time as the discovery of gold in the Yukon."

CHIKOOT PASS

membership and win the right of collective bargaining, often against the determined opposition of employers. But strikes did occur and these were sometimes long, often bitterly fought, and usually won by the employers. Working-class leaders concluded from their repeated defeats that only direct political action could win the workers their just share of the nation's wealth. But political action was very slow in developing, for in the prosperous years before the First World War most wage earners were satisfied to give their support to one of the existing parties. Conscious of the growing strength of labour, the Liberals established a Department of Labour in 1900, and in 1907 provided for arbitration of disputes under the Industrial Disputes Investigation Act. These were small concessions which indicated that labour was not yet well enough organized to make its voice effectively heard at Ottawa.

The farming community was more vocal, effective, and better organized, and its demands won sympathetic attention from the Laurier government. In the early years of the century the chief demand of the farming community was for cheap transportation. This demand was at least partially met by the construction of new railways and lower freight rates under the Crow's Nest Pass agreement of 1897. In return for government assistance to aid in the construction of a railroad through the Crow's Nest Pass, the Canadian Pacific Railway agreed to reduce its freight rates on agricultural products and machinery carried for farmers. The farmers also believed that a railway to Hudson Bay would provide cheaper transport and further reduce freight rates. After much controversy, Laurier agreed to begin the project in 1910, though it was not until 1931 that the Hudson Bay Railway was finally finished.

The farmers' sharpest criticisms, even in these prosperous years, were directed against the protective tariff. The tariff, the farmer maintained, raised the cost of the manufactured goods he had to buy; his grain, on the other hand, was sold on the free international market and faced fierce competition. The tariff served to fatten the eastern industrialist, but swallowed the farmers' profits. It also encouraged the growth of cities which attracted farmers' sons, destroyed the family farm, and undermined the rural community. By 1910, Grain Growers' Associations, Farmers' Unions, and farmers' newspapers like the *Grain Growers' Guide* were all loudly demanding a downward revision of the tariff. In the summer of 1910 Laurier made his first tour of the West and heard farmers everywhere clamouring for tariff reductions, and in December a delegation of eight hundred farmers converged on Ottawa from the West and Ontario. The leaders of this "march on Ottawa" demanded that the government negotiate a reciprocity treaty with the United States and increase the British preference. Their petition concluded: "Believing that the greatest misfortune that can befall any country is to have its people huddled together in great centres of population, and that the bearing of the present customs tariff has the tendency to encourage that condition and realizing also that the constant movement of our people away from the farms, the greatest

One of the main charges against the Canadian protective tariff was that it gave special privileges to the business interests at the expense of consumers and farmers who were forced to pay higher prices for the necessities of life. The Canadian government, so the proponents of tariff reductions maintained, was controlled by the business interests. A resolution passed by the United Farmers of Alberta in 1910 declared: "Having suffered for so many years under the bondage of a protective tariff which has been maintained by the Government and is but the levying of a tribute upon the people . . . and as in its practical operation the present Canadian tariff works unfairly in favour of the manufacturing industries and to the prejudice of the agricultural industries, we therefore ask for a general move towards freer trade."

problem that presents itself to the Canadian people today is the problem of retaining our people on the soil, we come doubly assured of the justice of our petition."

The Canadian farmers' demand for freer trade coincided with a renewal of interest in the subject by President Taft of the United States. Early in 1911 Canada and the United States concluded an agreement which provided for a free exchange of a wide range of natural products like grain and raw materials and lowered rates on some manufactured products. The reciprocity agreement won the immediate approval of the farmers, but when the Liberals appealed to the country to support the agreement in the election of 1911, Laurier discovered, too late, that powerful business interests were completely opposed to any lessening of their tariff protection against their American competitors. In Toronto, eighteen influential Liberal businessmen led by Laurier's former colleague, Clifford Sifton, denounced reciprocity. Their number included the President of the Canadian Bank of Commerce, the Vice-President of the Canadian Northern Railway, department store presidents, food manufacturers, insurance company directors and others. The treaty, they claimed, would destroy the Canadian economy which had developed on an east-west axis, and lead eventually to Canadian absorption into the United States. After the Liberal defeat, one westerner wrote: "The moment he [Laurier] showed signs of putting real Liberal doctrine into effect, the interests combined and crushed him." In their attack on reciprocity, however, the industrial and financial community found powerful allies among those Canadians who differed with Laurier's Imperial policy.

CHAPTER 30

Canada, the Empire and the United States

The similarities between the domestic policies of Sir John A. Macdonald and Wilfrid Laurier showed that both men were guided by a desire to expand, develop and unite the nation. When their policies differed, the differences were in approach, and in the times in which they governed, rather than in the goals they hoped to attain. The same is true of their attitudes to Canada's relations with the outside world, for both Macdonald and Laurier were nationalists who wanted their country to develop as a strong self-governing nation within the framework of the British Empire.

1. CANADA AND NATIONALISM

Both men realized that a small nation like Canada needed outside support if it were to preserve its independence. Without such assistance, Canada would always be in danger of slipping into the control of the United States. Laurier expressed this fear in 1903: "I have often regretted . . . that we are living beside a great neighbour whose people I believe . . . are very grasping in their national actions, and who are determined on every occasion to get the best in any agreement which they make." Since Canada had developed out of a British colony, it was natural that outside assistance, whether military or financial, should come from Great Britain. Nevertheless, neither Macdonald nor Laurier allowed the British connection to limit the growth of Canadian powers of self-government. Since their years in office witnessed different types of external problems, some of the methods the two men used were different. But their aims remained the same: the development of a self-governing nation.

Macdonald had looked upon the United States as the most serious threat to Canada's national existence. For him, Great Britain was a counterweight against the United States. He talked often of the need for a "permanent alliance" between Canada and Great Britain, a phrase which suggested some form of equality between Canada and the mother country.

In 1880 he had created the office of Canadian High Commissioner to Great Britain, because he believed that Canada "had ceased to occupy the position of an ordinary possession of the Crown." The appointment of a High Commissioner implied a diplomatic status greater than that of a mere colony. While Canada had no direct diplomatic relations with foreign countries, Macdonald did secure for Canada the right to negotiate commercial treaties. Macdonald did not regard the Empire as a closely integrated organization that should have common trading policies or automatic mutual military obligations. His National Policy turned upon an independent tariff policy made in Canada for the benefit of Canadians. The Conservatives also guarded jealously Canada's right to make its own decisions in military affairs. In 1885 a suggestion that Canada be asked to give military aid to help the British Prime Minister Gladstone's government in a quarrel in the Sudan, received a sharp reply. "Why should we waste our men and our money in this wretched business?" Macdonald asked. "Our men and our money would be sacrificed to get Gladstone & Co. out of the hole they have plunged themselves into by their own imbecility." On the whole, however, external and Imperial affairs did not cause the Conservatives much difficulty during their years in office.

2. LAURIER AND THE NEW IMPERIALISM

Laurier faced more difficult problems, but his solutions followed the lines that Macdonald had already laid down. Laurier came to office when the great powers of Europe and the United States were competing with one another for new empires and new sources of power. After nearly a century of industrial supremacy and "splendid isolation" Britain realized by the 1890's that the rapidly growing military and economic power of Germany and the United States threatened her position. Her Empire, long regarded with indifference, suddenly became a possible source of strength. The chief British advocate of Imperial consolidation and unity was Joseph Chamberlain who became Britain's Colonial Secretary in 1895. Chamberlain belonged to a new school of British politicians who looked upon the Empire as a valuable asset. With fanatical single-mindedness Chamberlain tried to bind the Empire into a military, economic and political federation.

Although some Canadians sympathized with Chamberlain's schemes for Imperial federation, the majority, and especially the French Canadians, opposed every plan that would limit Canada's freedom of action or increase her military obligations. As a French-Canadian Prime Minister, Laurier was caught between the powerful Imperial sentiments of English-speaking Canada, especially Ontario, and the vigorous opposition of Quebec to active participation in Imperial affairs. Thus he found it necessary to follow a cautious middle course which he hoped would satisfy a majority in both cultural groups. "I am neither an Imperialist nor an anti-Imperialist but a Canadian first, last and always." This middle course of compromise

ONE FLAG, ONE ARMY, ONE COUNTRY.

While Laurier began his "everlasting no" at the Imperial Conference of 1897, the Liberals were to use his warm reception and knighthood to counter Conservative charges that he was disloyal and anti-British.

was neither easy nor heroic, but Laurier knew it was necessary. He wrote to a disgruntled supporter: "Our existence as a nation is the most anomalous that has yet existed. We are British subjects but we are an autonomous nation; we are divided into provinces, we are divided into races, and out of these confused elements the man at the head of affairs has to sail the ship onwards, and to do this safely, it is not always the ideal policy from the point of view of pure idealism which ought to prevail, but the policy which can appeal on the whole to all sections of the community."

The year after he became Prime Minister, Laurier was invited to attend an Imperial Conference in London which was to be part of the celebration of Queen Victoria's Diamond Jubilee. Ten years earlier at the Queen's Golden Jubilee there had been an informal meeting of colonial leaders, but in 1897 these discussions were put on a formal basis. Joseph Chamberlain hoped to use this festive occasion to promote Imperial solidarity and to encourage the first step toward Imperial federation. The visiting statesmen were lavishly entertained; as Laurier wrote: "I am not sure whether the British Empire needs a new constitution, but I am certain that every Jubilee guest will need one." Chamberlain's plan of persuasion also included granting Laurier a knighthood, which the French-Canadian Prime Minister accepted with reluctance. But he refused to accept Chamberlain's proposal for the establishment of a permanent Imperial Council on the grounds that such an institution might limit Canada's powers of self-government. "Colonies are born to become nations," he told a British audience. "Canada is a nation. Canada is free, and freedom is nationality. Canada is practically independent; in a few years the earth will be encircled by a series of independent nations, recognizing, however, the suzerainty of England. The first place in our hearts is filled by Canada." Moreover, Laurier asked, how could Canada's devotion to the Empire be questioned when it had granted Britain a trade preference under the Fielding tariff of 1897? Imperial preference was the key to Laurier's attitude to the Empire; commitments must be voluntary, and not imposed by any outside body, whether it be the British government or an Imperial parliament in which Canada might be represented.

While Laurier escaped from the Imperial Conference of 1897 without accepting any new obligations, the Boer War, which broke out two years later, posed a more difficult problem, for it aroused the Imperial emotions of English-speaking Canadians, particularly in Ontario. Chamberlain tried to take advantage of this sentiment to promote his goal of Imperial unity. He suggested through Lord Minto, the Governor-General of Canada, that Canadian troops might be sent to fight in South Africa. While Laurier found it easy enough to resist the Imperial authorities, he found it impossible to withstand the pressure which built up in English-speaking Canada to send a Canadian contingent to South Africa. Yet while English-speaking Canada favoured sending troops to aid the Imperial cause, French Canadians were adamantly opposed.

As usual, Laurier attempted to find a compromise that would save the country from a division along cultural lines. He agreed to equip and transport one thousand volunteers to South Africa, where Britain would then assume full responsibility for them. But this action was not to be regarded as a precedent for a Canadian contribution to every British war. "Whilst I cannot admit that Canada should take part in all the wars of Great Britain," Laurier explained, "neither am I prepared to say that she should not take part in any war at all. I claim for Canada this, that in future she shall be at liberty to act or not act, to interfere or not interfere, to do just as she pleases." In 1899 the government sent a second contingent of Canadian troops to South Africa, which, coupled with private enlistments in the British army, brought to seven thousand the number of Canadians who served in the Boer War.

Laurier's compromise was not completely successful in preventing conflict between Ontario and Quebec. In Ontario, Conservatives denounced him as an enemy of the Empire; in Quebec, some French Canadians criticized him as an Imperialist. One of Laurier's young supporters, Henri Bourassa, resigned his seat in Parliament in protest against Laurier's action and was triumphantly re-elected as an Independent by his constituents. Bourassa was a brilliant young French-Canadian politician who was sometimes regarded as Laurier's successor. But, as his resignation in 1899 indicated, Bourassa was not a party man. Consistently placing principle above party, he found it impossible to submit to the inevitable compromises that democratic politics demand. Like his great-grandfather, Louis Joseph Papineau, Bourassa was a staunch defender of French-Canadian rights. Yet he was also a Canadian nationalist who insisted that Canada should acquire full powers of self-government and remain aloof from Imperial wars unless her own interests were directly involved. After his protest against Canadian participation in the Boer War, he gradually became one of Laurier's sharpest critics. In 1907 Laurier wrote: "No one recognizes Bourassa's talents better than I do. But he has one capital defect: he does not know how to keep within bounds." However, in 1899 Bourassa's popularity in Quebec was a warning to Laurier against close involvement in Imperial affairs.

The election of 1900 emphasized that Laurier's compromise during the crisis over the Boer War had not entirely satisfied Ontario either, for the Liberals lost eight seats in that province. But most moderate Canadians, British and French, approved Laurier's compromise. At an Imperial Conference in 1902 he again refused to commit Canada to schemes that he feared would involve permanent military obligations and unified political direction of the Empire. Faced with the Canadian Prime Minister's persistent refusal to support any plan for Imperial consolidation, one frustrated Imperialist remarked that Laurier should change his name from Sir Wilfrid to "Sir Won'tfrid."

3. THE BIG STICK

No sooner did the pressure for Imperial commitments temporarily relax than Laurier's government faced serious difficulties with the United States over the Alaska boundary. The Yukon Gold Rush in 1898 brought the long-standing dispute to a head, for both Canada and the

The brilliant Liberal cartoonist, Bengough, satirizes the difficulties of Sir Charles Tupper, the leader of the Conservative party in the election of 1900. The question of whether Canada had done too much or too little to aid the British in the South African war was one of the major issues in this election. Bengough, illustrating the division of the Conservative party, shows Tupper in Ontario declaring that Laurier and the Liberals had not done enough for the Imperial cause, while Tupper in Quebec maintains that "Sir Wilfrid Laurier is too English for me." In the election Laurier took this position, which he declared in Toronto: "If we are to become a nation, we must once and for all cease these appeals to creed and race. We must fight upon lines which appeal to all races, to all creeds, and which appeal to all Canadians. Have we not been separated long enough?"

YUKON TERRITORY

Dyea
Chilkoot Pass
White Pass
Skagway
Lynn Canal
Stikine R.
ALASKA
Pacific Ocean
Portland Canal
N
0   100   200
Canadian claim
U.S. claim
Settlement of 1903
QUEEN
CHARLOTTE
IS.

The Alaska Boundary Dispute

United States wanted control of the Lynn Canal, which gave the best access to the Yukon. Canada wanted the matter to be submitted to a board of arbitration composed of impartial outsiders. But the United States refused to accept this proposal, and Canada reluctantly agreed to the American suggestion of a judicial tribunal composed of three jurists appointed by each side.

In 1903 the tribunal was established, and from the outset it was clear that it would divide along national lines. Even before it met, President Theodore Roosevelt bluntly declared that he would reject any decision that did not accept all the American claims and he brazenly appointed three men whose reliability was greater than their impartiality. Canada appointed two members to the tribunal and Britain selected the third, all "impartial jurists of the highest repute" as the agreement had demanded.

The two Canadian delegates were caught between the determined Americans and the unfortunate Englishman who was anxious both to preserve friendly Anglo-American relations and to see the boundary properly defined. As it turned out, the Americans had the sounder case, and, with the British member supporting it, the tribunal rejected Canada's arguments and granted almost all of the American claims.

Announcement of the tribunal's decision produced violent protests in Canada directed primarily against the British delegate who was charged with sacrificing Canada in Britain's interests. In the heat of the debate Laurier even suggested that the time had arrived for Canada to assume full control over her foreign affairs. "The difficulty, as I conceive it to be," he stated, "is that so long as Canada remains a dependency of the British Crown the present powers that we have are not sufficient for the maintenance of our rights." But once Canadian tempers had cooled, the suggestion was forgotten. Indeed, the Alaska affair seemed once more to underline the necessity of maintaining the British connection for fear that without it, Theodore Roosevelt's "big stick" might be used more often. Perhaps the most lasting result of the Alaska dispute was the hardening of anti-American sentiment in Canada, a sentiment which was to play an important part in Laurier's downfall in 1911.

4. IMPERIAL DEFENCE AND RECIPROCITY

Both the Boer War and the Alaska boundary dispute had shown Canada that the role of a young country in a world of great powers is a difficult one. As the powers of Europe moved along the road to the First World War in 1914, Canada found herself involved, sometimes willingly and sometimes unwillingly.

Laurier's personal inclinations were to remain outside what he once called "the vortex of European militarism," even though he knew that Canada derived benefits from her membership in the Empire and that if a serious crisis arose she would have to help in its defence. Naturally some English-speaking Canadians felt that Canada should commit herself wholeheartedly to policies of Imperial defence, while other Canadians, especially but not only, French Canadians, felt that Laurier was not firm enough in his opposition to Imperial commitments. This division of Canadian opinion was both a strength and a weakness for Laurier. If he could keep the extremists separated and preserve his hold on the moderates, his leadership would remain unchallenged. But if issues were to arise which united the extremists and shattered the confidence of the moderates in his government, Laurier's days would be numbered.

As competition between Britain and Germany increased in the years following 1902, Britain began to turn more often to the Dominions for assistance in the defence of the Empire. This policy seemed reasonable to the British for the colonies benefited both economically and militarily from membership in the Empire. Surely, it was argued, the British taxpayer should not have to bear the entire burden of Imperial defence. Many Canadians felt, however, that they could contribute best to the strength of the Empire by developing their own country and its defences. Since Laurier shared this view, he refused to make any direct military contribution to Imperial defence in peacetime. Moreover, although Canadian military plans and practices were designed to conform with Imperial needs, Laurier's policy was to place Canadian military services completely under Canadian

Prior to the election of 1911, Prime Minister Laurier toured the prairie provinces—the provinces that had been heavily settled during the Laurier years. Everywhere he went he met delegations of farmers protesting against tariff regulations.

command, and in 1904 the British commander of the Canadian militia was replaced by a Canadian.

The most controversial issue of Imperial defence arose over naval policy. As the naval competition between Britain and Germany intensified in 1909, pressure mounted both in Britain and in Canada for the establishment of a Canadian navy. In keeping with his policy of maintaining Canadian control over Canadian affairs, Laurier decided in 1910 to establish a small navy owned, manned and directed by Canada. At first the policy seemed to win unanimous approval, but suddenly serious opposition emerged. In English-speaking Canada the Conservatives cried that Laurier's plan would merely provide a "tin pot navy," and that the best way of assisting the Empire would be a direct financial contribution to the British navy. In Quebec, a group of French-Canadian nationalists led by Henri Bourassa opposed the establishment of any navy at all, claiming that having a navy would cause Canada to be dragged into every Imperial war. These two extremes united in opposition to Laurier's naval policy. But after a long battle against the Conservative opposition, the Naval Bill was finally made law.

The controversy over the Naval Bill joined the wrangle over reciprocity as the major issues in the 1911 election. Cloaking their economic interests in patriotic fervour, opponents of reciprocity charged that it was a sell-out to the United States and, like the naval policy, ample proof that the Liberals with their French-Canadian leader were betraying Canadian and Imperial interests. In Quebec, Henri Bourassa, supported by the Conservatives, led the campaign against Laurier. In his newspaper, *Le Devoir,* Bourassa condemned the Liberal naval policy as a victory for Imperialism: "It is time for the people of the province of Quebec to prove to M. Laurier that if they admired him when he served the interests of the country well, today he has prevaricated, today he has duped us." In English-speaking Canada, on the other hand, the Conservatives maintained that Laurier's policy was not Imperialistic enough. They argued that the Liberal naval policy was a threat to the unity of the Empire, while reciprocity would break the Imperial connection by pushing Canada into the arms of the United States. Conservative orators made effective use of the indiscretions of some United States politicians, including a letter written by President Taft which noted that "the amount of Canadian products we would take would produce a current of business between Western Canada and the United States that *would make Canada only an adjunct of the United States. . . .* I see this

argument made against Reciprocity in Canada, and I think it is a good one."
The Liberals replied that rather than being a danger to Canada, reciprocity
would make her stronger economically, and therefore more independent
politically. But after fifteen years in office, the Liberals had lost their
vigour, and were constantly kept on the defensive by the office-hungry
Conservatives.

When the votes were counted on September 21, 1911, Borden's strange
coalition of Quebec nationalists and English-Canadian Conservatives had
triumphed, Only in the Maritimes and the prairie provinces had reciprocity
won the day. Defeated and despondent, Laurier summed up his position:

> I am branded in Quebec as a traitor to the French, and in Ontario
> as a traitor to the English. In Quebec I am branded as a Jingo,
> and in Ontario as a Separatist. In Quebec I am attacked as an Im-
> perialist, and in Ontario as an anti-Imperialist. I am neither, I am
> a Canadian.

His policy had been one of moderation, an attempt to preserve unity by
leading both his party and the nation along a middle course between the
extremes. For fifteen years he and the Liberals had succeeded. Now it
was Robert Borden's turn to struggle with the difficulties of governing a
small power in the face of an increasingly critical international situation.
The union of extremes which had made his victory possible now made more
difficult the formulation of policy.

5. THE COMING OF WAR

Robert Laird Borden was a Nova Scotian, who in 1901
had succeeded Sir Charles Tupper as leader of the Conservative party. As
a politician, Borden was quite unlike either of his two great predecessors,
Macdonald and Laurier. He lacked the warm affability and shrewdness

LIST NOT, JACK CANUCK, TO A BOLD EAGLE'S SCREAM;
A BIRD AND A BEAVER MAKE NOT A GOOD TEAM.

which had made Macdonald the master manager of men; nor did he have Laurier's brilliance as a speaker or his French-Canadian charm. Borden's strengths were those of a hard-working and careful lawyer. Although he was a good debater, his judiciousness made him somewhat uncomfortable in the rough-and-tumble of Canadian politics.

From the beginning Borden faced the problem of keeping English and French Canadians working together—the central problem of all Canadian Prime Ministers. Like Laurier before him, Borden soon discovered that events in the outside world, which by 1914 would sweep Canada into war, created his most difficult problems. Moreover, Borden was only in power a short time when the rosy glow of prosperity which had lasted through the years of Liberal government began to fade. Foreign investment in Canada declined, world wheat prices fell, business activity diminished, and unemployment increased. The war was to halt the recession temporarily, but while it lasted, the recession nourished the seeds of urban and rural discontent which were to flower in the post-war years.

Borden's immediate problem was to find a solution to the naval question. Before winning power, his party had taken the position in English-speaking Canada, that the Imperial emergency was so serious that Canada should make a direct financial contribution to the British navy. But Borden knew that this view was not held by his French-Canadian supporters and he therefore found it necessary to tread very carefully in devising a new naval policy.

One of the most difficult tasks that Prime Minister Borden faced after forming his government in 1911 was to ensure that his Imperially-minded supporters from English Canada and his nationalist supporters from Quebec would be kept working together. Borden's decision to have Canada contribute $35,000,000 to the British admiralty for the construction of three dreadnoughts drew serious criticism from Quebec and nearly, though not as completely as the cartoon suggests, caused the nationalist horse to stumble. Though Borden insisted that the financial contribution was designed to aid Britain in a time of emergency, the Liberal opposition claimed that the "Real Emergency" was in the dissension between the Imperialists and the nationalists in the Conservative government.

In 1912 Borden visited England to discuss the naval question with the Imperial authorities. He returned home convinced that the European crisis was so grave that Canada must take immediate action to help Britain. While in Britain he had argued that if Canada were to contribute to the military strength of the Empire, she should have some control over its foreign policy, but the Imperial authorities had been unresponsive to the idea. On his return, Borden put forward a plan which called for a Canadian contribution of thirty-five million dollars to the British navy for the construction of three dreadnoughts. This, he insisted, was a temporary expedient. No permanent policy could be settled upon until there was further discussion in the matter of giving Canada a voice in the determination of Imperial foreign policy. "When Great Britain no longer assumes sole responsibility for defence upon the high seas," Borden pointed out, "she can no longer undertake to assume sole responsibility for and sole control of foreign policy which is closely, vitally and constantly associated in that defence in which the Dominions participate."

Despite assurances that the direct contribution was merely a temporary policy to meet an emergency, some of Borden's French-Canadian colleagues refused to support it. Nevertheless, the bill passed the House of Commons, only to be rejected by the Senate, which contained a majority of Liberals. Thus it happened that when Canada entered the war in August 1914 her naval defence was composed of two old cruisers, the *Rainbow* and the *Niobe*. The long, bitter debate on naval policy had ended in a stalemate.

Few Canadians in the years before 1914 had taken much interest in world affairs. Even fewer had any clear understanding of the issues involved in the complicated events which preceded Britain's declaration of war on Germany. Even the government, with its tiny Department of External Affairs, set up in 1909, lacked the detailed information that independent states need in deciding such important issues as declarations of war. But in 1914 Canada was not an independent state and Britain's declaration of war was made on behalf of all the Empire, including Canada. Few Canadians resented this fact. If Britain declared war, most Canadians automatically accepted the view it was a just war. If the Empire was in danger, Canada must help to defend it. Sir Wilfrid Laurier summed up this feeling when he eloquently declared: "When the call goes out, our answer goes at once, and it goes in the classical answer of the British call to duty: 'Ready, Aye Ready'."

31

The Trials of War

"There are no longer French Canadians and English Canadians," declared the Montreal *La Patrie,* on August 3, 1914. "Only one race now exists, united by the closest bonds in a common cause." Unfortunately, the sense of common purpose evident at the outbreak of the war gradually weakened. As the national and personal sacrifices exacted by the war steadily increased, some sections of the Canadian community lost their enthusiasm for the war effort. By the summer of 1917 the national unity which had been so apparent in 1914 had almost completely disappeared, and Canada faced her most serious crisis since Confederation.

1. CANADA'S WAR EFFORT

In the autumn of 1914 these storm clouds had not yet appeared on the horizon. The Prime Minister, Sir Robert Borden, immediately summoned parliament and with no dissent the members approved the War Measures Act which gave the government broad powers to deal with wartime emergencies without the usual limitations of parliamentary debate and approval. Without hesitation the government then decided to raise a fighting force of twenty-five thousand men to bolster Canada's tiny regular army. Under the leadership of the energetic, if erratic, Sam Hughes, the Minister of Militia, the troops were recruited and trained. Within two months after the declaration of war Canadian soldiers set sail for Britain. Soon afterwards the Canadian Corps was created by the addition of a further two divisions. By 1918 over six hundred thousand Canadians had served in the army, while the navy enlisted nine thousand sailors mainly to man a one hundred and thirty-four vessel fleet responsible for patrolling the Atlantic coast. Canada had no air force of her own, but Canadians took readily to the air and contributed twenty-four per cent of the pilots in the Royal Air Force. Among the Canadian aces was "Billy" Bishop, who set a wartime record by destroying seventy-two enemy aircraft.

Canada's major military contribution, however, was in the brutal and

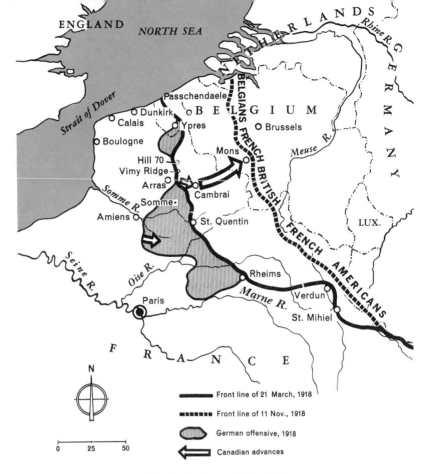

The War in France 1914 - 1918

costly trench warfare in France. In April 1915, shortly after arriving in France, Canadian troops among others were victims of the first German poison gas attack at Ypres. As the French troops on their flank broke and fled the Canadians fought bravely and blocked the gap through which the Germans hoped to drive towards the English Channel ports. An American war correspondent wrote of this exploit: "The Canadians made a stand which was to be remembered as one of the heroic episodes of the war." A year later the Allies launched an offensive at the Somme where the Canadians again won honours but at the cost of many casualties. The Germans soon learned the fighting qualities of the Canadian infantry. The British Prime Minister, David Lloyd George, declared: "The Canadians played a part of such distinction that henceforth they were marked out as storm troops; for the remainder of the war they were brought along to head the assault in one great battle after another." Their most famous and costly single engagement was at Vimy Ridge in the spring of 1917, by which time the Canadian Corps was under a Canadian commander, Sir Arthur Currie. The victory at Vimy was followed by a bitter struggle at Hill 70. Then the

Canadian forces moved into the bloody inch-by-inch, man-to-man struggle in the mud at Passchendaele. In 1918 the tide began to turn decisively in the Allies' favour. On August 8, at Amiens, the Canadian army, flanked by Australian and French troops, broke through the enemy lines on what was known as the "black day of the German army," and from then until the end of the fighting continued to spearhead Allied attacks.

Although the Canadian army was small in comparison with those of the British and French, and later the United States, it won a great reputation. "Whenever the Germans found the Canadian Corps coming into the line," Lloyd George wrote, "they prepared for the worst." So respected was their fighting quality that the Canadians were often thrown into the bloodiest battles where casualties were the heaviest. The loss of 60,661 killed was a price higher than that paid by the much larger United States. With justice Sir Robert Borden could write at the end of the war: "It is a glorious history, and I am extremely proud of it."

The military contribution was matched by the economic efforts at home. Agricultural produce, Canada's leading staple product before the war, provided a large part of the food consumed by Allied troops and civilian populations. The heavy demand for Canadian grain caused the price to rise so rapidly that the government in 1917 established a Board of Grain Supervisors to handle grain sales and fix prices. Lumber, another staple product of long standing, experienced a boom as a result of wartime demand. Even more important for the future was the stimulus which the war gave to the development of industry. Canadian metals, copper, lead, zinc and especially nickel, were greatly in demand. But instead of shipping these valuable minerals abroad to be processed, as would have been done before the war, Canadians developed their own heavy industry to turn out finished products. New industrial plants were designed to produce shells and guns which were manufactured under the direction of the Imperial Munitions Board. The growth of industry during the war, and its retooling for peaceful purposes afterwards, rapidly transformed Canada from an agricultural into an industrial nation.

The demands of war made it necessary for the federal government to assume powers that would have been unthinkable in times of peace. The greatest difficulty faced by Sir Robert Borden's government was to find sufficient men to keep Canada's armed forces supplied with reinforcements; the next was to finance the war effort. Before the war Canadian development had always been heavily dependent on British investment. The war cut this source of funds off. While the American money market helped to fill the gap, the Canadian government found it necessary to depend more heavily than ever before on domestic financial resources. This meant heavier taxes, and in 1917 the first Federal Income Tax Law was passed. In 1915 the government had turned to the people for loans in the form of Victory Bonds. The more than two billion dollars raised in this fashion during the war was a clear indication of the growing financial strength of the country.

Although both Liberals and Conservatives had united in 1914 to commit Canada to active participation in the Great War, by 1916 party politics were again growing bitter. The Liberal opposition anticipating an election in 1916, charged that the Conservative party, riddled with corruption, was collapsing. They pointed to the defeat of Conservative provincial governments in British Columbia, Manitoba and Nova Scotia. In fact, by 1916 the Liberals had great hopes of driving Sir Robert Borden's government from office. By the spring of 1917, however, the question of conscription for overseas service swept all other questions aside, providing the basis for a coalition Union government, and the defeat of the anti-conscriptionist, anti-coalition remains of the Liberal party in the wartime election of 1917.

The economic prosperity brought about by the demand for Canadian products was accompanied by rising prices and food shortages, but it was not until 1916 that growing public discontent forced the Borden government to introduce measures for control by the appointment of Cost of Living Commissioners, and later the establishment of a Food Controller and a War Trade Board. None of these agencies was really effective, for the government was reluctant to depart from the traditional Canadian view that government controls and restrictions were an unjustified interference in the lives of citizens. But as a result of wartime inflation, farmers and wage earners suffered severely and stored up discontents that were to explode in strikes and political radicalism after the war.

2. CRISIS 1917

By 1917 Borden faced a manpower problem which was far more serious in its implications than an inflationary economy; for it was a problem whose solution demanded very drastic interference with the rights of private citizens. The army and war industries absorbed Canada's manpower on a scale for which there was no precedent. Until the spring of 1917, when casualties on the battlefields of Europe rose to unexpected heights, the government had managed to find enough reinforcements. But by the middle of 1917 declining enlistment figures and mounting casualties showed that new recruiting methods would have to be adopted if reinforcements were to be found to fill growing gaps at the front. All efforts to stimulate voluntary enlistment failed and the government was compelled to revoke its promise not to introduce compulsory military service. When this decision was announced the always uneasy relations between French- and English-speaking Canadians took a turn for the worse. At the beginning of the war Quebec, like the rest of Canada, supported the Allied cause. Even the nationalist Bourassa stated that it was Canada's duty "to contribute within the bounds of her strength and by means which are proper to herself, to the triumph, and especially to the endurance, of the combined efforts of France and England." But Bourassa and most other French Canadians believed that Canada's contribution to the war should be a voluntary one. No one suggested in 1914 that the conscription of men would be necessary to win the war.

Unfortunately for the country and for the war effort, the revival of the controversial school question in the early years of the war undermined the goodwill and co-operative spirit that had existed in Quebec in 1914. This time the centre of the dispute was in Ontario where a rule known as Regulation 17 confined teaching in the French language to the early grades and appeared to restrict the establishment of new French-language schools. The French Canadians immediately attacked the regulation as an attempt to limit minority rights, and once the argument over language rights had begun the eyes of most people in Quebec turned away from the battlefields of Europe towards the cultural conflict in Canada. Bourassa put the French-Canadian view in its most extreme form when he wrote: "In the name of religion, liberty and faithfulness to the British flag, the French Canadians are enjoined to fight the Prussians of Europe. Shall we let the Prussians of Ontario impose their domination like masters, in the very heart of the Canadian Confederation, under the shelter of the British flag and British institutions?" In the end, the courts found the Ontario language regulations valid, but this did nothing to dispel the French Canadians' belief that an injustice had been done to them, particularly when Manitoba also abolished bilingual schools in 1916.

By 1917, as the Ontario school controversy reached its peak, the need for manpower became critical. English-speaking Canadians pointed to low enlistment figures in Quebec as the cause of the manpower shortage. To some extent the charge was true. The French Canadians as a whole were never as deeply committed to the war as were most English-speaking Canadians. They had no strong emotional tie with either Britain, which had conquered them, or with France, which had deserted them. However, when the enlistment record was carefully examined, it was obvious that the largest number of recruits from English-speaking Canada came from among the most recent British immigrants. Native-born English-speaking Canadians, like French Canadians, were somewhat more reluctant to volunteer for overseas service. Finally, the French Canadians were still largely an agrarian people, and farmers in *both* sections of the country had been slower to join the military services than had urban dwellers.

It was not merely the habits of an established way of life, however, that kept French Canadian enlistments lower than those from English-speaking Canada. The inept handling of recruiting by the Borden government also discouraged French-Canadian volunteers. The government showed little understanding of the language difficulties faced by French-Canadian recruits

in training camps commanded by English-speaking officers and was slow
to create French-Canadian regiments and to promote French-Canadian
officers. Moreover, the appointment of at least one Protestant clergyman
as a recruiting officer in Quebec did nothing to soothe the uneasiness of the
French Canadians. At the centre of this problem was the Minister of
Militia, Sam Hughes. Ever since the bitter debates of the 1890's, Hughes
had been in the forefront of the anti-French and anti-Catholic crusade.
During the war he suppressed his real opinions, although in an unguarded
moment in his home town of Lindsay, Ontario in 1916 he declared that
Quebec "has not done its duty as it should and would if the young manhood
of the Province had been taken in hand by the proper people, who have
benefited so much from British institutions in days gone by." Such statements did nothing to remove the French-Canadian suspicion that Hughes
was a prominent Imperialist, anti-French and anti-Catholic Orangeman.

As complaints and criticism of the French-Canadian contribution became more intemperate in English-speaking Canada, the stubbornness of
the French Canadians increased. Prime Minister Borden returned from a
visit to the Western Front in the spring of 1917 convinced that a policy of
compulsory enlistment would have to be adopted, if Canada's fighting men
were to be adequately reinforced. To the French Canadians, conscription
was unacceptable. To avoid a disastrous racial division, Borden proposed
that Laurier and the Liberals join a coalition government.

Laurier enthusiastically supported the war effort and had many times
appealed to his countrymen to volunteer for service. In August 1916, he
declared:

> There are many people who say we will not fight for England: will
> you then fight for France? I speak to you of French origin. If I
> were young like you and had the same health that I enjoy today, I
> would join those brave Canadians fighting today for the liberation
> of French territory. I would not have it said that the French Cana-

This 1916 caricature of Laurier in a
Prussian uniform by the French-Canadian
cartoonist Julien was a satirical comment
on the views of English Canadians about
their French-speaking compatriots. Not
untypical was the opinion of John W.
Dafoe, a Liberal, who wrote a French-
Canadian friend: "The trouble between
English and French Canadians has become
acute because French Canadians have
refused to play their part in this war—
being the only race of white men to quit.
They try to excuse themselves by alleging
that they have domestic grievances which
should first be righted. The excuse, if
true, would be quite contemptible. In
the face of an emergency like this
domestic questions have to stand."

dians do less for the liberation of France than the citizens of British origin. For my part I want to fight for England and also for France. For those who do not want to fight either for England or for France I say: will you fight for yourselves?

But Laurier had repeatedly promised that he would oppose conscription. In 1917 he realized that if he joined a coalition government whose purpose was to impose conscription he would give control of Quebec to Bourassa and the Nationalists. Moreover, he believed that conscription would split the country and so harm the war effort.

Despite Laurier's refusal to join a coalition, Borden and many Liberal leaders in English-speaking Canada were determined to form a union government that would enforce conscription. The temper of English-speaking Canada had been roused, and much of the anger was directed against Quebec. One Liberal newspaper announced:

> The authentic voice of Quebec today is that of Bourassa. He has been stating his views with perfect frankness. He says Quebec is against the war. Laurier is at best a moderating, not a controlling power in Quebec. If he came into a coalition government he would leave Quebec behind him. This is why the problem now before the people of Canada must be solved, if there is any solution, without the assistance of Laurier or Quebec.

Under the leadership of Sir Clifford Sifton, N. W. Rowell, the Liberal leader in Ontario, and a number of western Liberals, the movement for coalition government gained widespread support in English-speaking Canada. Pushing Laurier aside, these Liberals began negotiations with Borden. Before the negotiations were completed the Conservatives enacted two new electoral laws giving votes to the soldiers overseas and their female relatives at home (women in 1914 had not the right to vote) and disfranchising all immigrants who had come to Canada from enemy countries after 1902.

When women were enfranchised posters such as these appeared soliciting their votes. The caption under the picture on the right urged women to make good use of the weapon put in their hands and, by supporting the Union government, to defend themselves against the fate of their Belgian sisters.

Women of Canada
Remember Your Sisters in Belgium

THE KAISER and his war lords have repeatedly said: "We must leave nothing to the women in the countries we vanquish but their eyes to weep with."

Yet Laurier and Bourassa say we must QUIT the fight against these inhuman monsters.

Our boys in France are giving their lives to save the women and children of France, Great Britain,—yes, and of Canada—from the same brutal violence with which the Huns violated Belgium.

To hold back the Germans our boys send an urgent call for reinforcements. Union Government is pledged to raise the reinforcements at once, and is actually doing this now under the Military Service Act, 1917. Women of Canada, now is your opportunity to revenge your sisters in Belgium and help your boys in France.

Vote for the Union Government Candidate

This legislation helped to ensure an electoral victory for supporters of conscription and no doubt helped to bring the negotiations for coalition government to a successful conclusion. In October 1917, Prime Minister Borden announced the formation of a Union government of Conservatives and English-speaking Liberals.

Before conscription was enforced an election was called for December 1917. The campaign was a bitter one. In English-speaking Canada election posters warned that "Laurier is the tool of Bourassa," and that "a vote for Laurier is a vote for the Kaiser." In Quebec, conscription was denounced in equally vigorous terms. But the result of the election was never in doubt. Laurier and his followers won eighty-two seats, all but twenty of which were in Quebec. The Unionists swept English-speaking Canada, carrying one hundred and fifty constituencies, but won only three in Quebec. Canada was split along cultural lines as never before, and was governed by a cabinet which, for the first time since the achievement of responsible government, included none of the recognized leaders of French Canada.

Gradually tempers cooled, but it was a long time before French Canadians were willing to forgive English-speaking Canada, and especially the Conservatives, for conscription. The conscription policy raised about 120,-000 men, of whom about 47,000 were sent overseas before the war ended. The disruption of national unity was a high price to pay for these reinforcements, but in the spring of 1918 the war was in its most critical phase and neither Borden nor anyone else realized that Germany would collapse in November. Furthermore, like Macdonald and Laurier, Borden was a nationalist. He regarded Canada's war effort not only as an expression of maturing Canadian nationalism, but as an opportunity to advance her national status. If he were ever to convince Great Britain and the world that Canada deserved to be recognized as a nation, he could not allow his country's war effort to slacken.

3. IMPERIAL DEVELOPMENT AND PEACE

In 1914 Canada was automatically at war because Great Britain had declared war. Canada had played no part in pre-war diplomacy, since direction of the foreign policy for the Empire was entirely in the hands of the British government. Yet Canada suffered the consequences of policies which she had played no part in making. Prime Minister Borden and many other Canadians found this situation most unsatisfactory. As the war dragged on the feeling grew stronger that Canada should have a larger measure of influence and control over policies that touched Canadian interests.

Canadian subordination to British control was most evident in military affairs. From the beginning of the war, Borden and Hughes insisted that Canadian soldiers should be kept together as a Canadian army, rather than being divided up and dispersed among British troops. Although a Canadian Corps was formed, it was at first commanded by a British officer, Sir

LA PRESSE

Le plus fort tirage des journaux du Canada tout entier, plus de 140,000 copies par jour

FETE DU JOUR: Saint Thomas

BEAU ET FROID
TEMPS PROBABLE:

31me ANNEE—No 42   EDITION QUOTIDIENNE—MONTREAL VENDREDI 21 DECEMBRE 1917   PRIX | UN CENTIN à Montréal

POUR FAIRE SORTIR QUEBEC DE LA CONFEDERATION CANADIENNE

(Spécial à la "Presse")

Québec, 21.—A la séance d'aujourd'hui, à l'Assemblée Législative, M. J.-N. Francoeur, député libéral de Lotbinière, a donné avis qu'à la prochaine séance de l'assemblée législative, il proposera la motion suivante:

"Que cette Chambre est d'avis que la province de Québec serait disposée à accepter la rupture du pacte fédéral de 1867, si, dans l'opinion des autres provinces, la dite province est un obstacle à l'union, au progrès et au développement du Canada." M. Francoeur est le président du comité des bills privés.

Following the bitter wartime election of December 1917 which left Quebec almost completely isolated from the rest of Canada, Mr. J. N. Francoeur, a Liberal member of the Quebec legislature, proposed a motion which declared, "This Chamber is of the opinion that the Province of Quebec would be disposed to accept breaking of the Confederation pact of 1867 if in the other provinces it is believed that she is an obstacle to the union, progress and development of Canada." The motion never came to a vote but most of the members agreed with the Quebec Premier, Sir Lomer Gouin, who concluded the debate by declaring, "It is to preserve my country's greatness, to cherish in the hearts of our children all their hopes, to hand down to them, in a word, the heritage which we received from our fathers, that we should struggle fearlessly against the passing storm, that we should labour ceaselessly and untiringly to develop and maintain the Canadian Confederation."

Julian Byng. By 1917 Borden's insistence compelled the British to appoint a Canadian commander, Sir Arthur Currie. But Borden was not content with this small concession. He was anxious to gain some voice in the determination of policy. The British authorities were unwilling even to keep the Canadian government fully informed about military policy, but Borden was a stubborn fighter and did not give up easily. "It can hardly be expected," he warned, "that we should put 400,000 or 500,000 men in the field and willingly accept the position of having no more voice and receiving no more consideration than if we were mere toy automata. Any person cherishing such an expectation harbours an unfortunate and even dangerous delusion." Towards the end of 1916 Borden's complaints won a more sympathetic hearing in London. David Lloyd George, the new British Prime Minister, saw the justice of these complaints and established the Imperial War Cabinet, a body composed of the chief British ministers and the Prime Ministers of the Dominions. Since the Prime Ministers of the Dominions could only spend a small amount of time in London, this method of consultation was not entirely satisfactory. For the first time, however, Canada had a seat in the inner circle of the policy makers.

Borden hoped that the new status of the Dominions as equal partners in the Empire would receive formal recognition after the war. At the Imperial War Conference of 1917 he introduced a motion known as Reso-

Sir Robert Borden was leaving Whitehall when this picture was taken. Along with the Prime Ministers of the other British Dominions, he took part in the meetings of the Imperial War Cabinet and their views were considered in the making of war policy. In 1917 the Canadian Prime Minister spoke of the significance of these meetings when he said, "The Imperial War Cabinet as constituted today has been summoned for definite and specific purposes publicly stated which involve questions of the most vital concern to the whole Empire. With the constitution of that cabinet a new era dawned and a new page of history has been written. It is not for me to prophesy as to the future significance of these pregnant events; but those who have given thought and energy to every effort for full constitutional development of the overseas nations may be pardoned for believing that they discern therein the birth of a new and greater Imperial Commonwealth."

lution IX, which recommended that a Conference should be called after the war to draw up a declaration which would recognize the self-government of the Dominions in domestic affairs, and their position as "autonomous nations" with "an adequate voice in foreign policy." Resolution IX expressed Borden's belief that Canada and the other Dominions had reached a position of equality with Britain as members of the Empire.

Sir Robert Borden's objective was not merely to have Canada's status as a nation recognized by Britain. That was only the first step. Equally important was his desire to have nations outside the Empire accept Canada as an independent nation. This aim was made clear in Borden's attitude when it came time to draw up a peace treaty at the end of the war. He believed that since Canada and the other Dominions had made large contributions towards the Allied victory, they should be allowed to participate individually in drawing up the terms of peace. Once more Borden had to overcome British opposition, but in the end each of the Dominions took part in the Peace Conference at Paris in its own right and as members of the British Empire delegation. Moreover, each Dominion signed the treaty for itself and, again on Borden's insistence, each Dominion parliament ratified the treaty separately. Thus Britain was no longer acting alone in implementing the foreign policy of the Empire. Each Dominion now had a voice in determining the collective policy of the Empire. This was not the same as each Dominion having its own foreign policy, but it was a step beyond the pre-war position when Imperial foreign policy was the exclusive responsibility of Britain.

While Canada had asserted and obtained a right to take part in the peace negotiations, she played a very small part in deciding the precise terms that would be imposed on the defeated powers. Borden's main concern was with the new international organizations, the League of Nations and the International Labour Organization, which were created by the peace treaty. Borden insisted again that the Dominion should be given separate representation in these bodies. This struggle for international recognition of Canada's new status was Borden's greatest battle, for he had to fight the United States and France, both of whom suspected that votes for the British Dominions in these international bodies would be nothing more than additional British votes. The usually mild Borden argued that "the Dominions have maintained their places before the world during the past five years through sacrifices which no nation outside Europe has known" and were entitled to full recognition. The justice of this claim was difficult to deny, and in the end Canada and the other Dominions were accepted as independent members of the League of Nations.

Canadian nationalism had been given a sharp stimulus by the war. When peace returned, the country was no longer ready to accept a position of subordination either within the Empire, or Commonwealth as it was now being called, or in international affairs. Borden's greatest achievement was that through dogged persistence he was able to win for his country a new status in the eyes of the world. At home, however, serious problems awaited the attention of Canada's political leaders at the end of the war. The economic and cultural strains which the war had produced meant that national development would be more difficult than it had ever been before.

CHAPTER 32

The Triumph of
Mackenzie King

The First World War had a powerful impact on every aspect of Canadian life. Not least important was its effect on politics. By 1919 there was no truly national party in the country that could claim support from all sections of the Canadian community. The Union government, which continued in office after the war, was without support among the French Canadians, and was losing ground among Ontario and western farmers who hated its high tariff policy. The Liberal party was strong only in Quebec, because it had opposed conscription in 1917. It had some followers in the Maritimes, and hoped that Liberals who had supported the Union government in 1917 would return to their old party when the war ended. In western Canada and rural Ontario no party held the allegiance of the voters, who opposed the tariff policies of the Unionists and the anti-conscription policy of the Liberals in 1917. With neither of the old parties able to gain a following, the way was clear for a new party, the Progressives, to win the support of Canadian farmers.

1. NEW LEADERS AND A NEW PARTY

Immediately after the war three new political leaders competed for the support of the electorate. Following the death of Sir Wilfrid Laurier in February 1919, representatives of the Liberal party met in Ottawa in August to select a new leader. The chief contenders for the position were two former cabinet ministers: the elderly, experienced W. S. Fielding, and the young, ambitious William Lyon Mackenzie King. Fielding had been one of Laurier's most trusted colleagues, but in 1917 he had broken with Laurier and had supported conscription. King, the grandson of the rebel leader of 1837, had become Canada's first Minister of Labour in 1909, after spending many years studying economics and sociology and working in the civil service. Only forty-five years old in 1919, King knew that he had one distinct advantage over Fielding and the other candidates. As he wrote in his diary: "All the Liberal members of the Union government failed in a moment of crisis, at a time of great need. They left their leader when the popular tide was rising against him." By standing with Sir Wilfrid in the conscription crisis, King had ensured himself of the support of Quebec in his quest for the party leadership. After three ballots, the Ottawa Liberal convention elected Mackenzie King.

Dumpy and undistinguished in appearance, King lacked the personal grace and warmth of Laurier, but he possessed the patience and capacity for compromise that were necessary for a leader whose first task was to mend a party shattered by the conscription issue in 1917. On the surface King was calm, and his manner ponderous, but in times of crisis he could act with deliberation and ruthlessness. Since he remained a bachelor and developed few non-political interests, he devoted his life almost entirely to managing his party and governing the country. His personal life was lonely and marked by a deep devotion to the memory of his mother. He possessed a strong religious conviction which, in later life, included a mystical belief in spiritualism. King never lost the conviction that the hand of destiny guided his actions. On his election to the party leadership he wrote: "My thoughts were of dear mother and father and little Bell all of whom I felt to be very close to me, of grandfather & Sir Wilfrid also. I thought: it is right, it is the call of duty. I have sought nothing, it has come. It has come from God."

By the summer of 1920 the Unionist, or Conservative party as it was again being called, also required a new leader, for Sir Robert Borden had seriously undermined his health during the trying war years and now retired from political life. The new Conservative leader, Arthur Meighen, was selected, not by a convention, but by the Conservative members of parliament. Like King, Meighen was born in Ontario and the two men had attended the University of Toronto together. But here the similarity ended. While King did post-graduate studies in the United States, Meighen went West to set up a law practice in Portage la Prairie, Manitoba. In 1908 Meighen was elected to parliament where he soon impressed the members with his great abilities as a parliamentary debater. When war broke out he held only a minor post in the government, but rose rapidly to become Borden's chief lieutenant. His quick mind, his sharp tongue and his superb skill in detailed argument won the admiration, though seldom the affection, of many members of parliament. Recognizing his ability and industry, Borden made him responsible for some of the heaviest tasks that the government had to perform. Meighen was the government's chief defender of conscription in 1917, and also the architect of the complex and controversial legislation authorizing the nationalization of the nearly bankrupt Grand Trunk Railway in 1919.

Meighen was straightforward, direct and sometimes arrogant. He enjoyed debate and argument, but did not work easily with men whose minds moved more slowly than his. He was a formidable foe for Mackenzie King, and attacked the Liberal leader with characteristic sarcasm in a speech in 1919:

I have one suggestion to offer to the fair rose of expectancy of His Majesty's loyal Opposition; it is that when we have a concrete subject before the House for debate he would be good enough to offer some remarks which really bear upon the issue and leave out of consideration, if he possibly can, these old hackneyed phrases "democracy," "autocracy of executives"—all of the rest of it which have no more relevancy to the discussion than were he to discuss the merits of the government of Japan.

It was no wonder that King feared and even hated Meighen! But the new Conservative leader suffered from two serious handicaps: in Quebec his name was associated with the conscription policy, while in the West his high tariff views made him unpopular.

The most popular politician in the West at this time was Thomas A. Crerar, the leader of the new Progressive party that sprang up among the farmers immediately after the war. Crerar was a natural leader for the farmers' political movement. He had business experience gained as the President of a farmer-owned grain-buying organization, and political experience as a member of the wartime coalition government. His popularity among the farmers increased greatly when he resigned from the Union government in 1919 in protest against the continuation of a high tariff. In January 1920, when the National Progressive party was launched, Crerar's political experience as well as his knowledge of western problems made him the obvious choice as leader.

The appearance of Crerar and the Progressive movement on the Canadian political scene was one of many signs that the country was in a state of economic dislocation and social discontent in the years immediately after the war. It was this disturbed situation which made the three-cornered struggle for power among King, Meighen and Crerar a vigorous and exciting one.

2. POST-WAR PROTEST MOVEMENTS

The earliest and most dramatic signs of discontent came from the urban working class. Conscription had never been popular among this group, for they felt that wealth as well as manpower should have been conscripted. There seemed to be rank injustice in a system that sent a worker to the front while his employer fattened on lucrative war contracts. The attack on these "war profiteers" gave an edge to the growing tension between capital and labour. Moreover, the cost of living had raced far ahead of wages, despite the government's attempts to control prices. Trade union membership doubled between 1914 and 1918 and once the war ended union leaders attempted to gain the right of collective bargaining. The end of the war also brought servicemen home to find jobs, at a time when the end of wartime demands caused a business recession, wage cuts, and unemployment. In Canada, as in the United States, the year 1919 was marked by a wave of fierce strikes and new and alarming talk of socialism, the forma-

Headlines from the strikers' newspaper provide a graphic outline of the course of the Winnipeg General Strike.

tion of One Big Union of all workingmen, and a general strike to reveal its power.

The main centre of urban discontent in Canada was Winnipeg. In May 1919 the Winnipeg Trades and Labour Council called a general strike to display sympathy and solidarity with the members of the metals trades union who had been denied the right to bargain collectively by their employers. The strikers' success in paralyzing the economic life of the city brought a strong reaction from businessmen and professional people. By the end of May the latter were describing the strike as "a serious attempt to overturn British institutions in this western country and to supplant them with the Russian Bolshevik system of Soviet rule." It should be recalled that the Russian Revolution had occurred only two years earlier. Sympathetic strikes broke out across Canada, and, as hysteria mounted in the business community, provincial and federal authorities intervened. On June 17 the Royal Canadian Mounted Police arrested key men among the strikers on very slim evidence. Among those arrested was James Shaver Woodsworth, a former Methodist minister who, as temporary editor of the *Western Labour News*, had quoted a Biblical text which the authorities considered subversive. On June 21, "Bloody Saturday," armed policemen broke up a peaceful parade and troops dispatched by the federal government guarded the street corners.

By such tactics, the back of the strike was broken. Many strikers had been reduced to near starvation. When the Manitoba government promised to appoint a Royal Commission to investigate labour grievances, the strike was called off. The Royal Commission later reported that the strike had not been called with revolutionary intentions, however radically some of the strikers had talked, but had sought only the right to collective bargaining and an improvement in what the Commission agreed were deplorable working conditions.

While labour's immediate grievances disappeared with the return of prosperity, later in the 'twenties, the bitterness engendered by the strike had lasting effects. Labour leaders were convinced that direct political action was necessary to protect their interests. Woodsworth was elected to the House of Commons as a Labour member soon after his release from jail, while four others were elected to the Manitoba legislature as Labour spokesmen.

Unrest among the farmers in Ontario and on the prairies erupted in a less violent fashion, but it was no less startling, and brought more immediate results. The Union government had broken its promise not to conscript farmers' sons, and this, together with wartime profiteering and corruption, high prices, indifferent incomes, and rural depopulation, shattered their confidence in both the economic order and the traditional political parties. J. J. Morrison, an Ontario farm leader, wrote in 1919:

> We have passed through an orgy of corruption that is a disgrace to true Canadians and was only made possible by the utter failure of machine party politics to defend the rights of the people. I have followed partisan politics long enough and am disgusted. Something better must be found.

To many farmers the only solution to the uncertain economic situation was a farmers' political party. As one agrarian leader said: "Go into politics, or go out of farming." Ever since Confederation, the farmers believed, the country had been governed by men who supported economic and tariff policies which benefited only the industrial East. Their basic grievance was the tariff which, by protecting industry, forced the farmers to pay high prices for farm machinery and other essential manufactured goods. Yet their agricultural products had to be sold on a free and competitive international market. Since both the Liberals and the Conservatives supported a high tariff policy, the farmers concluded that they would have to form their own political party. In 1916 the Canadian Council of Agriculture issued a programme, The New National Policy, which by 1919 was accepted as a statement of aims for an agrarian political movement. Its main demand was for a lower tariff, but it also advocated political reforms such as the initiative, referendum and recall, all demands for direct democracy similar to those advocated earlier by the American farmers. The New National Policy also demanded public ownership of railways and lower freight rates. The platform was in effect a vigorous denunciation of the old National Policy, which encouraged tariff-protected industries, restricted railway competition, and nurtured monopolies and combines, and of the political parties that supported it. The Winnipeg Free Press explained the farmers' platform in this way: "It is the common acceptance of an economic policy which makes the encouragement of the basic industries of Canada— agricultural, mining, forestry, fishing—the first charge upon the interest and sympathy of the state."

By 1919 the farming community was organized and optimistic, as their battle song "The Day of Right" (sung to the tune of "The Battle Hymn of the Republic") suggests:

The first, and most surprising political success of the organized farmers came in Ontario in 1919. Out of a heated campaign among Conservatives, Liberals, the United Farmers of Ontario, and Labour, the one clear fact that emerged was the defeat of the Conservative Henry government. The U.F.O. won forty-three seats, the Liberals twenty-eight, the Conservatives twenty-six, Labour twelve, Independents two. Not the least surprised at the result were the U.F.O. leaders. After much debate, E. C. Drury was chosen to lead the new government which received the support of the Labour members. "May we not hope," said Premier Drury, "that before long this movement, which has had its birth in our particular class, may expand and broaden till it shall become, not merely a Farmers' Party but, in a very real sense, a People's Party?"

> The farmers of the prairie lands are massing in their might,
> Exulting in a Principle, a Cause for which they fight,
> The sacred cause of Justice, the establishment of Right,
> And Equal Rights to all.

Their confidence was justified. In 1919 the United Farmers of Ontario swept into power in the most industrialized province in Canada. Two years later the United Farmers of Alberta began a fourteen-year tenure of office, while the farmers of Manitoba were catapulted into office in 1922. Federally, these provincial farmers' movements gave vigorous support to T. A. Crerar and the National Progressive party.

These events provide the background for the exciting federal election of 1921. Prime Minister Meighen asked the electors to approve not only the government's wartime record but also the nationalization of the Grand Trunk and Canadian Northern railways. This railway policy was based on the report of a commission appointed in 1916 to examine the financial problems of the two railways. Rather than allow the railways to flounder in bankruptcy, the Union government had decided in 1919 to combine the two systems under government ownership. This decision drew criticism both from businessmen who opposed the principle of government ownership, and from others who believed that the government had paid too large a price for the near-bankrupt railways. As an issue in 1921 the tariff was more important than any other single question because of the farmers' intense interest in it. Meighen believed that Canada could only thrive and grow with the aid of "a tariff system made by the Canadian people, made on a clear, sound, impregnable principle, and that system must not rest on

"*I stand for Unity In Canada. My aim and object will be to hold the balance fairly and firmly among all classes.*"

"I Stand opposed to the platform of CRERAR. I have not the slightest 'doubt if it is put into effect it will bring disaster to the whole country."

"I stand against the KING Liberal platform against it from the first line to the last."

"To start in at this date to reverse Canada's Tariff policy and abandon the protective system would be, to my mind, as obvious and arrant a folly as was ever committed by an intelligent nation."

"I have the responsibility to lay the case of the Government before the people. That done, my responsibility is at an end. The other responsibility is yours. It is for you to decide what is best for the people of this great Dominion, competing in the world with other great national entities; it is for you to rise to the stature of Canadian citizenship and choose. Whatever your decision is I will abide by the result.

The National Liberal and Conservative
Publicity Committee.

This campaign poster for the 1921 election outlined the Conservative platform succinctly.

the insecure foundation of arrangements with the United States." Meighen's view was in complete contradiction to the farmers' demand that the tariff, especially the tariff against the United States, should be lowered.

Mackenzie King's viewpoint was not as clear-cut. He argued that it was "time for a change," and criticized the Conservatives' railway policy. On the crucial tariff question, however, his position was vague, for King was unwilling to adopt any policy that would alienate either the low-tariff westerners or the high-tariff eastern industrialists and financiers. Meighen was right when he charged that King's statements on the tariff were "just the circular pomposity of a man who won't say what he means."

Like Meighen, Crerar believed that the tariff was the main issue in the election. "I stand opposed to the principle of protection," he said, "and I trust I ever shall. Our policy rests on this consideration: that the wealth of Canada can best be developed or added to by developing the natural resources of the country."

The result of the 1921 election clearly revealed the divisions within the nation. Mackenzie King's Liberals won the largest number of seats, one hundred and seventeen, nearly half of which were in Quebec. Arthur Meighen's following was reduced to a mere fifty members, thirty-seven of them from Ontario. The surprise was the election of sixty-five Progressives, forty-one from the West and twenty-four from Ontario. Mackenzie King had won a narrow victory in the first round of the three-cornered fight with Meighen and Crerar.

3. KING, THE PROGRESSIVES, AND THE DEFEAT OF MEIGHEN

The new Liberal Prime Minister's natural caution was increased by the narrowness of his majority in the House of Commons. During the four years after the 1921 election his major objective was to win the support of the Progressives, whom he chose to regard as "Liberals in a hurry." "This is a moment for great generosity," he wrote in 1921, "and all the conciliation that is possible towards those who, believing in ideals which are strongly Liberal, have nevertheless been a powerful opposing force in the campaign just concluded. I want, if I can, to have the West feel that I am its friend." To the westerners King offered some slight tariff reductions and attempted to meet their demands for lower freight rates on shipments of western grain. But his main strength was the Progressives' realization that if they defeated King they would return Meighen to office, and with him high tariffs.

Moreover, internal divisions weakened the federal Progressive party. Most members, especially those from Ontario and Manitoba, were moderate in their demands for reform and concentrated almost exclusively on the tariff and freight rates. Many of them looked forward to an alliance with those members of the Liberal party who also favoured a lower tariff. But one wing of the farmers' movement had more radical ideas. The strength of this group lay in Alberta where Henry Wise Wood guided the United Farmers organization. Wood attacked the basic structure of the party system and parliamentary government, for he believed that representation should be on an occupational basis. Within the parliamentary party Wood's followers carried on a running battle with Crerar and the moderates, and denounced every suggestion of co-operation with the Liberals. In 1922 Crerar resigned from the leadership of the Progressive party. His successor, Robert Forke, was another moderate but he lacked Crerar's strength and after Crerar's resignation the Progressive movement began to disintegrate.

By 1925 these internal divisions had weakened the party, while the return of prosperity and higher wheat prices had taken the edge off agrarian discontent. Only twenty-four Progressives, mainly of the radical wing, were returned to parliament in the election of that year. Mackenzie King's conciliatory policy enabled him to capture Progressive seats in the West, but his party suffered heavy losses in Ontario and the Maritimes and won only one hundred and one seats. Meighen and the Conservatives made a comeback in the East and increased their standing to one hundred and seventeen seats to make them the largest party. The stage was set for the last round of the political struggle of the 'twenties. Crerar had withdrawn from the fight, leaving only King and Meighen in the ring.

Although Prime Minister King's government was defeated at the polls in 1925, no party had won a clear majority. King therefore decided to meet parliament rather than resign. Thus began one of the most complicated episodes in Canadian political and constitutional history. King had hoped to carry on government with the support of the twenty-four Progressive members. But early in the parliamentary session of 1926, a committee uncovered evidence of serious corruption in the Customs Department. This revelation made it impossible for the Progressives to continue supporting the Liberals, for it confirmed their worst suspicion of corruption in the two old parties. Before a motion of no confidence could be passed against his government, King asked the Governor-General, Lord Byng, for a dissolution and a new election. Since it was less than a year since an election had been held, and because the Conservatives actually had more seats in parliament than the Liberals, Lord Byng rejected King's advice. King resigned and Byng called upon Arthur Meighen to form a government.

In asking the Conservative leader to form a government, Lord Byng had acted in a completely constitutional manner. But he may have been unwise, for Meighen's prospects of holding office for any length of time were very small since to do so he would have to depend upon the support of the Progressives who had never trusted him. The expected defeat came within four days. Now there was no alternative but to call another election. In the campaign that followed the Liberals charged that Lord Byng's refusal to grant King a dissolution in the first place was unconstitutional, and that Meighen was responsible for the situation, since he had agreed to form a government. "If that is not anarchy and absolutism in government, I should like to know what category political philosophy would assign government carried on under such conditions. I know of nothing in British history comparable to this since the days of Charles the First," Mackenzie King maintained. Moreover, claimed King, the refusal of a British official to obey the advice of his Canadian Prime Minister was an infringement on Canadian autonomy or national status. Arthur Meighen rightly argued that the Governor-General's action was entirely constitutional and had nothing to do with autonomy or status. "It is ridiculous to assume that he [the Governor-General] sought in any way to establish gubernatorial autocracy, or to menace self-government," Meighen stated. Moreover, he added, the Liberals had attempted to create a constitutional issue to cover up the mismanagement and corruption that had been revealed in the Customs Department.

Advice to the little partisan politician — DON'T!

In the election of 1926, the Liberal leader, W. L. Mackenzie King charged that Lord Byng, the Governor-General, had overstepped his understood powers in refusing him a dissolution when he had been advised to do so. The Toronto **Globe** commented on the danger of making an issue of the Governor-General's action: "Is there anything to be gained, under these circumstances, by making the Governor-General an issue in a political campaign—by staging in the halls and on the hustings all over the land heated partisan controversies between self-appointed defenders of the Crown? There is much to be lost. This sort of thing can create only dissatisfaction and disturbance, and provide fuel for those agitators and disloyalists who are constantly plotting national or Imperial arson."

But the Canadian electorate, which suspected that Meighen had been over-anxious for office when he attempted to form a minority government accepted King's appeal to their nationalism and returned a large Liberal majority in the election of 1926. In this election the Progressives were almost completely wiped out as the West joined the Liberal fold. The election of 1926 marked the triumph of Mackenzie King over his bitter enemy, Arthur Meighen. Though possessed of a sharp mind and brilliant debating skill, Meighen had appeared as a cold and sometimes arrogant politician. The colourless and cautious Mackenzie King proved more to the electorate's liking. In 1927 Meighen resigned from the leadership of the Conservative party, and was replaced by a millionaire lawyer from Calgary, Richard Bedford Bennett.

4. ECONOMIC GROWTH, SOCIAL CHANGE AND DEPRESSION

In the late 1920's Canadian politics resumed a more normal course as the nation's economy expanded and prospered. The rapid development of new staples like gold, nickel, copper, pulpwood and newsprint gave better balance to an economy that had formerly depended so heavily on grain exports. This development altered the pattern of Canadian trade which before the war had been carried on largely with Britain and Europe. The new staples fed the developing Canadian industries and supplied the enormous United States demand for raw materials.

In the post-war decade, pulp and paper mills expanded in northern Ontario, British Columbia, Quebec and New Brunswick. Asbestos from eastern Quebec, copper and nickel from Sudbury and Copper Cliff in Ontario, oil from Alberta's Turner Valley fields, lead, zinc, and copper from Trail in the Kootenay Mountain regions of British Columbia provided new sources of wealth and new areas for employment and settlement. The processing of these metals increased the demand for electrical energy, and several provinces, including Saskatchewan and Manitoba, followed the pattern established in 1905 by Ontario in setting up publicly-owned power commissions.

The prosperity brought by these new economic developments was not evenly distributed across the country. Ontario and Quebec benefited most from the mining developments, with Toronto and Montreal providing the finances necessary for the development of new mineral deposits. The prairies and the Maritimes were less favourably affected by the surge of prosperity. Grain, and especially wheat, remained the great source of western wealth, and competition on the international market was keen. The farmers' political protest movements in the 1920's were in part a reflection of economic problems which resulted from the gradual shift in the Canadian economy from agriculture to industry, from the country to the city. In their battle for lower tariffs and lower freight rates, the farmers were attempting to save the agricultural way of life that was being displaced by the growth of cities and industry.

The depression struck the prairie farmer with particular harshness. As world markets for his products disappeared, as the hordes of grasshoppers and drought ravaged his crops, the farmer found that even the bare necessities of life, let alone mortgage payments and farm improvements, slipped nearly beyond his reach. Between 1929 and 1933 the export price of Canadian wheat fell by 55%, while the prices of goods that farmers had to buy declined only 14%. In these same years, goods produced by the farmer fell 49% in market value. In these circumstances it was no wonder that the net income of the farmer declined over 50% in relation to the total national income in the first four years of depression.

The new prosperity almost completely by-passed the Maritime provinces, which had never fully recovered from the late nineteenth-century decline in their shipbuilding industry. Like the farmers, the Maritimers also felt that Canada's tariff structure was designed primarily to benefit people living in the central provinces. While increased federal subsidies to the Maritime provinces and assistance to the coal industry in Nova Scotia eased economic difficulties temporarily, the Atlantic provinces remained economically poorer than the other parts of the country.

The years of prosperity came to an abrupt end in the autumn of 1929, with a great crash, when the world-wide economic depression began. In Canada the impact of the depression was severe. Not only were there weak spots in the economy, especially in the important agricultural sector, but Canada's prosperity depended heavily upon foreign trade. The impoverishment of international markets as the world succumbed to the depression meant economic disaster for Canada.

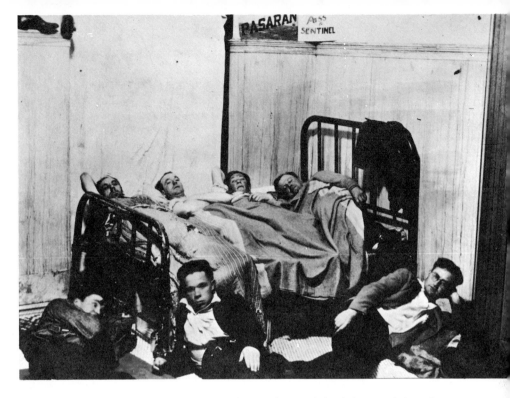

The disappearance of foreign markets for Canadian products and the drying up of domestic purchasing power resulted in the curtailment of production and, frequently, the shutting down of Canadian factories and businesses. The prices of seventeen major Canadian exports fell by 53% between July 1929 and December 1932, industrial production dropped 48%, and only 67% of the labour force employed in 1929 was still at work at the end of 1932. Of these years the Rowell-Sirois Commission reported, "Canada's political, public finance and economic organizations were not adapted to deal with sharp and prolonged economic reverses. When a specific and co-ordinated programme was required, there was bewilderment; when positive action was needed, there were only temporizing and negative policies; when a realization of the far-reaching effects of the altered circumstances was demanded, there was but faith in the speedy return to the old conditions of prosperity."

Though the depression affected the whole country, it was most serious in those areas that had gained least in the economic boom of the late 1920's. Such regions as the western provinces were also those most heavily dependent upon declining world markets. Although the same was true of some of the newly opened mining areas, the hardships were particularly severe in western Canada where the economic depression was aggravated by natural disaster. In the 1930's few prairie crops escaped the ravages of drought or grasshoppers, and many farmers saw their only source of income disappear under the destructive attacks of one or the other or both. In Saskatchewan the average personal income fell from four hundred and seventy-eight dollars to one hundred and thirty-five dollars, and Alberta and Manitoba were little better off.

The impact of the depression and the collapse of the prairie farm economy was soon felt throughout the Dominion. In eastern Canada factories began to close their doors or reduce production. Thousands of men had no means of supporting themselves or their families. Since there was no unemployment insurance in these years, men without work were forced to depend on direct government relief or local charities. Some "hopped freights" and "rode the rods" across the country hoping to find some kind of work that would enable them to become self-respecting citizens again. Few succeeded, and as the ranks of the unemployed reached half a million, people looked for new political means of solving their economic problems. The depression struck while Prime Minister King was still in power in Ottawa. The Liberal government insisted that unemployment was temporary, and that the depression would soon yield to the traditional policies of cutting government expenditures and balancing the budget. The Conservative opposition claimed that the economic collapse was serious, demanded that jobs should be provided by public works projects and that tariffs be raised to stimulate Canadian industry. In the spring of 1930, the argument was carried out onto the hustings when Prime Minister King called an election.

R. B. Bennett launched a vigorous campaign to convince the people that the Conservatives had a solution to the country's economic difficulties. The major Conservative campaign plank was a demand that Canada should raise the tariff in order to make it plain to other countries, especially the United States, that Canada would reduce its tariff only if other countries did so. Canada should "blast her way into the markets of the world," Mr. Bennett declared. The Conservative campaign found a sympathetic response throughout the country, for many people felt that the Liberals had failed and that the Bennett party should be given a chance to try to restore the country to prosperity. When the votes were counted the Conservatives were elected by a majority of thirty-one seats. J. W. Dafoe, editor of the *Winnipeg Free Press*, wrote after the Conservative victory: "No doubt what beat the government was the very feeling that something better might come out of a shake-up. . . . I don't think the bolters, whose defection beat the government candidates, gave a thought to the effect of their vote on policy— what they wanted was to hit someone in the eye, in retaliation for hard times, low prices of grain, disappointment at the failure of the wheat pool to deliver the goods, losses suffered through speculation, lack of cash, the indignity of having to put up with the old car, and for a hundred other causes, just as profound."

In the autumn of 1930 R. B. Bennett was sworn into office as Prime Minister, and the country awaited his magic solution to the hardships and difficulties that the depression had brought.

CHAPTER 33

Depression Decade

Speaking to a radio audience in January, 1935 Prime Minister Bennett pointed out that "in the last five years great changes have taken place in the world. The old order is gone. It will not return. We are living amidst conditions which are new and strange to us." Most Canadians agreed that great changes had indeed taken place since the "Great Crash" of 1929. The depression had brought unemployment, worsened living conditions and frustrated ambitions. It had also raised fundamental questions about the traditional political and economic institutions of the country. Why had such a serious economic collapse taken place? Why had it not been prevented? Why was so little being done to cure it? Probably the most disturbing question was why there was .such obvious poverty in a nation so rich in human and natural resources as Canada.

By 1935 even Prime Minister Bennett was remarking: "Canada on the dole is like a young and vigorous man in the poorhouse. The dole is a condemnation, final and complete, of our economic system. If we cannot abolish the dole, we should abolish the system." But not everyone was satisfied that either the Conservatives or the Liberals could really find the answers to Canada's economic problems. Thus there developed a series of unusual political movements, offering new answers to the problems of a country where poverty existed in the midst of plenty.

1. BENNETT AND THE CONSERVATIVES

During the first four years of his term of office, Prime Minister Bennett attempted to meet the hardships of the Canadian people by following traditional policies. He was not the kind of man from whom radical policies were expected. Born in modest circumstances in New Brunswick, Bennett had gone west to Calgary where he had rapidly prospered as a corporation lawyer. He had always regarded his business career as a first step towards entering public life. In 1911 he was elected

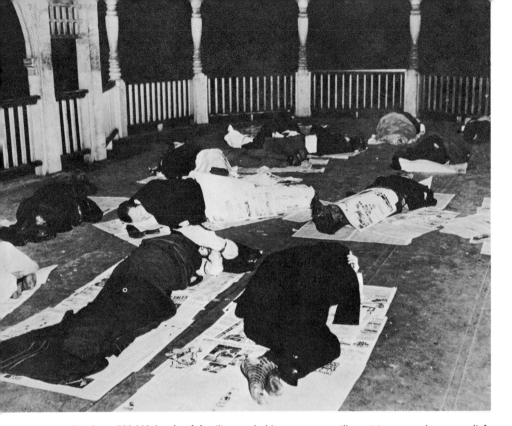

"At least 200,000 heads of families, probably more, are still receiving unemployment relief; . . . over 20,000 able-bodied employable men are in relief camps; . . . hordes of homeless young graduates of the business and technical schools, and of the colleges and universities, unplaced, idle, are drifting to dependence." Some of these people, described by Prime Minister Bennett in January 1935, found it necessary to take shelter wherever they could, sometimes covering themselves only with newspapers while spending the night in the open bandshell in Queen's Park, Toronto.

The plight of the unemployed can be seen in two case histories. John McKinnon told a **Toronto Star** reporter in 1930: "I have tried every means to get a job—but no luck. I have tried to keep straight, but I had to bum money from people in the streets to get something to eat. . . . The police gave me a ticket for a night's lodging at a King Street lodging house, and I changed my name three times to get more, so I could have shelter. . . . Last Friday night I went to the hostel again, but at three o'clock I had to get up. The place is running with bed-bugs." Six years later, Raymond Wandless told the **Star:** "We have been all over Ontario and a good bit of Quebec. By hitch-hiking, riding freights, and just tramping, we have covered hundreds of miles, but steady work just seems as far away as ever." His young wife, Alice, was clad in a cheap, threadbare cotton dress, no stockings; her red swollen feet stuck out between the uppers and soles of an old pair of shoes. The man was as poorly clothed—no socks, battered shoes.

to the federal parliament as a Conservative; in 1927 he was chosen leader of his party. His great capacity for hard work raised him to the top in both business and politics, just when the kind of society that had produced him was on the edge of collapse.

As Prime Minister, Bennett immediately called a special session of parliament to pass emergency measures increasing federal unemployment relief, and establishing a public works programme to create employment. But the government's most important proposal to cure the depression was the traditional Conservative one, a higher tariff. The Conservative argument was that since Canadian trade had been seriously injured by foreign tariff barriers like the American Hawley-Smoot Tariff of 1930, Canada should retaliate. Higher Canadian tariffs, Bennett believed, would at least protect the domestic market for Canadian manufacturers and perhaps force other countries to lower their tariffs against Canada.

The new Canadian tariff law of 1930 established the highest tariff in Canada's history. It protected not only goods already being produced in Canada, but goods that might be produced in the future by Canadian manufacturers. With this tariff as a lever, Prime Minister Bennett hoped to persuade the other countries of the Commonwealth to set up an Imperial preference which would turn the British Commonwealth into a trading area protected against the rest of the world. In 1932 Prime Ministers from all the Commonwealth countries met in Ottawa to draw up trading agreements. Though the British government, which had followed a policy of free trade for nearly a century, was reluctant to adopt the Bennett plan for a tariff ring around the Commonwealth, agreement was finally reached. Britain promised to allow a large number of Canadian manufactured and agricultural goods to enter Britain duty-free in return for a reduction of the Canadian tariff on British goods. In addition, bilateral agreements providing for special tariff treatment were worked out among all the members of the Commonwealth.

The Bennett tariff policy had some worth-while results. It protected Canadian manufacturers against foreign competition and thus created some new jobs in Canadian factories. More important, Imperial preference increased Canadian trade both with Britain and with the other members of the Commonwealth. But two facts remained unchanged by the tariff revisions. Domestic purchasing power, the money that Canadians had to spend, remained too limited to allow them to buy all the goods produced at home, for tariff protection also increased the cost of these goods. Moreover, Canada could not survive without access to the enormous markets of the United States and Europe. These markets remained largely closed to Canada, partly because the United States and many European countries had high tariffs, and partly because Canadian tariffs prevented foreign nations from selling goods in Canada. Thus, while Canada suffered from the strangulation of world trade caused by high tariffs in the 1930's, she also contributed to it by her own trade policies.

By 1932, when the Imperial economic agreements were coming into effect, depression conditions were growing more serious in Canada. J. S. Woodsworth, a Labour member of parliament, described the situation when he pointed out:

> For two generations we had an outlet in western Canada but that outlet is not only closed, the people are drifting back to the East from that

country. In the old days we could send people from the cities to the country. If they went out today they would meet another army of unemployed coming back from the country to the city; that outlet is closed. What can these people do? They have been driven from our parks; they have been driven from our streets; they have been driven from our buildings, and in this city [Ottawa] they actually took refuge on the garbage heaps.

With unemployment increasing and drought destroying the crops in the West, a mood of despair seized many Canadians. In the West, farmers rode in automobiles drawn by horses, because gasoline was too expensive, and derisively called them "Bennett buggies." In the cities, the tar-paper shacks that housed evicted families were christened "Bennettburghs." It was in this atmosphere that new parties of political protest made their appearance.

2. THE NEW PARTIES

The main centre of political discontent in the 1930's, as in the 'twenties, was western Canada where the depression hit hardest. The first new group to appear was the Social Credit movement in Alberta, organized and led by a school teacher and fundamentalist preacher, William Aberhart. A man of immense energy, Aberhart was gifted with powers of oratory and the ability to dramatize issues in a manner that quickly attracted a mass following. Moreover, he was one of the first Canadian public men to recognize the value of radio in political campaigning. He learned this first as a revivalist radio preacher, and his name and voice were well known throughout Alberta before his political movement was founded. In 1934 he began applying the same technique to politics.

Aberhart's political views were based on the writings of an English engineer, Major Douglas, who had evolved the doctrine of Social Credit. The theory, reduced to its simplest form, was expressed in the "$A + B = C$" equation. In this crude mathematical formula "A" equals wages and dividends paid to producers, "B" the other costs of production, including raw materials, bank charges and profits, and "C" the total cost of the product. Douglas maintained that since the cost of production (C) always exceeds the producer's buying power (A), "poverty in the midst of plenty" was bound to exist, for there would never be enough money available to buy the available goods. His solution was for the government to issue a "social dividend" or cash payment to all citizens. Aberhart read Douglas' book, and was convinced.

Before long Aberhart was mixing Social Credit and religion in his Sunday morning radio talks. His growing legion of supporters willingly listened to his vigorous attacks on the country's financial system, for many Alberta farmers were experiencing difficulties in obtaining credit or meeting mortgage payments. Climaxing his campaign in 1935, Aberhart de-

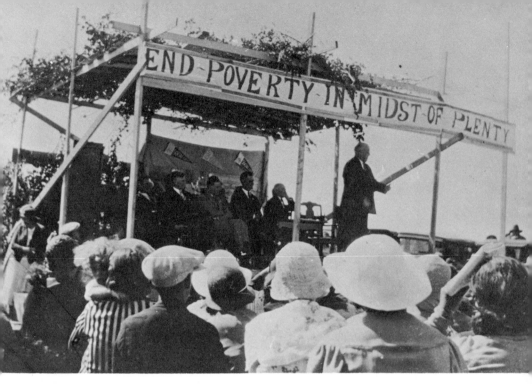

An Alberta farmer described the appeal of "Bible Bill" Aberhart: "Us farmers, being the producers of real wealth, were the first to feel the pinch and we felt it the hardest as the years went by. When we were all feeling down and out, Mr. Aberhart began to show the link between the economic injustices of today and the economic injustices of Christ's time. He linked these two up and showed how Christ had cleared the money changers out of the Temple. Then he showed us how the money changers of today had everything cornered . . . the tie-up between religion and economics made me realize that Social Credit was the answer to all our problems. Once I realized this, I went out and talked up Social Credit and organized groups among farmers all through our district."

clared: "You remain in the depression because of a shortage of purchasing power imposed by the banking system. If you have not suffered enough, it is your God-given right to suffer more." But he added, "We have still one free hand with which to strike—to mark our ballot on election day. Let us strike then with all our might at this hideous monster that is sucking the very life-blood from our people." This was the kind of spell-binding oratory that brought the people flocking to Social Credit meetings in the summer of 1935.

From the meetings, the people of Alberta carried their enthusiasm to the voting booth. In the provincial election that summer, Social Credit, previously without a seat in the legislature, won power. But Social Credit was easier to preach than to practise. Aberhart soon discovered that most of his ideas and promises, especially those that had to do with the field of banking and finance, lay outside the constitutional powers of the provincial government to make good. Attempts to control banking, finance and credit were rejected by the courts because they interfered with the federal power over banking and currency, and after several unsuccessful

"The shortage of purchasing power which results from the operation of the money system would be made good **by putting new money directly into the hands of the people.**" To fulfil this plank in its platform Premier Aberhart's government in 1936 issued "prosperity certificates" or "funny money," as the opponents of Social Credit called them. In taking this unusual step the Alberta government was found by the Supreme Court to have exceeded its powers and the certificates, which had been received suspiciously by most Albertans, were withdrawn from circulation.

experiments with "social dividends," Aberhart was content to give the province good government while his followers dreamed of the day when Social Credit would capture Ottawa.

Social Credit was not the only new party born during the depression. The apparent collapse of free enterprise created new interest in the socialist movement which had possessed a small following for many years. Since the days of the Winnipeg general strike in 1919, J. S. Woodsworth had led a small Labour party in the House of Commons. A former Methodist minister, Woodsworth had come to believe that the principles of Christianity could only be applied to politics and economics through some form of democratic socialism. A vigorous critic of Marxian communism, he nevertheless believed that the capitalist system gave too much power to too few men. The solution, he and the socialists declared, was to increase government authority over economic life.

Woodsworth had found few converts in the prosperous 1920's. His most important achievement lay in convincing Mackenzie King in 1926 that the country needed government-sponsored old age pensions. But when the 1929 depression struck, Woodsworth's views about the weaknesses of the capitalist system found a much more sympathetic audience. Farmers, labour leaders and some middle-class intellectuals agreed that the time had come to establish a socialist party.

In 1932 representatives of these groups met in Calgary where they established the Co-operative Commonwealth Federation, or C.C.F. A second conference at Regina in the following year approved a platform which came to be known as the Regina Manifesto. The aim of the party was summed up in part of the platform which read: "We aim to replace the present capitalist system with its inherent injustice and inhumanity by a social order from which the domination and exploitation of one class by another will be eliminated, in which economic planning will supersede unregulated private enterprise and competition, and in which genuine democratic self-government based upon economic equality will be possible." Woodsworth appealed to the delegates to support the new policy. "The C.C.F. believes in bringing about the changes our country needs through orderly and peaceful means. I believe that in Canada we must work out our own salvation in our own way. There are all kinds of socialism—Christian Socialism, Utopian Socialism, Russian, Marxist, German, American Socialism. Why not a Canadian Socialism?" Woodsworth's "Canadian Socialism" advocated government planning of the economy through the nationalization, or government ownership, of the largest and most important enterprises in the Canadian economy—the railways, banks, insurance companies, and other industries of large scale economic importance.

In Quebec in the 1930's political unrest combined social radicalism with French-Canadian nationalism. Since the war, Quebec had been passing through an industrial revolution which transformed the province from an agrarian to an industrial society. Most of the capital which financed this transformation came from English-speaking Canadian, British and American investors. Many French Canadians became concerned about the domination of their economy by English-speaking capitalists. When the depression threw thousands of French Canadians out of work, smouldering resentment exploded into anger against "foreign" employers.

Two groups sought to take advantage of these disturbed social conditions in Quebec. One was the tiny Conservative party which hoped to regain office by appealing to the nationalism of the French-Canadian voters. A second group, composed of radical Liberals who were dissatisfied with the provincial Liberal government, devised a programme which called for the nationalization of some industries owned by English-speaking investors, and the introduction of social welfare measures. These two groups united to form a new party called the *Union Nationale* led by a former Conservative, Maurice Duplessis.

By 1936 Duplessis and his radical allies succeeded in driving the corruption-ridden Liberal party from power. But once in office Duplessis outmanœuvred the sincere reformers and quickly forgot the promised reforms. The government provided assistance for farmers, but ignored the needs of the working people and did nothing to restore control of Quebec's economic life to the French Canadians. Instead, Duplessis cleverly turned the eyes of his compatriots away from local problems by declaring war on the federal government which, he claimed, was trying

Powerful oratory, always an important characteristic in Quebec politics, was one of Maurice Duplessis' strengths. But he had many other characteristics as well, not the least of which was a strong will and an ability to dominate those around him. A Montreal newspaperman who knew the Premier well wrote: "Duplessis left no one indifferent. People looked upon him either as an antichrist or as a messiah, depending on whether they were opponents or supporters. Few men in our history have aroused as many passions as did this authoritarian leader, at once generous and vindictive. He dominated Quebec for a quarter of a century and friends and foes alike trembled before him."

to undermine provincial autonomy, and was therefore threatening French-Canadian rights. This appeal to nationalist sentiment was successful, for, in the troubled atmosphere of international affairs in the 1930's, many French Canadians were reminded of the conscription crisis of 1917, and exhibited a strong hostility toward the government at Ottawa.

Ontario also produced a radical who, like Duplessis, rose to power on promises of reform. In 1934 Mitchell Hepburn brought the Liberals back to power in Ontario, after twenty-nine years in the Opposition, with promises to fight the depression by a reduction of government expenditures and by aid for the farmer, the worker and the unemployed. In his first years as Premier he introduced legislation to raise agricultural prices for farmers and to provide legal protection for the growing trade-union movement in the province. But within a few years he, too, began to lose his zeal for social reform. In 1937 he attempted to prevent the United Automobile Workers union from gaining recognition during a long and bitter strike in Oshawa and declared that the American labour organization, the Committee for Industrial Organizations, would enter Ontario only over his dead body! Like Premier Duplessis, he was soon to carry on a bitter battle against the federal government and Mackenzie King.

In British Columbia T. D. Pattullo's Liberal party had won the provincial election of 1933 with a promise of "Work and Wages," which echoed Roosevelt's New Deal. Unemployment was especially heavy in the Pacific coast province not only because it depended on exports, but also because, as Pattullo himself wrote, "by reason of its diversity of interests, its salubrious climate and general attractiveness [British Columbia] is the

Mitchell Hepburn, who led the Liberal party to victory in Ontario in 1934, on a platform of social and economic reform had, by 1937, developed a strong opposition to labour unions, especially labour unions with affiliations in the United States. When the United Automobile Workers, backed by the Committee for Industrial Organizations in the United States, called a strike at the General Motors plant in Oshawa in 1937, Premier Hepburn unequivocally voiced his support for the company against the union. Messrs. Croll and Roebuck, later Canadian Senators, resigned from Hepburn's cabinet on the issue, saying they "would sooner walk with workers than ride with General Motors." While most Ontario voters sympathized with the Premier's opposition to American-sponsored unions, the efforts of the province's workingmen to organize themselves into unions proved nearly irresistible. Premier Hepburn found he could no more prevent union organization than he could sweep back the sea!

mecca of those who suffer from misfortunes, mischance or ill health." After his victory, Pattullo raised the level of relief payments, set maximum hours of work and minimum wages, provided financial assistance for the mining and fishing industries, and began public works projects to create employment. While Premier Pattullo's reforms helped to revive the economy they also cost a great deal of money. To meet the rising deficit Pattullo appealed to Ottawa for financial assistance, and by 1935 was engaged in a bitter quarrel with the federal authorities over financial policies.

The appearance of new parties and leaders willing to use the power of government to fight the depression was a clear warning to Prime Minister Bennett that more vigorous action by the federal government was necessary. In 1934 he attempted to bring some order into the country's financial system by establishing the Bank of Canada, whose purpose was to regulate currency and credit, to provide financial services to private banks, and to act as a financial adviser to the government. To aid the farmers, Bennett re-established the Canadian Wheat Board, first used during the First World War, to regulate the sale of grain. Bankrupt provinces were given federal loans. The Canadian National Railways, which had suffered serious financial losses during the depression, was reorganized. In air transport, Bennett laid the basis for the establishment of the government-owned Trans-Canada Airlines. In the field of broadcasting, the Conservative government in 1932 established the Canadian Radio Broadcasting

Prime Minister Bennett's opponents refused to believe that the "New Deal" was anything other than an effort to bribe the voters in order to win the rapidly approaching election of 1935. The **Winnipeg Free Press** declared: "If Capitalism is corrupt, avaricious, predacious, heartless, regardless of human suffering, greedy and whatnot, how does it come that Mr. Bennett did not find out until December 1934 when, the millions having been safely amassed and salted down, Mr. Bennett turned his ambitions not to further triumphs of capitalism, but to the capture of a political position that will make him just as much the dictator of Canada as Mussolini is the dictator of Italy?"

Corporation, which four years later became the national radio network known as the Canadian Broadcasting Corporation.

Some of Bennett's colleagues pressed him to more radical adventures in government regulation. By 1934 H. H. Stevens, the Minister of Trade and Commerce, was insisting that the government should control business practices. Stevens was especially concerned about the way large retail stores used their buying power to force small manufacturers to sell to them at low prices, with the result that the manufacturers had to pay low wages to their employees. Stevens also believed that farmers received prices too far below those charged by meat packers and canners for the retail product. In short, he felt that large profits were being made by some large retailers who were underpaying producers, overcharging consumers, and forcing small businessmen out of the market. After Stevens had made his views public, Bennett agreed to establish a Royal Commission on Price Spreads with Stevens as Chairman. Unfortunately, Stevens was somewhat indiscreet in his public speeches on the price spreads problem, and some of his colleagues, closely connected with large companies, complained. Stevens resigned from the cabinet and in 1935 created the Reconstruction party, whose platform included a demand for stricter government regulation of business.

The price spreads investigation and Stevens' resignation were further warnings to Bennett that unless his government stepped up the pace of reform, its defeat was certain in the 1935 election. Meanwhile, from Washington, his brother-in-law, W. D. Herridge, Canadian Ambassador to the United States, urged Bennett to imitate Roosevelt's New Deal. He wrote: "Declare for the new Toryism, for it means government in business [which] is the only fulcrum powerful enough to lift us from the wreck of capitalism . . . [the people] want action, and if government does not give it to them, action they will nevertheless have, and it will be action of their own making." By January, 1935 Bennett had decided that the

When Prime Minister Bennett announced the sweeping measures for social security in 1935 some of his critics charged that he had borrowed his programme from the platform of the newly founded Co-operative Commonwealth Federation party. J. S. Woodsworth and his associates, A. A. Heaps from Manitoba, Agnes MacPhail from Ontario, William Irvine and E. J. Garland from Alberta were pleased with the Bennett "New Deal" but as socialists felt that it did not go far enough. "Capitalism still stands as a menace to the Canadian people and to the world," Woodsworth maintained.

time had come for action. In a series of radio addresses he announced his plans for a Canadian "New Deal." "The economic system must be reformed," he told the people. "Great social and economic changes have taken place in the life of all the nations, and these have gravely disturbed the operation of the system. What we call the crash of 1929 was simply the crash of the system." This was radical talk coming from a Conservative Prime Minister. The measures which followed were designed to reduce farm debt, control the export trade, regulate business practices, set up a system of unemployment insurance and establish minimum wages and maximum hours of work.

Bennett's "New Deal" caused great excitement. Within his own party there was opposition to this radical departure from traditional Tory principles. But it was accepted. The Liberals, too, were shocked. In parliament they argued that the measures were beyond the powers of the federal government and that they should be tested in the Supreme Court before being put into practice. But Bennett could not delay his programme, for an election was due in the summer of 1935.

In the election campaign the Conservatives defended the "New Deal." The Liberals accepted the need for social reform but on platforms across the nation insisted that the Bennett legislation was a farce because it went beyond the powers of the federal government. The Liberals also argued that the government's high tariff policies harmed the Canadian economy by stifling international trade. Finally, the Liberals charged that Bennett was a dictator and ran a "one-man government" in which ministers were mere puppets, and parliamentary rights ignored. "What the country needs is not the fist of the pugilist but the hand of the physician," declared

Mackenzie King, although his prescription for curing the sick nation was not clear.

The election results showed that Bennett's decision to adopt drastic measures had come too late. Most people were disillusioned with Conservative government and wanted a change. However, the results also showed that the Liberals, who won one hundred and seventy-one seats, had gained very few supporters, for their popular vote was almost unchanged from 1930. Bennett's defeat was largely due to the million voters who decided to support the three minor parties. The Conservatives won only thirty-nine seats, while Social Credit gained seventeen, the C.C.F. seven, and the Reconstruction party one—for its leader, H. H. Stevens. It remained to be seen whether King had any effective plans to meet the country's continuing economic difficulties.

3. KING AND THE ROWELL-SIROIS COMMISSION

The first action of Mackenzie King's new government in 1935 was to refer Bennett's "New Deal" legislation to the courts. While awaiting the courts' decision, King was able to take action in the field of trade with the United States. Bennett had already begun negotiations with Washington before his defeat. The King government resumed these negotiations and successfully concluded a bilateral trade agreement which gave Canadian agricultural, mining and industrial products freer access to the American market, while the Canadian tariff against goods from the United States was also reduced.

Success in finding new markets for Canadian products was important, but it had little immediate effect on the hardships created by the depression. In 1936 the Supreme Court ruled that the most important parts of the Bennett "New Deal" were unconstitutional. This left the federal government almost powerless to adopt measures to fight the economic and social disaster that lay all around. Obviously, if this were due to the constitution, the constitution needed to be amended. In 1937 Prime Minister King announced the appointment of a Royal Commission on Dominion-Provincial Relations to investigate the constitutional and financial relations between the federal and provincial governments. Five Commissioners and a host of assistants were given the enormous task of studying the history of the Canadian federation and of recommending solutions for the constitutional obstacles that stood in the way of any effective action to remove the worst hardships of the depression. This Commission, usually called the Rowell-Sirois Commission after its two chairmen, worked for three years before submitting its conclusions to the government.

From its extensive investigations the Commission concluded that since Confederation in 1867 two developments had taken place in Canadian life which affected the constitution. First, a series of court judgments handed down by the Judicial Committee of the Privy Council had restricted the legislative authority of the federal government to the enumerated powers of Section 91 of the British North America Act, and had completely undermined the effectiveness of its residual authority except in periods of "national emergency" such as wartime. At the same time, the responsibilities of the provinces had been expanded beyond the limits originally contemplated by the Fathers of Confederation, as education, highway construction and social services became the responsibility of the provincial governments. Yet the major powers of taxation remained with the federal government, so that the provinces had wide responsibilities, but lacked the funds necessary to fulfil them.

The second point emphasized by the Rowell-Sirois Commissioners was that since Canada was gradually changing from an agricultural to an industrial nation, it was desirable that the federal government should have broader powers over the economic life of the country and authority to enact social security measures that would be uniform for the whole country. "Canada's present and prospective economic condition," the Commission reported, "makes it clear that we can neither continue to afford the friction and waste of conflicting policies, nor the greater loss due to paralysis of policy arising from a possibly obsolete division of governmental responsibilities and powers."

After a thorough examination of the existing conditions the Commissioners recommended that the Dominion government should be given exclusive powers of direct taxation, in return for which the Dominion would pay the provinces national adjustment grants to provide a minimum standard of government and social services throughout the country. The purpose of this recommendation was to ensure a more equitable distribution of the national wealth among the provinces. It was particularly designed to meet the needs of the Maritimes and the prairie provinces, which, because of their lack of industry and natural resources, had not the sources of revenue that were available to the wealthier provinces. This was an admission that the national policies, which successive Canadian governments had followed, had not benefited all the sections of the country equally. Central Canada had grown rich at the expense of the Maritimes and the West. The national adjustment grants were designed to rectify these inequalities. A further important recommendation was that the federal government assume responsibility for unemployment relief and insurance, and that a system of social security be established by the provinces aided by financial grants from the Dominion government.

The Commission believed that these recommendations would bring the Canadian federal system into line with the developments and changes that had taken place since 1867. As the Report remarked: "The financial proposals are, in terms of the economic conditions of 1939, very similar to what the provisions of the British North America Act were in terms of the economic life of 1867."

The Commissioners hoped that the recommendations would find general acceptance throughout the country, and argued that they preserved the basic structure of a federal system in which both the Dominion and

An observer at the Dominion-Provincial Conference of 1941 wrote of it as follows: "The opening day of the Conference was fully occupied by the opening address of the Prime Minister and the nine replies by the provincial premiers. By adjournment time that evening the country had a cross-section of official reaction to the Sirois Plan. Certain provincial governments were on record as endorsing the proposals enthusiastically, others were mildly for it, or non-committal. Three were outspokenly opposed to continuing the conference at all, so long as it continued to take the Rowell-Sirois proposals for its basis of discussion." The three opposing provinces were Ontario, British Columbia and Alberta.

the provincial governments had important roles to play. "The Commission does not consider," the Report concluded, "that its proposals are either centralizing or decentralizing in their combined effect, but believes that they will conduce to the sane balance between these two tendencies which is the essence of a genuine federal system and, therefore, the basis on which Canadian national unity can most securely rest."

Unfortunately, the Commissioners were too optimistic in their expectations. While the poorer provinces were heartily in favour of a plan which would give them a larger share of the national income, the richer provinces, Quebec, Ontario and British Columbia, felt that they would lose by the suggested redistribution of powers and revenue. The government of Quebec, led by Maurice Duplessis, had opposed the Commission from the beginning, while Hepburn in Ontario and Aberhart of Alberta had been reluctant to co-operate. This staunch provincialism meant that the Commission's recommendations would be difficult to implement.

When the Rowell-Sirois Commission presented its report to the King government in the spring of 1940, Canada was again at war. Clearly the war effort would require increased federal authority if Canada were to contribute its share to allied victory. Prime Minister King called a meeting of the leaders of all the provincial governments in January, 1941 to consider the recommendations of the Commission. By the time the

Dominion-Provincial Conference met, Premier Duplessis had been turned out of office by the Quebec Liberals, and there was reason to believe that the new government of Adélard Godbout would be willing to accept a reorganization of the financial structure of Confederation. But vigorous opposition came from three other provincial premiers. Led by Mitchell Hepburn, Ontario, Alberta and British Columbia refused even to discuss the recommendations of the Rowell-Sirois Report. After two days of wrangling, the Conference ended and three years of hard work by the Commission was set aside. Nevertheless, the strains of war made it necessary for the federal government to conclude with each of the provinces separate taxation agreements which allowed the federal government access to the largest proportion of their tax revenues. This provided the federal government with the additional sources of revenue necessary to pay for the costly war effort. Thus the Conference of 1941 had not been a complete failure. Prime Minister King noted in his diary: "While to appearances it has been a failure, in reality it has served the purpose we had in view, of avoiding attack for not having called the Conference, and particularly what would certainly have followed, invasion of provincial sources of revenue. We have now got the pledge of the Provinces to let us take their revenues if we need them—a tremendous achievement." Moreover, even before the Dominion-Provincial Conference met, the federal government had secured a constitutional amendment giving it power to establish unemployment insurance.

By 1940, of course, all eyes were turned to the terrible events which were convulsing Europe. Although the demands of war soon had the Canadian economy working at full strength again, the strains imposed on the country by the depression were not easily overcome. In addition, the war also caused the reappearance of old tensions and conflicts and illustrated once more the difficulty of governing a geographically and culturally divided nation like Canada.

CHAPTER 34

Nationalism and Isolation

Canada's entry into the Second World War on September 10, 1939 ended a twenty-year period of intense debate about the Dominion's relations with the outside world. Despite the divisions which existed among races, classes and sections in 1919, participation in the First World War had given Canadians a new sense of national identity. This national feeling was difficult to define, except as a sense of belonging to a separate nation, and a desire that that nation should exercise all the powers of an independent state. There were still some Canadians who felt that the country should continue to follow Britain's policy in international affairs, and there were others who felt that Canada should be completely independent of the mother country. But these groups represented the extremes. The majority of Canadians felt that Canadian independence should be worked out within the structure of the British family of nations.

1. THE ROOTS OF CANADIAN FOREIGN POLICY

As Canada gradually moved towards full nationhood, it became evident that there were enduring factors in public opinion which guided the formation of Canadian foreign policy, regardless of which party was in power. In the first place, there was a strong sentiment which opposed any step that would increase Canadian commitments to the outside world. Some groups even wished to reduce the responsibilities that Canada had assumed as a result of her membership in the Commonwealth and the League of Nations. The groups which most firmly opposed an active Canadian role in international affairs were of a kind with the isolationists in the United States. French Canadians were especially isolationist in their outlook because they feared that foreign responsibilities would result in another crisis like the one that had split the country in 1917. Many Canadians of both races were isolationists because they believed that

Canada was secure in North America and had no reason to get involved in what appeared to be other people's quarrels. Senator Raoul Dandurand, a Liberal, expressed this sentiment when he told the League of Nations in 1924 that Canadians "live in a fireproof house far from inflammable materials." Every Canadian government in the inter-war period had to consider this isolationist sentiment when formulating policy.

There were two other groups in Canada whose views were also important in influencing foreign policy. There were those people, though their numbers were decreasing, who supported the idea of a common Imperial foreign policy. Then there were the internationalists who gave vigorous support to the League of Nations and held that the peace of the world depended upon the successful implementation of collective security through the League. The most influential spokesman for this group was John W. Dafoe, editor of the *Winnipeg Free Press*.

Although no Canadian government in the inter-war period adopted completely the point of view of any one group, it was the widespread isolationist sentiment that came nearest to controlling government policy, especially in the late 'thirties.

In addition to these domestic considerations there were also three constant external factors that played a role in shaping Canadian foreign policy. First, there was Canada's membership in the British Commonwealth. While membership involved no specific commitments or responsibilities, it did at least imply that if any member were threatened with war, the other members would come to its aid. Secondly, there was Canada's close relationship with the United States. Since the United States had refused to join the League of Nations, Canada had to tread carefully in its international activities in order to avoid upsetting Canadian-American relations. Finally, there was Canada's membership in the League of Nations. Canada had fought for membership because it would bring further recognition of nationhood. But few Canadians believed that membership in the League should involve Canada in heavy responsibilities for preserving the peace of the world.

No sooner had Canada joined the League than the government began to wonder whether the commitments it had made were too binding. The "heart" of the League Covenant, Article X, called upon the member nations to "undertake to respect and preserve as against external aggression the territorial integrity and existing political independence of all the members of the League." This article meant that if a League member were attacked, the other members would be obliged to come to its assistance. Even at Paris, while the Covenant was under discussion, the Canadian delegation attempted to have Article X weakened so that Canada could not be drawn into international disputes everywhere in the world.

When the Liberals came into office in 1921, their attitude towards the League and Article X was the same as Sir Robert Borden's had been when

OPERATION SUCCESSFUL, BUT THE PATIENT DIED

—*Winnipeg Free Press*

From the foundation of the League of Nations in 1919 Canada had been critical of the institution as a means of coercing aggressor nations. As Europe began to slip down the road to war in the 1930's, Canada's desire to be free of League commitments grew stronger. Speaking before the Assembly of the League of Nations in 1936, Prime Minister King defined the Canadian position when he said there was "a widespread conviction, born of experience, that at this stage in the evolution of the League, emphasis should be placed upon conciliation rather than upon coercion. There is a general unwillingness of peoples to incur obligations which they realize they may not be able in time of crisis to fulfil, obligations to use force and to use it at any place, at any time, in circumstances unforeseen, and in disputes over whose origin or whose development they had little or no control."

the Covenant was being framed. In 1924 the Liberals succeeded in securing an interpretative resolution concerning Article X which stated that in asking for military assistance the League would take into account the size and geographical position of member states. This really meant that Canada would be involved only if aggression occurred in the Americas. Henceforth, Liberal spokesmen, including Prime Minister King, repeatedly informed the League that while Canada favoured and supported the League as an instrument of arbitration and conciliation, it had strong doubts about the League as a body for enforcing peace by coercion. In 1936 King told the League Assembly: "Our attachment to this idea is as strong today as it was at the inception of the League. At the same time there is general concurrence in the view which has been expressed by leaders of all political parties since the beginning of the League, that automatic commitments to the application of force is not a practical policy." In effect, Prime Minister King was saying, as others had said before him, that Canada was no more willing to commit herself to supporting a common foreign policy devised by the League of Nations, than she was to a common foreign policy set out by the members of the British Commonwealth. A belief that Canada should assume no binding commitments whatsoever was the essence of Canadian foreign policy between the wars.

2. THE GROWTH OF NATIONAL STATUS

After the First World War, the first task in external affairs that the Canadian government faced was to define the relations between Great Britain and the Dominions. This family of nations which, before the war, had been called the British Empire, was by 1919 in the process of changing its name and its structure and was soon to emerge as the British Commonwealth of Nations. In 1919 the question before Canadians was how to increase Canadian independence without destroying the bonds which held the family together. Since Canada had already largely achieved self-government in domestic matters, the problem in the inter-war period centered mainly on whether Canada should have an independent foreign policy, or whether there should be a common foreign policy for all the members of the Commonwealth.

Both the supporters of a common Imperial foreign policy and of an independent foreign policy had an opportunity to test their views in the 1920's. Prime Minister Meighen's Conservative government followed the procedures which had been established by Sir Robert Borden during the war and at the peacemaking. At Paris in 1919 Borden had represented Canada as part of the British delegation. Moreover, he had insisted that Canada should be given individual representation in the League of Nations. The implication of Borden's policy was that the Dominions would have separate representation at international conferences, but that there would be a common Imperial policy worked out beforehand. After Borden's retirement in 1920, Meighen, Borden's successor, and his Conservative supporters continued to look upon Borden's approach as a satisfactory solution to the problem of allowing Canada a share in formulating foreign policy without breaking the united front that the British nations would present to the world. As Borden suggested in Resolution IX of the Imperial War Conference, "continuous consultation" would provide the machinery to devise a common foreign policy. "By tradition, by the sense of common inheritance and of common ideals, the Dominion of Canada aspires to one destiny, and one only—a destiny than which there is no nobler—a nationhood within the British Empire," declared Arthur Meighen in 1921.

Mackenzie King and the Liberals agreed that Canada should aspire to nationhood within the British Empire; but they disagreed about the means of attaining this end. They felt that nationhood meant that Canada should have complete freedom to formulate her own foreign policy, even if that policy differed from the policy of the other members of the Empire. As the *Winnipeg Free Press*, an independent Liberal newspaper, put it: "The only system that will work is one by which each British nation will attend to its own foreign affairs and accept responsibility therefor; reserving for a common policy only those questions—relatively few—in which we are all interested. When these questions arise there will be no difficulty about securing common action, as in war." Thus the Liberals believed that

This Austrian cartoon graphically illustrates the dilemma that faced Arthur Meighen, who also knew that continued good relations with the United States would be difficult, if not impossible, if the Anglo-Japanese alliance were renewed.

Canadian foreign policy should be primarily concerned with Canadian interests. The Conservatives believed that Canada's interests were the same as the interests of the Empire and that therefore there should be a common foreign policy for all the members of the Empire.

The Conservatives under Arthur Meighen were in power when the first opportunity arose to test their views of a common Imperial foreign policy in a practical fashion. The most important issue facing the Imperial Conference in 1921 was the renewal of the Anglo-Japanese alliance originally negotiated in 1902. Fearful of the rising power of Japan in the Pacific, Australia and New Zealand were determined to have the alliance renewed. Realizing that she could no longer maintain a fleet in every theatre of war equal or superior to any other nation, Britain also wished to keep the alliance with Japan. With the United States withdrawing from world affairs, Britain felt that the alliance was the only alternative to a ruinous naval armament race in the Pacific and a disruption of the balance of power.

The United States, however, was adamantly opposed to renewal. The Anglo-Japanese alliance, the Americans felt, could only be directed against them, for there were no other important powers in the Pacific. Moreover, renewal of the alliance would encourage the Japanese to expand in the Pacific, a course of action which alarmed the United States as much as it did Australia and New Zealand. To the United States non-renewal was viewed as the acid test of Anglo-American goodwill.

Canada was deeply affected by American feeling. Situated as she was in the North Atlantic Triangle, Canada was convinced that good relations between Britain and the United States lay at the foundation of her foreign policy. Thus when Meighen went to London he was determined to prevent renewal of the alliance at all costs. During the debates he spoke powerfully and eloquently of the need for good relations between the Empire and the United States. He explained the American position so well and so forcefully that the irate Prime Minister of Australia exclaimed that he was really speaking for the United States and not for Canada. Meighen answered that in any matters affecting the United States Canada's voice must be heard. "It has developed through the years, not as a matter of sudden departure or acquisition, but as a matter of growth out of the very necessities of the case," he said, "that in the determination of questions affecting not the Empire as such and the United States, but affecting the United States and Canada, the Dominion should have full and final authority." While this was a matter affecting the whole Empire, it was also a question that bore directly on Canada, whose position would be extremely uncomfortable if serious trouble arose between neighbour and mother country. Meighen's determination and logic prevented the alliance from being renewed. His suggestion of a multi-power discussion of Pacific affairs and naval disarmament in the Far East was grasped as an alternative. And at that precise moment President Harding of the United States, who had watched the proceedings of the Conference with great interest, invited the Pacific powers to a conference at Washington, where a disarmament treaty was signed and the Anglo-Japanese alliance was allowed to lapse.

The Imperial Conference of 1921 revealed that the members of the Empire had widely divergent interests in foreign policy. These fundamental differences had been overcome in 1921 when an alternative that all could accept, however reluctantly, was found. But such an alternative would not always be available. What would happen if no agreement could be reached? Would the Empire break up? Such were the questions that remained unanswered in 1921.

3. KING AND AN INDEPENDENT FOREIGN POLICY

The 1921 Imperial Conference was the only meeting of the leaders of the British nations that succeeded in formulating a common foreign policy. Shortly after the Conference the Conservative government in Canada was defeated at the polls. The victorious Liberals had never made any secret of their opposition to the principle of a common foreign policy for all the Commonwealth. Moreover, the Liberals were the party most strongly influenced by the attitudes of the French Canadians, and to French Canadians a common Imperial foreign policy meant Canadian involvement in Imperial wars.

The first opportunity for the new King government to give practical expression to these views came in September 1922, when the British government publicly appealed to the Dominions for assistance in a crisis at Chanak in Asia Minor where it appeared that Britain might be drawn into a war with Turkey. Prime Minister King read of the request in a newspaper before he received the official message from the British government. Understandably, the Prime Minister was furious. His cabinet agreed that most Canadians had no desire to engage in a war in Asia Minor that had no connection with Canadian interests. In his private diary King wrote: "Surely all that has been said about equality of status and sovereign nations within the Empire is all of no account if at any particular moment the self-governing Dominions are to be expected, without consideration of any kind, to assume the gravest responsibility which any nation can as-

sume, solely and wholly upon an inspired dispatch from Downing Street." King was extremely suspicious of the motives of the British government. The British request, he wrote, "is drafted designedly to play the Imperial game, to test our centralization vs. autonomy as regards European wars. I have thought out my plans. No contingent will go without parliament being summoned in first instance." King had no intention of asking parliament to send a contingent. No doubt his suspicion was exaggerated, for the British were only acting on the theory of a common foreign policy which had been accepted at the 1921 Imperial Conference. But the Chanak crisis, and Canada's reaction to it, indicated that the theory was a weak one.

When a crisis like Chanak arose there was no time for consultation and the formulation of a common policy. As a result, British policy would have to become the policy of the Empire. Prime Minister King, however, did not believe that a common policy was desirable. But even those who did were faced with an insoluble problem in circumstances similar to the Chanak crisis. The Canadian Conservatives argued that Canada should have agreed to the British request and sent troops. "When Britain's message came, Canada should have said, 'Ready, Aye Ready'," stated Arthur Meighen, who now led the Conservative Opposition in Parliament. Perhaps Meighen's proposal was the more heroic, but in 1922 the Canadian people were not in a heroic mood. With the Great War still vivid in their memories, they wanted no part in any war and agreed with Mackenzie King that Canada must decide issues for itself.

The Chanak crisis and Canada's refusal to send troops to Asia Minor really killed the idea of a united foreign policy for the Empire. The next steps in asserting Canada's right to formulate her own foreign policy came in quick succession during the next ten years. In 1923 Ernest Lapointe, the Canadian Minister of Justice, signed the Halibut Treaty with the United States. This treaty, which governed United States fishing rights in Canadian coastal waters, was significant because it marked the first time that Canada had signed an international treaty alone. Previously, a British representative had always taken part in the negotiation of diplomatic treaties affecting Canada and signed the document on Britain's behalf. After 1923 this was no longer done. Four years later Canada took a further step in asserting her diplomatic independence when she appointed a Canadian representative to Washington to take charge of the relations between Canada and the United States, which, until then, had been handled by the British Embassy.

The most important step in Canada's gradual achievement of complete independence in foreign affairs was taken at the Imperial Conference of 1923. At this Conference the members of the Commonwealth agreed to the principle that each member nation should have the right to negotiate its own international treaties. Moreover, the Conference struck another blow at the idea of a common Imperial foreign policy, and again it was Mackenzie King who wielded the axe. He strongly objected to a suggestion that the meeting should issue a statement indicating that the Conference had arrived at agreement about a common foreign policy. The Canadian Prime Minister insisted that he could not agree to a policy that did not have the sanction of the Canadian parliament. "We believe that the decision of Great Britain on any important public issue, domestic or foreign, should be made by the people of Britain, their representatives in Parliament, and the Government responsible to that Parliament," King told the Conference. "So the decision of Canada on any important issue, domestic or foreign, we believe should be made by the people of Canada, their representatives in Parliament, and the Government responsible to that Parliament." In short, King's policy was one of no commitments, and his method of stating that policy was to say that "Parliament will decide in the light of existing circumstances."

The practical result of the Imperial Conference of 1923 was the acceptance of the view that each Dominion had the right to complete control over its own foreign policy. This view was not written into any constitutional document, but it was admitted in a section of the Report of the Conference that had been included to satisfy Prime Minister King. This section declared: "This Conference is a Conference of the several Governments of the Empire; its views and conclusions on Foreign Policy, as recorded above, are necessarily subject to the actions of the Governments and Parliaments of the various portions of the Empire and it trusts that the result of its deliberations will meet with their approval."

Tuesday, November 6. Returned from Paris last night. Early this morning Skelton telephoned me to go over as important matters had developed. . . .

The business before the Conference was to agree to a statement about the Conference and Empire foreign policy which Curzon had prepared. Skelton showed me this report. It was a remarkable document. Not only did it represent the Conference as giving its general approval to the conduct of joint common affairs since the last Conference, but it announced that the Conference had laid down policies for the future which the foreign office would be authorized to carry out. It meant the acceptance in its most unqualified form of the doctrine of the joint foreign policy with joint responsibility. . . .

According to Skelton King rather went up into the air upon the conclusion of this statement and gave Curzon a piece of his mind. He said that he thought that he had made it quite clear that Canada did not subscribe to the theory of joint policy and joint responsibility in foreign affairs and would take no part except in matters of direct concern to her. He also insisted upon the Conference being regarded as a Conference between governments not having power to bind governments and commit them even to moral obligations. Yet at the close of the Conference he was asked to agree to a statement which ignored these Canadian declarations of Canadian policy and committed Canada definitely to courses to which she objected. He intimated that this was an illustration of tactics which made these Conferences not very pleasant prospects for Canadian governments. . . . He said flatly that unless there was an acceptance of the fact that these Conferences were only conferences Canada would in future decline to take part in them.

John Dafoe attended the 1923 Imperial Conference as a representative of the Canadian press. His recently discovered diary has thrown new light on the significance of the Conference.

Two years later the control of the Dominions over their own foreign policy was further emphasized when the Locarno Agreements were negotiated. By these treaties Germany and France promised not to use force in settling any disagreements that arose between them, and Britain guaranteed to aid either against aggression by the other. The Locarno Treaties were important in Imperial relations, too, for there was a clause inserted into the agreements, largely at Canada's insistence, which exempted the Dominions from their terms unless the Dominions accepted them by their own decision. The fact that none of the Dominions did so indicated that while Britain had one policy, the Dominions had another, and that the Dominions did not share responsibility for Britain's policy. Thus the idea of a common Imperial foreign policy was completely undermined.

The Imperial Conference of 1923 and the Locarno Agreements of 1925 clearly revealed that a united Empire with a common foreign policy had been transformed into a Commonwealth of Nations in which each member had its own foreign policy. This development was formally recognized in 1926 when another Imperial Conference issued a famous declaration named after its author, Arthur Balfour, a former Prime Minister of Great Britain. The Balfour Declaration described the Commonwealth as an association of "autonomous communities within the British Empire, equal in status, in no way subordinate to one another in any aspect of their domestic or external affairs, though united by a common allegiance to the Crown and freely associated as members of the British Commonwealth of Nations."

A number of legal anomalies remained to be removed before Dominion autonomy was as complete in law as it had become in practice. This was done by the Statute of Westminster in 1931, the final coping-stone on the development of self-government. The Statute gave the Dominions power to enact extra-territorial legislation, repealed the Colonial Laws Validity Act of 1865, which had declared British law supreme in any conflict with colonial law, and declared that no British law would extend to the Dominions. Britain retained some authority over Canada after 1931, for the Judicial Committee of the Privy Council was still the final court of appeal for some Canadian cases, and amendments to the Canadian constitution still required the approval of the British parliament. But Britain retained these powers only because Canadians were unable to agree on a more satisfactory way of dealing with judicial appeals and constitutional amendments.

Thus, in 1931, the British Commonwealth obtained legal definition as an association of self-governing or autonomous nations. Canada had not been alone in effecting this transformation for strong support had come from other Dominions, especially from South Africa and Ireland. Moreover, it was not just one party in Canada that had favoured this evolution. Although there had been differences of opinion between the parties on matters of detail, the gradual growth of Canadian powers of self-government received support from all. Macdonald, Laurier, Borden, Meighen and King had each played his part, and it was the Conservative government of R. B. Bennett that accepted the Statute of Westminster. "We are all autonomists now," one Canadian nationalist rightly claimed in 1931.

4. ISOLATION AND WAR

As war clouds gathered over a world united by technological and military advances, Canadians, like Americans, continued to believe that they could hide their heads in the sand like ostriches and remain untouched by explosions in Europe and Asia. One Canadian politician summed up the view of most of his countrymen in the 1930's when he wrote: "The more I see of the whole thing, the more I am certain that our destiny is on the North American continent and that if Europe is going to insist on destroying itself, it is no part of our mission to destroy ourselves in attempting to prevent it."

In 1931 the military dictators of Japan put the League of Nations to its first critical test when they launched an attack on the Chinese province of Manchuria. The attack was well timed, for most League members, including Canada, were giving their undivided attention to the domestic effects of the economic depression and had no desire to rush to China's assistance. At Geneva, the representative of R. B. Bennett's government to the League left no doubt that Canadians were unwilling to go to war over Manchuria. "I had to tell them," he explained to the House of Commons later, "that I did not believe that under the then existing circumstances the parliament of Canada would appropriate a single dollar toward maintaining a single company of troops in the Far East for that purpose." That was exactly the position taken in private by the governments of England and France and by the governments of the chief European states.

The failure of the League members to act against Japan gave a green light to other would-be aggressors. In 1935, the Italian dictator, Benito Mussolini, sent his Fascist battalions into the nearly defenceless country of Ethiopia. Here was an opportunity for the League to redeem itself. The League Assembly condemned Italy for aggression and imposed economic sanctions by which League member nations were forbidden to supply Italy with goods she required. But these sanctions did not include oil, a product essential to Mussolini's mechanized army. Despite the Italian dictator's warning that the imposition of oil sanctions would mean war, the Canadian delegate at Geneva, Dr. W. A. Riddell, acted without instructions and proposed that oil sanctions should be imposed. Riddell's action caused a sensation, particularly in Ottawa. Within a few days Mackenzie King's government repudiated Dr. Riddell. Most Canadians

The Canadian government objected to the initiative taken by its representative, Dr. W. A. Riddell, in suggesting that League sanctions against Italy should include coal, oil, iron and steel. Ernest Lapointe insisted that the Canadian government refused to take the initiative in proposing the extension of the measures with regard to the prohibition of exportation to Italy and did not propose to take the initiative in such measures. While most Canadians agreed with this stand, some believed that Lapointe was guided by pressure from Quebec. The Toronto *Evening Telegram* remarked: "If Canada's attitude is that this country is entitled to contract out of the League's collective efforts when it suits Quebec, that it is bound only to agree to sanctions that are agreeable to the aggressor, and that it is satisfied to have a spokesman at Geneva who does not speak for the Canadian government, then Mr. Lapointe's position is readily understandable. But that position is not, we think, the position of the Canadian people."

preferred King's caution to Riddell's courage. King accurately measured their temper when he asked: "Do honourable members think it is Canada's role at Geneva to attempt to regulate a European war?" They did not, and from the repudiation of Riddell to the outbreak of war in September 1939, King continued to avoid international commitments.

Mackenzie King was obsessed with the nightmare that foreign affairs could sharply divide Canadians again as in 1917 and he believed that the only way to prevent the country from splitting in two was to avoid positive actions. "A strong and dominant national feeling is not a luxury in Canada, it is a necessity," King claimed. "A divided country can be of little help to any country, least of all to herself." Probably the majority of Canadians agreed with their Prime Minister. Only a few, like John W. Dafoe in Winnipeg, realized that if the League were to fail Canada would inevitably be drawn into war.

In Germany, the dictator Hitler rearmed in defiance of the Treaty of Versailles and moved to expand his country's borders by force. Prime Minister King's chief hope was that somehow the German dictator's demands would be satisfied without provoking a war. In September 1938, at Munich, Hitler won the acceptance of Prime Ministers Chamberlain of Britain and Daladier of France for his plan to help himself to most of Czechoslovakia. Prime Minister King, and with him most of Canada, hoped that with this territorial acquisition the savage German dictator's appetite had been satisfied. From Ottawa the Prime Minister cabled Chamberlain: "The heart of Canada is rejoicing tonight at the success which has crowned your unremitting efforts for peace." In the columns of the *Winnipeg Free Press* John Dafoe's solitary voice cried out, "What's the cheering for?" He realized that Hitler's appetite for conquest was insatiable and that world war was just around the corner.

Throughout the inter-war years, while successive Canadian governments were rejecting commitments to the League and to the Commonwealth, the unity of the country which had been shattered by the events of the First World War was gradually being restored. But this unity was only achieved at the cost of avoiding steps which might have helped to prevent another war. At no time in these dangerous years was Canada's military budget raised to a level that would have placed the country in a state of preparedness. It was only in 1937, when warnings of war were already obvious, that Prime Minister King took steps to add to the country's defences. Even then the Canadian government refused to co-operate with the British in the establishment of an air-training plan for the Commonwealth countries. It was only after the war broke out that this plan was put into effect and the task of serious rearmament began.

Canada's course in foreign affairs during these years had been cautious and even shortsighted, but it was of a kind with the policy of her closest friends and allies, Great Britain and the United States. Like Canada, the United States refused to be drawn into world affairs, even rejecting membership in the League of Nations. Though the British played a more active role, they too failed to fulfil the commitments they had assumed in

As the war clouds gathered in Europe in the late 1930's, relations between Canada and the United States grew closer. Since Canada was a member of the League of Nations and of the British Commonwealth, her possible involvement in a European war was more likely than that of the isolationist United States. This situation was watched carefully by President Roosevelt. The joint cutting of the tape at the International Bridge over the St. Lawrence near Kingston in August, 1938 was a symbol of the Canadian-American friendship, a symbol which the American President transformed into words when he told an audience at Queen's University the same day, "The Dominion of Canada is part of the sisterhood of the British Empire. I give you an assurance that the people of the United States will not stand idly by if domination of Canadian soil is threatened by any other Empire."

joining the League. Britain, like Canada, was unprepared for war when the Nazi armies struck Poland in early September 1939.

When war finally came, Canada's position was different from what it had been in 1914. In the earlier world conflict, Britain had declared war for all the members of the Empire. In 1939 Canada controlled her own foreign policy and therefore declared war independently. On September 10, one week after Great Britain, the Canadian government, with parliament's approval, declared war on Nazi Germany. Although there were some opponents, including J. S. Woodsworth and some groups in Quebec, the country seemed united. The years of caution and careful avoidance of issues and actions that might have divided the country ended in solemn, but united, support of the war. Concern to preserve the country's unity had always been Mackenzie King's justification for his unheroic course in international affairs. In supporting the declaration of war in 1939, he pointed out: "I have made it the supreme endeavour of my leadership of the Government of this country, to let no hasty or premature threat or pronouncement create mistrust and divisions between the different elements that compose the population of our vast Dominion, so that, when the moment of decision came, all should see the issue itself that our national effort might be marked by unity of purpose, of heart and of endeavour." It remained to be seen whether this carefully nurtured unity would survive the test of another war.

CHAPTER 35

Canada and the
Second World War

"If today, I am prepared to continue to lead a Government charged with the awful responsibility of prosecuting a war, it is because, contrary to every hope and wish I have ever entertained, I have been compelled to believe that only by the destruction of Naziism, and the resistance of ruthless aggression, can the nations of the British Commonwealth hope to continue to enjoy the liberties which are theirs under the British Crown, and the world itself be spared a descent into a new and terrible age of barbarism." This was the message that Mackenzie King delivered to the Canadian people in October 1939. It was a message that only hinted at the terrible years of warfare that lay ahead.

Few Canadians realized in the autumn of 1939 that the new conflict would be longer and more costly than the First World War. The Second World War eventually spread from Europe to Africa and Asia and took Canadians to every battlefront in the world on land, on sea and in the air. At first, Canadians thought that their role would be limited mainly to providing materials and machines necessary to ensure the victory of the British and French fighting forces in Europe. But it soon became apparent that Canadian troops would be required too. By the end of 1939 the first Canadian contingent had been established in the military camps which transformed Great Britain into an island fortress. The "phoney war" ended in the spring of 1940, with the German invasion of Denmark and the Low Countries followed by the fall of France in June. It now became clear that the war would be long and bitter and that every Canadian resource would be needed if Hitler's massive, well-trained armies were to be defeated.

The magnificent prose of the British Prime Minister, Winston Churchill, best indicated the hard road that lay ahead. On June 4, 1940 in the House of Commons at Westminster, his defiant message steeled the spirit of his countrymen and buoyed up the hopes of free men everywhere.

We shall go on to the end, we shall fight in France, we shall fight on

the seas and oceans, we shall fight with growing confidence and growing strength in the air, we shall defend our Island, whatever the cost
may be, we shall fight on the beaches, we shall fight on the landing
grounds, we shall fight in the fields and in the streets, we shall fight
in the hills; we shall never surrender, and even if, which I do not for a
moment believe, this Island or a large part of it were subjugated and
starving, then our Empire beyond the seas, armed and guarded by
the British fleet, would carry on the struggle, until, in God's good
time, the New World, with all its power and might, steps forth to the
rescue and liberation of the old.

But as Churchill's inspiring words emphasized, the defeat of Hitler would
not be easy.

1. CONSCRIPTION IN THE SECOND WORLD WAR

The realization that the war would be long and difficult
recalled to Canadians the disagreements that had split the nation during
the last years of the First World War. Although the memory of these
events was especially vivid among the French Canadians, they supported the declaration of war in 1939. But they made it clear from the
outset that they opposed any form of military conscription for overseas
service. To French Canadians conscription was much more than a military matter; it emphasized their minority position in a bicultural society.
If the majority of English-speaking Canadians united against Quebec, as
they had in 1917, they could force their decisions upon the French-speaking minority as effectively as if they had been a conquering army. Thus
the conscription question was a harsh reminder to French Canadians that
the country explored and settled by their ancestors had been conquered
by the British in 1759. To defend their native soil, the French Canadians
were prepared to submit to any measures, including conscription. But
they insisted that the war overseas be fought on a voluntary basis.

Fully aware of Quebec's attitude towards conscription, Ernest Lapointe, Minister of Justice and the leader of the French Canadians at
Ottawa, stated the position of the Liberal government, and especially of
his French-speaking colleagues: "The whole province of Quebec will never
agree to accept compulsory service or conscription outside Canada. I
will go farther than that: When I say the whole province of Quebec I mean
that personally I agree with them. I am authorized by my colleagues in
the Cabinet for the province of Quebec to say that we will never agree to
conscription and will never be members or supporters of a government that
will try to enforce it." Having made this position clear, Lapointe then
concluded by noting that "we are willing to offer our services without limi-
tation and to devote our best efforts for the success of the cause we all
have at heart." Thus Quebec's position, and the position of the Liberal
government, was defined: complete support for the war effort, with the
provision that military service overseas would be kept on a voluntary basis.

The pledge to fight the war on a voluntary basis came none too soon,

This cartoon was taken from publicity issued by the National Government party for the 1940 election. In an attempt to revive the Conservative party and to enlist the support of anti-Mackenzie King Liberals, the Conservative leader, Dr. Manion, changed the name of his party to the National Government party before the 1940 election. Dr. Manion, who had succeeded R. B. Bennett, also promised that if elected he would draw his cabinet from all parties and form a truly national government to fight the war. Only thirty-nine Conservatives were elected. The cartoon was an example of their campaign, with the Liberals being attacked for raising the conscription issue. In fact, conscription had been raised throughout Canada long before, and was an issue.

for Premier Duplessis of Quebec called an election in October 1939. The campaign focused on the question of participation in the war. The Union Nationale leader claimed that Canadian participation in the war would lead to conscription. Duplessis' campaign was denounced as "an act of national sabotage" by Ernest Lapointe and the federal Liberals, who appealed for the defeat of Duplessis as a vote of confidence in themselves as men strong enough to prevent the introduction of conscription. The provincial Liberals were victorious, but their victory was based on a reiteration of the "no conscription" pledge. In the spring of 1940 a federal election was held. Once more the Liberal party was victorious; and once more it had repeated its pledge to fight the war without adopting conscription for overseas service.

It was fortunate for the government that the federal election had taken place before the gravity of the European situation was fully apparent. The disastrous defeat of France in the summer of 1940 immediately revived the conscription question in Canada. Naturally, it was from English-speaking Canada that the demand for compulsory enlistment came, and some Conservatives took up the cry. To silence the agitation for conscription, the Liberal government passed a law, which provided for conscription for home service only. For a short time the conscription issue slept, until the entrance of the United States into the war on December 8, 1941 once again brought the matter to a head. The United States had adopted a policy of compulsory military service and many Canadians felt that Canada could not play its part in fighting the war on the basis of voluntary service alone. Because of the mounting pressure for conscription in English-speaking Canada, the government decided to submit the question to the people. In a national plebiscite, in April 1942, the government asked the voters to release it from its promise not to apply conscription for overseas service. The plebiscite was not a vote on conscription, but a request by the government for a free hand in dealing with the problem. The vote showed that most Canadians were in favour of releasing the government from its pledge. But, equally important, the returns revealed that while English-speaking Canada had voted eighty per cent in favour of giving the government a free hand, seventy-two per cent of the voters in Quebec opposed the motion. The racial split of 1917 had reappeared. Mackenzie King wrote in his diary: "As I looked at the returns, I thought of Durham's report on the state of Quebec when he arrived there after the Rebellion of 1837-38 and said he found two nations warring in the bosom of a single state. That would be the case in Canada, as applied to Canada as a whole, unless the whole question of conscription from now on is approached with the utmost care."

Prime Minister King did not interpret the result of the plebiscite as a demand for the immediate enactment of conscription, but rather as a decision to allow the government to enact compulsory service whenever it was thought necessary. "Not necessarily conscription, but conscription if necessary," was the cautious way that King described his government's policy after the plebiscite. By adopting this non-committal attitude, King hoped to prevent, or at least to postpone, the crisis.

While the government's cautious policy completely satisfied no one, it did at least have the virtue of partially satisfying everyone. But the end had not yet been reached. The government made every effort to keep Canadian troops at the front reinforced, but the invasion of France in 1944 created a new manpower crisis. When it became clear in the autumn of 1944 that voluntary enlistments were not providing enough reinforcements, Colonel J. L. Ralston, the Minister of Defence, insisted that conscription was now necessary. But King was still convinced that more vigorous recruiting efforts could produce the needed men; Ralston resigned from office.

To succeed Ralston, King chose General A. G. L. McNaughton, the recently retired commander of the Canadian army overseas. McNaughton, who had at first believed that conscription was unnecessary, soon realized that voluntary enlistment could not provide the necessary recruits. In November 1944, King and his cabinet, which was on the verge of breaking up, decided that a measure of limited conscription for overseas service was necessary. Sixteen thousand men who had already been conscripted for home service only were now placed on the general duty rolls and became eligible for overseas service.

Although this policy of limited conscription threatened to divide the Liberal supporters of the government, the danger soon passed. Some French-Canadian members of parliament voted against King, but there was no permanent division either in the party or in the country. Mackenzie King's moderation and caution paid dividends, for by trying to understand the French-Canadian point of view he had won their trust. Moreover, he had obtained the support of strong leaders from Quebec. When his close colleague, Ernest Lapointe, died late in 1941, King had appointed a relatively obscure Quebec lawyer, Mr. Louis St. Laurent, as Minister of Justice, and to him must be given a great deal of the credit for the harmonious solution to the conscription crisis of 1944. St. Laurent stood by King throughout the crisis and accepted conscription when he saw that it could no longer be avoided. As he told the House of Commons: "The will of the majority must be respected and it must prevail. But I trust that, here in Canada, the majority will always, as it is doing in this case, assert that will only after giving due consideration to the feelings and views of the minority." Thus, by the end of 1944, the spectre of conscription had at last been faced and successfully laid. With a sense of satisfaction and pride, Prime Minister King could write: "I shall never be able to say how grateful I was and ever will be to my colleagues of French origin who kept so close to my side as we ran into and safely beyond the cataract which threatened to engulf us all."

As war approached, the anti-war and anti-conscription forces in Quebec became increasingly vocal. Their position was succinctly stated by Maxime Raymond in the House of Commons in April 1939 when he said: "Every Canadian citizen has the military obligation of defending the soil of his motherland and those of the province of Quebec have never shirked that duty, nor shall they ever do so, but no one is entitled to ask them to go and shed their blood in Europe, or in Africa, or in Asia for the greater glory or power of any other country, even if that country should be England or France. And if ever a majority of the people of this country should desire to compel an important minority thereof to take up arms in defence of a foreign land, whichever it may be, that would be the end of confederation." Three years later he explained his opposition to the plebiscite in the House: "A compromise was made on September 9, 1939, by virtue of which you have agreed not to demand conscription for overseas service, if those who opposed participation in the war, notably the Province of Quebec, would consent to participate in this war. On the faith of this engagement, this important part of the population, opposed to the war, consented to participate. Were you sincere then? I dare not doubt it. Did you wish to obtain this consent under false pretensions? I dare not think it. Now those who opposed the war have fulfilled their obligation, freely, generously—and God knows the ardour and devotion Mr. Lapointe put into the fulfilment of his engagement—are you going to refuse to fulfill yours?"

The aircraft on the assembly line at the De Havilland factory are the famous Mosquito. This high-flying and extremely fast bomber was made of wood, and thus was a natural product for Canadian manufacture. The Mosquito has been ranked by some observers as second only to the Lancaster as the great bombing aircraft of the war. It was used largely for specific bombing tasks rather than the massive raids on large targets. It was also used extensively for reconnaissance, photography, and pathfinder work.

2. THE WAR EFFORT AT HOME AND ABROAD

Though the conscription issue was the most dramatic problem in Canadian politics during the war, it was not the only difficulty that Canadians faced. The government's main task was to mobilize the nation's resources for war. Many of the country's natural resources were of the kind necessary for the manufacture of war weapons. Iron and steel production was greatly increased to feed the factories that were turning out guns, munitions and ships. These activities in turn increased the pace of hydro-electric development which was necessary to run not only the older industries but the new ones like the giant aluminum industry that grew up in Quebec. By the end of the war, Canada's industrial exports were exceeding the export of staple products for the first time in the country's history. The war had transformed Canada into a major industrial nation.

Mining and manufacturing were not the only industries that flourished because of the war. Increased demand for food products raised wheat prices, and, blessed by years of high rainfall, the prairie farmer once more produced bumper crops. British Columbians prospered on wartime demands for their timber and mineral resources, while the Maritimes benefited from shipbuilding and the great use made of east-coast ports by the Atlantic convoys carrying men and materials to the war fronts.

The government supervised much of the economic development of the war period. Under the guidance of C. D. Howe, who earned the title "Minister of Everything," the economic production drive was highly successful. Where private industry could not meet the demands of the war effort, the government stepped in to provide publicly-owned and operated corporations. Scientists employed by the government in war agencies and at the National Research Council developed new materials, such as synthetic rubber, to meet the multiplicity of demands made by modern warfare. The government controlled prices and rationed foods, to ensure that the men at the front were properly fed and equipped and to prevent war profiteering. These controls, and heavy wartime taxation, affected all Canadians.

But the war's most immediate effect was on the thousands of young men and women who served in the armed services on the battlefronts of the world. By the end of the war Canada had raised a military force of over a million persons from a population of only twelve million. At the beginning of the war Canadian troops sailed for England where they played an important, if undramatic, role in deterring the Germans from attacking the British Isles. Once the threat of a Nazi invasion of Britain passed, Canadian troops settled down to await the day when they were needed to take part in the invasion to liberate the European continent. Canadian troops had lost heavily in the fruitless attempt to defend Hong Kong against the Japanese in 1941, but it was not until August 1942 that Canadian troops first saw action in Europe. To test the German defences and to divert the enemy's attention while preparations were being made for landings in North Africa, five thousand troops of the Canadian Second Division landed at Dieppe on the French coast. It was a costly experiment. The Canadians held their ground for ten hours against heavy German fire, but were forced to retreat after suffering over three thousand casualties, of whom about half were taken prisoner.

In 1943 a Canadian division in the Mediterranean theatre assisted in the hard-fought conquest of Sicily and Italy. Then, on June 6, 1944, the long-awaited D-Day appointed for the invasion of Europe across the English Channel arrived. Canadian, British and American forces, all under the supreme command of United States General Dwight D. Eisenhower, stormed the Normandy beaches to begin the liberation of France. Led by General G. D. H. Crerar, the Canadian troops distinguished themselves in a year of long, hard fighting against some of Hitler's crack divisions.

Sweeping through France, the Allied forces cut off the Germans in the Falaise Gap in Normandy, and moved into Belgium and the Low Countries. In the Scheldt estuary, where the Germans were well dug in, the Canadian troops played a major role in freeing this important entrance to Europe from the enemy forces. When the Allied victory came in May

The town and ridge of Regalbuto was one of the key positions upon which the German defence of Sicily rested. After a fierce four-day battle in 1943 Canadian troops gained their objective. The scene that greeted the Canadians, like these tankmen from the Three Rivers regiment, was one of unprecedented devastation. The official Canadian war history stated: "Rubble completely blocked the main thoroughfare. . . . For once there was no welcome by cheering crowds, with the usual shouted request for cigarettes, chocolate or biscuits. The place was all but deserted; most of the inhabitants had fled to the surrounding hills or the railway tunnels. They were only now [after the battle] beginning to straggle back, dirty, ragged and apparently half-fed, to search pitifully for miserable gleanings among the debris of their shattered homes."

1945 it was the Canadian command that accepted the surrender of the Nazi forces in the Netherlands.

Six years of war had cost Canada 41,700 men, dead or missing. While Canada's contribution to the victory was naturally smaller than that of her allies, Britain, France, the Soviet Union and the United States, the quality of her armed forces had been high. In the words of the official historian of the Canadian Army, Canada's record "might command respect even by the standard of the greater powers."

It was not only the Canadian Army that emerged from the war with a proud record. The Royal Canadian Navy played an heroic and efficient role in the supremely important task of protecting Allied convoys from the Nazi submarines that lurked beneath the cold Atlantic. At the beginning of the war the Canadian naval service was only five thousand strong, but by 1945 it had increased to nearly one hundred thousand men. By the end of the war, the Royal Canadian Navy had assumed the main responsibility for ensuring the safe passage of Atlantic supply convoys to Britain. It was cold, tedious work, often punctuated by an encounter with a Nazi U-boat. But its work was of the greatest significance for neither Britain, in the early years of the war, nor the Allied armies after the invasion of Europe had begun, could have survived without the supplies shipped from North America.

Canadians also won distinction in the air. The air force increased from four thousand to two hundred thousand men. Forty-five Royal Canadian Air Force squadrons fought in Europe, the Mediterranean, India and

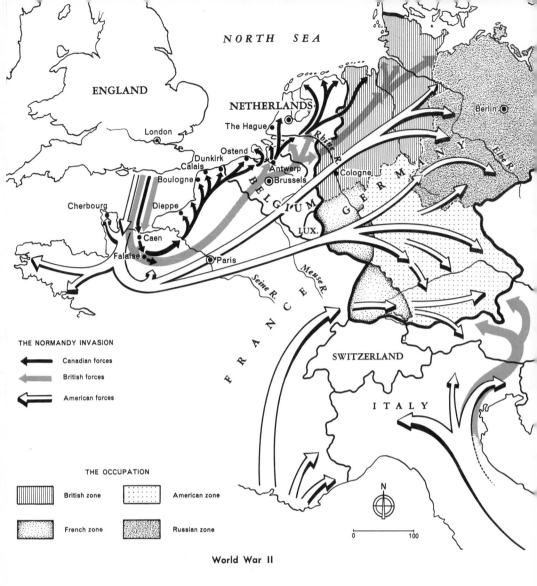

World War II

Burma. The Arctic Command aided the Canadian navy in convoy activities. As important as the actual engagements of the fighter and bomber squadrons was the air training programme carried out in Canada under the British Commonwealth Air Training Scheme. From 1939 to the conclusion of the war men from all parts of the Commonwealth and Allied nations came to Canada to receive their training before departing for the war theatres. The Air Training plan gave practical expression to the value of the Commonwealth association in defence matters. In this and many other ways the Commonwealth, which had faltered in the face of the German menace in the inter-war period, gave definite proof of determination to prevent the spread of totalitarianism.

It would be a mistake to overestimate the importance of Canada's contribution to the defeat of the Axis Powers, Germany, Italy and Japan. Canada was still a small country compared to her mammoth southern neighbour, or even to the heavily populated British Isles. Yet, in co-operation with these two countries, the rest of the Commonwealth and the Soviet Union, Canada played a role of more than minor importance. During the dark days after the collapse of France and before the Japanese had forced the United States into the conflict, Canada was Britain's major ally. At the level of diplomacy Canada was particularly important in working as a link between Great Britain and the United States, helping to ensure, even while the Americans remained neutral, that necessary materials and weapons were obtained by the hard-pressed British. This role held important political implications as the years of defeat began slowly to turn into victory.

3. PREPARATIONS FOR THE POST-WAR WORLD

During the war Canada's relations with her two powerful allies, Britain and the United States, were always close, but not always uncomplicated. Prime Minister King believed that Canada had a special role to play as the mediator between Britain and the United States, but he did not find it an easy one. Nor did he feel that the two big countries were properly appreciative of the contribution that Canada was making to the winning of the war. In 1943 he wrote in a somewhat irritated mood: "It was perfectly clear to me that, so far as Britain and United States were concerned, there was little thought of giving credit except in very general terms to what was being done by Canada."

But despite these momentary irritations, King worked very hard at his self-imposed role of mediator between Britain and the United States. By the end of the war Canada had probably come to deserve the description that Winston Churchill had earlier given when he wrote that Canada was "a magnet exercising a double attraction drawing both Great Britain and the United States towards herself, and thus drawing them closer to each other. She is the only surviving bond which stretches from Europe across the Atlantic ocean." The war made this bond more important than it had ever been, for it is unlikely that Hitler could have been defeated without the military and economic resources of the United States.

During the late 1930's relations between Canada and the United States had begun to grow closer. As Europe moved towards war, both Canada and the United States began to give serious thought to the defence of North America. When war came the United States remained a neutral, but a neutral interested in the outcome, especially as it might affect North America. In August 1940, Prime Minister King and President Roosevelt decided that the defence of North America required careful examination and mutual policies between the two neighbours. The result was the signing of the Ogdensburg Agreement which established the Permanent Joint Board on Defence. The purpose of this Board was to work out plans for the co-operative defence of North America in the event of any attack. This agreement was followed quickly by the announcement of an arrangement that had been worked out between Britain and the United States, with Canada as the go-between, whereby the United States was given permanent leases on a number of British naval bases in North America, including three in Newfoundland, in return for fifty over-age but badly needed destroyers. This agreement, King believed, vindicated his "whole life's work for better international relations, particularly between the United Kingdom and the United States." Thus Canada was playing the role of mediator, and at the same time moving closer to the United States. The construction of the American military road through Canada to Alaska, begun in 1940, also demonstrated the strengthening of the physical links between the two countries.

One of the Canadian government's problems from the outset of the war was a serious shortage of American dollars with which to pay for materials purchased from the United States. To find a solution, Prime Minister King paid an official visit to the American President in April 1941. The result of this meeting was the Hyde Park Declaration which provided for increased American purchases of war material in Canada and defence production sharing. In this way the economies of Canada and the United States were

In August, 1943 Prime Minister King played host to Prime Minister Churchill and President Roosevelt at the Citadel in Quebec. The three war leaders discussed plans for the continuance of the war effort, and also considered the prospects for preserving peace in the post-war world. But it was not only important matters of state that passed through Prime Minister King's mind for he wrote in his diary, "There comes to my mind the changes that are wrought by the whirligig of time. Little could my grandfather have seen while he was in prison and in exile, or my father and mother when they were making their sacrifices for the children's education, that some day one of their name would be entertaining the President of the United States and the Prime Minister of Great Britain at the Citadel of Quebec."

tied more closely together, just as North American defence was established on a co-operative basis. The growing friendliness between Canada and the United States was revealed by the informal manner in which President Roosevelt signed the original draft of the Hyde Park Declaration. He scrawled across the document, "Done by Mackenzie and F.D.R. at Hyde Park on a Grand Sunday, April 20, 1941." When the Japanese attack on Pearl Harbor on December 7, 1941 brought the United States actively into the war, co-operation between the neighbours grew even closer.

Some Canadians feared that their country was moving too readily into the well-intentioned but overpowering embrace of the United States. The enormous population, industrial might and material wealth of the United States could be a serious threat to Canada's independence. Was not the Canadian economy becoming too dependent on the United States? Was not Canada too closely tied to defensive arrangements in which the United States was the dominant partner? Was not the culture of English-speaking Canada becoming only a pale image of her neighbour's to the south?

These were questions which remained unanswered at the end of the war. During the war itself, when every effort was concentrated on defeating the Axis Powers, there was little time to worry about long term problems. Although Prime Minister King was aware of the dangers that threatened Canada through too close an association with the United States, he felt that the dangers were counterbalanced by the benefits that would result from close co-operation between the nations of the English-speaking world. At the time of the Hyde Park Declaration he wrote in his diary: "I, personally, would be strongly opposed to anything like political union. I would keep the British Commonwealth of Nations as intact as possible. Canada, in time, and sooner than we expect perhaps, will become its centre. It is better to have two peoples and two governments on this continent understanding each other and reciprocating in their relations as an example to the world, than to have anything like continental union." Not even Mackenzie King could foresee that the events of the post-war world would push Canada even further along the road of co-operation with the United States.

When the surrender of Japan in August 1945 brought the war to an end, Canada was a greatly altered country. She had become a fully-fledged industrial and urban nation. Moreover, most Canadians were now convinced that their country would have to play an active role in the affairs of the world if future wars were to be prevented. And the prevention of war now seemed more necessary than ever, for the dropping of the atom bomb on two Japanese cities in the summer of 1945 gave support to the fear that man could invent a weapon powerful enough to destroy himself. It was with good reason that the Canadian parliament passed a resolution in the spring of 1945 which emphasized that "the establishment of an effective international organization for the maintenance of peace and security is of vital importance to Canada, and, indeed, to the future well being of mankind."

CHAPTER 36

Canada in a
World of Super Powers

Canada emerged from the Second World War far more united than it had from the First. Mackenzie King's careful handling of the explosive conscription issue in 1944 avoided the dangerous racial crisis of 1917. More thorough-going and rigid government controls prevented the serious regional and occupational grievances which had existed during and immediately following the 1914-18 period. The war lifted the country from the miseries of depression by prompting full mobilization of the economy to feed and supply the Allied forces. By 1945 Canadians were anxious to turn their energy to the constructive task of national development and reconstruction.

1. ECONOMIC GROWTH

The steady and insistent demands of war had given a tremendous stimulus to the expansion of the Canadian economy and this continued after the war. Between 1941 and 1962 Canada's population increased from 11,500,000 to 18,500,000. This increase was partly due to a high birth-rate, but it was also the result of renewed efforts to attract European immigrants to help meet the labour needs of an expanding economy. As usual, the heaviest inflow came from Great Britain, which provided nearly a third of the total number. Italians, Germans, Americans, Hungarians who fled their country during the 1956 rebellion, and many others from western, northern and central Europe brought the total immigration to 1,500,000 by 1957.

The newcomers, or "New Canadians" as they were soon being called, seldom went into agriculture as they had during the great immigration boom prior to 1914. Instead, they found opportunities for their skills in the growing industrial cities. By 1962 almost sixty per cent of the population of Canada lived in cities, thus marking the final and unmistakable transformation of Canada from an agricultural to an urban and industrial nation.

The nation's productive capacity increased with its population. Between 1939 and 1962, the Gross National Product leaped from five billion, seven hundred million dollars to over thirty-six billion dollars. This rapid economic expansion after 1945 was partly due to the fact that Canada was particularly attractive to foreign investors; the nation's political stability and economic potential together gave investors assurances of security and growing profits. Foreign capital financed the exploitation of natural resources like oil, natural gas, iron and uranium, and financed expansion of steel production, pulp-and-paper milling, aluminum processing, and secondary manufacturing of all kinds. By the 1950's aluminum from Kitimat, British Columbia, oil from Leduc, Alberta and iron from Steep Rock, Ontario and Ungava, Quebec, found ready sales on domestic and world markets.

The agricultural sector of the economy also expanded and flourished. Wartime demands and the return of favourable food-growing conditions had already revived the wheat economy before 1945. In the post-war years Canadian farmers raised their wheat output to an average of five hundred million bushels annually. Until 1952, when a seven hundred million bushel wheat crop was harvested, there was no serious difficulty in finding markets for Canadian grain. But by 1952 the revival of European farming, combined with high Canadian prices and the disposal of United States agricultural surpluses at low prices, left a growing quantity of unsold grain in Canada in the years 1952-57. This situation produced dissatisfaction among western farmers who, by 1957, were ready to turn against the Liberal government in Ottawa.

The extensive economic developments of the post-war period created a demand for new transportation and communication facilities. A complex system of pipelines reached out from the oil wells in Alberta west across the Rockies, east across the prairies, and south into the United States, carrying crude oil to refineries and natural gas to feed industries and homes far from the western oil fields. As usual in Canada, the construction of new methods of transportation brought public money and private enterprise into co-operation. The decision of the Liberal government to provide public money to aid in the construction of the trans-Canada pipeline in 1956 occasioned a political quarrel that added to the growing unpopularity of the Liberal administration.

The largest and most adventurous enterprise in the field of transportation and communications during the post-war decade was the construction of the St. Lawrence Seaway and hydro-electric project. Designed to transform the inland cities on the Great Lakes into major oceanic trading centres, the enterprise had been in the planning stages for many years. In 1932, Canada and the United States had negotiated a treaty for the joint construction of the inland water-way. But lobbies, or pressure groups, representing railway, coal and coastal-port interests had been able to prevent ratification of the treaty in the American Senate. By 1950, however, Canada felt strong enough to construct the Seaway alone and her

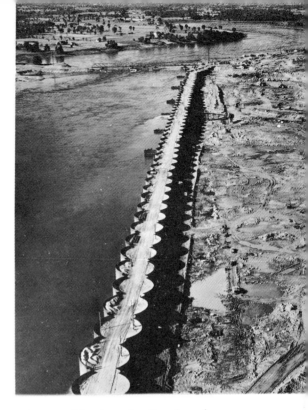

The St. Lawrence Seaway and hydro project ranks high among the great engineering feats of this century. Giant cofferdams, like this 3,200-foot one stretching from Barnhart Island to the Canadian shore, served as bulwarks against the St. Lawrence while the river was diverted to enable engineers to build the giant dams and powerhouses. The Seaway represented the fulfilment of the dream of the early merchants of Montreal, who hoped that the St. Lawrence would become the artery for the trade of the interior of the entire continent.

threat to do so was sufficient to overcome objections in the American Senate. As President Truman told Congress in 1952: "The question before Congress now is whether the United States shall participate in the construction and thus maintain joint operation and control over this development, which is so important to our security and our economic progress." Finally, in 1954, the last details were arranged and five years later this vast oceanic highway was opened to traffic. But, as Lester Pearson, at that time the Minister for External Affairs in the Liberal cabinet, told an American audience, "to be perfectly frank, many Canadians didn't think too highly of this last-minute participation—either of its timing or of its nature."

This slight feeling of resentment at the attitude of the United States to the Seaway was part of a growing anxiety in Canada about the degree of influence which the United States seemed to exercise in Canadian affairs. Canada was, of course, a close ally of the United States in international affairs. But of more immediate concern to many Canadians was the increasing dependence of the Canadian economy on that of its southern neighbour. Not only was the United States Canada's most important market for exports and source of imports, but it was the source of a large proportion of the foreign investment which had financed Canada's economic expansion. This latter state marked a great transformation in Canadian economic life. Before the First World War, about sixty per cent of all foreign capital invested in Canada came from Great Britain. But during the inter-war years Britain's economy declined, and American capital gradually replaced British. In 1956 non-residents, mainly American, controlled fifty-seven per cent of the total investment in Canadian manufacturing, and sixty-six per cent of the total in mining, smelting and oil. By 1959, seventy-five per cent of all foreign investment in Canada came from the United States.

There was no doubt that the great economic advances of the post-war years would not have taken place without the large inflow of American money. But many people were disturbed by the degree of control that foreign capital had gained over Canadian economic life. Moreover, there was a growing feeling that the United States often ignored Canadian interests. A committee of the United States Congress summed up this feeling when it reported in 1959: "The United States and its citizens have frequently adopted a patronizing assumption that Canada, like a poor relation, would remain at our beck and call, and that no matter what the provocation, Canadians would not object to any step we might take. This lack of interest, this ignorance of the Canadian heritage and Canadian problems, and this patronizing air have been displayed by the people, the press and the Government of the United States." Although there were obviously no easy solutions to these problems, many Canadians believed that methods should be found to encourage increased Canadian investment and more frequent employment of Canadians in managerial positions in foreign-controlled industries.

Despite such misgivings and fears, most Canadians enjoyed a high degree of material well-being in the prosperous decade after the Second World War. More homes were built, more domestic comforts purchased, more automobiles sold, and higher wages paid than in any comparable period of the country's history. And while the economy boomed, the non-material side of Canadian life was also expanding. Schools and universities bulged with students seeking every variety of education. Signs of a developing Canadian tradition, or rather traditions, French and English, in the arts, music and theatre began to appear. The Massey Commission, established in 1949 to investigate Canadian culture, reported: "We were conscious of a prevailing hunger existing throughout the country for a fuller measure of what the writer, the artist and the musician could give." The opening of the annual Shakespearean Festival at Stratford, Ontario in 1953 was one sign of the new cultural awakening. Such government-sponsored agencies as the National Film Board and the Canadian Broadcasting Corporation continued to support artistically creative Canadians. But the main aid for these activities came in 1957 with the establishment of the Canada Council, whose one hundred million dollar endowment was to be used to aid universities and to provide scholarships and grants to Canadian students, writers and artists. Thus the dozen years following the war were years of expansion and progress in many areas of Canadian life. The darkest cloud on the Canadian horizon was the tense international situation, for Canada was now involved in world affairs as it had never been before.

2. CANADA AND THE COLD WAR

The Second World War was a harsh warning to countries like Canada and the United States that the peace of the world could only be preserved if all nations worked together to provide collective security. Despite their isolationist policies in the inter-war period, both Canada and the United States had become involved in the struggle to defeat the Axis Powers. Neither country wanted to see a repetition of these events. Both nations, therefore, became founding members of the United Nations Organization that succeeded the old League of Nations. As Louis St. Laurent, the Canadian Minister of External Affairs, put it: "The choice we face today is the choice between isolationism and its certain weaknesses, and the hope through collective action of preventing another war."

Canada's role in the post-war world was a minor one compared with that of such powerful nations as the United States. Still, it was the view of the Canadian government that small and middle powers had much to contribute. "Power is not exclusively concentrated in the hands of any four or five states," Prime Minister King claimed in 1945. "Experience has shown that the contribution of smaller powers is not a negligible one, either to the preserving of peace or to its restoration when peace has been disturbed." With the assistance of the Minister of External Affairs, Louis St. Laurent, and later through the work of Lester B. Pearson in the same office, the Liberal government formulated a foreign policy designed for the needs of a middle power like Canada.

The United Nations was the chief hope of all those who believed that world peace could best be preserved through an organization that had a world-wide membership. But the success of the United Nations, like that of the League before it, required the co-operation of the great powers who held permanent seats on the Security Council. On these nations, especially on the United States, Britain and the Soviet Union, rested the heaviest responsibility for the enforcement of United Nations' decisions. Shortly after the founding of the world organization it became tragically clear that the wartime allies, and especially the United States and the Soviet Union, who dominated the Security Council, rarely agreed on issues that disturbed the world's peace. In fact, the effectiveness of the United Nations was often nullified by the use of the veto power which had been given to the major powers. Although the Soviet Union was rarely able to muster a majority of votes in the General Assembly where all the member nations were represented, its use of the veto in the Security Council prevented the United Nations from playing the part in world affairs that its founders had hopefully assigned it.

By the late 1940's, the activities and growing hostility of the Soviet Union caused the nations of western Europe, the Commonwealth and the United States to investigate additional means of mutual protection and collective security. In 1946 Canadians were shocked to learn from Igor Gouzenko, a cipher clerk in the Soviet embassy in Ottawa, who deserted his post, of the operation of a Russian spy ring in Canada. When the Russian position in eastern Europe was further consolidated by a Communist seizure of power in Czechoslovakia in February 1948, the western powers determined to form a new defensive alliance to prevent further expansion by the U.S.S.R.

The western response to the growing fear that the Soviet Union intended to use her military strength to gain control of western as well as eastern Europe was the North Atlantic Treaty Organization, formed in 1949. Canada was one of the founding members of this treaty of mutual defence. In suggesting such an organization Louis St. Laurent, the Canadian Minister of External Affairs, emphasized the need for "the creation and preservation by the nations of the Free World under the leadership of Great Britain, the United States and France, of an overwhelming preponderance of force over any adversary or possible combination of adversaries." But Canada also insisted that the organization should be more than a military alliance. "It must be economic; it must be moral," St. Laurent stated. As a result the treaty contained a clause providing for the social, cultural and economic co-operation of the member nations. However, the ideal of an Atlantic Community has proven easier to describe than to achieve. Since 1949 nothing has been achieved in transforming this section of the treaty of alliance into a reality.

Canada's membership in N.A.T.O. has meant the assumption of far-reaching military responsibilities. The scope of the alliance, originally limited to western Europe, was later expanded to include Greece and Turkey. In 1954 West Germany was permitted to rearm and join the Western Alliance. Under the N.A.T.O. agreement Canada has provided a brigade of infantry for service in Germany, twelve air squadrons, and some forty ships.

Two launching sites, one at North Bay, Ontario and a second at La Macaza, Quebec, have been established for the Bomarc missile. As part of the North American defence system, the nuclear-tipped weapon is designed as an interceptor to be fired at bombing aircraft. The missile is forty-seven feet long, with a wing span of eighteen feet.

It was not only in Europe that Canada assumed military commitments in the 1950's. Under the authority of the United Nations, Canadian troops served in the Korean War which broke out in June 1950 when North Korean forces moved against the American-sponsored government of South Korea. During three years of war Canada suffered one thousand six hundred and forty-two casualties, including four hundred and six dead. Canadian diplomats and soldiers also served on an international commission supervising the ceasefire agreement between warring Communist and non-Communist forces in Indo-China.

Canada's willingness to join N.A.T.O. and to assume widespread military and diplomatic responsibilities reflected her awareness of the dangerous position of a country sandwiched between the Soviet Union and the United States. One result of this situation was the growth of an increasingly close relationship between Canada and the United States. The two governments not only continued the wartime arrangements for continental defence; they organized new measures for mutual defence which included three lines of radar stations reaching into the Canadian north to detect any attack that might be launched over the northern wastelands. In addition to this warning system the governments in 1957 signed a new defence arrangement known as the North American Air Defence Agreement (N.O.R.A.D.) which placed Canadian and American air defence in North America under a united command.

As well as reflecting the pressures of the Cold War, the growing military dependence of Canada on the United States revealed the declining influence of Britain in world affairs. Having borne the heaviest responsibility for fighting two major wars in the twentieth century, Britain was on the verge of economic exhaustion in 1945. Nevertheless, the Commonwealth remained an important factor in the formulation of Canadian foreign policy. It was not the same Commonwealth that had existed in the inter-war years, for in 1947 the first Asian members were admitted to membership. One of these members, India, insisted on becoming a republic, and it was only after long negotiations, in which Canada played a leading role, that a formula was worked out whereby a republic could join an organization composed of monarchical states. The inclusion of India, Pakistan, Ceylon, Ghana, Nigeria and other non-white nations transformed the Commonwealth into a multi-racial organization. Moreover, since most of these new states were heavily populated and economically underdeveloped, Commonwealth members organized the Colombo Plan in 1950 to give them economic and technical assistance. By 1962 Canada had provided almost $400,000,000 in foreign aid under the Colombo Plan. These funds helped to finance a wide variety of developments: massive dams for power and irrigation, cement plants, an atomic reactor in India, fishing vessels, locomotives, raw materials and schools. The Colombo Plan also supplied teachers and technical experts.

Commonwealth relations were sometimes complicated in the post-war years. The most serious crisis occurred in 1956 when British and French

At Colombo, Ceylon, in 1950, the members of the Commonwealth resolved that "steps should be taken urgently to raise living standards and promote social welfare amongst the people of South and Southeast Asia, thus enabling this area, with its vast potential resources, to play an increasing part in fostering well-being and furthering world prosperity."

troops invaded the Suez Canal zone in Egypt to prevent the government of Colonel Nasser from taking over full control of this vital communications artery. Britain's action in Suez, unquestionably a violation of the United Nations Charter, placed Canada and other Commonwealth nations in a difficult position. India and other former British colonies regarded the action as blatant imperialism and contemplated withdrawal from the Commonwealth.

At the United Nations, Canada agreed with the United States and Russia in condemning the Anglo-French action. But with the aid of Lester Pearson, the Canadian Minister of External Affairs, the United Nations reached a settlement which brought the intervention to an end and prevented the break-up of the Commonwealth. The solution involved the establishment of a United Nations Emergency Force, which included Canadian troops and was under a Canadian Commander, Major-General E. L. M. Burns; the duty of the force was to supervise the evacuation of the invading armies from the canal zone. This successful action by the United Nations prevented what might easily have been an outbreak of

At the end of the Second World War many people expected that the King government would suffer the same fate that the Conservatives had experienced after the Great War. The question was whether the electorate would turn to M. J. Coldwell and the C.C.F. or to the Progressive Conservative party, now led by John Bracken. Prime Minister King's greatest fear was that the voters, anxious for measures of social security, would turn to the C.C.F. To meet this threat to his power, the Prime Minister began to plan for post-war social security measures.

THE CHIEF COOK COMES THROUGH

more general hostilities. For his contribution towards this peaceful solution, Lester Pearson was awarded the Nobel Peace Prize in 1957. Although Commonwealth feelings ran high over the Suez episode, the trouble was finally smoothed over without any of the Asian members withdrawing from the organization.

Thus the post-war years saw Canada moving closer to the United States, while at the same time preserving and strengthening relations with the members of what was now a multi-racial Commonwealth. New leaders were to emerge in Canadian domestic politics to guide the country through these years of change and international tension.

3. THE END OF THE KING ERA

When the war ended in Europe in the spring of 1945 Mackenzie King's Liberal government was nearing the end of its five-year term of office. There were signs that the C.C.F., which had won power in Saskatchewan in 1944, and the Conservatives, who had taken office in Ontario in 1943, were both serious challengers to replace the Liberal government in Ottawa. But the Liberals had prepared for the post-war years, anticipating the need for social reform and economic planning to prevent the return of the conditions of the 'thirties. A Liberal brains-trust drew up a programme including price supports to guarantee stable prices for agricultural products, children's allowances, hospital insurance, government-sponsored housing developments, and a scheme of public works projects to provide employment for returning servicemen and counteract any decline in economic activity. It was this programme that the Liberals offered the country in the election campaign of June 1945.

The election showed that the majority of the Canadian people approved the wartime policies of the King government and were prepared to entrust the Liberals with the tasks of post-war reconstruction. The Liberals had been particularly worried about their ability to retain the support of

Quebec, for the French Canadians had resented the conscription policy of 1944. One sign of Quebec's distrust of the federal government had been the re-election of Maurice Duplessis and the Union Nationale in 1944. But in 1945 the French Canadians once more supported Mackenzie King. The French-Canadian newspaper, *Montréal-Matin*, gave the best explanation of the King victory when it pointed out that the Liberals' "policy has been sufficiently elastic to adapt itself to the wishes of the people, while other parties sought to impose their programme and doctrine."

Back in office the Liberals found that most of their plans for post-war reconstruction could not be implemented. Post-war prosperity weakened the popular demand for social security measures and government economic planning. More important, the King government came up against the problem of "provincial rights" as it had done in the late 1930's. The leading opponent of any expansion of federal powers or functions was Premier Duplessis of Quebec, who met every federal proposal for social security measures, federal assistance to higher education, or revenue-sharing agreements that would spread the national wealth more evenly among the provinces, with the charge that provincial autonomy was being threatened. Nevertheless, the last three years of Mackenzie King's long term of office contained some notable achievements. It was a tribute to his political genius that when he gave up the leadership, he left his party in such a healthy state that it was able to retain office for another nine years.

The main domestic achievement of the last King government was the successful completion of Confederation. Since 1867 the island colony of Newfoundland had rejected every Canadian invitation to unite with Canada. But increasing contacts during the war, the decline in British power and the growing prosperity and strength of Canada, together with attractive financial inducements, enabled Joseph Smallwood, leader of the pro-Confederation forces, to persuade the Newfoundlanders to become Canada's tenth province in 1949.

By the time the Newfoundland agreement was settled and the Island's people had somewhat reluctantly given up their centuries of independence for the economic advantages of Canadian citizenship, King had left the political scene. The new Prime Minister was the man whom King had brought into his cabinet at the height of the conscription crisis. He was the dignified, wealthy, and bilingual Quebec lawyer, Louis S. St. Laurent, soon to be known as "Uncle Looie" by the Canadian electorate.

Unlike King, Louis St. Laurent had never considered himself a career politician, and had planned to return to private life as soon as the war was over. But he had stayed on, moving from the position of Minister of Justice to that of Minister of External Affairs in 1946. In the shrewd judgement of Mackenzie King, St. Laurent, the French Canadian, was his natural successor as leader of the Liberal party in 1948.

St. Laurent was a worthy successor to Laurier and King as Prime Minister. He lacked Laurier's spellbinding oratorical powers and the

In 1948, after twenty-nine years as leader of the Liberal party and twenty-two years as Prime Minister, W. L. Mackenzie King announced his resignation. Frank Underhill, one of Mr. King's sharpest critics, wrote on the Liberal leader's retirement: "In the long run of history it will not matter much that he never won the passionate personal devotion of his followers and associates, as Macdonald and Laurier did of theirs. Whatever they may have said of him individually, when they tried to give articulate expression to their feelings, the majority of the Canadian people have instinctively recognized that Mr. King is the leader who divides us least, and they voted for him accordingly."

deft political acuteness of King, but he was intellectually keen, an efficient administrator, and gave the appearance of a kind, elderly uncle whose integrity was beyond question. Like Laurier, he placed his Canadianism before his French Canadianism, and even quarrelled publicly with Quebec's autonomy-minded Premier, Maurice Duplessis, over such matters as federal taxing powers.

Under St. Laurent's leadership, and with the able assistance of such men as C. D. Howe, Minister of Trade and Commerce, the country's economic development moved ahead rapidly. In the field of international affairs, St. Laurent found an able minister in Lester B. Pearson, who moved from the civil service to active politics in 1948. Despite the emergence of such difficult problems as the growing grain surplus, increasing American control of the Canadian economy, and the dangers of the Cold War, the Canadian people showed their continued confidence in the policies and the administrative competence of the Liberals by re-electing them in 1949 and again in 1953 with overwhelming majorities.

Throughout the years of Liberal ascendancy, three opposition parties continued an apparently fruitless competition for the support of the electorate. Since R. B. Bennett's defeat in 1935 the Conservatives had suffered numerous setbacks. Three successive leaders had tried without success to revive the party's fortunes, and by 1948, when George Drew took over the leadership, the Conservatives had been reduced to little more than an Ontario party. The C.C.F., led by M. J. Coldwell after Woodsworth's death in 1942, had its main strength in the prairies, especially in Saskatchewan where T. C. Douglas had won office for the C.C.F. in 1944. The Social Credit party, led by Solon Low, drew its chief support from Alberta, which had maintained its allegiance to the party ever since 1935. In 1952, British Columbia joined Alberta and elected a Social Credit administration. On the national level, however, none of the opposition parties was able to find the formula that would bring an end to the long years of Liberal rule.

But by 1956 the Liberal government was beginning to show signs of weakness and old age. Accustomed to wielding power, the Liberals developed a careless attitude towards public opinion, clearly revealed during the bitter parliamentary debate in 1956 over the construction of the trans-Canada pipeline. The Liberal policy was to provide public money to aid in the construction of this pipeline, which would be owned by a private company controlled by American investors. "Canada, through the agency of this government, will put up the money," George Drew charged, "and then an organization owned in the United States to the extent of eighty-three per cent is going to get the benefit of the Canadian investment." This

SOMEBODY TURNED OFF THE GAS!

"If the Liberal government is beaten at the next election—a prospect less unlikely now than it has been for twenty-one years —this session of Parliament will appear in retrospect as a 'Gritterdammerung' or 'Twilight of the Grits'," a parliamentary reporter wrote in 1956. "Political historians may well conclude that the Liberals fell, not because of any one policy, and certainly not a pipeline policy of which the average voter knew little and cared less, but because they failed to observe the proper limits of power." George Drew, leader of the Conservative party in 1956 led the Opposition attack on the Liberal government's pipeline policy and especially its use of closure in the debate.

was a charge that won the sympathy of many Canadians who were growing uneasy about the degree of American control over Canada's economy. The Liberals weakened themselves further by attempting to force the pipeline measure through the House of Commons by the introduction of closure, a parliamentary device designed to limit debate. The Conservative and C.C.F. parties fought the measure with a vigour that seemed to restore their vitality. The government measure finally passed, but throughout the nation the pipeline affair was taken as a sign that the Liberals had held office long enough.

In the same year, the Progressive Conservatives elected a new leader, John G. Diefenbaker, a prairie lawyer who had been a member of parliament since 1940. By the time a new election was called in 1957, this evangelical orator had instilled in his party a new spirit. Campaigning strenuously and playing upon national fears of undue American influence in Canadian affairs, Mr. Diefenbaker succeeded in dislodging the Liberals. But the Diefenbaker victory was so slim that a new election had to be called in 1958, when the Progressive Conservatives, with two hundred and eight seats, were swept into office with the largest parliamentary majority in Canadian history.

In 1958, a new era opened in Canadian politics. After twenty-two years of Liberal government, the country had turned to the Progressive Conservatives and their new leader, John Diefenbaker. After the 1957 defeat, the Liberals too chose a new leader, the internationally known Lester B. Pearson. For the first time since 1921, national minor parties were nearly erased in 1958. The C.C.F., which had won only eight seats, looked towards a future in which its identity would be submerged in the New Democratic Party formed in alliance with the Canadian Labour Congress. The Social Credit party, though it was far from dead, was left without representation at Ottawa.

4. PROGRESSIVE CONSERVATIVES IN POWER

During the first four years of Progressive Conservative government the pace of economic expansion gradually slowed down. Both Canada and the United States experienced economic recessions during 1959, and by 1962 unemployment figures in Canada reached a level that was higher than any year since the depression. Among the reasons for the country's economic difficulties was the gradual decline of American investment which had been so important in financing the developments of the early 1950's. In addition, Canadian products were harder to sell in overseas markets, since the countries of Europe whose industrial power had been destroyed by the war were now once again operating at full capacity. With declining exports the country experienced financial difficulties which included a balance of payments problem caused, in part, by a failure of export sales to balance the imports of goods and capital.

Though the industrial sector of the economy suffered from stagnation,

John G. Diefenbaker's greatest strength as a politician was as a campaigner on the hustings. His technique was that of the courtroom lawyer pleading a case before judge and jury. This was natural, for the Conservative leader's early life was spent as a defence counsel and criminal lawyer. During his courtroom career he defended twenty people against the charge of murder and his plea was successful in all but two cases. Mr. Diefenbaker's early career as a politician was not a successful one and he failed several times to win election to public office before finally gaining a seat in the House of Commons in 1940. Sixteen years later he was chosen leader of his party, and the following year campaigned strenuously and successfully for the Conservative party which had been out of office for twenty-two years. In the following year, 1958, the Conservative party won more seats than any previous party in Canadian politics. Throughout his speeches Mr. Diefenbaker gave expression to a belief in a Canadian nationality. "As a nation of North America," he once remarked, "we have deep roots in two European cultures, the British and the French, and also in the cultures of all the other races of men that have come to us."

agricultural prosperity revived. Not only did the Conservative government give generous aid to the farmers, but the large wheat surpluses which had piled up during the late 'fifties gradually disappeared, when poor harvests in 1959 and 1960 reduced grain production. Moreover, the Conservatives succeeded in finding new markets for Canadian grain, especially in eastern Europe and Communist China. The political result of this agricultural prosperity was the transformation of western Canada, once the fortress of protest movements, into a Conservative stronghold.

Elsewhere, too, the Diefenbaker government made some notable innovations. To meet the problems of slack trade and unemployment, the government established a National Productivity Council in 1960, whose function it was to advise the government on methods of increasing Canadian productivity and trade. In social welfare the government increased the pensions of the aged, the disabled and the war veterans. One action for which the Prime Minister made himself personally responsible was the enactment in 1960 of a Bill of Rights. This Act, unlike the American Bill of Rights, was not a constitutional amendment. It was simply a parliamentary statute declaring that Canadians have a right to enjoy such traditional liberties as freedom of speech, association, religion and the press, and also the right to a fair trial, habeas corpus, and legal counsel. Though the Bill of Rights applied only to federal legislation and would have no effect during wartime, it represented an important reminder to Canadians that even the power of government was limited.

In foreign policy the Diefenbaker government faced several serious decisions. The Prime Minister, at a Commonwealth Conference in 1959, joined with the leaders of the African and Asian members in condemning the racial segregation practices of South Africa. The result was South Africa's decision to leave the Commonwealth in 1960. Another Commonwealth problem arose with Great Britain's announcement of her decision to seek entry into the European Common Market. The Diefenbaker government, naturally concerned about the possible loss of British markets for Canadian agricultural products, insisted that a Commonwealth Conference should be held before Britain made any final decision to join the E.C.M. With the breakdown of negotiations between Britain and the European trading partners early in 1963, Canadian worries were temporarily postponed.

No question of foreign affairs received more serious attention from the Diefenbaker government than disarmament. Mr. Howard Green, the Minister of External Affairs, made repeated attempts at both the Geneva Disarmament Conference, and at the United Nations, to break the deadlocked negotiations for controlled arms' reduction and a ban on nuclear testing. In 1963 his efforts remained unsuccessful. The Diefenbaker government's policy on disarmament raised some difficulties in the field of Canadian-American relations. Shortly after coming into office in 1957 the Conservatives signed an agreement with the United States establishing the North American Air Defence Command. This organization, with its headquarters at Colorado Springs, Colorado, provided for an integration of the Canadian and American air forces and air defence weapons under joint command. Despite the agreement, the Conservative government refused to accept nuclear weapons either for missiles or aircraft based in Canada, or for Canadian forces under N.A.T.O. command in Europe. The government, and especially Mr. Green, argued that for Canada to accept nuclear weapons, would be to jeopardize the world disarmament negotiations. By 1963 the indecision on the question of nuclear weapons was one cause of the growing criticism of the Diefenbaker government.

By the end of 1962 there were several other signs that the Diefenbaker party was losing its popularity. Though the party had won a majority of the seats in Quebec in 1958, its strength in that province had almost immediately begun to decline, partly because the Prime Minister was unable to find a French-Canadian lieutenant who could convince his compatriots that the Conservative government was sympathetic to their needs. Moreover, in 1960, the Union Nationale government, cautious ally of the Conservatives, was defeated by a vigorous Liberal party led by Jean Lesage, a former member of the St. Laurent government. The provincial Liberal platform called for reforms that would root out the political corruption that had grown up during Duplessis' long tenure of office, modernize Quebec's educational system, and increase French-Canadian control over the economic life of the province. Some French Canadians were convinced that these reforms could not be carried out unless Quebec seceded from Confederation. These extreme French-Canadian nationalists, or separatists, argued that Quebec was a colony of English-speaking Canada and like other colonies in the world, should be given full independence. While only a minority of Quebec people accepted this view, the existence of the vocal separatist movement was another sign that Canada, and the Diefenbaker government, was entering a difficult period.

Another sign of political discontent was the formation of the New Democratic Party. Negotiations between the C.C.F. and the Canadian Labour Congress had begun shortly after the election of 1958, and as unemployment increased so did the desire of many trade unionists for direct political action. In the summer of 1961 the New Democratic Party was born of the trade union-C.C.F. alliance. The platform of the New Democratic Party was less socialist than that of the C.C.F. had been, but it advocated government planning and control of economic development, and such social security measures as a national medical insurance scheme. As its first leader, the New Democratic Party chose T. C. Douglas, the colourful Premier of Saskatchewan.

The Social Credit party, too, underwent a reorganization during the summer of 1961. While the party continued to hold office in Alberta and British Columbia, it had lost all its federal representatives in 1958. The party's 1961 convention chose a new national leader, an inexperienced politician from Alberta, Robert Thompson. With a view to attracting

In the election campaign of 1962 the parties vied with each other in what many observers called "give-away programmes" in an attempt to secure votes. Duncan Macpherson, the brilliant satirist for the **Toronto Star** was moved to draw this cartoon of Messrs. Diefenbaker, Pearson and Douglas.

THE BALLOTEERS

support in Quebec, where the party was beginning to show signs of growth, the convention chose as deputy leader Réal Caouette, a fiery orator and enthusiastic organizer.

When a new election was called in 1962 the Conservatives asked for a vote of confidence and a renewed mandate to continue their policies of national expansion, including the development of Canada's northland. The Opposition leader, Lester Pearson, and the Liberal party charged that the government had mishandled the country's economic affairs, created increased unemployment and weakened the value of the Canadian dollar. The New Democratic Party agreed that the Conservative record was one of failure, but argued that only a policy of government control and increased social security could guarantee full employment and economic growth. The Social Credit party's chief campaign argument was that the country's economic difficulties were the result of the heavy national debt that had grown up under the Conservative government. In Quebec, Réal Caouette coined the improbable but appealing slogan, "You have nothing to lose, vote Social Credit."

When the ballots were counted on June 18, no party had won a clear majority. The Conservatives retained only one hundred and sixteen of their two hundred and eight seats. But the Diefenbaker government was not turned out of office, for despite a gain of over fifty seats, the Liberals had elected only one hundred of their supporters. The New Democratic Party won nineteen seats, while Social Credit was victorious in thirty, twenty-six of them in Quebec. Clearly, Mr. Caouette had succeeded in capitalizing on the dissatisfaction many people in his province felt with both the Conservatives and the Liberals.

The election held on June 18, 1962 was only the first step in the collapse and defeat of the Diefenbaker administration. Others followed quickly. Six days after the election the Prime Minister admitted that the country faced a serious economic crisis. Steps taken to meet the crisis included the devaluation of the Canadian dollar to 92.5 cents in terms of American currency, but despite this measure the dollar continued to decline in value and the nation began to run short of foreign exchange. On June 24 the Prime Minister announced to the nation the terms of an austerity programme which included the borrowing of a billion dollars from the International Monetary Fund, the United States and the United Kingdom; increases in the tariff on a wide range of goods; and reductions in the value of goods tourists could bring back to Canada. These measures were designed to reduce Canadian imports, expand exports, and maintain an adequate supply of foreign currency.

When parliament assembled in September, Prime Minister Diefenbaker, with the aid of the Social Credit members, was able to defeat motions of non-confidence. But the anticipated legislation to deal with the economic crisis and to fulfil his election promises did not materialize. The House of Commons drifted and reporters coined for it such names as the "Do-nothing Parliament." The government's defeat was inevitable, but before it came the simmering dispute over Canada's defence policy had boiled over.

As part of her N.A.T.O. and N.O.R.A.D. commitments, Canada had accepted weapons like the Bomarc missiles in Canada and the CF-104 aircraft and the "Honest John" rockets in Europe, all of which were effective only with nuclear warheads. Despite constant prodding by the opposition parties, however, the government refused to state whether it would accept nuclear weapons. In January the Liberal leader, Mr. Pearson, reversing his previous position, called for the acceptance of nuclear weapons to honour Canadian commitments. The Liberal party's endorsement and statements by United States government officials, which reflected impatience with Canada's lack of policy, set off a debate in the Conservative party which led to the resignation of the Honourable Douglas Harkness, the Minister of National Defence, who favoured acquisition of the weapons. On February 5, 1963 the government was defeated on a general non-confidence motion. The debate over nuclear arms became one of the major issues in the ensuing campaign.

After the defeat of the Diefenbaker government a group in the Conservative cabinet attempted a *coup d'état*, whose purpose was to replace Mr. Diefenbaker as leader of the party. The revolt failed, but two more ministers, Mr. Hees, Minister of Trade and Commerce and Mr. Sévigny, Associate Minister of National Defence, resigned, and several other ministers decided to retire from federal politics. It was a tattered remnant of a great party that Mr. Diefenbaker led into the campaign.

The electoral war was vigorous and bitter. Casting himself in the role of the underdog, the Prime Minister, in the hope that he could imitate Borden's success in 1911, lashed out at the Liberals, at the traitors within his own party, at the press barons in the big cities who had deserted the party, and at the Americans. The Liberals attacked Conservative mismanagement of the nation's economic and financial affairs, indecision on defence policy, the fading image of Canada abroad, and appealed above all for the return of a stable government with a majority. Mr. Douglas and the New Democratic Party hoped that their opposition to nuclear weapons and their extensive programmes of economic planning and social security would attract voters. The Social Credit party was divided between Robert Thompson's English-speaking wing, which advocated nuclear weapons for Canadian troops in Europe, and Réal Caouette's followers in Quebec who rejected any idea of nuclear weapons. All of the opposition parties, in an effort to lay the basis for better relations between French and English-speaking Canadians, promised the establishment of a Royal Commission on biculturalism to examine the role of French Canadians in the civil service, government-owned businesses like the C.N.R. and other areas of Canadian life.

On April 8 the national jury returned its verdict. No party gained a clear majority. The Liberals won one hundred and twenty-nine seats and forty-one per cent of the popular vote. Conservative representation fell to ninety-five seats and thirty-three per cent of the total vote. Social Credit lost six seats in Quebec and returned twenty-four members, while the N.D.P. retained fourteen per cent of the popular vote but elected only seventeen members. With increased support in the Maritimes, Quebec, Ontario and British Columbia, the Liberals emerged as the party with the best claim to national representation. Its largest measure of support came from the cities, for in the farmlands of Ontario and the West the Conservative defences were impregnable. Only in Calgary and Winnipeg were the Liberals successful.

Two weeks after the election Mr. Diefenbaker resigned and Mr. Lester B. Pearson became Canada's fourteenth Prime Minister. Four years before its centennial, the nation he was called on to govern faced serious economic problems at home and abroad, was sorely divided between city and country, between French and English, and still had not solved the pressing problems of foreign and defence policy. Whether the national birthday in 1967 would be a joyous occasion depended on the new Prime Minister's success in coming to grips with problems that taken together seemed to challenge the continued and healthy existence of the nation itself.

INDEX

NOTE: Italicized figures indicate captions.

Abbott, John, 383
Aberdeen, Lord, 383
Aberhart, William, 438, *439*, *440*, 448
Acadians, expulsion of, 12
Adams, John, 18-22, 32, 46, 50-1, 53
Adams, John Quincy, 60, 67, 70, 72, 73
Adams, Samuel, 17-19
Agriculture
    in Canada, 282, 392-3, 395, 398, *399*,
      413, 426-7, 429, 431, *432*, 433, 441, 476,
      488
    in New France, 9-11, 267-8
    in United States, 84-5, 139-40, 143, 155,
      156, 157-61, 205, 214-15
Aix-la-Chapelle, Treaty of, 11
Alamo, battle of, 91
Alaska
    annexation, 140, 163
    highway, the, 473
Alien Act, The, 50, 52
Allan, Sir Hugh, 361
Amendments to U.S. Constitution, 32, 51,
    101, 117, 119-20, 123-4, *125*, 127-8, 152,
    157, 178, 184, 201, 203-4, 242, 246
American Federation of Labour, 153-5,
    184, 189
"American System", the, 60, 61, 64, 65
Amnesty Act of 1872, 125
Anglo-American relations, 66, 90, 115,
    185-91, 231, 341-3, 459-60
    -French rivalry in North America, 8-9,
      10-13, 46-7, 54-60, 267
    -Japanese Alliance, the, *454*, 455
    -Saxon race in the United States, 148
Annexation,
    and Canada, 163, 328-31, 334-5, *336*,
      341, 349, 358, *360*, 376-7
    Manifesto, the, 328-9
Antietam, battle of, 111
Anti-Trust Act, 155, 158
Appomattox, agreement at, 113
Arizona - and union, 140
Arthur, Sir George, *317*
Attlee, Clement, 250

Bagot, Sir Charles, 323-4
Baldwin, Robert, 310, 318, *322*, 323-7,
    337
Balfour Declaration, the, 459
Baltimore, Lord, 7-8
Banks and Finance - in United States, 26,
    41-3, 60, 62, 64, 75, *76*, 77-8, 114, 211
Barnett, Ross, 247, *248*, 263
Batista, Fulgencio, 261
Bennett, R. B., 431, 434-5, *436*, 437, 443,
    444, *445*, 446, 459-60, *465*, 486
Berlin and Milan decrees, 55
Biddle, Nicholas, 75, *76*

Bill of Rights,
    Canadian, 488-9
    U.S., 38, 51
"Black codes", 121-2
Blaine, James, G., 126, 148
Blake, Edward, 362, 364
"Bloody Assizes" at Ancaster, 287, 303
Bond Head, Sir Francis, 310, 313
Boston Massacre, 16
Boston Tea Party, 17
Borah, William, 193-4
Borden, Sir Robert, 408, *409*, 410, 411,
    413, *414*, 415-19, *420*, 421, 423, 451,
    453, 459
Boundary agreements, 18, 66-7, 90-2, 99,
    270-1, 275, 290
    disputes, 48, *58*, 60, 92, 95, 106, 163,
      268, 334-5, 359-60, 404-6
Bourassa, Henri, 403-4, 407, 415, 417-18
Bourget, Bishop, 362-3
Bowell, Mackenzie, 383-4, *386*
Boxer Rebellion, the, 171
Bracken, John, *483*
"Brain Trust", the, *210*
Breckenridge, John C., 104-5
British-American Land Company, 295
British claims in America, 66, 91-2
    Commonwealth of Nations, 450-3, 455,
      457-9, 461, *462*, 463, 471-2, 474, 481-3,
      489
    conquest of New France, 267
    Indian relations, *58*
    North America Act, 349-52, 447
Brock, General Isaac, 287-8, *289*, 303
Brown, George, *337*, 338, 339, 343-6, 354
Brown, John, 104, 273
Bryan, William Jennings, *160*, 161-2, 181-
    182, 186, 199
Buchanan, James, 101, 105, 107
Buller, Charles, 317-18, 323, 325
"Bull-Moose" party, the, 182, 183, 187
Bull Run, Battles of, 111
Bureau of the Interior, and Indian affairs,
    136
Burma Road, *230*
Burns, General E. L. M., 482
Burr, Aaron, 41, 46, 51
By, Colonel, *300*
Byng, Lord Julian, 418-19, 429, *430*

Cabot, John, 4
Calhoun, John C., 56, 60-1, 72-4, *74*, 75,
    95, 97
California Gold Rush, 94
Canada (Que.) and the thirteen colonies,
    269-73
Canadian Tenures Act, the, 306

Caouette, Réal, 491-2
Carleton, Sir Guy, 20, 268-74, 279
Carnegie, Andrew, 133-4, *149*, 150
"Carpetbaggers", *123*, 124-5
Cartier, Georges Etienne, 338-9, 341, 343-344, 347, 354, 361, 373
Castro, Fidel, 261
Cattle Kingdom, the United States, 137-139
C.C.F. party, 441, *445*, 446, *483*, 486-7, 490
Champlain, Samuel de, 4
Chanak incident, the, 455, *456*, 457
"Chateau Clique", the, 303, 306-7, 318-19
Checks and balances (separation of powers), 32, *33*, 34-6, 46
Chiang Kai-shek, 256, 258
Church - in North America, 4-9, 18, 45, 152, 240, 267-70, 285, 288, 303-4, 357, 362-4, 379, *381*, 382-5, *386*, 387, 389, *390*, 394
Churchill, Winston, 226, 231, 233, 236, 250, 463-4, 472, *473*
Clay, Henry, 56, 65, 67, 70, 75-6, 77, 78, *96*, 97
Clayton Act, the, 184
Clergy reserves, 296, *298*, 304, 338
Cleveland, Grover, 146, 148, *149*, 150, 155, 163-5
Coldwell, M. J., *483*, 486
Colombo Plan, the, 256, 481, *482*
Colonial policy, British, 6, 8, 10, 14-19, 267-72, 278-9, 281-2, 302-8, 310-13, 315, 316-19, *320*, 321-6, 328-30, 332-3, 335, *336*, 340-3, 352, 355, 358, 401-3, 406, 418-19, 444
Commerce and Industry in Canada, *269*, 280-1, 291, 295, 298-301, 329, *330*, 334, *367*, 395-6; 431-2, 443-6, 468-9, 474-8, 488
Commerce and Industry in United States, 41-3, 64, 79-88, 90, 114-15, 131, 133-4, 151-2, 164, 196, 201-2, 238
Communications in North America, 83, 135, 159, 476
Communism, 197-9, 243, *244*, 245, 251-2, *253*, 254-7, *259*, 260-2, *263*
Compromise of 1850, *96*, 97, 99
Confederate States of America, 105-6, 109, 116, 120-1, *122*, 123
Confederation
  in Canada, 341, *344*, 345, 346, *347*, 348-351, 353-9, 379, 388, 484
  in United States, 24-7, 117, 140
Conkling, Roscoe, 126, 148
Conscription, 190-1, *414*, 415-18, 422, 464, *465*, 466, *467*, 468
Conservative party in Canada, 303, 310, 320, 324, 326-7, 329, 338-9, 343-4, *365*, 366-8, 373-9, 381-5, 387, *402*, 403, *404*, 408, *409*, *414*, 417-18, 423-4, 426, *427*, *428*, 429-31, 434-7, 441, 445-6, 453-5, *456*, 459, *465*, *483*, *486*, 487, *488*, 489-493

Constitution of United States, 27, *28*, 29-31, 37-8, 278, 302, 304-6
Continental Congress, *18*, 19-20, 22, 272-4
Convention of 1818, the, 91, 290, 329
Coolidge, Calvin, 200-1, 205, 208, 212
Credit Mobilier scandal, the, 126
Crerar, Thomas A., 424, 427-9
Crysler's Farm, 289
Crittenden Proposals, 107
Cuba, *see* Latin America

Dafoe, John W., *416*, 434, 451, 458, 461
Davis, Jefferson, 106, 109
Dawes Act of 1887, 137
Debs, Eugene V., 154-5, 217
Debt Assumption Act, the, 42
Declaration
  of Independence, 20-22, 45
  of Rights, 1774, 18
Democratic party, 70-3, 75, 77, *78*, 81, 83, 89-92, 94, 98-105, 115-16, 124-7, 146-8, 150, 159-62, 181-4, 187, 193-5, 201, 203, 208, 216, 218, 236, 238, 242-3, 245, 248
Detroit and War of 1812, 286, 288
Dewey, Thomas E., 235, 242-3
Diefenbaker, J. G., 487, *488*, 489, *490*, 491-493
Dieppe raid, the, 469
Douglas, Stephen A., 96, 99, 101-5
Douglas, T. C., 486, *490*, 492
Dred Scott case, 101, 103, 123
Drew, George, *486*
Drury, E. C., *427*
Dulles, John Foster, 257; *258*, 260-1
Duplessis, Maurice, 441, *442*, 448, 449, 465, 484-5, 489
Durham, Earl of (John Lambton), 316-19, *320*, 321, 325-7, 379
Durham's Report, 318-21
Dutch colonies in North America, 8
Duties, *see* Tariffs

Economic conditions in Canada
  depression, 312, 364, 368-70, 376, 409, 435, *436*, 437-9, 441-2, 446-7
  expansion, 366-8, 413-14, 468-9, 475-8, 485
  prosperity, 290, 369, *389*, 390, 393, 395-6, 426, 429, 431-2
  recession, 424-5, *432*, *433*, 434, 487, 491
  unemployment, 312, 424-5, *433*, 434-5, *436*, 437-9, 441-2, 446-7, 487
Economic conditions in United States
  depression, 56, 64, 69, 73, 77, *78*, 102, 119, *120*, 141, 150, *156*, 159-60, 205, *206*, 207, *208*, 211, 214-15, 218, 248
  expansion, 26-7, 43-4, 60-2, 64, 73, 75-83, 89-90, 129-34, *140*, 143, 145-6, 148, 202-6
  prosperity, 61-3, 117, 134, 143, 189, 195, 201-3, 238-41

Economic conditions in U.S. (cont'd.): reconstruction, 121-2, 125-7, *211*, 212-13, 215-16, 238-41
unemployment, 102, 206-8, 211-12, 216, 218, 238, *239*
Education
in Canada, 285, *297*, 350, 382-6, *387*, *390*, 394, 415
in the United States, 88, 145
Eisenhower, Dwight D., 232, 245-9, 257, 258, 259-61, 469
Elgin, Lord, 326, *327*, 329
Emancipation Proclamation of 1863, 115, *116*
Embargo Act of 1807, 56
Emerson, Ralph Waldo, 88, *103*, 104
Emigration from Great Britain, 80-3, *84*, 142, 280, 282, 294-5, 316-17, 473
Employment, *see* Economic conditions
English Canadian - French Canadian relations, 267-9, 281-2, 288
Confederation, 347-50
conscription issue, 411, 414-15, 416, 417-418, *419*, 422, 464-6, *467*, 468
co-operation, 322-4, 337-9, 343-4, *409*, 492-3
economic development, 300-1
isolationism, 401, 403, 406-7, 450-1, 455, 461
minority rights, 304-8, 319, 328, 381-2
nationalism, 441-2, 489-90
responsible government, 319-21, *327*
Riel's rebellions, 357, 372-3, 376, 379
separate schools, 383-7, 394
Espionage Act of 1917, 188
Expansion, Canadian, 331, 334-6, 370, 392-396
United States, 26-7, 58, 65, 83, 89-92, 94, 98, 105
Exploration, in Canada, 291-3, 331, 334-6, 392-6
in early America, 3-5, 8-10, 55

"Fair Deal", Truman's, 243
"Family Compact", the, 303-4, 308-10, 318-320
Farm Loan Board, United States, 184
Farmers' Alliances, 156, 157, 158-9
Federalist party in United States, 37-8, 41, 44-8, 50-4, 59-60
Fenian raids on Canada, *350*, 359, *360*
Fielding, W. S., 375, 388, *389*, 390, 403, 422
Fifteenth Amendment, the, 124, *125*
Fifth Amendment, the, 101, 157
Finance - United States, *see* Banks
Force Acts, 75, *125*
Ford, Henry, 202, *203*
Fordney - McCumber Act, the, 202
Foreign affairs, *see* International affairs
Fort Garry, 335-6
Fort George, *289*
Fort Vancouver, 334

Fort William and North West Company, 294
Four Freedoms, the, 226
Fourteen Points of President Wilson, 191-192, *194*
Fourteenth Amendment, the, 123-4, *125*, 127-8, 157, 246
France vs England in United States, 46-7, 54-8
Franco-American Treaty, 1778, 21, 47
Franklin, Benjamin, 22, 27, 29
Free Soilers, 94, 95, 97, 98, 99, 100, 107
Freedmen's Bureau, *122*, 125
Freeport Doctrine, the, 103
French-British rivalry in North America, *see* Anglo-French rivalry
French Canadians vs English Canadians, *see* English vs French Canadians
French Revolution, 45-7
Frick, Henry, 133, 149-50
Fugitive Slave Law, 97-8, 107
Fur trade in North America, 4-5, 8-11, 14, 48, 55, 267, 270, 274, 282, 286, 291, 293-4, 298-9, 334

Gallatin, Albert, 45, 52
Galt, A. T., 330-2, 339, 343-4, 347, 354, 367-8
Garrison, William Lloyd, 95, 105
Gênet, Citizen, 46-7
George III, *19*, 21, 273-74
Gettysburg, 111, *112*
Ghent, Treaty of, 60, 290
G.I. Bill of Rights, 240, *241*
"Gilded Age", the, 129, 150
Gold rush of '49, *94*, 95
Gompers, Samuel, 153, 184, 189
Good Neighbour Policy, the, 222-3
Gould, Jay, 125, 131, 153
Government
in English Colonies, 6-8
in Northwest Territory, 6, 25
in Quebec, 9, 18, 270
in Upper Canada, 283, 287, 303, 307-8, *309*, 313, 315
of thirteen colonies, after 1775, 22
federal in Canada, 268-70, 278-9, 302-12, 317, 322-3, 326, 328, 330, 337-9, 343, 346, 349-50, *351*, 352, 353, 360-4, *365*, 366-70, 373-6, 384-6, 388-9, 400, 416-17, 426, 434, 444-9, 451, 457, 459, 464-6, 489-92
federal in United States, 24-5, 29-32, *33*, 34-5, 38, 40-51, 52-6, 60, 62-5, 66, 68-73, *74*, 75-6, 79, 98-100, 102-8, 114, 121-4, 127, *132*, 135-6, 146-52, 155, 158, 176-84, 196-205, 207, 209-11, 215-18, 220-1, 235-6, 238, 240-6
provincial in Canada, 323-4, 350, *351*, 352-3, 374-5, 381-2, 384-7, 426-7, 429, 439-43, 446-9, 484
representative in Canada, 311-12, 318, 321, 323, 352

Government (cont'd.):
  responsible in Canada, 318-21, *322*, 323-324, *325*, 326-7, 330, 337, 341, 364, 400, 407, 455-9
  state, 24-8, 30, 32, 51, 53-4, 59, 62-4, 72-3, 75, 96, 100, 103, 107, 148, 152, 155, 157, 159, *176*, 217
Grangers, the, *156*, 157
Grant, General Ulysses, 112-13, 124-6, 148, 200
"Great Barbecue", the, 129, 131-4, 137
"Great Coalition", the, 344

Hamilton, Alexander, 27, 38, *40*, 41-2, *43*, 44-8, 52-3, 62
Harding, Warren G., 195, 196, 199, 200, 221-2, 455
Hawley-Smoot Tariff Bill, the, 202, 483
Hay, John, 169, 170-1
Hayes, Rutherford B., 126-7, 148
Hayne, Senator Robert, 74
Hepburn Act of 1906, 180
Hepburn, Mitchell, 442, *443*, 448-9
Hiroshima, *234*, 235
Hitler, Adolf, 209, 224, 225, 461, 463-4, 472
Holmes, Oliver Wendell, 199
Holy Alliance, the - and Spanish Revolution, 67-8
Homestead Act - U.S., 114, 137, 139
Hoover, Herbert, 196, 201-2, 205-8, 212, 222
Hopkins, Harry, 210, 212
Howard - Wheeler Act, 137
Howe, C. D., 469, 485
Howe, Joseph, *325*, 326, 348, 355
Hudson's Bay Company, 55, 91, 293-4, 334, 355-6, 367
Hughes, Sir Sam, 411, 416, 418
Hungarian Revolt, The, 260

Immigration Act of 1864, 114
Immigration - into Canada, 268, 276-8, 280, 282, 294-6, 268-9, *370*, *390*, 391-4, 475
Immigration - into United States, 64, 83-4, 114, 142-3
Imperial Conference of 1897, 402-4
Income tax - in the United States, 114, 184
Indians - and the Americas, 5-11, 15, 20, 26, 48, *58*, 67, 72, 129-30, 135-7, 286, *358*, 370-2
Industrial Revolution - in the United States, 80, 81, 82, 83, 84-5, 87-8
Industry, *see* Commerce
Integration, *see* Segregation
International affairs, Canada in,
  1867-1900, 359-60, 376-7, 400-3
  1900-1914, 404-8, 409-10
  1914-1918, 411-21
  1918-1939, 450-62
  1939-1945, 463-74
  1945-present, 477-8, 479-83, 489

United States in,
  1775-1800, 27, 31, 46-50
  1800-1848, 54-5, 55-60, 60-8, 90-3
  1848-1865, 115-16, 341-3, 345
  1865-1914, 163-74
  1914-1918, 185-8
  1918-1945, 191-5, 221-35, 472-4
  1945-present, 235-7, 250-63
Interstate Commerce Act, 158
"Intolerable Acts", The, 17, 18, 272
Isolationism - Canadian, 450-1, *452*, *456*, 458-59, *460*, 461, *467*
Isolationism - United States, 224-5, 450, 454, 459, 461

Jackson, Andrew, 59, 67, 69-71, *73*, 74-5, *76*, 77, 91, 158, 209
Jackson, William, 373
Japanese-American trade treaty, 1854, *83*
Japanese conquest of Manchuria, 222, *223*
Jay, John, 22, 27, *28*, 48, 286
Jay's Treaty, 48, 50, 291
Jefferson, Thomas, 20-1, *40*, 42-3, *44*, 45, *46*, 47-8, 50-1, 52-6, 158
Jesuit Estates Act, 381-2
"Jim Crow" laws, 127, 147-8
Johnson, Andrew, 116, 121, *122*, 124
Johnson, Lyndon, 248
Joint Board on Defence, the, 225, 472
Judiciary Act of 1789, 53
Julien, Henri, *386*, *416*

Kansas - Nebraska Act, 98-9, 100
Keating-Owen Act, the, 184
Keelboats, *61*, 62
Kellogg-Briand pact, the, 221-2
Kennedy, John F., 248-9, 259, 261, *263*
Kentucky and Virginia Resolves, 51, 59, 73
Khrushchev, Nikita, 259, *263*
King, W. L. Mackenzie, 225, *389*, 422-4, 428-31, 434, 440, 442, 445-6, 448-9, 453, 455-67 *passim*, 472-5, 479, 483-5
Knights of Labour, 152-3
Knights of the White Camellia, 125
Knox, Henry, *40*
Ku Klux Klan, 125, 198-9
Kuomintang, the, 256

Labour, conditions of
  in Canada, 425
  in United States, 80-1, 85-7, 129, 149, 152-3, 155
Labour party in Canada, 426, *427*, *456*
Labour unions in Canada, 396-8, 424, 442, *443*
Labour unions in the United States, 81, 143, 152-7, 202, *213*, 214, 239, 242
LaFollette, Robert M., *176*, 177-8, 181, 184, 200
LaFontaine, Louis, *322*, 323-4, 326-7, 337-8
Lambton, John, *see* Durham, Earl of
Lapointe, Ernest, 457, *460*, 464-6, *467*

Latin America and the United States, 67-68, 92-3, 98, 105, 125, 163-4, 167-70, 171-4, 222-3, 237, 255-6, 261-3
Laurier, Sir Wilfrid, 363-4, 372, 377, 385-399 *passim*, 400, 401-10 *passim*, 416-418, 422-3, 459, 484-5
League of Nations, the, 187, 193, *194*, 195, 221, 236, 421, 450-51, *452*, 459-60, *461*, *462*
Lee, Robert E., 111, *112*, 113
Liberal government in Great Britain, 321
Liberal party, 354, 361-3, 365-7, 374-6, 384-5, 387-91, 398-9, *402*, *404*, 407-8, 410, *414*, 416-19, 422-3, 426-31, 434-5, 441-3, 445-6, 451-5, 464-6, 476, 479, 483-93
Lincoln, Abraham, 92, *98*, 102, *103*, 104-9, *112*, 114-15, *116*, 117-18, 120-1, 341
Lindbergh, Charles, *205*, 225
Lloyd George, David, 192, 412-13, 419
Lodge, Henry Cabot, 167, *169*, 193, 194-5
Long, Huey, 216-17
Louisiana Purchase, the, 54-55
Loyalists, the, *19*, 21-3, 48, *275*, 276, 277, 278-9, 282-3, 286, 296
Lundy's Lane, battle of, 288
Lusitania, 186

MacArthur, Douglas, 229, 232, 257
Macdonald, Sir John A., 338-9, 343-61 *passim*, 365-78 *passim*, 379, *380*, 381, 382-3, *386*, 388, 389, 394-5, 400-1, 408, 409, 418, 459
Mackenzie, Alexander, 291, 362, 364, *365*, 389
Mackenzie, William Lyon, 308-9, 310-13, 314-15, 317, 394
Macon Bill, the, 57
Madison, James, 27-9, 38, 44, 46, 51-2, 56, *58*, 59
Mahan, Capt. A. T., 166-8
Maine incident, *168*, 169
"Manifest Destiny", 55, 89, 163, 167
Manitoba Act of 1870, 382
Manitoba and Confederation, 357
Maritimes, the, 280-1, 289-90, 360, 366, 375-6, 431-3, 447
and Confederation, 344-6, 348-9
Marshall, George C., 234, 245
Marshall, John, Chief Justice, 46, 53, 62-4, 72
McCarthy, D'Alton, *381*, 382
McCarthy, Joseph, *244*, 245, 256, 263
McKinley, William, 149, 161-2, 167, 168-9, 170-71, 179
McNaughton, Gen. A. G. L., 466
Meade, George C., 111, *112*, 113
Meighen, Arthur, 396, 423-24, 427-9, 430, 431, 453, *454*, 455, *456*, 459
Melville, Herman, 88, 118
Mercantilism, 10, 281, 325
Mercier, Honoré, 373-4, *381*
Meredith, James, *248*

Merrimac, the, 111-12
Merritt, William Hamilton, 299, *303*
Metcalfe, Sir Charles, 324, 326
Métis, 356-7, 370-3
Mexican War, 92, *93*
Michilimackinac, 48, 288-9
Milan and Berlin decrees, 55
Missouri Compromise, 66, 96-7, 99, 101
Molotov Plan, the, 251
Monopolies and trusts, 132-4, 151-2, 155, 158, 176, *377*, 396, 426
Monroe Doctrine, 68, 163-4, 174, 193, 222, 261
Monroe, James, 46, 54, 66, 67, 68
Montcalm, Marquis de, 12
Montgomery, Richard, *273*, 274
Montreal - history of, 4-5, 13, 268, 274, 282, 338
Morgan, J. P., 131, 133, 184
Morrill Act, the, 145
Morse, Samuel, 83
Munich pact, the, 461
Murray, (Gen.) James, 268, *269*
Mussolini, Benito, 209, 224, 232, 460

Napoleon Bonaparte, 54-5, 57, 289
Nationalism in Canada, 339, 379, 400, *404*, 408, 417-18, 421, *456*
Nationalism in United States, 57, 62, 150-1
Nativism - in the United States, 84, 142-3, *147*, 148, *198*
NATO, *254*, 255, 480-1, 489, 492
Naval Act of 1890, 167
Navigation Acts, 10, 15, 281
Neilson, John, 306, *307*, 308
Neutrality Acts of 1935 and 1937, 224-5
New Brunswick and Confederation, *344*, 348-9
"New Deal", the, 208, *211*, 212-15, *216*, *217*, 218, *219*, 220, 231
"New Deal", in Canada, *444*, *445*
New Democratic Party in Canada, 487, 490-93
Newfoundland, discovery, 4
and Confederation, 346, 348, 354, 356
and U.S.A., 66
New France, early history of, 4-5, 9, 11, 12-13
New Mexico, 92, 95, 97
and Union, 140
Ninety-two Resolutions, 308
Nixon, Richard, 249
"NORAD", 481, 489, 492
North West Company, the, 293-4
Northwest Ordinance, 25
Nova Scotia - and Confederation, *344*, 348-349, 355
Nova Scotia - and the thirteen colonies, 272-3, 278
Nuclear weapons, 233, *234*, 235, 253-4, 259-60, *263*, 474, *480*, 489, 492
Nullification, Doctrine of, 73, 75
Nye, Gerald P., 223, 225

O'Callaghan, E. B., 313
Olney, Richard, 155, 163
Ordinance of Secession of 1860, 105

"Pacific Scandal", the, 361
Paine, Tom, *19*, 20, 46
Panama Rebellion, The, 172
Pan-American Union, the, 164
Panic of 1837, the, 77, *78*
Papineau, Louis-Joseph, 306, *307*, 308, 309, 311, 312, 313, 314-15, 362, 403
Paris, Peace Conference of, *192*, 193
"Parti rouge", 339
Patrons of Husbandry ("The Grange"), 156-157
Pattullo, T. D., 442-3
Payne-Aldrich Tariff bill, 181
Pearl Harbor, *227*, 228, 231-2, 474
Pearson, Lester B., 477, 479, 482-3, 485, 487, *490*, 491, 492-3
Pendleton Act of 1883, 148
Perry, Matthew C., 83, 164
Philadelphia - and American Government, *16*, 18-19, 27-36, 111, 346
Philadelphia Conference of 1787, 27-32, 346
Pierce, Franklin, 98
Pilgrims, 6, 7
Pinckney, Charles, 48, 51
Pitt, William, 12
Platt Amendment, 223
Platt, Thomas, 178-9
"Pocket Veto", 35
Point Four Programme, The, 256
Polk, James K., 91, *92*, 97-8, 335
Pond, Peter, 291
"Popular sovereignty" (squatter sovereignty), 96, 99, 102, 103
Population - of British North America, 331-2, 337
Population - of Canada, 280-3, 295, 297, 319, 368, *369*, 392-5, 475
Population - of New France, 9, 11
Population - in the United States, 286
Populist party, 159, 160-2, 175, 184
Prevost, Sir George, 288, 289, 305
Prince Edward Island - and Confederation, *344*, 346, 348, 354, 356, 359, 375
Proclamation of 1763, the, 15-18, 268-9
Progressive party - in Canada, 422, 424, 427-31
Progressive party - in United States, 175, *176*, 177-8, 180-5, 187, 194-5, 197, 202, 209, 215, 242-3
Pulitzer, Joseph, 145
Pullman Company, the, 154-5
Pure Food and Drugs Act - United States, 180
Puritans, 6-7

Quebec Act of 1774, 17-18, 270-73, 278, 306

Quebec City,
    Confederation Conference at, 344-6, *347*, 348
    history of, 4-5, *12*, 13, 20, 268, *273*, *330*, 338
Queenston Heights, battle of, 59, 288, *289*

Radical Reconstruction, 121-2, *123*, 124, *125*, 127
Railways
    in Canada, 331, *332*, *333*, 334, 338-9, 358-359, 361, 364-9, *374*, 394-5, 398, 423, 427, 443
    in United States, 82-3, 85, 99-100, 104, 114, 117, 119, 126-7, 129, *130*, 131, 135-9, 148, 153-5, *156*, 157-8, 179, 201-202, *332*
Randolph, Edmund, *40*, 48
Rebellions in Canada, 304, 311, *312*, 313, *314*, 315, *317*, 318, 326, *327*, 356-7, *358*, 368, 370-2,· *373*, 374
Reciprocity
    British, 300, 316, 325, 328, 340
    Canadian, 181-2, 329, 359-60, *365*, 376-7, *389*, 399, 407-8, 446
Reconstruction Act, American, 1867, *123*
Reconstruction party in Canada, 444, 446
"Red Scare" in United States, 197-9
Redemptionists, Southern, *125*
Reform party in Canada, 303-4, 306-11, 313, 318, 320, 322, 324-7, 337-9, 343-4, 348
Republican party, 44-8, 50-6, 60-1, 69, 99-105, 107, 113-15, 117-18, *122*, 124-127, 146-9, 160-2, 180-3, 187, 193-5, 201, 205, 208, 217-18, 236, 238, 241-3, 245, 248-9, 256
Reserve Act, United States, 184
Richmond and the Civil War, 111, 113, *120*
Riddell, Dr. W. A., 460-1
Rideau Canal, *300*
Riel, Louis, 357, 368, 371, 372, *373*, 374, 376, 379, *380*
"Robber Barons" of United States, 131, 133-4, 141, 151-2
Robinson, John Beverley, 303
Rommel, Marshal, 229
Roosevelt, Franklin D., 204, 207-9, *210*, 211-18, *219*, 220, 222-4, *225*, 226-7, *228*, 229, 231, 233, 235-7, 250, 253, *462*, *473*, 474
Roosevelt, Theodore, *169*, 170-2, *173*, 178-179, *180*, *181*, 182-4, 405-6
Rowell, N. W., 417
Rowell - Sirois Report, the, *433*, 446-9, *448*
Rush - Bagot Treaty, 66, 290
Rusk, Dean, 261
Russell, Lord John, 311, 321, 323, 325-6
Russian claims in America, 55, 67, 75
Russian Revolution, 1917, 187, 191
Ryerson, Egerton, 290, 304, 310, *314*, 324

San Juan Hill, battle of, *169*, 170
St. Laurent, Louis, 467, 479-80, 484-5
St. Lawrence Seaway, the, 246, 476, *477*
"Scalawags", 123, 125, 126
Scott, Thomas, 357, 372
Secession in Canada, 375, 489-90
Secession in the United States, 74-5
Sectional conflict in the United States, 79, 86-8, 91-5, *96*, 97-109, 115-20, 122, 125, 127, 341, 344
Sedition Acts, 50-2, 188-9
Segregation, 71, 122, 147-8, 158-9, 246, *247*, *248*
Selkirk, Lord, 280, 282, 293-4
Senate Committee on Foreign Relations, 193
Separation of powers (checks and balances), 32, 33, 34-6
Settlement in Canada, 4-5, 282-4, 293-5, *296*, *298*, 335, *336*, 356-7, 370-2
Settlement in the United States, 48, 50, 55, 58, 64, 85, 114, 134-5, 137, 139, *140*
Seven Oaks, battle at, 294
Seventh Report on Grievances, 310
Seward, William, 97, 163, 341
Shays' rebellion, 27
Sherman Anti-Trust Act, 155, 158, *180*
Sherman, General (William), 113
Sifton, Clifford, 389, *390*, 391, 394-5, 399, 417
Silver Purchase Act, the, 149
Simcoe, John Graves, 282, *283*
Slavery, 25, 30, 45, 64-6, 79, 85-6, *87*, 88-99, *100*, *101*, 102-5, 107-8, *110*, 114-15, *116*, 117, 120, 122, 124-5, 128, 146
Slidell, John, 92, 115
Smallwood, Joseph, 484
Smith, Alfred E., 201, 208
Social Conditions in Canada, 284-5, *295*, *296*, *297*, 298, *309*, *436*, 445-6, 475, 488
Social Conditions in United States, 71, 79, 80, *81*, 86-8, 119-23, 125, 129-30, 134-5, 137-43, *144*, 146, *147*, 148, 150, *151*, 152, 156-7, 159, 176, 197-9, 202-8, 238-240
Social Credit party, 438, *439*, *440*, 446-7, 486, 490-93
"Social Darwinism", *147*, 150, 166, 175, 199
South Carolina Exposition and Protest, ·72, 75
Spanish claims in America, 3, 8, 26-7, 48, 54-7, 66, 67-8, 125
Spanish Revolution, the, 67
"Spoils System" in U.S. Politics, 37, 71, 77
Stalin, Joseph, 236-7, 250, 259
Stamp Act of 1765, 15-16
Stevens, H. H., 444, 446
Stevens, Thaddeus, 115, *123*

Stevenson, Adlai, 245, 248
Stimson, Henry L., 222, 253
Stowe, Harriet Beecher, *98*
Strachan, Bishop John, 303-4
Strikes in Canada, 424, *425*, 442, *443*
Strikes in United States, 81, 148, *149*, *153*, 197, 200, *213*, 241-2
Strong, Josiah, 167
Suez Crisis, the, 482-3
Suffrage in Canada, 308, 417
Suffrage in the United States, 70, 127, 137, 152
Sumner, Charles, 97, 115, *360*
Sydenham, Lord, (Charles Poulett Thompson), 322-3

Taft-Hartley Act, the, 241-3
Taft, William H., 174, 181, *182*, 183, 399, 407
Talbot, Colonel Thomas, 284
Talon, Jean, 9
Tammany Hall, 84, 127, 176
Taney, Chief Justice, 77, 101, 123
Tariffs in Canada, protective, 299, 328, 330, 340, 366, *367*, 374-7, 389-90, 395, 398, *399*, 426-8, 434, 437, 445
Tariffs in United States, protective, 30, 44, 61, 64, 72-5, 78, 100, 102, 108, 125-6, 147, 149-50, 155, 181, 202, 205, 300
Tarte, Joseph Israel, *386*, 389
Taxation in Canada, 350, 413, 447, 449, 469
Taxation in the colonies, 15-17, 19
Taxation in United States, 24, 26-7, 29, 31, *43*, 44, 52, 126, 202, 217, 242, 245
Taylor, General Zachary, 92-5
"Teapot Dome" Scandal, the, 200
Tecumseh, 58, 286, 288
Ten Resolutions, Russell's, 311
Tenth Amendment, the, 32
Tenure of Office Act, 124
Texas
  settlement and annexation, 90-3, 97
Thirteen colonies (*see also* British claims in America), 8, 14, 15, 18-20
Thompson, Charles Poulett
  see Sydenham, Lord
Thompson, Robert, 490, 492
Thoreau (Henry David) 88, 104
Tilley, Leonard, 345-6, 349, 354, 360
Tippecanoe, 58, 78, 286
Townsend, Dr. Francis, 216
Townshend Acts, the, 16, 17
Trade
  in British Colonies, 316, 329-30
  in Canada (*see also* International affairs), 281, 298-300
  in United States (*see also* International affairs), 55-6, 58-9, 67
Trade Commission Act,
  United States, 184
Trade, free, *see* Reciprocity
Trade restrictions, *see* Tariffs

Trade unions, *see* Labour unions
Trades and Labour Congress of Canada, 396
Transcontinental Treaty of 1819, 67
Transportation in Canada, 62, 67, 283, 294, *298*, 299, *300*, 305, 319, 328-9, 331-2, *333*, 334, *336*, 338-9, 343, 348-9, *358*, 359, 361, 364-5, 366-8, 374-5, 394-395, 398, 443, 476, *477*, *see also* Railways
Transportation in the United States, *61*, 62, 63, 72, 79, 82-3, 85, 119, 131, *332*, *336*, *see also* Railways
Treaty of Paris, the, 22-24
Treaty of Portsmouth, the, 171
Treaty of Rio, the, 255, 261
Trent incident, the, 115
Truman Doctrine, the, 251
Truman, Harry S., 233-5, 240-2, *243*, 244-246, 250-1, 255, 257, 259, 477
Trusts in United States, 132-4, 139, 158, 179, *180*, 184, 196, *see also* Monopolies and trusts
Tupper, Sir Charles, 345, 348, 354-5, 374, 383, *404*, 408
Tyler, John, 78

Underhill, Frank, *485*
Union gov't. in Canada, 418, 422-4, 426
Union in Canada, 321, 337, 340-1, 343-5, 347-9
Union Nationale party, 441-2, 465, 484, 489
United Farmers' parties in Canada, *427*, 429
United Nations Organization, the, 236-7, 479, 481-3
Upper Canada, 280, 282, *283*, *284*, 287-8, *289*, 296-7, 300-1, 303, 307-9, 313, 315, *317*, 319-21, 323

Van Buren, Martin, 77-8, 94
Vandenberg, Arthur H., *225*, 254
Vanderbilt, Cornelius, 131, 141
Vermont border incident, *345*, 346
Versailles, Treaty of 1783, 275, 286, 291
Versailles, Treaty of 1918, *194*
Virginia and Kentucky Resolves, 51, 59, 73
Volstead Act, the, 203-4

Wade-Davis Bill of 1864, 121
Wagner Act, the, 213-14
Wakefield, Edward Gibbon, 317, 319

Wallace, Henry A., 210, 220, 242-3
War Hawks, 56-8, 60
Warren, Chief Justice, 246
Wars
American Civil War, 37, 89, *100*, 107-119, *120*, 121, 123-5, 127-8, 132, 148, 152, 163, 341-2, 346, 349
American War of Independence, *19*, 20, *21*, 22, 24, 272-9
Boer War, 403, *404*, 406
"Cold" wars, 252, *253*, 255-62, 485
Korean War, 245, 256-8, 481
Mexican War, 12-13
Napoleonic, 55
of Austrian Succession, 11
of 1812, 57, 59-60, 280, 282, 286-8, *289*, 290-1
Russo-Japanese War, 171
Seven Years', 11-13
Spanish-American, 167-70
World War I, 184-191, *192*, 193-5, 406, 410-13, *414*, 415-21
World War II, 195, 225-7, *228*, 229, *230*, *231*, 232, *233*, 234-7, 250-1, 450, 461, 462-74
Warsaw Treaty of 1955, 255
Washington, George, 19-20, *21*, 22, 27, *28*, *39*, 40, 42-3, 45-8, 50
Washington, Treaty of, 360
Webster, Daniel, 73, *74*, 90, 97
Wheeler, Burton K., 200, 226
Wheeler - Howard Act, 137
Whig party in the United States, 71, *76*, 77-9, *81*, 91-2, 94, 98-100, 114
Whitney, Eli, 64, 85
Willkie, Wendell, 216, 220
Wilmot Proviso, the, 97-8
Wilson, Woodrow, 174, 176, 178, *182*, 183-185, *186*, 187-191, *192*, 193, *194*, 195, 207, 236
"Wisconsin Idea", *177*, 178
Wolfe, General James, 13
Wood, Henry Wise, 429
Woodsworth, J. S., 425-6, 437, *440*, 441, *445*, *456*, 462, 486
Workingmen's party, *147*

XY Company, the, 293

York, 283, *284*, 285, 288
Yorktown, battle of, 22
Yukon Gold Rush, 395, *397*, 404

Zimmermann, Alfred, 187-8